Dedication

In the late 1960s, I spent hour upon hour reading car magazines that belonged to my dad, Al Gunnell. They were filled with stories and photos about rare muscle cars that we collect now. *Motor Trend* columnist Mike Lamm used to write, way back then, that muscle cars were rare and would be collected in the future. Now, the future is here!

Mike Mueller

Credits & Acknowledgments

It would have been impossible to compile *Standard Guide to American Muscle Cars* without the help of many people who helped gather facts and photos for the book.

Bob Ackerson, Tom Brownell, John Gunnell, Phil Hall, Jerry Heasley, John Lee, Jim Lenzke and Terry Parkhurst are responsible for the muscle car histories. The majority of the color photos—which are new to this edition—were contributed by Jerry Heasley, a Texas photographer who has specialized in capturing America's "supercars" on film for nearly three decades. Other photos were supplied by individual car owners who responded to advertisements in *Old Car Weekly* soliciting photo contributions. The rest of the photos are from the giant *Old Cars Weekly* photo archives.

As for general encouragement, enthusiasm and spreading of knowledge about muscle cars, we greatly appreciate the support of Bill Bartels of Supercar Showdown, Reeves Callaway, Chevrolet Motor Div., The Chrysler Historical Foundation, Richie Clyne of the Imperial Palace, Tom Collins, Dodge Div. of Chrysler Motors, Helen Early (Oldsmobile Historical), Brian Earnest, Gary Esse of Madison Classics, Ford Motor Co., Alex Gabbard, GM Media Archives, Greg Grams of Volo Auto Museum, Jesse Gunnell, Phil Hall, Jerry Heasley, Craig Jackson of Barrett-Jackson, Gary F. Jole, Glenn Klobuchar, Ron Kowalke, John Lee, Jim Mattison of Pontiac Historic services, George McNeilus, Johnathan K. Meyers, Chip and Bill Miller of Carlisle Productions, Jack Miller, Joe Molina Public Relations (JMPR), Drew Phillips, Pontiac Motor Div., Ed Reavie of Nostalgia Productions, Vince Rufolo, John Sawruk, Marty Schorr, photographers Doug Mitchel, Phil Kunz and Tom Glatch, Carroll Shelby, Bill Siuru, Tom Stephani (Nickey Chevrolet), Angelo Van Bogart, Gordon Van Vechten, Robbie J. Wadzinski, Jim Wangers and Don Williams of Blackhawk.

We think this book will be successful as a reflection of the ever-growing interest in muscle car collecting and invite everyone who reads it to submit additional information and photos to make future editions bigger and better.

Jerry Heasley

Contents

Doug Mitchel

Introduction

Unlike the "Little Old Lady from Pasadena," I do not have a brand-new-shiny red, Super Stock Dodge in my garage. In fact, people are surprised to learn I never owned a really hot muscle car. I have 12 vehicles in my car building – antiques, sports cars and '50s fin-mobiles—but no LS6, no Thunderbolt, no Road Runner! The hottest cars I've owned included a '63 Chrysler Sport 300, an '84 Camaro Z28 and my '89 Caprice 9C1. (In case you don't know, that last one—cop-car collectors call them "box cars"— is a full-size police package Chevy, an ex-Wisconsin State Patrol supervisor's car).

If you ask me, the fact that I don't own a muscle car is the reason I love them and love writing about them. By putting together books like this one, I can "experience" over 400 muscle cars without laying out any cash. I formed a very deep appreciation of these machines in the '60s when I absorbed stories about them in the magazines that my dad, Al Gunnell, collected. I read Mike Lamm's column in *Motor Trend* and listened when he told me that muscle cars would be the Duesenbergs of the future. How right he was!

Modern enthusiasts are collecting muscle cars in a big way. Judging by the sales of early editions of *The Standard Guide to American Muscle Cars*, there's a lot of demand for good information about such models.

Actually, the term muscle car wasn't heard as much back when these vehicles were first hitting the market. In those days, the enthusiast magazines favored the term "supercar."

This probably came from Super-Stock drag racing terminology. Dodge had Super Stocks, Chevy had Super Sports and Plymouth had the Superbird. Therefore, the term supercar was a natural.

Some big and mid-sized supercars also raced on NASCAR's superspeedways. As you'll see in this book, stock car drivers spun the wheels of everything from Hudsons and Chrysler Letter Cars to Road Runners and Torino Talladegas. The big wings and droopy snouts used on the Dodge Daytona and Plymouth Superbird evolved from the desire to win Grand National races.

Early supercars had solid-color vinyl interiors, hood scoops, consoles, mag wheels, floor shifts and red-stripe tires. Many had a massive engine in a small body, which made them great for drag racing.

A few years later, the same big motors were shoehorned into even smaller cars: compacts, senior compacts and sports compacts (or pony cars). These were also drag raced. Then, people noticed that certain muscle cars were well suited for sedan races in the Sports Car Club of America's (SCCA) Trans-Am Challenge series.

There were also some huge cars that proved to be quite fast when big engines were stuffed into them: Thunderbirds, Marlins, Pontiac 2+2s and Chrysler Letter Cars come to mind. These machines were muscular, too, but they weren't the same as supercars like the GTO.

Eventually, the term "supercar" disappeared. "Muscle car" took its place and stuck like an F60-14 RWL tire on hot asphalt. Nowadays, collectors use it to refer to just about any of the types of cars mentioned above.

After 1982, genuine muscle cars started returning to the market. These smaller-sized, lower-weight, higher-tech performance machines were far different from '60s supercars, except that they also went fast. Now, we have a new millennium with turbocharged V-6s that can outrun yesterday's hottest factory hot rods.

This fourth edition of *Standard Guide to American Muscle Cars* has been expanded in three ways. First, we are taking a time-capsule ride back into the '50s to see some "mid-century muscle." These historic muscle cars were included in our early editions, but only in black-and-white. Now, you'll get to see some of them in full color. We are also adding several previously overlooked models from the 1964-1972 era of "real" muscle cars. In addition, our coverage of "Modern Muscle" now includes some of the latest factory hot rods.

As before, *Standard Guide to American Muscle Cars* incorporates research done for *Old Cars Weekly* and *Old Cars Price Guide*. In total, over half a century of high-performance machines are covered in these pages.

We hope you enjoy this book. Send us a nice picture of your muscle car and you might see it in future editions of *Standard Guide to American Muscle Cars*.

—John Gunnell, editor

The 1951 (white convertible) and 1952 Hudson Hornet might not have looked fast, but racers liked them and turned them into formidable forces on the track.

AMC & HUDSON

1951-1952 Hudson Hornet

If there was ever a car that was unlikely to dominate American stock car racing, it was the "Step-Down" Hudson Hornet. With a 124-inch wheelbase, a 77-inch width and a shipping weight around 3,600 lbs., the Detroit-built Hornet was a *big* car. Under the hood was an inline, L-head six—not a V-8.

The Hornet had made its bow in 1951, the same year that the Chrysler Firepower Hemi V-8 was introduced. Few observers thought that, even with 308 cubic inches, the new Hudson product could ever set the pace in the recently formed sport of stock-car racing.

Marshall Teague, the owner of a garage in Daytona Beach, Florida, saw the Hornet's potential. He figured out that the car's low center of gravity, its great handling and its big, "torquey" six were just what was needed to beat the racing-winning Olds 88.

Teague outran the Olds drivers and was then able to get the attention of Hudson's top brass. He convinced management to add "heavy-duty" parts to their options list. With extras like "Twin H" carburetion (a setup using two single-barrel carburetors) the Hudsons were virtually unbeatable on the nation's racetracks.

The Hornet got only minor changes in 1952, but by then the "roundy-round" boys had all they needed to keep the Hudsons out front. A number of top NASCAR drivers switched to the brand and 27 out of 34 Grand National races went to Hudson Hornets that year.

Teague took the checkered flag at Daytona. He then switched to AAA-sanctioned racing up north and won half of the 14 races on the schedule. Other Hudson drivers took five more, giving the nameplate 39 wins in 48 major 1952 events.

Hornets were not low-priced cars. The popular coupe sold for $2,742, the Hollywood two-door hardtop cost $3,095 and the convertible was priced at $3,342.

For those not involved in stock car racing, the Hudsons didn't seem all that fast in straight-line acceleration testing. *Motor Trend* magazine reported a 0-to-60 time of 16.8 seconds. However, ace automotive writer Tom McCahill tested a Teague-tuned Hornet and found it could achieve the same speed in 12.8 seconds. McCahill recorded a maximum speed of 107 mph, versus *Motor Trend's* under-100 mph top speed.

Hudson's success on the racetrack did not translate into showroom sales records. Model-year production for 1952 totaled only 70,000 units, only half as many as in 1951.

The wildly successful Hudson Hornet race cars were still going strong in 1954.
This is a replica of Herb Thomas' 1954 NASCAR champion car.

1954 Hudson Hornet

The last of the Step-Down design Hudson Hornets—the 1954 model—upheld the winning record established by the 1951-53 models on the nation's stock-car ovals, but it eventually lost the bigger battle, which was to remain in production.

This year the big cars were restyled to look more like the compact Jet introduced the year before. The grille had a heavy, bowed molding tracing the upper radiator opening. There was a full-width, flat horizontal loop surrounding the wedge-shaped parking lights at each end. The main bar (top of the loop) was ribbed towards the middle and held a triangular Hudson medallion in a finned housing at its center. Behind this bar was an angled plate with four additional, wide-spaced ribs. Block letters spelled out the Hudson name below the scoop on the nose of the hood. Despite a new one-piece curved windshield, new sheet metal from the belt line down, a modernized interior and the most powerful flathead sixes ever installed in a passenger car up to that time, the public and the critics voted that the Hudson was outdated and sales were dismal.

After long talks, Hudson and Nash-Kelvinator merged on May 1, 1954, to form American Motors Corporation. Nash was the strong partner, relatively speaking, and it was decided that current Hudson production would end in October, with the name being transferred to a variation of the Nash.

Even with the midyear introduction of the low-priced Hornet Special series, sales did not pick up. In all, 24,833 Hornets were made. Only 11,603 of the smaller Wasps were put together.

The base Hornet engine, still at 308 cubic inches, was rated at 160 hp and the Twin-H option brought that figure to 170 hp for $86 more. However, the stock-car racers used the specially built 7-X engine, which was available through the company's parts operation for $385. This high-performance engine reportedly produced 210 hp.

Hudson won 17 out of 36 NASCAR Grand Nationals, again more than any other make, and driver Marshall Teague wrapped up another AAA title with five wins.

Other Hudson drivers took three more victories to account for half the AAA events that season. Ironically, Teague's last win came September 12, at Milwaukee, Wisconsin, not far from where the 1955 Hornets would be constructed in Kenosha.

Hornet prices in 1954 ranged from the Hornet Special Club Sedan at $2,571 to the convertible Brougham at $3,288.

Doug Mitchel

With its 327-cid engine, the Rambler Rebel was AMC's first true high-performance car.

1957 Rambler Rebel

For 1957, American Motors made a sensational high-performance car called the Rebel. Under its hood was an enlarged version of the V-8 introduced a year earlier. The 4.00 x 3.25-inch bore and stroke, 327-cube engine featured five main bearings, a forged-steel crankshaft and a 9.5:1 compression ratio. Large cast-iron exhaust manifolds were hooked to dual exhaust pipes with straight-through mufflers.

AMC had originally planned to use a Bendix "Electrojector" electronic fuel-injection system in the Rebel. The system proved problematic and it's unlikely that any fuel-injected Rebels were ever turned out. A Carter WCFB four-barrel carburetor was used on 1,500 production units instead. Instead of 288 hp and fuel injection, the cars that left the assembly line had 255 carbureted horses.

Another thing in the original plan was limited production. AMC expected to manufacture Rebels on a made-to-order basis and to offer only two options: EFI and Hydra-Matic transmission. Extras added later included Solex tinted glass and 6.70 x 15 Goodyear Blue Streak racing tires.

The Rebel's standard transmission was a three-speed manual gearbox, with overdrive, linked to a Borg & Beck 10-inch clutch. The extra-cost "Flashaway" Hydra-Matic transmission was essentially the same unit used by Oldsmobile and Pontiac. A 4.10:1 rear was used with stick-shift cars and a 3.15:1 axle was added with Hydra-Matic.

Among the items included in the Rebel's price of $2,786 were reclining seats, power steering, power brakes, a "continental" tire carrier, windshield washers, a radio, back-up lights, full wheel discs, a padded instrument panel and sun visors.

The Rebel came only as a four-door hardtop and only in a solid silver-gray color scheme. Its special full-length body side trim featured a bronze-gold anodized aluminum insert with a "Rebel" nameplate on each front fender. A silver-and-black interior trim designed exclusively for the Rebel harmonized with the monotone body paint.

AMC promoted "amazing acceleration and speed" for the new car and road testers substantiated such claims. *Motor Trend* said that the only car capable of outrunning the Rebel from 0-to-60 was the fuel-injected Corvette.

A Rebel with overdrive and the 4:10 axle was made available for short acceleration runs at Daytona Beach in February 1957. *Motor Trend's* Joe Wherry reported a best time of 7.5 seconds from 0-to-60. *Hot Rod* magazine obtained a 9.4-second 0-to-60 time in a Rebel with Hydra-Matic and reported that the stick-shift version with 4.10 gears could break 8 seconds flat. The car with Hydra-Matic did the quarter-mile in 17 seconds at 84 mph.

Viewed in retrospect, the first Rebel ranks as one of the finest muscle cars ever made. It was offered in this format for just the single season and is now a rarity that AMC enthusiasts covet for their collections.

AMC & HUDSON

11

AMC & HUDSON

The 1965 AMC Rambler Marlin had a unique fastback roofline.

1965 Rambler Marlin

A muscle car from American Motors? The '65 1/2 Marlin had the hot fastback look of the Mustang 2 + 2, but did it really match the fastback Ford in appeal to high-performance lovers? Ramblers were supposed to be e-c-o-n-o-m-y cars. The Marlin looked different, but could it change what the initials AMC implied to most car buyers?

The Marlin roofline bowed on the 1964 Tarpon show car, which utilized the compact Rambler American's 106-inch stance. The Tarpon seemed to take aim at Plymouth's Valiant-based Barracuda and the '65 Ford Mustang, but the AMC brass blew Dick Teague's design up in size and sat it on the mid-size Rambler Classic chassis. From the beltline down, the two had the same body.

The 112-inch-wheelbase Rambler Classic was restyled for 1965 and grew about 5 inches longer. It now had distinctions from the upscale Ambassador, which got four additional inches of wheelbase and more individual styling.

Instead of stressing go-power, the Marlin emphasized comfort and roominess. It featured an Ambassador instrument panel and could be had with individually reclining front seats or slim bucket-type seats with a center console or center cushion.

Tucked under the hood was the same new 232-cid/155-hp Torque Command six used in the Ambassador. A pair of Gen-I AMC V-8s were optional. The first was a mild 287-cid 198-hp version. The second was the 327-cid/270-hp V-8 that

had been around since the days of the 1958 Ambassador.

In the transmission department, a three-speed standard shift came as the base unit. On cars without buckets, overdrive or three-speed Flash-O-Matic was optional. Those with the console and buckets had an interesting option called Twin-Stick overdrive, which boasted five forward speeds. You could also get Shift-Command Flash-O-Matic, which could be shifted manually if preferred.

AMC retained the outdated torque-tube-drive system with its enclosed drive shaft. There were coil springs at the rear. However, power disc front brakes and flanged rear drums were standard.

Not a screamer, the 327 Marlin was capable of average intermediate performance. *Mechanix Illustrated's* Tom McCahill found such a Marlin, with automatic transmission, capable of 0-to-60 mph in 9.7 seconds.

The factory base price for the Marlin was $3,100. There was sufficient curiosity in it to draw 10,327 orders in the short first-year run that followed its February 1965 introduction. That would be a high-water mark, so to speak, as the 1966 Marlin, minus the Rambler nameplate, some previously standard equipment and with the addition of an optional four-speed manual gearbox, found only 4,547 customers. It was in that model year that the 1966 1/2 Dodge Charger was introduced. It used the same formula with a fastback body on an intermediate chassis and sold better.

"Do Rogues really come with rally stripes?"

"No, but with the new engine
they drive that way."

'66 Rambler American Rogue

AMC & HUDSON

**The 1966 AMC Rambler Rogue sported a 290-cid V-8 and began a run of
several years' worth of interesting muscle cars from AMC.**

1966-67 Rambler Rogue V-8

Shaking up conservative Kenosha, Wisconsin, the Rambler Rogue Typhoon V-8 arrived on April 7, 1966. A year earlier, the first V-8 powered U.S. compacts had been made, but the near-300-hp Rogue was a definite "break-the-mold" machine for AMC.

A V-8 stuffed in the 106-inch-wheelbase Rambler American was exciting enough. On top of that, it was the debut of the newly designed AMC V-8, an engine that would be a standard bearer for the independent automaker in coming years.

The old AMC V-8—not used in Americans—dated back to 1956 and didn't have much room to grow. It was somewhat heavy and generally didn't take well to attempts to extract more ponies. In fact, 270 hp was the max for the 327-cid version of 1958-1966.

The new 290-cid "Typhoon" V-8 had a 3.75 x 3.28 bore and stroke, giving it plenty of growing room. It was rated at 200 hp with a two-barrel carburetor and 225 hp with a four-barrel. Eventually, 304-, 343-, 360-, 390- and 401-cid V-8s came out of the same thin-wall-casting design. This

engine gave both satisfactory service on the road and a good accounting of itself in racing and street performance. It wangled its way into some of the most interesting AMC muscle cars made after 1966.

The 290-cid V-8 was first slated to go into 1,500 special Rogue two-door hardtops with black tops and rear decks and Sungold lower bodies. For $2,961.60 you got the choice of Shift Command automatic or the American's first four-speed manual gear box—a Borg-Warner unit. Also included were spinner wheel covers, a blacked-out grille, V-badges on the rear fenders, power steering and power brakes.

Fewer than 1,500 Rogue V-8s were made. Since the option came in other Rambler Americans, there were leftover Rogue Typhoon pieces that went on six-cylinder cars and this doesn't help those finding or restoring these cars today.

Since any size V-8 would now fit in an American, they were used a couple of times for performance models. The 1969 SC/Rambler was the ultimate example and arrived just before AMC produced the last domestic car to carry the Rambler name.

13

The beefy Marlin was not a big hit among muscle car buyers in 1967, but its low production numbers make it a nice collector find today.

AMC & HUDSON

1967 Marlin "343"

The big-engined '67 Marlin was a "Walter Mitty" muscle car. Mitty was a book character who lived out his dreams, and the dreamy Marlin gave "Joe Lunchbox" a ticket to buy a sporty two-door fastback with a 5-liter V-8 for just over $3,000.

The new 343 V-8 was a bored-out version of the AMC's 290 and cost just $91 extra in a Marlin. It had a single four-barrel carb and generated 280 ponies at 4800 rpm with 365 ft.-lbs. of torque at 3000 rpm. While it wasn't the hottest car-and-engine combination on the road, the power was up, up, up from the previous year's 327-cid V-8.

Hot Rod wrung out a Marlin with this engine and compared it to the Dodge Charger. The car turned in a 0-to-60 mph time of 9.6 seconds and a 17.6-second quarter-mile at 82 mph. The writer compared this to the performance of a Charger with the base 383-cid two-barrel V-8. The same article mentioned a 343-cid 320-hp heavy-duty equipment option for the Marlin, indicating a hairier engine was available on special order. If any cars were sold this way, they are extremely difficult to find today.

The '67 Marlin's extra horsepower was handicapped by the fact that the size and weight of the car grew. For 1967, the "fish model" gained 6 inches in wheelbase and spanned 118 inches. Overall length got a 6 1/2-inch stretch. This added approximately 350 lbs. and did little for the car's power-to-weight ratio.

Styling-wise, the '67 model was cleaner and smoother looking. A new front-end treatment incorporated rally lights into a horizontal grille. The rear fenders had a "Coke bottle" shape characteristic of other muscle cars of the period.

Unlike the Mustangs, Barracudas and Chargers that it competed with, the Marlin did not come standard with bucket seats. They were $177 extra. A center console, priced at $113, was mandatory when the reclining buckets were ordered. Even vinyl upholstery was optional at $25. By the time a Marlin was all dressed up, the price tag was in the $3,500 range.

Perhaps it was predictable that AMC would run into problems marketing such a big car to anyone, let alone muscle-car buffs. The company had firmly established the image of being an expert in the small-car field. So the Marlin actually represented a double leap—one into muscle and the other into the large-car market. When the jump was first made, the Marlin got off to a good start. More than 10,000 were delivered in 1965, but the wind went out of its sails quickly. In 1966, production tapered off to just over 4,500. It bottomed out at 2,545 units for 1967, the nameplate's third and final year.

AMC would eventually tap the high-performance market with smaller models, such as the SC/Rambler and AMX, that better fit the AMC compact car image. For a time, things looked promising. It was not too little, just too late.

While the Marlin 343 wasn't a commercial success, it became a unique and rare automobile. Total production of cars with the optional "big" engine was counted in the low hundreds. That makes survivors desirable to AMC muscle car fans wanting to preserve models that reflect the company's high-performance history.

The 1968 AMX was a smaller sibling of the Javelin and had plenty of punch for a "little brother."

1968 AMX "390"

AMX stood for "American Motors Experimental." The car with that name was Step 2 in AMC's image revitalization program. The goal was to attract young car buyers who were scooping up high-performance models from other automakers. In the attempt to do this, designer Dick Teague created the first steel-bodied, two-seat American production model since the '57 Ford T-Bird.

From its inception as a prototype in '66, through its 2 1/2-year production run, to its ever-rising status as a collector muscle car today, the two-passenger AMX has always blazed new trails for a gets-no-respect corporate parent,

The first AMX was a non-running fiberglass concept car that let auto show attendees know that ultra-conservative AMC could design a car with pizzazz. A later running model had a "Ramble Seat" in place of the rear deck.

The AMC Javelin pony car bowed in the fall of 1967 as a 1968 model. The two-place AMX—which was a foot shorter in

A 390-cid motor stuffed into a tiny car with a 97-inch wheelbase made the AMX a mighty mite.

wheelbase and length—came out as a 1968-1/2 model. It bowed to the press at Daytona Beach, Florida and the Chicago Auto Show on February 24, 1968. Along with it came a 390-cid Gen II AMC V-8, which was rated at 315 hp.

The short 97-inch wheelbase cut the 390-powered AMX's curb weight to 3,205 lbs. That gave the little coupe a 10.8 lbs.-per-horsepower ratio when equipped with the 315-hp version of the 390-cid V-8. *Car and Driver* found this combination good for a 6.6 second 0-to-60 mph time. The 390 AMX did the standing-start quarter-mile in 14.8 seconds at 95 mph. Top speed was an estimated 122 mph.

Reclining bucket seats, carpeting, wood-grain interior trim and E70 x 14 Goodyear Polyglas tires were standard. Also included were a four-speed gearbox and heavy-duty suspension. Many buyers were happy with the performance of the standard 290-cid 225-hp V-8 or the one-step-up 343-cid 280-hp V-8, but the "390" was the most muscular engine option.

The '68 AMX was base-priced at $3,245, but *Road & Track* estimated the price of the 390-cid version at $3,500. Each AMX built in calendar year 1968 had a metal dashboard plate bearing a special serial number from 000001 to 006175. However, the first 550 cars, which were assembled in 1967, did not have this feature. That means that total production was 6,725 units.

In February 1968, on a test track in Texas, race driver Craig Breedlove established 106 world speed records with an AMX. About 50 special red-white-and-blue "Craig Breedlove" editions were then built. They had 290-cid V-8s and a four-speed manual transmission.

AMC & HUDSON

The Javelin SST got rave reviews for its handling, but it was not overly swift in a straight line.

1968 Javelin SST "390"

The SST was Dick Teague's handsome answer to the Mustang and Camaro. When the AMX "390" arrived at the Chicago Auto Show in February, the 390 Jav was right behind it. The 390 V-8 had the same outside dimensions as the AMC 290- and 343-cid V-8s and fit very easily into the SST. According to AMC expert Larry G. Mitchell, after the AMX came out, the 390 was put in other Javelins, too. "This engine doesn't show up in factory literature because it came out so late, but it makes sense," Mitchell says. "After all, it was just a question of taking the engine from this pile or that pile."

Car and Driver got its hands on the original Javelin "390" and used it in a comparison test printed in March 1968. "Our Javelin was the first 390 ever built," the magazine said. "But its long suit was its handling. It felt very much like a British sports car." Out of the six cars tested—Javelin SST, Camaro SS, Mustang 2+2 GT, Cougar XR-7, Barracuda Formula S and Firebird 400 HO—the SST was the favorite of everyone on the test crew as far as handling.

Car and Driver noted that the engine option was so new that "AMC hasn't had any time to play with the 390, at least officially, so we didn't expect the car to tear up the pavement." This proved to be an accurate assessment, as it was the slowest of the six pony cars with a 15.2-second quarter-mile at 92 mph. Part of the blame fell to AMC for limiting early 390s, like the *Car and Driver* test car, to only a three-speed manual transmission supplied by Borg-Warner. For comparison, a "Go-Package" Javelin with the 343-cid/280-hp and four-speed gearbox (that *Motor Trend* said was one of the best production units around) was good for an 8.1-second 0-to-60 time and a 15.4-second quarter-mile.

The '68 Javelin SST tested by *Car and Driver* had a manufacturer's suggested retail price of $3,943 with the 390 Go-Package. Its curb weight was 3,560 lbs. Other Javelin performance extras included front disc brakes, a special handling suspension (with a larger-diameter sway bar and heavy-duty springs and shocks), 5 1/2-inch-wide wheels, traction bars and quick-ratio power steering.

While Pontiac's GTO was selected as *Motor Trend* "Car of the Year," the magazine offered category awards in 1968. It picked the Javelin as the winner in the sports-personal category, saying that it exemplified "the most significant achievement for an all-new car and is the most notable new entry in (its) class."

Motor Trend liked the Javelin so much that it carried out a "Light-ning" project in a car that it called the Javelin SL (for Super Light). As the name implied, the editors started with a stock, off-the-showroom-floor Javelin and turned it into a completely modified, lightweight bomb that any enthusiast could duplicate without much difficulty. By removing accessories they cut 306 lbs. from the car, which was then fitted with a stock 390-cid V-8. In the "1/2-mile drags" the car covered the distance in 23.96 seconds and had a top speed of 102.22 mph.

With an Offenhauser aluminum intake and hood scoop, along with some chassis modifications, the Javelin SL did half-mile runs at 118.26 mph in 23.35 seconds. Later, at the Orange County Raceway, with its headers uncorked, the car did the quarter-mile in 13.97 seconds at 104.25 mph! Only one Javelin SL was built. Production of other versions included 29,097 Javelins and 26,027 SSTs.

The AMX changed little in 1968, and was still a lot of muscle in a small package.

1969 AMX

The AMX created nearly instant respect for AMC and speed records set by Craig and Lee Breedlove were thrown in for good measure. The 1969 version had few changes. With a full model year, AMC sold 8,293 examples— the two-passenger AMX's best year.

Power train availability was the same as 1968, with the 290-cid four-barrel V-8 rated at 225 hp as standard equipment. Adding $45 to the $3,297 base price bought a 343-cid/280-hp V-8. The 315-hp engine was also back, at a reasonable $123 additional. The desirable "Go Package" cost $233 on the 343s and $311 on the 390s and included E70 red line tires on 6-inch rims, a handling package, power disc brakes, Twin-Grip differential and the visually identifying over-the-top stripes.

At midyear, several "Big Bad" option packages were introduced in wild (at least for AMC) colors. A Hurst Competition Plus shifter for the Borg-Warner four-speed manual transmission was added to the options list at the same time at $205 extra. Javelins also got midyear Big Bad options.

Though the AMX Big Bad option was only $34, sales were limited, with 284 orange, 283 green and 195 blue copies being made. The most interesting and sought after AMX of all was the AMX SS. Only 52—or by some reports 53—AMX SS examples were sent to Hurst for "legalization" as drag racing cars. The AMX SS 390 was topped by a pair of 650-cfm Holley four-barrels on an Edelbrock aluminum cross-ram intake. Doug's Headers and other modifications resulted in a conservative advertised output of 340 hp. The suggested retail price of $5,994 seems a steal today, but was nearly twice the regular sticker price in 1969.

The AMX SS models went to NHRA and AHRA competitors, with Shirley Shahan —known as the "Drag-On-Lady"— being perhaps the most famous.

Two-place AMX production ended with the 1970 model run, but the nameplate returned on Javelin, Hornet, Concord and (finally) Spirit models. It was finally put to rest at midyear in 1980.

The two-passenger AMXs were the first AMC muscle cars to be sought by collectors other than AMC purists. Prices continue to outpace those of other AMC machinery, with special editions—not counting the AMC SS—topping $20,000 in top condition. For the few fortunate enough to have an SS, their value continues to blaze new trails for cars that were made in Kenosha, Wisconsin.

The AMX SS is particularly rare, and hard to miss with its loud color scheme.

The AMX reached its high point in 1969 with nearly 8,300 cars sold.

Javelin SST in Matador Red.

The Javelin SST could be had with a burley 390-cid, 315-hp V-8.

1969 Javelin 390

For '69, Javelins got a twin-venturi grille and a few mechanical upgrades, but no major changes. Engines again started with a six and V-8s were optional. The 290 continued to offer 200- and 225-hp editions and the latter came with an optional Hurst-shifted four-speed. The four-speed could also be linked to the carryover 343. The "big muscle" on the options list was the 390/315 V-8. It was available with dealer-installed factory high-performance parts, "Isky," Edelbrock or Offenhauser speed equipment and a Doug's Headers exhaust system. AMC was careful to offer it with stick or automatic.

Javelin SSTs included special trim, reclining bucket seats and added chrome. Originally there were two more or less straight stripes on the beltline. On January 9, these were changed to "C" stripes starting right behind the front wheel opening and running back along the mid-body feature line.

The optional "C" rally stripe was also available on a new Big Bad Javelin introduced in the spring. It came in Big Bad Orange, Big Bad Blue or Big Bad Green and included painted bumpers. Options included E70 x 14 Goodyear Polyglas Red Line tires, mag-style wheels, air conditioning, an "airless" spare tire, an 8-track stereo tape with AM radio, power disc brakes, a 140-mph speedo and big-faced tach, Twin-Grip differential, Adjust-O-Tilt steering, a roof-mounted spoiler, a close-ratio four-speed with Hurst shifter and more.

A "Mod" Javelin came in the same colors as the Big Bad Javelin and many Mod Javelins were also marketed with a Craig Breedlove package that included a spoiler on the rear of the roof and simulated exhaust rocker mountings.

Offered again was the Go-Package, which included a 390 or 343 V-8, heavy-duty springs and shocks, a thicker sway bar, wide wheel rims, Twin-Grip and other goodies. Traction bars were a factory-supplied dealer-installed item. As part of a performance package, buyers could install a pair of overlay fiberglass hood scoops, plus a new air cleaner that AMC claimed added 12 hp to the 390 due to better breathing.

Standard rear-end gears in the Javelin with a four-speed transmission were 3.54:1 and 3.15:1 gearing was a no-cost option. Serious enthusiasts could trot down to their AMC

dealership and pay extra for 3.73:1, 3.91:1, 4.10:1 and 5.00:1 axle ratios, as well as a Twin-Grip differential.

Production totals for 1969 included 17,389 Javelins and 23,286 Javelin SSTs. AMC built 17,147 of the 390-cid V-8s, but some were used in cars other than Javelin models.

Some people have a love then marry the Rebel.

Our Javelin is a beautiful machine with a beautiful body.

And our Rebel is a beautiful machine with a body. Which means you've got to get under its skin to see its beauty.

If you do, the Rebel may get under your skin.

You'll find beautiful little things like Molybdenum-filled #1 compression piston rings, not ordinary chrome-filled rings. These expensive "Moly-Tops" help eliminate scuffing the cylinder walls, and

could save you the expense of a ring job.

Your Rebel has a transistorized voltage regulator. It is solid state. No moving parts to break down, and give you the headache of costly repair bills.

Front shocks can go because of road dirt, grime and stones.

We put a stone and dirt shield on the Rebel's front shocks. This could save you from putting out a lot of money for replacing damaged shocks.

The Rebel has a coil resistor system.

AMC enjoyed plenty of success with the 1969 Javelin, as more than 40,000 combined Javelins and Javelin SSTs left the assembly line.

Jerry Heasley

**The "B" type SC/Rambler was distinguishable by its narrow striping.
The first 500 made had the red body side panels.**

1969 SC/Rambler

When AMC trotted out its new products at the Chicago Auto Show in March 1969, one of the most eye-catching vehicles was a small hardtop with a patriotic color scheme and a massive scoop dominating the front portion of its hoods. This AMC Hurst SC/Rambler represented one of the company's most unique models and the swan song for the Rambler American compact car.

Every muscle car lover knows the name of Hurst Performance Products. So, in 1969, American Motors hooked up with the Pennsylvania performance parts company to surprise everyone with the SC/Rambler (or "Scrambler" as some folks call it). Hurst actually thought up the idea and AMC bought it.

Based on the two-door Rogue hardtop coupe, the SC/Rambler stressed the big-engine-in-little-car format to the max. Below the hood went a 390-cid 325-hp V-8 linked to a Borg Warner four-speed manual gearbox with a Hurst shifter. A 3.54:1 rear axle with Twin-Grip differential was included, too. With a curb weight of about 3,000 lbs., the hot little car had a power-to-weight ratio of 10.03 lbs. per horsepower. This made it eligible for drag racing in the National Hot Rod Association's F-stock class.

The AMC factory estimated low 14-second quarter-miles at 98 mph. *Road Test* magazine clocked 14.4 at 100.44 mph

and managed to hit 109 mph without topping out. Modified SC/Ramblers have run the quarter-mile in the 9-second bracket.

In addition to the power team, the SC/Rambler included a long list of extra-cost goodies like a big hood scoop for Ram-Air induction, fat dual exhaust pipes, a column-mounted Sun tachometer and Bendix front disc brakes. Blue-finished five-spoke mag-style wheels, 14 x 6-inch rims, wheel trim rings and fat red-striped Goodyear tires were also standard. The SC/Rambler interior was done in plain-looking gray vinyl, but it had red-white-and-blue headrests. This color scheme was carried onto the body, in several variations. Full carpeting was another selling feature.

The first 500 cars built had red center body side panels and thick blue horizontal racing stripes on the hood, roof and deck. A blue arrow pointed towards the scoop, which had large letters spelling the word "AIR" and calling out the engine size. This was the "A" type graphic treatment.

When the cars sold quickly, another batch was made with new "B" type trim. These had a mostly white exterior with narrow red and blue stripes. Then, a third batch of cars was made, reverting to the type "A" trim, but lacking all of the elements. The A-finished cars seem to be the more common of the 1,512 SC/Ramblers built.

The AMX was longer, lower, and had a bigger engine for 1970.

Jerry Heasley

1970 AMX

"We made the AMX look tougher this year because it's tougher this year," heralded advertisements for the 1970 edition of American Motors' two-seat sports car. It came with a new 360-cid V-8 as standard equipment. This engine developed 290 hp—65 more than last season's 343-cid base engine. Other standard features included courtesy lights, a heavy-duty 60-amp. battery, rear torque links (traction bars), a tachometer, a 140-mph speedometer, 14 x 6-inch styled steel wheels, fiberglass-belted Polyglas™ wide profile tires, an energy-absorbing anti-theft steering column, a Space-Saver spare tire, heavy-duty shocks and springs, an Autolite Model 4300 four-barrel carburetor and dual exhausts.

Base-priced at $3,395 (and advertised as "the only American sports car that costs less than $4,000") the new AMX had a production run of 4,116 units, which made it the rarest of the three two-seat editions—1968, 1969,1970—that AMC offered. The height of the fastback coupe was reduced about one inch. While the wheelbase remained at 97 inches, the car's overall length grew about 2 inches to 179 inches. The increase gave it a longer nose and made it look more like its Mustang-Camaro-Firebird-Cougar-Barracuda-Challenger competitors, which should have helped sales, but didn't. It sold better when it was a totally distinct car. At 3,126 lbs., it was the heaviest AMX yet, but only by 29 lbs., so with the bigger engine the effect on performance was negligible.

Appearance-wise, the AMX got new rear lamps and a completely restyled front end that was shared with Javelin performance models. The frontal treatment featured a grille that was flush with the hood and a redesigned bumper that housed the "mutant square" parking lamps. A horizontally divided, crosshatched grille insert with four very prominent, bright horizontal moldings was used. AMX lettering filled a gap at the center of the second and third moldings. The

grille also incorporated circular rally lights and the bumper included an air scoop system to cool the front brakes. The restyled hood had a large ram-induction scoop that took in cold air for the engine.

Inside the AMX cockpit were new contoured high-back bucket seats with integral head restraints and a completely redesigned instrument panel. An exclusive Corning safety windshield was also available.

An all-synchromesh "four-on-the-floor" transmission with a Hurst shifter was standard. Performance options included the AMX 390-cid V-8 with 325 hp and a close-ratio four-speed manual transmission. Very desirable today is the code 391-392 "Go-Package," that was available on 360-powered AMXs for $299 and on 390-powered AMXs for $384. It included power front disc brakes, F70-14 raised white-letter tires, a handling package, a heavy-duty cooling system and a functional Ram-Air hood scoop.

The metal dashboard plates affixed to 1970 models were numbered 014469 to 18584. This was the final year for the original type AMX. Although the nameplate was to be used again on Javelin- and Hornet-based models, the two-seater AMX was the true sports car and the real high-performance edition.

Eric Dahlquist wrote up the '70 AMX in the December 1969 edition of *Motor Trend* and summed it up as "one of the better constructed cars around." The test car had the optional 390-cid V-8 that produced 325 hp at 5000 rpm and 420 lbs.-ft. of torque at 3000 rpm. It drove through the Borg-Warner four-speed gearbox to a 3.54:1 rear axle. Zero-to-60 mph took 6.56 seconds and Dahlquist did the standing-start quarter-mile in 14.68 seconds at 92 mph. Top speed in fourth gear was recorded as 109 mph.

The 1970 Javelin was plenty muscular even without the spoiler of the special editions.

1970 Javelin SST

A full-page advertisement in the March 1970 issue of *Motor Trend* was designed to catch the eye of enthusiasts looking to buy a new car. "Starting now, you can buy a Javelin with a spoiler designed by Mark Donahue," said the copy. Depicted was the rear view of an orange Javelin with all the extras needed to give it the image of a Trans-Am racecar. On the right-hand corner of the spoiler was Mark Donahue's signature in chrome.

Donahue had made history with his racing Javelin. He and car builder Roger Penske teamed up to win Trans-Am championships in 1968 and 1969, then signed a three-year contract with AMC to drive Javelins in that road racing series.

One of the modifications they made to their Trans-Am Javelin was Donahue's spoiler. To make this appendage legal for racing, the spoiler had to be *homologated* through its use on at least 2,500 cars that the public could buy. That motivated AMC to release the "Mark Donahue" Javelin.

In addition to the spoiler, the special Javelin SSTs came standard with other extras including dual exhausts, power front disc brakes, E70 x 14 white-letter wide-profile tires, 14 x 6-in. wheels, a handling package and a Ram-Air induction system that incorporated the AMX hood. The signature of Mark Donahue was seen on the right side of the spoiler. A

"Mark Donahue Signature Edition" AMX was also offered. This model came with the choice of a 360- or 390-cid V-8. Buyers could also go with a console-shift automatic transmission or a four-speed manual transmission with a Hurst shifter. 2,501 cars were built this way.

Trans-Am editions were also offered in 1970. These were replicas of Ronnie Kaplan's racing cars, with a red-white-and-blue paint scheme devised by industrial designer Brooks Stevens. Standard, in addition to SST equipment (minus sill moldings and paint stripes), were front and rear spoilers, black vinyl seats, the 390 "Go Package," a four-speed gearbox with Hurst shifter, a 140-mph speedometer, 14 x 6-inch wheels, a heavy-duty cooling system, a 3.91:1 rear axle and Twin-Grip differential and F70-14 glass-belted tires. The Trans-Am edition had a $3,995 sticker price. It weighed 3,340 lbs. and only 100 copies were built, just enough to qualify for Trans-Am racing.

The 1970 Javelin SST with the 390-cid/325-hp engine had only 10.4 lbs. per horsepower and could move pretty well. Zero to 60 mph took 7.6 seconds and the standing-start quarter-mile could be done in 15.1 seconds. Total Javelin production for 1970 dropped down to 28,210 cars (a 31 percent decline), of which 19,714 were SSTs, including the Mark Donahue and Trans-Am special editions.

The Trans-Am Javelin SST had the trademark spoiler and Mark Donahue signature.

Phil Kunz

The memorable Rebel "Machine" had few rivals when it came to getting noticed. Buyers could opt out of the patriotic color scheme, however, and get their Machine outfitted in a solid color.

1970 Rebel "Machine"

The AMC Rebel Machine was fast! It had AMC's biggest, most powerful 390 V-8. It produced 340 galloping ponies at 5100 rpm. The "standard stuff" list was filled with a four-speed, close-ratio tranny, a Hurst shifter, a lighted 8000-rpm hood tach, Ram Air, 3.54:1 or 3.91:1 rear axles, heavy-duty shocks and springs, a low-back-pressure dual exhaust system, front and rear sway bars, 15-inch raised white-letter tires, styled wheels, high-back bucket seats and power disc brakes.

"Standing before you is the car you've always wanted," AMC teased in a two-page introductory ad in the December 1969 issue of *Hot Rod* magazine. It showed the "Machine," that had actually debuted two months earlier at the National Hot Rod Association World Championship drag races.

The ad copy warned, "Incidentally, if you have delusions of entering the Daytona 500 with the Machine, or challenging people at random, the Machine is not that fast. You should know that. For instance, it is not as fast on the getaway as a 427 Corvette, or a Hemi, but it is faster on the getaway than a Volkswagen, a slow freight train, and your old man's Cadillac." Which meant it was plenty fast enough.

All this came at a price of $3,475 in a car with a 114-

inch wheelbase and curb weight of 3,640 lbs. and produced performance in the range of 14.4-second quarter-miles at a 98-mph speed. It also produced sales of 2,326 cars.

The first 100 "Machines" delivered from the AMC factory in Kenosha, Wisconsin, were finished in white. Hurst Performance Products did up the lower beltline stripes and hood in blue and then added red stripes on the upper body sides. At the rear, red-white-and-blue stripes ran across the fender tips and deck. Special "The Machine" emblems were tacked on the front fender sides and on the rear trim panel's right-hand side.

For buyers who didn't like the patriotic paint scheme, AMC advertised, "If you like everything about it except for the paint job, which admittedly looks startling, you can order the car painted in the color of your choice." When buyers did this, they got silver striping and a blacked-out hood. The original color scheme became a $75 option.

Although "The Machine" was a joint venture between AMC and Hurst, this association wasn't promoted to buyers. Customers were offered a chance to purchase "Up with the Rebel Machine" decals for 25 cents each. We wonder what those decals are worth now?

The 1974 Javelin-AMX was a nice-looking car, and its optional 330-horsepower mill was the most powerful motor ever offered by AMC.

1971-1974 Javelin-AMX "401"

From 1971 on, the AMX shared the Javelin four-seater body. "It's not really an AMX, it's a Javelin-AMX, taking over the top of the line in this series," said *Hot Rod* in October 1970. The new AMX was longer, wider and slightly lower than before. The front tread was the same, but the rear tread was three inches wider.

Exclusive to the AMX was a rear-facing cowl-induction hood, add-on spoilers, AMX emblems and special trim pieces. Standard 1971 V-8s were a 304/210 two-barrel job for Javelins (except police cars) and a 360/245 two-barrel version for the Javelin-AMX. A 285-hp 360 with a four-barrel carb was extra in Javelin-AMXs, but the muscle-car mill for the high-performance model was a new 401-cid V-8 that evolved from the 390. With 330 hp, it was the most powerful AMC engine ever offered.

In 1971, only 2,054 Javelin-AMXs were produced. In addition, the 1971 Javelin SST production total of 22,964 units included 100 Alabama State Police "Interceptors" with 401-cid V-8s. In 1972, Javelin-AMX output rose to 3,220.

Driver George Follmer took the '71 and '72 Trans-Am racing titles for AMC driving Javelins and a special "Trans-Am Victory" package was offered for 1973. It had a front fender decal pointing out that the model had won the SCCA race series in 1971-1972. Proving that racing helped sell cars, Javelin-AMX production rose to 5,707. The last year for the Javelin-AMX was 1974, when 4,980 were built.

The AMC 401-cid V-8 made the Javelin-AMX a real muscle car, despite its large four-place size and heavier weight. While the cars now had to move about 13 lbs. per horsepower, they were only a tad slower than the four-passenger Javelin 390s

offered from 1968-1970.

The 401 had a 4.17 x 3.68-inch bore and stroke, a four-barrel carburetor and a 9.5:1 compression ratio. It developed 330 hp at 5200 rpm and 430 lbs.-ft. of torque at 3300 rpm.

In 1972, a "401" Javelin-AMX was road tested. It moved from 0-to-60 mph in 8.3 seconds and did the quarter-mile in 16.1 seconds. Although 50 lbs. heavier, a 1973 Javelin-AMX with the same engine required only 7.7 seconds for 0-to-60 and 15.5 seconds for the quarter-mile.

Besides being the most powerful engine ever offered in a Javelin, the 1971 version of the 401 was the last to require premium gas. In 1972, it was de-tuned to fall into the low-compression category and its output rating went to 255 net horsepower.

The 1971 Javelin-AMX "401" was the last version of the 401-cid motor to require premium gas.

AMC & HUDSON

Adding the "Go Package" to the 1971 Hornet SC got the buyer a
285-hp motor stuffed into a small body for less than $3,000.

Jerry Heasley

1971 Hornet SC/360

American Motors thought that it was introducing a sensible alternative to the "money-squeezing, insurance-strangling muscle cars of America" when it advertised the all-new Hornet SC/360 in the December 1970 issue of *Hot Rod* magazine. Little did the company realize that it was also bringing out a rarity. Although it expected to make 4,000 of the cars and optimistically suggested that 10,000 sales might be possible, only 784 were ever made. That's what makes the SC/360 an especially interesting car. The model was never offered again, although a fairly mild version of the 360-cid V-8 was offered in other Hornets for a while.

The compact Hornet replaced the Rambler (formerly Rambler American) for 1970. It was efficiently sized with a 108-inch wheelbase and short 179.6-inch overall length. It was only 70.6 inches wide, despite having wheel wells that looked large enough to stuff in racing slicks. The largest engine at first was a 304-cid V-8, but that changed when the '71 SC/360 was introduced.

A 360-cid V-8 with 245 hp was standard for the base price of $2,663, along with: a "four-on-the-floor" all-synchromesh transmission, a heavy-duty clutch, D70 x 14 Polyglas tires,

14 x 6-inch mag-style wheels, a Space Saver spare, rally stripes and individually reclining seats. For $199 more you got the Go-Package with an AM 4300 model 1RA4 four-barrel carburetor, the 285-hp power plant with dual exhaust, a functional flat-black Ram-Air hood scoop, a handling package, raised white-letter tires and a big tachometer. A four-speed manual gearbox with Hurst shifter or a Borg-Warner Shift-Command automatic (for $237.85) and a choice of 3.15:1 (with automatic) or 3.54:1 and 3.91:1 rear axles with a Dana Twin-Grip differential were other options.

A *Hot Rod* road test of the SC/360 was printed in the December 1970 issue of the magazine. The virtually out-of-the-box car, fitted with the automatic, was put through its paces five times and turned in a top performance of 94.63 mph in the quarter-mile with a 14.80-second elapsed time. Can-Am driver Steve Diulo then wrung it out on a road racing course and summed it up as a great little car with slow steering that was "really a lotta car for the money!" Two other advantages were that it avoided a 25 percent surcharge insurance companies were levying on other muscle cars and that it got fuel economy as high as 17 mpg in freeway driving.

Roger Penske and Bobby Allison were among the big league
drivers who campaigned racing versions of the Matador X-2.

AMC & HUDSON

1977-1978 Matador X-2

You won't find it on old AMC option lists and it's not likely to be in the factory parts books, but there was an X-2 dress-up kit for the Matador coupe.

AMC totally redesigned the intermediate-sized Matador two-door for 1974 and super speedway stock car racing was one of the reasons the car was revamped. While the new Matador's fastback roofline and overall styling generated extremes of opinion, the new body was well suited, aerodynamically, for racetrack duties.

The Matador front end was less than sleek, however. The car's free-standing bumpers, huge headlight buckets and increasingly inward-sloping grille were all counter to basic aerodynamic principles in shape and appearance.

A formal rear window option cleaned up the back of the car, but help was still needed up front and AMC knew it. After Roger Penske and Bobby Allison gave up racing Matadors, early in 1976, Allison decided to race them on his own. He competed in 1977 NASCAR Winston Cup competition.

Some time during this period, a new front end was devised for the Matador. It featured lower body extensions under the headlights to smooth out the air flow. In addition, a 1975 grille was used. The end sections of the grille were cut off and the center section was turned upside down to meet the bumper.

AMC tried to get NASCAR to approve this aerodynamic package for racing, but the company's request was turned down. Allison didn't win NASCAR races with the Matadors in 1977, but he raced them in USAC and other events in 1978, using the new front end.

AMC made at least one Matador with the restyled front end. This "Barcelona Coupe" was seen parked in the garage area at Michigan International Raceway (MIR) during the NASCAR race in 1977. AMC used MIR to emission-test its cars during the week. The restyling on the car was all professionally done.

When Allison was questioned about the kit, he immediately knew what it was. "You mean the X-2. AMC made up a bunch of kits and we put 'em on cars for sale around my home town (Hueytown, Alabama). They sold right away," he said.

The X-2 nomenclature was no doubt derived from the Matador X package. How many X-2s were made? Who installed the kits? Are there any left today? These are some of the questions that AMC muscle car collectors ask about these cars.

AMC & HUDSON

American Motors revived the "AMX" moniker on a dressed-up 1978 Concord. The car was
probably more noteworthy for its exterior package and racey look than its 304-cid V-8.

1978 AMX

One of the distinctive facets of the mid-'70s automotive scene was that of "visual muscle" cars. These were cars that had the appearance of a muscle car even after government-mandated emissions regulations stifled the availability of true high-performance engines. Such machines combined rather wild graphics and styling with sedate, government-regulated drive trains. One such car was Ford's Mustang II Cobra. Another such car was the 1977 Hornet coupe with the AMX option.

This hot-looking AMC product revived the AMX name, which had last been seen on the top-of-the-line Javelin in 1974. The $799 AMX option package included front and rear wheel flares, bright body paint, body graphics, rear window louvers and the almost-mandatory large hood decal.

These add-on parts apparently weren't enough to raise sales and the AMX name returned for 1978. The racy-looking equipment was again offered for the two-door notchback body style, but this car was no longer called the Hornet. As an attempt to upgrade its image, AMC used the Concord name on the model in 1978. The AMX version was then marketed as a separate series.

The AMX used the Gremlin front end and its own blacked-out grille insert. Also, there was a front spoiler, painted bumpers, rubber-like wheel flares, rear window louvers, a brushed-aluminum "basket handle" over the roof at the B-pillars, slotted wheels and an assortment of bright colors.

Inside the AMX buyers found bucket-type seats, a center console, a Rally instrument cluster, a tach, a Soft-Feel steering wheel and other special trim items.

Under the hood, power offerings were no better than the year before, with the 258-cid/120-hp six as base engine. A 304-cid V-8 was on the options list. The federal version produced 130 net horsepower and the California-only version produced 100 nhp. The V-8 came only with automatic transmission.

Performance of the V-8-powered AMX was better than average for the era, although it was no challenge to '60s and early '70s AMC muscle cars. The six-cylinder AMX listed for $4,649 and the V-8 was $250 additional.

The move to the Concord name paid off for the 1978 model year with 121,293 Concords being ordered compared to 77,843 Hornets the year before. AMX production was broken out as 2,540 units. That was considered high enough to keep the model name around another year, although it was low enough to make the car rather hard to find and pretty rare today.

The Buick Special with a 236-hp V-8 was a forerunner to the many muscle cars that followed.

1955 Century

One of the best-selling performance cars of the '50s came from Buick. When Buick engineers stuffed the big Roadmaster V-8 into the small Special chassis, they created the '54 Century and it galloped to the front of the horsepower race.

Prior to World War II, the Century nameplate had been synonymous with performance and the formula was the same: big eight in a small chassis. The '54 model swapped the traditional straight eight for an overhead-valve V-8 and came in two versions: 195 hp with stick shift, and 200 hp with Dynaflow Drive.

That was a beginning, but the 1955 models took a big, power-packed jump up the power curve and delivered 236 hp from 322 cubes. That was the same number of ponies found under the hoods of the bigger and much heavier Super and Roadmaster models.

Motor Life magazine reported the Dynaflow-equipped Century Riviera Coupe could fly from 0-to-60 mph in 10.9 seconds. The only faster car the magazine tested that year was the diminutive two-seat T-Bird, which did 60 mph in 10.75 seconds.

Dynaflow—often dismissed as "Dynaflush"—wasn't known as a performance-type automatic transmission, but for 1955 the $193 option was reworked with a new Variable-Pitch Twin-Turbine setup and did a much better job in transferring power to the rear wheels.

Stock-car drivers and even drag racers noticed the Century in 1955 and it logged a pair of checkered flags in Grand National contests. Karl Kiekaefer's famed Mercury Outboard racing team had a few Buicks in its fleet, too. While not a dominator, the '55 Century was a worthy footnote in racing history because Buick's next win didn't come until 1981 (with Chevy power).

The '55 selling season was a high-water mark for the American automobile industry and Buick as well. The brand moved into third place in the national sales rankings and the Century drew 158,796 buyers, darn near twice as many as the year before.

The most popular Century was the two-door Riviera hardtop that listed for $2,601 and attracted 80,338 buyers. The convertible is worth the most today. It listed for $2,991 and only 5,588 were made. A Riviera sedan (America's first four-door hardtop) was added as a midyear model. With a base price of $2,733, it sold well and 55,088 were built.

The rarest model in the '55 Century series was the specially built two-door sedan. It was made exclusively for the California Highway Patrol, which ordered 270 cars, half with stick shift.

The Century series continued in the Buick lineup through 1958, but sales never matched 1955. Later, the name reappeared on a variety of different types of Buicks.

1957 Century

I had to add the '57 Century to this book because I own one and it's a blast to drive fast. It's got just the right rumble (thanks to a nasty dual exhaust setup) and it blasts away from a traffic light like a rocket-propelled grenade. My Caprice state trooper car might be a tad quicker, but the Century *feels* like the faster of the two. And it's a heavy four-door sedan, so imagine the kick you get in a coupe!

For 1957, Buick's styling changes from 1956 models were vast. A new grille insert brought the look of an electric shaver back to the Buick front end. As kids, we loved these cars because the round, red-white-and-blue badge in the center of the grille told you the model year. That emblem had handsome chrome wings protruding from it. Across the hood was the B-U-I-C-K name in bold chrome letters.

The grille looked much wider than before, with its massive "bumper bombs" spread to the outer edges. The headlights had neatly visored chrome bezels like a custom car out of the pages of *Motor Trend*. The portholes were again allocated by horsepower, three to Specials and four to other models. Parallel ridges were seen on the roofs of all hardtops and sedans, except on cars in the Super series. These sculpted creases added a crisp, aircraft fuselage look. New rear window treatments were seen, with rear window dividers in some Special, Century and Roadmaster models.

"Take off in the dream car to drive!" was a slogan that summed up the '57 Buick Century's market appeal. With the smaller body, it looked lean and low. With the Roadmaster V-8 it could really go. To the basic 364-cid Buick V-8, the Century added a four-barrel carburetor and a 10.0:1 compression ratio to get up to 300 hp. Buick said it had "the power-pack built right in at no extra cost."

Century trim included the Century name on the rear body sides (wagons said "Caballero), above the sweepspear dip, and a chrome check mark below the Century script. The trunk also displayed the Century name. A four-door sedan was reinstated in the Century series, while the deluxe four-door hardtop was dropped. The most expensive Century—and the series' only wagon—was the $3,831 Caballero model. The convertible, with 4,085 assemblies, had the lowest production of all Centurys. Model-year production of all Buicks totaled 405,086 cars representing 6.4 percent of all U.S. car sales. This included some 66,000 Centurys.

BUICK

1965 Riviera Gran Sport

It's said that GM styling chief William Mitchell used the Jaguar sports saloon as his inspiration for the first Riviera. But it wasn't until the 1965 Riviera Gran Sport arrived that the truly sporty side of this sports-personal car revealed itself. The "GS" had the gorgeous looks of the "Riv" combined with the heart of a true muscle car

Unlike other Buicks, including the youth-oriented Wildcat, the Riviera GS came with just one engine-and-transmission combination. This made it quickly apparent that Buick had a clear vision of what it wanted the model to be.

Powering the Riviera GS was a 425-cid V-8 with a 10.25:1 compression ratio. This engine produced 360 hp at 4400 rpm and 465 lbs.-ft. of torque at 2800 rpm. It put out .84 hp per cubic inch, very close to the legendary 1:1 ratio of Chrysler 300s and Corvettes.

Hooked up to the 425 was the latest GM three-speed Hydra-Matic. When *Car and Driver* tested the car in June 1965, it called this gearbox "without question, the best automatic transmission in the world."

A limited-slip differential with 3.42:1 gearing was used in the GS. It was combined with a 117-inch wheelbase to create a relatively compact and well-balanced car.

The Riviera GS was definitely hot with its dual four-barrel Carter AFB carbs, a dual exhaust system with large-diameter pipes and bright metal engine accents (including a large, chrome-plated air cleaner and polished, ribbed valve covers). Full wheel covers and Gran Sport lettering below the Riviera script on the deck lid and on the front fenders helped set the car apart visually.

A *Motor Trend* test at Willow Springs Raceway, early in 1965, yielded a quarter-mile run in 16.2 seconds, with a terminal speed of 87 mph. More importantly for a grand touring-type car, the top speed was 123 mph. *Car and Driver* reported a 7.2-second 0-to-60 time and an even better quarter-mile run of 15.5 seconds at 95 mph.

In muscle car fashion, the GS package also included a heavier front anti-roll bar than the standard Riviera, stiffer

A 360-hp Wildcat V-8 isn't all that's new with Riviera Gran Sport. But what a start.

You can easily spend a party or two talking enthusiastically about the engine in Buick's new Riviera Gran Sport. But after your friends have heard all there is to hear, you can start in on some of the Gran Sport's extra added attractions. A limited-slip differential. Power steering and brakes. If you specified them, the heavy-duty springs, shocks and stabilizer bar. Better than talking, though, is driving. You can start that at your Buick dealer's. After all, wouldn't you really rather have a Buick?
One of the new Gran Sports from Buick
You need not be a professional driver to qualify.

BUICK MOTOR DIVISION

With a 425-cid V-8 under the hood, a driver in a hurry could wind their 1965 Riviera GS up to over 120 mph.

shock absorbers, stiffer springs at all four wheels, stiffer bushings in the rear suspension and a higher-capacity exhaust system designed to give less back pressure and eliminate exhaust noise. *Car and Driver* said it "had that stumbling, sort of Chris-Craft V-8 rumble, much beloved of small boys—and ex-small boys—all over these United States."

The real significance of this car was the fact that Bill Mitchell and the engineers at GM achieved the goal that Mitchell had set quite well. *Car and Driver* loved the car and called it, "indecent luxury, but nice."

Buick described its 1965 GS as "a howitzer with windshield wipers."

BUICK

1965 Skylark GS

Buick responded to the mid-'64 introduction of the GTO with the new midyear '65 Skylark GS. "There is mounting evidence that our engineers have turned into a bunch of performance enthusiasts," said one ad. "First they stuff the Wildcat full of engine. Then the Riviera Gran Sport. And now this, the Skylark GS, which is almost like having your own, personal-type nuclear deterrent."

With a 400/325 V-8, a four-barrel carburetor and a 10.25:1 compression ratio, the Skylark GS tested by *Motor Trend* in May 1965 cranked out .81 hp per cubic inch and fed it through a two-speed Super Turbine 300 automatic transmission with a floor-mounted shifter. (A floor-mounted three-speed stick shift was standard.) The magazine reported that its 3,720-lb. test car reached the 60-mph mark in a mere 7.8 seconds. It did the quarter-mile in 16.6 seconds at 86 mph and had a top speed of 116 mph.

Buick engineers said that the Skylark GS was completely different than the regular Specials because all three body styles—coupe, hardtop and convertible—used a beefed-up convertible-type frame that resisted torque flexing. Naturally, it was fitted with heavy-duty shocks and springs and a stiffer anti-roll bar up front. Buick's marketing people claimed that the Skylark GS was like "a howitzer with windshield wipers."

Other features of the first Skylark GS included heavy-duty upper control arm bushings, dual exhausts, 7.75 x 14 tires and a choice of 2.78:1, 3.08:1, 3.23:1, 3.36:1, 3.55:1 and 3.73:1 rear axle ratios. To show what a Skylark Gran Sport

The sturdier convertible frame was used in all three 1965 GS cars — the coupe, hardtop and convertible.

could do set up with 4.30 gears and cheater slicks, *Motor Trend* mentioned that Lenny Kennedy's race-prepped example clocked a 13.42-second, 104.46-mph quarter-mile run at the Winternational Drags.

"It seems to us that Buick has another winner in the Skylark Gran Sport," said Bob McVay, *Motor Trend's* assistant technical editor. "The point is that better cars are being built—and Buick is building them!"

Jerry Heasley

At 4,375 lbs., the 1966 Riviera was definitely among the biggest muscle cars ever built.

1966 Riviera Gran Sport

For 1966, the Buick Riviera was treated to a major redo, sharing a new "E-body" with the Oldsmobile Toronado. "Though the details are different, they do have the same taut look," said *Road & Track* in its February 1966 road test. The Rivera had a smoother and cleaner look than the Toronado without its exaggerated wheel humps or cluttered hood.

The new Riviera's 119-inch wheelbase was 2 inches longer than before. It boosted overall length up to 211 inches and curb weight to 4,375 lbs. As a result, the Riviera engine was enlarged. The 425-cid V-8 had a bore and stroke of 4.31 x 3.64 inches. With the factory single-barrel carburetor and a 10.25:1 compression ratio it produced 340 hp at 4400 rpm and 465 lbs.-ft. of torque at 2800 rpm.

To turn the larger, heavier Riviera into a true muscle car, you really had to add a dealer-installed dual four-barrel carburetor setup. *Road & Track's* test car had this option and others that raised the window sticker from the basic list price of $4,424 up to $5,940! The optional version produced 360 hp at 4400 rpm and 465 ft.-lbs. of torque at 2800 rpm.

With the 360-hp job, the Riviera Gran Sport was moving about 13.1 pounds for each unit of horsepower and moving faster as well. It took 8.1 seconds to get up to 60 mph and 16.7 seconds to cover the quarter-mile, with an 86.7-mph terminal speed. The magazine pointed out that while the Riviera seemed "too big," it was actually 2 inches shorter than a Chevy Impala and 10 inches under a Pontiac Bonneville.

Road & Track thought that the Gran Sport equipment package was a real bargain for its $176.82 installed price. The option included dual exhausts, a 3.23:1 ratio rear axle with positraction, 8.45-15 Red Line or White Line tires and a stiffer-than-stock suspension. "Considering everything you get in size, speed, power, comfort, luxury, prestige and, yes, even road manners, the Riviera Gran Sport has to be in a class by itself," said the magazine.

Jerry Heasley

The Riviera GS was a long, smooth muscle car with a big 340-hp V-8 under the hood and great road manners.

This is what mountain country looks like to the tuned car.

What makes a car a car is styling, performance, ride and handling. Only when they're all tuned together is the car a Buick. Like this '66 Skylark Gran Sport.

As a matter of fact, it's what miserable traffic looks like to the tuned car. And twisty, winding roads. And a "ROAD UNDER CONSTRUCTION," too.

For the tuned car makes a habit of making unwelcome sights disappear.

Which makes the tuned car a most welcome sight indeed.

The **Skylark Gran Sport**—one of the tuned cars. The Skylark GS in the picture is, like every tuned car, a beautiful blend of styling, performance, ride and handling. Which means it rides as smoothly as it performs. (A suspension designed specifically for the GS sees to the ride. A 325-hp Wildcat V-8 sees to

the performing.) And it handles as briskly and responsively as you'd expect a car that looks like this to handle. (Alas, some cars don't live up to the way they look. The tuned car always does.)

How the tuned car works its wonders. If you're intent on making mountains evaporate, you've got to get out of the test lab, we say. So we do a lot of our product development out in the real world, on real roads, where real people drive.

For instance, in the mountains of West Virginia. (The residents of Pott's Mountain are getting used to seeing Buicks running up and down, up and down.) For another instance,

at Pikes Peak. (A lot of cars are tested in daring drives *up* Pikes Peak. Ours are tested in heroic drives *down* Pikes Peak. That's one of the best ways we know to learn about ride and handling and braking.)

All this means you aren't likely to run into a driving situation that we haven't already seen. And *that* means the tuned car is tuned to your kind of driving.

Tuned safety equipment, even. Built and blended into every Buick are padded sun visors and a padded dash. Two-speed electric wipers and windshield washers. A shatter resistant mirror inside and a rear-view mirror outside. Back-up lights. And seat belts all

around, which we exhort you—nay, plead with you—to buckle on. (Is there nothing we won't do to make sure you're in fit shape to come back for more Buicks? Nothing.)

How to turn your country into tuned car country. The only thing standing between you and the tuned car is your Buick dealer. And an easier obstacle to surmount you've never met.

Unless you count mountains.

Wouldn't you really rather have a Buick?

**1966 Buick.
The tuned car.**

The mid-season addition of a 401-cid/340-hp engine option made the Skylark GS a contender for the title of best heavyweight muscle car around.

1966 Skylark Gran Sport

Sports car racer Masten Gregory changed his mind after driving a '66 Skylark GS around Bridgehampton racecourse for *Car and Driver*. " I didn't like the car at first, because I thought it was too soft," he admitted. "But as I got used to it, I started liking it quite a bit."

Skylark GS became a separate high-performance series in 1966 and took Buick one step closer to a real muscle car image. *Motor Trend's* Steve Kelly also had an awakening. "Now and then, we select a car to test which at the outset promises nothing spectacular, but by the conclusion of the testing program, has shown itself to be an automobile of many virtues and few vices," he said. "This is the story, in part, of the Buick Gran Sport."

The 1966 Gran Sport had most of the plusher features of the Skylark models, plus bright simulated air scoops, side paint stripes, a blacked-out grille, specific GS badges on the grille and deck and a black-finished rear beauty panel. It also featured a heavy-duty suspension, an all-vinyl interior with a standard notchback bench seat up front (bucket seats were optional), carpeting and full wheel covers. Buyers could chose from White Line or Red Line tires in size 7.75 x 14. Unlike other Skylarks, the GS-400 had no hood ornament.

The standard GS V-8 was the 401/325 "Wildcat" with 10.25:1 compression and a four-barrel carburetor. It developed 445 ft.-lbs. of torque at 2800 rpm. To placate the

General Motors brass, the engine was advertised as the "400," which made it "legal" for use in an intermediate-sized GM car under corporate rules. In mid-season, a 340-hp engine option was released.

Three models were offered. The coupe listed for $2,956, weighed in at 3,479 lbs. and had a production run of 1,835 units. Tipping the scales at 3,428 lbs. was the sport coupe or hardtop, which sold for $3,019 and saw 9,934 assemblies. The convertible sold for $3,167, weighed 3,532 lbs. and racked up 2,047 assemblies.

Motor Trend actually tested two Skylark GS hardtops, both with Super Turbine automatic transmission. One was loaded with all power options and the other had no power options and several mild upgrades, such a 4.30:1 rear axle, racing slicks, headers, shimmed front springs and a transmission kick-down switch. The stock version weighed 3,660 lbs. and retailed for $3,558.43. It did 0-to-60 mph in 7.6 seconds and covered the quarter-mile in 15.47 seconds at 90.54 mph. The upgraded car did 0-to-60 in 5.7 seconds and the quarter-mile in 14 seconds at 101 mph! *Car and Driver's* car—also a hardtop—had the 340-hp Wildcat 401 V-8, Super Turbine automatic and other options that raised its price to $3,978.04. It covered the quarter-mile in 14.92 seconds at 95.13 mph.

With a top speed of 125 mph, the 1966 Wildcat Gran Sport was a rare blend of size and performance.

1966 Wildcat Gran Sport

The one-year-only 1966 Buick Wildcat Gran Sport was a massive muscle car. In terms of character and specifications, it didn't seem to fit the "muscle car" image. However, when you consider its performance, it goes like a genuine muscle machine. *Mechanix Illustrated* reported that the Wildcat GS could move from 0 to 60 mph in just 7.5 seconds and it had a 125-mph top speed. That compared to *Motor Trend's* 7.6 seconds for the smaller, lighter 325-hp Skylark Gran Sport and 8.6 seconds for the smaller Riviera GS with the Wildcat-like 340-hp V-8 and 3.23:1 rear axle. Did someone make a mistake? Were the *Motor Trend* editors that much better drivers?

The Wildcat was Buick's middle-priced, full-sized car. It had a 126-inch wheelbase and stretched more than 18 ft. overall (the hardtop was 219.9 inches long and the convertible had 220.1 inches between its bumpers). Two-doors tipped the scale at just under 4,100 lbs.

The Gran Sport equipment package was available for either Wildcat or Wildcat Custom Sport Coupes or convertibles. Its ingredients included a chrome air cleaner, cast-aluminum rocker arm covers, dual exhausts, a heavy-duty suspension, positraction and GS identification plates for the front and rear of the car.

Standard under the hood was a 425-cid V-8 with a 4.31 x 3.64-inch bore and stroke. It had a single four-barrel Carter carburetor and a 10.25:1 compression ratio. Buick rated it for 340 hp at 4400 rpm and 465 lbs.-ft. of torque at 2800 rpm. It came only with a Super Turbine automatic transmission and a 3.23:1 ratio rear axle.

Prices for Wildcat GS models were $3,581 for the sports coupe and $3,735 for the convertible. The Wildcat Custom versions were $3,802 and $3,956, respectively.

Buick GS-340.
What the car enthusiasts are enthusiastic about.

We started out to build a car that would cost less than our fabled GS-400. We ended up with a very sporting machine in its own right: a 340-cubic-inch V-8, pumping out 260 horsepower. A whole new distinctive look, with hood scoops painted to contrast with the hood, broad striping on the rocker panel, special emblems. Inside, a clean, simple, black interior. And you know what? It still costs less than our fabled GS-400. A lot less.

No wonder the enthusiasts are enthusiastic.

The 1967 GS 340 was not eye-popping in its performance or horsepower, but it was a sporty car at a relative bargain price.

BUICK

1967 Gran Sport 340

It would be easy to dismiss the 1967 Buick Gran Sport 340 as a "pretend" muscle car if it had been introduced in a vacuum. However, it made a big-time debut at the Chicago Auto Show on February 25, 1967, as sort of a muscle car for the masses. Buick called it the "GS 400's running mate … for people who look for a large measure of sporting flavor at a low price." Unlike the GS 400, though, the GS 340 came only as a sport coupe.

The 340-cid V-8 that was standard equipment in the GS 340 had a 3.750 x 3.850-inch bore and stroke with a single four-barrel carburetor and 10.25:1 compression ratio. It developed 260 hp at 4200 rpm and 365 lbs.-ft. of torque at 2800 rpm, which was nothing to write home about. It was the same engine a buyer could order for any other intermediate-size Buick that year, including wagons. However, in the GS 340, it did come attached to a four-speed manual gearbox at no cost. Buick's two-speed Super Turbine automatic was extra.

Among other "GS 340" features touted at the Chicago Auto Show were red rallye stripes along the sides, red non-functional hood scoops, red rallye wheels and GS ornamentation. Even Buick's real high-performance car of the time—the Gran Sport 400—didn't have the red decorative treatment. So, Buick offered its customers a choice between muscle-car image with the GS 340 or a genuine muscle-car motor in the GS 400. With a $2,845 window sticker—compared to $3,019 for a GS 400—price wasn't a major factor in selling a GS 340.

What probably made the GS-340 most interesting is that it came to market a half-year before the '68 Plymouth Road Runner. Buick and Plymouth both had the same idea of selling a high-performance car into the youth market for less than a top-line muscle car. The young buyers not only got image for less, but also saved on insurance premiums because of the lower horsepower rating. The Road Runner had more cubes and horses in standard form, but both cars came with plain bench seat interiors and a long list of good things on the options list.

GS 340 options included a Sport Pac suspension with heavy-duty underpinnings, a thick rear stabilizer bar and 15:1 steering. The list price was $2,850, but most carried enough extras to get over $3,000. Proving that the public pays attention to details, the GS 400 outsold the GS 340 darn near 4 to 1. Of course, the low production total of 3,692 units makes the GS 340 a lot more scarce and harder for today's collectors to find.

IN
'67 BUICK
Get in with the In Crowd in a GS-400
The In Crowd knows what's happening, and what's happening is Buick '67. Proof: GS-400, Buick's personal
sport car. It has a 400-cu. in., 340-hp V-8, a new brake system with dual master cylinders, energy
absorbing steering column, bucket seats, heavy-duty suspension and a list of standard equipment features—
including all the new GM safety items—so long it takes a Buick dealer to do it justice. (He'll also tell you
how four out of five new-car buyers pay Buick-sized prices to begin with.) The In Crowd's at your
Quality Buick dealer's right now. How soon can you join them?

The 1967 GS 400 got high marks from enthusiast magazines.

1967 Skylark Gran Sport 400

A new 400-cid engine helped the '67 GS 400 generate positive press reviews. It replaced the 1965-66 "401" that had been derived from Buick's old pent-roof V-8. That design dated back to 1953. The new V-8 combined lightweight construction and better breathing characteristics to create a potent package.

This new 400 had a 4.040 x 3.900-inch bore and stroke, a single Rochester four-barrel carburetor and a 10.25:1 compression ratio. It produced 340 hp at 5000 rpm and 440 lbs.-ft. of torque at 3200 rpm. It was also available with the variable-pitch-stator Super Turbine 400 transmission, a $236.82 option previously used only in big Buicks.

"Before the wheels had made their first revolution we immediately noticed that the 1967 GS 400 was going to be an even far stronger performer than its 1966 counterpart—which itself was no slouch," said *Motor Trend* in its October 1966 report on the new Skylark muscle car.

In April 1967, *Motor Trend's* Steve Kelly got to road test a well-equipped GS 400 hardtop with automatic transmission. Kelly also drove a GS 400 with a four-speed manual transmission and fewer options. The automatic version did 0-to-60 mph in 4.6 seconds, which was 1 second slower than the four-speed car. Quarter-mile performance was 15.2 seconds for both cars, but the four-speed GS 400 was going 95 mph, as opposed to

93 mph for the car with the Super Turbine 400 gearbox.

This was the first year that the GS 400 was in a series separate from regular Skylarks and Skylark GS 340s. The series contained a coupe with a $2,956 base price, a two-door hardtop with a $3,019 sticker and a convertible that listed for $3,167. With 10,659 assemblies, the hardtop sold the best, even though it wasn't exactly plentiful. Only 1,014 coupes were made, along with only 2,140 ragtops.

Special GS 400 equipment included a hood with twin simulated air scoops, a rallye stripe, GS ornamentation, all-vinyl seating with foam-padded cushions, dual exhausts, White-Line wide oval tires and a heavy-duty suspension. Desirable options included the four-speed manual transmission for $184.31, limited-slip differential for $42.13, front power disc brakes for $147, a tachometer for $47.39, a full console for $57.93, a consolette for $36.86 and chrome-plated wheels for $90.58.

In addition to its acceleration and speed characteristics, *Motor Trend* said that the 1967 GS 400 had "the best road behavior of any car we've driven in quite a while." The editors credited this impressive muscle car with maintaining the Buick image of quality, while starting a new image for young, performance-minded buyers.

1967 Riviera Gran Sport

Motor Trend put five personal-luxury cars to the test in August 1967 and the Buick Riviera GS was the best performer of the group. It moved from 0-to-60 mph in only 7.8 seconds and completed its quarter-mile acceleration run in 15.9 seconds at 86 mph. No wonder, since it had a larger, more powerful engine.

The new 430-cid V-8 had a 4.19 x 3.90-inch bore and stroke. It produced 360 hp at 5000 rpm and 475 lbs.-ft. of torque at 3200 rpm. It carried a four-barrel carburetor and delivered a 10.25:1 compression ratio. A three-speed Super Turbine automatic (actually a Turbo-Hydra-Matic design) was standard and the gear shifter was on the steering column. Mounting the shifter on the console between the front bucket seats was a popular option.

The GS package also gave buyers a heavy-duty dual-inlet air cleaner, a stiffer-than-stock suspension, a positraction rear axle, wide-oval tires with a choice of white or red stripes and GS monograms on the front fenders and instrument panel. A tilt steering wheel and dual exhausts were included on all '67 Rivieras.

The Riviera sport coupe cost Buick dealers $3,210 and normally retailed for $4,469 with dealer markups and federal excise tax. Dealers had to kick in an additional $98.30 for the RPO A9 Riviera Gran Sport Performance Group, but sold it for $137.88. It is not known how many Rivieras had this option. In *Motor Trend*, the manufacturer's suggested retail price of the Riviera GS was given as $4,791.88. That seems high, but there may have been a midyear price increase.

The Skylark GS was a beefed-up version of the 1968 Skylark Custom.
The "California GS" was a mid-year addition for West Coast buyers.

1968 Skylark GS 350 and California GS

In 1968, the Skylark GS 350 Sport Coupe replaced the Skylark GS 340. At $2,926, the new budget muscle car was slightly pricier, but more popular. Production hit 8,317 units, compared to just 3,692 for the 1967 GS 340 hardtop.

The GS 350 was based on the Skylark Custom, but had a more muscular exterior look. Finned, simulated air intakes decorated the front fenders and a paint stripe replaced chrome trim moldings on the lower edges of the body. Bright wheel lip moldings were used, but fender skirts were not. GS plaques decorated the grille, deck lid and rear fenders. All-vinyl seats were standard and bucket seats were available at extra cost. The hood had a scoop at the rear and concealed windshield wipers were featured.

The 350-cid Buick V-8 had a 3.8 x 3.85-inch bore and stroke and was equipped with a GM Rochester Quadrajet. In the Gran Sport model, it ran a 10.25:1 compression ratio and brake horsepower was 280 at 4600 rpm. The torque figure was

375 lbs.-ft. at 3200 rpm. In basic form, the GS 350 came with a column-mounted three-speed manual transmission. Options included a two-speed Super Turbine automatic with column or console shifter or a choice of three- or four-speed manual gearboxes with a shifter on the column, floor or consolette. The only available axle ratio was 3.23:1, except on a special California GS model.

The California GS was a midyear addition to the Skylark line intended for California motorists only. It was dressed up with a vinyl roof, extra chrome trim, styled wheels, a special steering wheel and "GS California" emblems. The California GS used the same engine as the GS 350, but came only with the Super Turbine automatic transmission. Buyers could chose between a column- or console-mounted gear shifter and either a 3.42:1 or 2.93:1 rear axle. Buick manufactured 8,317 GS 350s, but there's no breakout for California GS sales.

Tom Glatch

**The Skylark GS got some styling revisions for 1968, but the same formidable
400-cid/340-hp motor returned under the hood.**

1968 Skylark Gran Sport 400

The 1968 Skylark had a 112-inch wheelbase. Styling revisions included an overall swoopier look with an S-shaped body side feature line. A huge air scoop was integrated into the trailing edge of the hood and chrome finned ornaments decorated the area immediately behind the front wheel openings. *Motor Trend* described the car's rear view as reminiscent of the limited-production 1954 Buick Skylark sport convertible.

The GS 400 again used the 400-cid/340-hp V-8 introduced in 1967 models. There were no changes in the horsepower or torque ratings. Standard equipment included a three-speed manual transmission and a 3.42:1 rear axle. A heavy-duty three-speed manual transmission was $84.26 extra and a four-speed manual gearbox was $184.31 extra. Cars with sticks had 3.64:1 and 3.91:1 rear axle options. Ordering the Turbo-Hydra-Matic automatic transmission added $205.24 to the price. A 2.93:1 rear end was standard with automatic transmission and options included 3.42:1, 3.64:1 and 3.91:1 axles.

"Buick makes all kinds of cars because there are all kinds of people in the world," said a two-page color advertisement appearing in the fall of 1967. "So we thought we'd cater to the person who truly gets a thrill out of driving. The GS 400 is our contribution to his hobby."

GS 400 equipment was now available on only two models,

a hardtop that was base priced at $3,127 and a ragtop with prices starting at $3,271. Buick built 10,743 of the 3,514-lb. hardtops and 2,454 of the 3,547-lb. convertibles. *Motor Trend* tested a convertible with a bunch of options. Its total weight was 4,300 lbs. At a drag strip it clocked 16.3 seconds at 88 mph. Zero-to-60 performance for the GS 400 hardtop was charted as a snappy 7.5 seconds.

Hot Rod magazine's Eric Dahlquist did a little bit better with a well-equipped hardtop he wrote about in January 1968. His car had an as-tested price of $4,505 and weighed 3,820 lbs. By using the hood scoop as part of a homemade cold-air package, Dahlquist got the car's quarter-mile performance down to 14.78 seconds and registered a terminal speed of 94 mph. He noted that beginning January 1, 1968, Buick would begin making two factory cold-air packages available. These Stage 1 and Stage 2 valve train packages were offered along with forged aluminum pistons, a special intake manifold gasket that blocked the heat riser, oversize rods, fully grooved main bearings, 6 percent richer carburetor metering rods, special spark plugs and exhaust headers.

Motor Trend found the '68 GS 400 to have "surprisingly good" performance and said it was "very tight and hard to excel." The magazine liked the construction, comfort and general quality of the car, but disliked the rear vision in hardtops and the automatic shift lever.

**A cold-air package and two 400-cid Hi-Po engine options
gave the 1969 Skylark GS plenty of horses under the hood.**

1969 Skylark Gran Sport 400

The 1969 Skylark GS 400 had minor styling revisions, but quite a few under-hood differences. A functional hood-mounted air scoop was standard. *Hot Rod* described this system as, "Two 'muffs' reaching up from twin air snorkels on the four-barrel air cleaner, compressing against the hood underside, directing only outside air to the fuel mixer." The cold air passed through chrome grille on the car's more prominent air scoop. The grille also had a thick horizontal center bar.

The cold-air package was only the start of the good news that 1969 brought Buick fans. As part of a Super Performance package, the Stage I and Stage II engine options really came into their own this year. Both hi-po versions of the 400-cid V-8 offered drag strip-style performance enhancements for the serious muscle car lover. The calmer GS 400 Stage I was promoted in regular Buick ads, while the "hairier" Stage II hardware had to be ordered from a dealer's parts department and installed by the car owner.

The Stage I "factory" package—designed for dealer installation—incorporated a high-lift camshaft, tubular push rods, heavy-duty valve springs and dampers and a high-output oil pump was rated for 345 hp at 4800 rpm. When it was ordered, the transmission was equipped with a 5200-rpm governor to protect against over-revving the engine and a 3.64:1 or 3.42:1 positraction rear axle was used. Also included were dual exhausts with big 2 1/4-inch tailpipes and a modified quadrajet carburetor. A heavy-duty Rallye suspension and front power disc brakes were available.

The Stage II option was an install-it-yourself package for all-out racecars and was not recommended for use on the street or on cars with mufflers. It included an even wilder cam and all the other goodies.

For the second year in a row, *Car Life* found the GS 400 to be the quickest muscle car it tested with a reported 0-to-60 -mph time of 6.1 seconds. When *Motor Trend* tested the 3,706-lb. convertible with the standard 340-hp engine, it got the opposite result and concluded that the ragtop was the slowest of six muscle cars. It ran from 0-to-60 mph in 7.7 seconds and did the quarter-mile in 15.9 seconds at 89 mph.

An interesting sidelight to 1969 GS 400 history was the fact that six of the cars were given away in a "Drive Like A Pro" contest jointly promoted by the Pit-Stop Co., Coca-Cola and Petersen Publishing Co. Doesn't it make you wonder if any of the giveaway cars survive today?

BUICK

The hot 1970 GS 455 could blaze sub-14-second quarter-miles
with either an automatic or four-speed transmission.

1970 Gran Sport 455

According to muscle car expert Phil Hall, the 1970 Buick GS 455 was one of the wildest of all Buicks on paper. Its 455-cid engine was derived from the earlier 430-cid V-8 and produced 350 hp at 4600 rpm. Torque output was a strong 510 ft.-lbs. at 2800 rpm. It featured a 10.0:1 compression ratio and a Rochester four-barrel carburetor. This engine could push one of the approximately 3,800-lb. well-equipped Skylark bodies from 0-to-60 mph in about 6.5 seconds.

Available once again was the Stage I option. In fact, *Motor Trend* opined, "Buick's Stage I was interesting in 1969, now with the 455 mill it's an engineering tour de force." In addition, with a price of just $199.95, the engine option package was a bargain. It included extra-large nickel-chrome stellite steel valves, big-port cylinder heads with special machining and valve relieving, stronger valve springs, a high-lift cam, a carburetor with richer jetting, blueprinted pistons (notched for valve clearance) and an advanced-performance distributor. As in the past, the Stage I V-8 was available with either a special shift-governed automatic or a heavy-duty four-speed manual gearbox with a beefed-up clutch.

A Stage I GS 455 with automatic transmission could do 0-to-60 mph in 5.5 seconds and took just less than 14 seconds to zip down the quarter-mile. One magazine did it in 13.39 seconds at 105.5 mph and *Motor Trend* clocked 13.79 seconds at 104.50 mph as it flew through the traps. The stick-shifted version was just a little slower in reaching 60 mph from a standing start.

On top of its super performance, the GS 455 was a real handler and hugged the road even better when equipped with Rallye Ride package for $15.80 extra. It gave *Motor Trend's* press car extra stability at high speed. The test car had four-wheel manual drum brakes that could slow it from 60 mph in 139.1 ft. Senior editor Bill Sanders said the brakes "held up exquisitely without fade after repeated stops from over 100 mph."

The Gran Sport 455 option could be ordered for two body styles. The two-door hardtop cost $3,283 and 8,732 were put together. Buick built only 1,416 of the convertible versions, which sold for $3,469 and up.

The 1970 GS 455 was one of the great muscle cars of its era, and one of the fiercest Buicks ever produced.

The 1970 Sklyark GSX was a head-turner in its day, and a rare find today.

1970 Skylark GSX

"Buick's GSX. A limited edition," said the teaser headline on a Buick ad in the April 1970 issue of *Motor Trend*. The automaker called it "another light-your-fire car from Buick." As things turned out, not too many people had their fires lit, but you have to admit that with a total production of 678 copies, the GSX is a limited-edition muscle car.

Deep down inside, there wasn't too much of a difference between a 1970 GS 455 and a GSX of the same vintage. The latter carried a $1,196 options package as standard equipment. The package included a 455 four-barrel V-8, a hood-mounted tach, a Rallye steering wheel, power front disc brakes, a four-speed manual transmission, a 3.42:1 posi-rear axle, G60-15 "billboard" Wide-Oval tires, a special front stabilizer bar, front and rear spoilers, black vinyl bucket seats, heavy-duty front and rear shocks, a rear stabilizer bar, rear control arms and bushings, Firm Ride rear springs and GSX

ornamentation. The hood-mounted tach was specific to the GSX model and the four-speed gearbox had a Hurst shifter. The GSX ornamentation included a special graphics package with hood stripes and side panel stripes.

For 1970, the GSX came only in two exterior colors, called Saturn Yellow and Apollo White. Buick built 491 of the Saturn Yellow cars. The other 187 cars were Apollo White. Black vinyl interior trim, code 188, was used with both colors. Other special features included a distinctive padded steering wheel, a trunk tension bar designed to support the spoiler and a baffle incorporated into the rear spoiler. Of the 678 cars manufactured, 278 had standard 455-cid/315-hp V-8s, and 400 had the 345-hp Stage 1 engine option. All of the cars were built between February and May of 1970, but the VIN numbering appears to be assigned randomly.

The GSX was a special-order muscle car that remains somewhat of
an oddity today. Only 168 of the cars were reportedly produced.

1971-1972 Skylark GSX

According to the Buick GSX Registry at www.buickgsx.net, a GSX package was an option for 1971-1972 Buicks and could be ordered for any Skylark GS from the GS 350 to the GS 455 Stage 1. To order a 1971 or 1972 GSX, customers had to get their Buick dealer to check off the Special Car Order, or SCO, section of the order form.

The 1971-1972 cars varied widely in color and came with an unlimited range of options. The Buick GSX Registry stated that very little is known about them. Apparently, the option was added to 124 cars in 1971 and 44 cars in 1972.

Like other 1971-1972 Buicks, the GSX editions used de-tuned engines, all of which had an 8.5:1 compression ratio and less horsepower and torque than in 1970. However, when equipped with Buick's potent 455 Stage 1 engine, the GSX was still one of the hottest muscle cars in town. In fact, Buick fans insist that the Stage 1s can run down the quarter-mile faster than an LS6 big-block Chevelle.

In 1971 it was possible to put the GSX package on a car with the 350-cid/260-hp four-barrel V-8 that was standard in Grand Sports. This motor generated 360 lbs.-ft. of torque at 3000 rpm. Another option was the standard 455-cid/315-hp V-8 with 450 lbs.-ft. of torque at 2800 rpm. The 1971 version of the 455-cid Stage 1 engine produced 345 hp at 5000 rpm and 460 lbs.-ft. of torque at 3000 rpm.

In 1972, the engines were further choked by government emissions rules and the output numbers looked even worse because they were presented in SAE net horsepower (nhp) terms. The 350 produced 195 nhp at 4000 rpm and 290 lbs.-ft. of torque at 2800 rpm. The base 455 produced 225 nhp at 4000 rpm and 360 lbs.-ft. of torque at 2600 rpm. The 455 Stage 1 produced 270 hp at 4400 rpm and 390 lbs.-ft. of torque at 3000 rpm. At the rear of the cars, 3.08:1 or 3.42:1 axles were standard, depending on the engine and transmission combination.

Both 1971 and 1972 GSXs used a special frame, a computer-designed rally-tuned-suspension and large-diameter sway bars. The use of side stripes and a rear spoiler was continued.

While nowhere near as muscular as 1970 editions, the 1971-1972 Skylarks with the GSX package and the Stage 1 engine option are still tremendous performance cars and, since they were rare when new, are extremely hard to find today.

Despite being de-tuned slightly to 345 hp in 1971, the Gran Sport 455 was still a muscular beast.

1971 Gran Sport 455

Sales of Buick Gran Sports with the 455-cid Stage 1 engine were not strong in 1970. As a result, Buick worked hard to improve a good thing, albeit with modifications responding to government-mandated clean-air standards.

Buick combined the Gran Sport and the GS 455 into one series for 1971. This gentleman's muscle car—the Gran Sport Buick—was one of the few potent performance packages that was tractable in all kinds of driving. It could even be ordered with air-conditioning. Gran Sport equipment included a blacked-out grille with bright trim, bright wheelhouse moldings and bright rocker panel moldings with red-filled accents. Dual, functional hood scoops sat in the center of the hood. GS monograms appeared on the front fenders, deck and grille. Cars equipped with the 455 or 455 Stage 1 options had additional engine identification emblems. Standard equipment was the same as on the Skylark Custom, but bucket or notchback front seats in vinyl trim were optional.

For 1971, General Motors listed all its engines with SAE net horsepower ratings, along with gross horsepower ratings that reflected a reading without accessories. The SAE method was known as the "installed" output—the final output figure of the engine within a car carrying all necessary operating accessories. This may have been GM's way of mollifying insurance companies that were starting to impinge on the salability of muscle cars.

The GS 455 cid V-8 had a gross rating of 330 hp and an installed rating of 265 hp. The 455-cid Stage 1 engine had a 275 SAE hp rating, but its gross output rating was 345 hp

at 5000 rpm. This 345-hp rating was down from that of the 1970 Stage 1, which produced 360 hp at 4600 rpm. The reason was a lower 8.5:1 compression ratio, which was down from a 10.0:1 compression ratio in 1970. A functional Ram-Air induction system helped feed the engine cold air.

Buick's trademark—a high torque rating—was also down from 510 lbs.-ft. at 2800 rpm in 1970 to 460 lbs.-ft. at 3000 rpm for 1971. Still, if one averaged all 1971 GS 455 road tests, the elapsed time for the quarter-mile was 14.25, which compares favorably to an average ET of 14.02 for the 1970 model.

The 455 cid V-8s used valve spring dampeners to reduce valve spring surging. Also, the exhaust lobe profiles were lengthened to reduce valve-opening acceleration and increase valve-opening overlap, which was 20 percent or more in the 455 cid V-8.

All exhaust valves were now nickel-plated, due to GM's requirement that all 1971 engines be able to run no-lead fuel. The primary side of the venturi on the Quadrajet carburetor was 1/8 inch larger on the 455-cid engine. A problem with this was that the 1971 models had lower (higher number) axle ratios and gas mileage suffered.

Production figures show that 8,268 GS and GS 455 two-door hardtops were built. Of these, 801 had the Stage 1 option. Convertibles accounted for 902 total GS and GS 455 assemblies. A number of highly desirable options were offered, such as a Hurst-shifted Muncie M20 transmission and code RPO E6 through-bumper exhaust extensions.

BUICK

Jerry Heasley

The 1972 GS 455 Stage 1 bucked the trend of declining horsepower in muscle cars. The high-powered Buick turned out to be a star on the drag strip.

1972 Skylark GS 455 Stage 1

A sedate-looking '72 Buick Gran Sport picked up a bunch of enviable timing slips at the National Hot Rod Association's "Winternationals" drag fest in Pomona, California. Though the car looked like your average "grocery getter," it was definitely in the "fast food" category, according to *Motor Trend's* A. B. Shuman.

"Buick, it seems, has an indisputable knack for making singularly sneaky cars," said his June 1972 report on the Buick GS Stage 1. The red GS with a white vinyl top and automatic transmission looked nothing like a drag racer.

The Skylark-based muscle car was champion in the Stock Eliminator category and went on to beat all the other stock class winners to become overall category winner. In Shuman's hands it did 0-to-60 mph in 5.8 seconds, while the quarter-mile took 14.10 seconds (with a 97-mph terminal speed). With open exhausts, fatter tires and a few "tweaks" allowed by NHRA rules, weekend drag racer Dave Benisek set an elapsed time record of 13.38 seconds, at Pomona, with the same car.

By coincidence, the 1970 GS 455 Stage 1 also did the

quarter-mile in 13.38 seconds, but that was because it had a higher compression ratio (10.0:1), more horsepower (360 at 4600 rpm) and a taller (numerically lower) 3.64:1 rear axle.

By 1972, the no-lead version of the car ran an 8.5:1 compression ratio, produced 275 hp at 4400 rpm and came linked to a 4.30:1 rear axle. This, of course, made its performance numbers even more impressive. "The amazing thing, considering all that's happened just in the area of emissions controls, is that a car that runs like the GS Stage 1 could still exist," noted Shuman. He called it "the best example of the Supercar genre extant."

Despite such a positive appraisal, Buick made only 7,723 GS hardtops and 852 GS convertibles in model year 1972 and that included GS 350, GS 455 and Stage 1 production. In addition to a 350- 455- or 455-cid Stage 1 V-8, all 1972 Gran Sports had four-barrel carburetors, dual exhausts, functional hood scoops, and a heavy-duty suspension. GS monograms appeared on the front fenders and rear deck and bright moldings trimmed the rocker panels and wheel lips.

1982 Regal Grand National

The first Buick Regal Grand National was introduced at Daytona International Speedway on February 10, 1982. This car marked a revival of the high-performance image that the Skylark Gran Sport models had fostered in the late '60s and early '70s. The GN was the first in a new series of *real* muscle cars from Buick.

The Grand National name came from stock car racing. Buicks took the NASCAR manufacturer's trophy, in Grand National stock car racing, in 1981 and 1982. "The New Grand National Regal is a luxurious commemorative version of the winning Grand National Vehicle," said a dealer bulletin issued two days before the car's debut at Daytona. "Buick designed this magnificent Regal to be a one-of-a-kind car. With its special GN styling treatment and appointments, it is a distinctive vehicle inside and out. Our objective in producing these Grand National Regals is to offer an attraction that will stimulate sales of all the 1982 Buicks. We also want to capitalize on the momentum being generated by the Grand National racing competition and take advantage of enthusiast's magazine coverage to increase Buick's penetration of the enthusiast market!"

Grand Nationals were built on an off-line basis by Cars & Concepts of Auburn Hills, Michigan. The prototype car that appeared at Daytona was produced in December 1981. It was then shipped to Daytona in February 1982 for the press introduction. Initially, a run of 100 units was planned, but actual production was only 216 cars, including the prototype. The Grand National package sold for $3,278, making it one of Buick's highest-priced options ever at that time.

Buick sent factory-spec Regals to Cars & Concepts for conversion into GNs. Factory-produced parts used on the cars included the black-out style grille and headlight covers, the wheel center caps that say "GN," the horn button, body moldings and the trim for the instrument panel and console.

Cars & Concepts added the front spoiler, Lear Siegler bucket seats (the press kit says they were gray Branson cloth, but the color was actually silver), the rear airfoil, special seat covers, silver paint, GN decals, pinstriping and door-pull appliqués. The regular clock was usually replaced with GN instrument panel inserts.

The press kit made it sound like all 1982 Grand Nationals were identical, but they were not. Regal coupes, Regal sport coupes and Regal Limited coupes were all used as the basis for the conversions. A small number of cars were made without the GN emblem in the dash and carried analog clocks in addition to the clock built into the ETR stereo.

Most of the 1982 Grand Nationals were powered by a normally aspirated 4.1-liter V-6 that made 125 hp at 4000 rpm and 205 lbs.-ft. of torque at 2,000 rpm. This engine had a 3.965 x 3.400 bore and stroke and displaced 252 cid. It used a four-barrel carburetor and had an 8.0:1 compression ratio.

About 10 to 15 of the first Grand Nationals had the 3.8-liter turbocharged V-6 that was used in the 1982 Regal sport coupe. This motor was not on the regular options sheet, but savvy buyers could get a Turbo Grand National by ordering a Regal Sport Coupe plus the Grand National package. The turbocharged 231-cid V-6 had a 3.80 x 3.40-inch bore and stroke. With a four-barrel carburetor and 8.0:1 compression ratio it developed 175 hp at 4000 rpm and 275 lbs.-ft. of torque at 2600 rpm.

The '82 is the only Regal Grand National that didn't have all-black finish. Two-tone paint was featured, with Silver Mist on the upper body and Charcoal Gray on the lower body. Red pinstriping set off the two-tone finish. A sunroof was also included. While the '82 did not have the performance of later Grand Nationals, it is rare and unique. In addition, it set the theme for the return of Buick muscle cars. The turbocharged versions are extremely rare.

BUICK

1982 Regal Sport Coupe

In the early '80s, Buick held proud memories of its muscle car heritage created by models like the GS-400, the GS-455 and the GSX. Buick engineers wanted to develop a muscle car that could turn in amazing performance while meeting the more restrictive emissions and fuel-economy standards of the '80s. They dusted off the V-6 engine that had first appeared in the 1961 Buick Special and began experimenting with high-tech upgrades to boost its go-fast potential. They found that, by fitting a turbocharger to the V-6, they could make it perform in the same neighborhood as a V-8.

By 1978, a turbo 3.8-liter V-6 with a four-barrel carburetor was made available for Regal and LeSabre Sport Coupes. It produced 165 hp, but the setup was far from perfected. It provided extra highway passing power, but little more. So, Buick then set up a Turbo Engine Group dedicated to

designing a V-6 with muscle-car-like performance. By 1982, the TEG had concocted a 3.8-liter turbocharged V-6 (RPO LC8)—still with a four-barrel carburetor—that generated 175 hp at 4000 rpm. It was available in a special model called the Regal Sport Coupe.

The turbo V-6 included a re-sized Garrett AiResearch turbo unit with a smaller, more efficient housing that shortened up the time required for full turbo boost. The oil capacity of both the engine and the turbo unit was increased and hot air, rather than the hot water used earlier, was used to warm the induction system. Buick engineers also relocated the knock sensor and linked it directly to the electronic control module (ECM). The diameter of the turbine outlet pipe was increased from 2 to 2 1/2 inches to nearly eliminate backpressure. Two other performance improvements were a

Turbo-Hydra-Matic (THM350c) automatic transmission with a lock-up torque converter and a lower 3.08:1 rear axle that improved acceleration, but not fuel economy.

The standard features of this car included its high-performance engine, sport mirrors, fast-ratio power steering, a voltmeter, a turbo boost gauge, a trip odometer, P205/70R14 steel-belted BSW tires, styled aluminum wheels and a Gran Touring suspension. To identify it as a modern muscle car, the 1982 Model K47 Regal sport coupe also had a special hood

and black body accents. It had a base retail price of $9,738 and only 2,022 were made, including 10 to 15 with the special Regal Grand National package.

When it was completely warmed up, the turbo Regal could do 0 to 60 mph in 9.6 seconds and covered the quarter-mile in 17.3 seconds at 81 mph. In the February 1982 *Motor Trend*, industry affairs editor Jim McGraw said of the turbo V-6, "Buick is leaning more toward V-6 performance and allowing the driver more motoring fun."

1983 Regal Turbo T-Type

Buick introduced the Regal T-Type in the fall of 1982, as a 1983 model. At the same time, the Regal Sport Coupe disappeared. Also missing was the Grand National option, which would re-appear in 1984 and last through 1987. The Regal T-Type had the same sporty image as the Regal Sport Coupe and a host of extra features. To make it into a real muscle car, Buick put a turbocharged V-6 under the hood.

Speaking of the hood, it was of a special design with a "power bulge" at its rear end. Standard equipment on the T-Type included the AiResearch blown 3.8-liter V-6, a new THM 200-R4 four-speed overdrive automatic transmission, a 3.42:1 performance rear axle, sport mirrors, fast-ratio power steering, a turbo boost gauge, a temperature gauge, a trip odometer, P205/70R14 SBR tires, styled aluminum wheels,

dual exhausts and a grand touring suspension.

The 3.8-liter turbo V-6 had cast-iron alloy cylinder head and engine block construction. It featured a 3.80 x 3.40-inch bore and stroke and displaced 231 cubic inches. A four-barrel carburetor was used and it had an 8.0:1 compression ratio. The 1983 version put out 180 hp at 4000 rpm and 280 lbs.-ft. of torque at 2400 rpm. New for the year was a computer-controlled EGR system that enhanced driveability. In addition, the "taller" top gear in the new overdrive transmission allowed a shorter axle to be used, thereby providing much better off-the-line performance.

The T-Type listed for about $10,350 in standard form. A total of 3,732 were built.

BUICK

The 1984 Grand National carried a turbo V-6 that produced 200 horsepower.

1984 Regal Grand National

After showcasing its turbo-engine technology at the 1984 new-car shows, Buick brought out a new model it advertised as "the hottest Buick this side of a banked oval." This new Regal Grand National coupe was, according to Buick, "produced in limited numbers for those who demand a high level of performance." Its stated purpose was to give young and young-at-heart Buick buyers much of the feeling of a NASCAR racer. Buick built 2,000 copies of this car.

"A little chrome and a lot of power in basic black attire, that's what the Buick Regal Grand National coupe is all about," said the ad copywriters. The cost of the option—$1,282—was quite modest, considering that it had a host of appearance and equipment extras. To begin with, Grand Nationals carried the 231-cid (3.8-liter) turbocharged V-6 with sequential fuel injection (SFI). This code LM9 engine produced 200 hp at 4000 rpm and 300 lbs.-ft. of torque at 2000 rpm. It came linked to a four-speed automatic transmission and a 3.42:1 rear axle.

Ingredients of the GN option included black exterior finish on the body, bumpers, bumper rub strips, bumper guards, front air dam, windshield wipers, rear deck lid spoiler, taillight bezels and aluminum wheels. The paint code was No. 19. Grand National identification was carried on the front fenders and the instrument panel. A sport steering wheel, a tachometer, a turbo-boost gauge, a 94-amp alternator, power brakes and steering, dual exhausts and a special hood with a turbo bulge were also included in the package. The code 995 Lear Siegler seats (sand gray cloth with charcoal leather inserts) were embroidered with the Grand National model's distinctive "6" (for V-6) logo.

Individual options available from Buick included a hatch top (RPO CC1), an Astroroof with silver glass (RPO CF5), a theft-deterrent system (RPO UA6), cruise control (RPO K34), electronic touch climate-control air conditioning (RPO C68), a rear window defogger (RPO C49), a remote trunk release (RPO A90), electronic instrumentation (RPO U52) and a lighted vanity mirror on the passenger-side sun visor.

The Buick Grand National retained its signature all-black look and uncommon performance in 1985.

1985 Regal Grand National

Why change a good thing? The Regal GN wasn't selling in big numbers (2,102 built in 1985), but it was pulling enthusiasts into Buick showrooms where some of them bought other models. With oodles of image and oomph, the "new" GN certainly did not require a drastic overhaul, but it still got a facelift.

The forward-slanting nose of all '85 Regals carried a new grille. On the GN, it was finished in black. So was nearly everything else, including the windshield wipers. There *were* minor updates to the upholstery and ornamentation. Still, the ultra-high-performance version of the Regal T-Type was basically unchanged on the outside.

Under the hood once again was the turbocharged 3.8-liter V-6 with sequential fuel injection. The system (introduced in 1984) provided more precise fuel delivery. Metered fuel was timed and injected into the individual combustion ports sequentially through six Bosch injectors. Each cylinder received one injection per every two revolutions, just prior to the intake valve opening. The '85 engine had some torque curve revisions.

A nine in the eighth position in the VIN number indicated the use of the 3.8-liter turbo, which carried option code RPO

LM9 as it did in 1984. This engine was rated for 200 hp at 4000 rpm and 300 lbs.-ft. of torque at a slightly higher 2400 rpm.

The '85 GN stuck with a monotone black exterior treatment and was identified by special model badges. The Grand National package retailed for $675, so prices for the high-performance model started at $12,640. The package included the turbo V-6, quick-ratio power steering, an instrumentation group, sport mirrors with left-hand remote control, a four-speed automatic transmission, air conditioning and P215/65R15 black sidewall tires.

There were some interior revisions for 1985. A new two-tone cloth interior with front bucket seats carried code 583 soft trim. Underneath the car was a specific Gran Touring suspension. In addition, the following individual options could be added to a Grand National at extra cost: hatch roof (RPO CC1), Astroroof (RPO CF5), GM theft deterrent system (RPO UA6), electronic cruise control (RPO K34), electronic-touch climate control (RPO C68), rear window defogger (RPO C49), electronic instruments (RPO U52) and electric trunk lock release (RPO A90). Buick reported production of 2,102 Regal Grand Nationals in 1985.

The 1986 Regal Grand National looked a lot like the previous models, but it performed even better.

1986 Regal and LeSabre Grand Nationals

The 1986 Buick Regal Grand National package was a $558 option for the sporty T-Type, which itself listed for $13,714. The Grand National package included all Regal T-Type features, plus black (code 19) finish on the body, bumpers, bumper rub strips, bumper guards, rear spoiler and front air dam, Grand National and Intercooler identification trim, front bucket seats (trim code 583), a full-length-operation console and a performance-tuned suspension. Buyers had a choice of new standard chrome-plated steel wheels or new aluminum wheels. A high-mounted stop lamp became a part of the standard General Motors safety equipment package for 1986. Regal Grand National production climbed to 5,512 during the model run.

While overall appearance of the '86 Regal Grand National was very similar to the second (1984) and third (1985) Grand Nationals, Ron Yuille and his Buick Turbo Engine Group worked out some significant engineering upgrades for 1986 models. They included the use of an intercooler that lowered the temperature of the air charge between the turbo and the intake manifold. Airflow was also improved over 1985 by using a two-piece aluminum intake manifold with an open-plenum chamber. This change alone was good for a 10-percent horsepower boost to 235 hp at 4400 rpm. Torque increased to 330 lbs.-ft. at 2800 rpm. Another new-for-1986 item was an electric, temperature-controlled cooling fan.

A very different kind of Buick bearing the Grand National seal was introduced in conjunction with the 1986 Daytona 500. The 1986 1/2 LeSabre Grand National also featured monotone black finish, a front air dam, Buick's Level III suspension system, Electra T-Type wheels, Goodyear Eagle GT tires, unique rear quarter window trim and special GN badges. The LeSabre Grand National was built exclusively for promotional purposes only. It did not have a turbocharged V-6 or the performance of a Regal Grand National. Only 112 were made.

BUICK

The memorable 1987 Buick GNX was the result of a plan to produce "the quickest GM supercar. Ever."

1987 GNX

BUICK

To commemorate the end of Grand National production in 1987, Buick joined with ASC/McLaren to build a high-performance car called the GNX. The concept behind the GNX was to merge basic high-performance techniques with the latest in electronics and turbocharging technology to create the ultimate production modern muscle car. It was to be the kind of car enthusiasts and collectors would want to own. Almost overnight, the GNX achieved a memorable spot in the "muscle car roll of honor."

Along with rear-wheel-drive Regals, the hot Grand National was to go out of production in June or July 1987. When enthusiasts realized these would be the last turbocharged, rear-wheel drive Buicks, orders picked up. The model got an extension on life and approximately 10,000 assemblies were scheduled between August 3, 1987 and December of that year. The 547 GNXs built were made as a part of this total.

Chief engineer Dave Sharpe dreamed up the idea of a special car to mark the series' farewell. Mike Doble, of Advanced Concepts & Specialty Vehicles, got the job and came up with an integrated high-performance machine that he saw as a modern-day GS-455/GSX Stage I. The car was outlined in an April 25, 1986, document detailing a plan to build the "quickest GM production supercar. Ever!"

ASC/McLaren (Short for Automobile Specialty Co./McLaren Engines) helped create the GNX in a joint venture with Buick after Buick General Manager Don Hackworth approved the program in July 1986. Brainstorming sessions helped develop two prototypes. A management change caused concern that a new general manager, Ed Mertz, might cancel the GNX. After a ride in a prototype, he gave it "thumbs up." Seven additional pilot cars were made from 1986 to 1987.

The heart of the GNX became a turbocharged and intercooled 3.8-liter SFI V-6 that developed 276 hp at 4400 rpm and 360 lbs.-ft. of torque at 3000 rpm. It was blueprinted and fitted with such things as special bearings, shot-peened rods and a high rpm valvetrain. The Garrett AiResearch turbo was

linked to a special intercooler. McLaren reworked the PROM (computer chip) to enhance fuel mix, spark control, boost characteristics and transmission functions. The Sequential Fuel Injection (SFI) system was designed by Buick.

A race-type chassis was developed for the GNX. It had features such as a longitudinal torque bar (bolted to special differential cover), a tubular steel Panhard rod, revised lower control arms and different size Gatorback tires front and rear. GNX program manager Lou Infante said, "The net result is a mid-13 second GNX that's at home on the drag strip, road course and interstate."

Outwardly, the GNX got a "high-intensity" image with glossy paint, low-gloss Vaalex fender louvers, cast aluminum wheels and flared fenders. The hood had a power bulge, the deck had an airfoil and the body had little identification—only two polished aluminum GNX badges on the grille and deck lid. A badge on the instrument panel showed a car's production number.

ASC/McLaren supplied the option package at a cost of $10,995, which gave the GNX an MSRP of $29,900. According to Buick, 0-to-60 performance was 5.5 seconds and the quarter-mile took 13.43 seconds at 104 mph. Top speed was a claimed 124 mph. *Car & Driver* published test results of 4.7 seconds for 0 to 60 mph and 13.5 seconds for the quarter-mile at 102 mph. The magazine reported top speed to be "120 mph limited by a cut-off."

The hairy 1987 GNX was capable of sub-14-second quarter-mile runs and screamed from 0-to-60 mph in 4.7 seconds—spectacular performance for a car of its era.

The 1987 Grand National was the final edition of Buick's all-black muscle car line,
and arguably the best of the bunch, excluding the GNX of the previous year.

1987 Regal Grand National

There are two main differences between the 1987 Regal Grand National and the 1986 edition. The newer car has an all-black grille and the top section of the grille has no flat surface. Inside, the black vinyl door-pull straps of the 1986 edition were replaced by gray pull straps that matched the gray door panel in color. Under the hood of the '87 model, the turbocharged and intercooled V-6 was tweaked a bit to give 245 hp at 4400 rpm and 355 lbs.-ft. of torque at 2000 rpm.

Standard equipment with the Grand National WE2 package was the same as in 1986 and again included a long list of appearance, convenience and performance features. Only five individual options were available: the RPO YF5 emissions equipment package, an RPO B88 body molding package, an RPO CC1 lockable hatch roof, an RPO WG1 driver's side six-way power seat and an RPO UA5 theft-deterrent system.

By the end of the summer of 1987, Grand National sales had practically doubled over those of the entire previous year. This was due largely to the massive publicity exposure the hot, high-performance model was receiving in enthusiast publications. Buick dealers then pressured the company to make more of the cars, since dealers were marking them up an additional $3,000 per unit.

Grand National production had originally been slated to halt in July 1987, when Buick was supposed to stop making rear-wheel-drive Regals. On August 3, company executive W.H. Lotts decided to extend production of only the Grand National model through December. By the end of the year, total production had risen to 20,193 cars.

All of the approximately 10,000 cars built after August 3 came with 17 required options. These included black exterior finish, gray interior trim code 583, the 3.8-liter turbocharged V-6, the Grand National equipment package, Soft-Ray tinted glass, door edge guards, two-speed wipers, an electric rear window defogger, a visor vanity mirror, remote-control mirrors, a limited-slip differential, a tilt steering column, tungsten halogen headlights, headlight warning chimes, a heavy-duty battery, an RPO UM6 Delco radio and a front license plate mounting bracket. Buyers could add two option packages and five stand-alone options, but other regular Buick Regal options were unavailable.

The 1987 Grand Nationals were capable of doing 0-to-60 mph in the low 6-second bracket. *Cars Illustrated* magazine published quarter-mile performance of 13.85 seconds and 99.22 mph. *Musclecars* magazine's test Buick was just a little slower, if you can call 13.90 seconds at 98.16 mph "slow." Collectors today like the superior performance of the 1987 Grand National model, even though the '86 is a whole lot rarer.

The 1956 Chevy Bel Air was definitely a "Hot One" for its time with an optional
small-block Corvette V-8 that could produce up to 225 hp.

1956 "Power-Pack"

CHEVROLET

"The Hot One's Even Hotter," said the Chevrolet's fiery ads. The American auto industry was having a horsepower race and Chevy was stepping up to the starting line. The Bow Tie brand transitioned, at least a little, from a "family" car to a performance car with the release of its 265-cube "small-block" V-8 in 1955. Even the Power-Pack version with a four-barrel carb topped out at 162 hp that season, but 1956 was a different story as Chevy twisted the burner higher.

The number of optional "small-block" V-8s was expanded to four—and two of those were rated above 200 hp. The Power-Pack engine of 1955 became the "Turbo-Fire 205" V-8, which had a 9.25:1 compression ratio, a single four-barrel carburetor and dual exhausts. It developed 205 hp at 4600 rpm and 268 lbs.-ft. of torque at 3000 rpm. The most powerful option was a Corvette engine that cranked up 225 hp at 5200 rpm and 270 lbs.-ft. of torque at 3600 rpm.

The Chevrolet V-8s weighed less than the division's six-cylinder engines, which resulted in an outstanding power-to-weight ratio—one reason why the 1956 Chevrolet V-8s were called the "Hot Ones." Jim Wangers, an advertising executive employed by Chevrolet's ad agency, Campbell Ewald, was an avid high-performance enthusiast. Wangers was instrumental in establishing Chevrolet's 1956 "The Hot One's Even Hotter!" advertising campaign. He promoted the idea of driving a '56 Chevy up Pikes Peak to set a new record.

Afterwards, Wangers wrote: "Just point this new '56 Chevy uphill and ease down on the gas. In the merest fraction of a second you sense that big bore V-8 lengthening out its stride. And up you go with a silken rush of power that makes a mountain road seem as flat as a roadmap. For nothing without wings climbs like a '56 Chevrolet!"

Chevrolet's sassy "Motoramic" styling for 1956 included a full-width grille, large rectangular front parking lamps, new front and rear bumpers and guards (except station wagons), inward angled dome-shaped taillights with back-up lights set into chrome-ribbed decorative housings and squarer

headlight visors. The left-hand taillight housing "hid" the fuel filler. Chevy promoted "Glide-Ride" front suspension, Anti-Dive braking, tubeless tires, "Outrigger" rear springs, new Precision-Aimed headlights and a new Longer-Life battery.

Base One-Fifty models had minimal trim, a two-spoke steering wheel with horn ring, one sun visor, a lockable glovebox, a dome light, cloth-and-vinyl upholstery (all-vinyl on station wagons), black rubber floor mats and small hubcaps. These "stripper" cars were plain-looking, but popular with high-performance buffs. Less equipment meant less weight, but you could still get any engine option. The hot ticket for weekend drag racing was the lightest model (One-Fifty two-door sedan) with the Corvette V-8.

The middle series was the Two-Ten line with more external chrome, two sun visors, ashtrays, a cigarette lighter and upgraded interior trims. In this line the Del Ray two-door sedan was worth a look from enthusiasts. It weighed just slightly more than the Two-Ten version and had deep-pile carpets and all-vinyl upholstery. While "all-vinyl" is passe today, it was the way to go in the '50s and '60s if you wanted a street performance car with the "right" look.

For those who wanted a "full dresser" with a little punch, the Bel Air two-door hardtop or sport coupe was the ride to be seen in. Bel Airs had lots of trim, full wheel covers, a three-spoke steering wheel, deep-pile carpets, an electric clock and a lighted, lockable glove compartment.

With a 115-inch wheelbase and 197.5-inch length, the Chevy V-8 was a well-balanced machine. The standard 6.70 x 15 four-plys were not performance tires, but the optional 7.10 x 15s gave you a bit more bite off the line.

Chevrolet model-year production of 1,574,740 units in 1956 was enough to give the brand the crown for being America's number one automaker. Performance on the street and on the track had a lot to do with achieving strong sales.

A 1957 Chevy Bel Air with fuel injection was a hot ticket.

1957 "fuelie" coupe

The youth movement was in motion and Americans weregetting "hipper" in 1957. American Bandstand, beatniks and Brigette Bardot were now part of the culture.

The 1957 Chevys were in tune with the times. They had a more youthful, tail-finned look that was "radical" for a once-upon-a-time bread-and-butter car. "'57 Chevrolet! Sweet, smooth and sassy," said one ad.

Triple-Turbine automatic drive, a bigger V-8 and a bevy of new ideas including fuel injection made the '57 Chevy seem revolutionary and sexy. True, it was based on the body introduced in 1955, but the latest version seemed more modern and sportier. Its oval-shaped front bumper grille featured "bomb-type" bumper guards. A horizontal bar "floated" across the delicately cross-hatched grille. Windsplit bulges with bombsight ornaments ran up both sides of the flat hood panel. The headlights had grilles around them. The rear fenders were shaped into broad, flat tail fins.

All V-8 models, except those with stick shift, carried a new 283-cid V-8, which offered up to 283 hp in "super" fuel-injected format. All Chevrolets with a V-8 had large, V-shaped hood and deck lid ornaments (which were gold on Bel Airs). Very few cars carried the "fuel-injection" nameplate.

Prices began as low as $1,885 for the One-Fifty "business coupe," which could be built with any engine, including the 283-hp job. The '57 Two-Ten followed the "sassier-for-'57" theme by looking more Bel Air-like, especially with optional two-tone paint. The dressier-inside Del Ray version returned. Extra rich in all ways, Bel Airs carried rocker sill, roof, window and tail fin outline moldings. Chevrolet scripts decorated the hood and trunk and gold Bel Air scripts and Chevrolet bow tie crests were on the rear fenders. Distinctive two-tone interiors were seen.

A total of seven V-8s were available and some were quite rare. Five of the 283s ranged from fairly hot to scalding. A four-barrel carburetor and dual exhausts gave the 220-hp Turbo-Fire 220 more muscles to flex. Dual four-barrel carbs were featured on the Turbo-Fire 245 V-8. Fitted with a Rochester mechanical fuel-injection setup, the Ramjet 250 version of the 283 engine was another choice. Next in horsepower was the Super Turbo-Fire 270, which combined dual Quadrajet carbs with a higher 9.5:1 compression ratio. Chevy's legendary one-horsepower-per-cubic-inch Super Ramjet 283 was the top option combining the Rochester F.I. system with a 10.5:1 compression ratio. It was awesome and Chevrolet promoted this solid-lifter fuel-injection V-8 as the first American production-car engine to provide one horsepower per cubic inch of displacement.

Chevy tried to stay conservative when hyping horsepower in 1957 and there was a good reason for this. On April 10, a New Hampshire state senator made national news with charges that the auto industry was "engaged in a ridiculous and dangerous horsepower race." By June 6, the board of directors of the Automobile Manufacturers Association recommended to member companies that they take no part in auto racing or other competitive events involving tests of speed and that they refrain from suggesting speed in passenger car advertising or publicity. So, Chevy ads mentioned "V-8s up to 245 hp" and then footnoted information about the 270-hp high-performance engine and 283-hp Ramjet fuel-injection engine in small print.

Model-year production for 1957 peaked at 1,515,177 cars.

The 1959 Chevy Bel Air two-door sedan.

1959 "big-block"

The "Slimline Design" 1959 Chevrolets were lower, wider and longer than ever before. Innovations included a new radiator grille, a "Spread Wing" rear treatment, increased glass area and flat-top roof styling on sport sedans. The "cat's-eye" taillights were very distinctive. Engine options were greatly expanded, offering 13 choices—including 12 "vim-packed" V-8s with up to 350 hp.

The Biscayne was the basic Chevy and the lightweight Biscayne "coupe" replaced the One-Fifty version as the darling of drag racers. Bel Airs became mid-priced models, taking the place of the one-step-up Two-Ten. Bel Airs had full-length side moldings, painted inserts and front fender top ornaments. The Impala was the new top-of-the-line series. Impalas had model nameplates and crossed-racing-flags emblems on the full-length side trim moldings. Closed cars had very cool simulated roof scoops.

Listing all the 1959 Chevy engines could be a book in itself. The base V-8 was again a 283 Turbo-Fire small-block with a two-barrel carburetor. Next came a 230-hp version with a four-barrel carb. There were also 250-hp and 290-hp Ramjet fuel-injected versions of the 283. The 348-cid big-block V-8 (first seen in 1958) offered 250-hp (four-barrel), 280-hp (Tri-Power), 300-hp and 305-hp (high-compression four-barrel), 315-hp (high-compression Tri-Power), 320-hp (11.25:1 compression four-barrel), 335-hp (11.25:1 compression Tri-Power) and 350-hp (11.25:1 compression Tri-Power) options.

A longer 119-inch wheelbase carried the 210.9-inch long '59 bodies. They were 79.9 inches wide and had heights between 54 inches and 56.3 inches. Most models had 7.50 x 14 tires.

Model-year production totaled 1,481,071 Chevys. Some sales were generated by Chevrolet successes in Grand National stock car racing.

Only 456 1961 Impalas were equipped with the SS package.

1961 Impala SS and 409

When it comes to big Chevy muscle cars the first Impala SS with optional 409-cube big-block V-8 might be the purest strain of the breed. A big engine stuffed in a small car is the classic formula for a muscle car and the '61 Chevy Impala was, in relative terms, a *downsized* car. This gave the big-block versions super-high-performance abilities. For example, the SS two-door hardtop with a 409-cid/360-hp engine was good for 0-to-60 mph in 7.8 seconds and a 15.8-second quarter-mile.

The very first SS option could be ordered for Impala two-door sedans, four-door sedans and hardtops and no "factory assembly" was required. The package was strictly a dealer-installed item, costing around $54 for a few basic ingredients like "SS" emblems, a padded dash, spinner wheel covers, power steering, power brakes, heavy-duty springs and shocks, sintered metallic brake linings, a 7,000-rpm tachometer, 8.00 x 14 narrow whitewall tires, a dashboard grab bar and a chrome shift housing for the floor-shifted four-speed gear box.

Two V-8 engines were available at prices between $344

and about $500. The Turbo-Thrust 348-cid big-block came with 11:25 compression in 340-hp (four-barrel carburetor) and 350-hp (three two-barrel carburetor) versions. A new 409-cid Turbo-Fire engine was available with 360 hp (four-barrel), 380 hp (three two-barrel) or 409 hp (dual quad) options. It had 11:1 compression. A four-speed close-ratio transmission was $188 extra.

Some Chevy experts warn that the 1961 Impala SS is not the easiest car to restore. Only 456 Impalas were fitted with the "SS" package (including 142 with 409-cid engines), so parts are hard to find. This is something to consider if you have your heart set on becoming a Super Sport buyer. But take heart, because a 409-cid '61 Chevy without SS equipment is also a desirable muscle car.

According to the Standard Catalog of Chevrolet 1912-2003, a 1961 Bel Air sport coupe with the 409-cid/409-hp engine zipped down the quarter-mile in 12.83 seconds. Don Nicholson was also Top Stock Eliminator at the 1961 National Hot Rod Association's Winternationals behind the wheel of a 409/409 Chevy.

An Impala convertible with a 409 under the hood was a nice combination of power and style.

CHEVROLET

Jerry Heasley

The legendary Bel Air 409 was a true American muscle car—lots of motor in an unassuming package.

1962 Bel Air 409

"She's so fine my 409!" Remember the song? "Gonna save my pennies and save my dimes. Gonna buy me a 409, 409, 409."

What yearning that Beach Boys pop hit lit in teenagers of the early 1960s. Save your pennies and save your dimes and buy yourself a 409, could it be true? Not really, but put in enough hours in the grocery store or as a pump jockey at the local Esso station, mow a few lawns on the side, get a little help from Dad on the down payment and maybe, just maybe, you could buy one. That is, if your dealer would sell a kid a 409. Most local dealers refused. They didn't want a kid getting killed in a car they had sold. A 409 was killer fast!

The 409 engine could be ordered in about anything Chevrolet built, even station wagons, but the heart-stopping combination was a 409 in a "bubble top" Bel Air two-door hardtop. This body style got its nickname from the vast sweeps of front and rear window glass and was a better pick than the imitation convertible Impala hardtop due to its lighter weight. Fit the 409 with a close-ratio four-speed manual transmission, and in the stoplight grand prix nobody else would even come close (unless you missed a shift or your contender had slipped a Chrysler Hemi into that chopped Ford coupe). Take that 409 to the Saturday night drags and you'd get your car's value, that and a documented race with some pretty impressive times—like 115 mph at the end of a standing-start quarter-mile.

A 409 would go! Its power rating? How about 409 hp for the dual four-barrel carburetor version. OK, so it's 1962 and you're not into drag racing. You're looking for a car to take out on the highway and eat up the miles. You'll stop a little more often to fill up the fuel tank, but a 409 fitted with tall gears, Chevrolet's optional heavy-duty suspension and sintered metallic brakes would easily cruise with the top European sports sedans. On a long straight stretch you might even get the speedometer needle to nudge the 150-mph mark (the bubble-top body was fairly aerodynamic).

With 360 horsepower, the fuel-injected Sebring 327 Corvette was ready to go racing.

1962 Corvette fuel-injected Sebring 327

The last straight-axle Vette was the first to offer a 327-cid small-block V-8. There were three versions of the engine and the hottest was part of a package nicknamed after the sports car races at Sebring, Florida. In this format, Vette enthusiasts got the sole fuel-injected version of the new engine. But, that was cause for excitement. It churned out an unbelievable—for the time—360 hp!

Some say that the high-performance equipment offered for Corvettes of this era were related to the AMA racing ban of 1957 and its effect on Zora Arkus-Duntov. As the story goes, with these competition restrictions, the Corvette's "father" could no longer continue his racing with official factory backing. Therefore, he began to slip some serious racing equipment into the options bin. The story seems plausible, too, when you look at the 1962 Corvette options list. You could not get power steering, power brakes or air conditioning. However, you could add hot "Duntov" camshafts, thermo-activated cooling fans and aluminum-cased transmissions.

Other competition-oriented Corvette "Sebring" extras included 15 x 5.5-inch wheels (no charge), a direct-flow exhaust system (no charge), a 24-gallon fuel tank ($118.40), a four-speed manual gearbox ($188.30), a positraction rear axle ($43.05), sintered-metallic brake linings ($37.70) and heavy-duty suspension ($333.60). The 327-cid/360-hp Rochester fuel-injection engine was $484.20 by itself.

With a 3,080-lb. curb weight, the fuel-injected '62 Vette carried just 8.6 lbs.-per-horsepower (the lowest ratio ever up to that point) and could scat from 0-to-60 mph in just 5.9 seconds. It did the quarter-mile in 14.9 seconds. Until the arrival of the Ford-powered Cobra in late 1962, Corvettes dominated B-production racing in Sports Car Club of America (SCCA) events. This period, in fact, has been called the first "Golden Age" of Corvette racing.

The high-performance image didn't hurt in the showroom. An all-time high of 14,531 Corvettes were manufactured in 1962. However, few had the ready-to-race Sebring package with all the competition-oriented options.

1962 Nova SS 327

Chevy's first compact was the Corvair, but it was off in a class by itself. Competitors like Studebaker's Lark, Chrysler's Valiant/Lancer combo and Ford's Falcon were a bit more conventional in design and Chevy had nothing directly comparable. The boxy 1962 Chevy II was the answer. It had its engine up front, a drive axle at the rear and nothing as radical as an air-cooled "pancake" engine or a transaxle setup

The original engine options for this economy compact were a ho-hum 90-hp four and a slightly sprightlier 120-hp in-ine six. Someone at GM must have also remembered how

the sporty Monza buoyed sagging Corvair sales and decided to put some sting under the Chevy II's bonnet with a dealer-installed V-8 engine option.

Around February 1962, GM announced that any Chevy II buyer wanting to transform the quiet little compact into a boulevard bombshell could do so by adding a dealer-installed Corvette V-8. Any of four Corvette engines—250-, 300-, 340- or 360-hp versions of the easy-breathing 327-cid V-8—could be selected. The conversion was not cheap, adding about $1,400 to the "economy" car's $2,200 base price. On the other hand, what performance the Corvette engine produced!

Fitted with a fuel-injected 360-hp Corvette power plant, the little Chevy II was capable of a top speed in excess of 130 mph. It could leap from 0-to-60 mph in just 7.3 seconds. A power transfusion of this magnitude presented two problems: keeping the rear tires from smoking with every blip of the accelerator and getting the car to go around corners. The Corvette V-8 and four-speed transmission outweighed the stock six and manual three-speed by 160 lbs.

Since almost all of this extra weight rested on the front wheels, heavy-duty front springs (included as part of the engine-swap kit) kept the Vette-powered Chevy II's nose at proper height. A front anti-roll bar helped with cornering.

Other upgrades included heavy-duty (metallic) brake linings and rear traction arms. Surprisingly, the conversion kit did not include a beefier rear axle.

No external markings (except for the telltale dual exhausts) betrayed the beast lurking under a stock-looking Chevy II's hood, but sliding behind the steering wheel put you in front of a 200-mph speedometer and gave notice that this wasn't your typical shopping cart.

Since the Corvette engine was a dealer-installed option, figures aren't available on how many conversions were performed. But if you ever spot an early Chevy II with a V-8 wearing Corvette valve covers under the hood, chances are you're looking at a real factory-inspired hot rod.

The optional 409-cid/380-hp V-8 turned the stylish 1962 Impala SS into a true muscle car.

Jerry Heasley

1962 Impala Super Sport 409/409

Chevrolet's top models were in the Impala line in 1962 and the Super Sport option was available again, but only for sport coupes and convertibles this year. Selling for only $53.80 extra, the SS package was basically a group of special badges, hubcaps and trim items. It was identified as RPO 240 and included swirl-pattern body side moldings, "SS" rear fender emblems, an "SS" deck lid badge, specific Super Sport wheel discs with simulated knock-off spinners, a locking center console and a passenger-assist bar.

The option really had nothing to do with high performance, although the SS name came from a hot drag-racing class and helped sell more cars to youthful buyers. You could even get SS goodies on an Impala hardtop or ragtop with a six-cylinder engine. If you wanted bucket seats, you had to add another $102.25 and you still didn't have a muscle car.

Things started to heat up if you were willing to part with an additional $428 for a 409-cid/380-hp V-8 with a four-barrel carburetor, dual exhausts, a high-lift camshaft and solid valve

lifters. However, if you really wanted muscular performance, you had to move one step up to the 409-hp version of the big Turbo-Fire motor, which included a special lightweight valve train. Its price tag was $484, which sounds reasonable now, but represented a small fortune back in 1962.

A basic V-8-powered Super Sport hardtop listed for $2,776 and the convertible cost $2,919. A well-optioned 409 version was probably $1,000 or more extra. Although a lighter-weight Bel Air Z11 is probably faster, a lot of today's muscle car collectors would rather have a brightly decorated Super Sport with the hottest 409. At least two car magazines printed road tests on sport coupes. The first car was a racing-type aluminum-front-end version that weighed all of 3,500 lbs. It carried 8.6 lbs. per horsepower and did 0-to-60 in 4 seconds and the quarter-mile in 12.2 seconds. The second car tipped the scales at 3,750 lbs., or 9.2 lbs. per horsepower. It needed 6.3 seconds to hit 60 mph from a standing start and did the quarter-mile in 14.9 seconds.

Phil Kunz

The Impala SS 409 was fast in its own right, but it was scary fast when equipped with the Z11 racing package that included a 430-hp V-8, dual four-barrel carburetors, and aluminum body parts.

1963 Impala Z11 427/Impala SS 409

The 1963 Chevrolets promised Jet-Smooth comfort, Jet-Smooth luxury and Jet-Smooth driving excitement. Then there was the Z11. It went like a jet, but it wasn't exactly smooth as it blasted from the "Christmas tree" and left other super stockers coughing in its dust. The Z11 was a monster and it gobbled up the quarter-mile with brutality, rather than the smooth sailing of normal, street-performance Chevy models.

Chevrolet dropped the Bel Air "bubbletop" in 1963. After that, the Impala coupe, with its squared-off roof, became the basis for the RPO Z11 drag-racing package. Only about 57 of these cars were built. All were made specifically for Super/Stock drag-racing competition. Twenty-five Z11s were released by Chevrolet on December 1, 1962. An additional 25 were released on New Year's Day. Seven more were sold later on.

The Z11 option included an aluminum hood, aluminum front fenders, aluminum fender brackets and other lightweight parts. The cars also had no center bumper backing and bracing. All extra insulation was deleted to cut total weight by about 112 pounds. Under the hood was a 427-cid/430-hp V-8 with dual four-barrel carburetors.

Also in 1963, Chevrolet built five Mark II NASCAR 427 "mystery" engines and used them in racing cars at Daytona Beach. The cars the engines went in won the two 100-mile preliminary races and set the track's new stock-car record. These engines were closely related to the Z11 engines and were also prototypes for the 1966 Chevy 396-cid V-8. The cylinder block deck surfaces were angled to parallel the piston domes. The engines also used a staggered or "porcupine" valve layout. Early in the 1963 model year, General Motors ordered

all of its divisions to halt factory support of racing and the mystery-engine project came to a close.

Since most Chevy buyers were not in the market for a Mark II "mystery" engine or a Z11 package, the best option for those interested in a muscular street car was the Impala SS with the extra-cost 409 V-8. The Super Sport equipment package, RPO Z03, was expanded to include all-vinyl bucket seats, swirl-pattern side molding inserts, matching cove inserts, red-filled "SS" overlays for the Impala emblems on the rear fenders, specific full-wheel covers, a center console with a locking storage compartment (with optional Powerglide or four-speed transmission), swirl-pattern dashboard inserts and an "SS" steering wheel center hub.

The package was again available for the Impala sport coupe ($2,774 with the base 283-cid V-8) and the Impala convertible ($3,024 with the base V-8). The Turbo-Fire 409 V-8 was available in three versions. The mildest one had a single four-barrel carburetor and 10.0:1 compression. The second one, selling for $428, came with a single four-barrel carburetor, dual exhausts, a high-lift camshaft, solid valve lifters and an 11.0:1 compression ratio. The wilder 425-hp version, for $484 extra, had dual four-barrel carburetors, dual exhausts, a high-lift camshaft, solid valve lifters and an 11.0:1 compression ratio.

Motor Trend technical editor Jim Wright tested two versions of the Impala SS in the magazine's March 1963 issue. One had the 327-cid V-8. The other had the 409-cid/340-hp engine hooked to a Powerglide two-speed transmission. Even at that, it did 0-to-60 mph in 7.7 seconds and covered the quarter-mile in 15.9 seconds at 88 mph. It was no Z11, but it was fast for 1963.

CHEVROLET

Jerry Heasley

Though it was eventually overshadowed somewhat by the Cobra, the Z06 Corvette was a superior performer and one of the great muscle cars of the 1960s.

1963 Corvette Sting Ray Z06

Chevrolet's all new Sting Ray for 1963 was hot. It had a glorious new body, broadened in scope with the first Corvette coupe. It had an independent rear suspension and fuel injection and even knock-off wheels. Plus, it had the Z06 racing option.

The Z06 Vette bore the mark of Zora Arkus-Duntov, but by no purposeful intent. In fact, Duntov's intention was to keep the racing package nondescript, since Chevrolet was supposedly out of racing.

The Z06 Corvette was impressive for its day and would possibly be as legendary as the L88 is today, except for the superiority of the Cobra, which unexpectedly destroyed Duntov's 1963 Sting Ray party. Ready for sale in October of 1962—and available strictly on the coupe—the Z06 option consisted of a fuel-injected 327-cid engine, a 36.5-gallon fuel tank, heavy-duty brakes, heavy-duty suspension and knock-off wheels.

The heavy-duty brakes consisted of drums with sintered metallic linings, power assisted and backed by a dual circuit master cylinder. "Elephant ear" scoops rammed fresh air to the drums and cooling fans spun with the hub. Early in the 1963 calendar year, Z06 was expanded to include the really necessary racing part, the 36.5-gallon fuel tank, which fit the back of the coupe body like a pea in a pod. Coded N03, the "big tank" helped make the Corvette competitive in long-distance endurance racing events, such as Daytona.

Curiously, the knock-off wheels, which have become almost synonymous with the 1963 split-window Corvette, leaked due to the porosity of the aluminum and poor sealing at the rims. No more than a dozen coupes and roadsters actually got them. Futhermore, only one Corvette has been documented original with original knock-offs. It was originally picked up at the factory by an independent racer. Edward Schlampp Jr. raced the car in the SCCA A-production class.

Later in the model year, N03 was not mandatory with Z06, so only about 60 of the 199 Z06 Corvettes ended up with the big tank. N03 Corvettes also came with their inner wheel well housings modified to fit larger-than-stock tires.

In 1963, no RPO option was hotter than Z06.

Jerry Heasley

Only about 60 1963 Corvettes carried 36.5-gallon fuel tanks.

The Impala SS became a separate model, rather than an option package, in 1964. The mid-sized Chevy had three 409-cid engine choices, including a 425-hp model.

1964 Impala SS 409

Back in the '50s, it was typical for carmakers to apply a popular model name to a line of cars a few years later. For example, Chevy's first hardtop, introduced in 1950, was called the Bel Air. Three years later, the Bel Air name was used on all models in Chevy's fanciest series. This helped sell more cars because people raved about their 1950-1952 "Bel Air" and then Chevy made a whole range of body styles Bel Airs, so even the person who did not want a hardtop could still have a Bel Air.

During the '60s, the same game was played, but in a different way. The '61 Impala SS was launched as an option package, rather than a model. Then the 1964 model lineup offered a separate Impala SS series. Later, as interest in the big SS started to wane, it became an option package again.

The list of standard equipment on the '64 Impala SS took up where regular Impala features left off. Super Sport buyers got leather-grained vinyl upholstery, individual front bucket seats and swirl-pattern dashboard and body molding inserts. They could also store their gloves or sunglasses in a locking center console. Naturally, there were red "SS" emblems all over the cars. In addition, the doors carried red reflectors and neat-looking wheel covers were included.

For 1964, due to the performance ban that GM brass put into effect the previous year, Chevrolet engine choices stayed about the same as in late 1963. Ban or no ban, that meant that the Impala SS 409 hardtop ($2,947) or convertible ($3,196) was still a big, fast car. The hardtop tested out at 7.5 seconds for 0-to-60 mph and 15.3 seconds in the quarter-mile.

The Turbo-Fire 409 V-8 was again available in three versions. The first had a single four-barrel carburetor and 10.0:1 compression. The second version, costing $428 extra, came with a single four-barrel carburetor, dual exhausts, a high-lift camshaft, solid valve lifters and an 11.0:1 compression ratio. The third 409 was a 425-hp version costing $484 extra. It had dual four-barrel carburetors, dual exhausts, a high-lift camshaft, solid valve lifters and an 11.0:1 compression ratio.

In 1963, a total of 16,920 big Chevrolets left the factory with 409s under their hoods, but in 1964 orders for these engines dropped and only 8,684 were installed. That makes the 1964 Impala SS 409 much harder to find than a 1963 edition. In both years, most 409-powered Chevys were Impala Super Sports.

The Chevelle first entered the muscle car game in 1964 with a Malibu SS
model with the 250-hp L30 or 300-hp L74 engine.

CHEVROLET

1964 Chevelle Malibu SS 327

Life started out simple enough for the 1964 Chevelle. It was the lowest-priced of the four all-new A-body intermediates from General Motors that model year. The others were the Pontiac LeMans, the Olds Cutlass and the Buick Skylark.

Inside and outside of the Chevrolet offices, comparisons were readily made to the late and already lamented 1955-1957 Chevrolets. The 115-inch wheelbase of the Chevelle's frame was the same as the 1955 model's. Other dimensions, except height, were close.

A variety of models was offered with the top-of-the-line Malibu two-door hardtop and convertible available with the $170 Super Sport option. This package included bucket seats, a console and appropriate SS badges.

Initial power-plant offerings included the standard 194-cid six, an optional 230-cid six and a pair of old reliable 283-cid V-8s. In V-8 models, the 195-hp two-barrel version was standard. An L77 220-hp version with a four-barrel carburetor was $54 extra.

Nostalgia for the earlier models was fine, but when Pontiac shoved its big 389-cid/325-hp V-8 into GTO-optioned Tempests, the pressure was on to keep up. Oldsmobile answered quickly with a 330-cid/310-hp "police" option for its F-85, which soon evolved into the 4-4-2.

GM had just been through one of its soul-cleansing anti-performance purges in 1963 and Chevrolet, at first, was turned down when it requested that the 327-cid small-block V-8 be approved for use in the Chevelle. GM brass relented and, in quick order, the 250-hp L30 and 300-hp L74 327 V-8s were added to the Chevelle options list at midyear. The former was only $95 over the base 283-cid V-8 and the latter added another $138. Chevy literature even advertised the 365-hp L76 out of the Corvette and some back-door drag racing specials most likely got them.

It seemed that the Chevelle lived right, from its introduction through its value today as a collectible car. A Malibu two-door hardtop listed for $2,484 in base, V-8 form and the convertible at $2,587. Today, show condition convertibles sell for over 10 times their original price and the hardtops only slightly less. Models with four-speed manual gearboxes and SS trim do even better.

Ordering the L84 engine option gave 1964 Corvette buyers a whopping 375 ponies under the hood.

1964 Corvette L84 "Fuelie"

The Corvette Sting Ray's styling was cleaned up a bit for 1964. On coupes, the previous year's distinctive rear window divider was replaced by a solid piece of glass. On all models, the fake hood vents were eliminated and the roof vents were restyled. A three-speed fan was available in the coupe to aid in ventilation.

Chevrolet made 8,304 fuel-injected Sting Ray coupes. They sold for $4,252 and up and weighed 2,945 lbs. The $4,037 convertible weighed in at 2,960 lbs. and had a 13,925-unit production run.

Seven exterior colors were available for 1964: Tuxedo Black, Ermine White, Riverside Red, Satin Silver, Silver Blue, Daytona Blue and Saddle Tan. All body colors were available with a choice of black, white or beige soft tops.

All Corvettes built in 1964 had a 327-cid V-8 block with a 4.00 x 3.25-inch bore and stroke. The base engine had a 10.5:1 compression ratio and developed 250 hp at 4400 rpm and 350 lbs.-ft. of torque at 2800 rpm. It used a single Carter WCFB four-barrel carburetor.

The optional L75 V-8 ($53.80 extra) developed 300 hp at 5000 rpm and 360 lbs.-ft. of torque at 3200 rpm. It had a Carter aluminum Type AFB four-barrel carburetor.

Next came Chevrolet's L76 V-8 with mechanical valve lifters, a high-lift camshaft and a Holley four-barrel carburetor. It had an 11.00:1 compression ratio and developed 365 hp at 6200 rpm and 350 lbs.-ft. of torque at 4000 rpm.

Of course, real muscle car fans had to order the L84 option. This was basically the L75 V-8 fitted with Ram-Jet fuel injection. It was good for 375 hp at 6200 rpm and 350 lbs.-ft. of torque at 4400 rpm.

Only 3.2 percent of 1964 Corvettes were sold with the standard three-speed manual transmission. Most—85.7 percent—were equipped with a four-speed manual transmission. An L84-powered 1964 Corvette could go from 0-to-60 mph in 6.3 seconds and from 0 to 100 mph in 14.7 seconds. It had a top speed of 138 mph.

The 396-cid engine was only available in Sting Rays in 1965. The following year saw the arrival of the 427 big block.

CHEVROLET

1965 Corvette Sting Ray

If the Sting Rays are the best of the Corvettes, quite possibly the 1965 model is the best of the Sting Rays. It is, most assuredly, a memorable Corvette.

Refinement was the key word again in 1965. The '64 Vette offered as improvements a higher horsepower "fuelie" engine option, smoother ride and better insulation. But the best was saved for 1965. The big news in '65 was the addition of four-wheel disc brakes as standard equipment. The small-block Vettes could always go. Now they could stop!

Styling changes were held to a minimum, although Corvette enthusiasts could immediately spot a new '65 by the functional front fender louvers, new wheel covers and restyled grille. With no depressions or trim, the 1965 hood was not interchangeable with the '63 or '64 units. The model range again included a choice of convertible or sleek fastback coupe. Sales reached a record 23,562, including 15,376 convertibles.

Corvette continued as Chevy's prestige leader and the inside story was a decidedly plush one in 1965. Newly styled bucket seats were offered and genuine leather seating surfaces were optional. Options few European sports cars could match included power steering, power brakes, power windows, air conditioning, AM-FM radio, telescopic steering column and a wood-rimmed steering wheel.

But the performance enthusiast was usually drawn first to the engine and power-train specifications sheet. Standard equipment—and meant for the boulevardiers—was Chevy's tried-and-true 327-cid/250-hp Turbofire V-8. The next step up was a 300-hp version of the 327 and new for '65 was the precursor to the famous LT1. This L79 version of the 327 developed an impressive 350 hp, combining "sizzle with calm, cool behavior." Up next was the most powerful carbureted 327, putting out 365 advertised horses.

A legend since 1957, Ram-Jet fuel injection made its final appearance in 1965. At $538, fuel injection was an expensive option, but it made the 327-cid V-8 a 375-hp world-class stormer. It was the ultimate small block.

The introduction, in April 1965, of the 396-cid big-block V-8 marked the beginning of a new era for the Corvette. The 396 was made available at the same time in full-sized Chevrolets and Chevelles. Rated at 425 hp and priced at only $292.70, the 396 made the fuel-injected Corvette seem superfluous in those days of cheap, high-octane gasoline.

The big-block Corvettes could be immediately identified by the "power bulge" on the hood. Introduced at the same time as the 396 was a new $134.50 option, side-mounted exhausts.

Although the fuel-injected Corvette remained through the end of the 1965 model year, it was not widely available and was quietly dropped when the '66s made their appearance. Interestingly, 1965 was also the only year of the 396-cid Corvette. In 1966, that engine was bored out to 427 awesome cubic inches.

1965 was a vintage, memorable year for Corvette. It was the only year you could buy a fuel-injected, disc-braked Sting Ray. It was the first year for the big-block and side-mounted exhausts. And with prices starting at $4,106, the 1965 Corvette Sting Ray was also quite a bargain.

Side-mounted exhausts were an option on the 1965 'Vettes. The big block-equipped cars were identified by the "power bulge" on the hood.

Lerry Mitchell

The big 1965 Chevy Super Sport was available with the 400-hp engine,
but the 340-hp version was more common.

CHEVROLET

1965 Impala SS 409

Car and Driver (December 1964) noted that things had changed, but stayed the same, since the early '60s, when the Beach Boys first sang "She's real fine, my 409." Engine displacements of over 400 cubes had been non-existent only half a decade earlier, but then 406-, 409-, 413- 425- and 426-cid motors had come along, consistently upping the ante for high-performance fans.

The 425 "porcupine-head" big block proved to be nearly a Chevy pipe dream, because after it put in a quick showing at Daytona in 1963, GM brass told all divisions to get out of racing and throw all their racing hardware away. Thus, the 425 became known as Chevrolet's "mystery engine."

As a result of this change, the 409 found its way to the top of the bow-tie options list again when the all-new '65 Chevys arrived. Chevrolet's full-size 1965 model was curvier and larger than its counterparts of 1963-1964. It gained nearly 4 inches of length, although using the same 119-inch wheelbase. Curb weights rose more than 125 lbs. over 1964

for most models. The fact that the new Chevys were larger was a good reason for adding the 409 engine.

For the first time this year, Impala SS models were in their own separate series. The V-8 sport coupe sold for $2,947 and weighed 3,570 lbs. The counterpart convertible was priced at $3,212 and weighed 3,645 lbs.

The 409-cid V-8 came in 340- and 400-hp versions. The more powerful one was available with a Muncie four-speed manual transmission. It had an 11.0:1 compression ratio. However, the 340-hp engine was a better seller by far and is the one that *Car and Driver* tested. This engine featured a single four-throat Rochester carburetor and a 10.0:1 compression ratio. In the 4,200-lb. test car it provided 0.83 hp per pound.

Equipped with a Powerglide automatic transmission and 3.31:1 final gear ratio, the 340-hp Impala SS sport coupe did 0-to-60 in 8 seconds flat. It took all of 16.4 seconds to scoot down the quarter-mile at 91 mph.

Jerry Heasley

The Z16 Chevelle was definitely a wolf in sheep's clothing. Its pedestrian looks concealed a smoking 396-cid/425-hp mill that conceded little to any muscle car on the street.

1965 Chevelle Z16

The '65 Chevelle Z16 was an awesome muscle car that kind of sneaked out in the style of the first GTO. At first, it looked like Chevy was ignoring the clamor for a big-block Chevelle when it made a new 396-cid engine available for two other bow-tie products.

The announcements took place at the General Motors Proving Grounds in Mesa, Arizona, Chevy's all-new Caprice luxury car got a 325-hp version. At the same time, a 425-hp, solid-lifter 396 was made optional in the Corvette.

It seemed like the Chevelle had been overlooked, but nothing could be further from the truth. Through a "secret" program, Chevrolet made a 375-hp 396 available in a special Chevelle Malibu SS 396 model. Chevrolet chose not to advertise this hot car at first, since extremely limited production was anticipated.

Why was production so limited, when the latest GTO was setting sales records and Chevy enthusiasts were wild for a 396-powered muscle Chevelle? Well, the new Malibu SS 396 (RPO Z16) was a hurry-up car that pushed the Chevelle into the big-block muscle car leagues, but its special engineering came at a high cost.

On the surface, the Z16 looked, quite simply, like a big-block Chevelle with the new porcupine-head 396 dropped in. In reality, the Z16 was much more. Underneath, it was a heavy-duty machine that was much more like a big car than an intermediate model. Chevrolet wasn't quite ready to turn it out in mass quantities.

The SS 396 coupe used a convertible frame filled with rear suspension reinforcements and two additional body mounts. Its big power-assisted brakes came from the larger cars, with 11-inch-diameter drums front and rear. The springs and shocks were stiffer than standard Chevelle components. The ball-joint studs were shot-peened and the wheel hubs had sturdy Arma-steel construction. The wheels were six inches wide, compared to the five-inchers on the standard Malibu SS.

Every Z16 came out as a Chevelle Malibu SS Sports Coupe (Fisher Body style No. 13837). All of the cars were coupes—there were no convertibles. The 375-hp 396 was the L37 engine option, with special left- and right-side exhaust manifolds to fit the engine bay. The engine was linked to a four-speed Muncie gearbox with a 2.56:1 first gear. No cars with an automatic transmission were built.

The clutch conformed to big-car specs, too. It was 11 inches in diameter with pressure of 2,300-2,600 lbs. The regular 8.125-inch ring gear from the stock Chevelle wouldn't do, either. Chevrolet installed an 8.875-inch ring gear in the Z16.

Many other features were unique to the Z16, including the air cleaner, which had crossed flags made of metal. There were "396 Turbo-jet" emblems on the front fenders, a special taillight board with an SS emblem and a unique ribbed molding with black paint. All Z16 Chevelles also had a 160-mph speedometer, an AM-FM Multiplex stereo with four speakers, an in-dash tachometer and a dash-mounted clock.

Exactly 201 of the Chevelle Z16s were built for 1965. In 1966, Chevrolet was "geared up" for regular production of a similar car. This SS 396 Chevelle was easier to order and was available to the general public.

CHEVROLET

The Chevy II Nova SS was another hot performer wearing plain clothes. Its handling characteristics were questioned, but its 327-cid mill gave it plenty of motivation in a straight line.

CHEVROLET

1966 Chevy II Nova SS

In the early '60s compact-car race, Ford's Falcon was hot and Chevrolet's Corvair was not. By '62, Chevy had a more conventional Chevy II to fight the Falcon with. A lot of folks compared it to the '55 Chevy, but it didn't have a hot motor to go with its just-right size and looks.

By '63, Chevrolet offered a Super Sport option for the Nova sport coupe and ragtop. The SS package included amenities such complete instrumentation, an electric clock, a deluxe steering wheel, bucket seats and full wheel covers, plus special interior and exterior trim and emblems.

The '66 Chevy II was significantly restyled and engines available for SS Novas included a 327-cid/350-hp V-8 with a staggering 11.0:1 compression ratio. In essence, this was a "factory hot rod."

Racecar tuner Bill Thomas had constructed a hot rod Nova two years earlier. He dubbed it the "Bad Bascomb." It had Corvette independent rear suspension. The factory car had a stock chassis, but it was still hot enough to make your eyes water.

The 327 was a small-block engine derived from the 283. It had a 4.00 x 3.35-inch bore and stroke. The 275-hp RPO L30 edition had a 10.51 compression ratio, hydraulic valve lifters and a single four-barrel carburetor. It generated 275 hp at 4800 rpm and 355 lbs.-ft. of torque at 3200 rpm. The hotter RPO L79 version featured an 11.0:1 compression ratio teamed with the hydraulic lifters and single four-barrel. It cranked out peak horses at 5200 rpm and developed 360 lbs.-ft. of torque at 3600 rpm.

Car Life magazine (May 1966) tested the L79 Nova equipped in true muscle-car-era fashion with a four-speed manual gearbox, limited-slip differential, power steering and brakes, heavy-duty suspension, air conditioning, deluxe bucket seats, a console and full instrumentation. The Corvette engine and other options raised the price from $2,480 to $3,662.

The car did 0-to-60 mph in 7.2 seconds and handled the quarter-mile in 15.1 seconds at 93 mph. The magazine criticized steering and braking, but not its all-out performance and top speed of 123 mph. In July 1966, *Motor Trend* tested an L30 Nova with Powerglide automatic. This car did 0-to-60 in 8.6 seconds and the quarter-mile in 16.4 seconds with a terminal speed of 85.87 mph.

CHEVROLET

Jerry Heasley

The '66 Chevelle SS 396 was basically a no-frills muscle car with three
different 396-cid engine options and a reasonable sticker price.

1966 Chevelle SS 396

The hot-performing '66 SS 396 was a Chevelle—not a Malibu. This kind of product positioning stressed "fast" over "fancy," which seemed most appropriate for Chevy's mid-sized muscle car. The SS 396 wasn't Spartan by any means, but it seemed to be built more for go than show.

Like other Chevelles, the SS models—coupe and ragtop—had a new cigar-shaped body with "lean-forward" front fenders. Two-door Chevelles rode on a just-right-size 115-inch wheelbase and had an overall length of 197 inches. The front and rear tread were both 58 inches wide.

The SS 396s were clearly aimed at muscle car fans willing to spend $2,276 for a sport coupe (two-door hardtop) or $2,984 for a convertible. Together, the two body styles accounted for 72,272 assemblies. More than one enthusiast magazine made comparisons between the SS 396 and hot-rodded '55 Chevys.

The 396-cid V-8 belonged to Chevy's big-block engine family. Essentially a de-stroked 409 with a 4.09 x 3.76-inch bore and stroke, this size engine was standard equipment in the muscular SS. However, it was offered in three configurations.

The standard SS 396 engine was the RPO L35 version with 325 hp at 4800 rpm and 410 lbs.-ft. of torque at 3200 rpm. It had a 10.25:1 compression ratio and single exhausts. The SS kit also included twin simulated hood air intakes, ribbed color-accented sill and rear fender lower moldings, a black-out style SS 396 grille, black rear cove accents and

"Super Sport" script plates on the rear fenders. Specific wheel covers were included, along with red-stripe tires. An all-vinyl bench seat interior was standard.

Next up the rung was the RPO L34 version of the 396, which shared its cylinder head and compression ratio with the L35 version, but had certain upgrades such as a forged-alloy crankshaft, dual exhausts, a higher-lift cam and chrome piston rings. These helped raise its output to 360 hp at 5200 rpm and 420 lbs.-ft. of torque at 3600 rpm. The 360-hp SS 396 Sport Coupe did 0-to-60 mph in 7.9 seconds and the quarter-mile in 15.5 seconds.

Top option in the SS 396 lineup was the RPO L78 engine, a midyear release that was probably installed in less than 100 cars. It had an 11.0:1 compression ratio, fatter tailpipes, a hotter slide-lifter cam and other go-fast goodies that jacked its output number to 375 hp at 5600 rpm and 415 lbs.-ft. at 3800 rpm. Cars with this engine could do 0-to-60 mph in about 6.5 seconds.

Any of the 396-cid engines could be ordered with the M20 wide-ratio four-speed manual transmission or the M-21 close-ratio four-speed. Also available was the M35 Powerglide automatic. Rear axle options included 3.31:1, 3.55:1, 3.73:1, 4.10:1, 4.56:1 and 4.88:1 depending upon the engine-transmission combination. You could get positraction on all but the 3.31 and 3.55 axles.

The big-block 427 Corvette was clearly one of the hottest cars around, especially if it packed the 425-hp mill.
Such a setup brought sub-14-second times on the drag strip.

Jerry Heasley

1966 Corvette 427

When *Car Life* magazine did a comparison between two '67 Corvettes, it picked one car with a 327-cid V-8 and automatic and a second car with the 427-cid big-block V-8 and a four-speed manual gearbox. The latter vehicle was accurately described as, "a muscular, no-nonsense, do-it-right-now hustlecar." The editors added, "A drive in the 427 can convince anyone with a drop of sporting blood in his veins that an over-abundance of power can be controllable and greatly invigorating."

The basic format of the Corvette Sting Ray had been established by the classic 1963 model. For 1967, the overall appearance was cleaned up and the front fender had five functional, vertical air louvers that slanted forward towards their upper ends. The roof pillar air vents used on earlier fastback coupes were eliminated.

The new 427-cid V-8 came in 390- and 425-hp versions. *Car Life* tested the heftier version and found that it had power peak at a lower rpm and a wider range of torque delivery. This made the maximum muscle option more compatible to everyday driving, but didn't seem to hamper its quarter-mile capabilities. The 425-hp engine featured strong cam timing, special exhaust headers, a transistorized ignition system, solid lifters and a big four-barrel Holley carburetor. The 390-hp big-block initially came hooked to a mandatory wide-ratio four-speed manual gearbox and the 425-hp job came attached to a close-ratio four-speed stick. A modified Powerglide automatic was scheduled as a midyear option for the 390-hp engine only.

Car Life's 427/425 Corvette was a ragtop to boot. Its as-tested price tag of $5,401 included a Positraction rear axle, tinted windshield, transistor ignition, AM/FM radio, telescoping steering shaft, 7.75-15 UniRoyal Laredo gold stripe nylon tires, the close-ratio four-speed, power brakes, power steering and power windows. With a curb weight of 3,270 lbs. it had an 8.5:1 weight-to-power ratio. Zero-to-60 mph came in just 5.7 seconds and the quarter-mile was covered in 14 seconds with a terminal speed of 102 mph.

1967 Camaro 427

Camaros fitted with big-block 427-cid Chevrolet V-8s were evaluated by Chevrolet's engineering department in early 1967, just a few months after the new model first hit the showrooms. At about that time, one of these creations was demonstrated to the press by Chevrolet technical projects manager Walter R. Mackenzie.

As you might guess, the experimental 427-powered Camaro topped the performance of even the hottest of the production versions of the car. Mackenzie's machine was able to accelerate down the quarter-mile at times in the 13.5 to 13.90-second bracket. This car was actually a pilot model of the drag-racing-only machines that car builders would soon be constructing in various parts of the country.

These cars were constructed as "semi-factory-built" racing cars by a small number of high-volume Chevrolet dealerships that had close links to drag racing and Chevrolet Motor Division's Product Promotion Network. The managers and salesmen at such dealerships became key players in the development, sales and promotion of the 427 Camaros.

The specialized Chevrolet dealers involved in such

CHEVROLET

programs included Don Yenko Chevrolet in Canonsburg, Pennsylvania, Baldwin Motion Chevrolet of Baldwin, Long Island, New York, Dana Chevrolet in South Gate, California, Nickey Chevrolet in Chicago, Illinois, and the Fred Gibb Agency of La Harpe, Illinois.

Don Yenko, Dana Chevrolet and Nicky Chevrolet all started selling Camaros fitted with L72 Corvette engines (the 427-cid, 425-hp V-8) in 1967. Dana's basic version listed for $3,995. In addition to the big motor, the package included a Muncie four-speed manual gearbox, a 3.55:1 Positraction axle, 14 x 6-inch wheels with D70-14 Firestone wide-oval nylon red line tires, metallic brake linings, headers and dual exhausts, heavy-duty clutch and pressure plate, a fat front stabilizer bar, heavy-duty shocks and a 17-quart radiator. *Motor Trend* tested a Dana 427 Camaro with a 3.73:1 axle and 9.00/9.50 x 14 tires. It did the quarter-mile in 12.75 seconds at over 110 mph.

Jerry Heasley

**Only 104 of the 1967 Camaro RS/SS Indy 500 Pace Cars
(far left) were built, but there were more versions to follow.**

1967 Camaro Indy 500 Pace Car

It was new! It was its first year in the market! It was Chevy's answer to the trend-setting Mustang! No wonder the '67 Camaro was treated to an aggressive sales campaign. To fend off competition from Ford's pony and Plymouth's Barracuda, there was a seemingly constant revision of first-year Camaro options and trim choices.

Initially, the Camaro line offered a base two-door hardtop or Sport Coupe and a convertible. You could add Rally Sport trim (including hidden headlights), as well as the SS 350, which added stripes around the nose, special badges and a 295-hp version of Chevy's new 350-cid small-block V-8.

Since the 350 Camaro didn't seem to be enough to pull many customers away from Ford's new 390-cid Mustang or Plymouth's 383-cid Formula S Barracuda, Chevrolet very soon added its Mark IV big-block 396 to the Camaro options list. This engine developed 325 hp in its L35 form. Additional power selections arrived when the L78 engine option was unleashed. It provided Camaro SS 396 buyers with a 375-hp option.

Chevrolet got the chance to show off its newest product at the Indy 500, where the Camaro paced the racing cars. However, marketing wasn't what it was to become in later years and the cars supplied were RS/SS 396 convertibles. Chevrolet employee and two-time 500 winner Mauri Rose (1947, 1948) drove the pace car and A.J. Foyt got to keep a Camaro for winning the event.

Instead of offering replicas to dealers, Chevrolet built only 104 of the Camaros and let Indianapolis Motor Speedway VIPs use them during the month of May. Most of these "Indy Pace Cars" were SS 350s with Powerglide automatics. The 396s used for track purposes had the new Turbo-Hydra-Matic installed. When the race was over, the replicas were sold, as used cars, through local Indianapolis dealers.

The first-year Camaro was a big success with 220,917 produced, but it did not quite beat Ford's Mustang. SS production for 1969 amounted to only 34,411 cars, making them rarer than those who viewed all the Chevy SS promotions realized. The Camaro would be the Indy 500 pace car again in 1969. That time around, the marketing was handled a little bit better.

CHEVROLET

Jerry Heasley

The first Camaro to join the muscle car wars was the SS model, which carried either 350 or 396 cubes under the hood. Great styling certainly added to the car's appeal.

1967 Camaro SS 350/SS 396

CHEVROLET

Sketches of a new GM car called the Panther filled car-enthusiast magazines in the mid-'60s. They were said to predict what Chevrolet's version of the Mustang would look like. When it bowed on September 29, 1966, the real-life Camaro seemed far different than the drawings. In this case, the reality was better!

Just as the Mustang was based on the Falcon, the Camaro was based on the Chevy II Nova. That meant it could accommodate all kinds of muscular Chevy V-8s. To Chevy lovers, the term Super Sport equated to a muscle car, so the high-performance Camaro utilized the same "SS" designation as its bigger brothers.

An extensive lineup of engines was offered for Chevy's late-breaking contender in the pony car market and the initial offering for muscle car maniacs was a hot new small-block RPO L48 V-8 with 350 cubic inches and 295 hp. You could order it only with the SS 350 package, which included a raised hood with non-functional finned louvers, a "bumblebee" nose stripe, special ornamentation, fat red-stripe tires and a stiff suspension. Best of all, you got all this for $211.

A heavy-duty three-speed manual transmission was standard in the Camaro SS and options included a two-speed Powerglide automatic or a four-speed manual gear box. There was also a wide variety of rear axle ratios including 2.73:1, 3.07:1, 3.31:1, 3.55:1, 3.73:1, 4.10:1, 4.56:1 and 4.88:1. *Car and Driver* tested an SS 350 at 0-to-60 mph in 7.8 seconds and the quarter-mile in 16.1 seconds at 86.5 mph. *Motor Trend* needed 8 seconds to get to 60 mph, but did the quarter in 15.4 at 90 mph.

On November 26, 1966, Chevy released a pair of 396-cid big-block V-8 options: The RPO L34, which was priced at $235 with the SS package, produced 325 hp. The RPO L78 ($550 including SS goodies) produced an advertised 375 hp.

Motor Trend tested an L35 SS 396 Camaro with four-speed gearbox at 6 seconds for 0-to-60 mph and a 14.5-second quarter-mile at 95 mph. *Car Life* (May 1967) drove a similar car with Powerglide and registered a 6.8-second 0-to-60 time and 15.1-second quarter-mile at 91.8 mph.

Since a total of 34,411 Super Sports were built and 29,270 were SS 350 models, that leaves 5,141 that were built as SS 396s.

The fledgling Z/28 was quick as a cat, despite sporting only a 302-cid small block. The car had a racing
pedigree, and its performance certainly didn't disappoint.

1967 Camaro Z/28

"Win on Sunday, sell on Monday" was the automakers' creed in the super '60s. In the Camaro's case, in '67, the Sports Car Club of America's new Trans-Am "sedan" racing series was the place to strut your stuff.

In Trans-Am Cup competition, engine size was capped at 305 cubic inches, so the various companies strived to develop the most muscular motor they could within this "formula." Chevy's Vince Piggins decided the answer was to create a Camaro powered by a maximum-output small-block V-8. The Z/28 was the result of this effort.

RPO Z/28 was a performance equipment package designed to make the Camaro a contender in Trans-Am events. It was introduced November 26, 1966, during the American Road Race of Champions at Riverside Raceway in California.

Chevrolet used a 283-cid V-8 in the pilot version, but that was too far below the 305-cid engine-displacement limit to be a winner. In the production car, Chevrolet combined the 327-cid block with the 283-cid crankshaft and came up with a 302-cid V-8. By playing with other high-performance parts

like a giant four-barrel carb, an aluminum high-rise intake and L79 Corvette heads, they got this motor to crank out about 350 hp and 320 lbs.-ft. of torque at 6200 rpm. However, to play it safe, the Z/28 was advertised at 290 hp at 5800 rpm and 290 lbs.-ft. of torque at 4200 rpm.

The basic Z/28 package listed for $358, but other options were mandatory with the car and jacked the price up to where a typical Z/28 sold for at least $4,200. The price included a heater, but air conditioning was not available. And for those with serious racing in mind, even the heater could be deleted.

The Z/28 performed very well and, since it was designed for competitive road racing, it had terrific handling and braking to go with its impressive straight-line acceleration. The 1967 first-year model could move from 0-to-60 mph in 6.7 seconds and did the quarter-mile in an amazing 14.9 seconds at 97 mph. Its top speed was 124 mph.

The 1967 Impala SS 396 was a smooth-riding, big-car alternative for buyers who preferred a bigger vehicle.

1967 Impala SS 396

Smaller cars went faster when fitted with big engines. First it was the Falcon, the Valiant and the Chevy II. Then along came mid-sized muscle like the GTO and SS 396. By the time the Mustang and Camaro made the scene, big muscle cars like the Impala SS were beginning to fade from popularity.

The SS package started life as a midyear option for the full-sized Chevrolet in 1961. It became a lot more available in '62 and by '63-'64, the Impala SS was a high-performance icon. In '65, the SS played a major role in Chevy's big-car efforts, but by '66 you could sense a change was taking place.

One of the model's spotlight years was 1967, when a revival of sorts took place. The '67 Impala SS 396 was not just a go-to-work car with a hood scoop. It offered gunboat lovers a "no-excuses-sir" big-car alternative to mid-size muscle.

This is not to say that all Impala Super Sports for 1967 were performance cars. Continuing a practice that started with the '62 models, you could get either a Sport Coupe or convertible with SS markings and an incongruous six-cylinder engine. However, Chevy's Mark IV-based big-block V-8s made the SS name mean something real.

The 396-cid/325-hp Turbo-Jet (L35) engine was a good option for starters. It had a 4.094 x 3.76-inch bore and stroke. With its four-barrel Holley carburetor and 10.25:1 compression ratio, the version used in the Impala SS cranked up 325 hp at 4800 rpm and 410 lbs.-ft. of torque at 3200 rpm. The standard transmission used with this engine in the Impala SS was a fully synchronized three-speed manual gearbox. Options included four-on-the-floor, a console-mounted two-speed Powerglide automatic or the three-speed Hydra-Matic.

The Impala was a big car in 1967. It rode a 119-inch wheelbase and was 213.2 inches long overall. Tread measurements were 62.5 inches up front and 62.4 inches at the rear. Regular equipment included 8.25 x 15 tires (or 8.15 x 15 tires if the optional disk brakes were ordered). The V-8-powered hardtop listed for $3,003 and weighed 3,615 lbs. The convertible with a base V-8 had a $3,535 list price and weighed in at 3,650 lbs. Nevertheless, these cars could move from 0-to-60 mph in about 8.5 seconds and did the quarter-mile in around 16.3 seconds.

While not a huge sales success, the 1967 Impala SS collected 66,510 orders for the hardtop and 9,545 for the convertible and most were SS 396s. The big Impala SS models returned to extra-cost-option status after 1967.

The SS 427 was large for a muscle car, but some racey options and available
425-hp engine gave it some solid performance numbers.

1967 Impala SS 427

In 1967, with Chevelle sales soaring on the SS 396's muscle reputation, Chevrolet concluded that high performance could help to sell big cars. This led to the Impala SS 427.

To understand the SS 427's role in the product mix, it's important to remember that the Chevelle SS 396 was more than a Malibu with Super Sport trim. Malibus were not available with the big Turbo-Jet V-8, while SS 396s came only that way. That made the SS 396 exclusive. Its real job was establishing a high-performance identity that would spur sales of the less costly Chevelles it resembled.

Similarly, the Impala SS 427 was intended to be an "image" car, though one of larger proportions. While the 427-cid engine was made available in other Chevrolets, only the SS 427 came with a full assortment of muscle-car goodies. They included special badges and engine call-outs, a Corvette-inspired power dome hood, larger wheels, a stiffer suspension and standard red-stripe tires.

When first introduced, SS 427 features were optional for two body styles in the separate 1967 Impala SS series. Regular Super Sport equipment included vinyl-clad Strato bucket seats, black grille finish, wheelhouse moldings, black lower body and deck lid accents, badges and specific wheel covers. A second option, coded RPO L36, turned the SS into an SS 427. This $316 package included the SS 427 trim and a 385-hp 427 Turbo-Jet V-8.

Ordering this option required the buyer to add at least the heavier-duty M13 three-speed manual gearbox. For additional go-power, an M20 four-speed or Turbo-Hydra-Matic could be specified, as could a more powerful 425-hp engine. Out of a total run of 76,055 Impala Super Sports, only 2,124 were SS 427s.

Viewing any SS 427 as a muscle car depends on one's definition of the species. The '67 version was road tested at 8.4 seconds for 0-to-60 mph and 15.8 seconds for the quarter-mile. That's just slightly slower than a 1970 SS 396 Chevelle with 350 hp, which isn't bad at all for a full-sized Chevy.

With all the fanfare being paid to the new Camaro, the 1967 Chevy II Nova SS was somewhat forgotten. Still, it packed a 327-cid V-8 and was a nice little performer for the money.

1967 Chevrolet II Nova SS

The Nova got only minor changes for its second year in the marketplace. There was a new anodized aluminum grille that had a distinct horizontal-bars motif with a Chevy II nameplate on the driver's side. The Super Sport -- or SS -- series continued to be available as an upper line in the Nova model range.

The Nova SS sport coupe had a suggested base price of $2,467 and weighed 2,690 lbs. Appearance items included with the SS ranged from a special black-accented grille and specific Super Sport full wheel covers to body and wheelhouse moldings. Naturally, there were SS badges in several locations. The interior featured all-vinyl trim with front Strato bucket seats, a three-spoke steering wheel and a floor shift trim plate.

This boxy, but neat-looking Chevy compact continued to make an excellent muscle car when equipped with the right extras. In the January 1967 *Motor Trend*, "Tex" Smith noted, "The fattest parts catalog of all is authored by Chevrolet, but with it comes the sad tale of yanking power options from some of the lines, notably Corvair and Chevy II, to the extent that one wonders if Ralph Nader has been secretly elected to the board of directors."

Smith pointed out that the maximum output engine for the '67 Nova SS was a 327-cid/275-hp V-8 that had 75 hp less than the top 1966 engine option. This four-barrel motor with 10.25:1 compression generated peak horsepower at 4800 rpm and put out 355 lbs.-ft. of torque at 3200 rpm. Tex did point out, however, that the Nova SS retained all of its 1966 gearing selections and was "surprisingly alert," despite all the changes Chevrolet had made.

The motivation for the power reduction was the new Camaro, which was actually based on the Chevy II/Nova. Chevrolet did not want a hot, Corvette-engined Nova stealing muscle car fans away from the new pony car. In the end, the people spoke and a lot of parts managers were kept busy ordering Camaro bits for smart Nova owners. Total production of the Nova SS was 10,100 units.

CHEVROLET

The popular Chevelle SS 396 came with 325-, 350- or 375-hp engine options. Even though production was off slightly for the model year, more than 63,000 SS 396s were built.

Jerry Heasley

1967 Chevelle SS 396

Chevrolet's mid-size 1967 Chevelle continued on with a cigar-shaped body and forward-thrusting front fenders. The radiator grille had more prominent horizontal bars. The prices for the SS 396 coupe jumped to $2,825 and the SS 396 convertible's price increased by the same amount to $3,033. Annual production of Chevelle SS 396s fell a bit, with 63,006 being made.

Chevelle Super Sport models again had twin simulated hood air intakes, ribbed color-accented sill and rear fender lower moldings, a black-out style SS 396 grille and rear cove accents and "Super Sport" script plates on the rear fenders. Specific SS wheel covers were included, along with red-stripe tires. An all-vinyl bench seat interior was standard.

The 325-hp engine (RPO L35) was carried over as the base choice in 1967. The RPO L34 version was also offered again, but its horsepower rating dropped to 350 hp at 5200 rpm. The L78 375-hp version of the 396-cid V-8 was not listed on

Chevy specifications sheets, but it was possible to purchase the components needed to "build" this option at your Chevy dealer's parts counter. The total cost of everything needed to upgrade a 350-hp engine to a 375-hp job was $475.80.

SS 396 buyers could get the 325-hp engine with a standard heavy-duty three-speed manual transmission, a four-speed manual gearbox, Powerglide automatic (or later in the year, Turbo-Hydra-Matic). There was a choice of nine axle ratios from 3.07:1 to 4.10:1, but specific options depended upon transmission choice. The 350-hp engine came with the heavy-duty three-speed manual, wide- or close-ratio four speeds or Powerglide. There were eight rear axle ratios from 3.07:1 to 4.88:1, but you could not get all of them with every engine and transmission setup.

The 1967 SS 396 sport coupe with 375 hp did 0-to-60 mph in 6.5 seconds and did the quarter-mile in 14.9 seconds.

The big forward-facing hood scoops were trademarks of the high-powered Corvette 427.

CHEVROLET

1967 Corvette 427

Some consider the 1967 the best looking of the early Sting Rays. Its styling, although basically the same as in 1966, was a bit cleaner. The same egg-crate style grille with Argent Silver finish was carried over. The same smooth hood seen in 1966 was re-used. The crossed flags badge on the nose of the 1967 Corvette had a widened "V" at its top. On the sides of the front fenders were five vertical and functional louvers that slanted towards the front of the car.

Minor changes were made to the interior. Most noticeable was the relocation of the parking brake from under the dash to the center console. The new headliner was cushioned with foam and fiber material. Four-way flashers, directional signals with a lane-change function, larger interior vent ports and folding seat-back latches were all new. At the rear there were now dual round taillights on each side (instead of a taillight and optional back-up light). The twin back-up lights were now mounted in the center of the rear panel, above the license plate.

Standard equipment included a new dual-chamber brake master cylinder, 6-inch-wide slotted rally wheels with trim rings, an odometer, a clock, carpeting and a tachometer. The optional finned aluminum wheels were changed in design and had a one-year-only, non-knock-off center. Ten lacquer exterior finishes were offered: Tuxedo Black, Ermine White, Elkhart Blue, Lyndale Blue, Marina Blue, Goodwood Green, Rally Red, Silver Pearl, Sunfire Yellow and Marlboro Maroon.

All convertibles came with a choice of a Black, White or Teal Blue soft top. The all-vinyl foam-cushioned bucket seats came in Black, Red, Bright Blue, Saddle, White and Blue, White and Black, Teal Blue and Green.

The Corvette "427," with its own funnel-shaped, power bulge on the hood, had been introduced in 1966. Its big-block V-8 was related to Chevrolet's 427-cid NASCAR "mystery" racing engine and the production-type Turbo-Jet 396. A 427-cid/435-hp 1967 Corvette convertible carried on 7.7 lbs. per horsepower. It could hit 60 mph in 5.5 seconds and do the quarter-mile in 13.8 seconds. Three four-speed manual gearboxes—wide-ratio, close-ratio and heavy-duty close-ratio—were optional. A desirable extra was side-mounted exhaust pipes.

Cars with 427s got a different power bulge hood and more top horsepower (435) when fitted with three two-barrel carburetors. The special hood had a large, forward-facing air scoop, usually with engine call-outs on both sides.

There were four versions of the 427 in 1967. The regular L36 was nearly unchanged from mid-1965. Next came the L68, with 400 hp. The Tri-Power L71 delivered 435 hp. Extremely rare (only 20 were built)—and off in a class by itself—was the aluminum-head L88. This powerhouse was officially rated at only 430 hp, but really developed nearly 600 hp!

CHEVROLET

The Camaro SS didn't change much for 1968—Chevy didn't need to mess with a good thing.
The hairiest engine option was the L89 mill that delivered 375 hp and went into only 311 cars.

Jerry Heasley

1968 Camaro SS 396

It takes an expert to tell the difference between the first Camaro and the second one at a glance. Only minor changes were made for '68. The front end received subtle changes and ventless side windows were introduced. A new Astro-Ventilation system was relied on to bring fresh air into the cockpit. Rectangular parking lamps replaced the square ones of 1967 and side marker lamps, required by new federal laws, were added. The grille insert was finished in silver instead of black. Front and rear spoilers were now optional.

Chevrolet expanded the number of Camaro SS options to five. The SS 350 had the same hood as in 1967, but the SS 396s had a unique hood with four non-functional intake ports on either side. The SS 396 represented the ultimate Camaro production car for muscle car lovers and it came in four versions. The L35, which produced 325 hp at 4800 rpm and 410 lbs.-ft. of torque at 3200 rpm, was the most popular with 6,752 installations. Second in popularity was the L78 edition, which 4,889 buyers ordered. It produced 375 hp at 5600 rpm and 415 lbs.-ft. at 3600 rpm. The L34 version,

which generated 350 hp at 5200 rpm and 415 lbs.-ft. of torque at 3600 rpm went into 2,018 cars. Rarest was the L89 version with aluminum heads. It was conservatively rated for 375 hp at 5600 rpm and 415 lbs.-ft. at 3600 rpm, but due to its high $896 price tag drew only 311 orders.

In 1968, the L35 option cost $63.20 over the base 350-cid Camaro SS engine. The L34 was $184.35 extra and the L78 was $316 extra. Other desirable SS options included the M20 and M21 four-speed manual gearboxes, both for $195.40, the M22 heavy-duty four-speed manual gearbox for $322.10, M40 Turbo-Hydra-Matic transmission for $221.80, a ZL2 cowl-induction hood for $79, a JL8 four-wheel disc brakes package for $500.30, a U16 tachometer for $52.70, U17 special instrumentation for $94.80 and G80 Positraction for $42.15.

Car Life magazine road tested a 375-hp SS 396 with cold-air induction and other muscle car hardware. It did 0-to-60 mph in 6.8 seconds and the quarter-mile in 14.77 seconds at 98.72 mph. Its top speed was 126 mph.

The Z/28 came only as a hardtop coupe in 1968.

Jerry Heasley

1968 Camaro Z/28

Even though only 602 copies were made, the Chevrolet Camaro Z/28 Special Performance Package made a strong impact on muscle car fans in 1967, especially considering that it was made primarily for road racing and had only half of a selling season in the marketplace. While it did not catch the Ford Mustang in sales, the Camaro was not that far behind the original, four-year-old pony car in racing results and that's something that rapidly enhanced the Z/28's appeal to enthusiasts.

In the hard-fought Trans-Am racing series, Roger Penske's Camaros had taken the checkered flag at Marlboro, Las Vegas and Kent, Washington, earning driver Mark Donohue some much-deserved recognition. The Camaro Z/28's image was mostly associated with this form of competition and the Z/28 was specifically designed to fit the Sports Car Club of America's small-cubic-inches formula.

As in its first year, the 1968 Z/28 came only as a two-door sport coupe. You could not order it with air conditioning or with an automatic transmission. In fact, you had to order a four-speed manual gearbox, as well as optional power-assisted front disc brakes. Also included was a dual exhaust system, deep-tone mufflers, special front and rear suspensions, a heavy-duty radiator, a temp-controlled de-clutching fan,

quick-ratio steering, with 15 x 6-inch wheel rims, E70 x 15 white-letter tires and special body striping.

Below its hood, the Z/28 featured the same hot 302-cid Chevy small-block V-8 that had been used in 1967. This engine had an easy-to-remember 4.0 x 3.0-inch bore and stroke. It carried a single 800-cfm Holley four-barrel carburetor on top of a special intake manifold and had 11.0:1 compression pistons. Maxium horsepower was 290 at 5800 rpm and it generated 290 lbs.-ft. of torque at 4200 rpm.

In addition to the standard Muncie four-speed, a Muncie close-ratio four-speed gearbox was the only option. A 3.73:1 rear axle was standard and six other ratios were optional: 3.07:1, 3.31:1, 3.55:1, 4.10:1, 4.56:1 and 4.88:1.

The 1968 Camaro Z/28 was road tested by three major magazines. It was written up in the June issue of *Road & Track*, which recorded a 0-to-60 time of 6.9 seconds and a 14.9-second quarter-mile at 100 mph. *Car Life* did its test in July '68 recording a 7.4-second 0-to-60 run and a 14.85-second quarter-mile at 101.4 mph. *Car and Driver* really caught the attention of enthusiasts, in June, with its 5.3-second 0-to-60 and a 13.77-second quarter-mile at 107.39 mph! No wonder Z/28 sales started to take off this year. Chevrolet put together 7,199 examples of its Camaro road racer.

CHEVROLET

Only 1,778 1968 Impala sport coupes had the SS 427 package.

1968 Impala SS 427

When it returned in 1968, the Impala Super Sport 427 reflected both styling and marketing changes from the previous season. Chevrolet Motor Division adopted a new technique of sculpting bodies by stretching cloth over a wire frame and blowing it out to create "fluid" shapes. The result was a smoother, softer appearance. Chevy also dropped the separate Impala SS series, replacing it with a new Z03 Super Sport option package. Priced at $179.05, it included essentially the same extras that cars in the 1967 Impala SS series had.

Another of Chevrolet's marketing changes involved making the performance option available for three Impala models, instead of just two. You could order it for the $2,968 sport coupe, the $3,021 custom coupe or the $3,197 convertible. The custom coupe had a more formal roofline and lower production total.

Making the SS an option made the SS 427 package an "option for an option." Coded RPO Z24, it had all of the basic SS features, plus a special performance hood, red-stripe tires, 15-inch wheel rims and the RPO L36 427-cid Turbo-Jet engine for $358.10. This "standard" version of the 427 had a 10.25:1 compression ratio. It developed 385 hp at 5200 rpm and 460

lbs.-ft. of torque at 3400 rpm.

Chevrolet buyers could also spend $542.45 to get a second SS 427 package featuring the L72 version of the engine with 11.0:1 compression. It was good for 425 hp at 5600 rpm and the same 460 lbs.-ft. of torque at a higher 4000 rpm.

Unfortunately, the 1968 Impala SS 427 proved ineffective in boosting big-car sales to enthusiasts. Total production of Impalas with Super Sport equipment took a big drop to 38,210 units. A mere 1,778 had the SS 427 option. Experts say the 1968s are the more desirable to collectors, but they also represent the easiest SS 427 model to fake. This is because they were not coded as an individual series model.

In September 1968, *Hot Rod* magazine published an article entitled "600-Plus Horsepower from Chevy's 427" that covered some 427-cid racing modifications that could produce 600 hp. It also talked about the availability of a "triple two-barrel" carburetion system option. According to editor Eric Rickman, this setup used primary No. 3925517 and secondary No. 3902353 in conjunction with the 1967 intake manifold No. 3904574. While perhaps not strictly stock, a 600-hp SS 427 would be a helluva muscle car.

Muscle car fans could have one of two 396-cid engines squeezed into their Nova SS in 1968. The first version delivered 350 hp. The second mill wasn't even advertised, but delivered 375 ponies.

CHEVROLET

Phil Kunz

1968 Nova SS 396

The "Gen II" Chevy II/Nova is becoming one of the hottest collectible Chevrolets in today's youth-oriented enthusiast marketplace. Starting in '68, Chevy's "senior compact" was restyled to resemble a small Chevelle. The re-skinned Nova was perched on a 111-inch wheelbase and you would need a 183.3-inch long measuring tape to gauge the distance between the front and rear bumpers. The new "Coke-bottle" body was 72.4 inches wide and 52.6 inches high. The coupe weighed about 2,850 lbs.

The new Nova appeared to be anything but a real muscle car when it made its first appearance in the fall of 1967. At that time, only two body styles were offered and Super Sport equipment was now considered an option package.

But the car's image began to change by the time the sales year was half over. The Nova's new stub frame was borrowed from the Camaro parts bin and, by January 1968, Nova buyers were being offered some new engine options, since big-block V-8s fit comfortably in the new power plant cradle.

For small-block performance fans, the milder 327-cid V-8 with 275 hp was carried over from the last two years. Joining it were two hotter small-block-based options. These were the new 350-cid/295-hp V-8 with a 10.25:1 compression ratio

and a 325-hp version of the 327 with 11.0:1 compression. However, the really big news was the availability of the 396-cid V-8, which was now being offered for serious muscle-car lovers.

Sharing 4.094 x 3.76-inch bore and stroke dimensions and a single four-barrel carburetor setup, the 396-cid big-block V-8s came two ways. The first version had a 10.25:1 compression ratio. It generated 350 hp at 5200 rpm and 415 lbs.-ft. of torque at 3200 rpm. The second version had an 11:1 compression ratio and delivered 375 hp at 5600 rpm and 415 lbs.-ft. of torque at 3600 rpm. Chevrolet didn't advertise this engine, which provided 6-second 0-to-60 mph performance and was good for 14-second quarter-mile runs.

The Nova's standard transmission was a column-mounted three-speed. Options included a three-speed with floor shifter, a four-speed stick (commonly ordered by muscle car fans) and Powerglide automatic.

The Nova SS had a base price of about $2,995. Chevrolet built a total of just 5,571 cars carrying the Nova SS package this year. Of those, only 234 had the milder 396-cid engine and 667 had the 396-cid/375-hp option.

CHEVROLET

Phil Kunz

The redesigned Chevelle ran as good as it looked in 1968 with a 396-cid mill as motivation. The L78 engine option was the top of the line and offered 375 hp.

1968 Chevelle SS 396

"To say Chevelle is all-new is an understatement," boasted the 1968 sales catalog for Chevy's hot mid-sized model. "It is brilliantly original for '68! Out-of-the-ordinary roof lines, front fenders and taillight arrangements. The latest look in long-hood/short deck styling. Two wheelbases: 112 in. for coupes and convertibles, 116 inches for sedans and wagons. An expansive grille to emphasize wider tread."

The new '68 Chevelle body had a "wrap-over" front end to give it a distinctive character. It also had the long-in-front-short-in-back styling that was all the rage in this era. As with other '68 GM intermediates, the use of two wheelbases allowed for sportier-looking Chevelle coupes and ragtops.

The high-performance SS 396 was a separate series in 1968. It included a sport coupe base-priced at $2,899 and a convertible priced at $3,102. Both had the shorter wheelbase, of course. Overall length, at 197.1 inches, was just a tad longer than in 1967, even though the wheelbase was downsized by 3 inches. Front and rear tread widths were also up an inch to 59 inches. The new Chevelle was also nearly an inch taller at 52.7 inches.

The SS 396 models were made even more distinctive by the use of matte black finish around the full lower perimeter of the bodies, except when the cars were finished in a dark color. Other SS features included F70 x 14 wide-oval red-stripe tires, body accent stripes, a special twin-domed hood with simulated air intakes, "SS" badges, vinyl upholstery and a heavy-duty three-speed transmission with floor-mounted shifter.

The standard engine was the RPO L35 version of the 396-cid V-8, which had an advertised 325 hp. The RPO L34 version with 350 hp was $105 extra and was the only option early in the year. That situation didn't last long, as competitors like the 375-hp Dodge Charger R/T and 350-hp Olds 4-4-2 were soon stealing sales away from Chevrolet based on horsepower alone.

At midyear, Chevy re-released the RPO L78 version of the 396 with 375 hp. This option cost $237 more than a base V-8. A '68 SS 396 with this engine and the close-ratio four-speed manual gearbox was road tested from 0-to-60 mph in 6.6 seconds and did the quarter-mile in 14.8 seconds at 98.8 mph.

As in the past, Chevrolet continued to offer the SS 396 with a wide range of transmission and rear axle options. Also standard were finned front brake drums and new bonded brake linings all around. About 57,600 Chevelle SS 396s were made and this total included 4,751 with the L78 engine and 4,082 with the L34 option.

Jerry Heasley

CHEVROLET

A handful of 1968 Chevy II SS's had the 427-cid engine installed for drag racers.
Details of these cars are a little sketchy, but it's a good bet that they were fast.

1968 Chevy II SS 427

Chevrolet's senior-sized compact underwent a basic styling change in 1968. The new Chevy II/Nova body was longer and wider. To give it more appeal to muscle car fanatics, the updated design featured a Chevelle-inspired semi-fastback roof line with wide, flaring sail panels.

Despite adapting the Chevelle image, the new Chevy II was actually more of a five-passenger version of the Camaro. Both of these Chevys shared the same basic platform floor, forward subframe and front suspension. Also common was the use of a rear suspension with staggered shock absorbers. The relationship between the Chevy II and the Camaro meant that all engines that fit in Chevy's "pony car" could also be stuffed into a Chevy II.

Based on a 1-inch longer 111-inch wheelbase, the new Chevy II was 187.7 inches long and 54.1 inches wide. When the car first arrived, it continued to use an in-line six as its basic (and most-ordered) engine. But V-8 options up to a 350-cid/295-hp engine were available at slight extra cost.

At midyear 1968, the 327-cid/325-hp V-8 was added. Cars with this engine were capable of doing the quarter-mile in under 16 seconds at around 90 mph. Since this didn't quite cut the mustard during the muscle-car era, it wasn't long

before the 396-cid Turbo-Jet V-8 with a choice of 350- or 375-hp was also offered.

It didn't take too long before well-known drag racers like Dickie Harrell and high-performance factory dealers (like Don Yenko Chevrolet of Canonsburg, Pennsylvania and Nickey Chevrolet of Chicago, Illinois) to realize that the Chevy II's Camaro-type engine bay could also accommodate a 427-cid Chevrolet big-block V-8. It wasn't long before a small number of such cars were constructed, mainly with drag racing in mind.

Since 427-powered Novas were not a factory-issued item, it's hard to pin down concrete information about cost, performance or rarity. When installed in Camaros, the 427 was made available in 410- and 450-hp versions and it's likely the output was roughly the same in the Chevy II.

A 427-powered Camaro sold for just under $4,000 in 1968, so logic suggests that a 427-powered Chevy II would have cost a bit less than that. The performance of both of these cars was probably in the same general bracket, which (documented in the case of the Camaro) was around 13 seconds for the quarter-mile at a bit over 100 mph.

The 1968 Corvette was all-new in the looks department, and plenty potent in the performance department with four available versions of the big-block 427. The L88 option was the most potent mill and was accompanied by a "power blister" hood.

1968 Corvette 427

"Corvette '68 . . . all different all over." That's what it said in the sales brochure. It was the Chevy sports car's first major restyling since 1963. The fastback was replaced by a "tunnel-roof" coupe. It featured a removable back window and a two-piece detachable roof section or T-top. The convertible's optional hardtop had a glass rear window.

The front end was more aerodynamic than those on previous Corvettes. As before, the headlights were hidden. They were now vacuum operated, rather than electrically operated. The wipers also disappeared from view when not in use.

Except for the rocker panels, the body sides were devoid of chrome. Conventional door handles were eliminated. In their place were push buttons. The blunt rear deck contained four round taillights with the word Corvette printed in chrome in the space between them. The wraparound, wing-like rear bumper and license-plate holder treatment resembled that used on the 1967 models.

Chevrolet's big-block, 4.251 x 3.76-inch bore and stroke, 427-cid V-8 was available in the Corvette in four different muscular versions. The least powerful was RPO L36. It had hydraulic valve lifters, a 10:25:1 compression ratio and a single Holley four-barrel carburetor. Its output was 390 hp at 5400 rpm and 460 lbs.-ft. of torque at 3600 rpm.

The second-most powerful 427 was the L68 version, which featured a 10.25:1 compression ratio and three Holley two-barrel carburetors. It produced 400 hp at 5400 rpm and 460 lbs.-ft. of torque at 4000 rpm. *Car and Driver* tested one of these cars, with a four-speed manual gearbox and 3.70:1 rear axle, in its May 1968 issue. It did 0-to-60 mph in 5.7 seconds and the standing-start quarter-mile in 14.1 seconds

at 102 mph. Its top speed was estimated to be 119 mph.

Next came RPO L71, which was a step up the performance ladder with its special-performance, solid-lifter camshaft, three Holley two-barrels and an 11.0:1 compression ratio. It was good for 435 hp at 5800 rpm and 460 lbs.-ft. of torque at 4000 rpm. The L71-powered Corvette could go from 0 to 30 mph in 3.0 seconds, from 0 to 50 in 5.3 seconds and from 0-to-60 in 6.5 seconds. An L71 with a four-speed manual transmission and 3.55:1 rear axle was tested by *Car Life* in June 1968. It did the quarter-mile in 13.41 seconds at 109.5 mph. Its top speed was 142 mph.

The ultimate option was the super-powerful RPO L88 aluminum-head V-8, a $947 option intended primarily for racing. The L88 had mechanical valve lifters, a special ultra-high-performance camshaft with .5365-inch intake and a single Holley 850CFM four-barrel. With a 12.50:1 compression ratio it produced an advertised 430 hp at 5200 rpm. However, some said its actual output was 560 hp at 6400 rpm. Advertised torque was 450 lbs.-ft. at 4400 rpm.

The L88 package also included a "power blister" hood. In addition, four heavy-duty options were required: RPO J56 heavy-duty brakes at $384.45, RPO F41 heavy-duty suspension at $36.90, RPO K66 transistor ignition at $73.75 and RPO G81 Positraction at $46.35. With a special high-performance Turbo-Hydra-Matic transmission ($290.40 extra) the L88 convertible sold for $6,562. With a 3.36:1 rear axle it did the quarter-mile in 13.56 seconds at 111.10 mph. "The tall gear in back made 13.56 seconds at 111 mph seem respectable," said *Hot Rod* in 1969. "But we know it's about 2 seconds from where it should be."

The 1968 Super Yenko Camaro could hit 115 mph in the quarter-mile.

Jerry Heasley

CHEVROLET

1968 Super Yenko Camaro 427

Ten pounds stuffed into a 5-pound sack. That describes the Yenko SC, a Camaro stuffed with 427 massive cubes of big-block V-8 power.

Don Yenko, of Canonsburg, Pennsylvania, operated Yenko Sportscars. He was one of the first Chevy dealers to turn Camaros into hot rods. Yenko had previously turned out race-modified Corvettes and Corvairs. After the Camaro was introduced, he dreamed up the "Yenko Super Camaro."

The Yenko SC was essentially a new Camaro V-8 that had the factory small-block replaced with an L72 Corvette engine. This 427 dropped right in the Camaro chassis, then Yenko's racing team mechanics added some heavy-duty bits and did some performance tuning.

Yenko Sportscars offered 427-powered Camaros with two horsepower ratings, 435 or 450. Most cars also received a Yenko data plate, special Yenko badges, 427 emblems and a clone of the "Yenko Stinger" Corvette hood. The basic '67 Yenko Camaro sold for about $3,800. The exact number made that year is unknown. For years, it was thought that 54 cars were made the first year, but some experts feel the total may have been closer to 100.

Don Yenko helped to establish a distributorship called Span, Inc., based in Chicago, that marketed the muscular Camaros nationally. It is likely that many of the cars were actually modified in Chicago. When they were shipped to Canonsburg, Yenko added decals, badges and other special features. To help sell the cars, Yenko supplied sales literature to other performance-car dealers like Fred Gibbs Chevrolet in LeHarpe, Illinois. Drag racer Dickie Harrell, who had

previously worked for Nickey Chevrolet of Chicago, became Yenko's Midwest distributor.

For 1968, Yenko started with cars that had the L78 version of the 396, which had become the top factory option. These units already had heavy-duty parts and Yenko merely dropped the L72 V-8 onto the stock motor mounts. Everything was a direct fit and the work went much faster. However, Yenko still couldn't keep up with demand for 427 Camaros,

Yenko and his Chevy dealer dad asked about getting cars with factory-installed big blocks. After some hesitation, the company's Special Projects Division agreed. To circumvent GM's policies against putting big engines into smaller cars, Yenko agreed to keep the project hush-hush. Some experts say only one "factory 427" was made. Others say all later cars had factory-installed engines. This kind of confusion exists because the cars were built on a special Central Office Production Order (COPO) basis, so traditional factory record keeping didn't apply. Most '68s are COPO 9561 cars. The rarest Yenko SC Camaro is a '68 built under COPO 8008.

Most of the '68s had a Yenko ID plate, Yenko badges, 427 emblems and a Stinger-type twin-ducted fiberglass hood. Other special features included a 140-mph speedometer, a larger Z/28-type front sway bar and 15-inch Pontiac Rallye II wheels. They could be ordered with a close-ratio four-speed manual transmission or an M40 four-speed automatic transmission. Again, the exact number built is unknown. Experts believe that between 68 and 100 of these cars were put together.

1969 COPO Camaros were very fast, and very scarce. What more could a muscle car lover want?

Jerry Heasley

1969 Camaro COPO/427

Chevy designers did a lot of work updating the styling of the '69 Camaro, and the result was a car that won instant recognition as a classic among the ranks of enthusiasts. With additional body sculpturing, raised feature lines streaming off the fenders and dummy rear brake cooling louvers just ahead of the rear wheel openings, this was an instant icon of the muscle car era. It is believed that a "retro" Camaro, with '69-inspired styling, is coming down the pike soon to fight the 2005 Mustang.

In '69, the Central Office Production Order (COPO) remained the key to doing an "end run" around GM's anti-performance policies. By quietly using this system, dealer Don Yenko was again able to offer his SYC (Super Yenko Car) Camaro in '69 trim. These cars could be ordered through Yenko's showroom or from two dozen other selected Chevy dealers. The '69s were built as COPO 9561 and 9737 cars.

The '69 edition of the big-block 427 Camaro could be ordered with either the M22 four-speed manual gearbox or the Turbo-Hydra-Matic transmission. In either case, it listed for $4,245. Yenko Camaros were available in a limited range of six body colors: LeMans Blue, Hugger Orange, Olympic Gold,

Daytona Yellow, Rallye Green and Fathom Green. Some had vinyl roofs. The base price was around $4,000.

Chevrolet first agreed to building 50 cars, but dealers asked for more and supposedly 69 of these monsters were made. In '69, $4,000 was considered a huge sum of money for any Chevy and the COPO cars were difficult to move. This was especially true of the famous ZL-1 version created by Fred Gibb Chevrolet. The ZL-1 carried a 430-hp factory rating (565 actual horsepower) and cost more than $7,000. Gibb ordered 50, but had to return them because he couldn't sell the cars. Some sat on the lot for over two years.

Experts estimate that between 199 and 201 COPO cars were built, but some enthusiasts believe that as many as 350 Yenkos were made. There is an old photo of Don Yenko standing in front of a transporter truck and he is holding a handwritten sign that reads "Our 350th Camaro." Hard evidence is lacking, though. The total of 350 could be for all cars built since 1967. No one knows for sure. However, people are beginning to research all of the high-performance dealerships more closely.

The 1969 Camaro Indy Pace Cars had RS/SS 396 options.

CHEVROLET

Jerry Heasley

1969 Camaro RS/SS 396 Indy 500 Sport Convertible Pace Car

Although not the hottest muscle Camaro of 1969, (some 427-powered COPO cars were also built by the factory) the 396-powered Indy Pace Car is one of the most collected Camaros of all time.

After making a hit at the Indianapolis Motor Speedway during the 1967 Indy 500 race, Chevy was invited to bring the '69 Camaro back for a repeat performance. This time the company decided to take better advantage of sales promotion opportunities by releasing the Z11 pace car replica option package for the model 12467 ragtop.

The genuine Indianapolis 500 Pace Cars were 375-hp SS 396 convertibles with "hugger" orange racing stripes, rear spoilers and black and orange hound's-tooth upholstery. About 100 were built to pace the race and transport dignitaries and members of the press around Indianapolis.

Chevrolet then released the Indy Pace Car replica option and sold 3,674 copycat cars to the general public. The Z11 was actually just a $37 striping package for convertibles only. But other extras, such as the $296 Super Sport option and the special interior, were also required. Buyers could order the pace car treatment on either RS/SS 350 or RS/SS 396 ragtops. The 350-powered versions are much more common. They had

300 hp.

To qualify as a collectible muscle car, a pace car replica has to have the big-block, which came in four variations. These were the L35 ($63) with 325 hp, the L34 ($184) with 350 hp, the L78 ($316) with 375 hp and the L89 ($711) with aluminum heads and 375 hp. It isn't hard to guess which is rarest and most valuable.

The 375-hp ragtops were good for 7-second 0-to-60 acceleration and could do the quarter-mile in just about 15 seconds, so they have some real muscle to go with their good looks.

Camaro club members have also documented the availability of a Z10 Indy Sport Coupe package in 1969. This car was offered only in Chevrolet's Southwst Sales Zone, which included the states of Arizona, Oklahoma, Texas and (for some reason) Wisconsin.

The Z10 option was similar to the Z11 package, but there were some differences such as black or ivory interior choices (standard, custom or houndstooth), an optional wood grained steering wheel or ComforTilt steering wheel and a vinyl top. The Indy coupes were all built at Norwood, Ohio, and about 200-300 may have been put together.

CHEVROLET

The Z/28 package for 1969 again came with lots of muscle car
goodies to go with a racing-inspired 302-cid engine.

Jerry Heasley

1969 Camaro Z/28

Chevrolet Motor Division built 602 Camaros with the Z/28 package in the first year of the option—1967. The Z/28 package was popular from the start and sales leaped to 7,199 cars in 1968. But even divisional brass weren't ready for 1969's larger increase to 20,302 assemblies of Camaros with the Z/28 Special Performance Package.

The restyled 1969 Camaro body featured more defined sculpturing and a squarish, race-car-like look. It was the perfect repository for the Z/28's redesigned high-output, small-block V-8. This 302-cid engine was created with Trans-Am racing in mind. It featured a 4.002 x 3.005-inch bore and stroke, big-valve heads, forged steel crank, new four-bolt-mains block with larger webbing, nodular iron main bearing caps, new pistons, 30/30 solid-lifter camshaft, 11.0:1 compression ratio and numerous other performance goodies.

The Z/28 package was offered only for the Camaro coupe. Some sources say that it came in a basic version priced at $458 and a version with dealer-installed headers for $758. However, there were actually at least six variations. The basic package released September 26, 1967, included the 302 V-8, dual exhausts with deep-tone mufflers, special front and rear suspensions, rear bumper guards, a heavy-duty radiator with a temperature-controlled fan, quick-ratio power steering, 15 x 7 rally wheels, E70 x 15 special white-lettered tires, a 3.73:1 rear axle and special hood and trunk stripes. Chevrolet mandated a four-speed manual transmission and power disc brakes and recommended a positraction rear axle.

On October 18, bright engine accents and Z/28 emblems for the grille, front fender and rear panel were added and rally wheels were no longer specified, but wheel trim rings were added. The price remained at $458. On January 2, 1969, a tachometer or special instrumentation was made mandatory and the price rose to $474. On April 1, the specs were changed to read "dual exhausts" only, wheel center caps were specified along with a front valance panel and rear deck-lid spoiler. The price increased to $507.

The 1969 model had an extended model-year run and on September 18, 1969, the package was revised again, with the price going to $522. New ingredients included bright exhaust tips. The final documented changes came on November 3, 1969, and were very minor.

There are many variations between Z/28s, as well as between original cars and the written factory specifications. For example, very-early-in-the-run cars were manufactured with the 1968-style stripes and 15 x 6-inch rally wheels. Buyers ordering a spoiler on the early cars got the 1967-1968 style spoiler. And these cars were the only ones to carry the chambered dual exhaust system.

A typical, well-equipped Z/28 set up for racing could be purchased for under $4,000. *Hot Rod* magazine drove a stock Z/28 through the quarter-mile in 14.34 seconds at 101.35 mph. The editors then bolted on some aftermarket hardware and did it in 13.11 seconds at 106.76 mph.

The 1969 Camaro ZL1 has been simply referred to by some enthusiasts as "the ultimate muscle car."

1969 Camaro ZL1

In 1968, Chevrolet dealer Fred Gibb was well known to drag racing enthusiasts for his energetic support of their sport. Gibb, the owner of the Fred Gibb Agency of La Harpe, Illinois, talked to Vince Piggins about constructing the "ultimate" muscle car. The idea was to use an all-aluminum 427-cid V-8 in the compact Camaro body to create a Super Stock racing car. Piggins, who is now a high-performance legend, was in charge of such projects for Chevrolet Motor Division.

National Hot Rod Association (NHRA) rules said that a minimum of 50 cars had to be built to qualify the super-hot ZL1 Camaros for competition. Chevrolet General Manager E.M. "Pete" Estes gave Fred Gibbs his word that Chevrolet Motor Division would build the first ZL1s before the end of the year, on the condition that the Illinois dealer would take 50 of the cars at a proposed price of $4,900.

Gibbs accepted Estes' offer and General Motors Central Office Production Order system was utilized to order the cars. The first ZL1s built were a pair of Dusk Blue cars made at the Norwood, Ohio, assembly plant on December 30, 1968. They arrived at the Le Harpe, Illinois, dealership the next day, covered with snow. Unfortunately, the factory invoice price had climbed to $7,269!

All 50 cars that were shipped to Gibbs were virtually identical, except for the choice of color and transmission. They had the COPO 9560 option with the aluminum 427 V-8. Nineteen additional cars were also built for other Chevrolet dealers around the country. The equipment on all 69 cars included the Z22 Rally Sport package, J50 power brakes, N40 power steering, a V10 tachometer, racing style outside rearview mirrors, exhaust resonators, a dual exhaust system with tailpipe extensions, a special steering wheel, F70-15 black sidewall tires with raised gold letters, special lug nuts, special wheel center caps, special identification decals on the hood, grille and rear panel, a special instrument cluster and an extra-wide front valance panel.

According to the February 1969 issue of *Super Stock* magazine, the ZL1 Camaro in racing trim could cover the quarter-mile in as little as 10.41 seconds at 128.10 mph. That was with the "stock" Holley 850-cfm carburetor. Driver Dickie Harrell, who raced for the Fred Gibbs dealership, traveled around the country campaigning a ZL1. He took four wins and registered a best performance of 10.05 seconds at 139 mph.

The ZL1 all-aluminum 427 Chevy was a fire-breathing motor that produced some spectacular quarter-mile times in the 1969 Camaro.

It was hard to find a more race-ready production car than the 1969 Super Yenko Camaro.

Jerry Heasley

CHEVROLET

1969 Super Yenko Camaro 427

In the early days of drag racing, enthusiasts modified old cars in their home garages (or even under the old shade tree) and raced them on the weekend. In many cases, the same machine provided daily transportation and weekend sport. After the factory muscle car was invented, interest in drag racing boomed and the sport grew more professional. Those getting into the field turned to specialized car dealers to get the hottest rides.

In 1968, Don Yenko Chevrolet of Canonsburg, Pennsylvania, decided to expand his high-performance car operation called Yenko Sports Cars by making SYC (Super Yenko Camaro) models available to enthusiasts through a small number of selected factory dealers nationwide.

The plan was to base these cars on 1969 Camaros ordered from Chevrolet via a COPO (Central Office Production Order) arrangement. This type of purchase allowed dealers to order special equipment on a Chevrolet as long as building the car did not upset the normal stream of output at the factory. Yenko's cars were produced under order number 9561 and were fitted with 427-cid/425-hp L72 V-8 engines, M21 or M22 four-speed manual gear boxes (or an M40 Turbo-Hydra-Matic), front disc brakes, a special ducted hood, a heavy-duty radiator, a special suspension, a 4.10:1 positraction rear axle

and a rear deck lid spoiler.

Originally, Don Yenko had planned to take all of the COPO 9561 cars, but other Chevrolet dealers wanted a piece of the same action and also placed additional orders. As a result, about 100 cars were sold. However, Yenko also ordered a batch of COPOI 9737 Camaros, which had 15-inch wheels, Goodyear Wide Tread GT tires, a 140-mph speedometer and a beefy 1-inch front stabilizer bar. So, in the end, between 100 and 201 Yenko SYC Camaros were made, depending upon which source you refer to.

Yenko's SYC Camaros came only in seven exterior body colors: Hugger Orange, LeMans Blue, Fathom Green, Daytona Yellow, Rally Green and Olympic Gold. The cars had a base price of $3,895, including shipping. Available options included front and rear bumper guards ($25), front and rear floor mats ($12), an AM-FM push-button radio ($134), heavy-duty Air Lift shocks ($45), traction bars ($50) and chrome exhaust extensions ($38).

On April 19, 1969 a Yenko Camaro with factory-installed headers and racing slicks, driven by Ed Hedrick, did the quarter-mile at a drag strip in York, Pennsylvania, in 11.94 seconds at 114.5 mph.

1969 Baldwin-Motion Chevrolets and Corvettes

Baldwin-Motion Performance Group was a marriage of Baldwin Chevrolet and Joel Rosen's Motion Performance, a speed shop. Both businesses were located in Baldwin, Long Island, New York. Starting in 1967, and running through 1974, Baldwin-Motion offered big-block SS and Phase III Camaros, Novas, Chevelles, Corvettes and Biscayne Street Racer Specials.

These cars were sold either by Baldwin Chevrolet or Motion Performance. They were converted by Motion and delivered as "new car deliveries" by Baldwin Chevrolet.

Phase III 427 and 454 cars came with a written money-

back guarantee that they would run the quarter-mile in the 11s. Nobody ever came back for their money.

The program behind these cars was created by Joel Rosen and automotive writer Marty Schorr. It was presented to Baldwin Chevrolet when the Camaro was introduced in 1967. Cars were built and dyno-tuned by Motion. Marty Schorr and his agency, PMPR, Inc., created all the aggressive, in-your-face advertising and promotional materials and was involved in product development.

Between 1967 and 1974, approximately 500 Baldwin-Motion and Motion branded niche market muscle cars were built for both domestic and export (Switzerland, Germany, Norway, Haiti, Jamaica, Mexico, Iran, Kuwait, Puerto Rico, Saudi Arabia) use.

The most valuable of the Baldwin-Motion muscle cars is the special bodied Phase III GT Corvette—10 built between 1969 and 1971.

Paint and striping on SS and Phase III Baldwin-Motion cars schemes were unique, as was badging and trim. A full range of decorative as well as high-performance chassis and engine options were available so that a purchaser could order exactly what he wanted on a brand-new Chevy. Popular options included three two-barrel Holley carbs, Phase III CD

ignition, Hone auxiliary overdrive transmissions, scooped hoods, mag wheels, etc.

Except for demonstration cars that were sold periodically, all Baldwin-Motion Chevrolets were built to order and could be powered by big-block engines ranging in horsepower to over 500. Baldwin-Motion never re-badged COPO 427 Camaros and Chevelles.

Unique product catalogs were produced in 1968 and 1969 and today they are rare and collectible. During the early 1970s they were included in the large Motion Performance mail-order catalogs.

Only two of the ultra-wild ZL1 Corvettes were ever built. Roger Judski of Maitland, Florida, bought this car for $300,000 at auction in 1991 and plans to keep it for life.

1969 Corvette ZL1

Perhaps the wildest, most exotic, highest-performance muscle engine ever offered to the public was the ZL1. It was an all-aluminum, 427-cid, Chevy "Rat" engine. Just 69 engines were installed in '69 Camaros, while two went into '69 Corvettes. That was it!

The use of the ZL1 in Camaros was intended to homologate the engine for National Hot Rod Association competition. A minimum of 50 had to be built for it to be eligible for "stock" class drag racing. But, in the Corvette, the ZL1 wasn't homologated. It was more a case of optioning the ultimate high-performance Chevrolet with the ultimate high-performance big-block.

You might say it was a matter of pride. There were 10-

12 engineering test Corvette "mules" built with ZL1s. They were used in magazine road tests, engineering and track evaluations and driven by the likes of Zora Arkus-Duntov and GM VIPs. Of course, these ZL1 evaluation vehicles had to be destroyed—eventually.

In the process, two 'Vettes went out the door as RPO ZL1s. They included a Canary Yellow car with side pipes and a Can-Am White T-top coupe with black ZL1 side stripes.

In 1989, the yellow car, also a T-top, was confiscated by the U.S. government. It had been in the possession of a convicted cocaine dealer serving a sentence in an Alabama prison. Earlier, someone had paid $225,000 for the car, which had 55,317 original miles. The government estimated its value

CHEVROLET

Jerry Heasley

at around $500,000 but sold it for the minimum reserve bid of $300,000.

Greg Joseph, a Ph.D of history at Long Beach College, in California, researched ZL1 history. This led him to *Hot Rod* magazine (December 1968), with a cover story on Chevy's new all-aluminum 427. The article told of a "painted-block ZL1" engine in a test Corvette driven by the automotive press. A parenthetical statement added: "And all those guys at the '69 Chevy preview thought it was an L88. Forgot your pocket magnets, right, guys?"

Chevrolet had painted the ZL1s, possibly to hide them from the press, as had been the case with one of the test cars spotlighted in *Hot Rod*.

To the journalists, the ZL1 (a $3,010 assortment of aluminum cylinder block and heads) was a $1,032.15 RPO L88 package. The L88 engine itself was a race option, but in ZL1 metal, it featured thicker walls and main webbing, along with dry-sump lubrication provisions.

The bottom end had four-bolt main bearings, with a forged steel crank and rods with 7/16-inch bolts, spiralock washers and full floating pins. The pistons were even higher domed than the L88's, yielding a titanic compression ratio of 12.5:1. The cylinder heads were also aluminum and featured open combustion chambers, round exhaust ports and 2.19-inch/1.88-inch valves (a configuration adopted by the L88 in mid-1969). The aluminum dual-plane intake was topped by an 850-cfm Holley "double-pumper" four-barrel carburetor featuring mechanical secondaries. The ZL1's solid-lifter camshaft was radical, so the engine could live in the upper revs.

It's hard to believe there was a step above the L88 in the muscle-car era, but the ZL1 filled the bill. It still ranks, today, as the wildest RPO engine option ever offered to the public.

The 1969 Impala SS 427 proved that big wasn't necessarily bad when it came to muscle cars.

1969 Impala SS 427

The Impala SS 427 was merchandised differently in each of three model years that it was offered: 1967, 1968 and 1969. This high-performance package for the fanciest full-size Chevrolet became a little more distinctive as it aged. In fact, the final version, offered in 1969, was the purest expression of the super-sized Supercar's reason for existing.

When Chevrolet Motor Division introduced its 1969 model, the regular Impala Super Sport was gone. There was not a Super Sport series and you could not get just a Super Sport option package. The only way that a buyer could get his or her hands on a Super Sport was to order the SS 427 option, which included both the big-block V-8 and the typical SS trimmings as a buyer-takes-all package. In other words, if you wanted to get a full-sized Chevy with a muscle car image, you had to go all the way!

The Z24 code was again used to identify the option.

It could be ordered for three Impalas: The Sport Coupe, at $3,033 (with V-8) was the low rung version. The custom coupe model listed for $3,085. Both of these cars were, technically, two-door hardtops, but the custom coupe had a more formal-looking roofline. The window sticker on the convertible was $3,261.

The SS 427 option package retailed for $422.35. It included power disc brakes, a special three-speed transmission, special ornamentation, chassis and suspension upgrades, 15-inch wheels, red-stripe tires and the 427-cid V-8.

This year the regular 427 with a single four-barrel carburetor and 10.25:1 compression ratio had a little more muscle. It carried ratings of 390 hp at 5400 rpm and 460 lbs.-ft. of torque at 3600 rpm. It had a Rochester four-barrel carburetor. There was also a special COPO (Central Office Production Option) version that featured an 11.0:1

compression ratio and an 800-cfm Holley carburetor. It put out 425 hp at 5600 rpm and 460 lbs.-ft. of torque at 4000 rpm. The '69 SS 427 was the most similar to the SS 396 Chevelle, since it was all-inclusive. If you wanted SS badges, you had to order an SS 427. Only 2,455 buyers did.

The '69 version was road tested at 8.4 seconds for 0-to-60 mph and 15.8 seconds for the quarter-mile. That's just slightly slower than a 1970 SS 396 with 350 hp, but not bad at all for a full-sized Chevy.

The Nova nameplate replaced the Chevy II in 1969. The top dog on the engine options list was the 396-cid/375-hp version.

1969 Nova SS 396

As the muscle car era raced through history, the intermediate-sized models and pony cars that made up the bulk of the model offerings got fatter, heavier and more expensive. That left slim pickings for very young buyers who read about high-performance cars in buff books, but found the manufacturers' suggested retail prices a bit hard to choke down on their bag boy budgets. On one hand, this led to the creation of value-priced packages like the Road Runner. These cars still weren't cheap, just a lot for the money. There was a still second niche for buyers who would be happy with a lot of "muscle" in a car not normally thought of as a performance car—like a Nova.

The Nova name, in fact, no longer suggested top-of-the-line trim. It was now the name for all of Chevy's "senior compacts" and the Chevy II designation was no longer used. Due to this change, a Chevrolet emblem was placed at the center of the upper grille bar in place of the previous Chevy II grille badge. Vertical louvers were also featured on the sides of the cowl, behind the front wheel openings. The front side marker lights were enlarged and moved closer to the body corners.

Nova Super Sport models still had "SS" emblems decorating the front and rear of the body, but the "Super Sport" lettering that had previously appeared on the front

fenders where the new cowl louvers were added had to be relocated.

The 327-cid small-block V-8 disappeared from the Nova's options list, but three hot engine options remained. They started with the 350-cid small-block V-8, which came from the Camaro SS and had five more horses (300 at 4800 rpm) than in 1968. It produced 380 lbs.-ft. of torque at 3200 rpm. The 396-cid big-block V-8 was available once more and came in the same power options offered in 1968, which were 350 hp at 5200 rpm and 375 hp at 5600 rpm.

The standard transmission for 1969 Novas was a special three-speed manual gearbox with a floor shifter. A four-speed Muncie gearbox with a floor shift was optional and was available with a center console. Buyers could also get a two-speed Powerglide or a three-speed Turbo-Hydra-Matic transmission with column- or console-mounted shifters. Standard rear axle ratios were 3.31:1 with manual transmissions or 3.08 with automatic. Options included 3.55:1 and 3.07:1 with manual transmission and 2.73:1 or 3.36:1 with automatic transmissions.

This season Chevy cranked out 17,654 Nova SS models, compared to only 5,571 the year before. Of those, 5,262, or 30 percent, had the 396-cid/375-hp V-8 and 1,947, or 11 percent, had the 350-hp version.

CHEVROLET

A buyer could turn a Chevelle into an SS 396 for an extra $440 in 1969.

Jerry Heasley

1969 Chevelle SS 396/SS 427

Except for the manner in which the Chevelle SS 396 was merchandised, Chevrolet Motor Division made no basic change in the design or configuration of its mid-size muscle car for model year 1969. There was no separate SS 396 series this year. The Super Sport equipment package became the Z25 option, which was ordered for 86,307 cars.

The popular high-performance option package included the 396-cid/325-hp engine, dual exhausts with oval tailpipes and bright tips, a black-painted grille, bright wheel opening and roof drip moldings, a black-painted rear cove panel, Malibu-style rear quarter end caps, Malibu taillights and taillight bezels, a twin power dome hood, special "SS 396" emblems on the grille (as well as front fenders and rear deck lid) and 14 x 7-inch Super Sport wheels with F70 x 14 white-letter tires. The interior featured a black steering wheel and steering column, a steering wheel shroud with a black-accented center area and a horn-blowing tab, an "SS" steering wheel center emblem, an SS 396 nameplate on the instrument panel, a black-accented instrument panel and SS 396 emblems on the door sidewalls. The price of the option was about $440.

Three regular production engine options were available and all of these were based on the 396-cid block. The mildest choice was the L34 version, which put out 350 hp and added $121 to the car's window sticker. Next came the L78 version of the 396 with 375 hp and a $253 price tag. A variation of the L78 was the new L78/L89, which was jokingly advertised at 375 hp. The engine's actual output was much higher, thanks to special hardware like a pair of high-performance aluminum cylinder heads.

An extremely rare 1969 engine was a 427-cid V-8 that was made available, in very limited numbers, on a special Central Office Production Order (COPO) basis. These engines came from GM's Tonawanda, New York, factory. Only 358 of the 427s were assembled and most or all of them went to dealer Don Yenko, who had them custom installed in cars sold at his Yenko Sports Car dealership in Canonsburg, Pennsylvania.

A road test of the 1969 SS 396 with 375 hp proved it to be a tad slower than earlier editions, probably due to a slight increase in the car's weight. It moved from 0-to-60 mph in 7.6 seconds and covered the quarter-mile in 15.4 seconds.

The L89 version of the 1969 Corvette had aluminum cylinder heads, solid lifters, and 435 hp.

1969 Chevrolet Corvette 427

After a year's absence, the Stingray name (now spelled as one word) re-appeared on the Corvette's front fenders in 1968. The back-up lights were now integrated into the center taillights. The ignition was moved to the steering column and the door depression buttons used in 1968 were swapped for a conventional key lock.

Front and rear disc brakes, headlight washers, a center console, wheel trim rings, carpeting and all-vinyl upholstery were now standard Corvette equipment. Buyers had their choice of 10 exterior colors: Tuxedo Black, Can-Am White, Monza Red, LeMans Blue, Monaco Orange, Fathom Green, Daytona Yellow, Cortez Silver, Burgundy and Riverside Gold. Convertibles came with a choice of Black, White or Beige soft tops. Interior colors were Black, Bright Blue, Green, Red, Gunmetal and Saddle.

The 427-cid/390-hp RPO L36 V-8 was again the starting-point engine for muscle car enthusiasts. Then came RPO L68 for $326.55 extra. It was the same 10.25:1 compression V-8 fitted with three two-barrel carburetors, which upped its output to 400 hp. The 427-cid 435-hp RPO L71 Tri-Power engine also returned in much the same form as 1968. Its price tag was $437.10.

Three ultra-high-performing options began with the RPO L88 V-8. It again included a "power blister" hood. *Hot Rod* magazine tested an L88 and described it as a "street machine with soul." This year the basic package was $1,032.15 and also required heavy-duty brakes and suspension, transistor ignition and Positraction. The test car—a Stingray convertible—was base priced at $4,583.45, but went out the door at $6,562 as an L88 with a beefy Turbo-Hydra-Matic and 3.36:1 rear axle. It did the quarter-mile in 13.56 seconds at 111.10 mph.

There was also the RPO L89 V-8 for $832.05. This was a solid-lifter version of the 427 with aluminum cylinder heads on the L71 block. It had a 12.0:1 compression ratio, a 435 hp at 5800 rpm rating and produced 460 lbs.-ft. of torque at 4000 rpm.

The ultimate 1969 power option was the aluminum block and aluminum heads RPO ZL1 V-8, which is listed separately. Other 1969 Corvette muscle options included an RPO M20 four-speed manual transmission for $184.80, an RPO M21 four-speed close-ratio manual transmission for $184.80, an RPO M22 heavy-duty close-ratio four-speed manual transmission for $290.40 and an RPO M40 Turbo-Hydra-Matic automatic transmission for $221.80. And of course, what muscle Corvette fan would be caught dead without an RPO N14 side-mount exhaust system, which sold for $147.45 in 1969?

For the top engines listed here, the L71 and the L88 were the closest in performance. The L71 made the trip down the quarter-mile in 13.94 seconds at 105.63 mph and the L88 did it in 14.10 seconds at 106.89 mph. The L88 had a top speed of 151 mph.

Looking for a fast muscle car? The L88 Corvette Stingray clocked in the mid 13's for the quarter-mile.

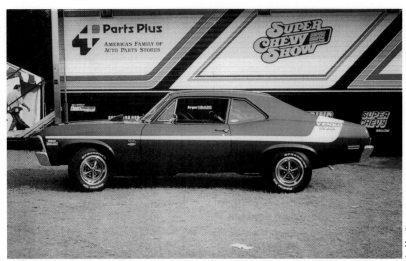

Joe Magglio

Don Yenko called his 427 Nova "a beast, almost lethal." As it turned out, the car was too lethal to insure, and only a few were built.

1969 Yenko "SYC 427" Nova

CHEVROLET

On paper, the SYC 427 Nova, built by Don Yenko Chevrolet in Canonsburg, Pennsylvania, is one of the most outrageous muscle cars to ever hit the highway and be street legal. It was a compact Nova with Chevrolet's monster 427-cid/425-hp V-8 stuffed into it. This RPO L72 solid-lifter big-block engine was made famous in the 1966 Corvette. In 1969, it was offered as a COPO (Central Office Production Order) option in the Chevelle and Camaro.

If a mid-sized Chevy 427 was a terror on the street, then a lighter 427 Camaro would have an even better power-to-weight ratio, second only to the Corvette. That's how things were until the absolutely wicked 427 Nova was produced. Don Yenko once said in an interview that his 427 Nova was "a beast, almost lethal." That is precisely why the insurance companies stepped in and virtually ended its production. They didn't want to insure it and, after 30 were converted at Yenko's Chevrolet agency, the other seven that had been slated to get 427s remained SS 396 Novas with 4.10:1 positraction rear ends.

SYC Novas supposedly started out as SS 396s, although at least one was a base Nova without SS equipment. The stock L78-optioned 396 engine, less heads, intake, carburetor, water pump and other top end components, was pulled and replaced with a crate-type 427 short-block. That's how easy the swap was, which is why it was so popular in the '60s. Many dealerships did these conversions for customers, but only certain dealers did them when the cars were brand new. In fact, Yenko went one step further and gave these cars special names. Every car—whether Camaro, Chevelle or Nova—was an SYC. The initials stood for "Yenko Super Cars." The center letter "Y" appeared larger than the other two letters on the badge.

A stripe kit—including SYC decals and Yenko badges—was installed, along with a unique tachometer atop the steering column. Each car was supposed to have had four options—a radio, Rally wheels, a vinyl roof and power steering. However, at least one car came minus each of these options and its history has been researched back to the original owner.

Greg Joseph, ex-curator of the former Otis Chandler muscle car collection in Oxnard, California, also believes that some of these Novas could have been COPO 427 cars with the larger engine installed at the factory. This is a distinct possibility, but the rarity of the vehicles is the reason that no broadcast sheets or original engines (with engine production code suffixes) or Protect-O-Plates (also showing a production code suffix) have yet been located.

Whether or not a Yenko SYC was COPO or not, it was still a 427 Nova and among just 30 built. Zero-to-60 mph times for such cars fell in the under-4-second bracket, according to Don Yenko, and the quarter-mile elapsed times were radical, too.

CHEVROLET

The Rally Sport option got the buyer the unique "split bumper" and other goodies on the 1970 Camaro. The SS option swapped the standard 350-cid engine for the more potent 396.

1970 Camaro RS/SS 396

Due to slow sales of the 1969 Camaros and delays in the design of an all-new replacement, the 1970 model arrived in showrooms very late in the game. In the fall of 1969, Chevrolet dealers had to continue selling leftover '69s until all of the cars were gone. Some of these units were delivered with 1970 titles (depending on state laws), but the true 1970 models—sometimes called "1970 1/2 Camaros"—did not go on sale until February 26, 1970.

When it arrived, the 1970 Camaro had completely revamped styling that made it seem like a GT coupe crafted in Europe. It featured high-intensity headlights, a semi-fastback roofline, a snout-style grille carrying an "egg crate" insert and a much smoother looking rear end. The convertible was gone and the only available body style was the sport coupe. Standard equipment included all General Motors safety features, Starto-Bucket front seats, an all-vinyl interior, carpeting, an Astro-Ventilation system, a left-hand outside rearview mirror, side marker lights and E78-14 bias-belted black sidewall tires. The base V-8 was a 307-cid small block V-8.

RPO Z27 was the Camaro SS option package. It included a 350-cid/300-hp V-8, bright engine accents, power brakes, special body ornamentation, a hood insulation pad, F70-14 white-letter tires, 14 x 7-inch diameter wheels, a black-painted grille insert, hide-away windshield wipers with black arms and Super Sport "SS" emblems. This package sold for $289.65 above the V-8 coupe's base price of $2,839.

RPO Z22 was the Rally Sport option package. It included a black-painted grille with a rubber-tipped vertical center bar and resilient body-color grille frame, a "split" bumper treatment with independent left and right front bumpers, a license plate bracket mounted below the right front bumper, parking lights with bright accents molded on the grille panel, hide-away headlights, bright window moldings, bright hood panel moldings, body sill moldings, body-colored door handle inserts, RS emblems, nameplates, bright-accented taillights and bright-accented back-up lights. It cost $188.35 and F78-14 or E70-14 tires were required.

The SS 396 Camaro substituted a big-block V-8 for the 350. The 396-cid engine had a 4.126 x 3.76-inch bore and stroke and actually displaced 402 cubic inches, although Chevrolet promoted it as a "396." It had a 10.25:1 compression ratio and a single four-barrel carburetor. This engine's advertised horsepower was 350 at 5200 rpm. Its torque rating was 415 lbs.-ft. at 3400 rpm.

Jerry Heasley

The 1970 Camaro Z/28 did the quarter-mile in 14.5 seconds at 100.22 mph.

1970 Camaro Z/28

Styling, engineering, performance and quality in the 1970 Camaro Z/28 were all high. On the other hand, its production total of 8,733 units was low enough to make owning one an uncommon treat. A good indication of this car's stature was its selection as the winner of *Car Life* magazine's first "Showroom Trans-Am Championship."

In this comparison, the magazine pitted pure stock versions of four American sports compacts against each other in acceleration, braking and cornering, rating the comparative performance of each according to a point system such as the Sports Car Club of America (SCCA) used. The cars were then run in the "main event"—a challenging road course—to see which could go the distance the fastest.

Engines in the four cars ranged from a 302-cid Ford V-8 to a 400-cid Pontiac, but the acceleration test proved that cubic inches didn't have a direct influence on performance. In fact, the Z/28, with its new-for-1970 engine of 350 cid, was the quickest on the drag pad. It did the quarter-mile in 14.50 seconds with a 100.22-mph terminal speed. This gave the Camaro five championship points.

Braking was the second performance aspect considered, with tests to measure stopping distances (from 80 mph) and fade. Credit for best braking went to the Mustang (which was third in acceleration). Coming in second gave the Camaro four more points, keeping it ahead of the pack, overall, with

nine.

In the steady-rate-cornering category, a skid pad at a California test facility was used to rate lateral acceleration, handling characteristics and tire grip. General Motors' two pony cars exhibited virtually neutral handling and the AMC product oversteered. With its neutral cornering, the Mustang also proved the best in handling, but the Camaro was again a close second.

As might be anticipated, the characteristics that showed up in individual tests were again revealed on the road course. This meant that the Camaro and the Mustang often led the pack. Each had its strengths and weaknesses. Traction proved to be a problem for the Ford, when it was pushed to the max. The Camaro exhibited rear axle hop while screaming through the switchback.

When the dust cleared, honors for the fastest average over the tricky course actually belonged to the Pontiac Trans Am, giving it 15 total points. The Camaro's average course speed (1:02.6) was the next fastest, giving it second place in the main event and 17 total points. The Mustang averaged 1:04 and wound up with 16 points.

"The winner is the Camaro Z/28 with 17 points," the magazine concluded. "One first, three seconds. The fastest car, and the more consistent."

The big Monte Carlo SS 454 had a lot going for it, and its limited
production numbers make it a nice collector prize today.

CHEVROLET

1970 Monte Carlo SS 454

Chevrolet's all-new Monte Carlo was a luxury-personal-performance car based on the 116-inch-wheelbase Chevelle sedan. Even though the Monte Carlo had its own 8-inches-longer frame, many of its chassis parts were interchangeable with those of the Chevelle. The reason for the longer frame was the Monte Carlo's 6-foot-long hood, which was there to enhance its classic look more than anything else. The length wasn't needed to accommodate optional big-block V-8 engines, which fit easily in the new car's engine bay.

Due to the body and frame changes, the Monte Carlo had different weight distribution characteristics than the Chevelle and Chevrolet engineers had to beef up the springs and shocks and install heavier stabilizers. The front stabilizer bar was larger than the Chevelle's and the rear stabilizer bar was of a type available only as an option on the Chevelle SS 396. The SS 454 version of the Monte Carlo came standard with an automatic leveling control system in which the rear shocks had pressurized air bags that extended the shocks as more weight was added to the rear of the car. The Monte Carlo's 60.3-inch front track and 59.3-inch rear track were both wider than those of the Chevelle.

The Monte Carlo was sheer luxury inside with comfortable seats, an electric clock, assist straps and simulated elm-burl dash panel inlays. There was a full complement of gauges, although *Motor Trend's* tester complained that they were "rather small" and hard for the driver to see. Standard equipment included all features found on Chevelle Malibus, plus power front disc brakes and G78-15B tires. Chevrolet's new 454-cid version of the Turbo-Jet big-block V-8 was available with the SS 454 package only.

The new 454-cid engine had a 4.251 x 4.00-inch bore and stroke, a 10.25:1 compression ratio and a single Rochester 4MV carburetor. It developed 360 hp at 4400 rpm and 500 lbs.-ft. of torque at 3200 rpm. *Motor Trend's* 3,575-lb. test car had a 3.31:1 axle and moved from 0-to-60 mph in 7.0 seconds flat. The standing-start quarter-mile took 14.9 seconds at 92 mph. *Car Life's* test car was a bit slower, doing the quarter-mile in 16.2 seconds at 90.1 mph.

With only 2.6 percent of the 1970 Monte Carlos built with the SS 454 option, total production for the year was a mere 3,823 copies of the muscle-car version. That's one reason why a 1970 SS 454 Monte Carlo is now almost worth its weight in gold.

A few more greenbacks in 1970 could turn a rather pedestrian 307-cid Nova
into a real mover with 396 cubes and 375 horses under the hood.

CHEVROLET

1970 Nova SS 396

Perfect for younger car buffs, high-performance versions of the Nova were real "sleepers" in the Stoplight Grand Prix. The Nova was a small, light basic car that normally appealed to factory workers and school teachers who wanted reliable, economical transportation. But since the car's underpinnings were derived from the Camaro, it was possible to stuff Camaro-type performance under the Nova's hood. Adding a few heavy-duty components and fat tires could turn the tiny "taxi" into a fairly respectable weekend cruiser.

For 1970 updates, the Nova got a new grille insert with squarer openings than the previous year's model. Chevrolet's

senior compact continued to use the 111-inch wheelbase platform introduced two years earlier. The "Coke-bottle" body shape had the popular long hood/short rear deck look and a trim overall length of 190 inches. Variable-ratio power steering was a new extra for 1970.

Of course, this was also the era of General Motors' infamous in-the-windshield radio antenna, which helped many youthful Nova owners tune in their favorite music while cruising the strip on Friday and Saturday night.

Chevrolet dealers had plenty of extra-cost options to sell Nova buyers to pump up the out-the-door price of the coupe model, which sold for $2,503 in the base V-8 series. Naturally, muscle car fans did not want the base 307-cid V-8. Most of them much preferred moving up to the RPO Z26 Nova Super Sport package. Its basic "SS" ingredients included a 350-cid/300-hp V-8, dual exhausts, power front disc brakes, a simulated air intake on the hood, simulated front fender louvers, bright accents, a black-finished radiator grille, a black-finished rear end panel, wide 14 x 7-inch wheels, E70 x 14 white-stripe tires, hood insulation and "SS" emblems. A four-speed manual or Turbo-Hydra-Matic transmission was mandatory with the $290.70 Super Sport option.

Two optional Turbo-Jet V-8s were available for those who wanted to compete either at a drag strip or on the downtown cruising strip. The first big-block package, coded RPO L34, came with the 396-cid (actually 402 cubic inches) 350-hp engine and was priced at $184.35 extra. The second package, coded RPO L78, included the 396-cid/375-hp engine at $316 above the cost of the base 350-cid V-8. Nova packages were added to a grand total of 19,558 cars in 1970, of which 1,947 had the L34 engine and 5,262 had the L78 engine.

1970 Yenko Deuce Nova

Sometimes it seems like every car that left Don Yenko's Chevy dealership in Canonsburg, Pennsylvania, (southwest of Pittsburgh) carried a big-block Chevy 427-cid V-8 ordered via the Central Office Production Order system. However, that's not quite true. The Yenko Sports Cars dealership actually started out modifying Corvairs with six-cylinder "pancake" engines. And in the later years of the muscle car era, Yenko turned out some hot small-block powered conversions as well.

A good example of the company's small-block artistry was the 1970 Yenko Deuce, a car that was based on the mundane Nova two-door sedan. Of course, the Deuce was treated to some rather busy-looking graphics treatments to set it apart from the pack. And under its hood was the 350-cid LT1 V-8, as used in Corvettes and Camaros.

Like its cousin the SS 396, the Yenko Deuce was based on the standard Nova without lots of bright metal trim. It did not start out as a Nova Super Sport edition, although it certainly had enough bolt-on goodies and decals to make it look pretty special.

The grille was treated to a trendy "black-out" appearance. Racing stripes ran up either edge of the hood like a pair of suspenders. These stripes carried LT1 call-outs. A hood-mounted tachometer, with flat black finish, was mounted on the driver's side, just ahead of the cowl vents. This put the rpm dial right in front of the driver and made it easier for drag racers to see. A "Deuce" decal decorated the forward section of the hood. Regular "350" engine badges sat atop the side marker lights.

A "hockey stick" decal ran along the sides of the car, then over the rear deck. At this point the decal grew wider. At the rear of the decal, the words "Yenko Deuce" were seen. Spoked mag-style wheels and fat white-lettered tires rounded out the Yenko Duece package.

The LT1 V-8 was pirated from the Corvette and the Camaro Z/28. It had a 4.0 x 3.48-inch bore and stroke. A single four-barrel 800-cfm Holley carburetor was mounted on top of the engine. Another high performance enhancement was an 11.0:1 compression ratio. The LT1 V-8 generated 360 hp at 6000 rpm and 380 lbs.-ft. of torque at 4000 rpm.

The Yenko Deuce cranked out a few more horses than the 350-hp RPO L34 Nova. However, even at that it did not quite match the 375-hp output of the factory available L78 version. It did, however, have a few things over the factory issued muscle car in that it was a lot more distinctive and had a much lower sales total.

Chevy gave the SS 396 a modest facelift for 1970.

Jerry Heasley

1970 Chevelle SS 396

Chevelles had a fatter, more sculptured appearance for 1970. A horizontally split grille with "blended" dual headlights was new. The SS 396 returned to the product line, but shortly after the manufacturing of 1970 engines started, the bore size of the big-block V-8 was increased from 4.094-inches to 4.125 inches. This increased the engine's actual displacement to 402 cubic inches. In spite of this change,

Chevrolet continued to identify the engine as the "Turbo-Jet 396."

The standard version of the "396" V-8 for 1970 was coded RPO L34 and. Despite the modest boost in displacement, it carried the same advertised power rating as in 1969: 350 hp at 5,200 rpm and 415 lbs.-ft. of torque at 3400 rpm. This motor was a $121.15 option.

Also available in the 1970 SS 396 was RPO L78. This optional version of the "396" big-block engine was advertised at 375 hp at 5600 rpm and 415 lbs.-ft. of torque at 3600 rpm. It added $250 to the cost of the car.

The L78/L89 V-8 with large-valve aluminum heads was a pricier ($647.75) option for the SS 396 only. It was also advertised at 375 hp, although that number was used to placate insurance companies and its real output was higher. This solid-lifter engine was rare and adds a lot to the collector value of a Chevelle SS 396 today.

A list of 13 items made up the content of the SS 396 package for 1970. In addition to the 350-hp engine they included: bright engine accents, power front disc brakes, dual exhausts with bright tips, a black-accented grille, wheel opening moldings, a black resilient rear bumper panel, a special domed hood, the F41 heavy-duty suspension, special chassis features, SS identification (including SS emblems on the grille, fenders, rear bumper, steering wheel and door trim), 17 x 7-inch Rally wheels (RPO ZL7) and F70 x 14 raised-white-letter tires.

The base price of a 1970 Malibu sport coupe was $2,809 and the cost of the SS package was $445.55. If you added the L78 engine it was $210.65 extra. Chevrolet produced 49,826 of its 1970 Chevelle models with the SS 396 option. With a curb weight of 3,990 lbs., one of the 350-hp cars had to carry about 11.4 lbs. per horsepower. In road testing it was found that it could move from 0-to-60 in 8.1 seconds and cover the quarter-mile in 15.5 seconds.

A convertible SS 454 is a rare find for muscle car collectors today.

1970 Chevrolet Chevelle SS 454

Only the good die young. The "bad" cars like the SS 396 kept going, but sometimes even they had to make adjustments to keep up with the competition. By 1970, the SS 396 was becoming a classic. It had been around since 1966 and was no longer the fastest muscle car in town. It was a snappy performer, but muscular newcomers from other automakers were proving to be a bunch faster on the streets and drag strips.

To keep the Chevelle in the muscle car race, Chevy had to do something to swing the balance back in its favor. After some brainstorming, the product planners came up with a simple answer—more cubic inches under the hood. Chevy announced that it would be releasing new 454-cid big-block V-8 for use in the Chevelle. The resulting model was called the SS 454 and is considered by many collectors to represent the pinnacle of the hot Chevelle SS series.

The 454-cid engine had a 4.250 x 4.00-inch bore and stroke. This monster was made available to the public in two different versions. The LS5 edition featured a 10.25:1 compression ratio and a 750-cfm Rochester Quadra-Jet carburetor. It was rated for 360 hp at 5400 rpm and 500 lbs.-ft. of torque at 3200 rpm. This engine was included in the SS 454 option, which had a $503.45 package price.

For a little bit extra, you could get the even more awesome LS6 version of the 454, which used an 11.25:1 compression ratio and a 780-cfm Holley four-barrel carburetor. It developed 450 hp at 5600 rpm and 500 lbs.-ft. of torque at 3600 rpm. To get an LS6 you had to pay the SS 454 package price, plus $263.30.

The LS6 was a super-high-performance engine featuring things like four-bolt main bearings, nodular iron bearing caps, heavy-duty connecting rods, big-diameter exhaust valves and a solid-lifter camshaft. A test car powered by the LS6 engine moved from 0-to-60 mph in 5.4 seconds and did the standing-start quarter-mile in 13.81 seconds at 103.8 mph. Those numbers were racked up with a Turbo-Hydra-Matic transmission and a 3.77:1 rear axle. You could also order either 454-cid engine with one of three available four-speed manual transmissions.

Only 3,773 of the SS coupes and convertibles built in 1970 had the 454-cid V-8s, and only a relative handful were LS6 editions.

CHEVROLET

Jerry Heasley

The 1970 Corvette was a hot car with two particularly hot engine options: a
350-cid/370-hp LT1 package, or the LS5 with a 454-cid/390-hp big-block.

1970 Corvette

The 1970 Corvette featured refinements on the basic styling used since 1968. There was a new ice-cube-tray design grille and matching side fender louvers, rectangular, amber-colored front signal lights, fender flares and square exhaust exits. The bucket seats and safety belt retractor containers were also improved.

Standard equipment included front and rear disc brakes, headlight washers, wheel trim rings, carpeting, a center console and all-vinyl upholstery (in either black, blue, green, saddle or red). Buyers had their choice of 10 exterior colors: Mulsanne Blue, Bridgehampton Blue, Donnybrooke Green, Laguna Gray, Marlboro Maroon, Corvette Bronze, Monza Red, Cortez Silver, Classic White and Daytona Yellow.

All Corvette convertibles came with a choice of black or white soft tops. Interior colors available were black, blue, green, red, brown and saddle. The 1970 version had a $5,192 base price and weighed 3,153 lbs. The convertible listed for a little less—$4,849—and weighed a little more at 3,167 lbs.

Chevrolet built 10,668 coupes and 6,648 ragtops. A total of 1,287 buyers interested in muscle-car-like performance separately checked off the LT1 engine.

In addition, 25 Corvettes with a ZR1 option package carried the LT-1 engine.

RPO LS5, a new 454-cid big-block V-8, featured a 4.251 x 4.00-inch bore and stroke. It had a relatively mild 10:25:1 compression ratio, a high-performance hydraulic lifter camshaft and a single Rochester 750CFM Quadra-Jet four-barrel carburetor. The LS5 Corvette had an advertised 390 hp at 4800 rpm and 500 lbs.-ft. of torque at 3400 rpm.

Another hot option was the RPO LT1 V-8, which was based on the 350-cid small-block V-8. This 4.00 x 3.48-inch bore and stroke motor had 11.0:1 compression, solid lifters and a four-barrel Holley carburetor on an aluminum intake manifold. It was good for 370 hp at 6000 rpm and 380 lbs.-ft. of torque at 4000 rpm.

A 454-cid/465-hp RPO LS7 V-8 was listed in some early 1970 Corvette sales literature, but never made it to the showroom. It had solid valve lifters, a high-performance camshaft and a Holley 800-cfm four-barrel carburetor. Only one car with the LS7 engine was ever built. *Sports Car Graphic* editor Paul Van Valkenburgh drove it 2,500 miles from a press conference at Riverside, California, to Detroit and raved about it. The car did the quarter-mile in 13.8 seconds at 108 mph. However, GM's policies against ultra-high-performance cars at the time led to the option being dropped.

The LT1-powered 1970 Corvette could do 0-to-30 mph in 2.5 seconds, 0-to-60 mph in 5.7 seconds and 0-to-100 mph in 13.5 seconds. It covered the quarter-mile in 14.17 seconds at 102.15 mph and had a top speed of 122 mph.

1970 Corvette "Ultimate" ZL1

The all-aluminum 427-cid ZL1 was the most-powerful engine ever offered in an American production car. It evolved from Chevy's Can Am racing experience of the late 1960s. To be "politically correct" in that era, Chevy rated the ZL1 V-8 at 430 hp, but its actual output was about 585 hp with tuned headers. The factory had a company named Kustom Headers build several sets of header and side pipes for ZL1 racers and made them available through Chevrolet parts departments at

101

a very high price. Later, Hooker Headers provided a popular-priced alternative that put the company on the map.

The ZL1's aluminum cylinder heads had some minor design upgrades. Engineers working in Chevrolet's high-performance engines group—including Gib Hufstaders, Bob Clifts, Tom Langdons and Bob Keithman—smoothed out the exhaust ports and double cut the valves and lapped them in. This resulted in a higher 11.45:1 compression ratio. The inlet manifold was shielded and had a steel pan under it to keep off hot oil. A bit of custom machining allowed the use of a Holley 4500 NASCAR carburetor with a flow rate between 1200-1400 cfm.

A special domed hood was used to accommodate the ZL1's intake manifold. The 1968-style L88 hood was adopted and cowl induction was used at the rear to improved airflow to the carburetor. This modification cut 7 seconds off the car's 0-to-140-mph time.

When *Motor Trend's* editors went to the 1970 Chevrolet

long lead press conference, they got to drive one of the hottest Corvettes ever made. The brilliant red coupe had been set up for drag racing by Corvette engineer Gib Hufstader. Its suspension was modified using a 2-inch spacer and 3-inch rubber to eliminate wheel hop. A set of 4.88:1 No. 4650 high-nickel alloy gears were installed in the differential. It had a "beefed-up" automatic transmission and 9-inch slicks. The car ran the quarter-mile in 10.6 seconds at 132 mph.

Chevrolet also built a white convertible that was designed for road racing by chief Corvette engineer Zora Duntov. It was equipped with an M-22 "rock-crusher" four-speed manual transmission and 3.70:1 rear end gears. On a drag strip, the white 'Vette could do the quarter-mile in 12.1 seconds at 116 mph. On a road racing course, with the right gears, it could hit 200 mph. Driver John Greenwood claimed racing victories, including the SCCA national title, with his ZL1-powered Corvette.

Chevrolet rolled out 4,862 new Z/28s for 1971.

Jerry Heasley

1971 Camaro SS, RS & Z/28

Since Chevrolet Motor Division didn't release the all-new 1970 Camaro until the middle of calendar-year 1970, no major design changes were made to the 1971 models. In fact, about the only way to spot the 1971 edition at a glance is to look in the front compartment for high-back bucket seats with integral headrests.

There were some equipment upgrades for 1971 models. The Camaro's standard features now included power front disc brakes and steel inner door guard rails, as well as the full complement of General Motors safety features, all-vinyl upholstery, bucket-style rear seat cushions, floor carpeting, a cigar lighter, Astro-Ventilation, E78-14 bias-belted black sidewall tires and a three-speed manual transmission with a floor-mounted gear shifter. The standard 1971 Camaro V-8 was a 307-cid small block engine.

The basic Camaro SS package included a 350-cid/270-hp V-8, a dual exhaust system, bright engine accents, power brakes, special ornamentation, hood insulation, F70-14 white-lettered tires, 14 x 7-inch diameter wheels, a black-finished grille, hide-away wipers with black arms and Super Sport "SS" emblems. The Rally Sport option package added a special black-finished grille insert with a rubber-tipped vertical center bar and a resilient body-color grille frame, independent left and right front bumpers, a license plate bracket mounted below the right front bumper, parking lights with bright accents molded on the grille panel, hide-away headlights, bright window moldings, bright hood panel moldings, bright body sill moldings, body-colored door handle inserts, RS emblems (deleted when the SS package was also installed), an RS steering wheel medallion, bright-

The cool Camaro SS package included a 350-cid V-8 with 270 hp under the hood.

accented taillights and bright-accented back-up lights.

The RPO Z/28 Special Performance package was a factory option that cost $786.75. Standard equipment included an exclusive 330-hp 350 Turbo-Fire 350 V-8, a beefed-up sport suspension, fancier wheels, a rear spoiler, heavy-duty radiator, dual exhausts and special decals and white paint stripes. The manual transmission Z/28 coupe cost $3,841 new, with the automatic version available for $100 more.

An M20 wide-ratio four-speed manual transmission with floor mounted gear shifter was standard with the 396-cid "big-block" V-8 and could be hooked to either a 3.73:1 or a 4.10:1 rear axle. The M21 close-ratio four-speed manual transmission was another possibility and was available with the same choice of axles.

Two automatic transmission options were also available for the Camaro SS. Both were based on the three-speed M40 Turbo-Hydra-Matic automatic transmission, which came with a choice of a steering-column-mounted gear shifter or a floor-mounted gear shifter.

The 1971 version of the 396-cid engine (which actually displaced 402 cubic inches) had a high-lift camshaft, hydraulic valve lifters, dual exhausts, an 8.5:1 compression ratio and a single Rochester four-barrel carburetor. Advertised horsepower was 300 at 4800 rpm. The torque rating was 400 lbs.-ft. at 3200 rpm.

1971 Monte Carlo SS 454

The muscle car era was winding to its untimely end in 1971, but it wasn't for lack of enthusiasts willing to buy such cars. Nor was it the doing of Detroit's "Big 3." New government rules about pollution and safety were forcing the issue, while insurance companies were using drastic rate hikes to make muscle cars prohibitively expensive to operate. The government requirements for product certification also absorbed money and time, making it harder and more expensive to do annual product revisions.

Chevrolet Motor Division made few changes in the Monte Carlo during its second year in the market. Well, it's true that the automaker did take the never-actually-made convertible out of its sales brochure. It also replaced the round 1970 front parking lamps with rectangular units and substituted a grille with an insert having a finer texture. Returning from the grave, so to speak, was the hood ornament, which was now designed with a spring-loaded attachment to avoid impaling pedestrians.

A touch of greater distinction was added to the Monte Carlo Super Sport option, which now featured a blackout-style rear beauty panel and "SS 454" identification on the lower front fenders. There was also an "SS" badge on the rear beauty panel. The best news was that muscle car lovers could now order two versions of the 454-cid V-8 in the Monte Carlo and both provided more horsepower, at least on paper. The standard version had a lower 8.5:1 compression ratio, but a higher 365 hp at 4800 rating (this doesn't make sense until you realize that, in 1970, Chevy actually rated the 454 at 390 hp in full-size cars). Torque was down a bit to 465 lbs.-ft. at 3200 rpm.

The LS6 version of the 454 was a new option for Monte Carlos. It was de-tuned to a 425 advertised horsepower rating from the 450-hp rating it carried in 1970 Chevelles.

Monte Carlo SS 454s came standard with a three-speed Turbo-Hydra-Matic automatic transmission. The only option was a fully synchronized four-speed manual transmission with a floor-mounted gear shifter, and this option was a special-order item only. The Monte Carlo SS 454 sold for $3,901 and weighed 3,488 lbs.

The 1971 SS 454 package included all of the same goodies it featured in 1970, such as heavy-duty front and rear springs, heavy-duty shocks with automatic level control and heavy front and rear stabilizer bars. Of course, with the government and the insurance industry breathing down its neck, Chevrolet didn't promote the Monte Carlo SS very heavily and production for the model year dropped nearly 50 percent to only 1,919 cars.

CHEVROLET

CHEVROLET

The "Heavy Chevy" wouldn't win many races against the muscle car big boys, but it looked the part of a tough customer and was affordable.

Jerry Heasley

1971 "Heavy Chevy"

Clouds were aplenty for the surviving muscle cars of 1971. High insurance rates for young drivers in fast cars ravaged the market. At the same time, emission standards imposed by the federal government cut output and compression for the top high-performance engines. American automakers were rapidly losing their enthusiasm due to the shrinking demand for muscle cars and rising manufacturing costs that evolved through satisfying an armada of coming federal safety and emission standards.

As the big-horsepower machines of the 1960s fell by the wayside, they were replaced by a growing number of "visual" muscle cars that looked much the same as real muscle cars, but were far tamer under the hood. Chevrolet announced a pair of these in March of 1971. They were called the Rally Nova and the Heavy Chevy.

The RPO YF3 Heavy Chevy option-created-model was

a version of the $2,980 Malibu V-8 two-door hardtop. The package added side striping, a blacked-out grille, base Rally wheels and appropriate front fender decals that read "Heavy Chevy." An air induction hood—complete with hood pins—was an option.

How "heavy" your Heavy Chevy got was up to you. Under the hood, options started with the standard 307-cid/200-hp small-block V-8 engine. You could check other boxes for the RPO L65 power plant, which was a 350-cid V-8 with a two-barrel carburetor and 245 hp. If you needed more than that, you could opt for a 270-hp four-barrel RPO L48 version of the 350-cid engine or go all the way up to the 300-hp/402-cid big-block. However, if you wanted the gangbuster 454-cid V-8, you had to go the Super Sport route. Production figures of the Heavy Chevy option came to 6,727 units, but very few of these cars still survive today.

Though the muscle car era was winding down by 1971, the
454-cid engine option was still popular in the Chevelle SS.

CHEVROLET

1971 Chevelle SS 454

Chevelle models received changes to the front end in 1971. A new twin-level grille was divided by a bright horizontal bar. The front parking lights were moved from the bumper into the fender tips. "Don't panic," says a 1971 Chevrolet sales brochure. Although the muscle car era was in decline, there were still some hot options left. "There's still an SS 454. Any car that was named the best of its kind in *Car and Driver's* reader's choice (the 1970 Chevelle SS 454) is sure to stay around."

There were changes, however. The early '70s was the era of low-cost muscle cars and "lick-'em-stick-'em" muscle cars that had the decals, but not the big-cube engines, of the recent past. Chevrolet set things up so buyers could order all of the Super Sport goodies on any Malibu as long as it had a 350-, 400- or 454-cid V-8.

With a V-8 engine, the Malibu coupe sold for $2,980 and weighed 3,342 lbs. The convertible, which came only with a V-8, was base priced at $3,260 and weighed some 3,390 lbs. Only 5,089 Chevelle convertibles were built in 1971.

The RPO Z15 SS package sold for $357. It included: power brakes with disc brakes up front, a black-accented grille, a special suspension, a special domed hood with functional hood lock pins, SS identification for the hood, rear deck and fenders, a driver's side remote-control sports mirror, gray-finished 15 x 7-inch five-spoke sport wheels, F60 x 14 white-lettered tires, a black-accented steering column and a steering wheel with SS nameplate.

If you wanted a 1971 SS 454 Chevelle, you had to order one of the two big-block engines as an add-on option. This year Chevrolet listed the net horsepower rating and gross horsepower rating for both engines. The LS5 version produced 285 net hp and 365 gross hp. The LS6 version generated 325 nhp and 425 ghp. Both came with a choice of a four-speed manual transmission or a three-speed Turbo-Hydra-Matic transmission.

Chevrolet put together an estimated 80,000 cars that carried the SS option this year. Of those units, 19,292 were equipped with 454-cid V-8s.

CHEVROLET

Jerry Heasley

**1971 Corvette buyers were given multiple hot engine choices, including
an LS6 version that blazed through the quarter-mile in 12.7 seconds.**

1971 Corvette

If you liked the 1970 Corvette, you liked the 1971 version. The two models were virtually the same car, at least on the outside. A new resin process (that supposedly improved the body) and a different interior were the major changes. Under the hood, the compression ratios were dropped a bit to enable Corvette engines to run on lower-octane fuel.

Standard equipment included all-vinyl upholstery, a dual-exhaust system, an outside rearview mirror, carpeting, a center console, wheel trim rings, an electric clock, a tachometer, a heavy-duty battery, front and rear disc brakes with a warning light and tinted glass.

Corvette buyers had their choice of 10 exterior colors: Mulsanne Blue, Bridgehampton Blue, Brands Hatch Green, Steel Cities Gray, Ontario Orange, Millie Miglia Red, Nevada Silver, Classic White, Sunflower Yellow and War Bonnet Yellow. All convertibles came with a choice of black or white soft tops. The interior colors were black, dark blue, dark green, red and saddle.

High-performance engine options included the RPO LS5 V-8. This $295 extra version of the 454-cid big-block now had an 8.5:1 compression ratio. It was rated for 365 hp at 4800 rpm and 465 lbs.-ft. of torque at 3200 rpm. It featured hydraulic valve lifters, a high-performance camshaft and a Rochester 750CFM Quadra-Jet four-barrel carburetor.

Corvette buyers willing to part with $1,221 could add the RPO LS6 V-8. It also had hydraulic lifters, a high-performance

cam, an 8.5:1 compression ratio and a four-barrel carburetor. However, the LS6 carb was a big 880-cfm Holley model. The motor was rated 425 hp at 5600 rpm and 475 lbs.-ft. of torque at 4000 rpm.

Another hot option available again to Corvette fans was the small block-based RPO LT1 V-8. This 350-cid engine had a 9.0:1 compression ratio. It generated 330 hp at 5600 rpm and torque was 360 lbs.-ft. at 4000 rpm.

A 1971 Corvette with the LS5 engine could go 0-to-60 mph in 5.7 seconds, 0-to-100 mph in 14.1 seconds and do the standing-start quarter-mile in 14.2 seconds at 100.33 mph. A 1971 Corvette with the LS6 engine and 3.36:1 rear axle was tested by *Car and Driver* magazine in June 1971. It moved from 0-to-60 mph in 5.3 seconds, from 0-to-80 mph in 8.5 seconds and from 0-to-100 mph in 12.7 seconds. The same car did the quarter-mile in 13.8 seconds at 104.65 mph.

An LT1-powered Vette with the M-21 four-speed manual transmission and a 3.70:1 rear axle was also tested by *Car and Driver* magazine in June 1971. It moved from 0-to-40 mph in 3.4 seconds, 0-to-60 mph in 6.0 seconds and from 0-to-100 mph in 14.5 seconds. The car did the quarter-mile in 14.57 seconds at 100.55 mph and its top speed was 137 mph.

Production for 1971 increased to 14,680 coupes and 7,121 convertibles. A total of 1,949 buyers separately checked off the LT1 engine option in 1971. In addition, eight ZR1 Corvettes carried the LT1 engine.

Phil Kunz

CHEVROLET

The Chevelle SS 454 wasn't quite as mean in 1972 as it had been in the previous years, but its 270 net horsepower rating was nothing to scoff at.

1972 Chevelle SS 454

There were very few differences between 1972 Chevelles and the models of the previous year. What stood out most were the single-unit front turn signals and side markers. In 1971, there had been multiple lenses "stacked" on one another, but this year there was a one-piece lens with horizontal lines molded on it.

Chevrolet buyers could again order all of the Super Sport goodies on any Malibu sport coupe or convertible as long as it had a V-8. That's right, you could even get an "SS 307" based on a base Malibu sport coupe this year. The 307-powered Malibu sport coupe cost $2,922.70. If you wanted a Super Sport convertible, a base V-8 was already figured in, since you could not get a Malibu ragtop with Chevy's in-line six-cylinder engine. The least expensive version of the open model retailed for $3,186.70.

The RPO Z15 Super Sport package included power front disc and rear drum brakes, a black-finished grille, a special domed hood with locking pins, a left-hand remote-control sport rearview mirror, Super Sport "SS" emblems, a sport suspension, 15 x 7-inch wheels with bright lug nuts, special wheel center caps, wheel trim rings and F60-15 white-lettered tires. The package listed for $350.15 for both body styles and required the optional V-8 engine and an optional transmission. The exact transmission used varied by engine.

If you wanted an SS 454 you got the LS5 version. It cost $272 and the SS equipment package and a heavy-duty battery were required. The battery was a $15 option. The 1972 version of the 454 had an 8.5:1 compression ratio and a single Rochester 4MV carburetor. It was rated for 270 SAE nhp at 4000 rpm and 390 lbs.-ft. of torque at 3200 rpm. Standard transmission with the 454 was a special four-on-the-floor manual with Turbo-Hydra-Matic optional at $231 extra. Chevrolet built 5,333 cars with the SS 454 setup this year.

Jerry Heasley

The Cosworth Vega emerged as a muscular car for its time in 1975. Just over
2,000 of the snappy unique aluminum-engine cars were built that year.

1975-76 Cosworth Vega

CHEVROLET

From the start of Vega production in 1971, Chevy capitalized on the new car's sporting character by offering a GT option. This package enhanced the Vega's handling, added a 100-hp engine and provided full instrumentation. By 1974, EPA regs and other factors had reduced the GT to 85 hp.

What the Vega needed was an "image" model that would appeal to high-performance buffs and weekend racers. The result was the Cosworth Vega. Cosworth was the name of a British firm that built racing cars. In August 1973, major car magazines reported that Cosworth would team with Chevy to make 5,000 special '74 Vegas. These cars wore consecutively numbered dashboard plaques for identification.

But the Cosworth package was much more than a plaque. It included twin camshafts and four valves per cylinder. The cams were hidden below covers with the Chevy bow tie, and the Cosworth and Vega names. They helped to boost performance to 140 hp at 7000 rpm. In fact, the hot 2.0-liter four produced 1.15 hp per cube. The torque rating was 105 ft.-lbs. of torque at 6000 rpm.

There were other upgrades as well. The engine was constructed totally of aluminum and weighed only 305 lbs. The special crankshaft was a hardened, tuftrided, forged unit. All of the con rods were forged, shot peened and magnafluxed. The special forged aluminum pistons had deep-dish tops to provide clearance for the valves. A higher-than-stock 8.5:1 compression ratio was used. The 16-valve cross-flow head differed from Cosworth's racecar version only in having cast combustion chambers and a different type of valve seat design.

The Cosworth suspension had stiffer springs and shocks and a torque-tube type rear suspension, developed for the Monza, was used. Mag wheels and fat tires set the package off. The cars were done in a distinctive Black finish with gold wheels and gold striping. Interior features included a gold-tone engine-turned dash panel and special instrumentation.

The launch of the Cosworth Vega was delayed by the EPA until after it passed a 50,000-mile emissions test. It finally arrived in March 1975. As a result, on 2,062 of these cars were built during that model year. All of them were constructed on the main line at General Motors Lordstown, Ohio assembly plant. Production supervisors put them together to help assure a high-quality product. With a base price of $5,916, the "Cosworth" had to be of top quality, since a Corvette coupe cost only about $900 more.

Special components of the 1976 Cosworth Vega engine were about the same as those provided in 1975, which is to say that everything was made to special high-performance standards. A computer-controlled induction system was employed, as well as an unusual low-lift cam and special exhausts. A Bendix electronic fuel-injection system was novel at the time.

Changes were also made to the drive train to go along with the engine's extra potential. Stiffer springs and shocks were used and the roll couple was redistributed to the front. The Monza-type torque-tube rear suspension was used again.

In proper tune, the Cosworth Vega could reach 60 mph in 8.7 seconds and do the quarter-mile in 17.6 seconds at a terminal speed of 80.1 mph. Besides going fast, it looked good. Even the engine compartment had a "designer" look with the cam covers finished in black crackle paint and the model names spelled out in raised letters.

For muscle-car history lovers, the Cosworth Vega has a lot of significance. It started a trend, for domestic car makers, towards modern high-performance sport coupes with double overhead cam four-cylinder engines.

Chevy needed something to spice up its mid-size car lineup in the
mid-1970s, and its answer was the sleek and sporty Laguna Type S-3.

1975-1976 Chevelle Laguna Type S-3

As more cars of the mid-'70s come to be appreciated by muscle car collectors, the value of the 1975 1/2 and 1976 Chevelle Laguna Type S-3 model will rise. This unique car has a lot going for it, including style, a standard V-8 power plant, low production numbers, an enviable racing history and the ability to perform on no-lead gasoline

After Chevrolet axed the convertible and two-door hardtop from the intermediate Chevelle lineup in model year 1973, the company started searching for ways to create a product for buyers remaining in the enthusiast market. For 1974, the bowtie brand's "trick" car was the Laguna Type S-3, which used a special soft urethane front end that Lagunas had carried in 1973.

Chevy's next move was even better, at least from a visual standpoint. The coupe body was treated to a racy-looking rear-slanting nose. This was used on the S-3, which was announced at the beginning of the model year but didn't become a production line reality until the time of the Chicago Auto Show, which opened on February 22, 1975.

The streamlined new nose made the 112-inch wheelbase Laguna S-3 look sharp for its time. A 350-cid V-8 with a two-

barrel carb was standard, except in California. On the "Left Coast," the 350 was fitted with a four-barrel carb. The 400-cid small-block V-8 was optional equipment. Also listed as a '75 Chevelle option – for the last time – was the big-block 454 V-8. However, it is not 100 percent certain that this engine was available when the S-3 model bowed.

What is known is that the S-3 had a base price of $4,113. For that the buyer got rally wheels, a radial-tuned suspension, louvered coach windows, sport mirrors, S-3 badging and a Monte Carlo instrument panel with round gauges. Bucket seats were optional, as were body-side tape stripes and a heavy-duty Sport suspension.

Only 6,714 of the 1975 1/3 models were built. Then, the S-3 returned for 1976 and drew an additional 9,100 orders. That was better, but not enough of an improvement to keep it in the lineup for another year.

Stock-car race drivers immediately took to the S-3. Its sloped nose was just what they needed to slice through the air at the superspeedways. Cale Yarborough used Laguna S-3s to help win the 1976 and 1977 NASCAR Winston Cup titles. NASCAR banned the S-3 from competition starting in 1978.

Jerry Heasley

The IROC-Z was inspired by a racing series that started in 1985.

1985 Camaro 5.0-liter IROC-Z

One of the most highly publicized forms of racing that Camaros took part in was the International Race of Champions, or IROC, race series. It originated in 1973, when drivers competed in 15 identically prepared Porsche Carreras. For several reasons, including a desire to expand the series to include oval track drivers, Camaros replaced Porsches in 1974.

The IROC series ran through 1980, with Roman numerals identifying each year. After the IROC VII competition in 1980, the series was dropped, but it returned in 1984 when the IROC VIII title was taken by NASCAR driver Cale Yarborough.

Thanks to television, the IROC series earned wide exposure and a strong link was created between the Camaro name and the IROC name. By 1985, this was strengthened even further by the release of a hot production version of the Chevy pony car called the IROC Z/28—more popularly called the "IROC-Z."

The IROC-Z was actually a sports equipment package (RPO B4Z). The standard engine was Chevy's LG4 190-hp version of the 305-cid (5.0-liter) V-8. This engine used a four-barrel carburetor and developed 240 lbs.-ft. of torque at 3200

rpm. A more muscular engine was available as the optional LB9 version of the 5.0-liter V-8, with electronic fuel injection and a tuned aluminum intake plenum with individual intake runners for each cylinder. This was dubbed "tuned port injection" and was good for 215 hp at 4800 rpm and 275 lbs.-ft. of torque at 3200 rpm.

The 5.0-liter H.O. engine also featured a hotter camshaft and a larger-diameter exhaust system. It came only with four-speed manual transmission attachments for 1985. A 3.42:1 rear axle was standard. Other IROC-Z equipment included a lower stance and center of gravity, re-valved Delco front struts, a faster spring jounce rate, front stabilizer bar, re-calibrated performance power steering, Bilstein rear gas shocks, fatter-than-normal rear anti-roll bar and unidirectional 245/50VR16 Goodyear Eagle tires mounted on 8 x 16-inch wheels.

In road tests, *Motor Trend* reported a 6.87-second 0-to-60 time and a 15.32-second quarter-mile run at 89.6 mph. *Popular Hot Rodding* took a little longer (7 seconds) to get up to 60 mph, but ran the quarter-mile in 14.94 seconds at 92.60 mph.

1986 Monte Carlo SS Aerocoupe

Chevrolet fans have NASCAR racing driver Bill Elliott to thank for the sharpest Monte Carlo SS of them all. It was called the Aerocoupe. The limited-run special was introduced in the middle of the 1986 model year and was designed to stress good aerodynamics.

During the 1985 NASCAR Winston Cup season, Elliott had driven a Ford Thunderbird. His "Blue Oval" racecar had captured a record 11 superspeedway wins, helping Elliott take a much-publicized $1 million bonus. This happened despite the fact that Darrell Waltrip (who drove Junior Johnson's Monte Carlo SS) took the driving championship and despite the fact that Chevrolet—which tied Ford (with 14 wins apiece)—had claimed the manufacturer's title for the third year in a row.

Although they wangled out the points championship, the bow-tie brand drivers howled because they couldn't catch the T-birds on the big tracks. To make matters worse, Ford went back and redesigned the Thunderbird for 1986 and it came out looking sleeker than ever.

With no new Monte Carlo model in the works, Chevrolet did the next best thing and improvised a solution to the problem. To keep costs to a minimum, Chevy simply extended the back window glass on the Monte Carlo SS. On December 18, 1985, the Aerocoupe option (B5T) was announced. It dropped the drag coefficient from .375 to .365.

To accommodate the 25-degree slope of the glass, a smaller trunk lid was used. Kits to turn the Monte Carlo SS racecars into Aerocoupes were readily available, but production models were not that common and only 200 Monte Carlo SS Aerocoupes were built for 1986.

The Super Sport option, which technically was a separate extra-cost package, came out in the middle of 1983. Unlike the Aerocoupe version, the regular Monte Carlo SS was an immediate hit in the showrooms, as well as on the racetracks. Its standard engine was a 180-nhp version of the 305-cid small-block V-8. The car's sloping nose, which was developed in a wind tunnel, was a key part of its high-performance image.

The American Sunroof Corp. (ASC) of Livonia, Michigan, turned a limited number of IROC-Z's into ragtop muscle cars.

1987 Camaro 5.7-liter IROC-Z

The 5.7-liter Camaro IROC-Z model arrived right on schedule for 1987. Chevrolet advertised the availability of the new engine by promoting the car as "a mean hombre in '87 with the arrival of the 5.7-liter TPI V-8 power plant roaring under the hood of the hot IROC-Z."

With the earlier 5.0-liter IROC-Z already accounting for nearly 25 percent of Camaro Z/28 sales (which in turn represented 47 percent of all Camaros sold), the 5.7-liter version was expected to have a strong influence on Chevrolet's overall business. A potential impediment, the unavailability of air conditioning on the 5.7-liter IROC-Z, was only temporary, since it was slated for production beginning in October 1986.

Except for its Camaro LB9 accessory drive belts, exhaust system and electronic control module, the new L98 IROC-Z V-8 was identical to the Corvette 5.7-liter TPI V-8 engine. Its power ratings were 220 hp at 4200 rpm and 320 lbs.-ft. of torque at 3200 rpm. With the exception of its 3.27:1 geared 7.75-inch Australian-built Borg-Warner rear axle, the 5.7-liter IROC-Z shared its running gear with the 5.0-liter version. All IROC-Z models had slightly revised suspensions for 1987.

The price of this engine, which was identified as RPO B2L, was $1,045 over the $13,488 cost of an IROC-Z with the base LG4 engine. Chevrolet required the purchase of a number of mandatory options. These included RPO MX4, a special version of the four-speed 700R4 automatic transmission with an upgraded torque converter, RPO B80, a limited-slip differential, RPO J85, four-wheel disc brakes and the RPO KC4 engine oil cooler. The cost of these features raised the price of the 5.7-liter engine to $1,924, which contrasted with the $707 list price of RPO LB9, the tunnel-port-injected 305 cid V-8.

The cost of the 5.7-liter IROC-Z paled before its exceptional performance. *Hot Rod* magazine, in its January 1987 issue, suggested that "it could be the closest facsimile to a full-bore road racing car you'll ever drive." Chevrolet's acceleration data underscored this perspective. Chevrolet test drivers achieved a 0-to-60-mph time of 6.2 seconds and a standing-start quarter-mile time of 14.5 seconds. Subsequent road tests essentially duplicated these figures.

Also available in limited numbers as a 1987 model was an IROC-Z Camaro convertible conversion done by the American Sunroof Corp. (ASC) of Livonia, Michigan.

The stylish 1987 Monte Carlo SS carried a sticker price of $13,463.

Jerry Heasley

1987 Monte Carlo SS

For 1987, the Chevrolet Monte Carlo coupe, model 1G, came in LS and SS versions. A V-6 was standard in the LS and the V-8 version listed for $11,746 or $440 more than the V-6. The V-8-only Monte Carlo SS (RPO Z37/Z65) had a base price of $13,463. A new SS feature for 1987 was aerodynamic composite headlights.

Also returning for 1987 was the Monte Carlo SS Aerocoupe package, which was technically an option (RPO Z37/Z16). Its big, slanting back window reduced the high-performance model's coefficient of drag from 0.375 to 0.365, but it also added $1,395 to the price of the Monte Carlo SS coupe. That brought the sticker on a production-type Aerocoupe to $14,838 without any add-on extras.

Powering the 3,528-lb. Aerocoupe was the high-output Super Sport version of the 5.0-liter (305-cid) small-block V-8, which produced 180 nhp. It came attached to a four-speed overdrive automatic transmission.

For its second season, the Monte Carlo SS Aerocoupe was made more readily available and Chevrolet wound up producing 6,052 copies. The main change between the original version and the 1987 edition was the placement of decals on the front doors.

Monte Carlo Aerocoupe production continued until December 11, 1987. When the short-run 1988 models were introduced, the Aerocoupe was no longer on the option list.

The Aerocoupe worked so well that Chevrolet drivers gave the factory manufacturer's championships in 1987 and 1988, along with a solid lead in May of 1989, when the stock car racing program switched over to the Chevy Lumina body.

Aerocoupes are still being raced successfully today on other racing circuits.

Jerry Heasley

By the time it finally rolled off the assembly line, the high-powered, and pricey, 1990 ZR1 had buyers standing in line.

1990 Corvette ZR1

Two things marked the Corvette ZR1's entry into automotive history in 1990. The first was its "super Corvette" image. This car had been conceived and built to compete in the marketplace with the top cars in the world—at a price that was noticeably higher than other Corvette stickers, but six figures less than the competition! The second thing was the length of time the car took to reach the market. Deadlines were missed and missed again, as Chevy refined the design and waited for necessary government approvals.

Finally, the car arrived! The first 1990 Corvette ZR1 was purchased by Glenn Ross of Marietta, Georgia. His car was the 114th ZR1 produced and the first delivered to a Chevrolet dealership. "The ZR1 is head and shoulders above the Ferraris and Lamborghinis," Ross said. "It drives like it's on silk." He added that he placed the order for his ZR1 14 months prior to its arrival in September 1989. Ninety-five percent of the first-year ZR1s were pre-ordered by March 1988.

The collectibility of the 1990 ZR1 went beyond initial demand for the car, which far outpaced supply. Subtle styling changes that set it apart from the 1990 Corvette coupe, along with low production numbers in its first year, marked the ZR1 as a car collector's target. Estimates from Chevrolet had only

2,000 ZR1 Corvettes being produced for 1990.

The ZR1, at first glance, looked similar to the Corvette coupe, but it was stretched 1 inch and was 3 inches wider to accommodate an increased rear tread width. The telltale difference between the base Corvette and the ZR1 was the high-performance model's revised rectangular taillights.

What really put a stamp of uniqueness on the ZR1, however, was its drive train. The ZR1's all-aluminum 350-cid LT5 V-8 produced enough thrust to launch the Corvette from 0-to-60 mph in 4.3 seconds. The LT5 was rated at 375 hp and was constructed by boat-engine specialists at Mercury Marine. An AZF six-speed manual transmission was mated to the engine. This transmission was also offered as optional equipment on 1989 Corvette coupes, but it was mandatory in the ZR1, which did not have an automatic transmission option.

The factory list price of a ZR1, as shipped with both the automatic climate control and one-piece removable top options, was $62,675. This was compared to the 1990 Corvette coupe's asking price of $37,900. But, because of the great demand for ZR1s, dealers asked for—and got—prices that were out of this world.

CHEVROLET

Tom Glatch

With only 2,044 built, the fabulous 1991 Corvette ZR1 will likely be a coveted collector car in the future.

1991 Corvette ZR1

The Corvette ZR1 was an amazing sports car. When the first Corvette arrived in 1953, the concept behind it was to grab a share of the market for sporty cars that developed after World War II. But until the ZR1 came along, the owner of Jaguar or a Mercedes could argue that the higher price tag on his car proved it better. Once the super 'Vette showed up, the debate was over! The ZR1 was "world class"—and at a fraction of the price of its competitors.

After the launch of the first ZR1 in 1990, the product planners got to relax for a short while. The 1991 version had very few changes from the original and really didn't need any. A long list of enthusiasts was lining up to buy the car.

The "super Vette" again had a convex rear fascia and two rectangular tail lamps on either side of the car. The ZR1 was attracting so much attention, that standard Corvettes were restyled at the rear to more closely resemble the hi-po model.

A new front end with wrap-around parking lamps was used on both the ZR1 and the standard Corvette. Both models also featured new side-panel louvers and wider body-color body side moldings. Although it was more like the standard 1991 Corvette in a visual sense, the second ZR1 continued to use different doors and had a wider rear end to accommodate

its 11-inch-wide rear wheels. Also, the high-mounted stop lamp went on the roof of the ZR1, instead of on the rear fascia as it did on other Corvettes.

All ZR1s were again equipped with ABS II-S anti-lock braking and a driver's side airbag, as well as the General Motors standard anti-theft system.

The ZR1 was again powered by a 32-valve DOHC 5.7-liter V-8 matched with a six-speed transaxle. Its "valet" power access system was offered again, but it was changed in that it now defaulted to normal power on each ignition cycle. The "full power" light was relocated next to the valet key.

On ZR1s, the fourth and fifth symbols in the vehicle identification number were YZ. The last six symbols indicated the sequential production number starting with 800001 for the ZR1, which came only as a hatchback coupe. The 1991 ZR1 listed for $64,138 and Chevrolet built 2,044 of them.

The ZR1's RPO LT5 Tuned-Port-Injected engine was a 90-degree overhead valve V-8 with four valves per cylinder and four overhead camshafts. The 350-cid (5.7-liter) engine utilized a cast-iron block and aluminum cylinder head. It had hydraulic lifters, an 11.0:1 compression ratio, 375 hp at 5800 rpm and 370 lbs.-ft. of torque at 5600 rpm.

The ZR1 remained an awesome car in 1992, but with only 502
built it performed better on the road than it did on the sales charts.

1992 Corvette ZR1

When model-year 1992 rolled around, it was evident that there was little change in the makeup of the Corvette model lineup. The zoomy ZR1 was basically a direct carryover from the previous year, except for the placement of new model badges above the rear fender vents. The "Super Corvette" was again powered by a 5.7-liter 32-valve DOHC 5.7-liter V-8 producing 375 hp at 5,800 rpm. The engine had a cast iron block and aluminum cylinder heads. It was mated to a six-speed manual transaxle.

Both the ZR1 and the regular Corvette had new rectangular exhaust ports. A new all-black dash treatment, a relocated digital speedometer and improved instrument graphics were adopted as well. General Motors' Acceleration Slip Regulation (ASR) traction control system became standard equipment, along with new Goodyear GS-C tires. The standard tires were Goodyear Eagle GTS, size P275/40ZR17 up front and P315/35ZR17 in the rear.

The 1992 Corvettes came in White, Yellow, Black, Bright Aqua Metallic, Polo Green II Metallic, Black Rose Metallic, Dark Red Metallic, Quasar Blue Metallic and Bright Red. Interiors came in Blue, Beige, Black, Light Beige, Light Gray, Red and White. The price tag for a ZR1 rose to $65,318. It weighed in at 3,465 lbs., but sales were light with only 502 of the muscle Corvettes built.

According to one enthusiast magazine, the 1992 Corvette ZR1 did 0-to-60 miles per hour in 4.3 seconds, while the standing-start quarter-mile took 12.9 seconds. That compared to 4.92 seconds for 0-to-60 in a base LT1 model, which did the quarter-mile in 13.7 seconds.

The all-new 1993 Z28 could do 14-flat quarter-mile with its 275-hp V-8.

CHEVROLET

1993 Camaro Z28

Despite the softening of the old pony car market, Chevrolet didn't look for any easy way out when it introduced its fourth-generation Camaro a few months into the 1993 model run. It featured an all-new body, reworked chassis and a Z28 that came only one way—fast.

While the 1982-1992 Camaro (and its close relative the Pontiac Firebird) stuck to rear-wheel drive and solid V-8 power in a changing automotive world of front drive and less cylinders, it still left room for improvement, mainly in handling and structural tightness. The new 1993 Camaro (and Firebird) improved on performance, handling and even comfort.

For the 1993 model year, only a hatchback coupe was offered. It came two ways, in a base model priced at $13,889 with a 3.4-liter, 160-hp V-6, and as a Z28 priced at $17,269.

The body, while much sleeker than the old style, featured a 68-degree raked windshield and steel structure to which composite (plastic) panels were attached. Only the rear quarters and hood were steel. Optional removable glass roof panels retailed for $895.

A new short-and-long arm coil spring front suspension and power rack-and-pinion steering replaced the old struts and re-circulating ball setup. The rear continued with coils with multi-link bars.

By checking the Z28 box on the order form you got a LT1 350-cid V-8 with aluminum heads. It was rated at 275 hp (up 30 from 1992). You also got a standard Borg-Warner T-56 six-speed manual transmission, four-wheel antilock disc brakes, 16 x 8-inch aluminum wheels and Goodyear GA P235/55R16 rubber. Z-rated GS-C Goodyears were optional at $144.

If you kept the standard tires, you also got a governed top speed of 108 mph, which you could hit in fourth, fifth or sixth gear. Going for the Z-rated doughnuts meant the Z28 could do what it wanted, which several magazines found

exceeded 150 mph.

The 1993 Camaro sat on the same 101.1-inch wheelbase as in the past. Length was up .6 of an inch to 193.2 inches while the car's width ballooned by 1.7 inches to 74.1 inches. Height was up nearly an inch to 51.3 inches.

Optional on the Z28 at $595 was the Turbo-Hydra-Matic 4L60 automatic. Like the LT1 engine, the transmission had seen service on the Corvette.

The no-excuses Z28 was an immediate hit with the car magazines. *Car & Driver* pitted it against the Ford Mustang Cobra and declared the Z28 the fastest with a 0-to-60 in 5.3 seconds and a quarter-mile romp of 14 seconds flat at 100 mph. *Motor Trend* tested several performance cars and noted that the Camaro—with a top speed of 151 mph—represented the "biggest bang for the buck" of the bunch.

Muscle cars had come a long when it came to interior creature comforts by 1993.

With a top speed of more than 150 mph, the 1993 Z28 was
more than capable of handling pace car duties at Indy.

1993 Camaro Indy Pace Car

The 1993-1995 Camaro Z28 models are essentially all the same cars. They differ mainly in small details, such as what type of fuel-injection system they utilize, type of engine management system, transmission choices (automatic or manual), axle ratios, colors of the numbers on the instruments and so forth. However, if you want one of these modern muscle cars that really stands out in looks, history and value, then grab yourself a 1993 Camaro Indianapolis 500 Pace Car replica.

Thanks to its excellent photo archive, the Indianapolis Motor Speedway has documentation of pace cars used at the "Brickyard" since 1911, when a Stoddard-Dayton paced the event. In 1953, on its 50th anniversary, Ford started the practice of producing quantities of special pace car replicas and using them to boost its sales totals. As the race cars got faster, the pace cars had to go faster, too, and that often led to a muscle car being selected for pace car duty, which is considered an honor in the auto industry.

A Camaro paced the Indianapolis 500-mile race for the fourth time in 1993. The previous years for Camaro pace cars were 1967, 1969 and 1982. Chevrolet provided the Indianapolis Motor Speedway with three "Official Pace Cars" and another

125 replicas for track officials. In addition, dealers were to get 500 copies, with another 20 reserved for Canada. The tally puts the 1993 Camaro Indy Pace Car replica squarely in the limited-production class, at least as far as Chevrolets go.

Only the Camaro hatchback coupe was available for 1993. The pace car replica came with a special black-and-white exterior and multi-colored accents. The special interior featured the same color combination with a new 3D knitting process for the seats and door panels. A gold hood emblem topped it all off. Mechanically, nothing special was needed, as the 350-cid/275-hp LT1 Corvette V-8 met Indianapolis Motor Speedway's performance requirements without modification. "Performance-wise, every 1993 Camaro Z28 is capable of pacing Indy," said Jim Perkins, Chevrolet general manager and driver of the pace car for the 500.

Camaro Indy Pace Cars were fitted with automatic transmissions. Chevrolet installed the 4L60 Hydra-Matic with a .70 fourth gear. The rest of the Z28 driveline and underpinnings were just fine for track duty. Camaro Z28s equipped with the optional six-speed manual transmission were clocked in the 155-mph range by magazines in 1993.

Jerry Heasley

The splendid LT1 Corvette was overshadowed perhaps only by
its ZR1 sibling when it came to fast American cars in 1993.

1993 Corvette LT1

First released as a 1984 model, the C4 Corvette picked up the trick ZR1 option for 1990 and a second-generation small-block LT1 base engine for 1992. This LT1 engine was so good that it reduced demand for the much more expensive ZR1 model. It came connected to a four-speed overdrive automatic transmission. A six-speed manual gearbox was optional equipment.

The LT1 was a 90-degree overhead-valve engine with a cast iron block and an aluminum cylinder head. The 350-cid (5.7-liter) hydraulic-lifter V-8 had a bore and stroke of 4.00 x 3.48 inches, a 10.5:1 compression ratio and multi-port fuel injection. It produced 300 hp at 5000 rpm and 340 lbs.-ft. of torque at 3600 rpm. The 1993 LT1-powered Corvette did 0-to-60 mph in 5.4 seconds.

For 1993, a great deal of interest was focused on the Corvette's 40th anniversary. To mark the occasion, a 40th Anniversary Appearance Package was offered for the $34,145 coupe or $41,745 convertible. Coughing over another $1,455 for the package got you Ruby Red paint, Ruby Red leather seats with special embroidery and appropriate badges. You did have to kick in $305 more for a power seat mechanism, whether you really wanted it or not.

The coupe sold for $34,595, weighed 3,333 lbs. and had a production run of 15,898 units. The convertible was priced at $41,195. It tipped the scales at 3,383 lbs. and 5,712 were built. Total model-year production was 21,590 cars. The RPO Z25 40th Anniversary Package was added to 6,749 cars with no body style breakout available.

Jerry Heasley

The amazing 1993 ZR1 Corvette was clocked at 178 mph by *Road and Track* magazine.

1993 Corvette ZR1

The ZR1 Corvette's 5.7-liter LT5 V-8 was upgraded this year and featured significant power and torque increases. Improvements in the designs of the LT5 engine's cylinder head and valve train included "blending" the valve heads and creating three-angle valve inserts, plus the use of a sleeve spacer to help maintain port alignment of the injector manifold. These upgrades added up to a 30-hp increase and also produced a higher torque rating.

In addition to the aforementioned improvements, the LT5 engine was now equipped with four-bolt main bearings, platinum-tipped spark plugs and an electrical linear exhaust gas recirculating (EGR) system. Improved airflow from the cylinder head enhancements and the valve train refinements boosted the engine's rating from 375 hp to 405 hp!

A special 40th anniversary appearance package was offered in 1993 and was available on all models. This package included an exclusive "Ruby Red" color exterior, a matching interior treatment and color-keyed wheel centers. The cars had special headrest embroidery. Bright emblems on the hood, deck and side gills were optional equipment on all models, including ZR1s.

The 1993 Corvette also introduced General Motors first Passive Keyless Entry system whereby simply leaving or approaching the Corvette automatically unlocked or locked the appropriate doors. The 1993 Corvette was also the first North American automobile to use recycled sheet-molded-compound body panels.

The ZR1 again used a six-speed transaxle. Arctic White, Black, Bright Aqua Metallic, Polo Green II Metallic, Competition Yellow, Ruby Red, Torch Red, Black Rose Metallic, Dark Red Metallic and Quasar Blue Metallic were the colors offered this year. Interiors came in beige, black, light beige, light gray, red, ruby red and white.

ZR1s were identified by a YZ in the vehicle identification number. The last six symbols indicate the sequential production number starting with 800001 for ZR1s. The engine code suffix ZVC identified the 350-cid/405-hp RPO LT5 V-8 used in the ZR1 model only.

The 1991 ZR1 Special Performance Package was actually a $31,683 option for the hatchback coupe and brought its base price up to $66,278. In standard trim, the ZR1-optioned hatchback weighed 3,503 lbs. Only 448 cars were built with the ZR1 option this year.

Motor Trend tested a 1993 Corvette ZR1 and found it could do 0-to-60 mph in 4.9 seconds. Quarter-mile performances were 13.1 seconds and 109.6 mph for the ZR. As for top speed, *Road and Track* did 178 mph in another ZR1.

CHEVROLET

With a 156-mph top speed, the Z28 was still the king of its class in 1994.

Jerry Heasley

1994 Camaro Z28

When the 1994s came out, there was mixed news for Camaro fans. A new convertible body style was added. It was the first factory built Camaro ragtop since since the 1969 model concluded the nameplates first generation. The open model listed for $22,565, compared to $19,235 for the coupe. At first, the convertible lacked some of the heavy-duty suspension parts used on the coupe and its top speed was governed at 104 mph.

Other 1994 changes included a new electronically controlled automatic transmission and a Computer Aided Gear Selection device for the six-speed manual gearbox that, similar to the Corvette, hit you with a first-to-fourth shift if you were not engaged in hard acceleration. Back to the good side, the Camaro's hot-running LT1 V-8 got sequential port fuel injection, which was a definite improvement over multi-port fuel injection.

All 1994 Camaros were equipped with improved brakes and the high-performance Z28 included four-wheel disc brakes. Ordering the 1LE special performance suspension package was simplified, as it now appeared on the Chevrolet order form as an RPO (regular production option) on the order form.

The Camaro interior had modest changes. High-contrast black knobs and white graphics were used in place of the gray knobs and yellow graphics of 1993. Camaro Z28s with optional speed-rated Goodyear tires had 150-mph speedometers substituted for the stock 115-mph type. Also new were inside sun visors with storage provisions, flood light type door illumination and an optional new keyless entry system. Flame Red was a new color of fabric available.

Highlights of the Camaro's standard equipment list included driver and passenger air bags, ABS VI anti-lock brakes, intermittent windshield wipers, a tilt steering wheel, left- and right-hand covered visor mirrors, side-window defoggers, a PASS Key II theft-deterrent system, cup holders, in-door storage pockets, a lighted console and a locking glove box. Two new exterior colors were Dark Bright Teal and Polo Green Metallic.

The newly bodied 1994 Mustang GT and Cobra were natural comparisons for the 1-year-old Camaro Z28, which had little trouble holding its class crown. Among other things, *Car & Driver* pointed to the Camaro's top speed of 156 mph (versus 137 mph for the Mustang) and noted "the Mustang got hammered."

Chevrolet built a total of 112,539 Camaro coupes and 7,260 Camaro convertibles in 1994, but it is not known how many cars had the Z28 package.

The 1994 Impala SS was a rare bird: a four-door muscle car that was both cool and fast.

1994 Impala SS

From a 1960s perspective, the 1994 Chevrolet Impala SS was an odd duck. It's a four-door sedan, it's big and it caters to comfort as much as performance. However, putting the SS back in context, it ranks as one of the last remnants of the old big-horsepower era. It combines a large-for-its-time V-8 with ample horsepower, rear-wheel drive and full-frame construction.

The last Impala SS had been the 1969 model. As domestic automakers converted to front-wheel drive, smaller engines and smaller bodies, big high-performance cars disappeared. Chevrolet continued offering a full-size, rear-wheel-drive car with V-8 power, but downsized it in 1977. The Caprice name was usually attached, but a few low-buck Impala models were produced through the 1985 model year.

There was a controversial restyling for 1991, utilizing basically the same chassis. The Caprice was popular with the police and taxi segments of the market, but "civilian" buyers tended to be on the senior side. All that changed in November of 1992 when Chevrolet tricked up a Caprice sedan for the Specialty Equipment Market Association (SEMA) show in Las Vegas. It had an LT1 350-cid V-8, 17-inch aluminum wheels, 50-series tires, full rear-wheel cutouts, slightly modified rear quarter windows and a blackout-style paint job.

Chevy went to its retired name farm and revived the Impala SS tag and reaction at the SEMA show and other previews that followed was the same: "Build it!" This is just what Chevrolet Motor Division general manager Jim Perkins wanted to hear and on Valentine's Day of 1994 the first of the new Impala SS models rolled off an assembly line in the GM Assembly Plant in Arlington, Texas.

Unlike some production versions of show cars, the SS was not a watered-down, wimped-out version. The 260-hp version of the 350-cid LT1 came standard and was attached to a 4L60-E automatic transmission. The wheels were special 17 x 8.5-inch units like those on the show car. They were wrapped with P255/50ZR17 tires.

Four-wheel ventilated disc brakes were used at all four corners, as were stiffer coil springs and DeCarbon shocks similar to those on the Camaro Z28. The result was a 20 percent stiffer suspension, much better handling and a still comfortable ride. From the police car parts bin came front and rear anti-roll bars and other hardware aimed at going fast on straight or curved roads.

Chevrolet listed a 0-to-60-mph time of 7.1 seconds, but a spirited *Car & Driver* crew got a 6.5-second run and a quarter-mile of 15 seconds with a 92 mph trap speed. A couple of SS examples were even quicker. GM put a 502 big-block in a test car and got 0-to-60 mph in 6.0 seconds and a 14.5-second quarter-mile at 98.2 mph. Horsepower was claimed to be 385. Reeves Callaway converted customers' Impalas into the SuperNatural SS with a 383-cid small-block with 404 horses. *Motor Trend* performance figures were 0-to-60 mph in 5.9 seconds and for the quarter-mile 14.0 seconds at 100.3 mph!

The late-model Impala SS cost $22,495 and turned out to be a small-volume niche car in the GM scheme of things. For the model's first year, 6,303 units were built. Of course, instant collector status was assured for the Impala SS. We may not see anything like it again, at least from General Motors.

The 1994 Corvette LT1 had a few goodies that the '93 version didn't have, including standard leather seats.

CHEVROLET

1994 Corvette LT1

Several product refinements that were focused on safety and smoother operation were the main updates to the 1994 Chevrolet Corvette. A passenger-side airbag was added to the interior and all Corvettes now offered dual front airbags. In addition, other interior changes included new floor carpeting, new door-trim panels, new seats, a new steering wheel, a redesigned instrument panel and a restyled center console. Among new equipment features were an optional rear-axle ratio, revised spring rates, a convertible backlight (rear window) with heated glass and several new exterior body colors. Corvettes now offered a brake-transmission shift interlock system. The 4L60-E electronic four-speed overdrive automatic transmission (standard equipment in the Corvette) was also refined to provide smoother shift points.

The 1994 Corvettes came in Arctic White, Admiral Blue, Black, Bright Aqua Metallic, Polo Green Metallic, Competition Yellow, Copper Metallic, Torch Red, Black Rose Metallic and Dark Red Metallic. Interiors choices included beige, black, light beige, light gray, red and white.

The Corvette's standard equipment included a removable body-color roof panel for hatchbacks or a convertible top. All Corvette convertibles—except those with Polo Green Metallic body finish—could be ordered with one of three convertible top colors: beige, black or white. The White convertible top was not available for Polo Green Metallic cars, but could be had in conjunction with all of the other colors. Leather became the standard seat upholstery material.

The hatchback coupe was $36,185 this year and weighed in at 3,317 lbs. The $42,960 convertible was a tad heavier at 3,358 lbs. The ZR1 now carried a manufacturer's suggested retail price of $67,443. Chevrolet built 17,984 coupes and 5,320 ragtops. Total model-year production, including ZR1s, was 23,330 units.

1994 Corvette ZR1

Several refinements that focused on safety and smoother operation were the order for all 1994 Corvettes including the hotter ZR1 model. Like the base model, the ZR1 got a new passenger side airbag, new carpeting, new door-trim panels, new seats, a new steering wheel, a redesigned instrument panel and a restyled console. The ZR1 also received new "non-directional" five-spoke alloy rims for 1994.

The ZR1 again used the LT5 5.7-liter V-8. It was teamed with a six-speed manual transmission. Arctic White, Admiral Blue, Black, Bright Aqua Metallic, Polo Green Metallic, Competition Yellow, Copper Metallic, Torch Red, Black Rose Metallic and Dark Red Metallic were the 1994 colors. Interiors came in beige, black, light beige, light gray, red and white.

Engine code suffixes for 1994 Corvette ZR1s were ZWC for the 350-cid/405-hp RPO LT5 V-8 with 11.0:1 compression and manual transmission.

The ZR1 option package actually saw a slight price reduction to $31,258 in 1994, but the cost of the base Corvette hatchback rose to $36,185. This made the total cost of the ZR1 higher at $67,443. The curb weight this year was 3,503 lbs. Production was, once again, 448 cars with the option.

The 1994 ZR1 package cost a whopping $31,258, which brought the total bill for the hot 'Vette to $67,443.

Jerry Heasley

The unique Impala SS could clock a 15-flat quarter-mile, which was
pretty nice performance from a mid-'90s American four-door sedan.

CHEVROLET

1995 Impala SS

It is almost an irony of automotive history that the first Super Sport packages for early '60s Impalas were available for four-door models. Later, the SS designation became associated with sporty two-door coupes and convertibles. Then, in its final revival in the mid-'90s, the Impala SS was exclusively a four-door sedan model.

The Impala SS four-door sedan returned for its second appearance in 1995. It was again a specialty entry in the Chevrolet's Series 1B Caprice Classic lineup. The Impala SS was coded as the L19/BL5 model. This year it had a base price of $22,910 and tipped the scales at 4,036 lbs. That was about $1,000 more and 200 lbs. less than in the previous season.

As in 1994, the Impala SS featured a host of special equipment as part of its standard price. The assortment included five-spoke 17 x 8.5-inch aluminum wheels, 17-inch B.F. Goodrich Comp T/A tires, quick-ratio power steering, air conditioning with CFC-free refrigerant, a unique grille, a rear deck lid spoiler, Impala SS emblems, reshaped rear quarter windows with inserts, four-wheel disc brakes, an anti-lock braking system, a center console, a leather-wrapped steering wheel, dual air bags, black satin-finished trim, gray cloth upholstery, an electronic tachometer, and a special ride and handling suspension system with DeCarbon shock absorbers. Gray leather upholstery trim was optional.

The Impala SS was powered by the 5.7-liter (350-cid) LT1 Corvette V-8 engine with platinum-tipped spark plugs and a stainless-steel exhaust system, which produced 260 hp. It was linked to a 4L60-E electronic automatic transmission with a floor-mounted gear shifter. Performance was in the same bracket as with the 1994 model. Different sources listed times between 6.5 and 7.1 seconds for 0-to-60 mph runs. (The 7.1-second figure was the official one from Chevrolet Motor Division). A typical quarter-mile trial was done in 15 seconds at 92 mph.

Several new colors were introduced and added to the original monotone black color scheme in 1995. Black, however, remained the most popular with 9,858 cars being finished in that shade. Dark Cherry was put on 7,134 cars. Another 4,442 Impala SS sedans were done in Dark Gray Green, another new-for-1995 color.

The LT1 Corvette was back as the Indy 500 Pace Car in 1995.

1995 Corvette LT1

While the price tag on the high-performance ZR1 kept going up, the "standard" LT1 Corvette just kept getting better. In fact, this would be the final year that both were offered, since there was not enough difference between the two cars to justify the difference in cost.

Changes on the 1995 LT1-powered Corvette included the addition of heavy-duty brakes with larger front rotors as standard equipment, along with new low-rate springs. De Carbon gas-charged shock absorbers were used for improved ride quality.

In addition to exterior color changes, Corvettes featured a new "gill" panel behind the front wheel openings to help quickly distinguish the 1995 models from predecessors. Other improvements included reinforced interior stitching and a quieter cooling fan. Engine and transmission offerings remained unchanged from the year previous.

The year's colors were Dark Purple Metallic, Dark Purple Metallic and Arctic White, Arctic White, Admiral Blue, Black, Bright Aqua Metallic, Polo Green Metallic, Competition Yellow, Torch Red and Dark Red Metallic. Interiors came in beige, black, light beige, light gray, red and white. Standard features included a removable body-color roof panel for hatchbacks or a convertible top.

All Corvette convertibles, except those with Dark Purple Metallic and Arctic White or Polo Green Metallic finish could be ordered with one of three top colors: beige, black or white. The Dark Purple Metallic and Arctic White combination was available only with a white convertible top, which was again not available for Polo Green Metallic cars. Leather seats were standard equipment.

The coupe sold for $36,785 and the convertible for $43,665. Weights for the two models were 3,203 and 3,360 lbs., respectively. Chevy built 15,771 coupes and 4,971 convertibles.

The 1995 Corvette LT1 was selected to serve as the official pace car for the Indy 500. An RPO Z4Z Indy 500 Pace Car replica option was released for convertibles only and had a $2,816 price tag. It was the third time (1978 and 1986 were the previous years) that a Corvette paced the race at the famed Brickyard. The Dark Purple Metallic over Arctic White Corvette Official Pace Car was driven by 1960 Indy 500 winner Jim Rathmann. Chevrolet built a total of 527 Corvettes in 1995 with the RPO Z4Z Indy 500 Pace Car replica package.

Chevy built almost 5,000 Corvette LT1 convertibles in 1995. They carried a base price tag of $43,665.

Jerry Heasley

The ZR1 bowed out in 1995. It was a super-fast car that built up a very loyal
following of fans, but its price tag was too much to swallow for most admirers.

1995 Corvette ZR1

The biggest news of all for Corvette fans in 1995 was the fact that the high-performance ZR1 model was making its final appearance after several years of availability. The last of these hot Corvettes was built on April 28, 1995, in the Corvette assembly plant in Bowling Green, Kentucky. It was then driven across the street to the National Corvette Museum, where it was put on exhibition.

Was the ZR1 a bad car? The answer is absolutely not! In fact, the ZR1 was easily the best Corvette ever made up to its time. It was also the most expensive production Corvette Chevrolet ever made. That put a built-in limit on the number of buyers willing to plunk down nearly $70,000 for a Chevrolet product.

Those who had the wherewithal to own a ZR1 are extremely loyal to the limited-edition model and are quick to point out the advantages of the car's docile driving personality, as much as its all-out performance. Unfortunately, not enough loyal buyers could be found to support the ZR1 program past 1995.

Part of Chevrolet Motor Division's motivation for dropping the car was that there was simply not much difference between the regular LT1 Corvette and the costlier ZR1. Commenting in *Car & Driver*, Chevrolet general manager Jim Perkins said, "It began to set in that there was no differentiation between the two cars except for the engine option."

The 1995 Corvettes came in Dark Purple Metallic, Dark Purple Metallic and Arctic White, Arctic White, Admiral Blue, Black, Bright Aqua Metallic, Polo Green Metallic, Competition Yellow, Torch Red and Dark Red Metallic. Interiors came in beige, black, light beige, light gray, red and white. Standard features included leather upholstery, a removable body-color roof panel for hatchbacks or a convertible top.

ZUF was the engine code for the 350-cid 405-hp RPO LT5 V-8 with 11.0:1 compression and manual transmission that was used in the ZR1 model only. This year the base Corvette coupe retailed for $36,785 and the ZR1 option price was unchanged, so it cost a minimum of $68,043 to buy one of the 448 made.

CHEVROLET

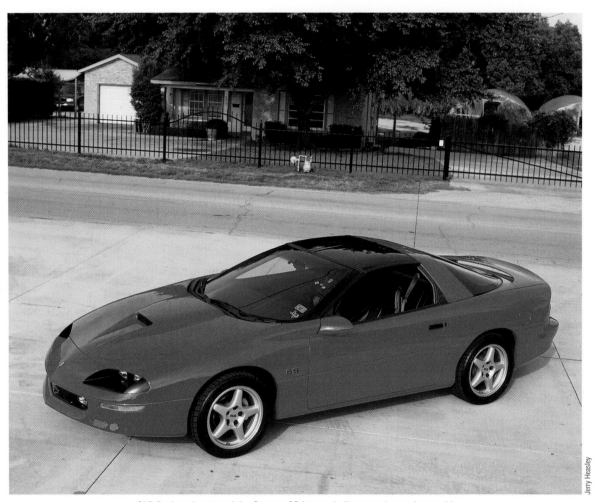

SLP Engineering turned the Camaro SS into a sizzling muscle car that could crack 100 mph in the quarter-mile.

Jerry Heasley

1996 Camaro SS

As the modern muscle car era progressed into the late 1990s, Detroit turned to smaller companies to help it create super cars for the enthusiast market niche. These companies were able to upgrade the looks and performance of regular production cars without jumping through all of the hoops the big automakers had to deal with. By "outsourcing" work to these companies, cars like the Camaro SS became available to those willing to pay a bit more to have a muscular ride.

The Camaro SS was built by SLP, which stood for "street legal performance." Ed Hamburger first got involved in the high-performance field by drag racing Mopars in the 1960s. Later, in the 1980s, he created SLP Engineering, in Red Bank, New Jersey. This company converted Pontiac Firebirds and Chevrolet Camaros into "street-legal performance" machines. His 1992 Firehawk version of the Firebird was a successful venture for SLP, as well as for the Pontiac dealers who sold the SLP package.

In 1996, Hamburger started working in conjunction with Chevrolet Motor Division to produce a Camaro muscle car that could be sold by Chevrolet dealers as a high-priced, factory-approved option package.

The secret of the 1996 Camaro SS was a special air-induction system which, when combined with an optional low-restriction exhaust system, boosted horsepower of the 10.4:1 compression 350-cid LT1 V-8 to 305 at 5000 rpm and torque to 325 lbs.-ft. at 2400 rpm. The engine had a cast-iron block and aluminum cylinder heads. It came with a sequential port fuel injection system and was hooked up to a six-speed manual transmission.

Like any real muscle car, the 1996 Camaro SS needed an image and a "feel" to suit its higher-than-standard performance capabilities. Therefore, the SS package also included a special composite hood with an "ant eater" air scoop, 17 x 9.0-inch Corvette ZR1-style wheels, BF Goodrich Comp T/A tires and special SS badges. It also featured a Torsen limited-slip differential, Bilstein shock absorbers, progressive-rate springs and performance-altered lower rear control arms.

The Camaro SS was roughly a $28,000 package. It weighed in at 3,565 lbs. and, while that didn't exactly make it a lightweight, it could accelerate from 0-to-60 mph in 5.3 seconds. It handled the quarter-mile in 13.8 seconds at 101.4 mph. Speaking of handling, it could brake from 60 mph in 117 feet and registered 0.88 gs in lateral acceleration testing.

1996 Impala SS

When the original Chevrolet Super Sport debuted in the mid-'60s "four on the floor" and a chrome-plated tachometer were the hallmarks of a "cool" car. Both of these features were found on the 1996 Impala SS, but with a high-tech twist. The Impala SS had a new floor-mounted shifter to control its sophisticated four-speed automatic transmission. A new analog tachometer kept tabs on its powerful LT1 V-8.

The heart of the Impala SS was again the Corvette-derived 5.7-liter LT1 V-8 with sequential fuel injection (SFI) recalibrated to deliver 260 hp at 5000 rpm and 330 lbs.-ft. of torque at 2400 rpm. It came mated to the GM electronically controlled 4L60-E four-speed automatic transmission, which harnessed the LT1's potent performance with smooth and precise shift points. A 3.08:1 final-drive ratio and a limited-slip differential helped provide quick acceleration.

The 1996 Impala SS was more than just a one-dimensional stoplight sensation. A special ride and handling suspension derived from the Chevrolet law enforcement package, coupled with quick-ratio power steering (12.7:1 vs. the standard 15.3:1 ratio), added an impressive level of agility for such a spacious sedan. Specially tuned de Carbon gas-pressure shocks—a luxury normally found only on Europe's finest cars—provided impressive dampening to maintain critical road feel. Tuned front and rear stabilizer bars were also fitted to help flatten cornering.

The Impala SS again wore aggressive P255/50ZR-17 speed-rated tires, along with lightweight 17 x 8.5-inch, five-spoke cast-alloy wheels. Standard four-wheel, ventilated disc brakes (12-inch diameter front and rear) and a four-wheel anti-lock brake system (ABS) allowed the Impala SS to stop as confidently as it went.

The 1996 Impala SS continued with the three monochromatic paint schemes of 1995 and production included 19,085 Black cars, 12,180 Dark Cherry cars and 10,676 Dark Gray Green cars. Body-color front and rear fascias, rocker moldings, door handles, key locks, tail lamp moldings and an antenna base were used. To add to its svelte style, body-side moldings, rear deck-lid moldings and external ornamentation were deleted. The Impala SS also sported a body-color grille, body-color 3-D Impala SS scripts along its flanks, a unique rear deck-lid spoiler and "stylish" Impala emblems on the sail panels and rear deck lid.

The interior was designed for driving enthusiasts. Deeply contoured front bucket seats were outfitted with gray leather seating surfaces, as was the full-width rear seat. The 1996 Impala SS incorporated a rugged steel safety cage that surrounded the entire passenger compartment, along with front and rear crush zones.

Impala SS filled a unique market niche for an affordable, full-size, highly styled performance sedan. Unfortunately, although the 1996 model enjoyed a nice sales boost, General Motors management decided to end production of rear-wheel-drive sedans at the end of the 1996 model year.

1996 Corvette Grand Sport/Collector Edition

Nineteen ninety-six was a landmark year for Corvette enthusiasts. With the demise of the ZR1 model, Chevrolet attempted to offset the void by introducing two new special edition Corvettes—the Grand Sport and Collector Edition models.

The 1996 Corvette Grand Sport evoked memories of its 1962-1963 racing predecessors. It sported Admiral Blue Metallic paint, a white racing stripe, red "hash" marks on the left front fender and black five-spoke aluminum wheels.

Powering the Grand Sport model (and also available as an extra-cost option in all other Corvettes) was a 330-hp 5.7-liter LT4 V-8 featuring a specially prepared crankshaft, a steel camshaft and water pump gears that were driven by a roller chain. The LT4 engine was offered only with the six-speed manual transmission.

The Collector Edition Corvette was produced as a tribute to the final year of production of the fourth-generation Corvette (the fifth-generation model was to debut the following year). The 1996 Collector Edition Corvette featured exclusive Sebring Silver paint on its sleek exterior. It also wore special "Collector Edition" emblems and distinctive five-spoke Silver aluminum wheels. A 5.7-liter LT1 V-8 was installed and was mated with a four-speed automatic transmission. The LT4 V-8 and six-speed manual transmission were both optional, in case you wanted to turn your Collector Edition Corvette into a muscle Corvette.

A Selective Real Time Damping system that employed sensors at each wheel to measure movement was new for 1996. Data retrieved from each wheel, as well as from the Powertrain Control Module, were processed by an electronic controller that calculated the damping mode to provide optimum control. The Sebring Silver Metallic (code 13) colored cars came only with black cloth tops. Admiral Blue (code 28) Grand Sports came only with white cloth tops.

The 5.7-liter (350-cid) LT4 was a 90-degree overhead valve job with four valves per cylinder and four overhead camshafts. It had a cast-iron block and a pair of aluminum cylinder heads. With sequential multiport fuel injection and a 10.8:1 compression ratio, it developed 330 hp at 5800 rpm and 340 lbs.-ft. of torque at 4500 rpm. According to manufacturer's test data, the LT4-powered Grand Sport did 0-to-60 mph in 4.7 seconds and the quarter-mile in 13.3 seconds at 109.7 mph.

The Z15 Collector's Edition was a $1,250 option and was installed on 5,412 cars. The Z16 Grand Sport Package option, which cost $2,880 to $3,250 depending on the body style of the car, was installed on 1,000 Corvettes.

CHEVROLET

CHEVROLET

The Collector Edition Corvette for 1996 was a tribute car that
celebrated the final year of production for the fourth-generation 'Vette.

The Admiral Blue Metallic paint, wide center stripe and red "hash" marks gave
the 1996 Corvette Gran Sport a custom racing look that was unmistakable.

The 30th Anniversary Camaro wore Hugger Orange stripes over
Artic White base paint patterned after the 1969 Indy Pace Car.

1997 Camaro Z28 SS and 30th Anniversary Edition

Thirty years is a long time for any car to survive in the automotive marketplace. For sure, there are Model T Fords, Volkswagens and Thunderbirds that seem to just go on year after year and decade after decade. But, for every long-lasting model or nameplate, there are dozens that stayed on the scene for just a couple of years.

The Chevrolet Camaro is another car that defied the odds by being a long-time survivor. Though gone at the moment (many say temporarily), the Camaro arrived on the scene in the '60s and survived through the New Millennium.

It was in 1997 that the Camaro observed its 30th anniversary and Chevrolet appropriately marked the occasion by offering a 30th Anniversary Package exclusively for the Z28 model. The $575 option package consisted of Artic White paint with Hugger Orange stripes, a combination patterned after the collectible 1969 Camaro Indy Pace car. Also included in the package were Artic White door handles, Artic White five-spoke aluminum wheels and an Artic White front fascia air intake.

The seats used only inside the 30th Anniversary Camaro were trimmed in Artic White with black-and-white houndstooth cloth inserts. This is another Camaro tradition that dated back to the classic '69 model. The floor mats and headrests had special five-color embroidery.

The Z28 came in coupe and convertible models for 1997. The closed car sold for $20,115 and weighed 3,433 lbs. The open car had a base retail price of $25,520 and weighed 3,589 lbs.

Standard equipment features of all 1997 Camaros included daytime running lights, four-wheel ABS disc brakes, dual airbags, an electronically controlled AM/FM stereo with cassette player, steel side-door guard beams and a reinforced steel safety cage. The Z28 included a 5.7-liter sequential fuel injected V-8 and a six-speed manual gear box.

The 350-cid engine was another marque tradition, as the Chevy "small-block" V-8 powered many Camaros over three decades. This latest version developed 285 hp at 5200 rpm and 325 lbs.-ft. of torque at 2400 rpm.

Also available, as an extra-cost option, was the Camaro SS Z28, which was powered by a 305-hp Corvette LT1 V-8. This car was specially built and sold through selected Chevrolet dealers. It featured a hood scoop, a high-performance exhaust system, a Hurst gear shifter and a sport suspension package with Bilstein shock absorbers.

The anniversary Camaro had black-and-white
seat cloth and standard dual airbags.

CHEVROLET

CHEVROLET

Jerry Heasley

The C5 Corvette finally arrived in 1997 after a 13-year wait.

1997 Corvette

It was another landmark year for Corvette in that the 1997 C5 model was the first all-new Corvette in 13 years and only the fifth or sixth (depending upon your viewpoint) major change in the car's 44-year history. The "fifth-generation" Corvette was offered only as a coupe in its debut year. It was designed under the direction of John Cafaro.

Among the equipment featured for the C5 was a new, more compact, 5.7-liter LS1 V-8 that produced 350 hp and 345 lbs.-ft. of torque. A rear-mounted transaxle opened up more interior space and helped maintain a near 50/50 front-to-rear weight distribution. An electronic throttle control system allowed engineers a limitless range of throttle progression.

The 1997 Corvette's underbody structure was the stiffest in the car's history and consisted of two full-length, hydro-formed perimeter frame rails coupled to a backbone tunnel. The rails consisted of a single piece of tubular steel, replacing the 14 parts used previously.

The cockpit of the all-new Corvette featured a twin-pod design reminiscent of the original 1953 Corvette. The instrument panel contained traditional backlit analog gauges and a digital "Driver Information Center" that comprised a display of 12 individual readouts in four languages. The new-design blunt tail section allowed for smoother airflow and resulting 0.29 coefficient of drag.

The C5 Corvette was offered with a 4L60-E electronic four-speed overdrive automatic as the base transmission and a six-speed manual transmission was optional. Corvettes came in Arctic White, Sebring Silver Metallic, Nassau Blue, Black, Light Carmine Red Metallic, Torch Red and Fairway Green Metallic. Interiors came in Black, Light Gray and Firethorn Red. Standard features included a removable body-color roof panel. Leather seats were standard equipment.

The C5 coupe sold for $37,495 and weighed 3,229 lbs. The car's SFI V-8 engine had a cast aluminum block and heads. Its displacement was 346 cu. in. or 5.7 liters. It had a 3.90 x 3.62-inch bore and stroke, a 10.1:1 compression ratio and 345 hp at 5600 rpm. Torque was 350 lbs.-ft. at 4400 rpm. An automatic transmission with floor-mounted gear shifter was standard equipment. Chevrolet built only 9,092 of these cars.

Jerry Heasley

Though the Camaro was on thin ice by 1998, it was still receiving significant updates. The SS was a $3,500 package that provided a 320-hp V-8 and some other performance and styling goodies.

1998 Camaro Z28 SS

At the tender age of 31, the Camaro may have seemed like it was 100 years old in "car years," especially to the GM big wigs, but Chevrolet wasn't ready to give up on its sports-personal car just yet. Some people were saying that the F-bodies (Camaro and Firebird) had passed their peak in popularity, but there were always enthusiasts within the company ready to fight for the cars' survival.

Chevrolet Motor Division treated the 1998 Camaro lineup to significant changes. For beginners, the RS coupe and convertible were dropped. That left the base coupe and convertible for buyers who wanted V-6 power and the Z28 sport coupe and convertible for diehard V-8 fans,

On the outside, all Camaros were restyled for the new model year. Obvious alterations included a redesigned hood, new front fenders, a newly styled front fascia and composite headlights with reflector optics. Fog lights were an option. A new four-wheel disc brake system was standard equipment, as was an all-welded exhaust system.

The standard Camaro Z28 was enhanced by making a "new-generation" 5.7-liter LS1 V-8 the base engine. The engine was the same aluminum block, 10.1:0 compression-ratio, sequential fuel-injected V-8 that came in Corvettes. It was rated for 305 hp at 5200 rpm and 335 lbs.-ft. of torque

at 4000 rpm.

Instead of the RS model, Chevrolet offered an optional Sport Appearance Package that was available on all models except the Z28 SS. The SS kit was changed from a "factory-approved" aftermarket option installed by an outside "partner" company to an extra added right at the Chevrolet factory.

Cataloged as the WU8 SS Performance and Appearance Package, it included an upgrade to a 320-hp V-8, a forced-air-induction hood, a rear deck lid spoiler, 17-inch aluminum wheels, a high-performance ride and handling package and special SS badging. The option was available only for Z28s. It retailed for $3,500. A six-speed manual gearbox was again used with V-8 engines.

Chevrolet built a total of 43,360 coupes and 3,858 Camaro convertibles for the 1998 model year. These totals included 2,397 coupes and 478 ragtops with the SS package. This muscular option included a special 320-hp V-8, a forced-air-induction hood, a unique spoiler, 17-inch aluminum wheels, P275/40ZR17 Goodyear Eagle F1 tires, a ride-and-handling package and SS badging. The SS (or Super Sport) package added $3,500 to the cost of the car.

CHEVROLET

Jerry Heasley

The Corvette convertible was back in 1998, and 1,163 of the hot ragtops wore the Indy Pace Car package.

1998 Corvette

In its 45th year, the Corvette returned to offering convertible and coupe models with the debut of a "topless" version of the C5 Corvette. The convertible's glass rear window was heated and the top had an "express-down" feature that released the tonneau cover and automatically lowered the windows part way at the touch of a button.

New for 1998 was a magnesium wheel option featuring lightweight wheels with a unique bronze tone. Standard features included a stainless-steel exhaust system, tires capable of running for 200 miles with no air pressure, dual heated electric remote breakaway outside rearview mirrors, daytime running lamps and 5-mph front and rear bumpers.

For the fourth time (1978, 1986, 1995, 1998) a Corvette was selected to pace the Indianapolis 500. Indy 500 veteran Parnelli Jones drove the Purple and Yellow pace car.

The LS1 V-8 and four-speed automatic transmission were again the standard offering, with the T56 six-speed manual transmission optional. Corvettes were available in Artic White, Sebring Silver Metallic, Nassau Blue Metallic, Black, Light Carmine Red Metallic, Torch Red, Magnetic Red II Clearcoat and Fairway Green Metallic. Leather seats were standard and came in Black, Yellow, Light Oak, Light Gray and Firethorn Red. Convertible tops came in Black, Light Oak and White.

The 1998 Corvette C5 coupe retailed for $37,495 and tipped the scales at 3,245 lbs. It had a production run of 19,235 units. The convertible could be purchased for a minimum of $44,425. It weighed just a pound more than the coupe. Chevrolet built 11,849 ragtops and 1,163 had the Indy pace car package.

Some neat performance options were on the C5 Corvette's list. They included the RPO F45 Continuously Variable Real Time Damping system for $1,695, an RPO G92 performance axle ratio for $100 (not available with six-speed), an RPO JL4 Active-Handling system for $500, the RPO MN6 six-speed manual transmission for $815, the RPO Z4Z Indy Pace Car package for $5,039 with automatic transmission and $5,804 with manual transmission and the RPO Z51 Performance Handling package with Bilstein's adjustable ride-control system for $350.

Corvette made its long-awaited return to Trans-Am racing successful by placing first in the 1998 season-opening event on the street circuit at Long Beach, California, in the AutoLink Corvette driven by veteran road racer Paul Gentilozzi.

The 1999 Z28 SS got high marks for its handling and road manners.

CHEVROLET

1999 Camaro Z28 SS

The 1999 Camaro Z28 SS was the top dog in a comparison test that *Car and Driver* magazine conducted in August 1999. The face-off pitted the convertible version of Chevy's muscular pony car against counterpart ragtops wearing Pontiac Firebird Trans Am and Ford SVT Cobra Mustang badges.

Powering the Camaro Z28 SS was a 346-cid 16-valve Chevrolet LS1 V-8 with an aluminum block and aluminum cylinder heads. It had General Motors' engine-control system with port fuel injection. This system generated 320 hp at 5200 rpm and 335 lbs.-ft. of torque at 4000 rpm. The available factory transmission options included a six-speed manual gearbox or a four-speed automatic.

The $33,955 fully equipped Camaro Z28 SS ragtop used in the road test did 0-to-60 mph in just 5.3 seconds, 0-to-100 mph in 12.8 seconds and 0-to-130 mph in 24.6 seconds. The quarter-mile took all of 13.9 seconds with a trap speed of 103 mph. The car's top speed was recorded as 160 mph.

The Camaro Z28 SS was not the fastest car in the *Car and Driver* test, but it was right up there and it really excelled where it came to roadability and handling. The original equipment P275/40ZR-17 Goodyear Eagle F1 GS tires were a big plus and it had a tight suspension, excellent steering and great brakes. The Camaro Z28 SS could stop from 70 mph in just 175 ft. and turned 0.86 gs on a skidpad. It also turned in the best performance when a professional driver, Paul Gentilozzi, put it through its paces on a road course.

Car and Driver said that the Camaro Z28 SS was the best car to drive on an everyday basis and suggested that ABS braking and traction control were important considerations when it came to daily driving in such a machine.

Wieck Media

The 1999 Corvette family.

1999 Corvette

In its second year of production, the C5 Corvette made *Car and Drivers'* list of the 10 best cars. The magazine said that the car possessed "a stellar blend of value, performance, practicality and extroverted personality, as well as a few enhancements." The car was a bit on the large side, with a 104.5-inch wheelbase and 179.7-inch overall length, but it could really fly despite a weight range from 3,150 to 3,250 lbs., depending upon the body style.

The C5's pushrod aluminum engine was a masterpiece of production engineering. The 16-valve 5.7-liter V-8 had a 10.1:1 compression ratio and put out 345 hp at 5600 rpm. Buyers had a choice of hooking it to a six-speed manual transmission or a four-speed automatic. Typically, the C5 turned in 0-to-60-mph times between 4.8 seconds and 5.3 seconds depending upon the transmission and rear axle combination. It did the standing-start quarter-mile in somewhere between 13.2 and 13.8 seconds. Top speed estimates recorded in various tests were from 162 to 175 mph.

A strong perimeter frame with a center backbone provided the C5 with a rigid platform that carried a host of innovative performance features including: ABS with four-wheel disc brakes, a rear-mounted transmission, a double wishbone suspension, lightweight aluminum alloy wheels, speed sensitive variable ratio steering, extended mobility tires and a choice of three different suspensions. The Corvette could brake from 70 mph in about 166 ft. and maintained

.086 to 0.90 gs on a skid pad, reflecting its outstanding road-holding characteristics.

New for 1999 was the first fixed-roof Corvette to see the light of day since 1967. It was a bit less expensive to buy than the regular coupe and the convertible, but included a few high-performance extras that did not come as standard equipment with the other models. Overall, the Corvette price range was $39,361 to $46,154 in 1999.

Jerry Heasley

With a top speed of 170 mph, the Corvette was still the measuring stick for domestic performance in 1999.

The wild, wooly and exotic Ligenfelter Twin-Turbo Corvette
was barely getting warmed up at 200 mph.

Jerry Heasley

1998-99 Ligenfelter Twin-Turbo Corvette

The 1999 Ligenfelter Twin-Turbo Corvette was a 650-hp muscle car that *Motor Trend* (March 2000) described as "The fastest, meanest, street-legal car we've ever tested." Race driver and car builder John Ligenfelter "remanufactured" these cars in his shop in Decatur, Indiana.

For $43,995 and up, Ligenfelter Performance Engineering would convert a new Corvette into a car with nearly double the factory model's price and performance. The conversion process started with the blueprinting of the stock Corvette LS1 engine. Then Ligenfelter installed a forged steel crankshaft, billet steel connecting rods and forged aluminum pistons, ported the cylinder heads, fitted larger stainless-steel valves, added a new roller-bearing camshaft and installed two Garrett turbos with up to 8.5 lbs. of boost pressure.

The 346-cid engine featured an aluminum block and heads, a 3.90 x 3.62-inch bore and stroke, a 9.5:1 compression ratio and sequential fuel injection. It produced 650 hp at 5800 rpm and 600 lbs.-ft. of torque at 5000 rpm. The engine was linked to a six-speed manual transmission.

Motor Trend tested the car with a 2.73:1 axle ratio for top speed and a 3.43:1 axle for acceleration runs. It also had some minor suspension changes like stiffer anti-roll bars, Penske adjustable shock absorbers, Baer brakes and thinner-than-stock Michelin Pilot Sport street tires (P235/235ZR18 up front and P275/235ZR18 in the rear) to improve its aerodynamics at 200-plus mph.

The Ligenfelter Twin-Turbo Corvette turned 0-to-60 mph in 3.3 seconds and went from 0-to-100 mph in 6.7 seconds (which would have been a great 0-to-60 time for any 1960s muscle car). The standing-start quarter-mile was covered in 11.8 seconds at 132.1 mph with street tires. The test was then repeated with drag racing slicks and the car did the distance in 10.8 seconds at 133.5 mph. Its top speed was 226 mph!

2000 SLP Camaro RS

Over the years, Ed Hamburger's SLP Engineering had grown successful building "Bandit" Trans Ams and Firebird Firehawks for Pontiac dealers to sell as a factory option. The company had started out in Red Bank, New Jersey, with such Pontiacs, but by 2000 it was operating in Troy, Michigan, and had added Camaro conversions to its line.

The SLP package for the 2000 Camaro RS was merchandised as an $849 Chevrolet dealer option with code Y3B. Ingredients of the SLP package included the Camaro Z28 dual-slot exhaust system and black longitudinal racing stripes, plus "RS" badges on the fenders and dash. A second SLP package costing $699 added 8 x 16-inch five-spoke alloy wheels.

The changes brought the price of the Camaro up to about $20,000 and added a little performance in addition to the appearance enhancements. Specifically, the 231-cid V-6 from the stock Camaro was tweaked to generate 205 hp at 5200 rpm and 225 lbs.-ft. of torque at 4000 rpm. *Car and Driver* (December 2000) found that good enough to produce a 7.5-second 0-to-60-mph time and a 15.8-second quarter-mile at 86 mph. The magazine pointed out that such performance wasn't likely to win any modern-day street races, but outdid the performance of the 350-cid V-8 used in the original "Bandit" Trans Ams that SLP created back in 1987.

CHEVROLET

Wieck Media

The 2000 Camaro SS was the high-output Camaro and served up 320 hp with its hot 5.7-liter engine.

2000 Camaro SS

Chevrolet's Camaro entered the new millennium continuing to play its traditional role as one of the greatest values among modern muscle cars. The 2000 Camaro was offered in a choice of coupe and convertible body styles with prices ranging from a low of about $17,500 to a high of $35,000. Regardless of where you purchased on the Camaro price spectrum, you wound up with a lot of car for your hard-earned bucks.

The base model came with a 3.8-liter 200-hp V-6 that was plenty adequate for the general public. A few rungs up the

ladder you got to the Z28, which used a 305-hp version of the venerable 5.7-liter (350-hp) V-8. However, for muscle car lovers, the hot ticket was the SS, which came stuffed with a tweaked 5.7-liter motor that cranked up 320 hp and promised 5.2-second 0-to-60-mph times, even with a 3,306-lb. curb weight.

Chevrolet offered a wide choice of convenience options and handling packages for the Camaro and those wanting to drive quick or fast were well advised to order the optional traction-control system and 1LE performance suspension.

The 2000 Corvette coupe, hardtop and convertible all came with
a 345-hp aluminum V-8. For production cars, they could fly.

2000 Corvette

Entering the new millennium, the Corvette represented a tremendous bargain in the muscle car market niche when you balanced what you got for each buck you spent and compared it to its international competitors. The base prices for the Sport Coupe, convertible and hardtop models ranged from $39,000 to $46,000 and bought you a world-class machine that could go from 0-to-60 mph in only 4.8 seconds.

The heart of the 2000 Corvette was a 5.7-liter 345-hp aluminum V-8 that rumbled like a '60s muscle car engine. It produced its peak power at 5600 rpm and could be had hooked to an RPO MN6 six-speed manual gearbox (for $815) or attached to Chevy's M30 four-speed automatic. A 2.73:1 axle was standard with the automatic transmission and a

3.15:1 performance axle was available for $500 extra. A 3.42:1 axle was standard on stick-shift cars. The 2000 Corvette took 13.2 seconds to cover the quarter-mile and its top speed was in the 165-mph bracket.

Introduced as a budget performance car, the $38,900 hardtop (a.k.a. "fixed-roof coupe") came standard with the six-speed manual transmission, Goodyear Eagle F1 tires and Chevrolet's Z51 high-performance suspension kit. It wound up being a rare car, too, since Chevy made only 2,090 of them. The sport coupe listed for $39,475 and had a production run of 18,113 units, making it the first choice of Corvette buyers. The ragtop was base priced at $45,900 and 13,479 were built.

The Z06 Corvette just kept getting better and faster in the early 2000s, and the 2001 version was no exception.

CHEVROLET

2001 Corvette Z06

Everyone has to have a goal in life, and for Chevrolet Motor Division's Corvette engineers it was to make the already great 2000 C5 Corvette even better for 2001. The C6 took the place of the previous model known as the hardtop, but it retained that body style as the sole platform for the Z06 model option. Basically, as compared to the 2000 hardtop, the Z06 gained 40 hp and lost 103 lbs. That added up to an amazingly muscular supercar. In fact, in performance terms the Z06 could speed from 0-to-60 mph in just 4.7 seconds.

The new 346-cid LS6 small-block Chevy V-8 under the hood of this impressive car produced 385 hp at 6000 rpm and 385 lbs.-ft. of torque at 4800 rpm. Its special features included modifications to the engine block casting to alleviate crankcase pressures, a special high-airflow intake manifold, a high-lift camshaft with increased duration, a 10.5:1 compression ratio and over-sized fuel injectors.

To lighten the cars, Chevrolet came up with a weight reduction of 6 lbs. for each tire and wheel, thinner glass in the windshield and backlight, and a titanium exhaust system that was 17 lbs. lighter than a conventional steel exhaust system. The increased power combined with the weight reduction added up to a car that carried just 8.09 lbs. per horsepower!

Other features of the $46,800 Corvette Z06 are a six-speed manual transmission, 12.6-inch-diameter vented disc brakes front and rear with ABS standard, forged aluminum wheels and Goodyear Eagle F1 SC tires size 265/40ZR18 up front and size 295/35ZR18 in the rear.

The interior of the Z06 included black seats with red pleated inserts and matching door panels, but all-black door panels could be substituted. However, you couldn't get any other seats but the red and black ones.

Wieck Media

CHEVROLET

The 2002 Corvette Z06 was yet another "fastest ever" Corvette.

2002 Corvette

Three Corvettes were marketed in 2002. The C5 coupe sold for $42,275 and weighed 3,221 lbs. A total of 15,861 were made. The convertible was priced at $48,800 and weighed 27 lbs. more. It found a slightly smaller total of 14,173 buyers. The rarest Corvette was the Z06 hardtop, which sold for $51,`075 and had a production run of 5,773 units.

All 2002 Corvettes had a second-generation Active Handling system as standard equipment. The automatic transmission cooler case was now constructed of lightweight cast aluminum, replacing stainless steel. Standard on equipment with the C5 coupe included alloy wheels, anti-lock brakes, a tachometer, automatic transmission and a Traction Control system. The Convertible came with the same standard equipment, plus a power antenna.

Chevrolet's LS1 SFI V-8 was standard in C5s. This 5.7-liter (346-cid) overhead valve V-8 had a cast aluminum block and heads. It used a 10.1:1 compression ratio. The engine developed 350 hp at 5600 rpm. Torque was 375 lbs.-ft. at 4400 rpm with the six-speed manual transmission or 360 lbs.-ft. at 4000 rpm with the 4L60-E four-speed automatic transmission.

The Z06 Corvette was aimed at true performance enthusiasts at the upper end of the high-performance market. For 2002, a 405-hp V-8 made the Z06 the quickest production Corvette ever. This improvement was the result of new hollow-stem valves, a higher-lift camshaft, a low-restriction mass airflow (MAF) sensor and a new low-restriction air cleaner. The Z06-specific FE4 high-performance suspension system featured a larger front stabilizer bar, revised shock valving, a stiffer rear leaf spring and specific camber settings. The Z06 also had new rear shock valving. The unique aluminum Z06 wheels were now produced via casting, rather than forging.

Hydroformed frame rails and a four-wheel independent front suspension with cast-aluminum upper and lower A-arms were other Z06 features. The Z06 (and C-5 Corvettes equipped with the Z51 package) now had aluminum front stabilizer bar links and reduced weight. The rear suspension had a transverse leaf spring system. A standard Head-Up Display (HUD) system projected the speedometer and many other gauges digitally on the windshield. New high-performance front brake pads on the Z06 provided improved lining durability and fade resistance in high-performance situations.

The 2003 Z06 Corvette was a loaded 405-hp rocket.

CHEVROLET

2003 Corvette

The sixth-generation 2003 Corvette was designed to deliver more power, passion and precision and a new standard of performance car excellence. Highlights included a 50th Anniversary Edition package, more standard equipment on C5 models and the availability of Magnetic Selective Ride Control. This feature used a revolutionary damper design that controlled wheel and body motion with Magneto-Rheological fluid in the shock absorbers.

All 2003 Corvettes featured a special 50th anniversary emblem front and rear. The Silver emblem featured the number "50" with the signature cross-flag design. In addition, Medium Spiral Gray Metallic exterior paint replaced Pewter. The C5 Coupe listed for $43,475 and 12,812 were built. The $50,375 Convertible was a bit more popular with 14,022 assemblies.

The 50th Anniversary Edition package, priced at $5,000, was available only on Coupes and Convertibles. It included special 50th Anniversary Red paint, specific badging, a unique Shale interior and Champagne anniversary wheels with special emblems. There were embroidered badges on the seats and floor mats, padded door armrests and grips and a Shale convertible top. The LS1 V-8 and Magnetic Selective Ride Control were standard.

A special 50th Anniversary Edition of the 2003 Corvette was the Official Pace Car of the Indianapolis 500 in May of 2003, marking the fifth time that a Corvette paced the race.

The three 2003 Corvettes provided to the Speedway for Pace Car duties were the only 2003 models in existence at the time. The Pace Car was virtually identical to the 50th Anniversary Edition Coupe made available at Chevrolet dealerships in the summer of 2003. It was equipped with the 350-hp 5.7-liter LS1 V-8. A few modifications were made to the 2003 Corvette 50th Anniversary Edition Pace Car to prepare it for pacing duties. They included special exterior graphics wrapped over the "Anniversary Red" exterior and a lower-restriction muffler system. A four-point racing safety belt setup and a safety strobe-light system were required by the Indy Racing League. A special heavy-duty transmission and a power steering cooler were also added to the three pace cars.

The Z06, now priced at $51,275, included the 405-hp Z06 engine, a unique six-speed manual gear box, hollow-stem valves, a high-lift camshaft, a low-restriction mass air flow sensor, a low-restriction air cleaner, a high-performance exhaust system, a FE4 high-performance suspension system, a fat front stabilizer, revised shock absorber valving, a stiffer rear leaf spring, specific camber settings, hydroformed frame rails, a four-wheel independent front suspension with cast-aluminum upper and lower A-arms, aluminum front stabilizer bar links, a transverse leaf spring system, the Head-Up Display (HUD) system and high-performance front brake pads. An AM/FM cassette/radio was optional in the Z06 and all 8,635 cars built had a manual gearbox.

Wieck Media

The 2004 Commemorative Edition Z06 wore Le Mans Blue paint
and special striping and badging. It also had a carbon fiber hood.

2004 Corvette

The C5 Corvette maintained its well-earned status as an American sports car icon that had been admired and sought after for a generation. It was in its final season, but Chevrolet continued to celebrate the nameplate's golden anniversary and keep the car fresh with technologies such as Magnetic Selective Ride Control, Goodyear EMT "run-flat" tires, active handling and a rear transaxle. Standard performance equipment included a 5.7-liter V-8, a four-speed automatic transmission, and a limited-slip rear axle.

The 2004 Commemorative Edition package recognized the success of the C5-R competition coupes campaigned by the Corvette Racing Team. The Commemorative Edition package included a Le Mans Blue exterior, a Shale interior, special badges, special seat embroidery and high-polished, five-spoke aluminum wheels with specific center caps. The Commemorative Edition package was only available with the 1SC package, which was a $3,700 option. It included a Shale convertible top with the convertible.

A 2004 Corvette convertible was selected to serve as the Official Pace Car at the 2004 Indianapolis 500. Very few modifications were made to the Corvette to prepare it for this role.

The Z06 Corvette remained for the extreme performance enthusiast. Z06 Corvettes featured revised chassis tuning for quicker, smoother response in challenging environments. The chassis enhancements were subtle in terms of physical parts, but significant in terms of the car's performance and feel. GM engineers refined the Z06's shock damping characteristics to provide improved handling in the most challenging conditions, while maintaining good ride control for the demands of daily driving. The Z06 Corvette also included a special engine, a unique six-speed manual gearbox, hollow-stem valves, a high-lift camshaft, a low-restriction mass air flow (MAF) sensor, a low-restriction air cleaner, a high-performance exhaust system, a Z06-specific FE4 high-performance suspension system, a fat front stabilizer, revised shock absorber valving, a stiffer rear leaf spring, specific camber settings, hydroformed frame rails, a four-wheel independent front suspension with cast-aluminum upper and lower A-arms, aluminum front stabilizer bar links, a transverse leaf spring system, the Head-Up Display (HUD) system and high-performance front brake pads.

The Commemorative Edition Z06 was also Le Mans Blue and also included a C5-R Le Mans stripe scheme, special badges, polished Z06 wheels and a lightweight carbon fiber hood. For 2004, the regular Z06 was given two performance-enhancing upgrades. A lightweight, race-inspired carbon fiber hood was used on Z06s with the Commemorative Edition option and all Z06s had the carbon fiber hood that weighed 10.6 lbs. less than the standard hood.

The sixth-generation Corvette was a slightly smaller and lighter package than the C5, and with a dizzying
array of performance and comfort features, it was definitely the most high-tech production 'Vette built to date.

2005 Corvette

The sixth-generation of the Corvette started with the 2005 coupe and convertible models. Featuring dramatic upgrades throughout, a new 400-hp 6.0-liter V-8 and dynamic new styling, the C6 Corvette brought more power and precision to America's performance icon.

The sixth-generation Corvette replaced the outgoing C5 Corvette (1997-2004), but the formula from the C5 era remained: Extremely high performance capabilities in a car that offered great style, value and quality, with surprising comfort for daily driving. The new Corvette added dramatic increases in performance and refinement, wrapped in a new design.

Thanks to an all-new chassis, a strong lightweight body structure and a new 400-hp LS2 V-8, the C6 Corvette raised the bar for performance, with outstanding handling and surprising ride quality. Equipped with the new Z51 Performance Package, the 2005 Corvette was offered in both coupe and convertible body styles and both nearly matched the Z06 model's track performance.

The sixth-generation Corvette convertible featured an optional power-operated soft top, a feature last seen in 1962. The convertible top reflected great attention to detail. In both manual and power versions, the canvas soft top was available in three colors: Black, Beige and Grey. In its closed position, the canvas top had a smoother, more contoured appearance that concealed the underlying structure better than traditional soft tops.

In an era in which most vehicles seem to grow ever more bulky, the C6 Corvette achieved a lower vehicle weight, even with the addition of numerous new features. The convertible had a base curb weight of 3,199 lbs., 49 lbs. less than the 2004 model. The manual top mechanism utilizes thin-wall castings for a weight savings of 8.6 lbs. The optional power top mechanism added just 14 lbs.

Both the coupe and convertible offered OnStar, XM Satellite Radio and DVD-Navigation. Likewise, three suspension choices—Corvette Standard Suspension, Magnetic Selective Ride Control and the new Z51 Performance Package—were available on the both body styles.

The Firepower V-8 developed 180 hp, good enough to make the Chrysler New Yorker the pace car for the 1951 Indy 500. The engine soon appeared in the racier Saratoga, which proved to be one of the earliest muscle cars to hit the street.

CHRYSLER

1951 New Yorker/Saratoga FirePower Hemi V-8

The contribution of the Chrysler FirePower hemispherical head V-8 to the domestic-car horsepower race of the 1950s is widely known and unquestioned. Lesser realized is the fact that, during the first year this engine was produced, Chrysler added a potential "factory hot rod" to its model lineup—the Saratoga.

The FirePower engine made its initial appearance when the new, mildly facelifted models were introduced in 1951. Replacing the flathead straight eight used in previous New Yorker and Imperial models, the engine was a plus in these large automobiles with their 131.5-inch wheelbase chassis that dated back to late-1949 models.

The 331.2-cid Hemi engine produced 180 hp. That was equal to the top rating available in the entire industry. The engine featured twin rocker shafts in each cylinder head, which allowed the valves to be canted on either side of the centrally positioned spark plugs. The early Hemi ran a 7.5:1 compression ratio and a Carter two-barrel carburetor, so operation required only regular-grade fuel.

At first it was the New Yorker that showcased the FirePower V-8. Automotive scribe Tom McCahill tested one of these cars. Despite its Fluid-Matic "semi-automatic" transmission, this car did just over 100 mph in the Flying

Mile run at Daytona Beach. *Motor Trend* reported the New Yorker's top speed at 106 mph.

Almost overlooked was the introduction of the Saratoga in July. It combined the FirePower V-8 with the smaller, lighter Windsor chassis. The series offered short- and long-wheelbase sedans and a Town & Country wagon, but the hot rod was the Club Coupe. It was 200 lbs. lighter than the New Yorker coupe with the same power. It was essentially Chrysler's version of the Rocket 88 Olds. Even with automatic transmission, *Motor Trend* got a 10-second 0-to-60 run out of the Saratoga.

The new car's racing potential wasn't overlooked. Stock car driver Tommy Thompson piloted a Saratoga to Chrysler's first NASCAR win August 12, 1951, at Michigan Fairgrounds, a dirt oval in Detroit. A bunch of auto industry brass were there and the Saratoga's go power impressed them all.

Saratogas were also the hot ticket in the La Carrera Panamericana or Mexican Road Race. Non-professional driver Bill Sterling finished third overall in his Chrysler, as well as first among strictly stock cars. Despite such performances, the '51 Saratoga gets little respect from muscle-car buffs or those bidding on high-performance models at classic car auctions. Too bad.

CHRYSLER

The 1960 Chrysler 300-F carried a 413-cid motor with either 375 or 400 hp.

1960 300-F "Letter Car"

When Chrysler took away the 300's Hemi in 1959, its performance image suffered. Even though the "Golden Lion" wedge-head V-8 was shown to be equally as potent (92 mph in the quarter-mile), the loss of the Hemi created a vacuum.

In 1960, the vacuum was filled by providing the 300-F with a ram-inducted 413-cid V-8 good for 375 hp in standard form and 400 hp in optional form. Engine hardware common to both included a hot cam, heavy-duty valve springs, low-back-pressure exhaust system, dual-point distributor, low-restriction air cleaner, special plugs and dual quad carbs.

The carbs were mounted on a wild-looking cross-ram manifold that put one air cleaner on each side of the engine. The stacks were 30 inches long and had to be crisscrossed to fit under the hood. At low speeds, the "long" rams worked

great, but they hurt performance above 4000 rpm. To solve the problem, engineers removed a section of the inner walls of the manifolds to create the optional 400-hp engine. On the outside, these "short" rams looked the same, but they were effectively 15 inches long.

This option was really intended only for Daytona-bound cars that competed in the Flying Mile there and about 15 "short" ram cars were built. The $800 option also included a rare four-speed gearbox made for the Facel Vega, a Chrysler-powered French luxury car. One of the 400-hp cars, driven by Greg Ziegler, set a Flying Mile record of 144.9 mph. In 1960, a total of 969 hardtops and 248 convertibles, all with ram manifolds, were made.

Robert Seroka

The 1961 300-G was a superb car with performance to match its good looks. One magazine wound it up to 131 mph in a test run.

CHRYSLER

1961 300-G "Letter Car"

Car Life called the Chrysler 300-G "the best road car on the market." Chrysler called it "the brand-new 1961 version of Chrysler's championship breed of rare motorcars. A limited-edition automobile, precision built for the connoisseur of careful craftsmanship and superb engineering."

The 300-G's suspension had front torsion bars that were approximately 33 percent stiffer than standard. The 60-inch leaf springs were 9 percent stiffer than stock. The 1.38-inch shock absorbers were considerably larger than units found on other Chryslers. The tires were 8.00 x 15 Goodyear Blue Streak Super Sport high-performance whitewalls.

The 300-G continued to use Chrysler's 413-cid wedge V-8 with 375 hp at 5000 rpm and 495 lbs.-ft. of torque at 2800 rpm. This engine had 30-inch ram-induction tubes that increased torque up to 10 percent in the mid-engine range. Dual Carter four-barrel carbs were carried over. As with the 300-F, Chrysler offered a 400-hp option for the 300-G. This V-8 had solid lifters, "short" induction tubes, slightly larger carburetors and a longer-duration (284- to 268-degree) cam. The short rams reduced maximum torque to 465 lbs.-ft. at 3600 rpm. The 300-G's standard axle ratio was 3.23:1. This change gave the G a slight top speed advantage over the F.

The push-button-controlled transmission gave test results 0-to-60 mph in 8.4 seconds and the quarter-mile in 16.2 seconds at 87.4 mph. Top speed of the 300-G was reported by *Car Life* to be 131 mph. At Daytona, a 300-G running with the optional 2.93:1 axle ratio won the NASCAR Flying Mile Championship with a two-way average of 143.0 mph. A 300-G also won the NASCAR Standing Mile Championship with a speed of 90.7 mph.

Replacing the four-speed Pont-a-Mousson manual transmission as an alternative to TorqueFlite was a heavy-duty three-speed Chrysler-built gearbox. A manual transmission 300-G had almost identical acceleration times as the TorqueFlite version.

The appearance of the 300-G was altered by the use of an inverted grille shape and the relocation of the taillights from the fins to above the rear bumper. Other revisions included a redesign of the headlights, reshaping the canted tailfins and replacing the (optional) Imperial-like trunk lid with a ribbed unit. Interior revisions were highlighted by a speedometer that read from 0 to 150 mph in single-mph intervals, a black finish for the painted sections of the dash and changes in the design of the dash panel padding and seat perforation. Numerous options were available, such as air conditioning, remote-control exterior mirrors, six-way power seat, power door locks and a "Sure-Grip" differential.

Letter Car production was the highest since 1955. A total of 1,617 Chrysler 300-Gs—1,280 hardtops and 337 convertibles—were manufactured. Respective prices for the hardtop and convertible were $5,413 and $5,843.

CHRYSLER

The 1962 300-H was the high-performance version of the Sport 300.

Phil Kunz

1962 300-H "Letter Car"

The Chrysler Letter Car was a legend in its own time. But after eight years, its time was beginning to run out. For 1962, Highland Park (Chrysler headquarters) decided to cash in on the 300's high-performance reputation by offering a series of non-letter Sport 300s. These cars used a milder 383-cid two-barrel V-8 as standard equipment and shared their 122-inch wheelbase with Chrysler's low-priced Newport line.

A real Letter Car was still offered. It was based on the same, smaller platform to hold down production costs. This 300-H came in the traditional two-door hardtop and convertible models. The shorter wheelbase actually shaved about 300 lbs. off its curb weight and therefore increased the horsepower-per-pound factor. At the same time, the standard 413-cid V-8 was boosted to 380 hp, five more than the 1961 300-G offered.

The lighter weight and higher horsepower resulted in an excellent performing car. With just 10.6 lbs. to move with each unit of power, the H had the best power-to-weight ratio seen in any Letter Car. It did 0-to-60 mph in the same 7.7 seconds as the Hemi-motivated 1957 300-C. And it covered the quarter-mile in 16 seconds. This tied the Ram-Tuned 1960 Chrysler 300-F for elapsed time.

Standard equipment for the 300-H didn't cut any corners, either. It included an interior with four bucket seats done in tan leather. Other colors of leather were available on special

order. Two big four-barrel carburetors sat atop the base engine, continuing a long-standing Letter Car feature. And a 405-hp Ram-Tuned engine was an exclusive-to-the-300-H option.

Push-button TorqueFlite transmission was standard in the Letter Car. Although an outstanding performer, the 300-H lacked the apart-from-the-crowd image of earlier Letter Cars. Its smaller size and close similarity to non-letter cars held down buyer interest. Some potential customers may even have opted for a loaded version of the Sport 300. The list of extras available for these non-Letter Car models included most of the goodies that came standard in the H.

Only 435 hardtops and 123 convertibles were made with 300-H trim. The hardtop sold for $5,090 and weighed 4,050 lbs. The convertible was $5,461 and 4,105 lbs.

Another big difference between the 300-H and earlier Letter Cars was its lack of tailfins. A management shake-up at Chrysler in the early 1960s inspired a move away from the design influences of stylist Virgil Exner, who was a big fan of fins. To make its purge complete, Chrysler simply shaved the rear end of the 1962 models.

Of course, no one single factor explained the low production of the 300-H. Rather, the combination of decreased size, less distinction and corporate changes in thinking teamed up to make the Chrysler 300-H a rare car.

Only 400 300-Js were produced, making them a rare prize today.

1963 300-J "Letter Car"

All Chrysler 300 Letter Cars deserve recognition as "beautiful brutes," but the 300-J has the added distinction of also being a rare beautiful brute when new. Only 400 were produced, so a sighting nowadays is worth celebrating.

Like the original C-300 and 300-B models, the 300-J was available only as a two-door hardtop. Chrysler adopted new styling for 1963 that it said possessed a "crisp, clean and custom look." As applied to the 300-J, a more appropriate description would be "restrained elegance." It's true that the 300-J shared much of its styling with lesser Chryslers, but the 300-J's lack of extraneous trim, its muscular profile and marvelously distinctive grille that evoked memories of earlier 300 models all contributed to make the 300-J one of America's most handsome automobiles.

The 300-J was available in five colors: Formal Black, Alabaster, Madison Gray, Oyster White and Claret. Adding a touch of class were the two pin stripes (in a contrasting color) that ran the length of the body and 300-J medallions situated on the C-pillar and the rear deck. The interior featured the controversial square steering wheel that many drivers found uncomfortable, but the outstanding design of the front bucket seats (finished in claret red leather), plus vinyl door panel trimming, color-coordinated claret carpeting and a center console with a built-in tachometer served as at least partial redemptions for this lapse of judgment by Chrysler.

A feature unique to Chryslers that was found on the 300-J were windshield wiper blades fitted with airfoils to press the blade against the windshield at high speeds. A great deal of equipment was included in the 300-J's list price of $5,184. A partial list includes: power steering/brakes/windows, front seat belts, padded instrument panel, windshield washers, variable-speed wipers, electric clock, remote control exterior mirror, four-way driver side power seat, 7.60 x 15 Blue Streak tires mounted on 6-inch-wide rims, TorqueFlite transmission, viscous fan driver and a 150-mph speedometer. Several options were available, including air conditioning, Sure-Grip limited-slip differential and a manual three-speed transmission.

Only one engine was offered for the 300-J—Chrysler's 413-cid wedge-head V-8. This engine, with mechanical lifters and a compression ratio of 10.0:1, had ratings of 390 hp at 4800 rpm and 485 lbs.-ft. of torque at 3600 rpm. Dual four-barrel AFB 3505S carburetors were used on a special cross-ram intake manifold. The dual-exhaust system was designed for maximum flow with minimum restriction.

Performance of the 300-J paralleled or exceeded that of many smaller and lighter vehicles. *Motor Trend*, April 1963, reported a 0 to 60-mph time of 8.0 seconds and a quarter-mile time and speed of 15.8 seconds at 89 mph in a TorqueFlite-equipped 300-J running with a 3.23:1 axle ratio. The true forte of the 300-J was its top speed, which was in excess of 142 mph.

The 300-J was a thoroughbred American grand touring car that maintained a tradition of excellence, which today gives it a status unique among performance automobiles. What a pity there aren't enough to go around!

CHRYSLER

Bob Schwartz

The classy 1964 300-K hid a 413-cid/390-hp V-8 under the hood.

1964 300-K "Letter Car"

The 1964 Chrysler 300-K was the most popular of the Chrysler 300 Letter Cars that started as 1955 models and ended with the 300-L for 1965. While it can be argued that the later Letter Cars lacked the performance that the earlier models abounded in, they were still among the fastest-accelerating cars of their era, although the competition was getting hotter and would soon pull ahead.

The 1963 Chrysler 300-J (there was no Chrysler 300-I to avoid confusing the "I" with a Roman numeral I) was completely restyled on a 122-inch wheelbase and came only as a hardtop. The 1964 Chrysler got only mild styling changes, but the Chrysler 300-K did get some much-needed attention.

A convertible returned and lower prices—$4,056 for the two-door hardtop and $4,522 for the convertible—did attract attention. This compared with regular 300 series models at $3,443 and $3,803, respectively. The 300-K's attractively styled interior also featured bucket-type seats and a console. Leather trim was now optional at just $93 extra.

The 300-K's standard engine was the 413-cid V-8 with a 360-hp rating, but for $375 you could order the 390-hp 413-cid power plant that featured twin Carter AFB four-barrel carbs on a short-ram intake manifold. TorqueFlite automatic was standard and a new four-speed manual transmission was optional.

When the counting of 300-K's was done at the end of the 1964 model year, 3,022 hardtops and 625 convertibles were turned out—a grand total of 3,647 units. That topped the 1957 Chrysler 300-C's record of 2,402.

The 1965 300-L ended the Letter series on a high note.

1965 300-L "Letter Car"

The last of the legendary Chrysler 300 "Letter Cars" was the 1965 300-L. It closed 10 years of milestone Mopar performance history. Some automotive historians and enthusiasts feel that the 1955 Chrysler C-300 was the first real "muscle car." If so, the last Letter Car has to be considered a significant automobile for serious collectors.

As the last edition of Chrysler's "beautiful brute," the 300-L was perhaps a bit tamed by old age. Nevertheless, the 300 Letter Car series did end with a car that was a capable performer. The Chrysler 300-L, with its standard 413-cid/390-hp engine, could hurl its 4,660 lbs. from 0-to-60 mph in 8.8 seconds. In the process, it coddled its passengers in beautiful vinyl front bucket seats and a notchback rear seat. The elegant dashboard used on all 1965 Chryslers was strewn prettily across the 300-L's interior and was complemented by a commanding center console between the bucket seats.

Aside from its massive, high-output power plant, the

300-L's only major distinction was a lighted medallion at the center of its silver crossbar grille. At night, the medallion glowed softly when the headlights were switched on.

Though lacking in individuality when compared to the standard Chrysler 300, the last of the Letter Cars moved just 11.8 lbs. per horsepower and could scat down the quarter-mile in 17.3 seconds. That was slower than a 396-cid/325-hp Chevrolet Caprice, but faster than a 390-cid/300-hp T-bird. It also managed to attract a good number of buyers, with 2,405 driving away in a 300-L hardtop and an additional 440 taking off in a rare 300-L convertible.

Even with such modest production totals, the Chrysler 300-L models were the second-best selling Letter Cars in history. Alas, this achievement went largely unnoticed and plans for the 1966 Chrysler 300-M were cancelled. A great Chrysler tradition had come to an end with the 300-L.

CHRYSLER

The Hurst 300 was definitely on the large side for a muscle car, but
its 375-hp motor turned the Chrysler into a big rig that could move.

1970 Hurst 300

George Hurst was much like the King Midas of motor heads—everything that he touched with his hands turned to muscle—even big boats such as the 1970 Chrysler 300. The Chrysler 300 came as a two-door hardtop with a 124-inch wheelbase. Its 224.7 inches of length made it look like an aircraft carrier. Yet, George Hurst convinced Chrysler Corporation that he could remake the car in the image of the legendary Chrysler 300 Letter Cars.

The heart of the 1970 Chrysler 300-Hurst was a TNT engine displacing 440 cid. It generated 375 hp thanks to a special hydraulic-lifter cam and a low-restriction dual exhaust system. The Hurst 300 included a heavy-duty suspension, power front disc brakes and H60-15 raised-white-letter tires.

Appearance features started with special Spinnaker White paint set off with gold accents. The fiberglass rear deck lid incorporated a recessed integral airfoil. There was also a power bulge hood, gold-accented road wheels with trim rings and fiberglass rear fender extensions. A brown leather interior was included. A TorqueFlite automatic was the only available transmission.

Hurst Performance Products Co. had one record indicating production of 650 cars, but another company document said that 501 were produced to the published specifications, plus one with a sunroof and one convertible. However, it has been discovered that two additional ragtops were possibly made, one by the factory and one by a dealer. One of these—the dealer-made car—was actually fitted with a 426-cid Hemi engine and appeared in *The Hurst Heritage* written by Bob Lichty and Terry Boyce. It even has Hemi hood emblems.

The normal Hurst 300 sold for $4,234. It could hit 60 mph in 7.1 seconds and did the quarter-mile in 16.8 seconds at 87.3 mph. Not bad for a 4,125-lb. "aircraft carrier."

The 300 package was available on the Chrysler Cordoba in 1979. It carried
a 360-cid V-8 at a time when few cars were offering muscular engines.

Phil Kunz

1979 Cordoba 300

Sometimes legends are best left alone, but the Chrysler Cordoba 300 is not one of those cases. These cars are coming on strong with MoPar collectors. In fact, one hobbyist just paid a bunch of money to have ace car hauler Guy Morice bring him a Cordoba with the 400-cid V-8 for a Cordoba 300 restoration project.

It was actually in November 1978 that the 300 option package was added to the list of extras. It added $2,040 to the Cordoba list price of $5,995. The package was designed to re-create the image of the famed Chrysler 300 Letter Car that had been offered for 11 glorious years.

The mid-size Cordoba bowed as a successful 1975 model and the 1979 model was the last to use the "Gen I" body on a 114.9-inch wheelbase. The 1978 Cordoba was the last in which you could get a big-block V-8 from the factory. The regular Cordoba tried to stress a luxury image, with actor Riccardo Montalban promoting its high-end virtues. This may be why a high-performance edition found few buyers waiting.

In any case, Chrysler literature proclaimed "Chrysler Recreates a Memory" and noted the similarities between the '79 Cordoba 300 and the '55 C-300. The limited-edition

Cordoba came in Spinnaker White with a red interior and featured leather bucket-type seats. The center console and dashboard had functional-looking engine-turned trim.

On the front, there was a cross-bar grille that recalled another Letter Car motif. Of course, it had a circular "300" medallion in its center. There were also fake front fender louvers, a 300 decal on the opera windows and tri-colored trim on the sides and special 300 logos on the aluminum and taillight lenses.

Standard engine in this model was the 360-cid V-8 with a 195 net horsepower rating. It was linked to a TorqueFlite automatic transmission. A special handling package kept the car properly balanced.

While it looked great, the 300 package was not a huge success at showroom level. The package was installed on just 3,811 cars. In 1980, an all-new Cordoba made its debut and a 300-like package was added at midyear. However, it was now called the "LS" package. Little did Mopar fanatics know, at the time, that the 300 name would come back and stick well several decades later. For 2004, the "300" was *Motor Trend*'s Car of the Year.

151

CHRYSLER

Wieck Media

**With a top speed of 145 mph, it was hard not to include the
Chrysler 300M in a conversation about late-90s muscle cars.**

1999 300M

This is a car that is hard to define. It's a specialty vehicle and it's chock full of luxury, but is it really a muscle car? With a 0 to 60-mph time of 7.8 seconds, you have to admit it's no rapid-accelerating Camaro SS, Mustang Cobra R or Corvette C5, but then it's not intended to be. On the other side of the coin, it has a top speed in excess of 145 mph.

In a way, that places it squarely in the tradition of earlier Chrysler Letter Cars, which also needed 8 seconds to get from rest to 60 mph, but then kept accelerating when the needle swept past double zeros! If the earlier "beautiful brutes" are muscle cars—and we think they are—the current one seems to fit the same image.

The front-engined, front-wheel-drive 300M first bowed in 1999. It featured a single overhead camshaft, 24-valve, 3.5-liter, all-aluminum V-6 that made it scoot pretty good.

In 1999, this engine produced 253 hp at 6400 rpm and 255 lbs.-ft. of torque at 3950 rpm. It came linked to an AutoStick dual mode manual/automatic transmission that permitted driver control on winding roads. Differentiating the $29,445 300M from other Letter Cars was an extra set of doors. It was a sedan, while all earlier Letter Cars were two-door hardtops or convertibles.

The 1999 Chrysler 300M's standard equipment list included heated leather seats, 16-inch tires, a premium four-disc changer Infinity sound system and a black-and-white analog clock and gauge cluster. Also featured was Chrysler's "cab-forward styling," driver and passenger air bags and all-wheel ABS disc brakes. Options included a pair of specific suspension settings and two different steering and braking levels that aided high-performance operation.

The 2000 Chrysler 300M was a four-door sedan that performed like a muscle car.

Wieck Media

CHRYSLER

2000 300M

After its 1998 introduction, the modern-day Chrysler 300M made it to *Car and Driver* magazine's "10 best" list two times in a row. Unlike its predecessors, the 300M did not change its "letter"—even though it was not only a different year, but also a new millennium. While its V-6 engine and extra set of doors made it a bit different in character than the original Chrysler 300 Letter Cars, the 300M has earned a following among collectors of the early, Hemi-powered and wedge-powered Chrysler 300s and, for that reason alone, it deserves at least an honorary spot in this muscle car book.

The 2000 model had a base retail price of $29,295. For that you got a big, stealthy looking, cab-forward, front-engine, front-wheel-drive four-door sedan on a 113-inch wheelbase with an overall length of 197.8 inches and curb weight of 3,600 lbs.

Below the hood there was a single overhead cam, 24-valve V-6 with an aluminum block and heads and a Chrysler SBEC III engine-management system with port fuel injection. The 215-cid engine developed 253 hp at 6400 rpm and 255 lbs.-ft. of torque at 3950 rpm. It came hooked to a four-speed automatic transmission with a lockup torque converter.

In testing, the Chrysler 300M moved from 0-to-60 mph in 7.8 seconds and did the standing-start quarter-mile in 15.9 seconds at 89 mph. It had a top speed of 139 mph. Was it a real muscle car? The answer is probably no, but it might be a great car for collectors of the original muscle car—the Chrysler 300 Letter Car—to use as an everyday driver.

The legendary Max Wedge was set up for drag racing and came in 415- and 425-hp varieties.

DODGE

1963-64 "Max Wedge" 426 Ramcharger

Dodge built high-performance Hemi-head V-8s from 1953 to 1958, by which time up to 320 hp was available in the Super D-500 version. There had been an even more brutal 340-hp D-501 option in mid-1957, before automakers were forced to apply brakes to the horsepower race. Also interesting was the 330-hp V-8 with electrionic fuel injection offered for a short time in early 1958. Cars ordered with this option were recalled and retro-fitted with "only" two four-barrel carbs.

A new, cheaper-to-build "wedge" V-8 arrived in 1959. It became well known in its early 383-, and 413- configurations. In the early '60s, it was available with wild-looking cross-ram intake manifolds in a 375-hp package. The 413 was the first Mopar engine to have an impact on drag racing. Chrysler's own factory literature said that it was designed for use in "acceleration trials."

The "Max Wedge" 413 was released in 1962. It had big intake and exhaust ports, stainless-steel head gaskets, big valves, a hot cam, dual valve springs, solid valve lifters and cast nodular rocker arms. A special aluminum ram-induction intake manifold with no heat crossover passage carried twin Carter AFB four-barrel carburetors. The engine was offered with two different compression ratios—11.0:1 or 13.5:1—and TRW built two types of special pistons for it. Other content included forged rods that were factory magnafluxed, free-flowing exhaust headers and a number of features usually associated with racing engines.

This potent big block could be hooked to a three-speed gearbox with a floor shifter or a beefy version of Chrysler's TorqueFlight automatic transmission. The 413 soon made drag racing history in cars such as Dandy Dick Landy's SS/S class Dodge. By the way, Dodge called it the "Ram-Charger 413" while Plymouth dubbed what was essentially the same engine its "Super Stock 413."

Also making its first appearance in 1962 was the 426-cid

Wedge-head V-8. That year, you could not order this engine in a Dodge (or Plymouth); it came only in big Chryslers. *Motor Trend's* "Spotlight on Detroit" column (June 1962) said, "You can now order 426 cubic inches on any Chrysler 300 or 300-H. Factory 413-cid blocks bored .060 are available on special order, with component combinations including forged pistons of 12-to-1 compression, 292-degree-duration cam with solid lifters, big exhaust valves, streamlined exhaust headers, and the original dual-four-barrel ram manifolds with passages shortened to "tune" above 4000 rpm. This top engine is rated 421 hp at 5400 rpm. Chrysler Division isn't going in for any dragging like Dodge and Plymouth, but they will supply the hot stuff if you want it."

Since the horsepower race was in full gallop, Mopar came out of the gate with the 426 "Max Wedge" V-8 in 1963. Like the 413 version, it came two ways. The tamer version had the 11.0:1 compression ratio and twin Carter four-barrels It stirred up 415 hp at 5800 rpm. The hairier "Max Wedge Stage II" Ramcharger V-8 used the 13.5:1 pistons. It was good for 425 hp at 5600 rpm. Both versions of the engine were designed strictly for racing. Dodge even supplied car buyers who ordered the Ramcharger V-8 with aluminum front end sheet metal to help make their cars lighter and faster. A functional aluminum hood scoop was part of the package, which dropped car weight by some 150 lbs.

In the spring of 1964, the first Dodge two-door sedan fitted with a complete, factory-installed Maximum Performance package, left the assembly line. It even had skinny front tires and real mag wheels. Car builders Don Beebe, Jim Nelson and Dode Martin used Dodge two-door sedans to create 800-hp drag cars that ran 480-cid versions of the 426 Ramcharger V-8 fitted with Hilborn fuel injection and GMC superchargers. The factory-backed "Ramchargers" drag racing team drew crowds, set records and sold Dodges.

Doug Mitchel

DODGE

The Polara 500 is an often overlooked muscle car that was fast off the line, especially for a big car.

1963 Polara 500

With its 119-inch wheelbase and 3,985-lb. curb weight, it is a bit hard to think of the 1963 Dodge Polara 500 convertible as a muscle car, until you see the results that Jim Wright recorded when he test drove such a car for *Motor Trend* magazine. His ragtop was equipped with the 383-cid/330-hp V-8 and managed to get from 0-to-60 mph in a mere 7.7 seconds. The quarter-mile took 15.8 seconds, by which time the big, open-top Dodge was moving at 92 mph. And we assume that a lighter Sport Coupe would have done even better.

With its 4.25 x 3.38-inch bore and stroke, the 383 was considered a Chrysler big-block engine and it was one of the best for all-around driving. It used 10.0:1 aluminum pistons and the 330-hp version had a Carter four-barrel carburetor that let the engine breathe deeply and rev to a 5,500-rpm redline above its 4,600-rpm horsepower peak. The torque output was a strong 425 lbs.-ft. at 2,800 rpm. Wright's

combination attached the 383 to a Borg-Warner T-10 four-speed with a 2.20.0:1 low gear, which didn't hurt its drag-strip performance one bit.

"Barring the all-out drag-strip engines, there aren't many that can stay with the 330-hp "383" in acceleration," Wright wrote in his article. He noted that the car's times through various speeds and the quarter-mile were "very impressive," especially considering that it used a 3.23.0:1 rear axle.

The 1963 Polara was considered the top trim level "Dodge" back in 1963, when the even fancier Custom 880 was thought of as, well, a Custom 880 instead of a Dodge. The basic Polara 500 convertible (which included four bucket seats) listed for just $3,196 and weighed 3,546 lbs. Wright's test car had some 340 lbs. of extras, including a Sure Grip differential, power steering, power brakes, electric windows, an AM/FM radio, a heater, a Sun tachometer and seat belts. The cost was $4,265.79.

The 1966 Charger was noteworthy for its shape and styling as it was for its performance.

1966 Charger 383

DODGE

The Charger was Dodge Division's answer to the fastback craze and it was dramatically different than all competitors when it arrived. It was big and wide, which gave it a distinctive "flat" look to distinguish it from other muscle cars. It combined MoPar's bright, clean interior styling with some of the company's best engine options to create a package that had no peers.

Dodge called its 1966 Charger a "Sports Sedan," even though it was really a Sport Coupe. This was an attempt to widen its sales appeal beyond the youth market and to stress its cargo-carrying abilities. With a full-size 117-inch wheelbase and 203.6 inches of overall length, the Charger was certainly roomy. And its 75.3-inch width didn't hurt either. With seating for only four on its front and rear bucket seats, the Charger was not really sedan-like in the passenger-carrying category, either. Its real appeal was its sporty flavor.

Nevertheless, young-at-heart American dads canny enough to convince their better half that the Charger was really a "kind of station wagon" were likely to go for the base 318-cid 230-hp V-8 or the one-step-up 361-cid/265 hp option, both fitted with two-barrel carburetors. Once you got to the big-block 383 or the even heftier 426-cid "Street Hemi," you were talking "muscle car" when you talked about a Charger.

The 383-powered Charger was honestly not the ultimate muscle machine, but it was entirely adequate for many buyers. The 383-cid V-8 had a 4.25 x 3.38-inch bore and stroke, a 10.0:1 compression ratio and a single four-barrel Carter carburetor. This added up to a package delivering 325 hp at 4800 rpm and 425 lbs.-ft. of torque at 2800 rpm.

A nicely outfitted Charger with power steering, power brakes, power steering, a limited-slip differential, a Rallye suspension, a few other goodies and the 383 hooked to a three-speed automatic transmission went out the door for just over $3,100. And two nice performance enhancements included at the regular price were dual exhausts and the well-known responsiveness of the Chrysler automatic gearbox.

On the test track, a '66 Charger 383 could move from 0-to-60 mph in 7.2 seconds and zip down a quarter-mile drag strip in 15.6 seconds at 89 mph. No one is saying that acceleration like that would win the NHRA Nationals, but the '66 Charger 383 was still a kind of "everyman's muscle car" that every man, woman or child could love back then.

Jerry Heasley

DODGE

With a dual-quad 425-hp Street Hemi stuffed under the hood, the 1966 Coronet was a muscle-flexing beast.

1966 Hemi Coronet

The Dodge Coronet was one of those automobiles capable of "wearing many hats." In its six-cylinder, four-door format it made a great grocery getter or salesman's "company car." When you reduced the number of doors by two and increased the number of cylinders by a like amount (packing them in a V-block format along the way), you got the makings of a muscle car. Then, by installing the ultimate V-8 and slapping "Hemi" badges on the sides, you wound up with a King Kong Coronet that could pound pavement with the best of them. This smooth-lined rendition of the classic big-engine-stuffed-in-small-body "factory hot rod" was a royal pain in the butt for GM and FoMoCo fans.

When it was introduced in 1965, the mid-sized Coronet immediately became the centerpiece of Dodge's muscle car fleet. An ad that ran that year asked "Why not drop a Hemi in the new Coronet 500?" The '65 Coronets had come only with the 12.5:1 compression ratio Race Hemi. That engine created more of a drag racing machine than a street-prowling muscle car.

This was corrected by making the 426-cid/425-hp dual-quad Street Hemi available in 1966. Displacement-wise and power-wise, it matched the race version, but the big differences

were a hydraulic lifter cam and a 10.5:1 compression ratio. The Hemi was the most powerful production car engine ever built until just recently, but it was still well suited to street use. In addition, the optional Hemi engine was a good deal for less than $500.

The Coronet was restyled for model year 1966. While it retained the 117-inch wheelbase used previously, overall length was reduced 1 inch to 203 inches. The new styling featured crisp, well-defined character lines, but the cantilevered roof was retained. The top-of-the-line Coronet 500 model had Charger-like bucket seats with a choice of all-vinyl or vinyl-and-fabric upholstery. Dodge offered a selection of 15 exterior colors in acrylic enamel finish.

A "500" designation on the car indicated the model, but not the engine. In fact, you really had to open the hood to see if there was a Hemi lurking underneath. Hemi Coronets could hit 60 mph in 6.1 seconds and do the quarter-mile in 14.5. Only 340 Coronet 500 hardtops (204 of them four-speeds) got the Hemi, along with just 21 convertibles (12 with four-speeds). Another 379 of the other Coronets also had this engine added to them.

DODGE

The 1966 Charger showed off a distinctive fastback roofline and
"electric razor" grille, but it was the 426 Hemi that made it a great car.

1966 Hemi Charger

Fastback styling was back in vogue in the mid-1960s and the Dodge Charger was a participant in the "Dodge Rebellion," an advertising and promotional campaign that pushed high-performance motoring. The Charger was really based on the Coronet platform and had essentially the same lower body styling, but with a more streamlined look and rich interior appointments and trimmings. With its low and wide roof line, the Charger showcased a drastic interpretation of fastback styling. Its "electric razor" grille was also quite distinctive looking.

Soon after the Charger arrived on the scene, almost every car enthusiast magazine rushed to take a test drive and publish the results. The Charger was new and exciting and having the car featured on the cover of a magazine was a sure way to pump up circulation and newsstand sales.

Most magazines tested Chargers with the 383-cid V-8, a big-block engine that cranked out 325 hp at 4800 rpm. This combination was actually quite fast, with *Car and Driver* registering a 7.8-second 0-to-60 time and doing the quarter-mile in 16.2 seconds at 88 mph. With the same engine and tranny, *Motor Trend* reported an 8.9-second 0-to-60 time and 16.3 seconds for the quarter-mile at 85 mph. The huffing-and-puffing Hemi could shave 2 seconds or more off acceleration times like those.

Though the car itself was large, lush and heavy, the availability of the optional 426-cid Hemi V-8 engine made the Charger a genuine contender for the hottest niche in the muscle car market. The 425-hp big-block V-8 featured a pair of four-barrel carburetors, extra-wide dual exhausts and all sorts of heavy-duty performance hardware. The Hemi package also included engine call-out badges, a heavy-duty suspension, larger brakes and 7.75 x 14 Blue Streak racing tires. The use of either a four-speed manual gear box or a TorqueFlite automatic transmission was mandatory. Dodge specified that the Hemi's short 12-month or 12,000 miles warranty would be invalidated by "extreme operation" or driveline modifications.

Total production of 1966 Chargers hit 37,300 cars. Of these, only 468 had Hemis, of which a mere 218 featured TorqueFlite. NASCAR drivers thought the fastback roof would enhance the Charger's aerodynamics in Grand National stock car racing. However, they actually tended to lift at the rear, a problem that the race car builders solved by adding a small rear deck lid spoiler. After that, the Chargers won 18 races.

Phil Kunz

**Dodge production numbers show only 283 Hemi Coronet R/Ts were built
for 1967. Better have deep pockets if you want to own a nice survivor today.**

1967 Hemi Coronet

You could get the new-for-1966 Street Hemi in the 1966 Dodge Coronet 500, as well as in the Dodge 440 and base models. So when the 1967 pre-production publicity photos showed a couple of Coronet 500 hardtops with 426 Hemi badges, it led to a bit of confusion because press kits and literature said the Hemi engine would only be available as a limited-production option for the top-line Coronet R/T and also for the Charger fastback.

Production figures bear out the limited-production concept, since they show that only 283 Coronet R/Ts and 118 Chargers with Street Hemis were built and seem to indicate that you couldn't get a Street Hemi in any other Coronet. However, that's incorrect.

On January 23, 1967, Dodge announced that the Coronet 440 two-door hardtop was being built on a production basis to meet National Hot Rod Association's (NHRA) Super Stock B rules. The WO23 cars—as they are known—were the latest in the Mopar tradition of special lightweight models built for drag racing. A shipping weight of 3,686 lbs. was given for

Dodge 440s with Street Hemi engines.

There were two versions of these drag-racing-only Dodges. One came with a modified TorqueFlite automatic using a 2,300 to 2,500-rpm-stall-speed torque converter and 4.86:1 Sure-Grip Chrysler-built 8 3/4-inch differential. The second had a four-speed manual transmission with Hurst linkage, reinforced gearing and clutch and an explosion-proof clutch housing. This second combo drew a 4.88 Sure-Grip Dana differential.

The S/S-B cars could be ordered through your friendly Dodge dealer and came without a warranty of any kind.

To meet the rules, Dodge had to build at least 50 of the cars and when 55 went out the door, enough was enough. Plymouth was also allowed to build 55 similar Plymouth Belvedere II two-door hardtops (RO23).

At least the availability of S/S-B Dodge Coronets was of some consolation to those who missed the Coronet 500 and other lesser-model Hemis. Prices for nice survivors are in the stratosphere today.

DODGE

The R/T package could be ordered on either the Coronet
coupe or ragtop. The convertible was much less common.

1967 Coronet R/T

One of the things the muscle car era did was to bring high-performance driving to streets and drive-ins across America. One no longer had to set aside Saturday or Sunday for a trip to the drag strip to see cars that could get up to 60 mph in under seven seconds! And there was nothing like the thrill of pulling up to a gas pump or a root beer stand and hearing a muscle machine rumble up alongside you.

Many "street" muscle cars were also weekend drag racing cars in the 1960s and the R/T badge was intended to emphasize street-and-strip nature of such beasts. The R/T stood for road-and-track, and we're not talking about a sports car magazine! A Charger-like "electric shaver" grille distinguished the hot mid-size Dodge, although it did not utilize the fastback model's retractable headlights. Other Coronet R/T features included simulated rear fender air vents and non-functional hood scoops.

Standard under the hood was the 440 Magnum V-8 linked to either a four-speed manual gear box or TorqueFlite automatic transmission. The Magnum engine had a 4.32 x 3.75-inch bore and stroke, a 10.1:1 compression ratio and a single four-barrel carburetor. It developed 375 hp at 4600 rpm and 480 lbs.-ft. of torque at 3200 rpm. One 440-powered R/T did 0-to-60 mph in 7.2 seconds and the quarter-mile in 15.4 at 94 mph. *Motor Trend* drove the same car with racing slicks mounted and did the 0-to-60 test in 6.5 seconds. The fat-tired car required 14.7 seconds for the quarter-mile with a 96-mph terminal speed.

The R/T hardtop listed for $3,199 and a convertible

was $3,438. The package also included a stiff suspension, heavy-duty brakes and 7.75 x 14 Red Streak tires. Production amounted to 10,181 cars, including a mere 628 ragtops.

For $907.60, the Hemi V-8 could be special ordered for a Coronet R/T. This powerful V-8 had a 4.25 x 3.75-inch bore and stroke, a 10.25:1 compression ratio and two four-barrel carbs. It produced 425 hp at 5000 rpm and 490 lbs.-ft. of torque at 4000 rpm. *Motor Trend's* stock-tired Hemi-powered Coronet went 0-to-60 in 6.8 seconds and ran the quarter-mile in 15.0 seconds at 96 mph. When shod with racing slicks, it went 0-to-60 in 6.6 seconds and did the quarter-mile in 14.8 seconds at 99 mph.

The 1967 Coronet R/T came standard with a 440
Magnum V-8—it wasn't a Hemi, but it wasn't bad.

DODGE

Jerry Heasley

The optional powerhouse 425-hp/426-cid Hemi engine was available for $877.55 on the 1968 Charger.

1968 Hemi Charger

By 1968, Dodge had its go-fast fleet in high gear. The King Kong Coronet was its mid-size muscle machine and the jumping-ramp-roofed Charger arrived in '66 to offer the family man with Hi-Po pretensions a good-looking brute of a car that had ample storage space. Out on the streets, when performance was spoken, Hemis could be heard rumbling under the air-scooped hoods of Mopars and Chargers had no problem digesting 426 cubes of bonsai big-block in their engine bay. Then Dodge sealed its deal with the devil and unveiled the second-generation '68 Charger. It was like beauty-and-the-beast combined in one fabulous fastback.

Taking its bow at the Chi-Town Auto Show, the Charger chuckled when Dodge general manager Robert B. McCurry called it "a full-sized sports car featuring semi-fastback design and jet-age aerodynamic styling." Hey guys, the Hemi Charger wasn't any giant MGB-GT—it was a quarter-mile rocket meant to go straight from point A to point B in the absolute minimum amount of time.

Compared to the '66-'67 Charger, the swoopy '68 was slimmer and smoother. With a 117-inch wheelbase, the Charger was no compact, but it didn't look like Haystacks Calhoun either. A new "Coke-bottle" profile drew your attention to the rear quarters like a mini-skirted gal in the Dodge white-hat ads. The sheet metal tapered to the front and gave the car a thrusting image that made it look fast standing still. A recessed rear window and curved roof pillars gave an airplane look, as did the slanting of the instruments towards the driver.

The hood was lower. A spoiler blended smoothly into the rear deck. The integrated bumper-grille had an aluminum molding and incorporated hidden headlights. Simulated "waste gates" in the hood and sides and a quick-fill gas cap were other fighter-jet touches. Rally-style parking lights hid in the bumper.

A handful of six-cylinder '68 Chargers were built, but the great majority were V-8-powered. The standard V-8 was the 318-cid/230-hp small-block engine. Options included the 383-cid/335-hp two-barrel V-8, the 440 Magnum V-8 with 375 hp at 4,600 rpm and 480 lbs.-ft. of torque at 3,200 rpm and the 426 Hemi V-8 with 425 hp at 5,000 rpm and 490 lbs.-ft. of torque at 4,000 rpm. Performance numbers reported for the '68 Hemi Charger included 0-to-60 mph in 5.3 seconds and a quarter-mile run in 13.8 seconds at 105 mph.

Carrying the high-performance torch was the new R/T (Road and Track) which came standard with a 440 Magnum V-8, heavy-duty suspension and brakes, dual exhausts and fat tires. "Bumble bee" stripes made the R/T buzz louder. The stripes ran around the rear deck and down the quarter panels. The popular new look pushed Charger production to 96,108 (including 908 six-cylinder cars) and 18,307 had the R/T package. Only a scant 475 Chargers came stuffed with the 426 Hemi. The Charger accounted for 16 percent of Dodge car sales in 1968. Its share of the total was up 460 percent from '67.

DODGE

Doug Mitchel

The Chargers got a new design in 1968, and the R/T model certainly had the raciest look.

1968 Charger R/T

Dodge's R/T designation meant "Road/Track. "The '60s was a time when youthful car enthusiasts drove their car to work at the grocery store five days a week just to earn enough to pay the loan they took out to by a muscle car. Then, on Saturday, they took their supercar to the drag strip for some "track time." The Charger R/T was pushed as a machine that was well suited for both purposes.

Motor Trend magazine summed up the look of the R/T model as "a Charger with a set of mag wheels, wide oval tires and a bumblebee stripe around its rear end." Appropriate name badges, heavy-duty underpinnings and a 440-cid/375-hp Magnum V-8 put extra emphasis on the car's split personality. The engine had a 4.32 x 3.75-inch bore and stroke, a 10.1:1 compression ratio and a single four-barrel carburetor.

All Charger models underwent a vast amount of change in 1968. Dodge stylists did a great job of adopting the popular late-1960s "Coke-bottle" shape to the more smoothly rounded 1968 Charger body, which was shared by the R/T version.

Neat details styling details of the R/T version of the Charger included an integral rear deck lid spoiler and a competition-type gas filler cap. Chargers retained a 117-inch wheelbase, but the rear track was widened from 58.5 inches to 59.2 inches in 1968.

Merchandised as a model with a base price of $3,480 (including TorqueFlite automatic transmission), the standard R/T could move from 0-to-60 mph in 6.5 seconds and zip down a drag strip in 15 seconds at 93 mph. This was the only Charger model that you could get a Hemi in during 1968.

The Charger R/T's Hemi engine option cost $604.75 in 1968 dollars, which might explain why only 475 such cars were put together. Of the total, 211 had the four-speed manual gearbox, which was a no cost option. Other available extras included a limited-slip differential for $42.35, a tachometer for $48.70, custom wheels for $97.30, a console for $52.85, power brakes for $41.75 and front disc brakes for $72.95. Bucket seats and high-performance tires were standard.

One of the most famous 1968 Chargers was the stealthy looking one that actor Steve McQueen drove in the motion picture "Bullitt."

The restyled 1968 Coronet R/T was praised for its comfort, ride quality and roominess.

DODGE

Robert Seroka

1968 Coronet R/T

The mid-size Dodge Coronet underwent a transformation for model-year 1968. It was completely restyled from stem to stern. This was a high-volume series for Dodge and production rose from 159,781 units in 1967 to 189,500 in 1968. In the Coronet R/T line, 10,900 cars were turned out—up from 10,181 the year before.

Two body styles were available in R/T format. The two-door Sport Coupes was base priced at $3,353 and convertible prices started at $3,613. The R/T equipment included bucket seats, dual exhausts, a stiff suspension, heavy-duty brakes and other goodies, including a 150-mph speedometer. TorqueFlite automatic transmission was the standard setup.

Bumblebee stripes—or alternatively no-cost optional body side stripes—were provided to set off the 1968 model's appearance. There were R/T emblems on the grille and R/T medallions on the fenders and rear trunk latch panel. Coronet R/Ts used the same interior as Coronet 500s, but had a special "power bulge" hood with simulated air vents.

In a *Motor Trend* comparison of eight 1968 super cars (Plymouth Road Runner, Dodge Charger R/T, Pontiac GTO, Buick GS 400, Chevelle SS 396, Olds 4-4-2, Ford Torino and Dodge Coronet R/T) the Coronet was said to have a "good engine" and "easily the best in comfort and in room." Its

quality of construction was rated "surprisingly good" and the magazine liked its comfort, roominess, engine and boulevard ride.

The standard 440-cid Magnum V-8 was the same as in 1967 with its 4.32 x 3.75-inch bore and stroke, 10.1:1 compression ratio and single four-barrel. Horsepower (375 at 4600 rpm) and torque (480 lbs.-ft. at 3200 rpm) remained unchanged. A four-speed manual or automatic transmission were also standard again. What did vary very slightly was the published performance numbers: 6.9 seconds for the 0-to-60-mph test and 15.1 seconds for the quarter-mile at 94 mph. The bad news was the 440-motivated Coronet R/T got 9.6 to 12.1 mpg fuel economy (if you could call that economy).

High-performance options for the Coronet R/T included a limited-slip differential for $42.35, custom wheels for $97.30, front disc brakes for $72.95 and a console for $52.85. High-performance tires and bucket seats were standard. This season, the optional Street Hemi V-8 cost $604.75 and was ordered for 94 Coronet R/Ts with four-speeds and 136 with TorqueFlite automatic transmissions. Experts believe that one stick-shift car and eight automatics were convertibles. Hemi cars came with a special heavy-duty suspension, but air conditioning couldn't be ordered.

DODGE

The cool 1968 Coronet Super Bee could be driven home new from the dealer for less than $3,500.

Doug Mitchel

1968 Coronet Super Bee

Mopar invented the bargain basement muscle car in the late '60s. When the GTO started the muscle car craze, only a few fancy (and expensive) options were standard. It fact, the base car came with "bottle cap" style wheel covers. However, as muscle car mania caught on, the emphasis switched to bucket seats, consoles, mag wheels and even luxury features like air conditioning. This sent the prices of many muscle cars beyond the budgets of the young drivers most interested in the breed.

Plymouth introduced the Road Runner as a reaction to rising prices. It wasn't a *cheap* car, but it was a car that gave you great value for the price and emphasized muscle over chrome and convenience options. The "Beep-Beep!" car was designed to fit a young man's budget—if he wanted to spend his money for go-fast equipment, rather than tinsel.

Dodge Division's corresponding entry was the Coronet Super Bee, which was introduced in February 1968 with a price tag in the $3,395 range. It was based on the Coronet 440 two-door sedan. This was done because a "post coupe" was needed to accommodate the non-lowering rear windows that

swung open on hinges mounted to the center pillar.

Base Super Bee engine was the big-block 383-cid V-8 in 335-hp format. It came linked to a heavy-duty four-speed gear box with a Hurst "Competition-Plus" floor shifter. Fat dual exhausts, fat F40 x 14 tires and a heavy-duty suspension with fat torsion bars were included. Everything was fat except the price tag. The Super Bee was only slightly fancier than the Plymouth Road Runner, with which it competed for customers.

Also part of the Super Bee look was a dummy hood "power bulge," bench seat interior, wide wheels and rear bumblebee striping with a bee inside a circular decal emblem. You couldn't get a vinyl roof, but for $712, you could add the legendary Hemi engine.

A total of 166 Hemi Super Bees were produced—92 had four-speed transmissions and 74 had TorqueFlite attachments. Cars equipped with the standard engine went from 0-to-60 mph in 6.8 seconds while the Hemi Super Bees made the same speed in 6.6. Quarter-mile times were 15 seconds and 14 seconds for the two engines, respectively.

DODGE

Phil Kunz

The '68 Dart GTS had an available 340-cid/300-hp V-8 and
sporty styling, and was a lot of muscle car for the money.

1968 Dart GTS

GTS meant GT Sport. It was the name of a sexy new-for-'68 "sawed-off shotgun" that was a whole bunch more than a sporty compact car. "Not to take the edge off the Road Runner, the GTS might be a more sensible package," said *Hot Rod* magazines's Steve Kelly in the publication's April 1968 issue. "The base price is higher, but you get things like carpet on the floor, fat tires, bucket seats and a few other niceties that can make Saturday night roaming more comfortable. The engine's smaller, but that could prove an advantage for drag racing classes."

Two hefty V-8s were available. A 340-cid small-block engine was standard. It was derived from the 273-318-cid Chrysler family of engines and had a 4.04 x 3.31-inch bore and stroke, a 10.5:1 compression ratio and a single four-barrel carburetor. The 340 engine cranked out 275 hp at 5000 rpm and 340 lbs.-ft. of torque at 3200 rpm. A 383-cid big-block engine with a four-barrel carburetor and 300 hp was optional. The 383 added 89 lbs. to the car if you got a four-speed gearbox and 136 lbs. if you got an automatic transmission. A standard 3.23:1 rear axle was supplied, but 3.55:1 and 3.91:1 ratio axles were also available as optional equipment.

Other technical enhancements included a low-restriction dual exhaust system with chrome tips, a heavy-duty Rallye suspension, 14 x 5.5-inch wheels and E70-14 Red Streak tires. Although a column-shifted three-speed manual transmission was standard, most Dart GTS models had either a four-speed manual gearbox with a Hurst floor shifter or a competition-type TorqueFlite automatic transmission.

Also identifying the GTS were hood power bulges with air vents, body side racing stripes, special GTS emblems and simulated mag wheel covers. A bumblebee stripe to decorate the car's rear end was a no-cost option. Vinyl front bucket seats were standard in the $2,611 hardtop and optional in the $3,383 convertible.

In 1968, the production of the GTS models was lumped into the total of 24,100 Dart GT series V-8s produced. The 1968 Dart GTS hardtop with the 340-cid/270-hp power train tested out with a 0-to-60 time of 6 seconds. It did the quarter-mile in a "Scat Pack" time of 15.2 seconds. *Hot Rod* magazine published even better numbers for its 340-cid TorqueFlite-equipped Dart GTS, which ran down the quarter-mile in 14.38 seconds at 97 mph.

DODGE

The 1969 Charger 500 was a limited production model based on the restyled 1968 Charger. Either 32 or 35 of these cars were outfitted with a Hemi, depending on who you believe. Either way, they are extremely valuable today.

1969 Charger 500

Sleek, beautiful new styling had characterized the '68 Dodge Charger and had helped to boost the model's sales to 96,100 units—from only 15,800 in 1967. Wind-tunnel testing revealed that the good-looking body's recessed grille and tunneled-in rear window created wind turbulence on the high-speed NASCAR superspeedways. Dodge engineers figured out that a flush grille and flush-mounted rear glass could reduce this wind resistance. Some say that a prototype car with these changes—which was actually the first Charger 500—was really a modified 1968 model.

The production–type 1969 Charger 500 was issued as a special limited-production model based on the style of the Charger 500 prototype. It was released to the public on September 1, 1968, but as a 1969 model. Dodge Division literature said it was offered specifically for high-performance racing tracks and available only to qualified race drivers. In reality, that was a great promotion, as muscle car lovers flocked to Dodge dealerships trying to buy one of the cars. Chances are pretty good that, if they didn't get one, they at least drove away in another Charger or a jazzy Coronet.

The Charger 500's handcrafted body modifications were actually the workmanship of a company called Creative Industries, which was an aftermarket firm from Detroit, Michigan. A minimum of 500 such cars had to be sold to the public to authorize the changes and make the Charger legal for racing under NASCAR rules. The Charger 500 model designation was based on the number of cars scheduled to be made.

Even though some books say Hemi engines were standard in the Charger 500, at least 392 of these cars have been researched and only about nine percent have turned out to have Hemis. If you didn't get the monster motor, at least you did get a heavy-duty suspension, a four-speed manual gear box (or TorqueFlite automatic transmission), a rear bumblebee stripe, "500" model badges, a special shorter-than-stock rear deck lid and a custom-made rear window package shelf.

Officially, 32 Hemi-powered Charger 500s were built, though experts have tracked down serial numbers for 35 such vehicles. About 15 cars had four-speed manual gearboxes. Charger 500s with automatic transmission covered the quarter-mile in 14.01 seconds at 100 mph. Cars with the optional four-speed manual transmission were significantly faster. They did the quarter-mile in 13.60 seconds at 107.44 mph.

Tom Glatch

DODGE

The unmistakable Charger Daytona was obviously created with
racing in mind—a role it eventually served with great success.

1969 Charger Daytona

One of Chrysler's famous "winged warriors" was the Dodge Charger Daytona—the ultimate expression of the Charger 500's built-for-racing inspiration. Shortly after the Dodge Charger 500 bowed in 1969, Ford Motor Co. launched the Torino Talladega and Mercury Cyclone Spoiler models. Both FoMoCo products had superior aerodynamics, which helped them to outrun the slippery Charger 500s in enough races (including the Daytona 500) to take the National Association of Stock Car Automobile Racing title. The '69 Charger Daytona was designed to get the NASCAR championship back.

A company named Creative Industries received the contract to build 500 Daytonas to legalize the 200-mph body modifications for stock car competition. The rear window was flush, rather than tunneled. The front fenders and hood were lengthened and dipped lower in front. The front air intake was lower. Reinforced-plastic parts were used on the front-end extension and hood parts. The concealed headlights popped up like bug eyes. The hood featured a fresh air intake similar to the NASA inlets employed on aircraft. The hood and fenders had cooling vents. At the rear was an airfoil/spoiler of fin-and-wing that provided greater aerodynamic

stability. Dodge press releases noted the modifications had been submitted to NASCAR for approval.

Richard Brickhouse won the Talladega 500 with an average speed of 153.778 mph. Jim Vandiver was second in Ray Fox's Dodge Charger 500. Brickhouse ran laps as high as 197 mph. Dodges took the first four places and a Plymouth was fifth. For the year, the Daytonas and Superbirds won 14 races on the big tracks. Buddy Baker's Daytona was also first to officially hit the 200-mph closed-course mark, at Talladega, on March 24, 1970. The winged cars won so many races that NASCAR outlawed the Hemi as well as wedge engines with piston displacements over 305 cubic inches.

Experts say that total production of Daytonas was 503 units. Officially, 433 cars with base 375-hp 440 Magnum V-8s were built for the streets and 70 were turned out with Hemi V-8s under their snout. The breakout as to how many of the Hemi Daytonas had four-speed manual or automatic transmissions was 22 and 48, respectively. One yellow Daytona, with 5,000 original miles, has been documented to be a car with a dealer-installed 440 Six-Pack V-8. Dodge did not, however, offer this set up as a *factory* option.

Don Bowser

Not much changed between 1968 and 1969 on the Charger R/T. The car was still available only
as a coupe, and came standard with a 440-cid Magnum V-8. For $648 more, a buyer could go
for the gusto and order the Hemi.

1969 Charger R/T

The 1969 Dodge Charger didn't change much from the 1968 model. As *Motor Trend* magazine put it, "That brute Charger styling, that symbol of masculine virility, was still intact." (Of course, those were the good old days when you could say things like that, which would be considered "politically incorrect" today, in the pages of a national magazine!)

For 1969, the Dodge Charger grille was divided into two sections and the taillights were modified a bit. However, the fastback Dodge was basically the same good-looking beast as before on the outside. Amazingly, you could get the big fastback with a six-cylinder engine, but only about 500 of those were made. The balance of the cars carried some type of V-8, usually a muscular version.

Inside the Charger, the interior treatment, including the well-designed instrument panel, also had very few changes. There was a large-faced tachometer and the instrument panel gauges were done in white on black to make them stand out very distinctly.

The R/T was the high-performance version of the Charger. The name once again implied its reliability as a street car and its adaptability to weekend dragstrip use. The Charger R/T came only as a two-door hardtop coupe with a base price of $3,592 and a factory shipping weight of 3,636 lbs. That included the 440-cid Magnum V-8, with a four-barrel carburetor, hooked to a three-speed TorqueFlite automatic transmission. Also included as part of the R/T package were low-restriction dual exhausts with chrome tips, heavy-duty manually adjusted drum brakes, F70-14 Red Line tires, the R/T heavy-duty handling package and bumblebee stripes.

With a 3.55:1 rear axle, the standard-equipped 440-powered model (which came with a column-mounted gear shift lever no less) was found capable of running down the quarter-mile in 13.9 seconds at 101.4 mph. The R/T was the only Charger available with the Hemi V-8 engine again this year. The 426-cid/425-hp powerhouse had a $648 price tag in 1969.

Charger R/T production went from the 1969 total of 17,582 units up to 20,057 units. A new option package for Chargers that was also available on the R/T models was the SE (or Special Edition) interior with leather bucket seats, lots of extra lights and wood-grained trim pieces. Sinking in popularity to 400 production units was the Hemi Charger R/T. Around 192 of the Hemi-powered cars had four-speed manual transmissions in 1969.

Ordering a "Six-Pack" on your 1969 Coronet R/T would
put 390 horses under your hood. A Hemi was also optional.

DODGE

Phil Kunz

1969 Coronet R/T

Back in the 1960s, thousands of young car enthusiasts looked forward to weekends at the drag strip—and they didn't go there to watch other muscle car owners run. Instead, they spent Saturday night in the garage, tuning the engine of the car they had driven all week for a couple of quick runs on Sunday afternoon. After that, it was re-tuned for additional street use until the following weekend. The "Dodge Boys" were well aware of how the car world worked, so they used the R/T designation to identify the cars best suited for dual-purpose use. The mid-sized Coronet was one of the favorites.

In 1969, the Dodge Coronet R/T continued to play its traditional role as the high-performance model in the Coronet series. It included all of the features of the upscale Coronet 500 model, plus the Magnum 440-cid V-8, TorqueFlite automatic transmission, a light group option, body sill moldings and R/T bumblebee stripes across the trunk lid and down the fender sides. Two simulated hood air scoops located on the rear fenders, just ahead of the rear wheel openings, were optional equipment.

The Coronet R/T two-door hardtop was designated model WS23. In standard format it listed for $3,442 and tipped the scales at 3,601 lbs. Also available was the model WS27 convertible, which carried a $3,660 base sticker price and weighed in at 3,721 lbs.

A "Six-Pack" arrangement of carburetors was the big news for the Coronet R/T in 1969. Three two-barrel Holley

carbs sat on top of a 440 Magnum V-8 that harnessed 390 horses and 490 lbs.-ft. of torque. A fiberglass performance hood covered the three carburetors. Also available was a Ramcharger fresh-air induction system, which was standard on Hemi-powered cars and extra-cost equipment on others. It included twin air scoops on the hood that fed cold air into a fiberglass plenum bolted to the underside of the hood. There was also a wider choice of rear axle ratios. Standard equipment was a 3.23:1 unit but 3.54:1, 3.55:1, 3.91:1 and 4.10:1 performance axle packages were also available.

Obviously, Dodge was placing additional emphasis on the "Track" portion of the *Road and Track* model designation by adding more performance to its Coronet muscle car. Overall styling was similar to 1968, except that the previous front fender medallion became a large decal that appeared as part of the rear bumblebee stripe. The four-barrel 440-cid was, of course, the standard motor.

A Hemi was an additional $418 option for 1969 Coronet R/Ts. Model year production totaled 7,238 hardtops and convertibles combined. This included 97 two-door hardtops (58 with a four-speed manual transmission) and 10 ragtops (six with TorqueFlite) fitted with 426 Hemis.

One magazine test-dragged a '69 six-pack R/T (complete with dummy rear fender scoops) to a 105.14-mph 13.65-second quarter-mile run. The Dodge's 0-to-60 time was a scant—or should we say "Scat"—6.6 seconds.

Don Bowser

The 1969 Coronet Super Bee had plenty of stuff to make it go fast, including three two-barrel Holly carburetors.

DODGE

1969 Coronet Super Bee

A two-door hardtop with a $3,138 starting price joined the Coronet Super Bee line in 1969. The Sport Coupe returned with a $3,076 sticker. There were few changes in appearance or standard equipment. They included a single, wider rear bumblebee stripe and a Dodge "Scat Pack" badge on the grille and trunk, plus front fender engine call-outs.

Three two-barrel Holley carbs on an aluminum Edelbrock manifold were the heart of the new "six-pack" performance option. Cars so equipped generated 390 hp and 490 lbs.-ft. of torque. The Six-Pack option included a flat black fiberglass hood that locked in place with four chrome pins so that it could be entirely removed for access to the engine.

There was also a new Ramcharger cold-air induction system (standard with cars having the optional Street Hemi V-8) that featured two large hood-mounted air scoops, an under-hood air plenum and a switch to select between warm and cold air. The Super Bee Six-Pack came with a choice of a four-speed manual gearbox or a TorqueFlite automatic transmission linked to a 9 3/4-inch Dana 60 Sure-Grip axle with 4.10:1 gears. A total of 27,800 Super Bees were built. This included 166 Hemi-powered cars, 92 of them with four-speeds.

In a January 1969 comparison of six "econo-racers" *Car and Driver* magazine got its hands on a new Super Bee with: a 3.55:1 limited-slip differential ($102.15 extra), power disc brakes ($93.10), head restraints ($26.50), foam-padded seats ($8.60), automatic transmission ($40.40), a remote-adjustable mirror ($9.65), three-speed windshield wipers ($5.40), undercoating ($16.60), rear quarter air scoops ($35.80), rear bumper guards ($16), a tachometer and clock ($50.15), cold air induction ($73.30), AM radio ($63.35), power steering ($97.65), styled wheels ($88.55), F70 x 14 tires and the base 383-cid/335-hp V-8.

The car, which listed for $3,858 fully equipped and weighed 3,765 lbs., could go from 0-to-60 in 5.6 seconds. It did the quarter-mile in 14.04 seconds at 99.55 mph. However, the magazine found the car to have a dual-point distributor and large-diameter exhaust pipes, which seemed at first to be "stock" but later proved to be tweaks made by Chrysler. "We can't consider our test car's performance to be representative of a 383 Super Bee you would buy," said the editors. "From our experience, we would estimate a production car in good tune to run about 98.5 mph in the 14.20-second range." Even that's not too shabby!

The GTS or GT Sport was one of nine different Dart models that Dodge buyers could select in 1969. It combined a dressy look and assortment of upscale equipment with a 340-cid base engine and a powerful new big-block option. This year the hardtop was base priced at $3,226 and the convertible was $3,419. Bucket seats were optional in the ragtop.

The 1969 version of the GTS sported a new black grille with a bright horizontal center bar. There was also a new blacked-out rear body panel. Also included were E70-14 Red Line tires, TorqueFlite automatic transmission, a three-spoke steering wheel, dual exhausts, carpeting and an engine dress-up kit.

The 1969 GTS 383 was a kind of "sleeper" in muscle car circles because the optional 383-cid V-8 was up-rated to 330 hp. It came standard with a 3.23:1 rear axle. Optional 3.55:1 and 3.91:1 rear axles were also available and at no extra cost when the Sure-Grip differential was ordered, too. Also new for the GTS was a rear bumblebee stripe with a separate lower section and the GT Sport name written on it.

As in 1968, the production of 1969 Dart GTS models was a part of the total of 20,900 GT series V-8s produced, but hardtops and convertibles together came to 6,700 cars with the GTS goodies.

DODGE

Phil Kunz

The 1969 Dart Swinger 340 hardtop originally listed for a modest $2,853.

1969 Dart Swinger 340

Not every Mopar muscle machine that came down the pike was a fire-breathing, Hemi-powered, big-engine-in-small-body bomber that fit in better at the drag strip than at the strip mall. There were also some compact Dodges and Plymouths fitted with hi-po small-block V-8s that provided enough sizzle for the masses without going overboard on the "high-end" high-performance hardware. The 1969 Dodge Swinger 340 was one example of such a car.

This model qualified as a member of the hot Dodge "Scat Pack" and proudly wore its bumblebee stripes, even though it was really more of a swinger than a stinger. Designed to give muscle car fans more bang for the buck by emphasizing performance over luxury, the Swinger fit right into the "budget muscle car" trend that produced cars like the Plymouth Road Runner and Pontiac GTO Judge. It was like a small-scale counterpart to such models.

As muscle cars went, the Swinger 340 was a bargain and collector's today can still swing a pretty good deal on one of these cars.

"Play your cards right and three bills can put you in a whole lot of car this year," said an advertisement showing a red Swinger two-door hardtop with a black vinyl roof. "Dart Swinger 340. Newest member of the Dodge Scat Pack. You get 340 cubes of high-winding, four-barrel V-8. A four-speed Hurst shifter on the floor to keep things moving. All the other credentials are in order."

Standard equipment for 1969 included the 340-cid 275-hp V-8 engine, four-speed full-synchro manual transmission with Hurst shifter, a three-spoke steering wheel with a padded hub, a heavy-duty Rallye suspension, "Swinger" bumblebee stripes, D70 x 14 wide-tread tires, dual exhausts, a performance hood with die-cast louvers and fat 14-inch wheels. Seven colors were available for the car and four colors for vinyl roofs.

A total of 20,000 were built. Even today, muscle car collectors can find bargains in the Swinger 340 market, since these cars don't look as flashy as a GTS, although they are equally fast.

DODGE

The 1970 Challenger was available in a wide variety of colors, three body styles, and a lengthy list of power train combinations. The 1970 R/T with a 440-cid motor, with or without the "Six-Pack," was a classic muscle car.

Jerry Heasley

1970 Challenger R/T 440

In writing about the '70 Challenger R/T, *Car Life* magazine posed the unusual question, "What do you call a car with a 440 Six-Pack, four on the floor, purple metallic paint and an urge to challenge the world? Genghis Grape?"

The new-for-1970 Challenger was Dodge's answer to the Mustang, Camaro, Cougar, Firebird, Camaro and Barracuda. The sports compact model was offered in three body styles: two-door hardtop, formal coupe and convertible. Challengers featured a low, wide look with a full-width, scoop-like grille opening. The body sides had the familiar "Coke-bottle" profile with raised rear fenders tapering down at the tail end. Two large, rectangular tail lamps nearly filled the entire rear beauty panel.

For high-performance buffs, Dodge offered all three models in the Challenger R/T format. The terminology suggested "road and track" use of the car. The R/T package included everything on the base Chalenger's equipment list, plus a 383-cid V-8 with a four-barrel carburetor, an electric clock, a Rallye gauge cluster for the instrument panel, front and rear Rallye suspension hardware with a sway bar, heavy-duty front and rear drum brakes, F70-14 fiberglass-belted black sidewall tires with raised white letters, longitudinal tape stripes or bumblebee stripes and special R/T exterior ornamentation.

The 440-cid Magnum V-8 was an option for the R/T. The standard version of this overhead-valve V-8 was a $250 option. It featured a 4.32 x 3.75-inch bore and stroke, hydraulic valve lifters, five main bearings, a 10.0:1 compression ratio, a Carter AFB four-barrel carburetor and a 350 hp at 4000 rpm output rating. It produced 425 lbs.-ft. of torque at 3400 rpm. A dual exhaust system with reverse-flow mufflers was standard. A 375-hp version of the 440-cid V-8 with a hotter cam was $113 additional. There was also a "Six-Pack" version with three Holley two-barrel carburetors.

Dodge built a total of 14,889 Challenger R/T two-door hardtops, which had a base price of $3,266. The formal hardtop listed for $3,498 and 3,979 were built. Naturally, the convertible was the rarer model. The ragtop had a $3,535 window sticker and a mere 1,070 were made.

The Challenger convertible with the 440-cid 375-hp V-8 could move from 0-to-60 mph in 7.1 seconds according to *Muscle Car Field Guide*. The quarter-mile got covered in 14.64 seconds with a terminal speed of 97.82 mph. The Hemi-powered version of the hardtop was even faster. It did the quarter-mile in 14 seconds at 104 mph.

A muscle car fan could pick up a Challenger R/T hardtop for $3,266 new in 1970. It cost another $778.75 to get the Hemi version, which could propel this Mopar to 104 mph in the quarter-mile.

1970 Hemi Challenger R/T

The 1970 Dodge Challenger came as a beautifully styled two-door hardtop or a ragtop, plus a Special Edition (SE) formal-roofed hardtop. *Car and Driver* magazine once described the muscular Challenger as "Lavish execution with little or no thought towards practical application."

Quotations like that really sum up the Hemi Challenger. Nobody needed such a car to get to work or run out for a pack of cigarettes. In the winter (and maybe even the summer) you could burn out a set of rear tires without moving an inch. The Hemi Challenger was a race car. It was really fast! It didn't even have to look pretty—but it did! And that made it a very special product within the muscle car market niche.

The Challenger was the last of the pony cars to arrive on the market and that gave it something that counted. By the time it showed up, all such cars had a big advantage over the earlier models—there was room in the engine bay to accommodate a big-block V-8.

All three Challenger body styles were offered in the high-performance R/T (Road and Track, if you prefer) series and all R/T models had large-displacement V-8s. A 383-cid engine with a four-barrel carburetor was standard. R/Ts also came with all equipment found on lower-rung Challenger models, plus an electric clock, a Rallye instrument cluster, front and rear Rallye suspensions with sway bars, heavy-duty drum-type brakes, F70-14 fiberglass belted raised-white-letter tires, R/T emblems and bumblebee or longitudinal tape stripes.

The 1970 Challenger R/T hardtop listed for $3,266 and weighed 3,402 lbs. According to Chrysler records, 14,889 were built. The 3,498-pound convertible listed for $3,535 and

had a 3,979-unit production run. Only 1,070 Challenger SEs, base priced at $3,498, left the factory. The SE weighed in at 3,437 lbs.

Challenger buyers could add a 375-hp/440-cid Magnum V-8 to the R/T model for just $130.55 or they could get a 390-hp version for only $249.55 more. For those who wanted maximum performance, the Street Hemi was also available at a price of $778.75.

Hemi production included 287 hardtops (137 with four-speeds), 60 SE hardtops (23 with four-speeds) and nine convertibles (five with four-speeds). All Hemi Challengers were R/Ts. They could do the quarter-mile in 14 seconds at 104 mph. And during the week, you could make a very fast run to pick up eggs and milk!

Looking for a rare muscle car? Only nine 1970 Challenger R/Ts were Hemi convertibles.

DODGE

DODGE

Jerry Heasley

Drivers of the fast and loud 1970 Challenger had no problem getting noticed.

1970 Challenger T/A

The 1970 Dodge Challenger T/A was a kissing cousin to the Plymouth AAR Barracuda. Unfortunately, the "fish car" usually sees more of the limelight than its Dodge counterpart. Too bad. The Challenger T/A was a fast, fast machine that got up to 60 mph in only 6 seconds.

"Wild and woolly" is a good way to describe the '70 Challenger T/A Sport Coupe. Chrysler allowed the Dodge Division to schedule production of 2,500 copies of the model. The plan was to build just enough to meet the requirements for racing its new Challenger "pony car" in the Sports Car Club of America's (SCCA) Trans-American Sedan Championship series.

The Trans-Am was a competitive venue for small-block-V-8-powered two-door hardtops and two-door sedans (coupes). Chrysler's Pete Hutchinson used a de-stroked 340-cid V-8 block as the basis for a competition coupe that ran a small 305-cid V-8, but cranked out 440 hp. Ray Caldwell—who worked for a company called Autodynamics—built the Challenger T/A that driver Sam Posey piloted to fourth place in SCCA standings.

Street-ready T/As had the same snorkel-type hood scoop,

side-exit exhausts and lock-pin-secured flat-black hood as the all-out racing cars. Of course, if you raised the hood you could spot differences in the engine compartment. The street version carried some special underhood goodies including a 340-cid "Six-Pack" V-8 with three two-barrel carburetors. Buyers had a choice of TorqueFlite automatic transmission or a four-speed manual gearbox.

A ducktail rear deck lid spoiler was part of the Challenger T/A package, along with heavy-duty underpinnings. The package also included a Sure-Grip differential. Performance axle ratios, semi-metallic front disc brakes, semi-metallic rear drum brakes, a specific black body side tape stripe and mixed size tires (E60-15 tires were used up front with G60-15s mounted in the rear). To provide clearance for the pipes of the dual exhaust system with the fatter rear tires, the T/As were "jacked up" in the rear through the use of increased rear spring camber.

The 1970 Challenger T/As were good for 0-to-60 mph in a flat 6 seconds. They could hit 100 mph in 14 seconds and do the quarter-mile in 14.5 seconds.

The Charger 500 didn't have the Hemi V-8 or 440 Six-Pack as high-performance options, but its 383-cid mill
put out either 330 or 335 hp, which made this nice-riding car an attractive all-around machine.

1970 Charger 500 "383"

Writing about the Charger 500 with the 383-cid big-block V-8 in the December 1970 issue of *Motor Trend*, A.B. Shuman noted, "The engine is flexible; the transmission is easy to work." Shuman could sense that this "383" Charger was an outstanding drive-it-daily muscle car that combined above-average street performance with a fairly affordable window sticker and decent road manners.

It was logical that the attention-getting Dodge Charger 500, which had been introduced in 1969, made a return appearance for 1970. In the second season, it did not have any aerodynamic enhancements like a flush-mounted grille or flush rear window glass. It was even available with a six-cylinder engine for $3,139, but most buyers preferred at least the 318-cid base V-8, which brought the base price up to $3,246.

Still, neither of these models was a true muscle car. The second 500 model—at least in its standard format—was little more than a regular Charger with "500" badges. The main extras in the latest version of the 500 package were new vinyl front bucket seats, an electric clock and front and rear wheel lip moldings. New options included a pistol-grip gear shifter and an electrically operated sun roof.

The biggest regular-production engine option for the

'70 Charger 500 was the 383-cid V-8. It came in a two-barrel E61 version for $69.70, but this had only modest appeal to enthusiasts. The E63 version, with a single four-barrel carburetor added $137.55 to the price. The 383-cid four-barrel V-8 was offered in 330-hp and 335-hp options and the latter was significantly different than the former. The more powerful version used the 375-hp/440-cid engine's Plymouth Commando/Dodge Magnum camshaft and freer flowing heads. It had a new cast-iron intake manifold that carried a Holley four-barrel carburetor, rather than a Carter AVS carburetor.

The Charger R/T could be ordered with 440 Six-Pack and Hemi V-8s, but these weren't listed as regular production options for the Charger 500.

In addition to 13 standard exterior colors, Charger 500 buyers could special order Plum Crazy (purple), Sublime (green), Go Mango, Hemi Orange and Banana Yellow paint.

None of the 1970 Charger 500s were made with Hemi engines. This wasn't as much a muscle car as the '69 edition, but we felt that muscle car buyers should be aware of the big difference between the two years. Plus, there's the rare possibility that cars with special-order engine options were produced.

Jerry Heasley

The flashy 1970 Charger R/T certainly had performance to go with its eye-popping looks—it could go sub-15 seconds in the quarter-mile.

DODGE

1970 Charger R/T

The 1970 Dodge Charger continued to use the same semi fastback body that it had employed in 1969. Naturally, there were several minor trim changes to set cars of both years apart. The R/T (Road/Track) edition was again marketed as a higher-performance version of the basic Charger. It had a newly designed grille, a new loop-style front bumper, two hood scoops (one near each outside edge of the hood), big bolt-on side scoops (with R/T badges) on the rear quarter panels and a choice of longitudinal or bumblebee racing stripes on the rear. A new interior design and some wild new exterior body colors like Plum Crazy, Sublime, Go Mango, Hemi Orange and Banana Yellow were also featured.

The 440-cid Magnum V-8 engine was standard equipment, along with Mopar's sturdy TorqueFlite automatic transmission. Other Charger R/T features included a heavy-duty 70-amp/hour battery, heavy-duty automatic-adjusting drum brakes, heavy-duty front and rear shock absorbers, an extra-heavy-duty suspension, three-speed windshield wipers, all-vinyl front bucket seats, carpeting, a cigar lighter and F70-14 fiberglass-belted white sidewall tires (or black sidewall raised-white-letter tires). R/T model designations were also carried on the center of the rear escutcheon panel,

directly below the Dodge name.

All Charger R/T models included blacked-out escutcheon panels and large bumblebee stripes running across the trunk lid and down the rear fender sides. A hefty jump to $3,711 was seen in the price of the basic 440 Magnum-powered Charger R/T for 1970. Total production this year dropped to 10,337 units, including a mere 42 cars with 426-cid Hemi V-8s. *Car Life* reported, "They keep making the Charger go like stink and handle better than a lot of so-called sportsters."

For a big car, the Charger R/T packed a big wallop when it came to high-speed performance. *Motor Trend* did a comparison test between a 440-powered Charger R/T, a Mercury Cyclone GT and an Oldsmobile Cutlass SX in its April 1970 issue. The Charger test car had the standard equipment V-8, which produced 375 hp at 4600 rpm and 480 lbs.-ft. of torque at 3200 rpm. It also had a 3.55:1 rear axle. The car did 0-to-60 mph in 6.4 seconds and covered the quarter-mile in 14.9 seconds at 98 mph. It also averaged 14.9 to 15.7 mpg, which was much better fuel mileage than the two other cars. The magazine liked the Charger R/T's image and its race-bred heritage.

DODGE

A "Plum Crazy"-colored Coronet R/T convertible was a pretty cool ride for Mopar lovers in 1970.

1970 Coronet R/T

Like most automakers, Dodge offered several flavors of muscle in its mid-size cars and the basis for the hotter models was the Coronet, which was facelifted with a new grille and new delta-shaped taillights. Instead of using a conventional bumper running across the front of the car, Dodge switched to a bumper that consisted of heavy moldings that looped around the grille openings. The smooth split grille tapered towards the center.

The Coronet R/T was a high-performance version of the upscale Coronet 500. On the R/T, there were dummy rear fender scoops above and ahead of the front wheel openings and the air scoops wore R/T emblems. These emblems were repeated on the nose of the car and between each of the segmented, tapering tail lamps. A bumblebee stripe circled the rear end.

The Coronet R/T hardtop was base priced at $3,569 and had a production run of 2,319 units. Only 296 Coronet R/T convertibles (base priced at $3,785) were made. The hardtop had a shipping weight of 3,573 lbs. and the ragtop was about 65 lbs. heavier. It was the last year for the Coronet convertible body style and also the last year for the Coronet R/T model.

Standard R/T equipment included all Coronet 500 features plus the 440-cid Magnum V-8 engine, TorqueFlite automatic transmission, a heavy-duty 70-amp/hour battery, heavy-duty self-adjusting drum brakes, heavy-duty front and rear shock absorbers, extra-heavy-duty suspension, three-speed windshield wipers, all-vinyl front bucket seats, carpeting, a cigar lighter, F70-14 tires (whitewall or raised white letter) and twin hood air scoops. Buyers could substitute a four-speed manual gearbox for the TorqueFlite if they preferred to shift for themselves.

Engines were essentially the same as before with the "440 Six-Pack" back for the second year with its triple two-barrel carburetors. The 426-cid/425-hp Hemi was priced at $718 and only 14 Hemi R/Ts—13 hardtops and one convertible—were built. The R/T continued to come in an outrageous assortment of colors, like Plum Crazy (purple), Sublime (green), Go-Mango, Hemi Orange and Banana Yellow. Optional vinyl roofs came in black, white, green or "gator grain."

Five Scat Pack options were available to muscle car fans who wanted to dress up their Coronet R/T a little bit. They included the Showboat engine dress-up kit, the Read-Out gauge package, the Kruncher axle and Hurst shifter combination, the Bee-Liever high-rise manifold and carb setup and the Six-Pack option with a fiberglass hood and other hi-po goodies.

The 1970 Coronet Super Bee traded some style for substance, which made it a pretty good
performer for the money, though it probably wasn't going to win any beauty contests.

1970 Coronet Super Bee

The Dodge Super Bee was a genuine muscle car created with an emphasis on keeping the price down as low as possible, while still delivering some serious go-fast hardware. The Super Bee was not a "cheap" car. The hardtop version was in the same bracket as a top-of-the line Coronet 500 hardtop— in fact it was $26 more expensive. In the fancy 500 model, the buyer was getting more chrome, richer upholstery, carpets and a cigar lighter. In the Super Bee, the buyer got less of the comfort and convenience items and more muscle for the money.

Also available for an even lower price was the Super Bee coupe (two-door sedan), which listed for $3,012. Now, that was $167 more than a Coronet 440 Deluxe coupe, but you got a whole lot more under the hood. So the Super Bee was more of a "good value" car than it was cheap. You were just buying hardware, rather than tinsel.

Restyled for 1970 along the lines of the Coronet R/T, the Super Bee did not get the dummy rear fender scoops, at least as standard equipment. It also had horizontally divided (rather than individually segmented) tail lamps. New options included a hood mounted tach and a rear deck lid spoiler. Buyers could get the R/T-type bumblebee stripe or pipe-shaped upper and lower rear fender stripes with a circular Super Bee decal between them.

Still standard ingredients were the 383-cid Magnum V-8, a heavy-duty torsion-bar suspension and a three-speed manual transmission (last year's four-speed manual gear box was optional). Despite the price reduction, production dropped to 11,540 hardtops and 3,966 coupes. Hemis went into only 32 hardtops (21 with four-speed) and four coupes (all four-speeds). Wouldn't you love to own one today?

DODGE

Jerry Heasley

The snappy 1970 Dart Swinger 340 featured two distinctive hood
scoops and a wraparound stripe on the rear deck lid and fenders.

1970 Dart Swinger 340

Another member of the "Scat Pack" that returned to Dodge dealerships in 1969 was the Swinger 340 two-door hardtop. As our ace photographer Jerry Heasley once wrote in *Car Review*, way back in 1986, "If the Road Runner was the first econo-supercar, then the Dart was very much its counterpart in the compact lineup. Nobody built this car better than the 'Good Guys' in the white hats from Dodge."

When it came to the Swinger 340, the Good Guys advertised the car as "6000 rpm for under $3,000." With a short 97-inch wheelbase and overall length of just 178 inches, the Swinger 340 was a small, light car that used hot versions of the small-block V-8 to the best advantage.

The 1970 Dodge Darts shared revised front and rear cosmetics and the Swinger 340 version even got a slightly reduced $2,808 price tag. A three-speed manual gearbox was on the standard equipment list. Instead of small power vents, the mini Mopar muscle machine now carried two long, narrow hood scoops.

Other standard Swinger 340 features included a 3.23:1 rear axle ratio, Firm Ride shock absorbers, a Rallye type heavy-duty suspension and E78-14 fiberglass belted black sidewall tires. For identification purposes, neat looking Dart

340 nameplates were applied to the front fenders, just in back of the front wheel openings. Front disc brakes were also included as a standard equipment item.

Despite the introduction of the all-new Challenger "pony car" in 1970, the Swinger 340 remained popular enough to generate 13,785 assemblies. One reason for its popularity was that insurance companies considered it a "compact" car. As a result, the insurers charged lower premiums for a Swinger 340 than for other more obvious muscle cars. Of course, the Swinger 340 was also as fast as—or perhaps even slightly faster than—the 340 powered Dart GT Sport. It accomplished 0-to-60 mph in about 6.5 seconds and did the quarter-mile in around 14.5 seconds with a 98 mph terminal speed. At 3,179 lbs., the '70 Swinger carried about 11.4 lbs. per horsepower and proved to be highly motivated by the 340-cid V-8's "herd" of 275 horses.

Even today, in-the-know muscle car collectors will find tremendous bargains in the Swinger 340 market. These cars just don't share the flashy looks of the Dodge Dart GTS, although they are equally as fast. And you know that some people will pay silly money just to get a little flashiness.

CHALLENGER T/A
End of the road for the Do-It-Yourself Kit.

This is one car where the list of standard equipment is longer than the list of options. Hey, man, this isn't the beginning of something great, it's the driving end.

Big bias-belted skins in front, bigger ones in back. The good shift, Hurst style. Power discs up front; drums, heavy-duty, in the rear. Dual exhausts with low restriction mufflers, chrome side exit megaphones.

Challenger T/A. Just the way you'd do it yourself. If you had the time. And the money. Yeah, the money. Frankly, it would probably cost you more to do it yourself. So why bother

with do-it-yourself dreams? Check out this bargain for the man who'd rather be moving than building.

Check out the Standard Equipment List carefully. You'll find that everything is in order. From engine to drive train, Dodge puts it all together for you.

STANDARD EQUIPMENT

340 4-bbl. V8 □ TorqueFlite automatic transmission or 4-on-the-floor fully synchronized manual transmission □ Fiber-glass hood with Fresh Air Pack □ Hood pins □ Special Rallye Suspension (includes rear sway bar, larger front sway bar, heavy-duty shock ab-

sorbers, increased camber of rear springs) □ Rear duck tail □ Low-restriction dual side exit exhaust with megaphones □ Tires: E60x15, front; G60x15, rear; raised white letters □ 15x7.0JJ wheels □ Power front disc brakes with special semimetallic pads; 10" rear drums □ 3.55 axle ratio—8¾ ring gear □ Vinyl front bucket seats □ Deep-pile carpeting □ Simulated wood-grained door trim inserts □ Locking flip-top gas cap □ Flush outside door handles □ T/A body side tape stripes □ Grille and deck panel blackout.

The Challenger proved to be successful and popular model, but 1971 was the last year you could get the 426 Hemi in the Dodge pony car.

1971 Hemi Challenger

Dodge scored a hit with its first pony car, the 1970 Challenger. Up until then, Dodge had relied on special mid-size Chargers and Coronets and compact Darts to uphold its performance image. With the Plymouth Barracuda due for a total restyling in 1970, Dodge was handed the same package to create a 2 + 2 configuration to compete with Pontiac's Firebird and Mercury's Cougar.

The Challenger succeeded so well that it outsold the Barracuda 83,000 to 55,000 in its first year. The next season, though, sales fell off drastically and the Challenger sold 30,000 units. Still, the Barracuda's dropped to 19,000.

With the Challenger, Dodge was clearly selling performance in a package that looked the part. So it's not surprising that 93 percent of the 1971 model run was fitted with V-8 engines, even though the "Slant Six" was available. Nearly 17 percent were optional engines, ranging all the way up to the 425-hp Hemi.

Unfortunately, 1971 would be the last year for the 426-cid Hemi, as emissions, safety and insurance considerations put the horsepower race under a caution flag. However, in 1971, Dodge was definitely promoting power and performance.

The Street Hemi engine, a $790 option on the '71 Challenger, had continued unchanged after its introduction in 1966. It had a bore and stroke of 4.25 x 3.75 inches, a 10.25:1

compression ratio, hydraulic valve lifters and dual four-barrel Carter AFB carbs mounted inline.

On the Hemi Challengers, a flat-black finished air scoop was mounted to the carbs and poked through a hole in the hood. This was the impressive "shaker" hood, so named because you could watch the torque twist the engine as throttle was applied. Some cars also had chrome NASCAR-style hood hold-down pins.

The R/T (the initials stood for "Road/Track") was Dodge's high-performance car. The R/T package for the '71 Challenger included Rallye suspension, an instrument cluster with an 8,000-rpm tachometer and 150-mph speedometer, plus heavy-duty drum brakes, chrome exhaust tips and distinctive graphic stripes. On top of the R/T performance package, Dodge offered the SE (for Special Edition) trim package. It included a vinyl top and choice of leather or vinyl upholstery. Other extras included chrome wheel well and door edge moldings, twin outside rearview mirrors and an AM/FM/cassette stereo with rear speakers and a microphone.

For maximum visual impact, as well as an outward statement of purpose, many Hemi Challenger owners selected bright Hemi orange paint trimmed in white. After all, if you put the big engine under the hood, you might as well let the world know it.

DODGE

John Lee

**Only 71 Challenger R/Ts were ordered with the Hemi option in
1971. Better take out a second mortgage if you want one today.**

1971 Challenger R/T Hemi

Road Test magazine summed up the Mopar muscle car marketplace in 1971 when it said, "For the street racer who doesn't mind sticking close to 6 grand in his toy, the 440 Six-Pack or 426 Hemi will be very hard to beat in the stoplight grand prix." And this was especially true when you ordered the monster motor in the small-bodied Challenger. The result was a machine that was not only sportier, but also snortier, than anything else on the street.

For 1971, the Dodge Challenger R/T sub-series had only one model left. This was the two-door hardtop. It listed for $3,273 and weighed 3,495 lbs. With the muscle car fervor winding down, this rare car found a mere 4,630 buyers. Styling changes for model year 1971 included a new grille, color-keyed bumpers and two dummy scoops in front of the rear wheel wells.

Standard equipment on all 1971 Challengers included Chrysler's Air Control system, front and rear side armrests, a front ash tray, a cigarette lighter (except in the base Challenger coupe), an evaporative emission control system, color-keyed carpeting, ventless side glass, a glove box with a rotary latch (lockable in convertibles), dual headlights, a heater and defroster, dual horns (except coupe), dome and parking-brake system warning lights, a manual left-hand outside mirror, an inside day-night mirror, roof drip moldings, wheel opening moldings (except Coupe), bucket seats with foam front cushions, a three-spoke steering wheel with simulated woodgrain and a padded hub and electric windshield wipers.

A 198- or 225-cid six or Chrysler's 318-cid V-8 were considered the 1971 Challenger's base engines. The R/T model also included heavy-duty drum brakes, bright exhaust tips, a Rallye instrument cluster with simulated wood grain trim, a Rallye suspension, body side tape stripes, variable-speed windshield wipers, F70 x 14 bias-belted whitewall tires and a 383-cid four-barrel V-8. All of Chrysler's 1971 base engines had lower compression ratios. The Challenger R/T's standard 383-cid Magnum V-8 came with an 8.5:1 compression ratio and was rated for 250 nhp. However, the optional performance power plants were still available.

Only 71 of the Challenger R/Ts with the 426-cid Street Hemi V-8 were ordered this season. A dozen of these cars had TorqueFlite automatic transmission. The rest were equipped with a four-speed manual transmission. It was the last year for the Challenger R/T model. The handful of these cars fitted with Hemi engines really went out with a bang!

The 1971 Charger R/T with the 440 Magnum engine could run the quarter-mile
in 14.93 seconds. Cars with the Six-Pack were slightly faster.

DODGE

1971 Charger R/T 440/440 Six-Pack

According to Dodge Division, the 1971 Dodge Charger R/T 440/440 Six-Pack was designed "strictly for adults." It was good for 0-to-60 mph in under 7 seconds. Getting to the end of a drag strip took under 15 seconds. By that time you were moving almost 100 mph.

The Dodge Charger started life in 1966 as a semi-limited-production specialty car, but it caught on and grew to become an important part of the Chrysler division's line. In 1969, more than 70,000 Chargers were sold. For 1971, management decided that it was time to give the Charger an image of its own—one quite separate from that of the mid-sized Coronet.

"It was evident after the initial success of the '68-'70 Chargers, the Dodge stylists would have to burn some midnight oil to create a fresh approach that would again make the Charger something unique in an industry where very little is unique," said *Motor Trend* in December 1970. "As far as the *Motor Trend* staff is concerned, they succeeded."

The Charger name was now applied to two-door hardtops that had a 115-inch wheelbase, while the Coronet name was used only on 118-inch-wheelbase four-door sedans. The re-sized Charger was 2 inches shorter in wheelbase than the 1970 model and more than 3 inches shorter at 205.4 inches. However, it had nearly 3 more inches of front overhang and 3 1/2 inches more width.

The new Charger seemed to be the perfect size for a sporty performance car. The R/T model was the quintessential "muscle" model and technically represented a sub-series of the middle-priced Charger 500 series. It included all of the many features of the Charger 500, plus hot stuff like heavy-duty underpinnings and the 440-cid Magnum V-8.

This engine had the same 3.75-inch stroke as the 426-cid Hemi, but a larger 4.32-inch bore size. The base version,

with a single four-barrel carburetor, produced 370 hp at 4600 rpm and 480 lbs.-ft. of torque at 3200 rpm. It had a 9.1:1 compression ratio. In a four-Charger test in December 1970, *Motor Trend* drove a 370-hp 1971 Charger SE with automatic transmission and a 3.23:1 rear axle. It did 0-to-60 mph in a flat 7 seconds and covered the quarter-mile in 14.93 seconds at 96.4 mph.

Also featured in the same test was a 1971 Charger Super Bee with the 440 "Six-Pack" engine. This version added three two-barrel carburetors and a 10.3:1 compression ratio. The Six-Pack V-8 developed 385 hp at 4700 rpm and 490 lbs.-ft. of torque at 3200 rpm. The car it was in also had an automatic transmission, but it was hooked to a 4.10:1 rear axle. This cut the 0 to-60 time to 6.9 seconds. The quarter-mile required 14.74 seconds with a terminal speed of 97.3 mph.

The 1971 Charger Super Bee could be had in either 440 Six-Pack or 426-cid Street Hemi varieties. The Six-Pack version was rated at 485-hp and could do the quarter-mile in 14.7 seconds. The ultra-rare Street Hemi version was a full second faster!

DODGE

1971 Charger Super Bee Hemi

The Dodge Charger was completely restyled for the 1971 model year. It had a semi-fastback roofline with a flush rear window and an integral rear deck lid spoiler. Dodge's Charger Super Bee was manufactured only this one year and used the same restyled body. The Charger Super Bee was aimed at the same market niche as the Coronet Super Bee and represented a value-priced serious high-performance package.

Price-tagged at $3,271, the Charger Super Bee included a standard 383-cid Magnum V-8 that cranked out 300 hp. The engine used a single four-barrel carburetor and came attached to a three-speed manual transmission with a floor-mounted gear shifter. Covering the motor was a "power bulge" hood with flat black finish. The Charger Super Bee had tape stripes and bumblebee decals. The interior was similar to that of the Charger 500, but substituted a standard bench seat for bucket seats. The Rallye suspension components package was used. It included heavy-duty front torsion bars, heavy-duty rear springs, a front anti-sway bar, heavy-duty shock absorbers all around and heavy-duty brakes (11 x 3 inches up front and 11 x 2.5 inches in the rear). The standard tires were fat F70-14 black walls with white lettering. The Charger Super Bee's optional equipment list was fat, too.

All Charger Super Bees carried a Mopar V-8. Available engines included the 440 Wedge with "Six-Pack" carburetion or the 426-cid Street Hemi. Unlike the 8.7:1 compression base engine, these muscle car mills had high-test hardware and continued to offer 390 or 425 hp. Other neat extras were a first-for-the-Charger functional Ramcharger hood scoop, color-keyed bumpers, a Super Trak-Pack performance axle

(with up to 4.10:1 gearing), a four-speed gear box with Hurst "pistol grip" shifter, a dual-point distributor, heavy-duty cooling aids and bucket seats.

The 440 Six-Pack Charger Super Bee was advertised at 485 hp. It did 0-to-60 mph in 6.9 seconds and the quarter-mile took 14.7. With a Hemi V-8, this 3,640-lb. machine moved into the same bracket as the original Charger 500, needing only 5.7 seconds to get up to 60 mph and a mere 13.7 to reach the traps at a drag strip!

Not too many 1971 Charger Hemi Super Bees were built. In fact, the total was 22 cars, of which nine had four-speeds and 13 came with TorqueFlite automatic transmissions. In *Motor Trend*, A. B. Shuman wrote, "If the Super Bee SE was interesting, the Hemi car was remarkable. It was a Hemi and you knew it!"

DODGE

Jerry Heasley

**Like its sibling the Super Bee, the 1971 Charger had an optional engine
that made the car super fast in its day, and super collectible today.**

1971 Hemi Charger

The Dodge Charger was given a complete restyling for model year 1971. Its looks were updated with the goal of making it look more distinct from the Coronet. A new 115-inch wheelbase chassis was used to carry the Charger bodies, of which there were two distinct types: semi-fastback coupe and two-door hardtop.

Both models featured new rear quarter window styling that swept up from the fender to meet the sloping upper rear window frame. A full-width bumper and grille combination was seen up front. It was split in half by a large vertical divider and the rear end was set off with a small "lip" on the trunk lid that formed a short air spoiler.

The base Charger was still offered with the choice of a 225-cid Slant Six engine for $2,707. Most buyers preferred to add at least the 318-cid small-block V-8, which brought the price to $2,802. The hotter Charger 500 series included the Super Bee and SE models. The former retailed for $3,271 and up. The SE (or Special Edition) model had prices beginning at $3,422. The Charger SE came standard with a 383-cid "big-block" V-8.

For high-performance buffs, there was also a one-car Charger R/T series. The R/T (Road/Track) model listed for

$3,777 and included a 70-amp-hour battery, heavy-duty front and rear brakes, heavy-duty shock absorbers at all four corners, a pedal dress-up kit, an extra-heavy-duty Rallye suspension and TorqueFlite automatic transmission. A four-speed manual gearbox could be substituted for the automatic with no change in price. The R/T also featured a 440-cid Magnum V-8 and specific R/T identification pieces.

The 426-cid Hemi V-8 was available in Charger R/Ts for $707 extra and in Charger Super Bees for an additional $837. The "Street Hemi" had a 4.25 x 3.75-inch bore and stroke, a 10.25:1 compression ratio and twin Carter AFB four-barrel carburetors. It produced 425 hp at 5600 rpm! According to Mopar authority Galen V. Govier, Hemi Charger production was extremely low. The big engine was bolted into 22 of the 1971 Charger Super Bees and 63 Charger R/Ts.

With a Hemi stuffed under its hood, the Charger quickly developed a bad attitude, especially when GM and FoMoCo muscle cars rolled by. In December 1970, *Motor Trend* road tested a Hemi Super Bee with automatic transmission and a 4.10:1 ratio rear axle. The car did 0-to-60 mph in 5.7 seconds. The quarter-mile was covered in an elapsed time of 13.73 seconds at 104 mph.

DODGE

Jerry Heasley

The Dart Demon 340 was the mighty might of the Dodge lineup for 1971.

1971 Dart Demon 340

After Plymouth experienced a runaway sales success with its 1970 Valiant Duster, the Dodge Division of Chrysler Corp. couldn't wait to get its hands on the 108-inch wheelbase coupe. It became the base for a new mini-muscle car in the compact Dart lineup. Things started cooking in the fall of 1970, when the Dart Demon was added to the 1971 model range.

Like the Duster, the Demon came in two models. The base version had the 198-cid "Slant Six" and minimal standard equipment. It listed for $2,343, only $30 over the cost of a base Duster. More interesting was the Demon 340, which at $2,721 was a mere $18 upstream from the Duster 340. It came standard with a well-balanced 275-gross horsepower version of the 340-cid small-block V-8. A three-speed, fully synchronized floor shifter was standard along with a Rallye instrument cluster, heavy-duty suspension, E70-14 rubber, stripes and dual exhaust.

Playing the option list was the name of the game with domestic compacts and the 340 had some interesting extras. They included a dual-scoop hood complete with hood pins, rear spoiler and "Tuff" steering wheel. You could also order a four-speed manual gearbox, TorqueFlite automatic transmission or an upgraded interior.

The 340 was a card-carrying member of the 1971 Dodge "Scat Pack," which boasted many performance cars. It would be the final year for the Scat Pack, however. At midyear, the Demon Sizzler option package became available. It was on the base Demon and started with the base six, but it added some of the 340's pieces and stripes to the base model. Demons also became the vehicles of choice for Pro Stock Dodge-mounted drag racers. Though the basic body was used, the cars were highly modified.

All the tricks worked and the Demon was a success, with 69,861 base models built and the 340 adding 10,098 more. The Dodge Demon returned for 1972, but the name was scrapped after that, in part because the religious community was less than thrilled by the name. Dart Sport nomenclature sufficed from 1973 models through the end of production after the 1976 model year.

DODGE

The somewhat unheralded Demon 340 measured up well against its muscle car peers in 1972.

Joe Maggio

1972 Dart Demon 340

Back in January of 1971, *Motor Trend* writer Jim Brokaw described the first Dodge Demon 340 as a "reasonable alternative" for buyers who wanted an *insurable* muscle car with just enough extra spice to make it interesting. The 1971 Demon was essentially a clone of the popular Plymouth Duster with different paint options, different striping options, a little more styling flair and tougher quality control.

In *Motor Trend's* 1971 road test, the Demon was compared to the Mercury Comet GT, the Chevrolet Nova SS 350 and the AMC Hornet SC 360. Although it did not have the biggest engine of the four cars, it turned out to be the top performer of the group. With a modest base price of $2,721, the Demon 340 was very affordable and it still did the quarter-mile in 14.49 seconds at 98.25 mph. It also went from a standing start to 60 mph in 6.5 seconds, which was again the best performance of the four tested cars. *Musclecar Review* (June 1989) said, "Even with a shipping weight of less than 3,200 lbs., the 340 Demon was not to be taken lightly."

The 340-cid V-8 had a 4.04 x 3.31-inch bore and stroke.

It developed 275 hp at 5000 rpm and 340 lbs.-ft. of torque at 3200 rpm. The engine came as *standard* equipment in the Demon 340. It carried a single four-barrel carburetor and ran a 10.0:1 compression ratio. This mini Mopar muscle machine was the only one of the cars tested to feature an optional four-speed manual transmission. The others came with three-speed manual "stick shift" gearboxes (standard equipment in the Demon 340). Dodge used a 3.91:1 rear axle, along with E70-14 tires.

For 1972, the Dodge Demon received only minor trim and taillight changes. It remained on the same 108-inch wheelbase utilized the year before. Overall, it was 192.5 inches long, 71.6 inches wide and 52.8 inches high. Dodge used a 57.5-inch front track and a 55.5-inch rear track. If you ordered a 1972 Demon 340, Dodge would add heavy-duty shock absorbers front and rear, a front sway bar and heavy-duty torsion bars. The 1972 version of the 340-cid engine was set up for unleaded gas. It had a lower 8.5:1 compression ratio and carried an output rating of 240 *net* horsepower.

1992 Daytona IROC/RT

A revival of interest in American-built high-performance cars began to unfold by the middle of model year 1982. Led by mid-range performers like the early 5.0-liter Mustang and the Gen III GM F-cars, a new breed of factory hot rods began to come on the scene. These were not the big-block muscle cars of the '60s and '70s, as they relied more on technology than "King Kong" cubic inches to achieve outstanding acceleration and higher top speeds.

No single route was followed to unleash more power from the engines available at the time. Fuel injection, turbo-charging, ignition improvements and other advances were experimented with by different car companies, based on their varying approaches to power train engineering. There were performance cars with fours, V-6s, V-8s and—by the early '90s—even a promised V-10. That latter promise came from Chrysler's Dodge Division, which was hard at work on a new Viper sports car. But Dodge took an entirely different approach with the midyear introduction of the 1992 Daytona IROC/RT.

This new entry from what was becoming Chrysler's performance division fit between the Dodge Stealth sports car and the Dodge Spirit R/T four-door sports sedan. The initial appearance of the latter model, in 1991, struck a chord with auto enthusiasts.

At the heart of the Daytona IROC/RT was the same 2.2-liter, 16-valve, DOHC turbocharged four-cylinder engine that powered the Spirit R/T. This high-performance engine was exclusive to the IROC/RT model in the Daytona lineup.

While it shared the exterior refreshening applied to the entire line, the IROC/RT boasted a few aesthetic extras of its own. The suspension redesign introduced on the 1991 Daytona (and other Chryslers) in 1991 was re-tuned especially for the IROC/RT to accommodate its more aggressive character.

The IROC/RT 2.2 turbo engine, which included an intercooler and twin balance shafts, had the highest specific power output—100 hp per liter—of any production engine *ever* developed by Chrysler Engineering. It produced 224 hp at 6000 rpm and 217 lbs.-ft. of torque at 2800 rpm with an engine redline of 6500 rpm.

Some of the front-end Dodge performance cues from the Stealth and the then-yet-to-be-introduced Dodger Viper were incorporated into the IROC/RT model's appearance. A new Daytona hood treatment continued forward into a redesigned front fascia that replaced the previous grille opening panel. In addition, aero-style headlights displaced the former hidden headlights. The IROC/RT sported fascia openings for fog lamps, as well as an aggressive front air dam configuration. This two-door hatchback, which seated four passengers, also had stylish application of body side cladding.

Specific performance re-tuning in the IROC/RT afforded a better-balanced ride and more driver control. The spring rates were revised and stronger front struts and larger rear shock absorbers were employed.

DODGE

1992-93 Viper RT/10

It all started in a brainstorming session by Chrysler's president Bob Lutz, VP of design Tom Gale, VP of vehicle engineering Francois Castaing, and racing car legend Carroll Shelby. They thought it was time for a successor to the great American sportscars of the 1960s. Shelby's famous Cobra was used as a benchmark.

They envisioned a car that brought back all the memories and emotions of the 1960s roadster, but with the technology and refinement of the 1990s. Their concepts laid out the pattern for the Dodge Viper.

All involved agreed that the new car had to have a smooth, sensuous shape that appealed to enthusiasts who fondly remember the great Cobras. It had to fit equally well in someone's driveway or at the racetrack. It had to be more stunning and more refined than the original Cobra. And all this had to be incorporated into a package selling for under $50,000.

Gale used the analogy of remembering a high school sweetheart. "In the mind's eye, looking back, we always remember her as absolutely perfect. She was gorgeous, intelligent and courteous. Everything a perfect person could be. That's how the Viper had to be. In our minds' eye, the Cobra was perfect. So, we had to design Viper as we remembered Cobra."

The shape recalled the roadsters of the mid-1960s and featured an integrated sport bar and side exhaust pipes. The full-width sport bar contained both head restraints and high-mounted stop lamp. The instrument panel provided large, driver-oriented analog gauges.

Power for the concept car came from an aluminum V-10 engine that produced 400 hp and 450 lbs.-ft. of torque. It was mated to a six-speed transmission that featured a gated selector. The Viper rode on 17-inch wheels and tires.

The original Viper concept car made its debut at the North American International Auto Show in Detroit in January 1989. The reaction from both the press and the public was overwhelmingly positive. Letters started flowing into the Chrysler headquarters demanding that the car be developed for production. Enthusiastic customers mailed deposit checks directly to Chrysler Corporation for the car (the checks were returned).

Chrysler quickly formed a small task force to study the feasibility of producing such a vehicle for today's market. Chassis mules were built to study vehicle dynamics. Within a year, the first V-8 Viper prototype was completed. A second, this time powered by a V-10 engine, was completed by spring 1990.

In May 1990, Chrysler Chairman Lee Iacocca announced the official "go ahead" for the program. The task force grew to a team of 85 engineers, designers, finance experts, purchasing agents and manufacturing personnel representing every aspect of vehicle development. They worked side by side to bring Viper to market.

Although some minor modifications were made between its debut at the Indianapolis 500 and final production, the Dodge Viper Pace Car was nearly identical to the showroom version of the car. It was seen and driven for the first time publicly at Indianapolis Motor Speedway that May. The Pace Car retained all the design and engineering integrity that made it such a popular concept car. The shape remained intact and the performance lived up to its promise. In fact, the Viper needed no power-train modifications to pace the race. It was only the third vehicle in the race's 75 years able to make that claim.

A total of 285 Viper RT/10 roadsters were produced in 1992. All the cars were originally painted red. However, three Vipers used as factory development cars were repainted in three different colors: black, green and yellow. On one car, the standard grey interior was replaced with a black one.

The 1992 models had a retail price of $50,700, plus a $2,600 gas guzzler tax and a $2,280 luxury tax. The 488-cid (8.01-liters) V-10 engine had a bore and stroke of 4.00 x 3.88 inches. It produced 400 hp at 4600 rpm and 465 lbs.-ft. of torque at 3600 rpm.

Plans for Year 2 included several new body colors. Black, green and yellow were announced, although not all of them ultimately arrived in time. Dodge also talked about a special black-and-tan interior that was to be combined with the green paint. Originally, only a gray interior had been offered. In the end, however, only the black Viper became a reality in 1993. Green and Dandelion (the latter being the official name for yellow) were held over to be used as new features for the 1994 model year.

The 1993 Dodge Viper was not a car for the weak of heart (or pocketbook). Its wholesale price was $43,125 and the suggested retail price at your local Dodge dealership was $50,000. A $700 destination charge also applied. Uncle Sam collected a gas-guzzler tax of $2,100 on each car sold, plus a $2,280 luxury tax. Classic car auctioneers were, of course, asking even more for the few cars consigned to their sales.

Underhood motivation once again came from the same 8-liter V-10 engine. It was rated for 400 hp. Features of the power plant included a 9.1:1 compression ratio, an electronic direct ignition system and sequential multipoint fuel injection.

The fierce-looking Viper was a whole new animal for Dodge. The low-slung performance coupe was fast and expensive and produced in limited numbers.

The futuristic Viper RT/10 carried a $54,500 price tag, but its performance
was stunning: 12.9 seconds in the quarter-mile and a top speed of 165 mph.

1994 Viper RT/10

DODGE

Buying a 1994 model Dodge Viper RT/10 roadster was a more expensive proposition. The dealer wholesale price of the hot-looking Dodge climbed to $47,450 and the suggested retail price went up to $54,500. Even at that, many of the cars were sold for prices well above what it said on the factory window sticker. The destination charge remained at $700 and the gas guzzler tax was once again $2,100. However, the luxury tax (which was based on 10 percent of the price in excess of $30,000) rose a bit to $2,520.

An antitheft security system became standard equipment in 1994 Vipers and factory air conditioning was now a $1,200 option. As in the past, all Viper RT/10s still came "wired for air." Other 1994 changes were of a very minor nature, but they included such things as a transmission reverse lock-out function, mesh map pockets on the seats, a passenger-door grab handle and a Viper embossed heat shield and EMI protector attached to the under side of the hood. All cars built this year had a windshield mounted radio antenna and amplifier.

Production nearly tripled in the Viper's third season and Dodge produced a grand total of 3,083 Viper RT/10 roadsters in the 1994 model year.

The 1994 Viper RT/10 roadster accelerated from 0-to-60 mph in 4.6 seconds and did the quarter-mile in 12.9 seconds at 113.8 mph. It had a top speed of 165 mph. Chrysler estimated that 2,189 of the 1994 models were finished in Red, 678 were Black, 133 were Viper Emerald Green Pearl and 83 were Viper Bright Yellow.

The color schemes were new on the 1995 Vipers, but otherwise the car changed little from the previous year. A total of 1,577 RT/10 roadsters were built for the model year.

DODGE

1995 Viper RT/10

"New exterior design themes" was the terminology that Chrysler Corporation adapted in the fall of 1994 to promote the availability of several new color combinations for the 1995 Dodge Viper RT/10 roadster. In addition to the previously available colors—which were Viper Red, Black, Emerald Green and Viper Bright Yellow used in combination with the standard cast-aluminum directional wheels and forged aluminum wheel caps—buyers could now pick from three new color options. The first combined the Viper Red exterior color with Viper Bright Yellow five-spoke wheels. The second featured a Black exterior with a Silver central racing stripe. The third was a White exterior with a Blue center stripe.

The base retail price for the Viper RT/10 roadster remained at $54,500 and the car's standard equipment list again included the 8.0-liter V-10 engine, a six-speed manual transmission, four-wheel independent suspension, power-assisted rack-and-pinion steering, dual stainless-steel side exhausts and 17-inch wheels. There were now three factory options available: air conditioning, a California emissions system and a Massachusettes emissions system.

Production dropped nearly in half this season, with Dodge Division producing 1,577 Viper RT/10 roadsters during the 1995 model year. This included about 515 Black cars, 458 Viper Red cars, 307 Emerald Green cars and 298 Viper Bright Yellow cars. Grey-and-black interiors were used in 1,005 cars and an additional 572 Vipers had a tan-and-black interior.

The official factory-issued performance figures for the 1995 Viper RT/10 roadster were the same advertised for the 1992 to 1994 models: 0-to-60 mph in 4.6 seconds and the quarter-mile in 12.9 seconds at 113.8 mph. A top speed of 165 mph was also generally quoted again.

Although the 1995 model year didn't bring a great deal of exciting changes to the Viper line, it did register a couple of historical milestones. It was the last year that Vipers were produced in the new Mack Avenue assembly plant. It was also the year that the pilot model for the dramatic Dodge Viper GTS-R coupe was unveiled at the Pebble Beach Concours d'Elegance in Monterey, California.

If the RT/10 roadster was akin to Carroll Shelby's Cobra, the GTS was akin to Enzo Ferrari's "prancing horse" cars. "From the beginning, developing the GTS coupe was a more difficult task than the roadster, because the car evolved with a broader character," said Roy Sjoberg, the executive engineer with the Team Viper development group.

Magazine testers wound the RT/10 up to 173 mph and posted a blazing quarter-mile time of 12.6 seconds.

DODGE

Wieck Media

1996 Viper RT/10

The 1996 Dodge Viper RT/10 roadster received several enhancements including a removable hardtop, sliding rigid plastic side windows, a more robust differential, stronger drive shafts, aluminum suspension control arms and revised spring and shock absorber rates.

The 488-cid (8.0-liter) V-10 engine continued to power the Viper. The 90-degree V-10 had a cast aluminum block with cast iron cylinder liners, aluminum cylinder heads and an aluminum crankcase. It had a 4.00-inch bore and a 3.88-inch stroke and a 9.1:1 compression ratio. It was attached to a six-speed manual, fully synchronized transmission with electronic 1-4 skip-shift and reverse-lockout mechanisms.

A new rear-exiting exhaust system replaced the side-mounted pipes used on 1992 to 1995 models. In addition to a cleaner look and quieter operation, this change was partly responsible for extra horsepower, too. New spark tuning and fuel calibration also helped boost the engine's output to 415 hp at 5200 rpm and 488 lbs.-ft. of torque at 3600 rpm. *Motor*

Trend (November 1995) reported a 0-to-60 time of 5 seconds and a standing-start quarter-mile in 13.2 seconds at 113.4 mph. *Car and Driver* reported a 4.1-second 0-to-60 run and a 12.6-second quarter-mile at 113 mph and a top speed of 173 mph!

The resin transfer-molded composite body was mounted on a tubular space frame chassis with a separate cowl structure. The Viper roadster weighed in at 3,445 lbs., with the weight distributed 50/50 front to rear. It had double-acting gas-charged hydraulic shock absorbers with adjustable rebound rates, 16.7:1 power rack-and-pinion steering and al-wheel vented disc brakes.

For the model year, Dodge manufactured 721 Viper RT/10 roadsters. About 231 of the roadsters were black, about 166 were red and about 324 were white. A Dodge Viper was entered in the 24 Hours of LeMans and took a 10th place finish in the GT-1 class.

Jerry Heasley

The 1996 Viper GTS got some meaningful upgrades inside and out, and potential buyers lined up to get one.

DODGE

1996 Viper GTS

The original Dodge Viper RT/10 roadster had its roots in a visceral back-to-the-basics, uniquely American sports car, but the 1996 Dodge Viper GTS coupe reached into a new, more sophisticated arena, offering more in the way of comfort and amenities than its roadster sibling.

Like the RT/10 before it, the GTS coupe first stole hearts when it was introduced as a concept car. That was at the 1993 North American Auto Show in Detroit. The GTS program was given the green light in May 1993 and just 34 months later the first GTS production car started down the line at the Connor Avenue Assembly Plant in Detroit.

In August, 1995, Dodge displayed a GTS coupe prototype at the second annual Dodge Viper Owner Invitational in Monterey, California, and made an exclusive offer to current owners—a voucher for the first GTS coupes produced. More than three-quarters of the 1996 calendar-year production of 1,700 was instantly spoken for.

The base manufacturer's suggested retail price (MSRP) of the first GTS coupe was $66,700, including destination charge. Additional gas and luxury taxes added approximately $6,330.

While the GTS continued the look of the original Viper roadster, more than 90 percent of the car was new. To start, there was a new body, a new interior and a modified V-10 engine with less weight and increased horsepower.

Horsepower in the GTS was increased to 450 from 415 in the 1996 roadster and torque was boosted 10 additional lbs.-ft., bringing it to 490 at 3700 rpm. A NACA duct design on the hood of the car force-fed oxygen into the V-10's intake and E-type louvers above each of the front wheels prevented air pressure from building under the hood.

Enclosing the Viper necessitated a new weatherstrip system for the doors and glass. Cooling the closed body also required a more powerful air conditioning system. Other engineering challenges included packaging dropped glass in the doors and designing an innovative electronic entry system.

To improve the overall driving experience, the Viper team pioneered a unique adjustable pedal system that allowed the driver to move the clutch, brake and accelerator pedals up to four inches closer by simply turning a knob mounted under the steering column.

The roof was made from a resin transfer-molding process, as were most other body panels. The hood was made of sheet molding compound. The sweeping shape of the car resulted in improved aerodynamics, dropping the coefficient of drag to 0.39 from the roadster's 0.50. With the enclosed cockpit, the GTS had about 12 percent more torsional rigidity than the roadster.

Even with the addition of the roof, backlight and roll-up windows, the GTS was actually 60 lbs. lighter than that of the roadster. Other significant features that differentiated the GTS coupe from the roadster included a rear storage compartment designed to stow a full-size Viper tire and increase cargo capacity, redesigned interior trim, dual airbags, a new instrument panel with revised gauge locations and—on the exterior—a racing-style fuel filler cover a twin-bubble roofline that provides ample headroom and a one-piece glass bonded hatch with a defroster.

Dodge built 1,166 of the GTS coupes at the Conner Avenue assembly plant in 1996. Blue finish was on 1,163 of them and three were done in White. Five cars had white wheels and the rest had polished alloy wheels.

Wieck Media

DODGE

With 450 hp coming from its 488-cid V-10 motor, the 1997 Viper was the highest-horsepower domestic car around.

1997 Viper RT/10

The "second-generation" 1997 Dodge Viper RT/10 roadster that arrived in 1997 was powered by the same 488-cid V-10 engine originally engineered for the GTS coupe. It produced 450 hp at 5200 rpm and 490 lbs.-ft. of torque at 3700 rpm. It had, by far, the highest output of any American production automobile. The power was channeled by a high-performance six-speed gearbox and transferred to the road via independent front and rear suspension system.

Braking was provided by power-assisted, four-piston, caliper front disc brakes and a single-piston rear disc design. The Viper R/T10 roadster came with high-performance Michelin Pilot SX MXX3 tires on 17-inch rims.

In addition to the soft top, the Viper RT/10 roadster also featured a removable body-color hardtop that has been redesigned for 1997 for increased headroom. The hard top was a "delete option," meaning owners could choose not to equip their Viper with the hardtop for a lower base price. Air conditioning was also a delete option for 1997.

Like the Viper GTS coupe, the Viper RT/10 roadster had a smooth exterior design that was free of add-ons. It offered an electronically assisted remote entry system, and, for the first time, standard power glass windows. A manual override system could be accessed through the rear window, which had key locks.

To improve the overall driving experience, Team Viper pioneered a unique adjustable pedal system that allowed the driver to move the clutch, brake and accelerator pedals up to 4 inches closer by simply turning a knob mounted under the steering column. That system was featured on all 1997 Viper RT/10 roadsters, along with a tilt steering wheel and a seat that allowed a generous fore-and-aft adjustment of 5.2 inches.

While the Viper's interior had evolved since 1989, it remained a simple, cleanly styled cockpit with an emphasis on function. The instrument panel featured full analog instrumentation with a 7,000-rpm tachometer, 200-mph speedometer, engine coolant gauge, oil pressure gauge, fuel gauge and a voltmeter. Safety items included standard driver and passenger air bags and three-point inboard-mounted seat belts.

For the first time, both the Dodge Viper RT/10 roadster and GTS coupe were available in either Blue with White painted stripes or solid Viper Red. Silver wheels were standard on the RT/10 roadster in Blue, while Viper Red RT/10 roadsters featured standard Gold wheels. Also available as options were additional wheel choice colors and special badging.

Only 117 RT/10 roadsters were produced in 1997. Of those, approximately 53 were painted Blue and 64 were Viper Red. Black interiors were installed in 114 cars and three had a tan interior. There were also 114 cars with polished wheels and three with gold wheels.

DODGE

Dodge produced 1,671 of the exotic Viper GTS coupes for 1997. A total
of 965 were painted Viper Blue. The rest were decked out in Viper Red.

Wieck Media

1997 Viper GTS

Chrysler said that the 1997 Dodge Viper GTS coupe was for the "discriminating sports car lover whose particular devotion is to the ultimate performance road car."

The GTS coupe stayed true to the front-engine, rear-drive layout that excited so many sports car lovers. It was strongly evocative of the greatest GT cars, particularly the 1965 World Championship-winning Daytona Cobra coupes. The GTS's functional, race-inspired details—the polished alloy quick-release fuel filler, twin helmet blisters in the roofline and NACA-ducted hood—tended to draw the eyes of observers further into the car's athletic body work.

Inside, noise levels were pleasantly subdued, although one stab of the right foot could ignite the uneven-firing rasp of the 450-hp Viper V-10 engine.

The Viper's well-balanced chassis provided a feeling of stability and prodigious grip. During the 24 Hours of Daytona, one Viper GTS-R driver described his car as "built like a battleship." In their first season on the track, factory-backed

GTS-Rs finished both the grueling 24 Hours of Daytona and 12 Hours of Sebring. They then qualified for the 24 Hours of LeMans, at speeds well above 200 mph.

New features for the 1997 GTS included a clutch disc with idle damper springs, a revised unibelt seat belt system, a new energy-absorbing tilt steering column, new seats and tracks, a new interior multi-function switch, a new instrument panel, an improved HVAC system with re-circulation mode and a new indicator lamp module. Standard equipment included the 8.0-liter V-10, six-speed manual transmission, polished five-spoke aluminum wheels, driver and passenger air bags, an alarm system with integrated remote keyless entry, power windows and locks, a one-piece glass hatch with defroster, GTS badging and GTS blue pearlcoat paint with dual stone white stripes.

The 1997 GTS coupe had a production run of 1,671 units. Of these, 965 cars were the standard Viper Blue color and 706 were finished in Viper Red.

1998 Viper RT/10

Popular Mechanics said that the Viper was the quickest and fastest car it had ever tested. "Have any '60s muscle cars ever equaled that performance?" The magazine asked, then it answered its own query with: "Legend says the 1969 Z-1 Corvette (two were built), ZL1 Camaro (69 were built) and the 1966 427 Shelby Cobra could run such times, although no such times have ever been actually published. But think about it. The Viper GTS has air conditioning, power windows, dual airbags, a CD player and a sixth gear for somewhat respectable economy on the highway. And it'll sit there and idle smoothly for hours in Death Valley without overheating or fouling its plugs."

Like the latest Dodge Viper GTS coupe that *PM* pictured, the 1998 Viper RT/10 roadster delivered the most exhilarating driving experience of any regular American production car. The open version of Dodge's powerful sports car also raced into the new model year with a list of similar product enhancements and refinements.

They included the use of new, weight-cutting tubular exhaust manifolds, the change to a low-overlap camshaft, a new electronic radiator fan control, next-generation air bags with a passenger air bag cut-off switch, revised key locks, a keyless entry system, a new instrument panel with full analog instrumentation, new Viper Bright Metallic Silver and Viper Red colors, a leak-resistant battery case, a "response-enhanced" evaporative emissions system, improved windshield washer nozzles, an automatic interior lamp shut off (to save battery power) and a quieter alternator.

Specifications for the two-passenger roadster were also very similar to those of previous models. Power from the 8.0-liter V-10 was now up to 450 hp at 5200 rpm and torque was 490 lbs.-ft. at 3700 rpm. The 9.6:1 compression engine redlined at 6,000 rpm. It again drove through a standard six-speed manual gearbox to a 3.07:1 ratio rear axle. A frame-mounted, bevel-gear-with-clutch type limited-slip differential was also standard equipment.

With a 96.2-inch wheelbase, 175.1-inch overall length, 75.7-inch overall width and 44-inch height, the roadster tipped the scales at 3,319 lbs. With only 7.37 lbs. per horsepower to move, it was one very fast machine.

During 1998, Dodge issued demographic materials showing that current Viper buyers were 51-57 years old and 94 percent male with an average annual income of $225,000. The study also profiled the "target buyer" for 1998 models as a 52-58 year old in the 95 percent male category, also with an annual household income of $225,000.

The production total for the 1998 RT/10 roadster was 379 units. Of these, 252 cars were done in Viper Red and 127 were Viper Bright Metallic Silver.

DODGE

Wieck Media

The Viper was still pretty much in a league of its own in 1998. Viper owners were part of an exclusive club, as only 837 of the GTS coupes were produced.

1998 Viper GTS

The legend of the Dodge Viper—from the original RT/10 roadster to the Viper GTS coupe—had grown to near mythic proportions since the first concept car version was shown almost a decade earlier.

DODGE

"Motor Matters" columnist Tom Keane summed up the Viper coupe's personality when he gushed, " I have never been in a car so sensuously thrilling as the all-new Dodge Viper GTS Coupe. Everything about this car excites me beyond my wildest dream. The Viper is not an *ordinary* sports car. Other prestigious sports cars pale by comparison; collectively, all the other cars are nothing more than also-rans. "

The 1998 Viper GTS stayed true to the marque's heritage of delivering the most exhilarating driving experience of any regular American production car. The sleek coupe powered into its third calendar year with several product enhancements and refinements.

The curb weight had been further cut from the 1997 model through the use of new tubular exhaust manifolds. In addition, the use of a low-overlap camshaft helped to reduce emissions and improve fuel economy. A new electronic radiator fan control was adapted to help reduce cooling system noise.

In the safety area, the 1998 Viper GTS benefited from next-generation air bags and a passenger air bag cut-off switch. Security was improved with revised key locks and a keyless entry system. The instrument panel featured full analog instrumentation with a 7,000-rpm tachometer, 200-mph speedometer, engine coolant gauge, oil pressure gauge, fuel gauge and a voltmeter.

Colors available for the 1998 GTS coupe included White, Viper Bright Metallic Silver and Viper Red. The year's production total included 102 White coupes, 436 monotone Viper Red coupes, 11 Viper Red coupes with Silver stripes, 267 monotone Viper Bright Metallic Silver coupes and 21 Viper Bright Metallic Silver coupes with Blue stripes. Of the 837 GTS coupes made for the model year, 735 had the standard black interior and 102 had blue interiors. Optional GT-2-style wheels were used on only 102 cars.

The Viper could move from 0-to-60 in just over 4 seconds and did 0-to-100 mark in under 10 seconds, making it faster and quicker than a Ferrari. And when the prices of these two cars were compared, the Viper GTS looked like a bargain as well.

The 1999 Viper GTS received larger tires and wheels, but only 699 lucky buyers ever brought one home.

1999 Viper GTS

During 1998, an auto industry analysis firm named Strategic Vision took a focused look at how American car owners felt about their automobiles, both domestic and imported. In the nationally syndicated survey, Dodge Viper owners registered the highest level of passion about their new vehicle. Strategic Vision stated that this finding made sense, "Given the financial, and other, sacrifices Viper owners have to make for this raw, heart-stopping performance machine."

The 1999 Dodge Viper GTS was indeed a heart-stopping machine. The annual changes made to this sexy-looking coupe were mostly the same as those that the 1999 RT/10 roadster underwent for that model year. Larger 18-inch aluminum wheels were mounted front and rear. The front wheels were shod with P275/35ZR18 Michelin Pilot MXX3 speed-rated tires. The rear wheels carried the same type of tires in size P335/30ZR18. The wheel and tire updates enhanced the coupe's cornering ability without sacrificing other ride characteristics. Painted wheels were standard equipment,

while bright polished wheels were an extra-cost option.

Other 1999 changes included the reintroduction of a Black factory color choice and release of the new Cognac colored Connolly leather interior option. This Cognac interior was ordered for 128 GTS coupes. Three GTS coupes had a Red interior, which came on stream as a late-in-the-year option. Of the other GTS coupes made, 22 were trimmed in solid Silver, 77 were done in solid Black and 26 had a black interior with silver stripes.

A grand total of just 699 GTS coupes were built in 1999, with 549 going into the U.S. marketplace, 72 going to Canadian buyers and 78 being shipped to other foreign countries.

The 1999 Viper GTS coupe could move from 0-to-60 in 4.4 seconds and did 0-to-100 in 9.7 seconds. Quarter-mile acceleration was reported as 12.7 seconds. The car's top speed was tested at 185 mph. EPA gas mileage figures for the GTS Coupe were 13 mpg in city driving and 24 mpg on the highway.

Wieck Media

DODGE

The GTS-R was a racing-inspired special edition that sold for $82,500 in 1999. The GT2 version of the car came only in white with blue stripes.

1999 Viper GTS-R/GT2

Chrysler Corporation competed in and won races with its factory-sourced, factory-sponsored Viper GTS-R competition coupe. This ultra-powerful Dodge muscle car took the FIA's GT2 Manufacturer's Championship in 1997 and 1998 and had a hard-to-forget 1-2 class victory during the French Grand Prix at LeMans in 1998. Race wins like these inspired Dodge to produce the GT2 Championship Edition Viper Coupe for private buyers. This limited-edition Viper carried a hefty $82,500 window sticker and was not for the faint of pocketbook buyer.

The GT2 version of the Viper GTS-R racing car came only in one color combination— White with Blue stripes. The V-10 engine with an aluminum block and aluminum cylinder heads was a tweaked version of the standard GTS and RT/10 power plant that cranked out an additional 10 hp. The vital statistics showed a stock-looking 4.00 x 3.88-inch bore and stroke and 488 cubic inches of displacement, but didn't tell the whole story. The Dodge boys revamped the intake system with K & N low-restriction air filters, new hoses and an air cleaner housing that had been used on the 1992 to 1996 Vipers. However, the engineers sealed off the regular functional air scoop and the result was a rating of 460 hp at 5200 rpm and 500 lbs.-ft. of torque at 3700 rpm.

Included as part of the GT2 Championship Edition coupe was a special front air splitter, a ground effects package, "dive bomber" spoilers and a carbon-fiber rear deck airfoil that resembled that used on the actual racing cars. The interior featured black leather seats with blue accents. In 0-to-60-mph acceleration testing, the GTS-R coupe pulled a 4.0-second time. It did the quarter-mile in 12.1 seconds at 120.5 mph.

DODGE

Wieck Media

The 1999 RT/10 Viper had the same awesome formula as the previous years: power to burn and looks to kill.

1999 Viper RT/10 Roadster

The 1999 Viper RT/10 remained a classic "wind in your face" roadster. It stood out as the quintessential American sports-muscle car—fast, loud and untamed with a massive engine. Since it exploded onto the streets in 1992, there had been many modifications. The 1999 RT/10 provided 400-plus hp, overmatched steamroller tires and looks to kill.

The Viper's 8-liter aluminum V-10 makes it a unique muscle car that relies on sheer size, rather than high-technology for power-producing prowess. By 1999, Dodge swapped side-pipes for rear tailpipes to up the output. Lacking the GTS coupe's streamlining, the roadster was good for a top speed in the 170-mph bracket without going airborne. But with the springs and shocks close to the wheels, driver control at higher speeds was excellent.

On July 6, 1998, Dodge announced that with the beginning of 1999 model output late that year, the venomous Viper RT/10 roadster was about to receive even more enhancements aimed at bringing its appearance and road-biting ability up to even higher levels than before.

One new feature on Viper roadsters was larger wheels and tires to enhance the car's cornering ability without sacrificing other ride characteristics. Replacing the 17-inch wheels were 18-inch aluminum wheels with Michelin Pilot MXX3 speed-rated tires mounted on them. The tires were P275/35ZR18 in front and P335/30ZR18 at the rear. Painted aluminum wheels were standard and polished wheels were considered optional equipment.

Another change for model year 1999 was reintroduction of black as an addition to the existing factory color choices of Viper Red and Viper Metallic Silver. The RT/10 roadster was offered in all three colors without racing stripes. A total of 549 were built, with 498 going into the U.S. market and 51 going to Canadian buyers.

Several interior enhancements were made, including a new Cognac-colored Connolly leather option that was ordered for 169 roadsters. Three RT/10s had red interiors, 50 were trimmed in silver and 116 were done in black. The Connolly package included leather seats, a leather steering wheel, a leather-wrapped shift knob, and leather parking brake boot and grip. It was not offered for Red cars.

The 2000 Viper GTS had a top speed of 185 mph.

Wieck Media

2000 Viper GTS Coupe

As the spiritual reincarnation of the Shelby Daytona coupe, the Dodge Viper GTS quickly developed a passionate following and changed very little from one season to the next because there was little motivation to mess with near perfection. A new steel gray color was the main update for 2000.

The coupe—which first appeared at Dodge dealerships in 1996—was based on the original RT/10 roadster and had virtually identical specifications, although there were minor differences between the two body styles. The RT/10 was 175.1 inches long, while the GTS was 176.7 in length. Overall height was 44 inches for the roadster and 47 inches for the coupe. The closed car was also a little heavier, at 3,383 lbs., than the 3,319-lb. roadster.

Other minor dimensional differences were a 19.3-sq. ft. frontal area on the RT/10 compared to 20.5 on the GTS. The drag coefficient was 0.495 for the roadster without a top

and 0.46 with one. The coupe's was 0.35. The 2000 Viper GTS coupe had a base price of $67,225. You could add the $10,000 American Racing Club (ACR) package that added 10 hp, stiffened the suspension and deleted items like air conditioning, a stereo and fog lights.

The base aluminum-block-and-heads V-10 engine was rated at the familiar 450 hp at 5200 rpm and 490 lbs.-ft. of torque at 3700 rpm. With the ACR package it was 460 hp and 500 lbs.-ft. of torque! The engine was linked to a six-speed manual transmission. The 2000 Viper was easily capable of a 4.3-second 0-to-60 times and had a top speed of 185 mph.

Total production of 2000 GTS models was 949, with 804 marketed in the U.S., 92 sold in Canada and 53 going overseas. The most popular 2000 Viper GTS color—solid Black—was sprayed on 179 cars of which 66 had Cognac interiors and 113 had black interiors.

Wieck Media

Dodge made only minor changes to the 2000 version of the Viper RT/10.

2000 Viper RT/10

The Dodge Viper RT/10 roadster didn't undergo very many drastic changes since its original inception, in mid-1992, as a modern interpretation of the muscular Shelby roadster. When Carroll Shelby spoke to us about the Viper RT/10 prototype at the 1991 SEMA show in Las Vegas, he said, "This is going to be a real muscle car and your readers will love it." Of course, "Shel" was telling the truth, as he always does.

Fast forward to the 2000 model year. Steel Gray exterior finish was probably the most obvious change in the latest Viper RT/10 roadster. You could order up this new hue if you wanted the latest and greatest or, if you preferred, you could still get your car in Viper Red or Black.

The 2000 Viper RT/10 roadster continued with its longitudinal front engine and rear-wheel-drive power train layout. It again rode a 96.2-inch wheelbase and measured 176.7 inches front to rear. It was 75.7 inches wide with a uniform track width of 59.6 inches in the front and the rear. The roadster's height also remained at the same 44 inches.

The aluminum-block-and-heads V-10 engine was rated at the familiar 450 hp at 5200 rpm and 490 lbs.-ft. of torque at 3700 rpm. As usual, the engine drove to a six-speed manual transmission that had gear ratios of 2.66:1 in first, 1.78:1 in second, 1.30:1 in third, 1.00:1 in fourth, 0.74:1 in fifth and 0.50:1 in sixth. The 2000 Viper was easily capable of a 4.3-second 0-to-60-mph time and had a top speed of about 185 mph.

Total production of 2000 Viper RT/10 roadsters was 840 units, with 757 marketed in the U.S. and 83 sold in Canada. The last car retailed by a Dodge dealer had the VIN ZV606129. Viper Red finish was used on 255 cars, of which 76 had Cognac leather interiors and 179 had black interiors. The new-for-the-year Steel Gray finish was the most popular 2000 color and was used on 296 cars—99 with Cognac interiors and 197 with black upholstery. The second most popular 2000 Viper color—black—was squirted on 289 cars, of which 131 had Cognac interiors and 158 had black interiors.

DODGE

Among the cooler features on the 2001 Viper RT/10 was its foldable and stowable top.

2001 Viper (All Models)

Highlights of the 2001 Viper RT/10 included its lightweight, all-aluminum 8.0-liter V-10 engine with sequential bottom-fed multipoint electronic fuel injection, a foldable and stowable soft top, remote keyless entry and 4-wheel high-performance power-assisted brakes with ABS. The seat belt cluster lamp now remained on after engine start and until the driver buckled up. An inside emergency trunk lid release was added along with a user-ready child seat top tether anchorage in the front passenger seat. Next-generation driver and front passenger air bags with front passenger air bag on/off switch were another new feature. As usual, the Viper used a fully-independent suspension system and precise rack-and-pinion steering.

The Viper GTS coupe had the same basic features and updates as the TR/10 roadster in a somewhat more streamlined, but less open-air package.

The Viper ARC coupe had the same basic features and updates as the TR/10 roadster and GTS coupe, plus a couple of distinctions. Its resin composite body featured a sheet-molded compound (SMC) hood, special ACR Viper badging and graphics and an interior identification plaque. Unique 18-inch, one-piece BBS forged aluminum wheels were provided, as was a supplemental five-point restraint system.

After a 20-year absence from racing, Chrysler went back on track in the late-'90s with a full-scale motor sports effort using the production-based GTS-R coupe. The racing V-10s, assembled by Caldwell Development, were offered in

three forms. First came the "standard" 525-hp V-10 with a competition camshaft and Borla headers. The next step up was the 650-hp "endurance" engine including the same changes, plus a velocity-stack intake manifold with ported heads, solid-lifter roller rockers, higher-rate valve springs and chrome-moly Carillo connecting rods. The final step was the 700-hp "sprint" engine—an endurance engine with larger valves, a more aggressive camshaft and 7000-rpm-plus valve train upgrades.

The $82,500 GT2 Championship Edition Coupe was again a version of the GTS-R competition coupe intended for private buyers. It came in White with Blue stripes (and its sooty racing exhausts did tend to get the White body a bit dirty). The aluminum-block-and-heads engine was a tweaked version of the standard GTS and RT/10 power plant with 460 hp. Its revamped intake system featured K & N low-restriction air filters, new hoses, the 1992-1996 style air cleaner housing and a sealed-off hood scoop. Great-looking BBS 18-inch alloy wheels were mounted and shod with Michelin Pilot MXX3 tires. Included once again as part of the GT2 Championship Edition coupe was a special front air splitter, ground effects, "dive bomber" spoilers and a carbon-fiber rear deck airfoil that resembled that used on the actual racing cars. The interior featured black leather seats with blue accents. In 0-to-60 acceleration testing, the GTS-R coupe pulled a 4.0-second time. It did the quarter-mile in 12.1 seconds at 120.5 mph.

DODGE

Wieck Media

The 2002 GTS Viper carried a price tag of $72,225.

2002 Viper (All Models)

As model-year 2002 unfolded, things seemed quiet in Viperville. Dodge had already told enthusiasts about an all-new and significantly updated Viper for 2003. If this didn't scare buyers away in 2002, it at least limited the pool to those with a passion for the original-style "snake" car. The magazine writers and Internet content providers told Dodge fans it was their last chance to get a Gen I version.

Although an "elderly" 11-year-old in auto industry years, the Viper was still king of the snakepit with something that competitors like the Porsche 911 and Corvette couldn't quite match. "If the Porsche is Wagner, and the 'Vette is Jim Morrison, then Viper is Mettalica. Armed with sledgehammers," said Dan Carney on the "NewCarTestDrive" web site.

For the early 2002 model year, Dodge offered just two Vipers. The now-classic RT/10 roadster was priced at $69,225 (at least until midyear, when a removable hardtop became standard equipment). The GTS coupe, with a window sticker reading $72,225, was the other option.

The American Club Racing (ACR) competition package was a $10,000 option for the coupe. As in 2000-2001, it added 10 hp, 10 ft.-lbs. of torque and heavier-service underpinnings, while deleting some creature comforts. The ACR kit was for those with serious racing in mind. However, those who just wanted to look racy could drop a little more than a grand extra to tack on the Comfort Group package with a stereo and A/C.

A new Final Edition Group option was added at midyear.

To be precise, April 23, 2002, was the day that Dodge announced plans to produce a special GTS Final Edition model to commemorate the last 2002 Viper coupes to roll off the line at DaimlerChrysler's Conner Avenue Assembly Plant. The coupes were the last 360 cars built on the 2002 Viper platform and became the first production Vipers to wear Viper Red exterior paint with twin Stone White racing stripes.

The White-over-Red theme was the same one that carried the Viper GTS-R/T race car to motor sports acclaim with an outright win at the 2000 Daytona 24-hour sports car racing event and consecutive American Le Mans Series manufacturers championships.

Dodge said that the Viper GTS Final Edition was "expected to hold special appeal to sports car enthusiasts and Viper collectors as a landmark in the product's history" although it was also a way to keep sales of the "old" Viper from bogging down in the 11th hour. The car made its public debut in early February at the Chicago Auto Show.

In addition to the special paint striping, a number of other details distinguished the GTS Final Edition. Inside, a red-stitched black leather steering wheel and shift knob were unique to the model, with a sequentially numbered dash plaque (Nos. 1-360) recognizing each individual car from the series.

Wieck Media

DODGE

The new 2003 Viper SRT10 was available only as a convertible. Continuing updates showed
Dodge was not content to rest on its laurels with its jaw-dropping peformance car.

2003 Viper SRT10

The Viper SRT10 was first revealed to the public at the 2001 North American International Auto Show in Detroit, Michigan. It promised enthusiasts more than 500 cubic inches of engine that generated a minimum of 500 hp and 500 ft.-lbs. of torque, selling points that set it apart from any contemporary sports car. Following in the footsteps of the 2001 show car, the production version Viper SRT10 was available exclusively in convertible form.

Before Viper SRT10 was offered at dealerships, Dodge gave the owners of Gen I Viper models the first chance at placing orders for the new car. This worked like gangbusters and the entire first-year production run was sold out immediately.

The 500-hp/500 ft.-lbs. Formula was carried through in the production version, which did 0-to-100-to-0 mph in about 13.2 seconds, compared to the "old" Viper's time of 14.5 seconds. But Dodge emphasized that the new Viper could also stop faster than the old one.

The improvements didn't stop at that point, either. The new Viper was sleeker, more refined, quieter and better handling than the original. It was not whimpy, however. "Dodge said the car was tuned for tearing up pavement and rumbling out a cool exhaust note."

The 2003 Dodge Viper came only in a single roadster body style (although there were hints that a coupe was in the wings for 2005). Standard equipment for the SRT10 included a manual top with a glass rear window, a six-speed manual transmission with floor shift, four-wheel anti-lock brakes, a viscous limited-slip differential, power windows and mirrors, intermittent windshield wipers and bucket seats with leather seating surfaces. An alarm system with remote door locks was also included. The only engine available was the 8.3-liter 500-hp V-10.

The new Viper body featured a lowered hood line, swept-back fenders and deep-cut side scallops that took their cues from the original design, while bringing the Viper into the 21st century. Improved aerodynamics and a full-length undertray add functional performance enhancements. The Viper's visceral lines spoke volumes for the passion that Dodge designers could bring to their craft. The new Viper gave enthusiasts an American sports car offering all-out high performance. The SRT10 was truly a muscle car.

Wieck Media

The Viper SRT10, shown here with the Dodge Slingshot concept car, changed little for 2004 and was again only available as a convertible.

2004 Viper SRT10

DODGE

America's most-powerful production car returned as a carryover model with few alterations for 2004. Standard features included leather-and-fake-suede seats, a tilt steering column, power-adjustable foot pedals and xenon high- and low-beam headlights. New for 2004 were carpeting in the trunk and red-colored brake calipers.

Designing a modern American legend is a tall task, but Dodge engineers met the challenge head-on, creating a vehicle that stayed true to its heritage while adopting cutting-edge design and technology. The Viper again came only as a convertible with a fully convertible clamshell-design top featuring easy, single-latch operation and a heated glass rear window. The car's RIM (Reaction Injected Molded) fenders provided lightweight strength. With an aerodynamic shape and underbody pan, it registered a low drag coefficient.

The Viper cockpit was covered with leather trim and great-looking chrome accents. Satin chrome was featured on the gearshift lever and knob, the gearshift boot trim ring, the parking brake release handle, the door handles and the release levers. The instrument panel had a 7,000-rpm center-mounted tachometer, a 220-mph analog speedometer and a center stack with gauges for oil pressure, oil temperature, coolant temperature and voltage. In addition, the interior

included all the push-button controls and race-inspired sports car features you would expect. A push-button starter fired the SRT10 up, the wraparound seats kept driver and passenger in place and the adjustable pedals (including a dead pedal) ensured that the clutch, brake and throttle would be within easy reach.

The Viper's only engine was the 8.3-liter (505-cid) V-10. The intake manifold featured shorter runners and a single non-staged two-barrel throttle body that permitted a lower hood line and higher rpm peak. To squeeze 500 hp and 525 lbs.-ft. of torque out of the V10, Dodge engineers used a large-bore cast-aluminum block and a long-stroke crankshaft. The exhaust system ran across the car and exited on the opposite side, allowing the use of a less restrictive resonator.

The only Viper transmission was a Tremec T56 six-speed manual transmission controlled via a short-throw shifter. It was bolted to a heavy-duty clutch, heavy-duty pressure plate and heavy-duty flywheel for outstanding performance.

The Dodge Viper SRT10 is the kind of car you dreamed about having as a kid. Its low-slung stature bespeaks some of the finest performance characteristics on the road and allows it to handle better than your wildest dreams.

DODGE

The 2005 Viper SRT10 was an unobtainable dream car for most enthusiasts,
but it was a lot of car for the money compared to its competition.

2005-06 Viper SRT10

The 2005-2006 Viper SRT10 roadster carried a dealer invoice of $73,875 and a manufacturer's suggested retail price of $81,090. A typical car with options set the buyer back more than $87,000. Unlike muscle cars of the '60s, the Viper was not a car that the local supermarket box boy could hope to own, even if he worked very hard. Too bad. It was, however, a great bargain when stacked against competitors like the Acura NSX, Corvette Z06 and Porsche 911.

All-new in 2004, the Dodge Viper SRT10 was pretty much a direct carryover model for model-year 2005. The low-slung roadster shell, lowered hood line, swept-back fenders and side scallops returned. Designers were successful in carrying on traditional Viper styling themes, yet giving them a more modern touch.

Performance was again outstanding, a function chiefly of the car's engine size. The 8.3-liter, 505-cid V-10 engine was the new, more powerful version introduced in 2004. It generated 500 hp at 5,600 rpm and 525 ft.-lbs. of torque from 1500 to 5600 rpm. The side-exit exhaust system was among carryover features, along with the stiffer frame that enhanced quietness and handling. The four-wheel independent suspension again featured lightweight high-performance aluminum control arms and knuckles and revised geometry for outstanding road handling. Lightweight aluminum-bodied front and rear coil-over shocks with revised tuning and new springs, six-

bolt hubs and tubular stabilizer bars were incorporated. The Viper had the most sophisticated suspension of any car in the world.

The Viper's bi-fold clamshell top with a center latch made it a true wind-in-your-hair convertible. It came with polished 18 x 10-inch front and 19 x 13-inch rear forged aluminum wheels. Viper colors for 2005 included Black Clear Coat, Bright Silver Clear Coat Metallic and Red Clear Coat.

The SRT10's standard features included premium leather and suede-trimmed seats featuring integral head restraints, aggressive side bolsters and optimal high-back support, and power-adjustable throttle, brake and clutch pedals. A manually adjustable aluminum footrest was provided. The seats accepted a racing-style 5-point driver and passenger restraint system. The "stacked cluster" instrument panel included a center-mounted tachometer and a 220-mph speedometer. A Tire Pressure Monitoring System alerted drivers to any drop in tire pressure below 20 psi. A premium in-dash AM/FM radio with six-disc in-head CD changer was standard. It featured a seven-channel, 310-watt under-seat amplifier, two 3/4-inch instrument panel-mounted tweeters, two 6 1/2-inch low-mass full-range Alpine loudspeakers, one 6 1/2-inch subwoofer with ported enclosure and two 2 3/4-inch fill speakers mounted in the bulkhead.

DODGE

Wieck Media

The big change for the Viper SRT10 in 2006 is the arrival of the coupe body style.

2006 SRT10 Coupe

The Dodge Viper legend began with the 1992 Dodge Viper RT/10 Roadster and grew with the introduction in 1996 of the Dodge Viper GTS coupe. Starting in the fall of 2005, history will be repeating itself. Since the debut of the Gen III Viper in 2003, it was a convertible-only series. But on January 9, 2005, the all-new SRT10 coupe made its bow for the Detroit and Los Angeles Auto Shows.

The exterior of the SRT10 Coupe featured "double-bubble" roof styling and unique rear styling with wraparound taillights reminiscent of those on the Viper GTS Coupe. With the addition of a roof, the Viper SRT10 became more torsionally rigid than the already-sturdy convertible. Aerodynamically, the SRT10 coupe provides increased downforce and more high-speed stability with its sloping roofline and rear deck lid spoiler. The only bodywork that the new coupe shared with the convertible was the front fascia and fenders, the hood and the doors.

In addition to a new canopy and deck lid, the coupe had a special windshield surrounds, door side glass, rear fascia, quarter panels and taillights.

The deck lid for the Dodge Viper SRT10 coupe was designed for customer convenience as well as for structural integrity. The deck lid opening was deeply integrated into the rear fascia, which offered a low lift-over height for stowing cargo. Gas struts held the deck lid in place when it was open. When closed, the deck lid was secured with a lock that met federal regulations for latch safety.

The SRT10 Coupe was originally available only in Viper Blue with twin Stone White racing stripes. The interior

featured a distinctive two-tone color scheme and unique interior pieces in the coupe included various weatherstrip pieces, a headliner, the carpeting and the trim panels. The "double-bubble" roof was promoted as a way to give race drivers additional helmet room.

Under the coupe's hood was an aluminum-block 8.3-liter (505-cid) V-10 that generated 500 hp and 525 lbs.-ft. of torque. The engine was hooked to a heavy-duty six-speed manual transmission.

Braking power for the coupe was supplied by Brembo 44/40 dual-opposing piston calipers in the front and Brembo 42/38 dual-opposing calipers in the rear. They gripped on 14-inch brake rotors. An anti-lock braking system (ABS) prevented lock-up during hard braking. This resulted in a world-class braking performance of 60-to-0 mph in less than 100 feet.

The coupe relied on a race-bred, four-wheel independent suspension featuring lightweight, high-performance aluminum control arms and knuckles, damped by lightweight coil-over shock absorbers. Power was delivered to the pavement via a Dana 44-4 Hydra-Lok speed-sensing limited-slip differential.

The SRT10 coupe rode on unique forged aluminum wheels, size 18 x 10 up front and size 19 x 13 at the rear. Each wheel carried a Michelin-made zero-pressure run-flat tire with a low-pressure sensor in the valve stem.

1957 Supercharged "T-Bird Special"

If you had to name Ford Motor Company's earliest muscle car, you'd be safe picking the 1957 model with a supercharged 312 cid V-8 as a good candidate. It was the company's first over-300-hp out-of-the-box engine option. Officially, it was rated at exactly 300 ponies, but Ford general manager Robert McNamara was known as a conservative guy and race car builders estimated the real output of the street version at 325 hp. There was also a special NASCAR version of the engine that put out 340 hp.

Ford racecar driver "Fireball" Roberts proved the motor's muscle by averaging 107.9 mph to win the Rebel 300 stock car race at Darlington, South Carolina, that year. The 27 wins by Fords in Grand National events was an all-time high for the marque and tied Hudson's record.

During Ford's first year of racing, in 1956, the most powerful motor available in the showroom was the then-new 312 with a four-barrel and 225 hp at 4600 rpm. As the competition heated up, a dual four-barrel carburetion system bumped the numbers up to 260 hp at 4600 rpm. Both of these motors used an 8.4:1 compression ratio.

For 1957, Ford needed a car that could keep up with Chrysler 300 Letter Cars and fuel-injected Chevys. The compression of the 312-cid Ford V-8 was boosted to 9.7:1, giving 245 hp at 4500 rpm with one four-barrel carburetor and 270 hp at 4800 rpm with two four-barrel carbs. This was not quite enough, but in midyear, the supercharged Ford engine arrived. It had an 8.5:1 compression ratio with a McCulloch supercharger. (The dual-quad motor also got the higher compression and increased to 285 hp at about the same time.)

With 80 more ponies than the '56 V-8s, the latest Ford stockers really moved out. The big engine worked extremely well in the light Custom/Custom 300 Tudor Sedan, which had a 116-inch wheelbase and weighed just over 3,100 lbs. It was also a favorite for the convertible racing classes, where 118-inch Fairlane 500 Sunliners competed.

Neither body style had a whole lot of time to achieve its supercharged racing potential though. By June, the Automobile Manufacturer's Association issued a ban on advertising racing results and McNamara pulled the plug on factory support. Independent teams continued to run, but there would be no more special hardware coming from Dearborn to help them out, until the 1960s.

1957 Thunderbird "F-Code"

The 1957 Ford Thunderbird, like all two-seat Thunderbirds, is among the most collectible. And the '57 Thunderbird equipped with a supercharger as a factory option, heads the list of classic Thunderbirds for not only being the hottest Thunderbird on the road, but also on the auction block.

Engine options increased in 1957 with high-performance, racing and super-charger options. The supercharged version of the 1957 Thunderbird is the rarest. The first 15 production super-charged Thunderbirds were reportedly built in January, 1957, to homologate the engine for NASCAR competition.

The very first factory-sponsored supercharged Thunderbirds were actually 1956 models built by Peter DePaolo Engineering in Long Beach, California. Several 1957 Thunderbirds were then similarly modified for racing.

A modified, blown 'Bird with a 1/4-inch stroked crank, aerodynamic light body panels and a beefed-up gearbox and rear end, beat the Corvettes at the 1957 Daytona Spring Speed Week Trials. It blasted through the two-way Flying Mile on the beach at 138.755 mph. And later that year at the Bonneville speed trials, the same car topped 160 mph.

On the 1957 T-birds, the code letter of each engine type leads off the serial number. Supercharged cars could be either D or F cars.

The "D" cars came with a 312 cid V-8 with a four-barrel carburetor used with automatic and overdrive transmissions—90 percent of automatics.

Fifteen D-types were fitted with Paxton-McCulloch superchargers and are popularly referred to as "DFs." Their serial numbers will be near 30,000.

1957 Thunderbirds with a serial number of "F" featured the 312 cid V-8 with four-barrel carburetor and a Paxton McCulloch VR57 supercharger. A special head reduced compression to 8.5:1. Production of the 196 F engines began in spring. They were available at a factory invoice price of $340. There were three grooves on the crank pulley and the manual transmission cars used two belts for the supercharger. With an automatic transmission, the front groove was larger and drove the super-charger with a single belt.

Supercharged T-birds also boasted reinforced cylinder heads, modified combustion chambers with lower compression ratio and a dual-point distributor developed by Gus Davis of Peter DePaolo Engineering. Certain models also had a hotter camshaft of 290 degrees duration versus the stock unit of 256 degrees.

In order to deliver fuel to the carburetor fuel bowl, the fuel pump itself was modified; the metered combination of blower bleed air and carburetor vacuum pressure was injected into the atmosphere side of the fuel pump to obtain a pump pressure greater than the carburetor pressure. A supercharged Thunderbird couldn't have gotten its gas without this positive differential.

Horsepower ratings with fine-tuning ranged from 325 to 340.

The formal total of 211 superchargers in the D and F series is an approximation. Some of the Thunderbirds with an F letter don't have the blower, special heads or manifolds. Many original owners removed the superchargers because they were noisy and not oil-tight. Also a Ford dealer in 1957 would probably have been willing to add a supercharger to a D or E 312-cid engine, or remove one from an F-series car if the buyer wanted it.

FORD

The supercharged V-8 is a rare find under the hood of a 1957 Thunderbird.

Mike Mueller

The 1957 Thunderbird was a small car with a big engine
when it was outfitted with the F-Code with well over 300 hp.

John Gunnell

Cars like the 1958 Fairlane 500 convertible with an "Interceptor"
V-8 laid the groundwork for better muscle cars to come.

FORD

1958 "Interceptor" V-8

While not a big year for Ford Motor Company high-performance or racing, the 1958 season saw an important development which would become significant to the company's development of some great muscle cars in the future. This was the introduction of Dearborn's first "big-block" V-8s. This "FE" series of engines started with 332-cid and 352-cid motors, although the later-to-be-famous "390" had originally been planned.

The Automobile Manufacturers Association's ban on high-performance advertising and promotions led to shelving these plans until 1963. So, Ford lovers were left with three 1958 big-block choices. The Interceptor 332, with 9.5:1 compression, generated 240 hp at 4600 rpm using a two-barrel carburetor, and 265 hp at 4600 rpm using a four-barrel carburetor. The latter was called the Interceptor Special 332. Top option was the Interceptor Special 352, a 10.2:1 compression job rated for 300 hp at 4600 rpm.

Since Ford Motor Company was officially out of racing, all three engines were marketed only in a moderate state of tune for street use. Ford had not yet started to cheat on the AMA ban by making special speed equipment available on an under-the-counter basis, as GM had done right from the start. However, high-performance buffs liked the new motors and found them suitable for modifications. In stock car circles, many builders stuck with the 116-inch wheelbase Ford Custom models, which ran like scat with big-blocks shoe-horned in below the hood. These cars racked up 10 Grand National victories and six other checkered flags, even without official factory racing support.

At the drag strips, the big-engined Fords in stock 300 hp format took about 17.7 seconds to run the quarter-mile. Zero-to-60 was achieved in about 10.2 seconds. These cars had a better power-to-weight ratio than conventional '57 Ford engines, although they could not out-perform the supercharged motor.

Although the company halted racing support, its competition director, Jacques Passino, made a deal to get John Holman and Ralph Moody together to purchase the factory parts inventory. This kept Fords running as entries of independent teams and sustained the performance image without direct corporate involvement. Junior Johnson was the year's winningest Ford pilot, with eight victories.

FORD

Jerry Heasley

The 1960 Ford Galaxie was available with the 360-hp Thunderbird Super V-8.

1960 Galaxie 352/360 Special

"We like the way it looks, we like the way it rides, we like the way it corners, we like the way it stops and we especially like how it goes when equipped with the 360-horsepower engine." That's what *Hot Rod* magazine's technical editor Ray Brock said after road testing the 1960 Ford Galaxie 352/360 special. Back in the early '60s, this was the performer that Ford fans had been waiting for, with a tri-power V-8 engine capable of pushing a stock-bodied coupe way over the 150-mph mark.

As the 1960 full-sized domestic cars began appearing in the showrooms, it became quite apparent at the drag strips and on the racetracks that "performance options" was no longer the dirty term it had been for the past two or so years. Cubic inches, ram induction, multi-carburetor setups and different combinations of each were made widely available.

An exception at the start of the model year was the full-sized Ford. Its hottest option since 1958 was the 352-cid 300-hp V-8.

The big Fords were bigger than ever. Their wheelbase was up an inch to 119 inches. The overall length increased 5.7 inches to 213.7 inches. Overall width was the widest ever at 81.5 inches, an increase of 3.9 inches.

Styling departed radically from the popular and conservative 1959 Fords. Grille-mounted headlights and gull-wing fins gave deep meaning to the often-used term "all-new." At the top of the line was the sleek Starliner two-door hardtop and its convertible counterpart the Sunliner. Technically, they were in a Galaxie Special series. They came with six-cylinder engines or a variety of V-8s.

Ford got a late start in the new performance sweepstakes, but before the end of 1959 it had released its 360-hp Thunderbird Super V-8, which was based on the 352. It was also called the "Interceptor" or "Super Interceptor" and carried an "R" code. This engine was not initially available with Cruise-O-Matic, but only with a Borg-Warner T-85 three-speed manual gearbox, with or without overdrive. A Holley 540-cfm four-barrel carburetor, an aluminum intake manifold, new cast-iron exhaust headers, a cast nodular crank, solid valve lifters, a 10.6:1 compression ratio and a dual-point ignition system all helped.

The muscular combination was available on any full-sized 1960 model. *Motor Life* magazine got hold of a pre-production example and found it capable of going from 0-to-60 mph in 7.5 seconds with a top speed of 152 mph. Obviously, it had been modified a bit over the production version.

The most desirable combination for the 360-hp 352 is with a Starliner two-door hardtop or a Sunliner convertible.

FORD

Jerry Heasley

**In 1960, Ford said it was ready to return to support racing again,
and made waves with its 375- and 401-hp-equipped Starliner.**

1961 Galaxie Starliner 390

"In base form, the Ford 390 V-8 was nothing to write home about," admitted *Car Review* magazine in December 1985. "But by using some components from the earlier 352 Interceptor, Ford came up with the 375-hp 390 Thunderbird Special. Put that in your Galaxie and smoke the tires." Despite its spaceship name and looks, the '61 Galaxie had the underhood stuff to make a drag strip competitor feel like a tricycler with a CHP cruiser on its tail.

The year 1961 was a big one for Ford performance. Inspired by the "win-on-Sunday-sell-on-Monday" marketing mentality, the company released a 390-cid V-8 at the start of the year and a four-speed manual transmission near the end of the season. Both performance add-ons were hot options for the steamy Starliner hardtop.

In 1960, Ford had advised the Automobile Manufacturers Association (AMA) that it was suspending its support of the trade organization's 4-year-old ban on stock car racing. The company then showed up at the Daytona Motor Speedway with a 360-engined Starliner that ran 40 laps at an average of 142 mph.

By fall, similar cars had been put into the hands of racing car drivers and racked up 15 checkered flags in Grand National stock car competition. At the same time, a re-entry into factory-backed drag racing was made and a "three deuces" carburetor setup was legalized by the National Hot Rod Association.

The new-for-'61 Starliner was smaller, but had a bigger engine. Three versions of the 390-cid V-8 were offered. The standard rating was 300 hp. A police car variant was rated for 330 hp. Tops on the list was the 375-hp Thunderbird Super edition with a four-barrel carburetor. At midyear, when the triple two-barrel carburetor system was released, it pushed the big engine up to 401 hp. After it was approved for NHRA racing, Fords dominated their classes.

Both engines featured a 4.05 x 3.78-inch bore and stroke and 10.6:1 compression ratio. The Thunderbird Special generated 375 hp at 6000 rpm. The Thunderbird Special 6V gave 401 hp at 6000 rpm.

The V-8 Starliner had a base price of $2,713 and tipped the scales at 3,615 lbs. Prices on the engine options were about $199 for the 300-hp V-8, $350 for the 375-hp job and $425 for the 401-hp edition.

Performance-wise, the 6V (six-venturi) engine was capable of 7-second 0-to-60 mph runs and quarter-miles with ETs just over 15 seconds. This definitely put it into the "muscle car" category. Starliner production—including sixes and smaller V-8s—was 29,669 units. However, the number of 390-cid/401-hp and 390-cid/375-hp cars built was smaller.

FORD

Doug Mitchel

The 1962 Galaxie 500XL could nudge 140 mph with a 406-cid triple-carburetor V-8 that produced 405 hp.

1962 Galaxie 500/500XL

Certainly not the least significant attraction of the 1962 Fords was their appearance. They stand out as one of the best examples of Ford's competence level in car design.

With a 209-inch overall length they were large automobiles, but their clean lines—now totally free of fender fins and devoid of any overtones of General Motors influence—gave them a handsome appearance.

Ford got back into performance in 1960. It was more of the same in 1961. The results included the debut of the triple-carbureted 390-cid V-8 with 401 hp and a Borg-Warner four-speed gearbox for any 390 engines.

Shortly after New Year's celebrations ended in 1962, Ford piped on board a new 406-cid V-8 packing 405 hp at 5800 rpm. This "Thunderbird Special 406" carried over the triple carbs, special cam, valve gear, ignition, bearings and exhaust system of the 390-cid/401-hp engine. A 385-hp version with a single four-barrel carburetor was also available.

Despite the similarity to previous engines, there were some changes that reflected Ford's growing expertise in developing modern, high-performance automobiles. The 406-cid engine block, with its larger 3.78-inch bore, used a totally different casting that provided thicker cylinder walls.

To cope with the 406's added power, stronger pistons and connecting rods were installed and the oil relief valve

was set at 60 psi instead of 45 psi. Dual valve springs with greater maximum load were also used on the 406.

Included in the $379.70 price tag of the 406 engine (one of which was Ford's 30,000,000th V-8) was a comprehensive performance package. Its most obvious feature was an excellent Borg-Warner four-speed transmission with ratios of 2.36:1, 1.78:1, 1.41:1 and 1.0:1. Less apparent—until the 406 Ford got into motion—were its stiffer (by 20 percent) springs and shocks. In *Hot Rod* magazine, Ray Brock opined, "Anyway you look at it, this is a bargain-priced hi-po automobile. Ford should not have any trouble selling 10,000 of these items."

Ford didn't offer sintered metallic brake linings, but 3-inch brake drums fitted with harder linings did a respectable job of hauling the 2 tons of Ford down from a maximum velocity approaching 140 mph.

Ford also added substantial strength to its high-performance driveline. For example, a 9-inch-diameter ring gear was found at the rear, in place of the 8.75-inch unit used in 1961. A 3-inch diameter drive shaft was also fitted, along with a four-pinion differential.

With Ford's standard 3.56:1 ratio rear axle, the typical 405-hp Galaxie was capable of 0-to-60-mph runs in 7 seconds and of doing the quarter-mile in 15.5 seconds at 92 mph.

The 1963 Galaxies and Galaxie 500XLs were definitely ready to
run when equipped with one of two 427-cid engine options.

FORD

Jerry Heasley

1963 Galaxie 427

"The Chevrolets were fast but frail, the Pontiacs were strong, but not strong enough," wrote Brock Yates early in 1963. "When the flag fell on the fifth annual Daytona 500, there were five Ford fastbacks rumbling across the line in a hot, noisy formation." The 427-cid V-8 just didn't take no for an answer, and Ford proved it at Daytona that memorable year.

Ford realized that it was going to be necessary to support a racing program if it expected to compete in the muscle car market of the 1960s. That thinking was behind the company's late 1962 release of two powerful new engine options based on a 406-cid V-8. Version one used a single four-barrel carburetor to generate 385 hp. The second carried three two-barrel carburetors and was advertised at 405 hp.

Ford really got its act into gear around the middle of 1963. Its first step was the release of the good-looking 1963 1/2 Galaxie fastback. Then came a new 427-cid V-8 with massive muscle for the street, the drag strip and the NASCAR superspeedways.

To promote the 427-powered 1963 Galaxie, Ford manufactured 50 special cars at its factory in Atlanta, Georgia. These cars were "factory lightweights" made exclusively for going down the quarter-mile faster than the competition.

They had fiberglass doors, hoods, trunks and front-end components. The bumpers and other parts were made of aluminum. Virtually everything that wasn't needed for racing was left off the cars.

For motivation, the Galaxie lightweights got a 427-cid V-8 with two Holley 600-cfm four-barrel carburetors advertised at 425 hp at 6000 rpm. The actual output was much higher. The engine was attached to a special version of Ford's "top-loader" four-speed manual gearbox that had an aluminum case to cut even more weight off. These cars tipped the scales at below 3,500 lbs. and ran the quarter-mile in the low-12-second bracket at just under 120 mph!

In addition to the just-for-racing cars, FoMoCo produced 4,978 big Fords with one of two versions of the 427-cid V-8. One was the 425-hp engine tuned for the street. It had dual Holley 540-cfm carburetors on top of a cast-aluminum intake manifold and most owners who took these cars racing on weekends felt that the power rating was very conservative. The second street engine was a 427-cid V-8 with a single four-barrel carburetor. It produced 410 hp. Both of the big engines were available in Galaxie or Galaxie 500 XL two-door hardtops. The dual-quad engine was a $461.60 option.

Phil Kunz

**Fiberglass body parts and aluminum bumpers shaved weight off the
race-ready Galaxie Lightweight and made the car ideal for the drag strip.**

FORD

1963 Galaxie Lightweight

Although some people regarded 1963 Ford styling changes as "minor," it wasn't hard to identify the new models. For those interested in how the new Ford would "go," the car shined on race tracks early in the year, showing off both of Ford's new 427-cid V-8 and 1963 1/2 fastback body.

The 427-cid engine was based on the 406-cid V-8 with a 4.23-inch bore and 3.78-inch stroke. It encompassed design improvements outlined in Ford's "Total Performance" program.

Beginning with cross-bolted mains (numbers two, three and four), lighter-weight impact-extruding aluminum pistons and stronger connecting rods, the 427 had many advantages over the 406. With twin fours, the Thunderbird 427-cid high-performance V-8 produced 425 hp at 6000 rpm and 480 lbs.-ft. of torque at 3700 rpm.

Since NASCAR did not allow multi-carb setups to run on its superspeedways, Ford also offered a single four-barrel 427-cid/410-hp (at 5600 rpm) job with 476 lbs.-ft. of torque at 3400 rpm.

Although some questioned the use of the term "fastback" for Ford's 1963 1/2 model, there was good reason for its existence. By adopting the "sportsroof" for NASCAR competition, Ford had a car that could maintain 160 mph with 100 less hp.

The lightweight fastbacks were made to let it all hang out on the drag strip. Ford offered these hardtops only in a white-and-red exterior/interior color combination.

Although the drag model's steel body was identical to that of a stock Galaxie, all bolt-on items, such as the doors, trunk lid, hood and front fenders, were constructed of fiberglass. Aluminum was used for the bumpers. The interiors offered only the basics: skinny front buckets, cheap floor mats and absolutely no sound deadening.

With 425 hp, these Galaxies—which the NHRA declared eligible for both super stock and stock eliminator competitions—were capable of quarter-mile marks of 12 seconds and 118 mph.

Hot Rod (July 1963) asserted, "a tremendous improvement over 1962 … from the 352 high-performance of 1960 to this 427 engine, there has been a constant flow of improvement."

Before the competition season came to a close, Ford offered a "Mark II" version of the 427-cid V-8 with new cylinder heads. It had larger ports and valves, an aluminum high-rise manifold, stronger connecting rods, a forged-steel crankshaft and a 10-quart oil pan.

The tremendous performance of the 427-cid NASCAR Ford was demonstrated in a road test of a car that stock-car builders Holman & Moody had prepared. It was conducted by *Car Life* magazine. Although rated at 410 hp, the true output of the 427, after the Holman & Moody treatment, was closer to 500 hp. With a 3.50:1 rear axle, the Ford's top speed was approximately 155 mph. Even with this gearing, however, the Ford was a strong sprinter with *Car Life* (February 1964) reporting the following acceleration times: 0-to-30 mph in 2.3 seconds; 0-to-60 mph in 6.3 seconds and 0-to-100 mph in 13.2 seconds. The same car did the quarter-mile in 14.2 seconds at 105 mph.

Ordering the "K" Code in the 1964 Fairlane would get a
muscle-minded buyer 271 hp from his 289 small-block.

FORD

1964 Fairlane Hi-Po ("K" Code)

Along with new styling, the 1964 Ford Fairlane offered some neat engine options based on he 289-cid small-block V-8. The original version of this engine was the 221-cid V-8, which grew to 260 cid and then to 289 cid. The 289 was originally designed for use in the mid-sized Fairlane and was an option for Falcons and Comets. However, it was most famous as a Mustang power plant and the Mustang was marketed with the support of a "Cobra" parts program that could take the hot "K" code 271-hp of the 289 and make it even hotter.

In 1964, the basic "C" code version of the Challenger 289 had a 9.0:1 compression ratio and a two-barrel carburetor. It generated 195 hp at 4400 rpm and there was nothing "muscular" about that. There was an "A" code edition with a four-barrel carburetor and a 9.8:1 compression ratio, which generated 225 hp—acceptable for keeping up with traffic on the freeway. But for muscle car fans, the only way to order it was as a "K" code or "Hi-Po" version. This meant that you got a 10.5:1 compression ratio and 271 horses at 6000 rpm with a single Holley four-barrel carb.

FORD

Wieck Media

Fairlane "Thunderbolts" earned their reputation as no-frills tire-shredders. They were built for sprinting, but their production run, like their races, was over in a blink.

1964 Fairlane "Thunderbolt"

A few years back, we watched in awe as a pack of restored 1964 Ford Fairlane "T-Bolts" blasted down the track during the "Muscle Car Showdown" event at Quaker State Dragway in Ohio. Back in May of 1964, *Car Life* magazine's Allen Hunt said of the T-Bolt, "Obviously it's a racing car . . . and one calculated to Ford right back in the front row on the drag strips this summer."

These cars had fiberglass fenders, teardrop-shaped hood blisters, Plexiglas windows, lightweight bucket seats, a cold-air induction system, 8000 rpm Rotunda tachometers, modified front suspensions (to accommodate the 427), a long list of equipment deletions and many special competition equipment features. The 425-hp big-block V-8 actually cranked out more like 500 hp. It was linked to a beefed-up Lincoln automatic or a Borg-Warner T-10 four-speed manual transmission.

The 1964 Fairlane Special Performance drag vehicles soon adopted the Thunderbolt name and also became known as "T-Bolts." Demand was strong enough to prompt the ordering of a second batch of 54 all-white cars. Racing driver Gas Ronda dominated NHRA's 1964 World Championship with 190 points by running his T-Bolt through the quarter-mile in 11.6 seconds at 124 mph.

Ford records show that the first 11 cars left the factory painted maroon and 10 of them had four-speed transmissions. The 100 additional cars produced were painted white when they were built and 89 of them had four-speed gearboxes. At least one 1965 Thunderbolt-style car was raced by Darrell Droke. However, the new Mustang soon took over as Ford's best offering for drag-car enthusiasts and the short life of T-Bolts halted at that point.

The 1964 Galaxie 427 with the dragster option.

FORD

Jerry Heasley

1964 Galaxie 427

After their 1-2-3-4-5 finish at the '63 Daytona 500, 427-powered Ford Galaxies became a legend in NASCAR-land. But, despite their best-ever-for-Ford performances on drag strips and racetracks, the 1963 Galaxie lightweights had not dominated quarter-mile competition the way Ford hoped they would.

At first the hot Fords competed with Pontiac's powerful 421 Super Duty V-8, and later the Chrysler Hemi V-8 came along. To keep up with the Joneses, Ford changed its focus to mid-size muscle by launching its fleet of Fairlane-based Thunderbolts that could run down a drag strip in less than 12 seconds at close to 125 mph.

However, the 427-powered full-sized Fords were still the hot ticket for stock car racing and to get them sanctioned for NASCAR competition the company kept producing big muscle cars. "With performance a byword at Ford these days, it's not surprising that the plant's '64s look as though they should go places quickly," noted *Car Life* magazine.

In addition to looking fast, the new Galaxie offered a big-car-based lightweight drag package as well. The 1964 Galaxie A/Stock dragster package was offered for two-door models. Also available was a B/Stock Dragster package that added a low-riser manifold for the monstrous 427-cid V-8 engine.

These cars came in white with red interiors. Body sealer, sound deadening insulation and heaters were deleted. Lightweight seats and a fiberglass "power bubble" hood were added. The grilles were modified with fiberglass air-induction vents.

The 427-cid V-8 was also offered in two versions for production-type full-sized 1964 Fords. The "Thunderbird High-Performance" option carried code "Q" and was the 410-hp (at 5600 rpm) version. The specifications for this power plant included a 4.23 x 3.78-inch bore and stroke, an 11.5:1 compression ratio and a single Holley four-barrel carburetor. The "Thunderbird Super High-Performance" engine carried code "R" and added two larger Holley carburetors to boost output to 425 hp at 6000 rpm. A 427-powered stock-bodied Ford was basically good for a 0-to-60 time of just over 6 seconds and a quarter-mile time of just under 15 seconds.

By 1964, the full-sized Fords had grown a little big for even NASCAR racing. Dodges and Plymouths were not only lighter, but had the Hemi engine to help them set the pace in stock car racing. Ford tried to get an overhead-cam version of the 427-cid V-8 sanctioned, but NASCAR said that it didn't qualify as a production engine. Instead, a high-rise manifold and "high-rev" package were certified as production options and legalized for racing.

FORD

The Cobra 289 was a competition killer and an instant legend. Ford had its name on
the body, but the blazing-fast Cobra was actually a make and marque unto itself.

Jerry Heasley

1965 Shelby-American AC/Cobra 289

"When the Cobra is certified for production sports racing, a fox will have been dropped among the chickens," said *Car Life* magazine. Well, we don't know about feathers, but fiberglass was flying all around the hen house after the Cobra arrived in Ford dealerships.

The Cobra is perhaps the ultimate American road warrior because it brought this country its first and only World Manufacturer's Championship in auto racing. The year was 1965 and the car was the 289 Cobra roadster. Despite the British origins of its AC Ace chassis, which was highly beefed-up and modified to accept American V-8 power, the Cobra was by rights its own unique marque. It was built by Shelby-American of Los Angeles, California. Carroll Shelby contracted with AC of England for the chassis and body and put the dream together using engines from Ford.

When the Cobra became a reality, AC had its name on the car. So did Ford, thanks to the use of "Powered By Ford" fender badges. However, the Cobra vision belonged to Carroll Shelby and Cobra was officially the name of the marque. A Cobra is not an AC and it is not a Ford. A Cobra is a Cobra. Shelby built small-block-powered versions from 1961 to 1965

and big-block versions from 1965-1967.

The small-block Cobra, which weighed slightly over 2,000 lbs., was easily capable of speeds topping 150 mph, and was quicker than literally any other sports car sold to the public.

Shelby's original idea was to sell a street version of the race vehicle to finance the cars on the track, although any final accounting would certainly reveal that Ford Motor Company backed the Shelby-American racing program to benefit from the on-track publicity associated with its new small-block V-8.

Shelby accomplished the ultimate with his Cobra, beating archrival Ferrari for the World Manufacturer's Championship.

At the end of the production run of the small-block roadster, Shelby-American built about 30 cars with automatic transmissions. Carroll Shelby drove one, and still owns it to this day. He favored the automatic for everyday use, but still also owns a big-block 427 Cobra roadster. Sadly, most of the automatics were changed over to four-speeds, but a few do exist today.

Jerry Heasley

FORD

For a big car, the Galaxie 427 was plenty quick off the line and a nice all-around muscle car.

1965 Galaxie 427

Though the Mustangs and Malibus of the world were better suited to the budgets of the young car buyers most interested in muscle cars, there was always a substantial number of young-at-heart car enthusiasts who needed roomier cars and wanted them to go fast. They were "money-is-no-object" type buyers and Detroit had the hardware available to build what they wanted, as long as they were quite willing to pay for it. That big-block V-8 shoe-horned under a Fairlane's hood could fit into a Galaxie with a whole lot less hassle. In addition, this kind of full-size "squeeze job" was usually a lot more profitable

The 1965 full-sized Fords were billed as "the newest since 1949." Luxury and comfort were emphasized in the new Custom, Custom 500, Galaxie 500, Galaxie 500XL and Galaxie 500 LTD series. It was the first year for coil spring rear suspension and promotions were geared towards the new LTD being quieter than a Rolls-Royce.

Clean, sharp, square lines characterized the fresh new body styling that was set off by a radiator grille with thin, horizontal bars and dual headlights stacked on top of each other. There was a slight "Coke bottle" shape to the rear of the body.

Ford continued offering the 427-cid V-8 for the big cars to help maintain Ford's "total performance" image. It didn't fit into other models like the Falcon, Mustang and Fairlane without extensive modifications, but it was a drop-in for the big Galaxie. Fortunately for Ford, NASCAR had kicked the Chrysler Hemi V-8 out of stock car racing, so FoMoCo's 427-powered stock cars took a record of 48 Grand National wins.

The Galaxie 500XL series was the sport trim version of the Galaxie 500 two-door hardtop ($3,167) and convertible ($3,426) and included all Galaxie 500 trim plus bucket seats, a floor-mounted shift lever, polished door-trim panels and carpeting on the lower portion of the doors. It's likely that the majority of full-sized Fords fitted with the 427 (except for all-out race cars) were Galaxie 500XL models.

A Galaxie 500XL two-door hardtop with the 427-cid/425-hp Thunderbird Super High-Performance V-8 could be purchased for as little as $3,233 in 1965. And even though it was a big car with a 119-inch wheelbase, a 210-inch overall length and a curb weight of 3,507 lbs., it still carried only 9.6 pounds per horsepower with the big-block V-8 installed. It could fly from 0-to-60 mph in 6.8 seconds and did the quarter-mile in only 14.9 seconds.

The GT package made the already popular Mustang a truly exciting machine.

FORD

1965 Mustang GT

Though it was far from the fastest car of the '60s, the Mustang GT played a big role in building enthusiasm for muscle cars and rarely gets full credit for its contribution to muscle car history. As *Car Life* magazine put it, "Ford started a round-up of its state-of-the-Total-Performance art to produce the Mustang GT." But before getting into the go-fast details, let's review Mustang history a bit.

It is not often that a car comes along and gets to create its own market segment, but that is what happened when Ford introduced the Mustang sporty compact on April 17, 1964. Mustang initiated the all-new "pony car" segment, and the market for the cars was large and long lasting.

There is argument among purists over whether the Mustangs produced prior to September 1964 are 1964 1/2 or 1965 models. However, when it comes to the interesting and collectible GT equipment group, there can be no question, as it was introduced for the first anniversary of the Mustang's introduction on April 17, 1965.

The Mustang had already become a desirable commodity. Its standard equipment included bucket seats. It had the immediately popular long hood, short deck look. At first it came as a sport coupe (two-door hardtop) and a sporty-looking convertible. In the fall of 1964, a fastback model

called the 2+2 was added to the lineup. From the outset, the options list was important in marketing the Mustang. Buyers could add lots of appearance and convenience extras, plus some bolt-on high-performance hardware. However, being based on the low-priced compact Falcon, there was some room for improvement in the go-fast department.

Combining available mechanical features with new visual pieces made the GT package a fairly thorough upgrade. First, the buyer had to order an optional V-8 engine, which at the time included the 225-hp Challenger Special 289 at $157, or the high-performance 271-hp/289-cid engine for $430.

The GT option included quick-ratio steering, disc front brakes, chromed dual exhaust tips that exited through the rear valance panel, a new grille bar with fog lights built in and GT instrumentation—which replaced the Falcon-based instrument panel with five round dials. Throw in GT badging and lower body striping and you had a bargain for around $150.

Although the exact number of Mustangs built with GT equipment is not available, they had a massive following and the installation rate for this option increased even more when Ford later released the appearance items separately for dealer installation.

FORD

Jerry Heasley

Only 36 of the ready-to-race "R" Code Shelby Mustangs were built for 1965.

1965 Shelby Mustang GT 350 "R" Code

The "R" is for race, no joke. After serial number 34, Shelby-American began inserting an R as the second digit of the vehicle identification number (VIN). But in the early days, both Ford and Shelby-American were not entirely clear on the direction of this new high-performance Mustang.

Two things were certain. First, Ford wanted a higher-performance, specialty version of the Mustang. Second, it wanted a car that could compete with Chevy's Corvette. The latter suggested a two-seat car and this could be achieved by removing the back seat from a Mustang 2+2 fastback. Higher performance meant hopping up the 289-cid V-8, since Ford's big-block engines would not fit in the Mustang and because the small-block worked best for road racing.

Both jobs were turned over to Shelby-American of Los Angeles, which had taken the AC-based Cobra roadster and thrashed Corvettes in USRRC (United States Road Race of Champions) racing. At the same time, the Cobra completely overpowered the Corvette in SCCA A-production racing and beat out Ferrari for the World Manufacturer's Championship.

Ford felt that it made a lot of sense to hire Shelby to turn the Mustang into a car that could beat the Corvette in SCCA B-production racing. The automaker knew this would further reinforce the muscular image of Ford's new pony car.

Shelby-American proceeded to build a street version of a new GT Mustang, which Carroll Shelby himself named the GT 350. It was a rather obvious reference to the 350-cid small-block engine from Chevrolet, although Shelby gave the press some story about walking off 350 steps.

With racing victories a major goal, Shelby-American also built a race-ready competition model that was not meant for street use. It was called the R-model.

To satisfy SCCA regulations at least 100 cars (race and street versions) had to be built. Therefore, 100 white fastbacks—each fitted with 289-cid high-performance K-code V-8s with solid valve lifters and 271 hp—were lifted off an assembly line at the Ford plant in San Jose, California.

The R-model came with the high-performance features of the street GT 350—the 289-cid 306-hp small-block with a hi-rise aluminum intake manifold, four-speed transmission, No-Spin differential, lowered suspension and lots more—plus special R-model features. The GT 350 R code Mustang was so specialized that a mere 36 were sold. However, they were available to anyone willing to pay the base price of $5,950 to buy an out-of-the-box race winner. The 1965 GT 350 R was the SCCA B-production national champion in 1965, 1966 and 1967.

1966 Fairlane 427

The 427 Fairlane was the product of corporate thinking; an attempt to salvage some commercial benefit from the 1963 Thunderbolt drag-racing program. While the T-Bolts had been built for racing only, the later big-block Fairlanes were meant to excite showroom shoppers seeking the ultimate in street performance machines.

Ford did a total redesign of the Fairlane for 1966. The engineers specifically left enough room in the engine compartment so the 427 could be shoehorned under the hood. Nothing was held back because of the sales theme Ford wanted to push at the time. When *Hot Rod's* Eric Dahlquist reviewed a 427-powered Fairlane in the magazine's July 1966 issue, he pointed out that Charlie Gray of Ford's Performance Division and Bill Hollbrook of the company's Performance & Economy Section had helped to develop the car as part of the company's "Total Performance" program.

This program was aimed at taking the wind out of the sails of Mopar and General Motors. FoMoCo's 390 V-8 was eating the dust generated by Hemis, GTOs, 4-4-2s and SS-396 Chevelles. The fact that the 427 out-cubed Mopar's various 426s was no coincidence. It was an engine designed to turn on the hot rodders who wanted a Ford that could smoke the competition.

Identified by a big, long lift-off fiberglass hood with a huge scoop taking in air just above the grille, the Fairlane 500s and 500XLs equipped with the big-block came in 410-hp (single four-barrel) and 425-hp (with twin Holley four-barrel carburetors) configurations. The cars also featured NASCAR-style hood locking pins, chrome engine parts, 11.2-inch diameter disc brakes, a 2 1/4-inch diameter exhaust system, a heavy-duty suspension and a tachometer.

Hot Rod did not do a full road test of the 1966 Fairlane 427, but reported some figures quoted by "some of the mechanics on the project," which indicated quarter-mile runs in 14.5 to 14.6 seconds at 100 mph. Later, on drag strips with some tuning and racing slicks, the cars were found capable of doing the distance in just under 13 seconds at nearly 114 mph.

Only about 60 such cars were produced in 1966, but they gave the midsize Fords a muscle car image that boosted the entire line's market impact. In drag racing, the Fairlane 427s were so dominant that the rules were soon changed and they wound up in F/SX class, even though they were technically factory production models. In stock car racing, the medium-riser 427s were deemed legal and gave Ford a winning advantage over single four-barrel Mopars. (Dual-quad Hemis were not sanctioned to compete.)

1966 Fairlane GT/GTA

They could have written a song about this mighty muscle car. It would go, "Little GTA, you really give me a thrill, four-barrel and a Sport shift and a 390 mill . . . wind 'em up, wind 'em out, you wound up like the GTO." The Fairlane GT/GTA was Ford's "Tiger" and brand loyalty dictated that it would hit the streets to prove itself. *Car Life's* Gene Booth said, "The GTA (do you suppose it will be called 'GeeTAw') plants Ford firmly in the performance market."

The first production Fairlanes able to carry a big-block V-8 were the totally redesigned 1966 models. The size of the Fairlane body didn't change much on the outside, but the increased dimensions under the hood became important in the muscle car era. These cars served as Ford's factory hot rods when they were equipped with the monster V-8s. They competed head to head with the GTO and a Ford advertisement for the high-performance model was titled "How to cook a tiger!"

The Fairlane GT came with a 390-cid/315-hp V-8 as standard equipment. The Fairlane GTA included a 335-hp version of the 390-cid V-8, chrome-plated rocker covers, oil filter cap, radiator cap, air cleaner cover and dip stick, a high-lift cam, a bigger carburetor and the two-way three-speed Sport Shift automatic transmission that could be used like an automatic or like a manual gearbox.

A limited number of Fairlanes were sold with "side-oiler" 427-cid wedge engines. Some of these cars even hit the NASCAR ovals. The 427-powered Fairlanes were characterized by a big air scoop that gulped cold air at the front of the hood. Only about 60 Fairlanes with 427s were produced.

Both Fairlane GT models were part of the fancy 500/XL line. The two-door hardtop sold for $2,843 and 33,015 were built. With the production of 4,327 units, the $3,068 base-price convertible was much rarer.

Included in the GT package were badges, a special hood, body striping, engine dress-up parts, a heavy-duty suspension, front disc brakes, bucket seats, a center console and a sport steering wheel. The base 315-hp V-8 featured a hot cam, special manifolds and a single four-barrel carb.

A 1966 Fairlane GTA two-door hardtop with the 390-cid 335-hp V-8 carried only about 10.5 lbs. per horsepower. It could move from 0-to-60 mph in a mere 6.8 seconds and did the quarter-mile in 15.2 seconds.

FORD

The Fairlane GT was equipped with a 315-hp V-8. A convertible
like this could be had new for a base price of $3,068.

The chrome rocker covers distinguished the GTA from the GT. Under
the hood, the GTA featured the stronger 335-hp/390-cid engine.

FORD

223

1966 Galaxie "7-Litre"

The Galaxie "7-Litre" was a car that was truly out of this world. In fact, it belonged in the muscle car world, despite the fact that it was bigger than most of the other machinery in that universe.

While full-sized 1965 and 1966 Fords shared a similar overall design character, the hood is the only body panel that can be interchanged between the two years. The 1966 feature lines were a bit more rounded and the Galaxie 500 two-door hardtop with its semi-fastback roofline had particular eye appeal.

In the muscle car marketplace, at this time, the demand for big cars was declining. The mid-sized models, sporty "senior" compacts and pony cars like the Mustang were offering go-fast options designed to steal high-performance buyers away from full-sized models. In reaction to this, Ford decided to package the big-engine Galaxie as a separate, sporty model aimed at mature muscle car mavens.

The Galaxie 500XL "7-Litre" series offered high-performance versions of the Galaxie 500XL two-door hardtop and convertible with a 428-cid/345-hp V-8 engine as *standard* equipment. Also included was a Cruise-O-Matic automatic transmission, but a four-speed manual gearbox was optional at no extra cost.

Along with the 428-cid power plant, the features of this model included a sport steering wheel with simulated English walnut finish, bucket seats, a floor-mounted gear shifter, a low-restriction dual exhaust system, power disc brakes and a non-silenced air cleaner.

The code "Q" 428-cid "Thunderbird Special" V-8 had a 4.13 x 3.98-inch bore and stroke. With a single Holley four-barrel carburetor and a 10.5:1 compression ratio, it developed 345 hp at 4600 rpm. A "Police Interceptor" version (Code "P") with 360 hp at 5400 rpm was optional. With its small-bore, long-stroke configuration, the 428-cid V-8 was designed for smoothness rather than competition. The 1966 Galaxie 500XL "7-Litre" hardtop could do 0-to-60 mph in about 8 seconds and the quarter-mile in 16.4 seconds.

The 7-Litre fastback two-door hardtop had a suggested retail price of $3,596 and weighed 3,914 lbs. Ford records show that 8,705 were made. The convertible version had prices starting at $3,844 and weighed 4,059 lbs. Its production total was 2,368 units.

Ford did build 237 427-cid V-8s in 1966, but many of them were installed in Fairlanes, which had become wide enough to accept the big-block V-8 under the hood. Therefore, only a handful of 427-powered 1966 Galaxie 500XLs were produced.

The growing popularity of the GT package helped keep Ford riding high in the pony car race in 1966

1966 Mustang GT

For 1966, little change was made to Ford's hot-selling Mustang. You don't mess with success, so why change a good thing? Minor updates were all that were needed. A revised instrument panel that looked less like the Falcon's was used. The grille retained its now-familiar shape, but had the Mustang horse emblem "floating" in the "corral" in its center, with no horizontal or vertical dividing bars. A wind split ornament was added at the end of the "cove" on the

FORD

Jerry Heasley

224

Jerry Heasley

FORD

The growing popularity of the GT package helped keep Ford riding high in the pony car race in 1966.

body sides.

Federally mandated safety equipment that was formerly optional—including seat belts, a padded instrument panel, emergency flashers, electric windshield wipers (with washers) and dual padded sun visors—were made standard features. To cover the added cost of these must-have items, prices increased $44 for the two-door hardtop, $18 for the 2+2 and $49 for the convertible.

The GT Equipment Group continued to be available in 1966 as a $152.50 option package for Mustangs with high-performance V-8 power plants. The GT Equipment Group included a dual exhaust system, front fog lamps, special body ornamentation, front disc brakes, GT racing stripes (in place of rocker panel moldings) and handling package components. The handling package (normally $30.84 extra by itself) included increased-rate front and rear springs, larger-diameter front and rear shock absorbers, a steering system with a 22:1

overall ratio and a large-diameter stabilizer bar.

The Mustang's base V-8 engine for 1966 was the Code "G" 4.00 x 2.87-inch bore and stroke 289-cid with a 9.3:1 compression ratio and an Autolite two-barrel carburetor. It generated 200 hp at 4400 rpm. The performance options included the Code "A" 289-cid Challenger V-8 with a 10.1:1 compression ratio and four-barrel Autolite carburetor, which produced 225 hp at 4800 and the Code "K" Challenger High-Performance V-8. This version of the "289" featured a 10.5:1 compression ratio, a four-barrel Autolite carburetor and solid valve lifters, which helped it to make 271 hp at 6000 rpm.

A Mustang 2+2 with the Challenger High-Performance V-8 could do 0-to-60 mph in 7.6 seconds and needed about 15.9 seconds to make it down the quarter-mile.

The GT package proved to be twice as popular as it had been in 1965 and its sales increased from about 15,000 the earlier year to approximately 30,000.

FORD

Travelers could get where they were going in a big hurry (oftentimes
to the race track) in a race-ready Shelby GT 350H rental car.

1966 Shelby-Mustang GT 350H

"Rent-A-Race-Car" may seem like an oxymoron, but then, you might have forgotten about the Shelby GT 350H. The H stood for Hertz and it was a special version of Carroll Shelby's legendary conversion of the Mustang pony car into a true muscle car. The GT 350H was not Hertz's first venture involving rental cars that weren't totally ho-hum. Prior to 1965, Hertz had rented Corvettes.

In any case, during 1966 you could walk up to the Hertz counter in many major cities and ask for one of the hottest cars of the era. You did have to be a member of the Hertz Sports Car Club. You also had to be at least 25 years old and able to demonstrate "driving skills." The latter often involved no more than a quick spin around the block.

When Hertz switched its allegiance to Ford products, renting 'Vettes didn't seem appropriate. Carroll Shelby's astute sales manager saw the promotional possibilities in having the Shelby-Mustang replace the Corvette. This would be great advertising, as well as a way to get potential buyers in the driver's seat.

While Shelby initially hoped to sell a couple dozen cars to Hertz, the ultimate order was larger. The final tally came to 936 GT 350s out of a total run of 2,380 in 1966.

It came as no surprise—except possibly to Hertz—that these muscular rent-a-cars would create some maintenance headaches after being put into the hands of weekend racers. There are tales of "Rent-A-Racers" showing up at drag strips. When the remnants of a roll bar were found under the carpeting in one car, it was concluded that it had seen some track time in SCCA competition.

At a cost of only $17 dollars a day and 17 cents per mile

(still about twice the rate of a regular Hertz rental at the time) the GT 350H offered a cheap car to use for a weekend of racing. After the race, Hertz could take care of any needed repairs.

The original Borg-Warner T-10 close-ratio four-speed manual transmissions were a real problem . . . especially when used by inexperienced drivers. Hertz later switched to Ford's C-4 automatic, which became an option on all Shelbys for 1966. Although lacking a stickshift, this was still a rental car with over 300 hp.

With the automatic, the "Cobra-ized" 289-cid H-Po small-block V-8 was fed by a 595-cfm Autolite carburetor that replaced the regular 715-cfm Holley. Another running change was to Mustang-type front disc brakes and a revised master cylinder. This lowered the pedal pressure a bit with sintered metallic brake pads and linings. A warning that read: "This vehicle is equipped with competition brakes. Heavier than normal pedal pressure required" was displayed on the instrument panel.

The GT 350H had some visual differences from normal '66 GT 350s. Most were finished in black with gold decals (a color scheme Hertz had used when it built its own taxicabs in the 1920s.) A few GT 350Hs were painted white, red, blue and green. Most of these also got gold striping.

After serving Hertz, the GT 350Hs were returned to Ford for minor refurbishing. Then, they were resold to the general public through selected dealers. Unfortunately, during refurbishing, the high-performance parts sometimes got "lost." While there were no special Hertz models in later years, the company did rent GT 350s through 1969.

The Fairlane continued to be a versatile racing beast in 1967. Its optional 427-cid engine came in 410- and 425-hp varieties, and a multitude of racing gadgetry was available for these cars.

FORD

1967 Fairlane 427

There was nothing "middle-of-the-road" about Ford's mid-size muscle machines in 1967. If you wanted to go all the way when it came to building a high-performance Fairlane, your FoMoCo dealer had the vehicles and hardware you needed to create a street racer or a weekend dragster. Ford advertisements made this clear when they stated, "The 427 Fairlane is also available without numbers." They weren't talking about meter rates on the side of a taxi cab, either — they were talking about the numbers on racing cars that went brutally fast.

The stock 1967 Ford Fairlane continued to use the same body introduced in 1966 with only minor trim changes. The 1967 grille was a single aluminum stamping used in place of the two grilles that graced the previous model. The 1967 taillights were divided horizontally by the back-up light, instead of vertically, as in 1966.

The fire-breathing 427-cid "side-oiler" V-8 was again available on the Fairlane's options list. The 1967 edition of *Car Fax* indicated that it came only on non-GT club coupes (two-door sedans) and sport coupes (two-door hardtops). In the full-size Galaxie, the price for the 410-hp engine, when ordered without the 7-Litre package, was $975.09. Logic suggests that price is probably in the same general ballpark that the 427 would cost in the smaller Fairlane models.

The milder 410-hp single-four-barrel-carburetor version of the 427 was not the only choice. There was the hairier 425-hp version that carried two four-barrel Holley carburetors. Both of these engine options included a transistorized ignition, heavy-duty battery, heavy-duty suspension, extra cooling package and four-speed manual transmission. Also

mandatory on Fairlane 427s at $46.53 extra were 8.15 x 15 four-ply-rated black nylon tires. Fairlane 427 buyers could opt for 8.15 x 15 four-ply-rated whitewall nylon tires for $82.83 extra or for blackwall ($62.22 extra) or whitewall ($98.52) models of larger 8.45 x 15 four-ply-rated nylon tires.

Racing versions of the 427-cid V-8 were offered with goodies like a new eight-barrel induction system that put about 30 extra horses on tap. A tunnel-port version of the 427 was available as an over-the-counter kit, with a tunnel-port intake on special cylinder heads and a special intake manifold.

In NASCAR competition, the 427-powered Fairlanes swept a bunch of early-in-the-year races before Chrysler complained. The sanctioning rules were then changed again to handicap the midsize Fords. Similarly, NHRA placed the Fairlane 427s in SS/B class to keep them from totally dominating the quarter-mile sport.

Whether it had a 289- or 390-cid V-8, the 1967 Fairlane was a more-than-respectable looker and performer. The GT and GTA were again the fastest and sportiest cars in the Fairlane stable.

FORD

1967 Fairlane GT/GTA

In 1967, the Pontiac GTO was still the monarch of the muscle car kingdom, but Ford's rebellious Fairlane GT/GTA was back to try to topple royalty once again. As the "pappy" of supercars, the GTO was starting to get a little fat and fancy, while the muscle-building mid-size Fords were looking leaner and more lethal.

The basic '67 Fairlane continued Ford's trend toward sporty, youthful styling. In appearance, it was clearly moving away from the dowdiness of the model's earlier years. The hotter GT models carried a narrow-wide-narrow side stripe motif on both sides of the body, just above the rocker panels. A new deeply recessed radiator grille added to the midsize Fairlane's performance image and the vertically mounted dual headlights created instant Ford family identification.

For '67, standard equipment for the Fairlane GT included all Fairlane, Fairlane 500 and Fairlane 500XL features plus power front disc brakes, wide oval white stripe tires, a special GT hood carrying simulated "power domes" with integral turn signals, GT body stripes, GT fender plaques, a GT black-out style grille, deluxe full wheel covers, a 289-cid V-8, a left-hand remote-control outside rearview mirror and deluxe seat belts.

The 390-cid V-8 was optional in the hot Fairlane. For $78.25 you could get it with a two-barrel carburetor and 270 hp. For $158.08 you could get a 320-hp version with a single four-barrel carburetor, but only if you also ordered an extra-cost transmission.

The Model 42 Fairlane GT sport coupe (two-door hardtop) sold for $2,838.88. The Model 43 convertible version had a $3,063.67 sticker price. Only 18,670 hardtops and 2,117 convertibles were made. The 390-cid engine added $184 to the price of both models ($264 when it was fitted with a four-barrel carburetor).

A 289-equipped Fairlane hardtop could go from 0-to-60 mph in 10.6 seconds and do the quarter-mile in 18 seconds at 79 mph. The 390-cid/320-hp version required 8.4 seconds to reach 60 mph and did the quarter-mile in 16.2 seconds at 89 mph.

1967 Galaxie 500XL

By 1967, Chevrolet Motor Division had brought the huge, powerful Impala SS 427 on the market. This was not the time for Dearborn to rethink its so far futile attempt to sell the muscular "7 Litre" version of its full-size car in big numbers. However, there was no separate Galaxie 500XL "7-Litre" series this year. Instead, the 7-Litre engine and chassis goodies were offered as an option package for the Galaxie 500XL two-door hardtop and ragtop.

After two years of somewhat similar, but not identical styling, the big Fords were completely restyled for model year 1967. Though changed greatly in appearance, they continued to ride on a 119-inch wheelbase and retain a general "Ford" character. Overall length went up to 213.9 inches, making them nearly four inches longer than in 1966. This gave the cars a new sense of proportion from stem to stern.

The new models had even more rounded feature lines than the previous Fords, with rounder tops and rounder fenders. On the front end, dual stacked headlights were seen once again, but the grille was of a completely new design. It was a double-stamped aluminum piece featuring horizontal bars divided by five vertical bars. The center portion of the grille projected forward and this pointed shape was carried over on the hood.

FoMoCo stylists emphasized the "Coke-bottle" look even more in the body feature lines and the taillights were now vertically positioned rectangles with chrome trim and chrome "crosshair" moldings. In the big car's interior, Ford fans found a new energy-absorbing steering wheel with a thickly padded center hub that reflected America's growing consciousness of safety equipment.

**The full-sized Fords got a total makeover for 1967, and the Galaxie 500XL had
a host of big engine options that made the XL a cruiser that could move.**

Ford once again offered the Custom, Custom 500, Galaxie 500, Galaxie 500XL and LTD car lines. The basic Galaxie 500XL was the choice that appealed most to muscle car types. It featured sporty bucket seats, a center console, special exterior and interior ornamentation, courtesy lights, bright trim on the foot pedals, a 289-cid/200-hp V-8 engine and a SelectShift Cruise-O-Matic transmission. The 3,594-lb. fastback Sport Coupe sold for $3,243 and the 3,704-lb. convertible sold for $3,493.

Ford's 428-cid/345-hp "Thunderbird Special" V-8 was part of the 7-Litre option and could move the car in a fairly rapid manner. If you wanted to go even faster, you could order the 360-hp "Police Interceptor" version at additional extra cost.

Also continuing to be optional at extra cost was the hotter 427-cid V-8 in both the 410-hp "Thunderbird High-Performance" version and the 425-hp "Thunderbird Super High-Performance" version. There was even a tunnel port version of the 427 that was made available at Ford dealerships as an over-the-counter dealer kit. It featured a tunnel port intake on special cylinder heads and special manifolds.

1967 Mustang GT/GTA

For 1967, competition in the so-called sports-compact market was noticeably stiffer. Mercury introduced its fancy version of the Mustang—the Cougar—in 1967. Chevrolet, which had made little effort to respond to the Mustang with the dying Corvair, chose to develop its own, entirely new sports-compact model for 1967. It was called the Camaro. The Firebird was Pontiac's version of the Camaro. It bowed in mid-1967, six months after the Camaro.

Ford was hard pressed to improve on the "classic" Mustang it had introduced in 1964, but it had to. The competition was getting very keen, indeed. Iacocca and company did a great job with a tough assignment. The 1967 Mustang got a jazzy new body, a wider tread for better road grip and a wider range of engines. Option choices were widened, too. They now included a tilt-away steering wheel, a built-in heater/air conditioner, an overhead console, a stereo-sonic tape system, a SelectShift automatic transmission that also worked manually, a bench seat, an AM/FM radio, fingertip speed control, custom exterior trim group, and front power disc brakes. Styling followed the same theme, but in a larger size.

On the exterior, the 1967 Mustang was heftier and more full-fendered. Especially low and sleek was the new 2+2 fastback, which featured all-new sheet metal. The roofline had a clean, unbroken sweep downward to a distinctive, concave rear panel. Functional air louvers in the roof rear quarters were made thinner than before. The wheelbase was unchanged, but overall length grew by nearly 2 inches. Front and rear tread widths went up by 2.1 inches and overall width was 2.7 inches wider at 58.1 inches.

All Mustangs had bigger engine bays. This was very necessary because the first "big-block" option was among the many 1967 hardware upgrades. It was a 390-cid V-8 with 315 hp. This small bore-long stroke power plant was related to the Ford "FE" engine, introduced way back in 1958. It provided a good street-performance option with a low $264 price tag, lots of low-end performance and plenty of torque.

All of the 1966 engines were carried-over, plus there was a new 200-hp version of the Challenger 289 V-8 with a two-barrel carburetor. This motor was standard in cars with the GT option. A new designation used on cars with automatic transmission and GT equipment was "GTA."

Other technical changes included front suspension improvements. A competition handling package was released, but it cost quite a bit extra and didn't go into too many cars. The 1967 Mustang GT 2+2 with the 390-cid/335-hp V-8 could do 0-to-60 mph in 7.4 seconds and the quarter-mile in 15.6 seconds.

FORD

FORD

The stylish Mustang continued to evolve in 1967 in response to its tough muscle car competition. The sporty
1967 GT coupe and convertible were very appealing all-around pony cars.

The 1967 Shelby GT-500 was the top of the Mustang food chain and one of the great muscle cars of any year.

Jerry Heasley

FORD

1967 Shelby-Mustang GT-350/GT-500

For 1967, the Shelby GT-350 took on an appearance different from the stock Mustang. At the same time, the Shelby became mechanically more similar to its garden-variety cousin. Shelby dealers liked this change. It created a visually exciting product with as much creature comfort as a basic Mustang, but with no need for specialized maintenance equipment and training.

With the base Mustang redesigned for '67, Shelby created an entirely new appearance that made its fastback look longer and lower than stock Mustangs by the use of more fiberglass than in previous years. A twin-scoop fiberglass hood with racing-style lock-down pins, reached farther than the Mustang's all-steel piece and made the grille appear like a dark, menacing mouth. The grille housed two round high-beam headlights placed side by side in the middle.

The Mustang front bumper, minus the vertical bumperettes, looked like it was made for the Shelby. In front of each rear wheel well were fiberglass, forward-facing scoops that channeled air into the rear brakes. Stock Mustang rear vents were covered with a rear-facing scoop that helped draw air out of the passenger compartment. (Early 1967 cars had a red running light installed in this scoop, but the accessory was dropped later due to legal concerns.) A three-piece spoiler was applied to the rear of all '67 Shelby-Mustangs and accented by extra-wide taillights.

The Deluxe Mustang Interior in black, white or parchment was the only choice for the more luxurious '67 Shelby. A sporty, two- or four-point roll bar was installed. The bar was a mounting point for an inertia reel shoulder harness. All Shelbys received a unique wood-rimmed steering wheel with GT-350 or GT-500 plastic horn buttons. Fold-down rear seats, once an option, were standard. Stewart-Warner gauges were housed in a metal bezel under the middle of the dashboard. The Mustang's optional 8000-rpm tach sat next to a 140-mph speedometer.

Shelbys came with power steering and brakes. Suspension enhancements were largely stock Mustang, including the special handling package, front disc brakes, thicker front stabilizer bar, export brace, and adjustable Gabriel shock absorbers. The 15-inch stamped steel wheels had '67 Thunderbird hubcaps with Shelby center caps. Sporty Kelsey-Hayes rims were optional.

The 289-cid K-code engine was used again with very few changes. Tubular exhaust headers were dropped at the beginning of the year and Ford's high-performance cast-iron manifold, was used. The factory continued claiming 306 hp. Options included a Paxton supercharger, SelectAire air conditioning and the Hi-Po C-4 automatic transmission. For the second straight year, GT-350 prices decreased. Shelby dealers sold 1,175 units for $3,995 apiece.

With the new looks came a new family member: the GT-500. Shelby installed the 428-cid big-block V-8 in this top-line offering. It produced at least 50 more horsepower than the 390. This "Police Interceptor" engine featured hydraulic lifters and an aluminum, medium-rise intake manifold wearing a pair of 600-cfm four-barrel Holley carburetors. Ford's four-speed "toploader" transmission was standard. The stout "police spec" C-6 automatic was optional. The GT-500, available only in fastback form like the GT-350, retailed for $4,195 and sold 2,050 units.

231

1968 Fairlane 428-CJ

In the mid-to-late 1960s, Ford was doing all it could to promote the benefits of "Total Performance" throughout all of its car lines. This was largely reflective of the company's success in stock car racing, its European Grand Prix racing experience and the performance of certain FoMoCo products at drag strips across the nation. When you added up the numbers to get Total Performance, the Fairlane 428-CJ was one of the combinations you ended up with. As *Car Life* put it, "The Cobra may not eat all birds for breakfast, but when it does, it doesn't chew them with its mouth full."

The Fairlane grew in 1968. It retained a 116-inch wheelbase, but overall length grew by 4 inches to 201. Some enthusiasts felt that it looked almost like a full-size car, although the big Fords of the day were still a whole foot longer. In addition to the Fairlane, Fairlane 500 and Fairlane GT series, there was a new Fairlane Torino top trim level.

In 1968, the fastback version that muscle car fans favored did not come as a Torino, only as a Fairlane 500 (six or V-8) or Fairlane GT (V-8). The GT was usually the version that showed up at drag strips and not with the base 302-cid V-8

or the optional 390-cid "big block." At the start of the year, racing buffs could order the 427-cid monster mill in a detuned 390-hp state, but this option was soon replaced with a new 428 Cobra-Jet engine that came in two versions.

The 428-CJ had a 4.13 x 3.98-inch bore and stroke, which made it a totally different engine than the 427. The base version, code "Q," came with 10.7:1 compression heads and a single Holley four-barrel carburetor. It was advertised at 335 hp at 5600 rpm. The Super Cobra-Jet (SCJ) version, code "R," had a 10.5:1 compression ratio, a four-barrel with ram-air induction and advertised 360 hp at 5400 rpm.

The Cobra-Jet V-8 was basically the 1966 Ford "FE" big block fitted with 427-type cylinder heads. The factory grossly underrated the power of the Cobra-Jet V-8 in the mid-sized cars to give them an advantage in drag racing classifications. Later, it was revealed that the CJ-428 produced something like 410 hp in the 1968 Fairlanes and Torinos. No wonder they could run from 0-to 60-mph in just over 6 seconds and do the quarter-mile in 14.5 seconds.

1968 Custom/Galaxie/XL 427

For 1968, the full-sized Fords continued with the same basic body introduced in 1967, but there were some significant revisions to the front-end sheet metal that make the two designs look more different than they really were. The new grille work was less protruding and hidden headlights were used on the upper series. The new grille had a honeycomb texture with a single vertical division bar in its center. The Ford name in block letters and a Ford crest appeared. Roof lines were generally more formal looking and the taillights were divided horizontally (instead of vertically, as in 1967) by the back-up light lenses.

As far as underhood goodies went, this was the closing year of an exciting era. The legendary "side-oiler" 427-cid V-8 made its last appearance in big Fords in model year 1968. This version of the truly Hi-Po big-block V-8 was slightly detuned from the previous issue. It was advertised to have 390 hp at 5600 rpm and 460 lbs.-ft. of torque at 3200 rpm.

This year's full size Fords came in Custom, Custom 500, Galaxie 500, Ford XL and Ford LTD series. If you wanted a sport coupe or a convertible (like many buyers interested in big-block engines did) you had to shop in only the upper three series. In the Galaxie 500 line the prices were $2,964.55 for the sportier fastback sport coupe, $2,999.28 for the formal roof sport coupe and $3,215.20 for the ragtop. The Ford XL line offered just the fastback sport coupe at $3,068.94 and the ragtop at $3,320.65. The LTD came only as the formal roof sport coupe at $3,129.87. There was no LTD convertible. Of course, those with serious racing in mind could get the 427 in a $2,667.49 Custom two-door sedan and go lots faster without the eye appeal.

QUIET. STRONG. BEAUTIFUL. A GREAT ROAD CAR. '68 FORD

1968 Ford XL. Latest version of the Fords shown quieter than Europe's finest luxury cars, strong enough to leap off an Olympic ski jump. This year, Ford XL leaves its rivals farther behind than ever. No other car in its field offers disappearing headlamps as standard equipment. Or front power disc brakes at the XL price. Or a transmission like SelectShift on any model, with any engine. Or a 6-passenger fastback with XL's unique styling. Or the stripes that specially modified Ford cars won at LeMans, Sebring, Daytona. Ride this great road car.

See the light!

FORD ...has a better idea.

The 427-cid/390-hp V-8 was offered for any of the full-sized Fords in 1968, including the Galaxie XL Fastback.

The 427-cid engine had a dealer wholesale price of $449.53. Once the Ford dealer tacked on federal excise tax and his normal profit, the price tag for the monster motor was up to $622.97.

At midyear 1968, Ford Motor Company discontinued making the 427-cid V-8. In the Fairlane and Mustang series, the 427 was replaced by the equally famous and powerful Cobra Jet 428 and Super Cobra Jet 428 engines. The big cars got a new Thunder-Jet 429-cid V-8 that sounded formidable, but produced only 340 and 360 hp—not quite enough to turn the later big Fords into muscle cars.

FORD

Jerry Heasley

The 1968 SCJ (Super Cobra Jet) Mustang was a competition model that was one step up from its Cobra Jet sibling. The CJ-428 was fast for a production car, but the SCJ-428 was a pure racer.

1968 Mustang CJ 428/SCJ 428

The compact Mustang became a *really* fast car when Ford Motor Company decided to shoehorn the 428-cubic inch Cobra-Jet V-8 under its hood. Such a machine could move from 0-to-60 miles per hour in a mere 6.9 seconds. The quarter-mile took only 15.57 to do and the car's terminal speed at the end of such a run was about 99.5 mph. After one test drive at a drag strip, *Hot Rod* magazine declared the Mustang 428 CJ to be "the fastest running pure stock in the history of man."

Ford introduced the 428 Cobra Jet engine option on April 1, 1968. The new motor was the automaker's big-block performance leader. Production of the 428-CJ engine continued through 1970. Rated conservatively for 335 hp at 5200 rpm, the 1968 Mustang CJ 428 put out a lot more like 375 to 400 gross horsepower. The engine was hot competition for the SS 396 from Chevrolet, the 400 HO from Pontiac, the 440 Magnum from Mopar and literally any other muscle car on the street in 1968.

A high-performance variant of the basic 428-cid V-8, the main features of the Cobra Jet V-8 were revised cylinder heads. They were of a design that was similar to the Ford 427 "low-riser" type, but with bigger valve ports, a camshaft from the 390-cid GT engine, a cast-iron copy of the 428-cid Police Interceptor intake manifold and a 735-cfm Holley four-barrel carburetor.

For 1968 1/2, all Cobra Jets were coded "R" in the fifth digit of the vehicle identification number (VIN) and all were Ram-Air cars (featuring an air cleaner and flapper assembly mounted underneath the hood). A small scoop sat atop the hood to admit cold air to the Holley four-barrel.

The 428 SCJ (Super Cobra Jet) V-8s were built with drag-strip duty in mind, which is why Ford beefed up the bottom end and added an oil cooler, but left the top end alone. SCJs came with hardened cast-steel crankshafts (regular CJs had nodular iron cast cranks) and LeMans rods that were externally balanced with a large vibration damper. Of course, the CJ was already stock with a nodular-cased 9-inch differential and 31-spline axles.

SCJs did not have a unique engine code, but they were mandatory with either a 3.9:1 Traction-Lok (code V) or a 4.30:1 Detroit Locker (code W) axle.

The 1968 Mustang GTs were great-looking cars, and those outfitted
with big-block 390 engines are particularly prized by collectors today.

1968 Mustang GT/GTA and California Special

Ford invited 1968 car shoppers to "Turn yourself on, switch your style and show a new face in the most exciting car on the American road," in its advertising for the 1968 Mustang.

Only subtle changes were actually made to the new-in-1967 design. Bucket seats, a floor-mounted stick, a sports steering wheel and rich, loop-pile carpeting remained standard. Minor trim updates included a front end with the Mustang emblem "floating" in the grille, script-style (instead of block letter) Mustang body side nameplates and cleaner-looking bright metal trim on the cove. There was a new two-tone hood. Still, prices rose substantially, averaging about $140 more per model.

The $147 GT option included a choice of stripes. Either the rocker panel type or a reflecting "C" stripe could be specified. The latter widened along the ridge of the front fender and ran across the door, to the upper rear body quarter. From there, it wrapped down, around the sculptured depression ahead of the rear wheel, and tapered forward, along the lower body, to about the midpoint of the door. Other GT goodies included fog lights in the grille, a GT gas cap and GT wheel covers. The fog lights no longer had a bar between them and the "corral" in the grille. Disc brakes were usually extra, but made the

standard equipment list when big-block V-8s were ordered. A total of 17,458 GTs were made in 1968. A GT equipped with the 390-cid V-8 is considered a very desirable collector's car.

Many new engine options were offered in 1968. Some reflected midyear changes. There were no options with the base 289-cid/195-hp V-8. Instead, a 302-cid V-8 was added. This was initially seen with a four-barrel carburetor and 230-hp output rating. Later, a 220-hp version with a two-barrel carburetor came out. Big-block options included two "FE" series engines, the 390-cid V-8 (with 320/325 hp) and the 390-hp/427-cid V-8. This engine was used in only a handful of cars before it was phased out in December 1967. Starting in April 1968, a new 428-cid Cobra-Jet V-8 with 335 hp was put into about 2,817 Mustangs. Cars with four-speed transmissions included strengthened front shock absorber towers and revised rear shock absorber mountings. Ram Air induction was available.

About 5,000 GT/CS "California Special" Mustangs were produced in 1968. Their features included a Shelby-style deck lid with a spoiler, sequential taillights and a blacked-out grille. They had no Mustang grille emblem. The wheel covers were the same ones used on 1968 GTs, but without GT identification.

The spoiler and "CJ/CS" script identified the 1968 "California Special" Mustangs.

FORD

Jerry Heasley

The Shelby GT 500KR wasn't the fastest car on the road in 1968, but it was the fastest Shelby Mustang up to that time and a very desirable car.

1968 Shelby-Mustang GT 500KR

Somebody stole the Shelby GT 500KR that *Car Life* magazine was going to test drive. You couldn't blame them—the under-$5,000 fastback had a lot of appeal. With its 428-cid Cobra Jet engine, it was a big temptation to any car-loving cat burglar. After a rough three-day break-in, the LAPD recovered the car, but a Ford public relations guy had to call *Car Life* and admit it was in no shape for a national article. The magazine wound up with a replacement car and a good lead-in to introduce it.

Actually, the hot Mustang didn't need too much of an introduction. Everyone knew what Cobra meant and the GT 500 designation was well understood by 1968. As for "KR," the folks at Ford and Shelby said it stood for "King of the Road." With a 6.9 second 0-to-60 mph speed and 14.57 second-quarter-mile ET, the GT 500KR wasn't the undisputed king of drag racing. "But, there's more to life than the quarter-mile," *Car Life's* editors maintained.

Tucked below the hood was a 428-cid Cobra Jet V-8 with 4.13 x 3.98-inch bore and stroke, 10.6:1 compression, special hydraulic lifters, dual branched headers and one extra-big Holley four-barrel. It was rated for 335 hp at 5200 rpm and 440 lbs.-ft. of torque at 3400 rpm. True horsepower, however,

was 435-500.

The Shelby KR package, for a coupe or convertible, also included a fiberglass hood and front panels, functional air scoops and hot-air extractors. A big speedometer and tachometer were added to the instrument panel and other gauges were moved to the console. Vinyl buckets and thick carpeting were standard. There was wood-look dash trim, suspension upgrades (including staggered shocks), E70-15 Goodyear Polyglas tires, a limited-slip differential, engine dress-up items and special stripes and badges.

Large, but ineffective, air scoops were attached to the body sides to cool the disc/drum power brakes. During a test drive, the binders got so hot that they started pouring smoke out of the scoops. No wonder *Car Life* rated overall braking performance poor.

Although it was not the fastest car ever made, the GT 500KR was the fastest Shelby-Mustang made up to its time. Some racers registered ETs below 13 seconds and top speed was around 130 mph. The fastback model was base-priced at $4,473 and ran about $4,900 with a nice selection of options. Production counts were 933 units for the fastback and 318 for the convertible.

FORD

Tim Calvert

**The Torino GT package was a $622.97 option that turned the
1968 Fairlane into a 427-cid/390-hp card-carrying muscle car.**

1968 Torino GT

The 1968 Ford Torino GT was the sporty version of the Fairlane 500 and was based on that model. The Torino GT actually came in three versions. Model 65D was the two-door hardtop, which sold for $2,768.17, weighed 3,194 lbs. and had a production run of 23,939 units. The convertible—Model 76D—was much rarer and only 5,310 were made. Prices for the ragtop began at $3,020.40 and it tipped the scales at 3,352 lbs. in showroom stock condition. The real image car was the Model 63D two-door fastback, with its $2,742.84 window sticker, 3,208-lb. curb weight and 74,135 units produced. Dubbed the "SportsRoof" by Ford, this car had lots of buyer appeal in its era.

Fairlane standard equipment included government-mandated safety equipment, a 200-cid six or a 302-cid V-8 and 7.35-14 tires. The standard Torino models (sports coupe, sedan or wagon) added wheel covers and an electric clock. The sporty Fairlane GT included all this plus a vinyl bench seat, a GT handling suspension, argent silver styled wheels with chrome trim rings, F70 x 14 wide oval tires, GT body stripes, a gray GT grille, GT nameplates and a 302-cid/210-hp V-8. Power brakes were required if the optional 390-cid big-block V-8 was ordered.

The 390-cid engine came in two versions. The 265-hp edition with a single two-barrel carburetor added just $78.25 to the price of a Torino V-8. The 325-hp four-barrel version was $158.08 extra and also required an extra-cost transmission (either the heavy-duty three-speed at $79.20, a four-speed manual at $184.02 or Ford's Select Shift Cruise-O-Matic at $233.17).

Real muscle car lovers were probably more interested in getting a Torino GT with a 427-cid/390-hp V-8. It was a $622.97 option for all Fairlane two-door hardtops and you could not get it with Select Aire air conditioning, power steering, a 55-amp generator, a heavy-duty suspension or optional tires as extras either because it didn't make sense or these options were already required.

Motor Trend (December 1967) tested a 1968 Torino GT SportsRoof and liked most things about it, except the vision to the rear with the radical fastback styling. Other minor criticisms were made, but the overall impression was positive. "The new breed of super car from Ford is a full step ahead of its '67 counterpart," the magazine concluded.

The test car had the 390-cid four-barrel engine, which developed 335 hp at 4800 rpm and 427 lbs.-ft. of torque at 3200 rpm. It had a 10.5:1 compression ratio, three-speed manual attachment and 3.25:1 rear axle. *Motor Trend* reported 7.2 seconds for 0-to-60 mph and 15.1 seconds at 91 mph for the quarter-mile.

FORD

Jerry Heasley

With long, sleek looks, a big scoop in the hood, and 360 ponies on tap, the Super Cobra-Jet-equipped '69 Fairlane was a relative bargain. It came in notchback (above) and fastback varieties.

1969 Fairlane "Cobra" 428-CJ/SCJ

While most people think that Detroit is really a place where they make cars, the truth is that it's a giant genetic engineering laboratory. When one company creates an innovative product that fills a new niche in the market, the other carmakers immediately "clone" the idea and play copycat.

The hit of the season in Ford's mid-sized line for 1969 was a low-buck muscle car called the Torino Cobra. It was a clone of the popular Plymouth Road Runner, but a good one that was certain to steal sales away from the "beep-beep" MoPar machine.

The Torino Cobra was offered in both notchback and fastback models with the 428-CJ engine as *standard* equipment. Also standard was a four-speed manual gear box, a heavy-duty suspension and cartoon decals of the coiled-snake Cobra emblem. Ford people would say that this trumped the Road Runner which came only with 383 cubic inches—although it did include a four-speed and a campy cartoon character of its own.

At the time, the idea of a "stripper" performance car at a budget price had great appeal to many people, but there were those who liked their muscle cars with a bit more spit and polish, so Ford also offered the same goodies, as optional

equipment, in all 1969 Fairlanes—not just the Fairlane Torino models.

In all likelihood, few if any such engines made their way into base Fairlane models, since this series did not offer the fastback body style. This model was merchandised in the Fairlane 500 line with a base price of $2,674 for a V-8 version. Of course, you could also get a 428 CJ in the regular hardtop—which listed for $2,699—if you wanted a "sleeper" type muscle car.

As in 1968, the 428-CJ had a 4.13 x 3.98-inch bore and stroke. The base version came with 10.6:1 compression heads, a single Holley four-barrel carburetor and 335 hp at 5600 rpm. The Super Cobra-Jet (SCJ) version had a 10.5:1 compression ratio, a four-barrel with ram-air induction and 360 advertised horsepower.

One of the buff books tested a 1969 Fairlane Cobra two-door hardtop with the 428-cid 335-hp engine option. It gave the price of the car as $3,139. The hot Fairlane 428-CJ version moved from 0-to-60 in 7.8 seconds and needed 14.9 seconds for the quarter-mile at 95.2 mph. The even faster SCJ version did 0-to-60 mph in 6.3 seconds and did the quarter-mile in 14.5 seconds.

FORD

The 1969 Boss 302 Mustang had about everything a muscle car fan could want: great looks, a solid quarter-mile time, acceptable road manners, and a very cool name.

1969 Mustang Boss 302

In the slang of the '60s the word "boss" had a bundle of connotations. It meant "tough" or "awesome" (in the sense kids use the word today) and something that was "boss" was something every right-minded person aspired to. So, Ford picked it as a good name for its hot Mustang with the new 302-cid V-8.

Actually there were two Bosses. The first was a race-ready Boss 429 with Ford's NASCAR racing engine and completely redesigned front suspension. Then came the Boss 302, which was intended for high-performance street use.

The Boss 302 was Ford's answer to the Camaro Z/28 and was as likely to wind up in the hands of a hard-working kid as a middle-to-upper income youth who wanted to put a little excitement into his life.

What made the Boss special was a beefed-up 302-cid V-8 with four-bolt main bearing caps, a stronger crankshaft and—most important of all—redesigned cylinder heads that allowed dramatically better breathing. These "Cleveland" heads (as they are called) were also designed to sit atop Ford's 351 Cleveland V-8. In stock tune, a Boss 302 could turn in 0-to-60 times of under 7 seconds and nudge the century mark in a standing-start quarter-mile.

While a Boss 302 in the hands of a collector is likely to be driven a little more gingerly than the paces original owners put these cars through, Ford built an rpm limiter to keep lead-footed types from blowing up the engine. Basically, the limiter worked by counting ignition impulses and not allowing the engine to exceed 6,000 rpm.

Besides the special 302 engine, a Boss can be recognized by the matte black paint on its hood and trunk, Boss 302 name swatches on its sides, a front spoiler and styled steel wheels. Its performance equipment includes front disc brakes and a four-speed manual transmission. The optional rear spoiler was obviously decorative. (If this feature had been functional it would have been standard, right?)

Unlike other performance cars of the period, the Boss 302 had exceptionally good street manners—although the firm suspension did broadcast tar strips and other pavement irregularities.

Open the door and the Boss became just another Mustang. The interior is attractive, but it also features the infamous Mustang "park bench" rear seat. That's okay, though; the Mustang fastback wasn't really designed to be a four-seater.

If you've had a chance to own or drive one of these cars you'd probably agree with its original admirers: "Hey, man, this car is Boss!"

Jerry Heasley

The Boss 429 Mustang was the big brother to the Boss 302 in 1969. A total of 1,358 of these powerhouse cars were produced as Ford attempted to make a splash on the NASCAR scene with its big-block 429.

FORD

1969 Mustang Boss 429

Ford Motor Company was delighted to give birth to a set of twins in 1969—the ready-to-race Boss 302 and the Boss 429. Both of these special cars were built around state-of-the-art, high-performance power plants. The main difference is that one championed small-block performance, while the other was aimed at big-block V-8 competition.

From the driver's seat, Boss models were still basic Mustangs in layout. They had the same exterior styling and an interior with circular gauges, dash lights to monitor oil pressure and electrical systems and a tachometer. Two very desirable Boss options were an adjustable rear deck lid spoiler and rear window SportSlats.

The Boss 429 was born because Ford had a second engine, in addition to the 302-cid small-block V-8, that it wanted to place into race track competition. The Boss 302 was designed to compete with the Camaro in Trans-Am racing. The Boss 429 was created to legalize the 429-cid V-8 for use on the NASCAR circuit.

Ford considered doing a 429-powered Torino, but decided to offer the new-for-1969 429-cid "semi-hemi" big-block in the popular Mustang platform instead. Marketing experts felt that it would be easier to sell 500 big-block Mustangs than the same number of Torino-based supercars. Kar Kraft,

an aftermarket firm in Brighton, Michigan, was contracted to build Boss 429s. Since the Mustang's engine compartment was not designed to house such a wide power plant, the job required a big shoehorn and a lot of suspension changes and chassis modifications.

Body alterations included engine bay bracing, inner wheel well sheet metal work, and flared wheel housings (to accommodate a widened track and the use of seven-inch Magnum 500 rims). The hood received a huge, functional scoop, and a special spoiler underlined the front bumper. Power steering and brakes, a Traction-Lok axle with 3.91 gears, and the Boss 302's rear spoiler were also included. All Boss 429s had the fancy Decor Group interior option, high-back bucket seats, deluxe seat belts, wood-trimmed dash and console treatment, and Visibility Group option. Automatic transmission and air conditioning were not available, but the $3,826 price tag included all of the above.

Horsepower for the Boss 429 was advertised as 375, although real ratings were rumored to be much higher. A total of 1,358 Boss 429s were constructed during the 1969 calendar year. This included 859 of the 1969 models made in early 1969 and 499 1970 models built late in the summer.

The 1969 Mustang GT was available in both coupe and convertible body styles, with a host of engine options, again including the hot Cobra-Jet and Super Cobra-Jet 428 mills.

1969 Mustang GT and Mach 1 428/SCJ 428

FORD

For model year 1969, the Mustang got its third major restyling. Its new body wasn't drastically changed, but it grew 3.8 inches. There was no change in wheelbase, which was still the same 108 inches as in 1965. The windshield was more sharply raked and quad headlamps were used. The outer lenses were deeply recessed into the fenders and the inboard lenses were set into the grille.

Missing for the first time was a side scoop (or cove) on the body. This styling gimmick was replaced with a feature line that ran from the tip of the front fender to just behind the rear-most door seam, at a level just above the front wheel opening. On convertibles and hardtops there was a rear-facing, simulated air vent in front of the rear wheel opening on both sides. On fastbacks, this feature line lead to a backwards C-shaped air scoop above the main feature line.

The fastback was now referred to as the SportsRoof or Sports Roof (various Ford ads spelled the term differently). It had a 0.9-inch lower roofline than earlier fastbacks. Also, Mustang fastbacks were now true hardtops. The rear quarter louvers were gone. Instead, a small window abutted the door glass.

Though the styling theme remained Ford-like, the Mustang adopted GM-like models to suit the tastes of different buyers. Mustangs now came in basic, luxury, sporty and high-performance formats like a Camaro or Firebird. This may have reflected the influence of Semon "Bunkie" Knudsen, a longtime GM executive who became president of Ford on February 6, 1968. While he didn't have time to change the cars, it's just about certain he changed marketing ideas.

Knudsen's background included a heavy emphasis on high-performance cars. He liked the look of the SportsRoof and this body style became the basis for a series of hot-forming "buzz bombs" like the Mach 1 and the soon-to-be-released Boss 302 and Boss 429.

Mach 1's had the Mustang's fanciest interior with high-back bucket seats, black carpets, a rim-blow steering wheel, a center console, a clock, sound-deadening insulation and teakwood-grained trim on the doors, dash and console.

One nice performance option available to enthusiast

buyers in 1969 was a Mustang GT or Mach 1 with the Cobra Jet 428 engine. This motor was Ford's big-block performance leader. It came in Cobra Jet (CJ 428) or Super Cobra Jet 428 (SCJ 428) versions. The former was called the "standard Cobra engine" in the *1969 Performance Buyer's Guide*. It generated 335 hp at 5200 rpm and 440 lbs.-ft. of torque at 3400 rpm. The latter was the same engine with Ram Air induction, a hardened steel cast crankshaft, special "LeMans" connecting rods and improved balancing for drag racing. It had the same advertised horsepower.

A 1969 Mach 1 two-door hardtop with the 428-cid/335-hp engine carried just 9.6 lbs. per hp. It could do 0-to-60 mph in 5.5 seconds and cover the quarter-mile in 13.9 seconds according to one road test. *Car and Driver* tested a Mach 1 fastback with the regular Cobra Jet V-8, automatic transmission and a 3.91:1 limited slip axle. This combination produced 5.7-second 0-to-60-mph performance and a 14.3-second quarter-mile at 100 mph. The car had an estimated top speed of 115 mph.

The Mach 1's base engine was a 351-cid two-barrel Windsor V-8. This was essentially a stroked 302-cid Ford V-8 with raised deck height, which created a great street performance engine. The basic version cranked up 250 horses. Options included the 351-cid/290-hp four-barrel V-8 and a 390-cid/320-hp V-8.

The Mach 1 had some differences inside and out from its GT sibling. Among them were matte black hood, reflective stripes that decorated the sides and rear, and a small spoiler on the tail.

Jerry Heasley

The lack of hood stripes identifies this car as a 1969 vintage Shelby GT-500.

1969-1970 Shelby Mustang

The '69 Shelby's cosmetic camouflage relied on the extensive use of fiberglass. The use of this material for fender, hood, and rear cap panels allowed Shelby designers to make the GT-350 three inches longer than the factory-stretched Mustang.

The Shelby hood had five recessed NASA-type hood scoops. The leading edge was trimmed with a chrome strip that curved around and down to meet the unique Shelby bumper. A chrome strip formed a wide rectangle as it ran around the outside of the flat-black grille. Lucas driving lights that added a degree of nighttime safety were attached to the underside of the bumper.

The Shelby side stripes in the middle of the body were larger and ran the entire length of the car. The rear brakes were cooled through a scoop mounted just ahead of the wheel well. On convertibles it was in line with the body stripe, on fastbacks it sat just behind the door handle.

A set of 1965 T-Bird sequential taillights further removed the cars from their Mustang roots. Directly between the two taillight lenses sat a spring-mounted frame that displayed the license plate and concealed the fuel filler cap. A pair of rectangular exhaust tips, separated from the fuel filler only by the width of the rear bumper, were part of a fire-hazard recall later in the year.

Early in the year, Blue, Green, Yellow and Orange "Grabber" colors and Competition Orange were added to Black Jade, Acapulco Blue, Gulfstream Aqua, Pastel Gray, Candy Apple Red and Royal Maroon. Interiors came in Black, White and Red (less than 80) with high-back bucket seats, a vinyl-covered "Rim Blow" steering wheel and a center console appearing as part of the deluxe Mustang equipment. The door panels and dashboard had many fake wood inserts.

The '69 Shelby used heavy-duty Mustang components straight from the Ford factory. In order to keep the rear axle from suffering during the occasional hard launch, staggered shocks were standard on the GT-500. No longer was the Shelby Mustang a car that could be ordered as a Plain-Jane racing car. Instead of stamped steel wheels, Shelby buyers got 15 x 7-inch five-spoke rims shod with Goodyear E-70x15 wide oval tires (F-60x15 tires were optional). Some Shelbys wound up with Boss 302 "Magnum 500" wheels when a defect in the stock rim forced a recall.

Every GT-350 built in 1969 received Ford's new 351-cid 290-hp Windsor V-8 with a 470-cfm Autolite four-barrel carburetor. It came attached to Ford's four-speed manual transmission. Optional gear boxes included a close-ratio four-speed manual and the FMX automatic.

The GT-500 (the "KR" suffix was gone) retained the fire-breathing 428-cid Cobra Jet V-8. A close-ratio four-speed was standard, with the C-6 back as an optional automatic.

Sales were brisk, with 1,087 GT-350 fastbacks ($4,434); 194 GT-350 convertibles ($4,753); 1,534 GT-500 fastbacks ($4,709); and 335 GT-500 convertibles ($5,027) going to new owners.

In the fall of 1969, Carroll Shelby convinced Ford to end the Shelby GT program. Shelby could see that the American auto industry and federal government were tightening the screws on performance cars and that there would soon be no market for the type of vehicles he wanted to produce. Also, Ford was mass producing cars that competed directly with the GT-350 and GT-500, such as the Mach 1, Boss 302, and Boss 429. With several hundred cars still in the pipeline, Shelby agreed to update 1969 leftovers into 1970 models with new vehicle identification numbers, a set of black hood stripes, a chin spoiler, and a mandatory emissions control unit. The hands-on work of converting from one year to the next was handled directly by the factory, under the watchful eyes of representatives from the Federal Bureau of Investigation. There is no accurate count of how many 1970 Shelbys were created, but some reports say it was 789 units.

It came up the hard way, easy.

A pack of rough, tough supercars is hard to beat. Specially modified Torinos make it look easy. Won all 3 U.S. stock-car championships: NASCAR, ARCA, USAC. 22 major trophies so far.

Easy to get excited about, another nonstop winner: Torino GT SportsRoof. With new 428 Cobra Jet V-8 option. See Torino '69. Moving out fast.

On tracks.
On highways.
Off showroom floors.

Cobra Jet 428

FORD
It's the going thing!

TORINO Ford

Jerry Heasley

The SportsRoof body style proved to be the most popular among fans of the 1969 Torino GT.

1969 Torino GT

In the "clone-o-mobile" industry, if someone has a good idea, there's no use giving it a trademark or copyright. Another automaker is going to copy it and try to make some improvements. In the case of the Torino, it was like the cloned cloning the clone of the original.

In mid '63, FoMoCo went to a semi-fastback roof to make its racecars faster on the track. By 1965, the design was cloned for other production cars. In 1966, Dodge went fully fastback with the jumping-ramp-shaped Charger, and by '68 Ford had cloned the Charger look into the SportsRoof body, which was found in most of its muscle car lines. Torinos came in various other body styles, too, but it was always the fastback that created its image.

For '69, the Ford Torino GT lineup again offered three body styles. Model 65D was the two-door hardtop, which sold for $2,848, weighed 3,173 lbs. and had a production run of 17,951 units. The convertible—Model 76D—was much rarer than even the 1968 version and only 2,552 were made. Prices for the ragtop began at $3,073 and it tipped the scales at 3,356 lbs. in showroom stock condition. Still the most popular body style was the Model 63D two-door fastback, with its $2,823 window sticker, 3,220-lb. curb weight and 61,319 units produced.

The 1969 Torino GT included all Fairlane 500 features plus the 302-cid/220-hp V-8 engine, bucket seats, a center console, special GT nameplates, GT exterior trim, argent silver finished styled steel wheels, a heavy-duty suspension, wide oval fiberglass-belted white-sidewall tires, hood scoop

turn signals, lower body side stripes on sport coupes and convertibles and a C-style body side stripe on fastbacks. A power top was included on convertibles.

This year a 351-cid/250-hp two-barrel V-8 was the first option for Torino GTs (at $58.34 over the 302) and actually replaced the two-barrel version of the 390-cid Ford big-block V-8. The four-barrel version of the 390, now rated for 320 hp, was $163.24 extra and also required an extra-cost transmission (either the heavy-duty three-speed at $79.20, a four-speed manual at $194.31 or Ford's Select Shift Cruise-O-Matic at $222.08).

The 427-cid/390-hp V-8 was no longer available. Its replacement in the "Fairlane" models (including Torino GTs) was a new 428-cid 335-hp V-8 for only $287.53 extra. This option also required an extra-cost transmission and included a heavy-duty battery, a 55-amp alternator, dual exhausts, the extra-cooling package, bright engine dress-up parts, cast aluminum rocker covers and a 3.25:1 non-locking rear axle. This was the non-Ram Air version.

The 428 Cobra Jet Ram Air V-8 was an additional $420.96 for Fairlanes that were not already Cobra models. This included all of the same goodies as the "regular" 428 Cobra Jet option, plus a 3.50:1 non-locking rear axle and a functional hood scoop.

In one magazine test, the 1969 Torino GT with the 428-cid big-block V-8 turned in a 14.5-second quarter-mile run. It could also scat from 0-to-60 mph in just 6.3 seconds.

FORD

Jerry Heasley

FORD

The Cobra was its own model and a sub-series of the Torino lineup for 1969. This car
is the formal hardtop version. The Cobra was also available as a SportsRoof coupe.

1969 Cobra

Ford's sexy-looking Cobra had an Italian-sounding first name that meant "fast," plus looks that meant "muscle car" in any language. "Torque gives rubber big bite for fast acceleration," *Motor Trend* said to sum up the car in a few words. "Four speed helps and Ford has many hop up parts for the 428."

A new sub-series showed up in the 1969 Ford Torino GT lineup. This Cobra line included just two body types, the Model 65A formal hardtop base priced at $3,208 and the Model 6B SportsRoof-base priced at $3,183. The emphasis was on performance when you went Cobra shopping and the standard equipment included a 428-cid/335-hp Cobra Jet V-8, a four-speed manual transmission, competition suspension, wide oval-belted black sidewall tires and 6-inch-wide wheels with hubcaps.

The base Cobra engine featured a 4.13 x 3.98-inch bore and stroke, a 10.6:1 compression ratio, 335 hp at 5200 rpm and 440 lbs.-ft. of torque at 2600 rpm. You could get it with an optional 351-cid/290-hp V-8 if you wanted to save on gas, but few muscle car buffs did. Also optional on the Cobra

was the 428 Cobra Jet "Ram Air" V-8, which also carried a 335-hp rating but achieved it at a higher 5600 rpm peak. Its torque output was 445 lbs.-ft. at 3400 rpm and it had a 10.7:1 compression ratio.

The Ram Air engine featured a functional hood scoop to "ram" cold air into its single Holley four-barrel carburetor. This setup was only $133.44 extra on the Cobra, compared to $420.96 when ordered for other "Fairlane" models, including Torino GTs.

If you did not want to shift for yourself, a Select Shift automatic transmission was optional for $37.06 and it came with a floor shift and optional center console. The 3.25:1 rear axle was standard and optional axle ratios included 3.45:1, 3.91:1 and 4.30:1. Power disc brakes were also available for $64.77. A Traction-Lock differential was $63.51 extra and getting a factory tachometer added $47.92 to the price tag.

Motor Trend road tested a Cobra with the Ram Air engine and liked the car. The magazine charted 0-to-60 performance at 6.3 seconds and the quarter-mile at 14.5 seconds and 100 mph.

FORD

Jerry Heasley

Only 754 of the racing-inspired Talladegas were produced for the 1969 model year.

1969 Talladega

This fastback Ford is the perfect quarter-mile machine for the FoMoCo fan who wants to go drag racing against Starsky & Hutch rather than John Force. Though the Talladega was a bit heftier and weightier than other Torinos, the 428 CJ still pushed it to mid-14-second quarter-miles. However, it was much better suited to left hand turns on an oval-shaped racetrack.

At the time they were built, the fastback cars that became combatants in the "aerodynamic wars" on the 1969-1970 NASCAR Grand National superspeedways were more of a headache to their manufacturers than the worshiped treasures they are today. Requirements to "legalize" them for racing meant at least 500 examples had to be produced during the 1969 model year. That minimum production level was raised to one car per dealer for 1970.

Ford's hopes rode on the sloped-nosed 1969 Torino Talladega, which was part of the midsized Fairlane model lineup. A similar, but not identical, Mercury Montego counterpart was produced and called the Cyclone Spoiler II.

Ford called its fastback-styled two-door hardtops "SportsRoof" models at this point and the Talladega model was one of them. It was named after a town in Alabama where a new 2.66-mile NASCAR superspeedway was opening. The Talladega had an extended, sloped nose and a flush radiator grille. A revised Torino rear bumper was used in front of this model and the rocker panels were reworked a bit. The result was a car that was nearly 6 inches longer and 1 inch lower

than a stock Torino SportsRoof. Of course, NASCAR racing teams started from there and continued to enhance their Talladegas.

In the stock version, power came from a 335-hp Cobra Jet 428-cid "FE" block V-8, which was pretty potent, but came only with a C-6 Cruise-0-Matic automatic transmission. The racing cars ran the 427-cid big-block at the beginning of the season. Beginning in March, they were allowed to use the new 429-cid "semi-hemi" V-8. These engines were not installed in showroom Talladegas, however, since the Mustang Boss 429 was utilized to meet the requirements of the race-sanctioning groups.

Counting prototypes, Talladega production easily passed the required 500 units and wound up at 754. The cars came in Wimbleton White, Royal Maroon or Presidential Blue. They had Black interiors and came only with bench seats.

The idea behind the Talladega was to get the production work over with as quickly as possible and let the racers create a performance image for the Torino series. They did this, too. David Pearson won his second straight NASCAR Grand National championship driving for race team owners Holman and Moody.

The 1969 Talladegas proved very adept at racing. In fact, test drivers found that their 1970 replacements were some 5 mph slower on the big tracks. As a result, Ford's factory-backed teams ran year-old models at many tracks during the 1970 racing season.

There were a lot of muscular Mustangs to pick from in 1970. If you didn't wind up with a Boss 302 or 429, you could opt for the standard sport coupe or Mach 1 (pictured here) with a variety of engine options—including the fire-breathing 428 CJ and SCJ mills.

1970 Mustang CJ 428/SCJ 428

FORD

In Mustang enthusiast circles, the 428 CJ/SCJ Mustang is legendary for grabbing the Stock Eliminator title at the 1970 National Hot Rod Association's (NHRA) Winternationals. This was the race of the year for high-performance buffs and the Mustang was the monarch that season. In his book *Fast Mustangs*, marque expert Alex Gabbard observed, "The 428 Cobra Jet engine has been called the fastest-running pure stock in the history of man."

The 1970 Mustang had some distinctions to set it apart from the 1969 edition. The biggest change was a return to single headlights up front. The new headlights were located inside a larger new grille opening. Simulated air intakes were seen where the outboard headlights were on the 1969 Mustang models. The 1970 rear end appearance was also slightly restyled.

Standard equipment in the 1970 Mustang included wall-to-wall carpeting, bucket seats, belted bias-ply tires, a locking steering column, a full synchronized manual transmission, a sporty floor-mounted gear shift lever and a rear deck lid spoiler on SportsRoof models. Among the many muscle car options were power front disc brakes, a functional hood scoop, louvered sport slats for the rear window (which were very popular at the time), a Hurst shifter, a tachometer and a Drag Pack racing package.

In addition to the base sport coupe (two-door hardtop) and convertible, Mustangs came as the hot Mach 1 fastback, the luxurious Grande hardtop and the race-bred Boss 302 fastback. With different engine option selections, you could change the Boss 302 into a Boss 351 or a Boss 429. In total, Ford offered nine Mustang engines to pick from and the lineup was the same as 1969, except that the 390-cid V-8 was discontinued.

While the pre-packaged Boss models were the hit of the enthusiast magazines this season, the CJ 428 and SCJ 428 engines were both back. The former listed for $356 in all Mustang models except the Mach 1, which offered it for $311 over the price of its standard 351-cid V-8. The Ram-Air version was $376 extra in the Mach 1 and $421 extra in other models. A 2.32:1 close-ratio four-speed manual gearbox ($205) or a Cruise-O-Matic automatic transmission ($222) was required with both of the Cobra Jet engines. In addition, on base Mustangs F70-14 whitewall tires were required over E78-14 black sidewall tires when either of these engines was ordered. On Mach 1s, Boss models and convertibles, E70-14 whitewalls were required.

The 1970 Mach 1 featured the new year's front end styling and had its taillights recessed in a flat panel with honeycomb trim between them. Ribbed aluminum rocker panel moldings with big Mach 1 call-outs and a cleaner upper rear quarter treatment without simulated air scoops at the end of the main feature line were seen. A black-striped hood with a standard fake scoop replaced the completely matte-black hood. New twist-in hood pins held the hood down.

You could also get a shaker hood scoop on Mach 1s with the standard 351-cid V-8. A redesigned steering wheel was the big interior change. A larger rear stripe, larger rear call-out, mag-type hubcaps, wide 14 x 7-inch wheels and bright oval exhaust tips were also new. Black-painted styled wheels were a no-cost option.

Motor Trend tested a 1970 Mustang Mach 1 with the 351-cid four-barrel V-8. It had a 4.002 x 3.50-inch bore and stroke. With an 11.0:1 compression ratio it developed 300 hp at 5400 rpm and 380 lbs.-ft. of torque at 3400 rpm. With automatic transmission and a 3.00:1 axle the car turned 0-to-60 mph in 8.2 seconds and did the quarter-mile in 16 seconds at 86.2 mph.

FORD

The 1970 Torino Cobra was seen as a challenger to the fast-moving Mopars, but
it wound up playing second fiddle to the Mustang and its Torino GT sibling.

Doug Mitchel

1970 Torino Cobra

Though conceived as the answer to the winged Dodge Charger Daytona and Plymouth Superbird, the '70 Torino Cobra SportsRoof was more of a street muscle car. *Motor Trend* once said: "Maybe this shaped-for-the-wind thing is real," but if it was, it really didn't matter. These cars were not going to drive on NASCAR superspeedways and maximum aerodynamics didn't help much in the Stoplight Grand Prix.

Ford had its intermediate cars on a two-year styling cycle at this time, so no matter how good the 1968 and 1969 Fairlane fastbacks looked or how fast they were in stock car racing competition, by the time the 1970 model year rolled around, it was time for a new batch of sheet metal.

Ford also had its intermediates (and most other lines) on a growth binge and the wheelbase measurement for the new '70 Torino increased from 116 to 117 inches. The length of the car also went up half a foot and its width was increased by about two inches.

A full line of models was again available. At the top of the heap was the Torino Cobra. At $3,270 it had the most expensive base price in the line, even more than the sole remaining convertible—the GT at $3,212.

Part of the cost could be attributed to its new standard power plant, the 385 series big-block 429. The 428 was gone from the intermediates for the new year. Torinos got the milder 360-hp engine with a single four-barrel carburetor. Cobras came with Ford's top-loader four-speed manual transmission (capped by a Hurst shifter), a competition suspension with staggered rear shocks, 7-inch wide steel wheels, F70-14 wide oval tires, a black hood with locking devices, black-out trim and Cobra badging. Bench seats were standard. Engine options included the 370-hp Cobra 429 or Cobra Jet Ram Air 429 with the same rating. For $155 you could get the Traction-Lok differential, and for $207 the 4.30:1 Detroit Locker rear axle was available.

Production was 7,675, which was overshadowed by the 56,819 Torino GTs produced. The Torino GTs, which were flashier and cheaper at $3,105, thanks to a standard 302 cid V-8.

Torino Cobra was supposed to be the car of record for NASCAR Grand National racers, but it was slower than the 1969 Talladegas, forcing teams to run year-old cars. As an answer to the winged Dodge Charger Daytona and Plymouth Superbird, the King Cobra was stillborn.

Jerry Heasley

FORD

The 1971 351-equipped Boss Mustang could crack 14 seconds in the quarter-mile. Only about 1,800 of these highly acclaimed machines were made, which makes them collector trophies today.

1971 Mustang Boss 351

When you were "working for the man" back in 1971, a car like this could make you look forward to the weekend— especially your Sunday afternoon trip to the drag strip. *Road Test* magazine observed in March 1971 that the Boss 351 was the "Sophisticated Mustang." The magazine said, " The '71 Boss is 40 hp bossier than last year's 302 (and) still gives fine handling coupled to straightaway performance." With the base 330-hp V-8, the Boss 351 did 0-to-60 in 5.9 seconds and the quarter-mile in 13.98 seconds at 104 mph.

Ford Mustangs grew to their all-time largest for the 1971 model year. Wheelbase was up an inch to 109 inches, length increased 2.1 inches to 189.5 inches and width grew 2.4 inches to 74.1 inches. The latter was accompanied by a tread increase that permitted the 429-cid big-block V-8 to fit in the engine compartment with ease. Although the 429-powered cars were the most muscular, the Boss 351 was perhaps the most interesting.

The Boss 429 was curtailed early in the 1970 model run, and the Boss 302 was of no more use after it was gone. Racing rules had changed and engine size was no longer critical to racing legalization. As a result, the Boss 351's purpose was just to tap what was left of the declining high-performance market.

Like its predecessors, the Boss 351 was based on the SportsRoof or fastback model. It was considered an option package and brought the base Mustang price of $2,973 up to $4,124. The heart of the new Boss 351 package was a 351-hp Cleveland V-8 with four-bolt main bearings, solid valve lifters and a four-barrel carburetor. The 1971 models were the last for Ford high-compression engines and the last for gross advertised horsepower numbers, which were 330 hp for the Boss 351.

Other mechanical features included a four-speed "top-loader" manual transmission with a Hurst gear shifter, a competition-type suspension, power front disc brakes, 3.91:1 Traction-Lok gearing, dual exhausts with non-exposed tips and the infamous rev limiter. Visuals were plentiful with side and rear identification decals, a matte black hood with functional scoops and locks and side stripes.

Only about 1,800 Boss 351s were made, which adds up to rarity today. There was no 1972 Boss Mustang of any kind, but by playing with the options list, you could come close to "building" one. The last year for the "big" Mustang was 1973.

FORD

The 1971 Mach 1 Mustang had cool packaging, twin hood nostrils, rear
spoiler, new paint schemes and an optional 429 big-block. What's not to like?

1971 Mustang Mach 1

You may not be able to break Mach 1 in a Mustang Mach 1, but it's the kind of car that looks – and feels – like it could do just that if you pushed it real hard. "For those interested in owning a sporty car which reflects up-to-the-minute design, Mustang (Mach 1), an all-around vehicle without a significant flaw, can't be a bad choice," opined *Road Test* magazine in September 1970.

For 1971, Ford completed its fourth redesign of the Mustang. This created a bigger car. It had the basic Mustang look, with a longer wheelbase, a stretched length, more width, wider front and rear tracks and a heavier curb weight. A raked windshield, bulging front fenders and aerodynamic enhancements were evident.

The Mach 1 package returned. It included color-keyed mirrors, a honeycomb grille, color-keyed bumpers, sport lamps, a new gas cap, special decals and tape stripes and black or argent silver finish on the lower body perimeter. A special hood with NASA-style air scoops was a no-cost option with the base 302-cid V-8 and standard otherwise.

Available for the last time was a 429-cid big-block engine, which came in Cobra-Jet Ram Air and Super-Cobra-Jet Ram Air versions. Ford put together 1,255 of the CJ-R equipped Mach 1s and 610 of the SCJ-Rs.

Basically a de-stroked Thunderbird/Lincoln 460-cid V-8, the 429 had a wedge-head-shaped combustion chamber derived from up-to-date performance technology. The CJ-R version utilized large valves, a hydraulic camshaft, four-bolt main bearing caps, re-worked porting and a 700-cfm Quadrajet carburetor (sourced from General Motors). A Ram Air induction system was included. Advertised horsepower for the 429 CJ-R was 370 at 5400 rpm.

The 429 SCJ-R put out 375 hp at 5600 rpm. A Drag Pack option with either a 3.91:1 Traction-Lok differential or a 4.11:1 Detroit Locker axle was mandatory. The option also included an oil cooler for when things really got hot at the drag strip. Other 429 SCJ-R performance features included solid valve lifters, adjustable rocker arms, drop-forged pistons and a 780-cfm Holley carburetor.

Both Cobra Jet engines had 11.3:1 compression and produced 450 lbs.-ft. of torque at 3400 rpm. The SCJ-R had a bit more camshaft duration (200/300 degree versus 282/296 degrees).

Car Life (July 1969) tested a 375-hp Boss 429 with a four-speed manual transmission and 3.91:1 axle. It did 0 to 60 mph in 7.1 seconds. The quarter-mile took 14.09 seconds with a terminal speed of 102.85 mph. Top speed on the car was about 116 mph.

It might be a stretch to call the Mustang II "King Cobra" a muscle car, but it looked the part and stood out during a time when few cars offered much in the way of excitement.

FORD

Jerry Heasley

1978 Mustang II "King Cobra"

During the fuel shortage-scared, federal regulation-oppressed mid- to late-'70s, a number of "visual" muscle cars were offered by domestic manufacturers. Their mission was to drum up enthusiasm in the youth market and to snare what was left of the old performance buyers.

Exemplifying this was the 1978 Ford Mustang II King Cobra option. It dressed the not-universally-loved lines of the hatchback in its most garish (or garnished, depending on your point of view) trim yet.

Ford made numerous efforts to "trick-up" its Mustang II, which was introduced in the fall of 1973 as a 1974 model. The King Cobra option, named after the stillborn 1970 replacement for the Torino Talladega, would be the last as the 1979 models were going to be all new.

The King Cobra followed the Cobra II option that came out midyear in 1977. Huge side stripes, lettering, front and rear spoilers probably did more to anger purists of the order of the sacred snake than attract serious performance seekers.

The Cobra II returned for 1978, but at the start of the model year we got the King Cobra. It featured a more complete front air dam, similar rear spoiler, wheel flair treatment, the same fake hood scoop and different graphics from the Cobra II.

Subdued lettering on the sides and rear spoiler contrasted to the giant Cobra hood decal that the King carried. Its $1,293 addition to the hatchback's base $4,011 price also bought color-keyed dual sport mirrors plus black out grille and headlight door trim. Thankfully, it didn't include the window slats the Cobra IIs often got.

Mechanically, first the good news. Power front disc brakes, power steering and heavy-duty suspension were part of the package. Also good was a standard four-speed manual gearshift. Its clutch was attached to the 302-cid V-8, which came standard, too. Before visions of Boss and High Output 302s dance in your head, note that the 302 was the F Code version, which in 1978 breathed through a Motorcraft 2150 two-barrel carb and churned out a lazy 139 hp at 3600 rpm.

While scorned by today's standards, the King Cobra wasn't all that inferior compared to the rest of the visual muscle cars of its time. Not everybody wants, can afford or even relates to the muscle cars of the 1960s or the new ones out today. With around 5,000 KCs made, they are getting rare, offer somewhat unique styling touches, have salvage yards full of mechanical replacement parts and bring a 50 percent premium over the regular hatchback '78 Mustang II prices today.

FORD

Brad Bowling

**The 1979 Mustang Indy Pace Car featured a 5-liter engine,
lots of aerodynamic stuff, and a memorable paint job.**

1979 Mustang

This is one of those "coulda-shoulda-woulda" cars that came out when car collectors were still fighting the prewar-vs.-postwar battle. I was involved because I took my '54 Chevy to an old-car show and they turned me away at the gate. "The only thing that car is good for is making a hot rod," they said. That kind of mind could not envision the time when a car made after World War II would be worth more than a Model T, much less accept the fact that a late-model Mustang Pace Car would be collectible someday. So I coulda bought such a car, I shoulda bought such a car and I woulda bought such a car—had I had any money back then.

Thankfully things are changing now. In his book *Fast Mustangs*, high-performance Ford enthusiast Alex Gabbard states, "The appearance of the 5-liter Mustang in 1979 caused many enthusiasts to applaud. As usual, the segment of the market that likes the feel of brawn found in the torque of a V-8 was somewhat impressed. As the engine increased in power, impression grew increasingly until the modern version of the HO 5-liter had become a real muscle car by any definition."

A whole new breed of Mustang was presented for 1979. It was derived from the Ford Fairmont platform and featured unit-body construction. With dramatic new sports car styling, it had one of the most efficient, aerodynamic body designs of its era and also had 20 percent more interior space than the previous model.

The Mustang now had a 100.4-inch wheelbase, a 179.1-inch overall length and weighed around 2,600 lbs. Precise handling was delivered by a variety of suspension improvements. The two-door notchback model was priced at $4,858 with V-8 power and the three-door hatchback ran about $5,223 with the big engine.

The 1979 V-8 had a 4.00 x 3.00-inch bore and stroke for a familiar-sounding 302 cubic inches. With a single Motorcraft two-barrel carburetor and an 8.4:1 compression ratio, it was no muscle car compared to those of the '60s or those available today, but it was pretty snappy for 1979. The 5.0-liter V-8 generated 140 hp at 3600 rpm and 250 lbs.-ft. of torque at 1800 rpm. While this was obviously not a real drag racer, the Indy Pace Car model had the "look" of a genuine performance car and more or less honored the return of the V-8 that started the ball rolling to a lot better things in the years to come.

The V-8-powered Mustang three-door hatchback that paced the 63rd running of The Indianapolis 500-Mile Race on May 27, 1979, had a T-top and special silver and black finish with red-orange striping and Official Pace Car graphics. It wore stock, forged-metric aluminum wheels. A limited edition of Indy Pace Car replicas was marketed to the public.

The scarce SVO-McClaren Mustang broke the mold for
muscle cars by using a turbo-charged four-cylinder engine.

FORD

Jerry Heasley

1980 SVO-McLaren Turbo Mustang

The McLaren Mustang was created by Ford Motor Co.'s newly formed Special Vehicle Operations (SVO) group. The car represented a very obvious indication that Ford was finally turning the performance-car battleship around to chase the enthusiast market. "The bright orange police magnet was a bit too obvious to thrash about on residential roads," wrote Bob Nagy in *Motor Trend*.

This "semi-aftermarket" modern muscle car hit the market in late 1980. It represented the ultimate-for-the-era, small-displacement street performance car. Unfortunately, its price tag of $25,000 was anything but small.

Under the car's hood was a high-tech 2.3-liter turbocharged four-cylinder engine. It had a special variable-boost turbocharger that provided from 5 to 11 psi. This provided optimum road and track driving performance.

Compared to the stock Ford turbo four, with its set pressure of 5 psi (and an estimated 131 hp), the McLaren Mustang was a screamer. It was rated for 175 hp at 2500 rpm with the turbocharger boost running 10 psi.

Flared fenders and a functional air dam were among body changes that set the McLaren apart. Designers Todd Gerstenberger and Harry Wykes went after an International Motor Sports Association (IMSA) racing car image. They did a great job of achieving just the look they wanted. The air dam directed cold air to the front disc brakes through the hairy-looking wastegate hood.

Other features of the McLaren Mustang included BBS Euro-styled laced wheels shod with Firestone 225/55R-15 HPR tires, Koni shocks, Stewart-Warner gauges and Recaro seats. To complement the McLaren's competition look, there was a competition-type roll bar in the car's interior. A dress-up kit made the mighty little engine shine like a jewel.

Part of the SVO concept was to showcase high-performance components in cars such as the McLaren—which was virtually hand-built—and determine the most popular equipment. The favorites could then be made available through the performance parts aftermarket at a later date.

No one expected to see the production of thousands of McLaren-Mustangs. Instead, the idea was to get lots of enthusiasts interested in bolt-on hardware for thousands of late-model Mustangs. Consequently, production of the cars was extremely limited. No more than 250 examples—including the prototype—were believed put together. Some experts think that the real number was substantially lower than that.

Loaded with good looks and outstanding performance capabilities, the McLaren exudes collector appeal as well. It has always been a special and rare machine that few people have owned.

FORD

The 1984 Mustang SVO had Ford firmly back in the muscle car game. The car
scooted from 0-to-60 mph in 7.5 seconds and had a top speed of 134 mph.

1984 Mustang SVO

The release of the 5.0-liter V-8 in 1979 Mustangs was the beginning of the marque's high-performance revival. However, getting back to a traditional, high-torquing V-8-powered muscle Mustang didn't happen overnight. Ford reverted to a smaller 4.2-liter (255-cid) V-8 in 1980, but gas shortages during the 1970s had put the focus on finding ways to make smaller, more efficient cars go faster. Ford tried four-cylinder turbo power in its Cobra model and the limited edition 1980 McLaren Mustang and the company had no intentions of stopping there.

On April 17, 1984, Ford distributed a letter noting the Mustang's 20th birthday and mentioning two hot cars the company was offering that year. One was a more powerful midyear GT with a 5.0-liter V-8 that wound up being delayed. The other was the Mustang SVO, which was named after the automaker's Special Vehicle Operations team.

Featuring a touch of European-inspired technology, the $15,596 SVO model (about $6,000 more than a regular Mustang Turbo GT) was promoted as a "machine that speaks for itself." Special features included multi-adjustable articulated bucket seats, a performance suspension with adjustable Koni gas shocks and a 2.3-liter port-fuel-injected turbocharged four-

cylinder engine with an air-to-air intercooler. The engine had an 8.0:1 compression ratio and produced 175 hp at 4400 rpm and 210 lbs.-ft. of torque at 3000 rpm. A functional hood scoop designed to "ram" cold air into the engine was also part of the package.

The SVO engine was linked to a five-speed manual transmission with overdrive fifth gear and a Hurst shift linkage. It had a Traction-Lok rear axle with a 3.45:1 final drive ratio. Disc brakes were fitted on all four corners, as were Goodyear NCT steel-belted radial tires on 16 x 7-inch cast-aluminum wheels.

Only the three-door Hatchback body was delivered as an SVO. Identification features included unique single rectangular headlamps, a front air dam with integral spoiler, a functional hood scoop, rear wheel opening "spats" and a dual-wing rear spoiler.

According to Ford, the SVO could do 0-to-60 mph in 7.5 seconds and had a top speed of 134 mph. *Motor Trend* called the SVO "the best driving street Mustang the factory has ever offered." *Road & Track* said "the SVO outruns the Datsun 280ZX, outhandles the Ferrari 308 and Porsche 944 and it's affordable."

FORD

Brad Bowling

Saleen Autosport produced three of the unique Saleen Mustangs for 1984. The drive train was largely unchanged from the base Mustang, but the Saleens offered a long list of cool parts inside and out that made them run faster and look better than the garden variety Mustang.

1984 Saleen Mustang

Ford turbocharged the four-cylinder Mustang off and on, but high costs, low power when compared to the cheaper V-8 and reliability issues killed that program. It was the re-introduction of the 5.0-liter HO V-8 in the 1982 Mustang GT that put Ford back on the muscle car highway.

Steve Saleen, a business school graduate with a background in Sports Car Club of America (SCCA) Formula Atlantic and Trans-Am racing, was thrilled by Ford's first assault on the early '80s horsepower war. Saleen (pronounced like the last two syllables of "gasoline") had owned '65 and '66 Shelby GT-350s and a '67 GT fastback with a 390-cid V-8. He was aware of how Carroll Shelby had turned garden-variety Mustangs into world-class performance cars.

To meet federal laws, Saleen established a formula he applied, at least initially, to all of his Hi-Po Mustangs: Rather than make engine modifications that required expensive and extensive testing for emissions, fuel consumption and warranty standards, Saleen left the engines stock and enhanced performance through suspension, brake, chassis and aerodynamic improvements.

In 1984, Saleen Autosport produced three 175-hp Mustang hatchbacks with Saleen's own Racecraft suspension components including specific-rate front and rear springs, Bilstein pressurized struts and shocks, a front G-load brace and urethane swaybar bushings. He lowered the car and

improved the Mustang's handling to near racetrack levels. Those first three cars wore 215/60-15 Goodyear Eagle GTs wrapped around 15x7-inch Hayashi "basketweave" wheels. A custom front air dam, sides skirts, clear covers for the recessed headlights and a rather showy spoiler created a smoother aerodynamic package. The interior featured a Saleen gauge package, a Wolf Racing four-spoke steering wheel and an Escort radar detector.

The standard equipment list included a Saleen windshield graphic, deck lid emblem and serial-number plaque, a Ford Motorsport rear window graphic, tri-color racing stripes on the rocker panels, side window louvers, a chrome air cleaner with Saleen graphic, a 170-mph speedometer, a Cal Custom Hawk leather-covered shift knob, an Escort radar detector and a Cal Custom Hawk security system. The only option was a Sanyo AM/FM stereo cassette player with speakers. Because the first three cars were essentially prototypes, the tri-color stripes were hand-painted on two of the cars and not used on the third. In 1985 and afterward, tape was used.

For $14,300 ($4,526 more than a standard Mustang GT), the Saleen was quite reasonable when parked next to a comparably equipped Camaro Z-28 ($14,086), Pontiac Trans-Am ($15,100) or Toyota Supra ($16,853). Even the SVO Mustang was more expensive at $15,585.

At 210 hp, the 1985 GT brought the Mustang closer to its muscle car roots.

1985 Mustang GT 5.0-Liter HO

Robert L. Rewey took over as vice president of Ford Division in 1985. He enjoyed a great first year at the helm, as the company's sales increased for the third year in a row. At the start of the model year, Ford made a forecast of 128,000 Mustang sales, which turned out to be conservative. In reality, 156,514 units were produced a 31.7 percent had V-8s.

All 1985 Mustangs had a new frontal appearance with a 4-squares integral air dam below the front bumper. It was flanked by low, rectangular parking lamps. GTs also had integral fog lights. A grille that looked like the SVO grille, with one large slot and angled sides in a sloping front panel appeared on all Mustangs. Wide horizontal taillights wrapped around the rear body corners.

The 1985 5.0-Liter Mustang GT proved that powerful V-8s had a future under the Mustang's hood, even if Ford Motor Company wanted enthusiasts to think that cars with turbocharged four-cylinder engines were poised to take over in the enthusiasts' market niche. One reason for the popularity of the V-8 was its price. You could purchase a Mustang GT three-door hatchback with a 302-cid engine for $9,885, compared to the Mustang SVO's base window sticker of $14,521.

Ford had upgraded the 5.0-liter V-8 to a Holley four-barrel carburetor in 1984, a year in which the motor cranked out 175 hp at 4000 rpm and 210 lbs.-ft. of torque at 3000 rpm. In 1985, the news was a new HO (high-output) version of the 5.0-liter engine with 210 hp at 4400 rpm and 270 lbs.-ft. of torque at 3200 rpm. *Motor Trend* magazine said it had "lovely axle-creaking torque of another time."

In addition to having a Holley four-barrel carburetor like the previous year's model, the 1985 version of the Mustang GT 5.0-liter HO featured a high-performance camshaft, roller tappets and a two-speed accessory drive system. The small-block V-8 was connected to a floor-mounted gear shifter with a tighter shift pattern and new gear ratios. This engine was hot and as the word about it got out, the production of V-8 Mustangs leaped from 36,038 in 1984 to 45,463 for 1985.

All Mustang GTs had the V-8 engine as standard equipment. The three-door hatchback model sold for $9,885 and weighed 2,899 lbs. while the ragtop listed for $13,585 and weighed 3,043 lbs.

FORD

Jerry Heasley

Brad Bowling

Saleen revamped 140 Mustangs for 1985, including this car, number 85-0109.

1985 Saleen Mustang

The 1985 Saleen model was based on a new 210-hp Mustang, In Saleen format it featured larger 225/60-15 Goodyear and Fulda tires (the brand depended on time of the year the car was produced) and a slightly modified aerodynamics package. Metallic brake pads for the front binders were standard on the Saleen, which had a $16,900 window sticker. Sales were definitely improved for the year, with 140 units going to new owners, including two in convertible form.

The Saleen conversion for 1985 cost $4,195 on top of the factory-ordered LX V-8 hatchback or convertible. Standard colors included Ford's Black, Canyon Red, Medium Regatta Blue or Oxford White. Special-ordered paint cost an additional $150. If the buyer wanted the car to be built on a Mustang GT, instead of a standard Mustang, the cost was an additional $100.

Ford agreed to a bailment pooling arrangement with Saleen in 1985, meaning his cars could be sold through the company's established dealer network and were eligible for full warranty protection. Stock Mustangs were shipped from Ford's home factory in Dearborn, Michigan directly to the Saleen conversion facility in California. After the conversion work was done, they were distributed to ordering dealers.

Participating dealers were advised to order cars intended for Saleen conversion in the following manner: with the M-code 5.0-liter V-8, 3.08:1 limited-slip axle, five-speed transmission, and 225/60VR-15 Goodyear Gatorbacks. Equipment not to be ordered for conversion included: lower two-tone paint treatment and cruise control.

Because Saleen's production line was subjected to the same sort of component supply problems and customer demands Shelby had endured, running changes were common right from the start. Some 1985s were fitted with 16-inch wheels and German-made Fulda tires and several early units were built using the blockier 1984 spoilers and dams. Cars converted early in the year were modified in a shop in Petaluma, California, whereas the remainder of 1985 production took place at the Burch Ford dealership at 201 North Harbor Boulevard in LaHabra, California.

Production for 1985 included 133 hatchbacks (one was a special competition model), two convertible and five cars that Saleen listed as being of "unknown" body style. The convertible had an $18,900 windows sticker, while the price of the five unknown cars is not available. The regular 5.0-liter EFI V-8 was rated for 165 hp at 4200 rpm. The H.O. version had a four-barrel Holley carb an delivered 210 hp at 4400 rpm.

FORD

The Mustang SVO was back for a second year in 1985, again
sporting a high-tech four-cylinder engine that delivered 205 hp.

1985 SVO Mustang

Engineers in Ford's Special Vehicle Operations (SV) branch were no doubt pleased when their self-named Mustang model was revised in the middle of the year with a new look (primarily flush-mounted headlights) and an impressive 205 hp.

All of the cars were Model 28 three-door hatchbacks (Style 61B) with the Code W 2.3-liter turbocharged four. All were built in the Dearborn, Michigan assembly plant (Code F). The SVO models came in a choice of six colors: 1B=Medium Charcoal, 1C=Black,1Q-Silver, 2C=Canyon Red, 2R=Jalapena Red and 9L=Oxford White.

The in-line single overhead cam four had a 3.78 x 3.13-inch bore and stroke and 141 cubic inches of displacement. An electronic fuel injection (EFI) system fed it fuel. The compression ratio was 8.0:1. The 205 peak horsepower was achieved at 5000 rpm. Once again, hot rod met high-tech under the hood with a higher-performance cam, higher-flow exhaust system, reconfigured turbocharger, larger injectors, and greater boost accounting for the power increase.

The price of the all-out sports car dropped slightly, to $14,521, but sales also fell to 1,954 units. Available options included an engine block heater ($18), a heavy-duty battery ($27), California emissions ($99), high-altitude emissions (no charge), an electric rear window defroster ($140), all tinted glass ($110), a flip-up sunroof ($315), a single wing rear spoiler (no charge) and leather performance bucket seats ($189). A special SVO competition preparation package deleted the air conditioning and power locks, AM/FM/cassette and power windows and gave the buyer a credit of $1,417.

A total of 3,382 200-hp SVO Mustangs were assembled for 1986 before the car was discontinued.

1986 Mustang GT/SVO

There were not many changes made to the 1986 Mustangs. Ford increased its anti-corrosion warranty, added sound-deadening material and adopted a single-key locking system. A revised port-type fuel-injection system and a 200-hp V-8 for GT models were other changes.

Ford continued to offer an 88-hp four-cylinder engine and a 120-hp throttle body-injected V-6 in Mustangs, but the updated 5.0-liter HO V-8 was standard in GTs. It was revised from 1985's four-barrel carburetor induction system to a multi-port fuel injection system and lost 10 hp in the process, although performance was still quite impressive. The 302-cid cast-iron V-8 had a 9.2:1 compression ratio and produced 200 hp at 4000 rpm and 285 lbs.-ft. of torque at 3000 rpm.

Other standard equipment on GTs was oriented towards performance car buyers and included a five-speed manual overdrive transmission, Goodyear Eagle VR tires, quick-ratio power steering, a special heavy-duty suspension and articulated front sports seats. An automatic overdrive transmission was optional for $622.

The Mustang GT was available in two models. One was a three-door hatchback with a $10,691 price tag and curb weight of 2,976 lbs. The other was the convertible, which listed for $14,523 and weighed in at 3,103 lbs.

The computer-controlled 2.3-liter turbocharged and intercooled four-cylinder engine was standard in SVOs. The SVO included a five-speed transmission with Hurst shifter with short, quick throws, four-wheel disc brakes and all of the other special goodies that the previous SVO models came with.

For its final year of production, the SVO Mustang received more conservative programming of its EEC-IV electronic engine control system, which dropped its horsepower rating to 200 at 5,000 rpm. The SVO's appearance was essentially unchanged from 1985. Ford enhanced the anti-corrosion warranty, added more sound-deadening material and adopted a single-key lock system. The 1986 model came in a choice of four body colors and two of them were new. They were 1B Dark Gray Metallic, 1C Black, 2A Bright Red and 9L Oxford White.

The 1986 SVO Mustang carried a higher $15,272 price tag. In spite of this, sales increased to 3,382 units before it was dropped. That made the three-year total for the high-tech performer just 9,844 units.

FORD

Brad Bowling

The 1986 Saleen hatchback sold for $17,900. A total of 190 hatchbacks and 11 convertibles were made.

1986 Saleen Mustang

The factory-type Mustang V-8 gained electronic fuel injection in 1986 and Steve Saleen expanded the standard equipment list for his custom-built versions. With Saleen Mustangs taking to racetracks in Sports Car Club of America (SCCA) events, the cars saw high-performance improvements such as 16-inch wheels, a revised air dam and spoiler package, a short-throw Hurst shifter, a three-spoke leather-covered Momo steering wheel, GT front bucket seats, Koni adjustable gas rear shocks and a top of the line Kenwood stereo system. A race-style "dead pedal" for the driver's left foot—such as the one offered in the 1986 SVO Mustang—became standard equipment in 1986 Saleen Mustangs.

Other standard equipment included 225/50VR-16 Fulda tires, specific rate front and rear coil springs, Saleen-specific strut mounting bearings, Koni quad shocks, urethane sway bar pivot bushings, a Saleen aerodynamic kit (now built out of urethane), Lexan headlight covers, a 170-mph speedometer, a leather-covered gear shift knob, an Escort radar detector, articulated sport seats (with leather upholstery as an option) and a Saleen Mustang jacket.

The only option listed by the factory was the Kenwood KRC 6000 AM/FM cassette stereo system, although customers could make special requests for add-ons such as automatic transmission, a sunroof and certain aftermarket performance

enhancements. Running changes took place throughout the production year. Many cars were built without the Hurst shifter, a few were shipped with 15-inch wheels and many carried the 1985-spec aerodynamics package.

Exterior body colors available were Black, Canyon Red, Medium Regatta Blue, and Oxford White. On Canyon Red and Oxford White cars, the side louvers located just behind the triangular rear window were painted the body color. The tri-color racing stripes were available in gold, silver or blue.

Participating Ford dealers were required to order cars for conversion with the following specs: LX hatchback or convertible, 5.0-liter V-8, five-speed manual transmission, 3.08:1 limited-slip axle, 225/60VR-15 tires, radio delete, articulated sport seats, GT dash panel, SVO driver's foot rest and pinstripe delete. Two-tone paint and cruise control were not to be ordered on cars that would receiving the Saleen treatment.

Magazine testers were impressed with the package's 6.0-second 0-to-60 mph time and top speed of 142 mph. Corvette-caliber handling was a measured .88g of lateral acceleration. Sales continued to increase, with 190 of the $17,900 hatchbacks selling and 11 convertibles with a $19,900 price tag going to new customers.

FORD

Brad Bowling

The Mustang GT was a hot new car for 1987 and featured a more-than-respectable 225-hp 5-liter V-8.

1987 Mustang GT

Ford's Fox-bodied pony car received a fresh look for 1987, with the first significant restyling since its 1979 debut. No one outside Ford Motor Company could predict at the time that the Mustang's refreshed appearance would endure, with very little change, for the next seven years.

Ford actually had some plans to replace the rear-wheel-drive "Stang" with a Euro-style front-driver developed with its Japanese partner Mazda. The thinking was letting Mazda develop the company's next sporty car would save millions. When articles about the concept leaked out in car magazines, America's Mustang maniacs went ballistic. Ford switched tracks and rode to success with the long-lived but much-loved small-block V-8 version of its original pony car, while the Mazda-bred alternative became the Probe and had little appeal to the 5.0-liter crowd.

The well-thought-out and attractive styling revamp made the 1987 Mustang look more changed than it really was. Although it was not an all-new car, a package of new front and rear body fascias, aero style headlights and a prominent lower feature line with heavy moldings made it seem like a different car. It also sported a redesigned instrument panel, pod-mounted headlight switches and a center console.

With the Mustang SVO model and its sizzling turbocharged four-cylinder engine gone the way of the doo-doo bird, the 5.0-liter HO V-8 took over as the top Mustang performance option. The ante was upped with a pair of hot new cylinder heads that added 25 hp. The engine's compression ratio remained at 9.2:1, but the revised heads and sequential fuel injection system boosted output to 225 hp at 4000 rpm and 300 lbs.-ft. of torque at 3200 rpm.

The Mustang GT was again offered in two body styles. One was a three-door hatchback with an $11,835 price tag and curb weight of 3,080 lbs. The other was the convertible, which listed for $15,724 and weighed in at 3,214 lbs. GT models had a lower front air dam with integrated air scoops and "Mustang GT" lettering formed into the flared rocker panel moldings and rear fascia. Also added were so-called alert lights and a Traction-Lok rear axle. The GT hatchback also had a large spoiler with a high-mounted stoplight. The wide taillights on the GT models were covered by a louver-like appliqué. The sport-tuned exhaust system carried dual outlet exhausts.

An upgrade to four-wheel disc brakes was a nice improvement on the quick 1987 Saleen Mustangs.

Brad Bowling

FORD

1987 Saleen Mustang

Ford restyled and re-engineered its Mustang for 1987. With a 225-hp V-8 under the slightly more aerodynamic hood, the LX and GT moved up a step on the high-performance ladder.

In addition to benefiting from the factory improvements Saleen Autosport cars had a few improvements of their own. A big plus was the addition of four-wheel disc brakes and stronger five-lug rotors originally for the SVO Mustang. This labor-intensive change required the addition of a heavy-duty master cylinder. When tested, the new brakes stopped the car from 60 mph in 5 feet less and exhibited far less fade under extreme conditions.

Alloy American Racing "basket weave" wheels, measuring 16 x 7 inches (front) and 16 x 8 inches (rear), were wrapped by 225/50VR-16 General XP-2000 high-performance tires. Saleen's Racecraft suspension system included specific-rate front and rear coil springs, Koni shocks all around, special strut mounting bearings, urethane sway bar pivot bushing and high-performance alignment specs. The chassis was

tightened by a triangulated strut tower brace and a bar that ran under the engine's oil pan effectively making a strong box out of the front subframe.

The greatest boost to the Saleen's acceleration was the introduction in 1987 of the 3.55:1 rear axle ratio as an option. It was available to replace the standard Saleen 3.08:1 gearing and provided a substantial improvement in 0-to-60 mph and quarter-mile times.

Compared to previous years, there were very few running changes to 1987 Saleens. A few cars built early in the year were fitted with side window louvers (similar to what had come stock from Ford prior to 1987), but problems with the adhesive used to affix them ended their use.

One two-door coupe was produced for Austin Craig, co-founder of the Shelby American Automobile Club and account manager for Ford Motorsports. This added a third body style. Sales of the $20,999 Saleen hit 280 copies. This included 240 regular hatchbacks, six competition hatchbacks, 33 convertibles and the coupe.

1988 Mustang GT

After the extensive changes that it underwent in its 1987 makeover, the Mustang was little changed for 1988. The base-level LX models got a battery with more juice and it was about the extent of all revisions. Three basic body styles were offered in LX trim and a pair of Mustang GTS continued to be offered in hatchback and convertible styles. Prices jumped about $700 for the closed cars and $1,100 for ragtops.

The Mustang GT came once again in two body styles. One was a three-door hatchback, now with a $12,745 price tag and curb weight of 3,193 lbs. The other was the

convertible, which listed for $16,610 and weighed in at 3,341 lbs. GT models had a lower front air dam with integrated fog lamps and air scoops, "Mustang GT" lettering formed into the flared rocker panel moldings and rear fascia, a large rear spoiler with a high-mounted stop light on hatchbacks and wide tail lamps covered by a louver-like appliqué.

As in 1987, the GT shared the 100.5-inch wheelbase with other Mustangs and the 179.6-inch overall length was also the same. At 51.9 inches, the convertible sat slightly lower than the 52.1-inch tall hatchback. Both models were 69.1 inches wide and both GTs rode on P225/60VR16 Goodyear Eagle GT Gatorback tires. The front tread measured 56.6 inches and the rear tread was a tad wider at 57 inches. The GTs again added pressurized gas shocks and sway bars to the Mustangs four-bar link and coil spring suspension system. A Titanium lower body paint accent treatment was a no charge option for the GT.

Back again was the 5.0-liter V-8 with its 4.00 x 3.00-inch bore and stroke, five main bearings, hydraulic valve lifters

and sequential fuel injection system. Its compression ratio rose to 9.5:1 so that the peak of 225 hp came at a slightly higher 4200 rpm. Advertised torque remained at 300 lbs.-ft. at 3200 rpm. In *Motor Trend* magazine editor Tony Swan noted, "Ironically, the best all-out performer in the Ford power ladder is another yestertech 5.0-liter pushrod V-8, the one that's almost as venerable as those employed by General Motors."

Brad Bowling

Jeff Alexander owns this 1988 Saleen hatchback, number 88-0117.

1988 Saleen Mustang

The 1988 Saleen Mustangs were essentially carryover models from the previous year. They had minimal changes. Monroe shock absorbers replaced the Koni units after Monroes helped Saleen racecars turn faster lap times. Pioneer got the nod to replace Kenwood as the official stereo supplier to Saleen Autosport. The Escort radar detector was dropped from the standard equipment list.

Saleen's Racecraft suspension system included specific-rate front and rear coil springs, Monroe shock absorbers, special strut mounting bearings, urethane sway bar pivot bushing and high-performance chassis alignment specs. Other standard equipment included 225/50VR-16 General XP-2000V tires, Monroe quad shock absorbers, a Saleen aerodynamic kit, a 170-mph speedometer, a leather-covered gearshift knob, a Hurst quick-ratio shifter, articulated FloFit sport seats, a three-spoke Momo steering wheel and a Saleen jacket. The standard stereo was comprised of a Pioneer KEH

6050 AM/FM system with a cassette tape player, a Pioneer BP 880 graphic equalizer and six speakers.

The only option listed by the factory was a 3.55:1 rear axle, although customers could make special requests such as for automatic transmission, a sun roof and certain aftermarket performance enhancements. Running changes through the production year were minimal.

Participating Ford dealers ordered cars for Saleen conversions with the following specs: Mustang LX hatchback, coupe or convertible, 5.0-liter V-8, five-speed manual transmission, 3.08:1 limited-slip axle, 225/60VR-15 tires, radio delete, Custom Equipment Group and rear window defogger. Cruise control was not offered because it interfered with the addition of a custom steering wheel.

With enthusiasm and name-recognition building for Saleen's modified Mustangs, it was no surprise that 708 of them were sold in 1988, including 137 convertibles and 25 coupes.

FORD

Jerry Heasley

The 1989 5.0-liter Mustang GT convertible was a fast, cool car for a comparatively modest price of $17,512.

1989 Mustang 5.0-Liter HO

For the 25th anniversary of the Mustang nameplate in 1989, the 5.0-liter small-block Ford V-8 was back. Under the hood of the Fox-bodied Mustang, this power plant offered go-fast enthusiasts as much performance as the 5.7-liter Camaro IROC Z with less bulkiness and a lower price tag.

"It's a very hot package with a '60s ring and a torque curve that'll tighten your skin, all for the price of a Honda Accord," said *Motor Trend's 1989 Automotive Yearbook*. "Ford has vowed to keep the V-8 Mustang as you see it here through the early '90s. And you thought Santa had forgotten." Though cars like the '89 Mustang GT may not have shared the futuristic styling of the GM F-cars, they sure packed a punch when it came to street racing and drag strip action.

The Mustang GT came once again in just two body styles. One was the three-door hatchback, now with a $13,272 price tag and curb weight of 3,194 lbs. The other was the convertible, which listed for $17,512 and tipped the scales at 3,333 lbs. GT models continued to feature a lower front air dam with integrated fog lamps and air scoops, "Mustang GT" lettering formed into the flared rocker panel moldings and rear fascia, a large rear spoiler with a high-mounted stop light on hatchbacks, wide tail lamps covered by a louver-like appliqué; and P225/60VR16 Goodyear Eagle GT Gatorback tires.

The five-main-bearing 302-cid or "five-point-O" V-8 had a 4.00 x 3.00-inch bore and stroke and a 9.2:1 compression ratio. It produced 225 hp at 4200 rpm and 300 lbs.-ft. of torque at 3200 rpm. Other features of the code "M" powerplant were hydraulic valve lifters and an electronic fuel-injection system. The 5.0-liter Mustang could move from 0-to-60 mph in 6.2 seconds and did the quarter-mile in 14.5 seconds with a 96 mph terminal speed.

Brad Bowling

The 1989 Saleen SSC had a lot of flash and dash. Its paint schemes
were hard to miss, and under the hood was a 292-hp V-8.

1989 Saleen Mustang

FORD

Big things were happening at Saleen Autosport in
1989. The company's plans included record sales of its
popular Mustang conversion, another attempt at an SCCA
championship, an IndyCar campaign and the introduction of
the highly anticipated Saleen SSC supercar.

1989 Saleen Mustangs were essentially carryovers from
the previous year, with minimal changes. The only options
listed by the factory were the 3.27:1 limited-slip differential,
the 3.55:1 limited-slip axle, a heavy-duty radiator and cooling
system and a Panhard rod. Special five-spoke, 16-inch wheels
became available early in the year. For the first time, Saleen
buyers had the option of cruise control due to the availability
of a custom bracket.

Available exterior colors were Black, Canyon Red, Dark
Shadow Blue, and Oxford White, although other colors could
be arranged through the Ford dealer. New rocker panel-
affixed racing stripes (featuring the first re-design since their
debut on the 1984 model) were available in the same colors of
Gold, Silver or Blue. 1989 marked the first year for the Saleen
date tag to be affixed to the firewall with the last six digits of
the Ford vehicle identification number.

Sales for the standard conversion added up to 734 cars,
including four specially built hatchbacks for Pioneer (although
standard Saleens, they resembled SSCs), two ordered by Eagle
1 for giveaways, and one ordered by General Tire.

On the track, the SCCA campaign was still successful.
Unfortunately, Steve Saleen's attempt to move to open-wheel
Indy Cars ended when the team failed to qualify for the
Indianapolis 500.

On April 17, 1989 (the Mustang's 25th birthday) Saleen
introduced the SSC. It was built around a 292-hp, 5.0-liter V-
8 with EPA 50-state approval. Saleen modifications included

a 65mm throttle body (up from 60mm), a revised intake
plenum, enlarged cylinder head ports, wider rocker arm
ratios, stainless steel tube headers, heavy-duty cooling and
Dynomax mufflers.

A high-performance version of the Mustang's Borg-
Warner T-5 transmission was installed behind the new power
plant and controlled by a Hurst short-throw shifter. Standard
3.55:1 gears were housed in an Auburn "cone clutch"
differential for ground-scorching acceleration.

The SSC's three-way Monroe Formula GA electronic
cockpit-adjustable shocks were innovative at the time.
Massive 245/50-16 General XP-2000Z rubber sat on the
rear, with the front receiving 225/50-16Zs. SSC wheels were
beautiful 5-spoke, 16 x 8-inch DP models.

The SSC cabin combined luxury and performance
with leather FloFit seats and matching door panels. The
speedometer showed 200 mph. There was no back seat; that
area was taken up with 200 watts of Pioneer sound system,
a CD player and six speakers. A four-point interior chassis
support system ("roll bar") further stiffened the Mustang
platform.

There were no options available. All 161 SSCs produced
as 1989-only models were identical. They were White with
White wheels and Gray-and-White interiors. The only
differences lay in changes made by component suppliers, For
example, not all cars received the Momo steering wheel. The
asking price for this "unofficial" 25th anniversary Mustang
model was $36,500. Certifying, building, and selling a
modified engine package made Saleen customers happy and
gave the company a broader product range that included a
base model and a high-end supercar.

Jerry Heasley

The 1990 Mustang GT had a small-block V-8 that produced 225 hp.

1990 Mustang 5.0-Liter HO

For 1990, Ford Motor Company gave the Mustang a driver's side air bag and standard rear shoulder belts. Both of the features were the outgrowth of new federal safety regulations. Map pockets were added to the door panels, while tilt steering and an armrest on the console disappeared.

Since there had been no 25th anniversary model Mustang in 1989, the nameplate's quarter century of tradition was recognized in sales literature that emphasized that the first Mustang was a "1965" model. As you'll recall, the original version, though released at the New York World's Fair on April 1, 1964. Ford was correct that the 1964 1/2 Mustang was technically a 1965 model, but that doesn't explain why the automaker produced anniversary editions in 1984 and 1994. At the time, Mustang fans were saying things like, "C'mon Dearborn – you can't have it both ways just because you forgot you anniversary."

A two-door coupe, a three-door hatchback and the ragtop again came in the LX series and all could be had with the optional 5.0-liter V-8. Prices were $12,107, $12,950 and $17,681, respectively. The V-8-powered Mustang LX actually used the beefiest suspension available for the model year.

As before, only the hatchback and convertible came in GT trim, which primarily added spoilers, air dams and gas-pressurized shock absorbers. The small-block V-8 had a 9.0:1 compression ratio and again made 225 hp at 4200 rpm and 300 lbs.-ft. of torque at 3000 rpm. "225 horses are bound to kick something" said an advertisement for the Mustang GT. Once again, the Borg-Warner five-speed manual gearbox was linked to it as standard equipment.

Cars with the 5.0-liter EFI HO V-8 and the five-speed manual gearbox came standard with a 2.73:1 axle and a 3.08:1 Traction-Lok rear end was optional. With automatic overdrive transmission, the 2.73:1 axle was standard and a 3.27:1 Traction-Lok unit was optional. The wheels used on the Mustang GT and 5.0-Liter LX models were 15 x 7.0-inch aluminum rims compared to 14 x 5.0-inch standard steel wheels on the Mustang LX. They carried P225/60VR15 Goodyear unidirectional "gatorback" tires.

A limited-edition metallic Emerald Green convertible with a white interior was ultimately announced, in the spring of 1990, as the forgotten and long-awaited "25th anniversary" model. There were rumors that Ford was planning to build a Mustang "street racer" with a 351-cid V-8, but the automaker eventually dropped this idea because such a model would have been too costly to manufacture. Too bad . . . the world could have used another Boss 351!

Brad Bowling

FORD

This pristine 1990 Saleen convertible was numbered 90-0010. It was one of 62 convertibles built for 1990.

1990 Saleen Mustang

The 1990 Ford Mustang was not fundamentally changed. However, it did get a new driver's airbag and a front suspension with improved geometry as the only obvious updates. Saleen Mustangs were virtually a carryover from the previous year with just a few tweaks. The Racecraft suspension system now included variable rate front and rear coil springs (gone were the stiff, specific-rate units), Monroe Formula GP gas shocks all around, special strut mounting bearings, urethane sway bar pivot bushings and high-performance alignment specs. Due to changes by Ford, Saleen modified the shock tower brace this year.

Standard equipment was much the same as before, but among the few pieces of new content was a "split" front air dam, a two-piece rear wing and bolt-on subframe connectors. The only options listed by the factory were the 3.55:1 limited-slip axle, a Pioneer CD player and a leather interior. Some customer requests for automatic transmission, a sunroof or certain aftermarket performance enhancements were filled as before.

As in years past, participating Ford dealers were required to order cars for conversion with the following specs: Mustang LX hatchback, coupe or convertible, 5.0-liter V-8, five-speed manual transmission, 3.08:1 limited-slip axle, 225/60VR-15 tires, radio delete, Custom Equipment Group and rear window defogger. A Saleen Identification Code, 31S, gave the

Ford factory in Dearborn, Michigan a clear indication that a certain order was part of the unique bailment pooling/drop ship arrangement that Saleen Autosport enjoyed.

For 1990, the upscale SSC became known as the "SC" and continued giving Saleen enthusiasts power, handling and appearance upgrades. Continuous improvements and changes to the aerodynamic body pieces, wheels and tires and various other equipment proceeded deliberately during this period. The SC was lighter and more powerful (304 horsepower) than the SSC that preceded it. Only 13 of the Hatchback-only SC models were built in 1990.

The slowing sales led Saleen to find creative ways to continue production, including the subcontracting of its conversion work to Cars & Concepts in St. Louis, Missouri, at the end of 1990. A California-based spin-off company, Saleen Parts Inc., assembled the SCs.

Only 243 standard Saleen Mustangs were built in 1990. This included 173 three-door hatchbacks, 62 convertibles and eight two-door coupes. The list prices were $24,990 for the hatchback, $29,390 for the ragtop, $24,190 for the coupe and $32,000 for the SC hatchback.

The 5.0-liter H.O. EFI V-8 was the only engine used this year. It had a 4.00 x 3.00-inch bore and stroke, a 9.2:1 compression ratio and 225 hp at 4000 rpm.

FORD

Brad Bowling

Saleen sales were losing momentum by 1991. Only 92 of the 225-hp pony cars were turned out by Cars & Concepts for the model year.

1991 Saleen Mustang

All of the standard 1991 Saleen Mustangs were built by Cars & Concepts in St. Louis, Missouri. Once again, hatchback, coupe and convertible models were sold. Saleen Performance Parts, located in Long Beach, California, continued building the higher-priced and very rarely ordered SC model.

Once again, the Racecraft suspension system included variable rate front and rear coil springs. Monroe Formula GP gas shocks were fitted all around. The Saleen suspension upgrades also included special strut mounting bearings, urethane sway bar pivot bushing and high-performance wheel and chassis alignment specs.

The standard Saleen stereo was again a Pioneer AM/FM cassette unit with six speakers, a graphic equalizer and a remote controller. Other standard equipment included 225/50ZR-16 General XP-2000Z tires on American Racing rims (16 x 7 inches in front, 16 x 8 inches in rear), Monroe quad shocks, four-wheel disc brakes, a Saleen aerodynamic kit, a 170-mph speedometer, a leather-covered shift knob, a Hurst quick-ratio shifter, articulated FloFit sport seats and a Saleen Mustang jacket.

The only options listed by the factory were the 3.55:1 limited-slip axle, a Pioneer CD player and a leather interior, but customers could make special requests such as automatic transmissions, sun roofs and certain aftermarket performance enhancements.

Sales continued to decline, with only 92 standard Saleen Mustangs finding new homes in 1991 and 10 of the SCs being built. This included 58 base three-door hatchbacks, 30 base convertibles, four two-door coupes and 10 of the SC three-door Hatcbacks. In the same respective order, the advertised prices for the four models were $25,990, $29,990, $24,990 and $34,750.

The Code E 5.0-liter H.O. V-8 was the standard Saleen engine. Its output was 225 hp at 4000 rpm.

The Saleen Mustang remained a darn nice muscle car in 1992, but only
17 of the cars were ordered. This is one of five convertibles built.

FORD

Brad Bowling

1992 Saleen Mustang

Although it would go down as the company's worst-ever year for sales, Saleen introduced several improvements to its line of Mustangs in 1992.

Ford was in its sixth year with the identical base car, and Saleen had gone just as long with only subtle cosmetic changes. A new 17-inch wheel design gave the Saleen package a much-needed visual pickup. The 17-inch Stern wheels measured 8 inches wide in front and 9 inches in the rear, with Z-rated BFGoodrich Comp T/A radials all around (225/45ZR17 in front, 235/45ZR17 in the rear). Saleen also returned to a single-piece rear wing after two years of what proved to be an unpopular bi-level design.

The Racecraft suspension system included variable rate front and rear coil springs, Monroe Formula GP gas shocks all around, special strut mounting bearings, urethane sway bar pivot bushing, and high-performance alignment specs.

The standard stereo was again a Pioneer AM/FM cassette unit with six speakers, graphic equalizer and a remote control. Other standard equipment included Monroe quad shocks, four-wheel disc brakes, Saleen aerodynamic kit, 170-mph speedometer, leather-covered shift knob, Hurst quick-ratio shifter and new-for-'92 articulated Recaro sport seats.

The only options listed by the factory were the 3.55:1 limited-slip axle, Pioneer CD player and leather interior. Custom upgrades for specific customers were done on some cars.

Saleen's "Spyder" convertible package, featuring a soft tonneau cover that turned the rear seats into a convenient storage area, was new. Saleen teamed with Vortech in 1992 to offer one of its superchargers as an option (10 blowers were installed by customer request) and Recaro came on board to supply its legendary seats.

Only 17 standard Saleens were sold in '92. Of these, 12 were hatchbacks (base priced at $26,990) and five were convertibles (base priced at $30,990). There were no SCs produced. Because Cars & Concepts closed its St. Louis plant at the end of 1991, Saleen moved all of its Mustang production to the Long Beach-based Saleen Performance Parts for '92.

Outside the regular 1992 Saleen Mustang line were four non-serialized "entry-level" GT Sport hatchbacks modified with the lowered suspension and a few body upgrades, and one Ranger pickup given treatment similar to the 1988 Sportrucks.

The muscular 1993 Mustang Cobra was the first offering from Ford's Vehicle Team

FORD

1993 Mustang SVT Cobra

Model year 1993 could easily have been one in the "live bait" category for the Ford Mustang. It was in the last year of a long run (since 1979) before the all-new 1994 models bowed. Chevrolet's Camaro and Pontiac's Firebird were also redesigned and available in performance trim. Both shared a 350-cid 275-hp V-8 that could beat the Mustang's 302-cid 205-hp H.O. V-8.

Ford was well aware of Steve Saleen's hot Mustangs and other "tuner" versions of the Mustang that were much more powerful than production cars. However, the need to meet CAFE standards and warranty claims precluded production-line attempts to match such aftermarket creations. Still, the Cobra and Cobra R—introduced in mid-1993—turned out to be a great warm-up act for future performance Mustangs from Ford. In the end, the Camaro Z/28, Firebird Formula and Firebird Trans Am wound up leading the pony car class in ultimate performance numbers, but not by very much.

Ford had called on its legendary snake nameplate in the past when it needed an image to spice up its vehicles, but some summons were more for show than go, such as the Mustang II derivatives called the Cobra II and the King Cobra. This time it was a different story, as the show items were few and the go items were abundant, thanks to the effort of the new Special Vehicle Team. The "SVT" group was a sort of "skunkworks" that fit in somewhere between racing and production cars—and even trucks, a few years later on. The SVT method was to take a production car, go over it top to bottom and make it a better performing and handling vehicle, then add a few dress-up items to set it apart from the common models.

For the 1993 Cobra, they took the 302-cid V-8 and added GT-40 cast-iron cylinder heads with larger valves, stronger valve springs, a two-piece intake plenum and manifold, a hotter cam, higher-ratio rocker arms, higher-flow fuel injectors and air management and a less-restrictive exhaust system. The result was a conservative 235 hp at 5000 rpm.

Other mechanical improvements included stronger insides for the Borg-Warner T-50D transmission, much-needed four-wheel disc brakes, cast-aluminum 17 x 7.5-inch wheels (wrapped in 245/45ZR-17 Goodyear tires) and suspensions softened up a bit for more travel and better road contact.

"It is the hardest accelerating, quickest stopping, best handling pony car from Ford yet," said *Road and Track* of the Cobra.

Naturally, the Cobra had to go door to door with its GM counterparts. *Motor Trend* put one up against a six-speed Camaro Z/28 and wound up with a 0-to-60 time of 6.2 seconds for the Ford versus 5.6 seconds for the Chevrolet. The Camaro covered the quarter-mile in 14.0 seconds and 98.8 mph compared to 14.4 seconds and 97.4 mph for the Cobra. Considering Chevy's cubic inch and horsepower advantages, it was really a very close contest. As a comparison, *Motor Trend* tested a 1993 Mustang GT convertible that did 0 to 60 in 8 seconds flat and the quarter in 16.1 seconds at 85 mph.

Under the guidance of SVT—with help from road racer Paul Rossi—about 100 Cobra R versions were made for racing-only purposes, even though they met showroom emission and safety requirements. There were wind-up windows, no radio and no option for air or other power goodies, just like the lightweight drag cars of the 1960s. The price for the Cobra R was $25,692 compared to the base Cobra's sticker price of $18,555 plus $475 shipping.

Brad Bowling

**Buyers who were serious about going fast on the street could opt for
the 1994 Saleen S-351, which carried a roaring 371-hp V-8.**

FORD

1994 Saleen Mustang

There's nothing like a new model, Steve Saleen discovered, when he debuted the efforts of his rejuvenated company during the Mustang's 30th anniversary show at Charlotte Motor Speedway in April 1994. It calmed fears that Saleen Autosport (now Saleen Performance) had gone the way of Shelby. Ford's SN-95 (or '94 Mustang) gave Saleen a fresh canvas to create masterpieces on.

Saleen's "entry-level" V-6 Sport combined traditional Saleen equipment with a less-expensive power plant. Boosted by a standard supercharger (installed by delivering dealers), the Sport's 3.8-liter V-6 had 220 hp. The car had Racecraft suspension tuning, 17 x 8-inch wheels and Saleen aero body pieces. A short-throw Hurst shifter and leather-grained shift knob were the interior modifications. Listing for less than $22,000, the V-6 Sport was in the same price range as a loaded GT Mustang, but without the high insurance. Saleen saw it as a good entry-level car.

Saleen's all-new S-351 took the SSC/SC idea to a new level. Powered by an EPA-certified 351-cid/371-hp V-8 built by Saleen, the S-351 had the highest Saleen-unique content to date. Almost all of the 1994 to final-year 1999 V-6 coupes and convertibles were delivered to a new factory in Irvine, California where they were stripped to bare shells (except for certain components). A few cars were converted from GTs, but there is no discernible difference.

The S-351 V-8 featured high-po heads, bigger valves, hydraulic roller cam and lifters, 65mm throttle body, 77mm mass air sensor and other high-tech goodies. The unique V-8 was installed on new mounts (an inch further back and an inch lower than stock) and rewired to a new EEC-IV engine management system. Just about every part of the S-351 was replaced or massaged for 120 hours, making the prices ($34,990 coupe and $40,990 convertible) remarkable.

The S-351 offered options. The stock 235/40-18 (front) and 245/40-18 (rear) BFGoodrich Comp T/A radials could be upgraded to Dunlop SP8000s measuring 255/40-18 and 285/40-18. A Vortech supercharger was available. More acceleration could be dialed in with a 3.55:1 rear axle. Larger 13-inch brake discs could be ordered. The Speedster package, first seen as a '92 option known as the "Spyder," came with a rollbar-like "sport bar" and hard tonneau cover.

If the S-351 was a home run, then the third all-new Saleen model for 1994 was a World Series championship. The SR ("Supercharged Racer") was a barely legal package that dressed a Vortech-supercharged S-351 in FIA Group A competition clothing, including a dual-plane rear wing, carbon-fiber hood and scooped body side enhancements. Inside, the SR benefited from a rear race tray (taking the place of the back seat), four-point roll bar, four-point safety harness and racing Recaro seats. With its 351-cid supercharged V-8 rated at 480 hp, no one could say the SR was "all-show, no-go." Base price for the latest Saleen supercar was $45,990.

Saleen also announced that 75 Ford outlets were "stocking dealers" who had agreed to keep a minimum of two cars on the floor at all times. With only a few months of real production time in 1994, those 75 dealers managed to sell 29 V-6 Sports, 44 S-351s and two SRs.

FORD

Jerry Heasley

The scarce 1995 SVT Mustang Cobra came with a base 302-cid V-8, but lucky buyers who planned to race could get the Cobra R, which had 300 ponies and was built for competition.

1995 Mustang SVT Cobra/Cobra R

The 1995 introduction of the Cobra's second-generation "R" model signified a new high-water mark for late-model Mustang performance. Not since 1973 had a Mustang been available with 351 cubic inches of small-block V-8, but the Cobra R's slightly enlarged fiberglass hood scoop helped hide such a power plant.

Because demand for the 1993 Cobra R had easily exceeded the 100-car production run, Ford's Special Vehicles Team (SVT) increased the availability of the 1995 version to 250 units. Realizing that many of the first Cobra R's had gone straight into collectors' garages (bypassing the racetracks they were built to compete on), Ford insisted that sales of the 1995 model should be limited only to active, licensed competitors who planned to actually drive the cars in SCCA and IMSA series events.

Since the standard Cobra's 5.0-liter/302-cid V-8 and the Cobra R's 351-cid V-8 were part of the same engine family, emissions certification was easier to get than if a totally different engine had been used. A Ford marine engine block formed the basis of the super V-8. It had a special camshaft, aluminum alloy pistons, forged steel connecting rods, GT40 cylinder heads, a performance lower intake and a specially-designed upper intake manifold making up most of its performance gains.

Visually topping off the high-performance engine package was a "5.8 Liter Cobra" plate on the intake manifold.

With its greater displacement, the 351-cid V-8 produced 300 hp and 365 lbs.-ft. of torque.

SVT dropped the usual Borg-Warner T-5 transmission for a beefier Tremec five-speed, giving Ford's warranty department peace of mind concerning broken gears. Combined with a 3.27:1 rear axle ratio, the Cobra R power train delivered true neck-snapping acceleration.

To increase its performance potential, the Cobra R was stripped of many unnecessary components including the air conditioning system, sound system, rear seat, some sound-proofing materials and fog lamps. The suspension was built with ultimate road holding in mind and included Eibach springs, Koni adjustable shocks, firmer bushings, five-spoke wheels measuring 17 x 9 inchesa and 255/45-17 BF Goodrich Comp T/A tires.

Other race-oriented features on the $35,499 car (not including the $2,100 gas guzzler tax) included a fiberglass hood, a 20-gallon fuel cell and separate radiators for the engine oil and power steering fluid. All 250 cars were finished in Crystal White and fitted with Saddle cloth interiors.

Just about every Cobra R was quickly grabbed by serious racers, but *Motor Trend* got its hands on a 1995 Cobra R to test. The magazine reported that it was good for 151 mph, 0-to-60 mph in 5.4 seconds and a 14.0-second quarter-mile at 99 mph.

Brad Bowling

FORD

The S-281 version of the Saleen was a car for serious go-fast enthusiasts: it had the double
overhead-cam muscle of the Cobra and the eye-catching looks and handling of the Saleen.

1996 Saleen Mustang

The original Saleen formula made a dramatic return in
1996, in the form of the aggressive-looking S-281 that featured
minimal upgrades to the engine and interior (a new shifter and
gauge treatment), but maximum massaging of the suspension
and aerodynamics. Ford's new modular 4.6-liter 281-cid V-8,
with only minor tweaking from Saleen, provided motivation
for the bespoiled coupes and convertibles. Massive 245/40-
18 BF Goodrich rubber on 18-inch, five-spoke alloy wheels
belied the fact that the S-281 was the "entry-level" Saleen
at only $28,990 for the coupe. Options included 18-inch
magnesium wheels, Recaro seats, a carbon fiber hood and
a 3.55:1 rear axle. The convertible-only Speedster package
featured a hard tonneau cover for the back seat and a two-
point padded roll bar.

Although it was not listed as a separate model, customers
could have SVT's Cobra taken to the next level with a Saleen
S-281 conversion. Checking this option gave buyers the
double overhead cam Cobra V-8 with the looks and handling
of a Saleen.

Showing a crystal clear understanding of who the
company's most ardent supporters were, Saleen included one-
year memberships in both the Mustang Club of America and
the Saleen Owners & Enthusiasts Club with the purchase of
an S-281. The S-281 proved to be the most popular Saleen
model in many years, with 438 examples selling in the first
year of production—30 of which were convertibles sold to the
Budget rental car company for use at its premium locations
such as Las Vegas.

Twenty S-351s were sold in 1996, and two SRs were
built. The SR model was unofficially blended into the S-351
line on which it was based as the S-351 was now available
with the same 500-hp rating when ordered with the Vortech
supercharger option. 1996 S-351s received new Trick Flow
heads in place of the previous Edelbrock units.

The author had a chance to drive a Bright Orange S-
281 Spyder while attending the Mequiar's Award Committee
meeting in L.A. You could say that Gunnell "waxed
enthusiastic" about the car.

On one of his many side trips during a week away from
the Wisconsin winter, Gunnell drove the car to the Nethercutt
Collection in Sylmar, California. When he arrived, the top
was down and it was starting to rain. Curator Byrom Matson
allowed him to drive the car into the musuem's lower level
where a group of senior citizens was waiting to begin a tour
of the museum. When the tangerine-colored Saleen rolled in,
almost every one of the ladies in the group—most of them
well past retirement age—asked if they could go for a spin in
the "cool convertible." Luckily, the rain kept coming down.
The reaction of the ladies proved that the eye-appeal of Steve
Saleen's products knows no age barrier.

FORD

Brad Bowling

A record 10,049 SVT Cobra Mustangs were produced for 1997, providing more evidence that high horsepower was back in style by the late 1990s.

1997 SVT Cobra Mustang

It was business as usual for SVT in 1997. The only noticeable change in the Cobra was a slightly larger grille opening, which was shared by the entire Mustang lineup due to a wider and taller radiator design across the board. The galloping horse emblem replaced the coiled serpent this year in the grille, but the rear valance panel retained the embossed "Cobra" lettering.

Model 46 was the convertible and Model 47 was the coupe. The Code V 4.6-liter (282 cubic inches) double overhead-cam V-8 with aluminum block and heads was used again. The engine used a 9.85:1 compression ratio and electronic fuel injection with a dual 57-mm throttle body. The special intake setup featured equal-length thin-wall cast-aluminum runners and a cast aluminum plenum chamber. The special manifold type exhaust headers were made of high-silicon molybdenum cast iron. The engine put out 305 hp at 5800 rpm and 300 lbs.-ft. of torque at 4800 rpm. The power flowed through a Borg-Warner T45 five-speed gearbox to the 3.27:1 rear axle.

Up front was a modified MacPherson strut suspension with separate springs on the lower arm, 400/505 lbs./in. variable rate coil springs and a 29mm stabilizer bar. At the rear was a rigid axle, upper and lower trailing arms, two leading hydraulic links, 165-265 lbs./in. variable-rate coil springs, shock absorbers and a 27-mm stabilizer bar. The front brakes were 13.0-inch vented discs featuring PBR twin-piston calipers with embossed "COBRA" lettering. At the rear were 11.65-inch vented disc with single-piston caliper. A Bosch three-channel, four-sensor ABS system was used.

SVT established another sales record for its Cobra in 1997 by an additional 43 units. Of the 10,049 Cobras produced, 6,961 were coupes and 3,088 were convertibles. The closed car weighed 3,446 lbs. and sold for $25,335. The open car tipped the scales at 3,620 lbs. and had a $28,135 window sticker. Production according to factory color was 2,369 Black coupes, 1,180 Black convertibles, 1,994 Rio Red coupes, 925 Rio Red convertibles, 1,543 Crystal White coupes, 606 Crystal White convertibles, 1,055 Pacific Green coupes and 377 Pacific Green convertibles.

FORD

Brad Bowling

This is one of 10 supercharged 4.6-liter S-281 Saleen anniversary models made for 1998.

1997-1998 Saleen Mustang

For 1997, Saleen continued offering its S-281 with either a 220-hp version of the 4.6-liter SOHC V-8, or a 310-hp 4.6-liter DOHC (the SVT Cobra's 32-valve engine introduced the previous year). A six-speed manual transmission became standard on the S-351. Optional equipment available on the S-351 included outrageous "Widebody" front fascia, fenders, rear quarter panels, rear valance, a carbon-fiber hood, and dual-plane rear wing. All S-351s built in 1997 were supercharged. They also benefited from forged pistons, Saleen/Cosworth computers, and 36 lbs./hr. injectors.

An extra-cost tire upgrade on the S-281 and S-351 were Michelin Pilots measuring 255/40-18 (front) and a super-wide 295/35-18 (rear). All S-351s came standard in 1997 with magnesium wheels.

The company produced 327 S-281s, 40 S-351s and five SRs in 1997.

Various Ford colors were used on a per-request basis. The annual production breakdown showed seven variations with the following model codes, base prices and model-year output:

The 4.6-liter (281-cid) single overhead-cam V-8 had a 3.60 x 3.60-inch bore than stoke. It featured a 9.0:1 compression

ratio and an electronic fuel-injection system This Code W engine made 220 hp at 4400 rpm and 285 lbs.-ft. of torque at 3500 rpm.

A double-overhead camshaft design and large (37mm intake 30mm exhaust) valves were some of the secrets behind the aluminum-block Cobra version of the 4.6-liter V-8. It had EFI and a 9.5:1 compression ratio. This helped it to produce 310 hp at 5800 rpm and 300 lbs.-ft. of torque at 4800 rpm.

The top Saleen engine was the supercharged 5.8-liter (351-cid) V-8 featuring high-performance aluminum heads, hydraulic rollers and lifters and a supercharger. It put out 510 hp!

The 1998 Saleen models, based on a now five-year-old Mustang design, changed little. Saleen's efforts were aimed toward the Mustang facelift Ford was promising for the 1999 model year.

Sales of the S-281 slipped to 183 cars; the super-fast S-351 only found 22 purchasers; and there were only three SRs built in 1998. Ten of the S-281s were SA-15 anniversary convertible models produced with superchargers and available only in yellow, with black and white accents.

FORD

Wieck Media

The new-look SVT Cobras of 1999 had a top speed of 149 mph and a long-awaited independent rear suspension.

1999 SVT Mustang Cobra

Ford gave the Mustang a major facelift for its 35th anniversary year in 1999. In addition, a number of chassis and engine improvements were seen on all models. Ford's Special Vehicles Team (SVT) took the new-and-improved Mustang platform and turned it into one of the most awesome muscle cars of the 20th century.

The Cobra's 4.6-liter DOHC engine was given a different combustion chamber design and reconfigured intake port geometry that created a more efficient fuel-air mix. Improved combustion raised power and a coil-on-plug ignition system and a new type of knock sensor contributed to the Cobra's reliability and smooth power delivery.

The 281-cid 32-valve V-8 featured an aluminum engine block, aluminum cylinder heads and port fuel injection. It served up an advertised 320 hp at 6000 rpm and 317 lbs.-ft. of torque at 4750 rpm. An SVT Cobra Mustang with five-speed manual gearbox and 3.27:1 rear axle ran from 0-to-60 mph in 6 seconds flat, from 0-to-100 mph in 15.3 seconds and from 0-to-130 mph in 31.8 seconds. The same car covered the quarter-mile in 14.6 seconds at 98 mph and had a top speed of 149 mph.

The Cobra sat on a 101.3-inch wheelbase and stretched 183.5 inches bumper to bumper. It stood 53.5 inches high and weighed in at 3,588 lbs. The Cobra coupe, Model 47, was priced at a hefty $27,470. It tipped the scales at 3,430 lbs. and Ford built 4,040 of them. The $31,470 convertible was slightly more popular with 4,055 assemblies. It was Model 46

and weighed in at 130 lbs. more than the coupe.

Basic features of the Cobra included an independent-struts-type front suspension with coil springs and an anti-roll bar. The rear independent suspension used unequal-length control arms with a toe control link, coil springs and an anti-roll bar. The ABS brakes used vented discs at all four corners. Attaching the car to the ground were 245/45ZR-17 B.F. Goodrich Comp T/A tires.

Car and Driver magazine (August 1999) reported that the SVT Mustang Cobra had fresh-looking styling, a high-tech power plant, a top-notch independent rear suspension and outstanding brakes, as well as a very affordable price for this type of car. It rated the SVT "competent, quick and exclusive," but said the transmission could use an additional gear to win more races in the "Stoplight Grand Prix."

While testing the '99 Cobra, a number of magazines reported performance figures lower than those for the previous model. At first it was thought that the weight of the independent rear suspension might have been the problem, but dynamometer testing indicated the car was not hitting its advertised horsepower. On August 6, Ford stopped selling Cobras and recalled all cars in private hands. SVT then replaced in intake manifold, ECC and entire exhaust system from the catalytic converter back on every car Ford had made. A label indicating the "Authorized Modifications" had been made was placed under the hood. The recall impressed the media and Cobra buyers.

FORD

Brad Bowling

Not much changed on the 2000 Saleen Mustang. But when a car is fast, handles great, and looks like this, why change it?

1999-2000 Saleen Mustang

His creation of an in-house engine development and certification lab gave Steve Saleen a tremendous advantage in building high-performance cars and he started by adding another 25 hp to the stock V-8's rating for 1999. The company found 285 hp in the SOHC 4.6-liter V-8 through the use of a new premium fuel calibration, special under drive pulleys and a new exhaust system. Saleen offered a Roots-type supercharger option that boosted output from the Saleen S-281 to an advertised 350 hp. No longer the domain of the Ford service department, in 1999 the Eaton supercharger became a Saleen factory-installed option.

The Saleen S-351 again came standard with a Vortech supercharger and claimed 495 hp for 1999. That was down from the previous year. The standard, quick-ratio, six-speed manual transmission sent power to a 3.27:1 rear axle (3.08:1 and 3.55:1 axle ratios were optional). The 1999 model year was the last season for production of the Saleen S-351; its replacement, the S-281E, would be released in 2002.

The Saleen S-351 was initially advertised with a 22-gallon fuel cell and a trick center exhaust system, but the car would not pass evaporative emissions testing with these features in place. However, this change of plans did not put the hurt on business. The new Mustang design and the greater power offered in the base model gave Saleen Performance a spike in sales for 1999. By the time the year ended, 373 Saleen S-281 models and 45 Saleen S-351 Mustangs had found new homes.

With the end of S-351 production in 1999 and the SVT Cobra's one-year hiatus to work out power output issues (see the Cobra entry elsewhere in this book), 2000 was a one-flavor season for Saleen, but what flavor!

The supercharged version of the Saleen S-281 became known as the S-281 S/C, although the blower package was not actually considered a separate model. It was technically an option. With a sticker price of $29,900, the S-281 coupe settled in as the lowest-priced Saleen model, but it had few other changes. Normally aspirated cars came standard with Ford's 3.27:1 rear axle and the S/C was only available with the 3.08:1 axle ratio.

In tests on the drag strip, the $35,460 S-281 S/C coupe bested the 0-to-60 mph time of the normally aspirated 281 by 0.4 seconds (4.8 vs. 5.2) and both models burned up the skidpad at .93g.

Brad Bowling

The screaming 2000 Cobra R could probably outrun any Mustang that came before it, and certainly ranks as one of the best muscle cars to come off an American assembly line.

FORD

2000 SVT Cobra Mustang

In a move unprecedented in the auto industry, SVT cancelled its production of 2000 street-model Cobras in order to evaluate its gaff over the 1999 Cobra's power deficit and to fix all of the recalled cars. The company did, however, go ahead with plans to produce the most powerful, brutal Mustang since the Boss 429: the 2000 Cobra R.

SVT developed an all-new engine for the 2000 R. The cast-iron 5.4-liter DOHC, 32-valve V-8 was tweaked until it turned out an awe-inspiring 385 hp and 385 lbs.-ft. of torque. The 5.4-liter's bore was the same as the 4.6-liter's, but the stroke was 15.8mm longer. Peak airflow was increased by 25 percent over the standard Cobra. Stainless-steel short-tube headers led to a Bassani X-pipe, '98 Cobra catalytic converters, Borla mufflers and dual twin-pipe side exhausts.

New engine mounts and crossmember lowered the engine in the compartment by 12mm. Competition conditions dictated the use of an extra-capacity Canton Racing Products oil pan filled with synthetic lubrication. Redline for the R 5.4-liter was 6500 rpm, with a dual-stage rev-limiter shutting off fuel at 6800 and ignition at 7000.

A Tremec T56 six-speed manual transmission was specified to handle the 5.4-liter's tremendous torque. An aluminum driveshaft measuring 4 inches in diameter led to the 8.8-inch aluminum-case differential. Induction-hardened GKN halfshafts are the final link to the rear wheels. Final drive ratio was a short 3.55:1 for increased acceleration.

Suspension tweaks included Eibach coil springs that lowered the car 1.5 inches in front and 1.0 at the rear and made the chassis 30 to 40 percent stiffer than the 1999 Cobra. Brembo four-wheel disc brakes were activated through four-piston aluminum calipers. Air inlets designed into the Cobra

fog light openings were used to provide extra cooling for the R's front brakes, with air ducts shipped and installed by SVT dealers if requested by the customer.

Eighteen-inch five-spoke wheels were fitted with 265/40ZR-18 BFGoodrich g-Force tires, which contributed somewhat to the R's astounding 1.0g of lateral acceleration. The Cobra R's rear deck and fascia were from the base V-6 Mustang, as rear-exit dual exhaust cutouts were unnecessary with the R's side-exit setup. The front of the R included a specially designed front air splitter that, in concert with the large rear wing, reduced front lift and increased rear downforce. Because it also reduced ground clearance to a few inches, the splitter was shipped with the cars and installed at the customer's request by the dealer.

Racing Recaro seats, a thickly padded steering wheel, and a B&M Ripper shifter were used. Many stock Cobra pieces were left off the R to reduce weight, but the standard equipment list was still extensive. It included dual airbags, independent rear suspension, ABS, a 20-gallon Fuel Safe bladder-type fuel cell, full-size spare tire, front air splitter, seven-inch rear wing, power dome hood, SecuriLock passive anti-theft system, Recaro seats, tilt steering wheel, 180-mph speedometer, B&M Ripper shifter with leather-wrapped shift knob, Power Equipment Group (dual electric remote-control mirrors, power side windows, power door locks, and power deck lid release), dual illuminated visor mirrors, and keyless illuminated entry system.

The 3,590-lb. R could do 0-to-60 mph in less than 5 seconds, with a top speed of more than 170 mph. A total of 300 of the $54,995 SVT Mustang Cobra R models were sold.

FORD

Although it was largely unchanged from the previous year, there
was still a lot to like about the 320-hp 2001 SVT Cobra.

2001 SVT Cobra Mustang

The 2001 model Cobra was largely carried over from the package introduced in 1999. Minor exterior changes included the return of "Cobra" lettering imprinted into the rear fascia. The Model 47 coupe retailed for $28,605, weighed 3,430 lbs. and had a run of 3,867 units. The Model 46 convertible was priced at $32,605, tipped the scales at 3,560 lbs. and found 3,384 buyers. The total production of 7,251 units was down for the third time in a row.

Standard equipment included dual airbags, ABS, articulated sport seats (a new-for-2001 design with four-way power for the driver), Premium Sound (with a six-disc in-dash CD player), Power Equipment Group, rear window defroster, air conditioning, cruise control, front floor mats, dual illuminated visor mirrors, and remote keyless illuminated entry.

The all-aluminum 4.6-liter DOHC V-8 continued unchanged from 1999, except for fixes made by SVT in 2000 to the intake manifold, engine management computer and entire exhaust system from the catalytic converter back. The 2001 Cobra produced a true 320 hp at 6000 rpm and 317 lbs.-ft. of torque at 4750 rpm. The engine was again linked to a Tremec-built Borg Warner T45 five-speed gearbox that drove to a 3.37:1 ratio rear axle.

All 2001 Cobras were equipped with a standard traction control system. This hybrid system featured a power start innovation that allowed the driver to spin the drive wheels under acceleration as long as the car tracked straight. Once the system detected wheel slippage, it would engage and reduce power to that wheel. If the spinning continued, the engine management system cut off one or more cylinders, and the anti-lock brake system applied braking to the affected wheel, transferring power to the other drive wheel.

Once again, the SVT Cobra options list was short. In fact, there were only three items on it: polished wheels for $395, a rear spoiler for $195 and floor mats for $25.

The 2001 Bullitt Mustang was one that Steve McQueen probably would have liked a lot. With its souped-up
4.6-liter V-8, the Bullitt could turn the quarter-mile in 14.1 seconds.

2001 Bullitt Mustang

Ford Motor Company understood that the 2001 Bullitt Mustang had to be good. If you are going to name a specialty vehicle after one of America's hardest-nosed tough guys, you can't do the dirty deed half-heartedly. The car was actually named for the 1968 Mustang GT that actor Steve McQueen drove when he played detective Frank Bullitt in the cult-classic motion picture of the same name. The hot 2001 model was also based on a Mustang GT, but it came complete with $3,695 worth of upgrades.

Muscle Mustangs & Fast Fords magazine said, "In stock form, with nearly 1,500 miles on the odometer, the Bullitt (Mustang) turned out 239 rear-wheel horsepower, or about 275 to the flywheel." The $26,320 coupe-only special was tuned to move out from 0 to 60-mph in 5.7 seconds. The quarter-mile took 14.1 seconds and had the speedometer pegged at 98 mph at the end.

Ford's youthful styling chief J Mays, who created the retro two-seat Thunderbird, was also responsible for the "Bullitt" Mustang concept car. The car's body was modified to reduce the size of the rear quarter windows. It addition, to make it more ground hugging, it was lowered 3/4 inch all around. The traditional Mustang side scoops were covered

up, a crushed-aluminum flip-up gas filler was added and the Bullitt Mustang rode on Torq Thrust D-style wheels sourced from American Racing Wheels.

Under the hood, the 4.6-liter (281-cid) single overhead cam V-8 featured the SVT Cobra model's cast-aluminum intake manifold, a twin-bore 57-mm throttle body, special cylinder heads and a high-flow exhaust system. The power plant changes produced 265 hp at 5000 rpm and 305 lbs.-ft. of torque at 4000 rpm.

The engine was attached to a five-speed manual gearbox. It had heavy-duty shocks, special anti-roll bars and 17-inch diameter Goodyear Eagle tires. Its curb weight was 3,241 lbs.

The Bullitt Mustang interior had perforated black leather upholstery and matching trim, a black leather steering wheel, white-faced gauges and an aluminum gearshift knob. The car came in Dark Highland Green—just like the famous movie car—as well as optional True Blue or Black. Ford projected that it would build 6,500 of these cars in 2001, but wound up a tad short of that total. The actual production figure was 5,582, including 3,041 Dark Highland Green cars, 723 True Blue ones and 1,318 in Black.

Brad Bowling

FORD

This head-turner is one of 167 S-281 Saleen convertibles that left the factory for 2001.

2001 Saleen Mustang

The 2001 versions of the Saleen S-281 and Saleen S-281 S/C continued with only a few changes. Saleen engineers developed a new Roots-type blower for the Saleen S-281 S/C this year. Known as the "Series II" supercharger, it was essentially the previous year's model with a built-in bypass valve that allowed the supercharged 4.6-liter V-8 to develop 365 horsepower. Ford's slight increase in the GT's compression ratio let Saleen sell the S/C with a numerically higher 3.27:1 rear gear without incurring emissions or fuel efficiency penalties.

The biggest news for Saleen fans this year was the announcement of an all-new Saleen SR model wearing a $158,000 price tag. The now-familiar 351-cid V-8 was rated at 505 horsepower and 500 lbs.-ft. of torque with a six-speed transmission sending all that power back to a 3.55:1-geared rear axle by way of a shortened drive shaft.

Independent rear suspension components sat where a live axle had been for more than 35 years of Mustang history—a lesson learned from Steve Saleen and Tim Allen's RRR Speedlab racecars. Braking occurred through 14.4-inch front rotors with four-piston calipers in front and 13-inch metallic discs with four-piston calipers in the rear.

Beneath the wildly styled, Saleen-unique composite body panels lay a complete roll cage and suspension reinforcement system. The Saleen SR, available in coupe form only, was wind-tuned at Lockheed-Martin's full-size tunnel in Marietta, Georgia. Performance figures released by Saleen Performance claimed the hard charging SR model could reach 60 mph from a standstill in 4.0 seconds flat. The car could circle the skidpad at 1.09g.

The Cobra-based Saleen was once again offered, with the return of SVT's double-overhead cam 320-hp V-8. Saleen made no engine modifications to the Cobra package other than the addition of a performance exhaust system.

The standard S-281 coupe retailed for $32,099, with the convertible selling for $36,099. Prices for the S-281 S/C models were $37,499 for the coupe and $41,500 for the ragtop. When the Cobra platform was ordered, prices were $41,600 (coupe) and $45,500 (convertible).

Most popular among the Saleen Mustang models in 2001 was the standard S-281 coupe, which appealed to 262 buyers. The convertible version was built 167 times. The S-281 S/C coupe was, surprisingly, nearly as popular as the base model and 243 were built. The S-281 S/C convertible was right behind it with 223 assemblies. A handful of other Saleen products left the factory, including nine S-281 Cobra coupes ($41,600), six S-281 Cobra convertibles ($45,500) and one SR coupe.

FORD

Brad Bowling

Saleen produced 835 S-281 coupes and convertibles for 2002. This car is number 02-0002.

2002 Saleen Mustang

There were three 4.6-liter Saleens in the showroom in 2002, but no Cobra-based model. SVT skipped the 2002 model year in order to push the launch of its upcoming supercharged Cobra into the 2003 season.

Saleen continued to offer its "base" S-281 with a modified EEC-V computer strategy, under drive pulleys, a performance air filter, less-restrictive mufflers and freer-flowing exhaust pipes—all of which contributed to a 285-hp rating (up 25 from the GT). The naturally aspirated S-281 came with Ford's Tremec five-speed or optional four-speed automatic transmission—both working with a standard 3.27:1 rear axle or optional 3.55:1.

The S-281 S/C continued unchanged, with an Eaton M90 Roots-type supercharger (known as the "Series II" to Saleen engineers) and twin-gauge pod (displaying boost and intercooler temperature) as standard equipment. The S/C blower package proved to be extremely successful for Saleen, with 441 S-281s going out the door so equipped. Once again, S/C models came standard with a 3.27:1 rear axle ratio that could not be upgraded by the factory.

Pirelli PZero Neros measuring P255/35ZR18 (front) and P265/35ZR18 (rear) were standard equipment on the S-281, as were 18 x 9-inch five-spoke aluminum wheels, although an upgrade could be had to P265/35ZR18s (front) and P295/35ZR18s (rear).

The S-281 exterior was freshened up some in 2002, with all base and S/C models receiving a standard composite hood and new three-piece rear spoiler with "legs" that ran to the bumper line. An S-281 badge on the fender in place of the old

horse-and-bars emblem was new for this year.

A suitably powerful replacement for the S-351 was released this year, sporting an engine deserving of its "Extreme" label. The S-281 "E" took advantage of new power plant technologies Saleen had developed in its racing SR and S7 programs, including a Saleen-spec forged steel crankshaft, forged steel connecting rods, forged aluminum pistons and E-specific aluminum cylinder heads wearing high-performance valve springs and camshafts. Saleen installed its own version of a 90mm mass airflow sensor, inlet tube and intake manifold, with exhaust routed through a full 2.5-inch stainless-steel exhaust system with four-way catalytic converters and an X-configuration crossover pipe. Its development also provoked introduction of a Lysholm 1.6-liter "Series V" twin-screw supercharger compressor.

The result was 425 hp, which was backed by a standard six-speed manual transmission, 8.8-inch rear axle, 3.08:1 gears and MaxGrip limited-slip differential. The E was equipped with the company's premium brake package: two-piece, slotted front discs measuring 13 inches clamped by four-piston calipers. Wheels and tires were Pirelli's PZero Rossos (P265/35ZR18 in front, P295/35ZR18 in rear) on 18x9- and 18 x 10-inch five-spoke alloy rims.

When introduced, the automotive media declared it to be the ultimate iteration of the Mustang. There were virtually no options on the E, with sticker prices of $60,190 (coupe) and $64,089 (convertible). Unlike the S/C, the E was considered its own separate model by the factory.

The Mustang reached all new levels of power and performance with the 2003 SVT Cobra. With 390 hp and 390 lbs.-ft. of torque, this modern masher could melt blacktop with the hairiest factory machines ever made.

FORD

2003-2004 SVT Cobra Mustang

There was no 2002 Cobra model from Ford, since the Special Vehicles Team (SVT) delayed development of its next-generation supercar so long that it arrived at midyear and technically became an "early 2003" model.

Mustang fans were aware, through grapevine rumblings, that Ford Motor Company was planning an SVT Cobra model that was more powerful than any Mustang ever made—including the Boss 429s and Super Cobra-Jets of the 1960s. The 2003 Cobra not only met the high standards set by those tire-shredding muscle cars—it easily surpassed them.

Packing a supercharged 4.6-liter double overhead cam engine below its hood, the new SVT Cobra was in a league of its own. Factory spec sheets showed engine output rated at 390 hp and 390 lbs.-ft. of torque. Eaton supplied the Roots-type supercharger, which was tuned to produce 8 lbs. of boost. A water-to-air intercooler reduced the temperature of the charge for maximum mixture volatility in the combustion chamber. To strengthen the power train against such violent internal forces, the new Cobra engine was built around a cast-iron block. In the interest of saving weight and speeding up heat dissipation under the hood, SVT retained an aluminum cylinder head. A six-speed Tremec T-56 manual gearbox was the only transmission available. An accelerator-friendly 3.55:1 rear axle backed it up.

SVT's independent rear suspension system—introduced on the 1999 Cobra—was refined and retained.

With driver and passenger airbags, anti-lock braking on four-wheel discs, traction control and independent rear suspension all as standard equipment, the new Cobra was also safer and better handling than its legendary predecessors. (As a yardstick of how far the Cobra name had come since the dark days of the 1970s, realize that this model put out more than three times the horsepower of the 1976-1978 Cobra II and King Cobra V-8s and it more than quadrupled the output of the four-cylinder version.)

Just when fans of the nearly 40-year-old Mustang thought it couldn't get any better, SVT released its 10th Anniversary Edition SVT Cobra later that summer. It was available in either coupe or convertible body styles with 17 x 9-inch Argent Silver wheels, Red leather seating surfaces, carbon fiber-look interior trim, and special anniversary badging on the floor mats and deck lid. Only 2,003 of the anniversary Cobras—to be painted Red, Black or Silver—were produced.

In all, SVT produced 8,394 2003 Cobra coupes (at $34,065 each) and 5,082 Cobra convertibles ($38,405).

In 2004 every Mustang fan on the planet was eagerly awaiting the all-new Mustang design promised by Ford for 2005, so SVT carried its 390-horsepower coupes and convertibles into a second year without any serious changes.

In addition to a color-shifting Mystichrome appearance package, SVT offered two more traditional colors for its Cobras: Screaming Yellow and Competition Orange. Otherwise, the only options available were chromed wheels and a rear spoiler delete.

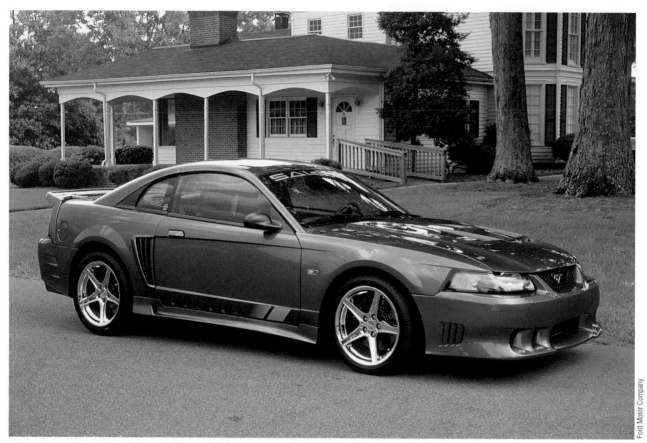

Ford Motor Company

There was nothing plain about the "base" S-281 2003 Saleen coupe. It had 290 hp and the customary lengthy list of Saleen cool stuff inside and out.

2003 Saleen Mustang

Saleen's entire line of S-281 Mustangs received a power increase for 2003.

The base car was bumped to 290 hp due to a new high-flow exhaust system with 2.5-inch diameter pipes and a reconfigured engine management computer. Carried over from 2002 were the performance air filter, under drive pulleys and less-restrictive mufflers. The S-281 came standard with a Tremec five-speed or optional four-speed automatic transmission—both working with a standard 3.27:1 rear axle, although the 3.55:1 gear ratio could be had at extra cost.

Base S-281s received white-faced gauges (including a 200-mph speedometer), performance pedals, a short-throw shifter, a new leather-wrapped shift knob design, floormats and a console plaque as standard equipment. A dash-mounted twin-gauge pod (standard on S/Cs, not available on base S-281s) was phased in during the middle of 2003.

Saleen returned to using Ford's stock GT hood on the non-supercharged S-281, unless ordered with the more expensive composite option. Although they looked like Ford parts, the non-functional scoop and plastic louvered insert were Saleen designs.

The S/C jumped to 375 hp through the addition of a new Lysholm screw-type supercharger similar to (but with smaller displacement than) the compressor introduced on the 2002 E. This "Series IV" blower was paired with a high-density water-to-air intercooler and 4.0-inch Saleen Power Tube low-restriction air intake. Standard rear axle on the S/C package had 3.55:1 gearing.

The incredibly popular S/C represented 61 percent of non-E S-281 production for 2003.

The E model became more extreme in '03, with a boost to 445 horsepower after engineers switched to a larger (75mm) throttle body and smaller supercharger pulley. The E received all of Saleen's regular S-281 interior and aerodynamic equipment, plus an S-351 rear wing, separate rear valance with integrated center exhaust system. The only options available on the $60,586 coupes and $64,504 convertibles were the Performance Cooling package, Speedster equipment and custom paint. Fourteen of the super-performance E's were built in 2003.

In April, Saleen began offering a "Hollywood Horsepower" package to commemorate the company's appearance in three big spring movie releases: *Bruce Almighty* (starring Jim Carrey and an S7), *2 Fast 2 Furious* (Paul Walker) and *Hollywood Homicide* (Harrison Ford). A Laser Red S-281 supercharged coupe was available for fans of 2F2F; a silver convertible represented the star car of HH.

Eleven SVT Cobras were converted to Saleens in 2003, and the company produced a line of 10 SA-20 anniversary models—all in white with black and yellow accents based on the S/C package.

The Lincoln Capri was a little on the plush side for a muscle car, but it was certainly a good performer for the time. Shown is a 1954 convertible.

1952-55 Lincoln Capri/Cosmopolitan

Lincoln, Ford Motor Company's luxury brand, was promoted as the "crowning achievement of Ford Motor Company's 50th Anniversary." The '53 Lincoln was also billed as "The one fine car designed for modern living—completely powered for modern driving." Modern muscle car buffs would probably be quite surprised to learn that the '53 Lincoln was considered a high-performance car in its day.

In those days, big cubic inch displacement meant big horsepower and only the biggest cars had both. As the decade of the 1950s progressed, so did Detroit's "horsepower race," a contest that became a game of numbers among the domestic nameplates to see which could advertise the biggest horsepower increases each model year.

Early in the decade, high-priced luxury cars boasted the highest numbers. Among the leaders in the 1953 model year was Lincoln, which extracted 205 advertised horses from its 317.4-cid overhead valve V-8. Its tally was second to Cadillac's 210 hp.

However, the 1953 Lincoln's reputation as a performance car was not built on horsepower alone. For 1952 it got all-new conservative styling, a solid 123-inch wheelbase chassis (which was not long for a luxury car) and most important, a modern ball-joint front suspension that made it a fine handler.

That year was also the first for Lincoln's new overhead-valve V-8, which replaced a heavy L-head unit. It produced 160 hp, which gave it average performance.

A four-barrel carburetor and boost from 7.5:1 to 8:1 compression made the whole package a balanced performer.

In the fall of 1952, Lincolns were entered in the Carrera Panamericana, or Mexican Road Race, and took the top four spots, assuring the "Road Race Lincolns" identification that sticks to this day. In the fall of 1953, Lincoln took the top four spots again, again using 1953 models. To follow it up, 1954 models took the top two sedan positions in the fall of that year.

Tom McCahill of *Mechanix Illustrated* found the 1953 models did 0-to-60 mph in 12.61 seconds compared to 14.8 seconds for the 1952. "The Lincoln is a high-priced car giving high-priced performance," he said, noting it was America's finest automobile.

McCahill backed up his word by buying a 1953 Lincoln Capri two-door hardtop. He later wrote that he regretted selling it.

The top-line Capri two-door hardtop had a base price of $3,549 and was the most popular model, with a production run of 12,916. A convertible listed for $3,699 and a lesser-trimmed Cosmopolitan hardtop started at $3,322.

The basic style remained in production through the 1955 model year, but the 1953 and little-changed 1954 Lincoln models are the most sought after today.

MERCURY

Mercury broke away from its traditional big car offerings when it unveiled the 1964 high-performance Comet Cyclone.

1964 Comet Cyclone

Mercury had long been highly regarded as a "factory hot rod" version of the Ford, but its image was always keyed to hot full-size vehicles. In fact, in the mid-'50s the cars carried the maker's first initial in their grille and were promoted as "Big M" models. By the early '60s, Mercurys were bigger and more powerful than ever, but that wasn't what the booming "youth market" wanted in a car. Big engines in a smaller body was the trend.

In the middle of the 1964 model year, Lincoln Mercury Division decided to bring out a real muscle car carrying the Mercury Comet nameplate. The new Comet Cyclone high-performance model arrived in showrooms soon thereafter. The Cyclone went for a "serious street performance" image and featured less chrome than other Comets. There were thin moldings over the wheel wells and under the doors and "C-O-M-E-T" lettering appeared only on the rear fins. "Cyclone" front fender badges, done in the same style used on the full-size Marauder, sat low on the fenders.

The standard engine provided in the Cyclone was the four-barrel, 210-hp version of FoMoCo's 289-cid small-block V-8 with a 9.0:1 compression ratio. The Cyclone also featured 14-inch chrome wheels. Camera-case-grained black vinyl

replaced wood trim on the instrument panel. The hot Comet also came with new, pleated black bucket seats and a center console with color-keyed vinyl trim in special colors. A special option was a "convertible" style vinyl roof covering. Cyclones offered a three- or four-speed manual transmission, plus Merc-O-Matic. Promotions for the car were tied into the 100,000-mile endurance run at Daytona.

As tested in *Car Life* (April 1964), the Cyclone priced out at $3,027 with a typical array of options. The magazine listed 0-to-60-mph times of 11.8 seconds with automatic transmission and 10.2 seconds with a four-speed gearbox. The quarter-mile was covered in 16.5 seconds at 73.8 mph by the Merc-O-Matic-equipped Cyclone and 16.4 seconds at 77 mph by the four-speed Cyclone. The car with automatic averaged 12 to 15 mpg in normal driving, while the stick-shift car did a bit better at 13 to 16 mpg. Top speed was listed as 109 mph.

There was also a fastback Comet "Super Cyclone" concept car that debuted at the New York Automobile Show. It had a special body with a Plymouth Barracuda-like glass back window.

The feisty 1965 Comet Cyclone came only as a two-door hardtop.

MERCURY

Jerry Heasley

1965 Comet Cyclone

Mercury's 1965 Comet Cyclone was as whiplashingly fast as the Coney Island roller coaster that it shared the Cyclone name with. Auto writer John Ethridge said, "The Cyclone's 225-hp engine had what you'd consider a healthy feeling at any speed between idle and 3000 rpm. Then it felt like four more cylinders were added and came on very strongly."

The Comet Cyclone series consisted of a single two-door hardtop priced at $2,683. That made it the second-most expensive Comet (the Villager station wagon was the priciest model).

The 1965 Cyclone had a special grille with only two groups of horizontal blades and blacked-out finish around its perimeter. Cyclones had all the equipment that came on Calientes, plus bucket seats in front, a center console, a tachometer, unique deluxe wheel covers, curb moldings and a 289-cid "Cyclone" V-8 engine with a two-barrel carburetor. A distinctive twin-air-scoop fiberglass hood was optional.

In May 1965, *Motor Trend* printed a road test titled "2 Comets: Hot & Cool" that compared the Caliente and Cyclone two-door hardtops. The Caliente had the 289-cid, 200-hp engine and Merc-O-Matic transmission. It did 0-to-60 mph in 11 seconds and ran down the drag strip in 18.1 seconds with a 76-mph terminal speed. Its top speed was 96 mph. The Cyclone had the 225-hp version of the "289" and a four-speed

gearbox. It trimmed 2.2 seconds off the other car's 0 to 60-mph time and the quarter-mile took 17.1 seconds at 82 mph. Its top speed was 108 mph.

The magazine liked the restyled Comet front end, the higher horsepower, its handling and its large trunk. The brakes (the Caliente's brakes had power assist and the Cyclone's did not) were both good. Stopping distance from 60 mph was 158 feet with assist and 161 feet without assist. Technical editor John Ethridge's major criticisms concerned the Cyclone's wheel-spinning ability and its rear axle hop (which hurt acceleration times). He also said that the Caliente's "hang-under-dash" air conditioner interfered with the driver's right leg.

The 195-hp "Cyclone V-8" engine was a $108 option for non-Cyclone models. It had a 9.3:1 compression ratio. In addition, there was a 220-hp "Super Cyclone 289" with a 10.0:1 compression ratio and a four-barrel carburetor. This engine cost $45.20 extra in Cyclones and $153.20 additional in other models.

A three-speed manual gearbox was standard with all engines. A four-speed manual transmission was $188 extra, and Multi-Drive Merc-O-Matic ran $189.60 additional. This was, again, a three-speed automatic, comparable to the Ford Cruise-O-Matic.

MERCURY

Jerry Heasley collection

With a 335-hp/390-cid V-8 as motivation, the 1966 Cyclone
GT was equipped to handle pacing duties at the 1966 Indy 500.

1966 Comet Cyclone GT

Dyno Don Nicolson's drag racing Comets brought many muscle car maniacs into Mercury dealer showrooms in '66. Few of them were disappointed with what they saw there. As Mercury once put it, "This one will start a glow in any red-blooded American driver." *Car Life* said that the newly redesigned '66 Cyclone provided "Supercar status for Lincoln's little brother."

After bidding itself into providing the mandatory matched set of Cyclone GT convertibles for the revered Indy 500, Mercury built some 100 Indy pace car replicas that found their way to Indiana. There they were used to transport parade queens and celebrities in conjunction with the pre-race festivities. Unlike other automakers, Mercury made no attempt to market the replica pace cars through its dealers.

The base Cyclone version of the midsized Comet had premiered in midyear 1965. The high-performance 1966 Cyclone GT came out in the fall of 1965, along with the rest of the new Comet line.

From its inception, the Comet and Cyclone body had grown almost every year. The 1966 version was based on Ford's Fairlane body shell. It rode on a 116-inch wheelbase. This moved it out of the compact category and into the intermediate size class. For performance buffs, this change

made the Cyclone a viable contender against the small-bodied, big-engined muscle cars of the period.

For 1966, Mercury went full blast and brought out the Cyclone GT. Powered by Ford's popular 390-cid/335-hp V-8, the Cyclone GT had an optional handling package, front disc brakes and optional four-speed manual or automatic transmission. (A three-speed manual was standard.) Also standard were dual exhausts, a fiberglass hood with twin non-functional scoops and GT identification and stripes.

The 390-cid V-8 used a four-barrel carburetor and had a 10.5:1 compression ratio. The optional Merc-O-Matic transmission only came with a GT Sport Shift enabling manual inter-range control via a floor-mounted lever. When so equipped, the Cyclone GT was capable of 0-to-60 mph in 7 seconds and quarter-mile runs in the high 14s. And this was in spite of the fact that the 390-cid engine added some 430 lbs. to the standard six-cylinder Comet.

Mercury's director of high-performance projects, Fran Hernandez, and his assistant, Paul Preuss, oversaw the 1966 pace car effort. The two actual pace cars that emerged were Candy Apple Red Cyclone GT convertibles capable of 115-mph cruising speeds.

Only 13,812 hardtops and 2,158 convertibles were built.

David Hooten

MERCURY

The Comet Cyclone again toiled largely in anonymity in 1967. It was a nice muscle
car, but was largely overshadowed by Ford's Mustang, Cougar and Fairlane.

1967 Comet Cyclone GT

Mercury had a hard time attaining a presence in the booming intermediate market in the 1960s. Its cars were always in the shadows of other Ford products. The Mercury Meteor and the Ford Fairlane were both introduced as intermediates for 1962. The Meteor died of lack of interest after the 1963 models were done, but the Fairlane continued on.

For 1966, the formerly compact Comet was upgraded to the same 116-inch wheelbase in the midsized Fairlane. Just when people were starting to get used to that, the mildly face-lifted 1967 models came along and the Comet name was only applied to the lowest-priced series, leaving Mercury awkwardly calling its offerings the Mercury intermediates. This changed for the better in 1968, when the Montego name was introduced. However, for 1967, not only were the intermediates lacking a name, but promotional backing as well, since the new Cougar—a luxury sports compact—was getting all the hype.

For the performance buyer, Mercury continued its Cyclone series. It again offered two-door hardtop and convertible models. While a rather meek 200-hp version of the 289-cid V-8 was standard, knowledgeable buyers selected the GT Performance Group from the Cyclone options list. Doing so substituted the 390-cid "FE" big-block V-8 with a

rating of 320 hp. That was down 15 hp from the 1966 version, but still fairly hot.

The Cyclone with the GT Performance Group also included a four-barrel carburetor, a dual exhaust system, an engine dress-up kit, a hood with two non-functional air scoops, 5 1/2 x 14-inch wheels, wide oval tires, heavy-duty shocks and springs, a thicker front sway bar, 3.25:1 gearing, body side stripes with GT badges and interior GT badging. Cyclones also came standard with front bucket seats. Options included a four-speed manual gearbox.

The recession of 1967 was not kind to car sales and the Mercury intermediates took a beating. A total of 6,910 were made compared to 24,164 for 1966. The 1967 models with the GT option included 3,419 hardtops and 378 convertibles, meaning the GT-embellished cars outnumbered the regular Cyclones. The 1967 Cyclone GTs, and all Cyclones for that matter, are rather rare today.

Racing promotion for the 1967 Cyclone was limited to its body lines being used atop funny cars for drag racing, but better things were ahead for Cyclones. They would become the NASCAR superspeedway stars of 1968 and beyond, finally helping Mercury's intermediate-sized models to establish a name for themselves.

MERCURY

The 1967 Cougar GT equipped with a 390 was a nice,
refined car that just happened to move pretty fast, too.

1967 Cougar GT 390

The '67 Mercury Cougar with the optional big-block 390 V-8 was a muscle car for the enthusiast on his or her way to a Thunderbird. "The Mercury Cougar's fascination is in finesse in fabrication," *Car Life* said of this well-built Merc.

Although the optional 390-cid/335-hp power plant was equipped with hydraulic lifters, a fairly mild cam and street-type valve timing, it produced a 1:10 power-to-weight ratio that was good for some driving excitement.

The Cougar, said *Car Life*, was best described as a "Mustang with class." It had a shapely, graceful appearance and jewel-like trimmings. Only the two-door hardtop was available at first. A convertible would come along later.

While based on the Mustang platform, the Cougar received some upgrades to its suspension componentry. They included a hook-and-eye joint in the lower front A-frames to dampen ride harshness, 6-inch-longer rear leaf springs and better-rated rear spring and axle attachments.

The GT, however, came more firmly sprung with solid rear bushings, stiffer springs all around, bigger 1.1875-inch shocks and a fatter .84-inch anti-roll bar. Power front disc brakes, 8.95 x 14 wide oval tires and a 390-cid 335-hp V-8 were included, as well as a low-restriction exhaust system and special identification features.

A Holley C70F carburetor with four 1.562-inch venturis and vacuum-operated secondaries sat on the 390-cid engine. With a 10.5:1 compression ratio, it required premium fuel. The horsepower peak came at just 4800 rpm. A husky 427 lbs.-ft. of torque was produced at 3200 rpm. Transmission choices included three- or four-speed synchromesh gearboxes or a three-speed Merc-O-Matic with manual shift capabilities for downshifting to second below 71 mph or to first below 20 mph.

The manual gearboxes used with the 390 were different from those used with the 289. The three-speed with the big-block had ratios of 2.42:1 and 1.61:1. For the four-speed attachment, 2.32:1, 1.69:1 and 1.29:1 ratios were provided. Smaller-engined "stick" cars used numerically higher gear ratios. In the rear axle department, the 390 came standard with a 3.00 axle. A 3.25 unit was optional. They called this the "power transfer" axle.

The Cougar GT 390 was good for 0-to-60 mph in 8.1 seconds and 16-second quarter-miles. Only 53 percent of all Cougars had four-speed manual gearboxes in 1967.

The 335-hp/427-cid "E" engine option officially put
the Cougar into the muscle car category in 1968.

1968 Cougar GT-E

The Mercury Cougar followed the pioneering Ford Mustang into the "pony car" marketplace. The Cougar came along three-and-one-half model years later than the Mustang and had a classier, more upscale image. I recall that, at the time it was first introduced, Mercury did a great job of promoting the Cougar as truly more car than the Mustang. However, when you look at the spec sheets for both cars, they are more alike than they are different. I hope they paid those Mercury PR guys very well!

When it bowed in model-year 1967, the Cougar (as well as its restyled Mustang cousin) had enough room under their hoods to accommodate Ford big-block V-8s between the front wheel wells. This was something that the original 1964-1/2 to 1966 Mustang could not do, although competitors bowing in 1967, like the Camaro, Firebird and new Barracuda, could.

The hottest engine showing up on the 1967 Cougar options list was the 390-cid big-block V-8 with a passable 320 advertised horsepower rating. Then, as model year 1968 bowed, the Cougar got its first real high-performance package with the 7.0-liter GT-E. The "E" kit became an option for both the base Cougar and the fancier XR-7. The option included the mild 390-hp E-code version of Ford's 427-cid engine,

plus a SelectShift Merc-O-Matic transmission, a performance handling package, styled steel wheels, power disc brakes and a non-functional "power dome" hood air scoop.

When the nose-heavy 427-cid V-8 was installed in the Cougar, which had an 111-inch wheelbase (3 inches longer than the Mustang), it produced average performance for the muscle cars of that era. A 7.1-second 0-to-60 time was published in the enthusiast magazines.

The mating of the 427-cid V-8 to the Cougar was a short-term offering because the 427-cid option was discontinued late in 1967. Later in the model year the Cougar—like Ford's other sporty and mid-sized cars—received an injection of Cobra Jet 428 power. To keep insurance agents and bean counters happy, the 428-cid big-block V-8 carried a rating of 335 advertised horsepower. Strangely enough, because it had a longer stroke, the 428-cid engine had an easier time with emission requirements. However, its actual power output was estimated to be closer to the choked-down 427E it replaced.

Although the Cougar concept was aimed at sporty luxury instead of high performance, the 1968 GT-E was the nameplate's first step into the muscle-car sweepstakes and would not be its last.

The Cougar XR-7G "Dan Gurney" model may have been a little pedestrian in the performance department, but its low production numbers make it a rare and collectible beast today.

1968 Cougar XR-7G "Dan Gurney"

According to *Muscle Car Field Guide: American Supercars 1960-2000*, "A Dan Gurney edition XR-7 with the 427-cid big-block motor must be just about the hottest and rarest Cougar any collector could own." The 427 Cougar did 0-to-60 mph in 7.1 seconds and could race down the quarter-mile in 15.22 seconds at 93.6 mph.

As any book collector knows, autographed copies of a literary work (or even a car book) are something special to look for. Signature models of high-performance cars were "in" during the late 1960s and early 1970s. AMC had its "Mark Donohue" edition Javelin and Mercury offered a limited-edition Cougar—now called the "Dan Gurney" edition. Both Donohue and Gurney were popular drivers in the Sports Car Club of America's Trans-Am racing series.

Today, signature editions like these are usually popular with car collectors even though they were not all that popular with the buying public when they were originally introduced years ago. Since they didn't sell all that well, they were produced in small numbers and now they've become rarities.

This certainly is the case with the 1968 1/2 Mercury Cougar XR-7G. This was actually an upscale Cougar XR-7 with a personalized option. The "G" stood for "Gurney," an

American racing hero of the day who was under contract to Lincoln-Mercury Division. Gurney was a member of the driving team that piloted the Bill Stroppe-prepared 1967 Cougars that raced in the Sports Car Club of America (SCCA) Trans-American sedan series competition.

The Cougar would be the first of two Mercury specials named for Gurney. The second was a version of the 1969 1/2 Cyclone Spoiler. After 1969, Gurney's racing and car-building services were contracted by Plymouth and the string of Gurney editions ended.

The Cougar's rather rare XR-7G option package was mainly an assortment of "gingerbread" and any available power plant from the base 302-cid V-8 on up could be used to power cars with the package. The features of the G option included a fiberglass hood scoop, road lamps, a racing mirror, hood pins and a new power sunroof (which could also be ordered for other 1968 Cougars).

At the rear of the car, four exhaust tips exited through the valance panel. New styled wheels held radial FR70-14 tires. Badges showing a special emblem decorated the instrument panel, roof pillar, deck lid and grille. The XR-7G Cougars were not widely promoted back in 1968 and very few were made, making the survivors highly prized by collectors today.

When Mercury rolled out the ferocious 1969 Cougar Eliminator with an optional 428,
it was clear that the company was getting serious about producing great muscle cars.

MERCURY

1969 Cougar Eliminator

This "Cat" car was crawling the streets from the moment the first one left the factory in 1968. The 428-cid/335-hp edition did the "60" thing in an amazing 5.6 seconds and the quarter-mile thing in 14.10 seconds with left you at the century mark at the end of the strip. "The Eliminator name was perfect for a muscle pony car," said *Car Review* in December 1986. "And the bright colors created the desired effect at the drive-in."

The 1969 Mercury Cougar that the Eliminator package was based on was wider, longer and heavier. Attractions for model year included the nameplate's first convertible. As a midyear muscle car offering the Eliminator came only in two-door hardtop form.

The new Cougar grille had horizontal pieces that protruded slightly at the center. Bucket seats and retractable headlights were standard. Rocker panel strips, wheel opening moldings and two parallel full-length, upper-level pinstripes decorated the body sides. The back-up lights wrapped around the rear fenders and the taillights were trimmed with concave vertical chrome pieces. A vinyl interior with foam-padded bucket seats and carpeting was standard.

The Cougar two-door hardtop ($2,999) and convertible ($3,365) were the base models. A GT appearance group option included: Comfortweave vinyl bucket seats, a rim-blow steering wheel, a remote-control left-hand racing mirror, turbine wheel covers, GT decals, a GT dash nameplate and F70 x 14 fiberglass belted tires for $168.40. The XR-7 looked like the basic Cougar outside. Its extras included a rim-blow steering wheel, a courtesy light group, a visual check panel, a left-hand remote-control racing mirror, an electric clock, deluxe armrests, a walnut-toned instrument panel with tachometer and trip odometer, leather-and-vinyl upholstery, vinyl door panels and special wheel covers.

Standard in the Eliminator was a four-barrel version of the Windsor 351 cid V-8, rated at 290 hp. Other Cougar options were available, including the last of the 390-cid V-8s and the 428 CJ with and without Ram Air. Both of these were rated at 335 hp, far under their true output on a dyno. Another notable engine option—the Boss 302—was new and came in "street" and "racing" versions. The former had a single four-barrel carburetor and was advertised at 290 hp, a fraction of its actual output. The latter had two four-barrel carburetors, but its horsepower rating was never advertised.

The Eliminator and Boss 302 were a curious combination. The term "eliminator" comes from drag racing and the Boss 302's forte was sports sedan racing. The wisdom of sticking it in the 3,500-lb. Cougar was questionable. Factory-backed Mustang Boss 302s were raced in SCCA Trans-American sedan events, but Cougar Eliminators were not.

Visuals with the Eliminator package included front and rear spoilers, a blacked-out grille, a hood scoop, argent styled steel wheels similar to the Torino GT type, appropriate side striping and a rally clock and tachometer. With the CJ 428-cid engine option you got a hood scoop, hood hold-down pins, a competition handling package and hood striping.

MERCURY

The 428 Cobra-Jet-equipped Cyclone GT of 1969 was a sub-14-second performer for about 3,200 bucks new.

Doug Mitchel

1969 Cyclone GT/CJ

I don't see muscle car lovers knocking down walls to buy my '48 Pontiac Streamliner, but when the fastback body style enjoyed a revival in the mid-1960s, they acted as if an aerodynamic roof was the latest and greatest invention since sliced bread. The fastback version of Mercury's hot Cyclone had outsold the two-door hardtop model by a wide margin in 1968, so Lincoln Mercury brass took the hint and dropped the notchback version for 1969. A slightly re-trimmed fastback returned for the new model year, while the Cyclone GT was reduced to only an appearance group option. There was also one very hot, all-new Cyclone CJ model.

The '69 Mercury Cyclone CJ included a trendy blacked-out grille insert that was framed with bright metal. There was a single chrome piece in the middle, running from each end of the grille. A Cyclone emblem in the center of the grille highlighted the CJ model's front end. Additional features included front and rear wheel opening moldings, a dual exhaust system, a 3.50:1 ratio rear axle, an engine dress-up kit, a hood tape stripe and a competition-type handling package. A Sports Appearance option group with bucket seats, a racing-style remote-control left-hand outside

rearview mirror, turbine-style full wheel covers and a rim-blow steering wheel was optional for the Cyclone CJ at $149 extra.

The Cyclone CJ was kind of a fastback Charger and bargain-basement Road Runner wrapped in one package. It came with Ford's big-block 428-cid/335-hp Cobra Jet V-8 as *standard* equipment. Also included were a four-speed manual gear box, a competition handling package and a plain front bench seat interior. The Cyclone CJ sold for $3,224. That was just a tad more than a regular Mercury Cyclone V-8 with the 302-cid base engine (which had a base retail price of $2,771).

The Cyclone CJ was aimed at the budget-priced super car niche that the Road Runner had carved out of the muscle car marketplace. It had a list price of $3,207 and only 3,261 copies were assembled. A Cyclone CJ with a 435-hp version of the 428-cid V-6 carried only 11.6 lbs. per horsepower. It could do 0-to-60 mph in 6.1 seconds and fly down the quarter-mile in 13.9 seconds.

The CJ might easily have been the most desirable Cyclone for 1969 and probably was at first. Then, at midyear the Cyclone Spoiler II came along. That changed the picture.

Doug Mitchel

MERCURY

**Mercury continued to hold its own in the muscle car wars in 1969
thanks to the Cyclone Spoiler II.**

1969 Cyclone Spoiler II

Cars like the Cyclone Spoiler II were designed to put some Viagra into Mercury's high-performance image in the muscle car era. When NASCAR Grand National stock car racing teams tested the new 1968 body styles, they found the Mercury Cyclone fastback to be a bit faster than its Ford Fairlane fastback counterpart. A more aerodynamic nose design was said to be the reason.

When Cale Yarborough drove the Wood Brothers' Cyclone to victory in the Daytona 500 in February 1968, the battle of the NASCAR noses was on. Dodge countered with the Charger 500 for 1969. Ford forces fought back with the Torino Talladega and Mercury Cyclone Spoiler II. Both featured flush grilles and extended noses.

The Talladega was fairly simple, but the Cyclone Spoiler was not. Mercury announced the Spoiler as a midyear model to go on sale in January 1969. The main feature in early information was a spoiler bolted on the trunk deck. It was nice, but the device was not legal in NASCAR at the time. Originally, an extended nose similar to the Talladega was to be an option.

After considerable confusion, the long-nosed Spoiler came to be known as the Cyclone Spoiler II. A total of 519 were made, all with the 351-cid four-barrel V-8 despite an

announcement that there also would be a 428-cid Cobra-Jet Ram-Air option. At least 500 needed to be produced to qualify the car as a production model so it could be raced.

Cyclone Spoilers came in two trim versions. A "Dan Gurney" Spoiler had a dark blue roof, dark blue striping and a signature decal on the white lower portion. A "Cale Yarborough" edition featured red trim similar to his Wood Brothers stock car. It, too, had a signature decal.

As it turned out, the Spoiler wasn't declared legal in NASCAR until the Atlanta 500 on March 30. This put Cyclone pilots in Talladegas for the Daytona 500 race, which was won by Lee Roy Yarbrough in Junior Johnson's Talladega.

Yarbrough turned out to be the year's hottest driver, but his Spoiler season was short since Ford was worried that it wouldn't win the manufacturer's title. As a result, the company put him back in a Talladega at mid-season. The aerodynamic wars got hotter late in the season when Dodge announced the Charger Daytona and later the cartoon-inspired 1970 Plymouth Road Runner SuperBird. The latter helped Plymouth snag Gurney to drive its racing cars.

The Cyclone II Spoiler was good for 0-to-60 mph in 7.4 seconds or a 14.4-second quarter-mile at 99 mph.

MERCURY

Jerry Heasley

**The "Boss 429" package provided the biggest engine for the 1970
Cougar Eliminator. This car had the optional "Boss 302" mill.**

1970 Cougar Eliminator

The term Top Eliminator was familiar to drag racing buffs, but to Mercury fans the term simply meant "hot Cougar." *Car Life* recommended, "Think of it as a family car with guts and you'll be happy with it."

Evolutionary design changes characterized the 1970 Mercury Cougars. They included a new vertical grille and a forward-thrusting front end. Promoted as "America's most completely equipped sports car," the new Cougar grille had a center hood extension and an "electric shaver" style insert. Its design was reminiscent of the 1967 and 1968 models' grilles.

Features for the basic Cougar models included upper body pin stripes, wheel opening moldings, roof moldings and windshield and rear window chrome accents. The sporty interior featured high-back bucket seats, courtesy lights, carpeted door trim panels, a vinyl headliner and a rosewood-toned dash panel. The Cougar convertible had a Comfortweave vinyl interior, door-mounted courtesy lights, a three-spoke steering wheel and a power top with a folding rear glass window. There was a two-door hardtop with a base retail price of $2,917. Prices for the convertible started at $3,264. Only 2,322 ragtops were made.

The Cougar XR-7 had distinct wheel covers, rocker panel moldings, a remote-control racing mirror and an emblem on the rear roof pillar. Interior features included vinyl high-back bucket seats with leather accents, map pockets on the seat backs, a tachometer, a trip odometer, a rocker-switch display, a burled walnut vinyl applique on the instrument panel, rear seat armrests, map and courtesy lights, a visual check panel, loop yarn nylon carpeting and an electric clock with elapsed-time indicator. The XR-7s came in the same body styles as the base Cougar, at $3,201, and $3,465, respectively. The XR-7 ragtop had a run of just 1,977 units.

The Eliminator returned for one final time. Now standard was the new 351 Cleveland four-barrel V-8 that was rated at 300 hp. There were options galore for the muscle car's engine compartment including the Boss 302, the 428 CJ and a new version of the 385 series big-block 429. This "Boss 429" package included Ram-Air induction and a 375-hp rating. "Call it the road animal," said Cougar literature. A rear deck lid spoiler, body graphics and a restyled scooped hood returned as part of the Eliminator's image.

One car enthusiast magazine of the era tested a 1970 Cougar Eliminator with the 290-hp version of the "Boss 302" V-8. It carried 12.4 lbs. per hp and did 0-to-60 mph in 7.6 seconds. The quarter-mile took 15.8 seconds.

The Spoiler was the top dog in the 1970 Cyclone lineup and came with a 370-hp/429-cid engine.

MERCURY

Jerry Heasley

1970 Cyclone Spoiler and GT

Mercury Cyclones got all kinds of things when they were restyled for 1970 after a two-season stint with a more radical fastback roofline. Some of the changes made for 1970 were good for muscle car fans.

"The Cyclone's racy looks are borne out in the accompanying specs," said *Motor Trend's* April 1970 report on the car. "The Cyclone has the looks and performance" the magazine said. The Spoiler model with the 429-cid/370-hp V-8 went 0-to-60 in 6.4 seconds and did the quarter in 14.5 seconds at 99 mph.

Though the same unitized chassis was used, the Cyclone wheelbase grew by 1 inch to 117 inches and the overall length of the car was extended by a hefty 6.7 inches. The latter alteration was due primarily to a protruding nose and fender design that produced somewhat questionable styling. Cyclones also got a gun sight-type design in the center of their grilles.

While their Ford Torino cousins got new fastback designs, Mercury intermediates did not. The Cyclone hardtops had trunk lines about halfway between the old notchback hardtop and a true fastback. There were three Cyclones for 1970: The base model that retailed for prices starting at $3,238, the Cyclone GT base priced at $3,226 and the Spoiler, which listed for $3,759 and up.

The base Cyclone came with the 429-cid/360-hp version

of the Ford 385 Series big-block V-8. Standard equipment included a four-speed manual transmission with a floor-mounted Hurst shifter, a competition handling package, a 3.25:1 ratio rear axle, a blacked-out performance styled grille with vertical running lights, exposed headlights, a silver- or black-finished lower back panel, loop carpeting, G70-14 fiberglass-belted tires and a bench seat. Options included the 370-hp CJ 429 engine, the 375-hp Super CJ 429 V-8 and—in extremely limited production numbers—the Boss 429.

The Cougar GT, which had once been the hottest Cyclone model, was now the mildest. It came with a 351-cid/250-hp V-8 with a two-barrel carburetor. Other standard features included a choice of seven unique exterior tone-on-tone color combinations, a three-pod taillight treatment, lower body side moldings, a non-functional performance hood with integral air scoop, a left-hand remote-control racing mirror, a right-hand manual racing-style mirror, concealed headlights, bright belt and trunk lid moldings, high-back bucket seats, Comfortweave vinyl upholstery, a three-spoke sports steering wheel with rim blow and unique door and quarter trim panels. The new 351-cid "Cleveland" V-8 was among the available engine options.

A Ram-Air equipped 370-hp 429 was standard motivation for the Spoiler. High-back buckets were also a part of the package.

MERCURY

Jerry Heasley

**Muscle cars don't come much bigger than the hefty 1971 Cougar GT,
but with a Cobra-Jet 429 on board, the big Cougar was no pussycat.**

1971 Cougar GT CJ 429

The '71 Mercury Cougar is an interesting automobile and the 429 CJ V-8 adds about as much performance as you might find—with few exceptions—in the waning years of the muscle-car era. "Driving the Cougar in whatever version you choose is still a fun proposition," *Motor Trend* opined in September 1970.

For 1971, the Cougars had the most dramatic changes seen since the marque's introduction in 1967. There was a lower silhouette, interior refinements and a muscular new GT option to fill up the gap left by the no longer offered Eliminator. The styling inspiration for the Cougar's thinner roof and windshield pillars was said to have come from European cars.

The 1971 models were "horse-sized" ponies, based on the big, new Mustangs. They were 4 inches longer (113 inches) in wheelbase and 7 inches longer (197 inches) in overall bumper-to-bumper length. With their new radiator-style grille, they looked even heftier than they actually were.

The Cougars had better manners than the Mustang, with more sound-deadening materials and nicer trim and interior appointments. Only big V-8 engines went under the hood. The power train options included a 351-cid engine with a two-barrel carburetor and 240 hp, a 351-cid V-8 with a four-

barrel carburetor and 285 hp and a 429-cid four-barrel job with 370 hp.

There were two Cougar series, each offering both hardtop and convertible body styles. The XR-7 was the sporty version with front bucket seats, full instrumentation and a vinyl half-roof. Cougar list prices started at $3,289 and went to $3,877.

The $129.60 GT package was available only for the base Cougar hardtop. It included a high-ratio rear axle, a competition suspension, dual racing mirrors, a hood scoop, a performance cooling package, a tachometer, a rim-blow steering wheel, F78 x 14 white sidewall tires, hub caps with bright trim rings, GT fender identification and a black instrument panel. The hood scoop was non-functional, except when the 429 CJ engine option was installed.

The 429 CJ V-8 engine listed for $310.90 in all Cougars with the Select-Shifter four-speed manual transmission (which cost $215.10 extra). This big-block engine also included cast-aluminum rocker-arm covers, a bright dipstick handle, a bright oil filler cap, a chrome radiator cap and shiny air cleaner (on cars without Ram Air) and a heavy-duty battery. Other options required with the 429 CJ package were power disc brakes and F70 x 14 or larger tires.

The 2004 Marauder was a full-sized modern cruiser with lots of room,
creature comforts and 302-hp double-overhead cam 4.6-liter V-8.

2003-04 Marauder

The 2003 Mercury Marauder was introduced at the Chicago Auto Show. A prototype convertible version with a supercharged engine was a one-off car that still survives (and which recently showed up at the Atlantic City Classic Car Auction). The convertible was never certified for street use and was created entirely for product evaluations and gauging customer response. However, the four-door sedan version was exciting enough to make it to the production line and into the hands of a few lucky buyers. Automotive writer Dan Lyons described the car as "a 300-hp black leather jacket." Others have compared it to a "police car without the gumball machine."

Designed to play the same role as the recently departed (1996) Chevy Impala SS, the Mercury Marauder's heartbeat was provided by an all-aluminum 4.6-liter double-overhead cam V-8 that cranked up 302 hp at 5700 rpm and 310 lbs.-ft. of torque at 4250 rpm. The engine had a hot Lincoln Aviator cam, a genuine dual exhaust system with fat pipes and a four-speed automatic overdrive transmission. The high-stall speed torque converter had shift points calibrated for top performance. The tachometer redlined at 6250 rpm and top speed was governed at 120 mph.

The Marauder, while based on the Marquis, had a 24 percent stiffer frame. The short-and-long arm front suspension incorporated coil-over-shock springs and monotube dampers. At the rear was a live rear axle with load leveling air springs and monotube dampers. The rear shocks were mounted in a more vertical manner than on the Marquis and police-car-type suspension hardware was used.

The ABS disc brakes were also police-car-like units and a new upgraded rack and pinion steering system was featured. Polished 18 x 8-inch five-spoke alloy rims carried BF Goodrich g-Force T/A tires, size 235/50WR18 up front and size 245/55WR18 at the rear.

Despite having two extra doors, the Mercury Marauder featured leather front bucket seats with embossed Mercury logos and came in a choice of solid black or two-tone black and gray. Gray dot matrix trim decorated the dash and doors. White-faced gauges monitored all functions. This was a family-oriented muscle car with a big back seat, a gigantic Grand Marquis-sized trunk and creature comforts like cupholders and a 6-CD changer.

Mercury expected to sell about 18,000 Marauders in the car's first year with a price tag in the $35,000 range. Unfortunately, that goal wasn't achieved. By the end of the model year, production was tabulated as 7,839 cars including 7,094 finished in Black, 328 in Blue and 417 in Silver Birch.

The 2004 Marauder had only modest changes from its first year specs.

One of the most important 2004 updates was a new 4R75W heavy-duty, four-speed automatic transmission with improved shift response, greater efficiency and increased low-end torque. Needle bearings and Teflon seals were added to the Marauder's new 11.25-inch high-stall-speed torque converter. The new transmission provided quicker upshifts and downshifts and allowed drivers to kick down into first gear at a higher speed.

Built in FoMoCo's St. Thomas, Ontario, Canada plant, the Marauder was again powered by the all-aluminum 4.6-liter, 302-hp V-8. Other features included rack-and-pinion steering, hydroformed front frame rails, monotube dampers and 18-inch wheels and tires.

OLDSMOBILE

The Oldsmobile Rocket 88 was a big engine that wound up in the
relatively small "A" body cars, like this 1949 Model 88 convertible.

1949 Rocket 88

The first domestic performance car to be in1troduced after World War II was the Oldsmobile Rocket 88. This hot-running "small" Olds came about as the result of an afterthought, rather than a master plan.

Oldsmobile developed its 303-cid overhead-valve "Rocket" V-8 for its top-of-the-line Series 98 models. The powerful engine was supposed to cap off the new "Futuramic" B-body styling that was first seen on the 1948 Oldsmobile models.

Not long before the introduction of the '49 models, the decision was made to put the Rocket V-8 engine in the smaller "A" body cars as well. The General Motors A body—shared with Chevrolet and Pontiac—was normally the home of the trusty, but slow, flathead six. Cars in this line formed Oldsmobile Motor Division's Series 76 offerings.

When the 135-hp V-8 went into the 119 1/2-inch wheelbase, the Futuramic Series 88 was born. It shared the same six body styles of the 76, but it rode on a 5 1/2-inch shorter wheelbase and weighed 250 lbs. less than the 98. Hydra-Matic drive was standard on both.

"The Series 88 combines Oldsmobile's new-high compression (7:25:1) Rocket engine with a new medium-weight body . . . the result is a highly favorable power-to-

weight ratio," a news release dated February 6, 1949 stated.

The high-performance implications of such a power-to-weight ratio weren't lost on members of the new breed of racecar drivers, those who piloted late model stock cars in NASCAR events. These contests were being held in some areas of the country and the Olds Rocket 88 was an instant success.

There was no factory backing of stock car racing at the time. If a driver wanted to race in such an event, he went down and bought his own car, put masking tape over the chrome and headlights, took the wheel covers off and raced it. The Rocket 88 proved to be just that and five of the first eight NASCAR Grand National races held in the initial 1949 season went to Olds 88s with the big engine. Series champion Red Byron was an Oldsmobile driver.

An Oldsmobile 88 convertible served as the Official Pace Car at the Indianapolis 500 that year and got the attention of even more race fans. It was dressed up with large rocketships and had a see-through hood panel to show off the hot V-8 engine.

Production cars and stock car racing would undergo many changes in coming years, but beating the Oldsmobile 88 became the target for both.

The J-2 Rocket engine option found its way into this Golden Rocket Holiday coupe Pikes Peak pace car.

OLDSMOBILE

1957 J-2

By model year 1957, it was getting more difficult to compete in the Detroit "Horsepower Race." This was the all-out effort by automakers to offer more cubic inches and more horsepower each season. The traditional techniques of upping engine displacement and raising compression each season were not doing the trick. In order to stay ahead of the competition, exotic fuel induction systems were needed. Among those utilized in 1957 were fuel-injection, supercharging and multiple carburetion.

Oldsmobile chose the multiple carburetor route to get more horses out of its Rocket V-8. It also upped displacement from 324 cid in 1956 to 371 in 1957. At the same time, compression rose from 9.25:1 to 9.5:1. However, even with those improvements, the Olds V-8's top reading was only 277 hp. That wasn't enough to match a Chrysler 300 or a fuel-injected Chevy with 283 ponies.

To get its horsepower figure up, Oldsmobile announced the J-2 Rocket option in January of 1957. This multi-carb setup featured triple two-barrel carburetors, a 10:1 compression ratio and a maximum rating of 300 hp. Buyers who plopped down an extra $83 could get the J-2 setup on any 1957 Olds from the $2,478 Golden Rocket 88 two-door Sedan to the $3,838 Ninety-Eight Starfire Convertible.

Less commonly available was a second version of the J-2 option rated at 312 hp. Legend has it that this option was sold only to drivers who had numbers on their car doors. It went for a cool $395.

Speaking of numbers on the doors, Oldsmobile signed driver Lee Petty to a contract to represent it in NASCAR Grand National and Convertible class racing. When the factories were forced to pull out of organized racing in June of 1957, most factory teams got to keep the cars and equipment they had. Petty, known for his frugal ways, made the Olds stuff last until the 1959 season. During that time he won several events, including the 1959 Daytona 500 and started his son Richard on his legendary racing career.

Engine size stayed the same, 371 cid, but compression on the top line models went up to 10:1, producing 305 hp in standard form. Therefore, the J-2 rating went up to 312 hp for its final appearance.

OLDSMOBILE

The 1962 Olds Jetfire has a definite claim to fame: It was the
first turbocharged car ever offered for public consumption.

1962 F-85 Jetfire

Oldsmobile won the race against its sister division, Chevrolet, to be the first American manufacturer to offer a turbocharged car with the introduction of the Jetfire in April 1962. Chevrolet's Corvair Spyder with its turbo engine would debut later that year.

In fact, the Oldsmobile Jetfire was the first turbocharged car ever offered to the public. Sure, turbo-diesel trucks were fairly common in 1962 and the turbocharger as a performance booster had been offered in airplanes for decades. And cars as far back as the '20s and '30s had used superchargers. But Oldsmobile was the first to use a turbocharger. (Interestingly enough, some magazine descriptions of GM cars using turbos that year called them "superchargers.")

The little Jetfire was based on Oldsmobile's F-85 series. As a result, it used the same aluminum-block 215-cid V-8 that survives to this day in the British Land Rovers and Range Rovers (albeit bored out a bit).

Oldsmobile added a waste gate, kept this engine's 10.25:1 compression ratio and suppressed detonation with a water-and-alcohol injection system. This system included a tank under the hood for "Turbo-Rocket" fluid. The turbocharger's boost was limited to 6 psi.

The Jetfire's engine was rated at 215 hp—numerically equal to its cubic-inch displacement. This was 30 horsepower more than the rating of the non-turbo F-85 engine with Rochester four-barrel carburetor. Torque was also increased to 300 from 230 lbs.-ft.

Oldsmobile claimed the Jetfire was the first car in the U.S. auto industry to offer one horsepower per cubic inch—the same claim Chrysler had made in 1956 for its 300B and Chevrolet in '57 for its fuel-injected 283 cid V-8. The Jetfire was, however, the first car to qualify as a regular production model, as opposed to a special production model, and at the same time offer the magical one horse per cubic inch.

The Jetfire could hit 60 mph in 9.2 seconds and do the quarter-mile in 17.5 seconds. Oldsmobile went conservative with this car, despite what its name suggested, putting the emphasis on the low-end torque and long-range reliability.

The Jetfire's major drawbacks, described in a *Car and Driver* report at that time, were dead-slow steering, a soft suspension and touchy, all-drum brakes.

The F.O.B. price for the 2,744-lb. Jetfire was $3,045. The production total for the year 1962 was 3,765 (according to the *Standard Catalog of American Cars 1946-1975*).

Sadly, given its potential and the prescient thinking on the part of Oldsmobile, turbocharging left the Oldsmobile F-85 line in 1964. For '64's substantially larger F-85, the aluminum V-8 gave way to cast-iron engines of larger displacement and turbocharging was no longer seen as necessary.

The 1964 Olds 4-4-2 got rave reviews from press and stacked up
nicely in both price and performance against the GTO and Mustang.

Phil Kunz

OLDSMOBILE

1964 4-4-2

The first Oldsmobile 4-4-2 was a 1964-3/4 offering for drivers who wanted just a bit more performance and handling than the standard midsize Oldsmobile delivered. On the official price sticker attached to the window, this $285.14 package was described as "Option number B-09 Police Apprehender Pursuit." One piece of Oldsmobile factory literature called *Product Selling Information for Oldsmobile Salesmen* explained the 4-4-2 like this, "police needed it—Olds built it—pursuit proved it." This literature clearly pointed out the original meaning of the 4-4-2 designation was as follows:

"4-BARREL CARBURETION—plus high-lift cams boost the power of the "4-4-2" Ultra High-Compression V-8 to 310 hp—up 20 hp over Cutlass V-8.

4-ON-THE-FLOOR—stick shift synchromesh transmission captures every power advantage both up and down the entire gear range.

2 DUAL EXHAUSTS—complete dual exhaust system features less back pressure for better performance ... aluminized for longer life."

Motor Trend tested an Oldsmobile F-85 Cutlass 4-4-2

two-door hardtop in its September 1964 issue. The car had a base price of $2,784 and an as-tested price of $3,658.74. Options on the test vehicle included power steering, two-speed windshield wipers, an electric deck-lid release, back-up lights, a crankcase ventilation system, an outside rear view mirror, a power front seat, simulated wire wheel covers and the Police Apprehender Pursuit package. The car had a 3.55:1 non-Positraction rear axle.

The car accelerated from 0-to-60 mph in 7.5 seconds. It could do the standing-start quarter-mile in 15.5 seconds at 90 mph.

"What Olds engineers have done, in the final analysis, is produce a car which at long last lives up to the claims of the company's advertising copywriters and top-level spokesmen," said *Car Life*.

The Oldsmobile sold for $2,734.57, compared to $3,120 for the Mustang and $3,161.31 for the GTO LeMans. Even the fancier Cutlass Holiday Coupe with the 4-4-2 package was only $3,144.46.

The 4-4-2 got a new 400-cid V-8 in 1965, giving it 345 hp and
giving Olds one of the best all-around muscle cars on the market.

OLDSMOBILE

1965 4-4-2

If you wanted to buy a muscle car that gave you the thrill of a GTO or an SS 396 without the headline-high pricing, the 4-dash-4-dash 2 was the way to go in 1965. A new engine was the year's big news. As *Car Life* put it, "Olds joins the bigger-inch crowd with another meaning for that first "4"— 400 cubic inches.

The F-85 Cutlass line was mildly face lifted for 1965 and the 4-4-2 performance and handling package gained in popularity. Noting the runaway success of the Pontiac GTO with its 389-cid engine, Oldsmobile engineers saw the need to cram more cubes into their creation. Reducing the bore of the new Olds 425-cid engine from 4.125 inches to an even 4.0 produced an engine ideally sized for the 4-4-2 at 400 cid.

This year the 4-4-2 package was offered with an optional Hydra-Matic transmission. Since the second "4" in the 1964 model designation had stood for "four-speed manual transmission," Oldsmobile had to explain the 4-4-2 name a different way. The company now said that the first four (4) stood for the new 400-cid V-8, the second four (4) meant four-barrel carburetor and the two (2) meant dual exhaust. This sounded a little awkward, since "4" and "400" aren't the same, but who cared?

With the 400-cid engine, power rose by 35 horses to a total of 345 hp at 4800 rpm and torque increased by 85 ft. lbs. to 440 at 3200 rpm. The new engine had a 10.25:1 compression ratio and a single Rochester four-barrel carburetor. *Car and Driver* magazine test drove a 1965 Olds 4-4-2 convertible with a four-speed manual gearbox and a 3.55:1 axle in May 1965. Its 0 to 60-mph time was recorded as 5.5 seconds and the quarter-mile run took 15.0 seconds at 98 mph.

Said *Car and Driver*, "Summed up, the Oldsmobile 4-4-2 is another one of those 'special purpose' American cars that should really be sold as the all-purpose car. It really isn't a sports car, and it isn't exactly like the imported sports sedans—even though that seems to have been the aim of its manufacturer—but it does approach a very worthwhile balance of all the qualities we'd like to see incorporated in every American car."

A standard 1965 Olds F-85 coupe with the 4-4-2 option sold for $2,605. The Cutlass version came in coupe ($2,799), hardtop ($2,940) and convertible ($3,139) versions. A total of 25,003 cars had the 4-4-2 package installed this year.

The 4-4-2 got a few updates and 5 more ponies under the hood for 1966.

Jerry Heasley

1966 4-4-2

When it was restyled for 1966, the Oldsmobile Cutlass F-85 took on a more massive, creased-edge look. The 4-4-2 high-performance option package now included seat belts, an instrument panel with a padded dashboard, a windshield washer system, two-speed windshield wipers, a left-hand manual outside rear view mirror, foam padded seat cushions, carpeting on the floor front and rear, chrome roof bow moldings, a deluxe steering wheel, front bucket or custom seats, deluxe armrests, a courtesy lamp package, 7.35 x 14 tires and seat upholstery in either all vinyl or cloth.

Under the hood of the 4-4-2 model, the 400-cid V-8 had been tweaked by another 5 hp (to 350 hp) thanks to a slight increase in compression ratio. Late in the model year, the 4-4-2 received another adrenalin injection (to 360 hp) with the one-year-only triple two-barrel carburetor setup. *Car Life* magazine took one of these screamers from 0-to-60 mph in a mere 6.3 seconds and called it the "civilized supercar." Quarter-mile runs were made in as little as 14.8 seconds with a terminal speed of 97 mph.

From the standpoints of both performance and rarity, the 1966 Olds Cutlass 4-4-2 equipped with the 360-hp factory Tri-Power installation is the most desirable example of these production years to a real muscle car enthusiast.

Today it matters little that the 1967 Oldsmobile 4-4-2 was only an option for the intermediate Cutlass Supreme series. It wouldn't be until the 1968 models bowed that the performance edition would get full model status.

OLDSMOBILE

Jerry Heasley

1967 Cutlass Supreme 4-4-2

If you've got a 1967 4-4-2, be it a two-door sedan, two-door hardtop or convertible, you've got a full-fledged muscle car that makes no excuses, unlike some of the later 4-4-2-badged cars that Oldsmobile turned out.

The original 1964 Cutlass 4-4-2 option was a quick, midyear answer to the GTO option for the Pontiac Tempest. It utilized parts and pieces from the police package available at the time. By 1967, Olds and its competitors were turning out nicely packaged hot intermediates with good looks and mechanical performance galore.

The 1967 Cutlass 4-4-2 option was available for the top-of-the-line Cutlass Supreme series, which grew from a single four-door hardtop in 1966 to a full model range for 1967. You could add the 4-4-2 package to all of the series' two-door models. Base prices were $2,694 for the sedan, $2,831 for the hardtop and $3,145 for the convertible. They came with a standard 330-cid/320-hp V-8.

Checking option box L78 brought the 4-4-2 option and added only $184 to your bill. For that small sum came the 440-cid 350-hp V-8, heavy-duty suspension, and other go-fast stuff.

While a standard rating of 350 hp was good for openers in 1967, it was necessary to have a trick setup a step beyond that. General Motors bureaucracy had undergone another of its periodic soul cleansings and banned Tri-Power in all cars except the Corvette. Oldsmobile's reaction was the W-30 option.

The flush hood louvers over the air cleaner were functional on the 4-4-2, but they did not have any ram-effect needed for added horses. Using factory ducting from the front of the car, the 1967 W-30-optioned version was advertised at 360 hp, the same as the 1966 Tri-Power Cutlass 4-4-2. Performance tests of the 1966 and 1967 Cutlass 4-4-2s, however, revealed nearly a second lost in the 0-to-60 runs and quarter-mile sprints were down about the same for the 1967s. However, that doesn't prevent a 30-percent price premium today for W-30-equipped 1967 4-4-2 examples.

Tom Glatch

OLDSMOBILE

The 1968 4-4-2 may not have been the most economical car to drive, but it was big, attractive,
handled great, was plenty fast, and could be driven home new for about 4 grand.

1968 4-4-2

Oldsmobile deserved congratulations for the '68 Olds 4-4-2. As one astute writer of the day noted in *Car Life*, "The 4-4-2 Holiday Coupe looked every bit as quick and strong as it really is. A true hi-po car and the best handling of today's supercars." The magazine also noted the car's lack of recognition due to the high-priced and luxurious Oldsmobile image that made a muscle car an odd fit in the product mix.

But Olds was trying. Along with the car's all-new General Motors A-car body, the 4-4-2 also had separate model status for the first time in 1968—it was no longer a Cutlass add-on. There were three models: Holiday hardtop, sports coupe (post sedan) and convertible in this first 4-4-2 series.

The new 4-4-2 had more curves than ever on its long hood and short deck body with razor edge fenders and a swoopy rear. Big 4-4-2 emblems and dual through-the-bumper exhaust made it easy to spot. On a 112-inch stance, the 4-4-2 was 201.6 inches long, 76.6 inches wide and 52.8 inches tall. Front and rear tracks were both 59 inches.

A coil spring front suspension with anti-roll bar was mated with a coil spring link-coil live axle rear suspension. The recirculating ball gear steering (with integral assist) had a 20.7:1 overall ratio and 4.3 turns lock-to-lock. Brakes were discs up front and drums rear. Tires were F70-14s.

As in 1967, a 400-cid V-8 was standard, but it was a totally new one with 3.87 x 4.25-inch bore and stroke (4 x 3.975-inch bore and stroke in 1967). There were three basic four-barrel versions of this 10.5:1 compression engine, the hottest with the W-30 Force Air package added. They gave

325 hp (automatic), 350 hp (stick) and 360 hp, respectively. However, a milder two-barrel "turnpike cruiser" economy engine with 9.0:1 compression and 290 hp (including Turbo Hydra-Matic) could be had, too.

Shift-for-yourself choices included a three-speed gearbox and wide- and close-ratio four-speed manual transmissions. A slew of rear axle options were available. Other popular extras included power steering, a high-voltage ignition system, a tilt-away wood-grain steering wheel, a so-called "Rocket Rally Pac," an AM radio, a center console and a remote-control outside rearview mirror. Bucket seats were standard.

Buyers who ordered the Force Air induction system got large 15 x 2-inch air scoops below the front bumper, a special camshaft for a higher torque peak, modified intake and exhaust ports, a free-flowing exhaust system and low-friction componentry.

Car Life's 4-4-2 Holiday listed for $3,127 f.o.b. in Lansing, Michigan, but went out the showroom door at $4,059. It had the 350-hp engine and took 15.13 seconds to do the quarter-mile at 92.2 mph. According to the magazine, overall braking was poor and fuel consumption was in the 11 to 16 mpg range for normal driving (12.2 mpg for the test). "A true high-performance car and the best handling of today's supercars," the editors wrote.

Production of the 1968 Olds 4-4-2 totaled 4,282 sports coupes, 5,142 convertibles and 24,183 Holiday hardtops for a total of 33,607 units compared to 24,829 the previous year.

Jerry Heasley

George Hurst took a 1968 4-4-2 and turned it into one of the great muscle cars of its generation.

1968 Hurst/Olds

"These executive supercars won't last very long," said *Super Stock* magazine's Jim McCraw about the '68 Hurst/Olds. He was right, too. Back then, Oldsmobile had a quality-car image that couldn't be beat and Hurst had a high-performance image that other aftermarket firms would kill for. Teaming up these two companies was a marriage made in heaven and produced one of the legendary muscle machines.

For 1968, what had formerly been the largest Olds engine offering, at 425 cid, was punched out to a full 455 cid. GM brass would not permit the cramming of the new 455 into the 4-4-2 platform, but this didn't stop George Hurst, of Hurst Performance Products, from trying it on his own. So successful was his effort that he—along with Olds officials— got entrepreneur and Oldsmobile supplier John Demmer, of Lansing, Michigan, to assemble clones of Hurst's car in his own facility on a limited basis. This is how the first Hurst/ Olds was born!

To power the Hurst/Olds, the 4-4-2's standard 400-cid engine was replaced with a Force Air 455 with a 10.5:1 compression ratio that was beefed-up internally to develop 390 hp at 5000 rpm and 500 ft.-lbs. of torque at 3600 rpm. The big W45 motor was based on the Toronado engine, but built with a special crankshaft, a custom-curved distributor,

special carburetor jets, a 308-degree camshaft with a .474-inch lift and hand-assembled Ram-Air cylinder heads. The power plant was hooked to a modified Turbo Hydra-Matic with a Hurst Dual-Gate shifter that could be shifted like a manual transmission or used like an automatic.

A heavy-duty rear end incorporated a standard 3.91:1 rear axle. Also included as part of the package were specially calibrated power disc-drum brakes, a heavy-duty suspension, a heavy-duty cooling system with a high-capacity radiator and viscous-drive fan and G70-14 Goodyear polyglas tires. The entire car was dressed up in a special silver and black trim package that looked very distinctive.

A total of 515 Hurst/Olds were built for 1968. Of these, 451 were based on the 4-4-2 Holiday two-door hardtop, while the remaining 64 were originally 4-4-2 coupes. No Hurst/Olds were produced in convertible form. In August 1968, *Super Stock* magazine road tested the 4-4-2 and reported a top run of 12.9 seconds for the quarter-mile at 109 mph.

The Hurst/Olds partnership proved to be quite an image-boosting program for the GM division and the two companies went on to team up on other Hurst/Olds models for many years.

A 1969 Olds W-30 4-4-2 sport coupe with the 400-cid V-8 could top out at 123 mph.

OLDSMOBILE

Phil Kunz

1969 4-4-2

"Built like a 1 3/4-ton watch" is how Oldsmobile described its 4-4-2 for 1969. Like the crocodile in "Peter Pan," the 4-4-2 ticked loud and precisely and was ready to snap its jaws at any horsepower pirate trying to steal its go-fast glory. The 4-4-2 was hotter than just about anything other than the Hurst model and it was a whole lot less money than that type of conversion.

A new pitchman named Dr. Oldsmobile prescribed image enhancements for the 4-4-2 in 1969. They included a bolder split grille, fat hood stripes and bright, new name badges. Also, the two-barrel "turnpike cruiser" option was eliminated to purify Oldsmobile's muscle car reputation.

When the W-30 kit was added, the car's advertised torque was 400 lbs.-ft. at 3600 rpm compared to 440 lbs.-ft. a year earlier. However, the 400-cid V-8's advertised horsepower rating was the same 360-hp at 5400 rpm V-8 and this motor could push the W-30 Olds to 123 mph tops.

Transmission options were also unchanged. Hurst shifters again came with stick-shift cars. Turbo Hydra-Matic buyers got a column shift, although a console mount was optional.

A divider between the halves of the grille, finished in body color, carried big 4-4-2 identifiers. W-30s had special hood stripes and front fender decal cutouts. Front parking lights were moved from between the headlamps to the front bumper. Strato bucket seats, red-stripe wide-oval tires, a juicy battery, dual exhausts and beefy suspension goodies were included. An anti-spin rear axle was mandatory.

The coupe ($3,404), hardtop ($3,467) and convertible ($3,658) with W-30 Force Air Induction accounted for 5 percent of production, or 1,389 cars. Total 4-4-2 output, by body style, included 2,475 coupes, 19,587 hardtops and 4,295 ragtops.

New for the year was a calmer W-31 Force-Air setup for the F-85 with Turbo Hydra-Matic transmission. This was a "for-the-street" extra for those with milder street use in mind and was aimed at the younger set where heavy breathing and heavy spending didn't co-mingle. At $310, the package was actually higher than the W-30 at $264. However, the car-and-equipment tab was lower. So was production. Only 1 percent of all Oldsmobiles were W-31s in 1969.

OLDSMOBILE

Jerry Heasley

**The 1969 Hurst/Olds was an intimidating beast with twin hood scoops and
a flashy paint job, and the car had performance to match its appearance.**

1969 Hurst/Olds

In George Hurst's "magic kingdom" the 4-4-2 that he built for Dr. Oldsmobile sat on the golden chair in the muscle car throne room. The famous red-and-black H/O badge reflected high-performance perfection. "Ah yes friends, there really is a supercar without lumps in it," advised *Super Stock* magazine in July of 1969.

Olds 4-4-2 styling was based on the mid-sized Cutlass and it was altered only slightly for the 1969 model year. Essentially, each pair of lenses in the quad headlight system was brought closer together. This, along with some modification of the central grille and bumper area contributed to an overall smoother, less-cluttered frontal appearance. This year the Cutlass taillights were recessed and took on a more vertical theme, as opposed to the horizontal orientation of the 1968 model.

The Hurst/Olds again rode a 112-inch wheelbase and had an overall length of 201.9 inches. With a shipping weight of 3,716 lbs., it was not the lightest muscle car in the mix, but the awesome power train made up for a lot of the added mass.

The number of Oldsmobiles that Hurst modified nearly doubled for 1969, with a total of 906 making it to the pavement. For this year, all Hurst/Olds were based on the 4-4-2 Holiday two-door hardtop body style.

Stimulated by a special 455-cid 380-hp "Rocket" V-8, this year's Hurst/Olds was slightly lighter (3,715 lbs.) than its '68 counterpart (3,870 lbs.) and therefore bettered the original version's 0-to-60-mph acceleration times (5.9 seconds versus 6.7 seconds). However, it took slightly longer to cover the quarter-mile (14.0 seconds versus 13.9 seconds). At least, that's what one publication said. A second car magazine had different numbers—6.0 seconds for 0-to-60 mph and 13.9 seconds at 102.27 mph for the quarter. Pick the ones you like best—the point is it was a fast car!

At a price that ranged from $4,500 to $4,900, the Hurst/Olds buyer had to part with a few more pennies than it took to buy Oldsmobile's factory hot rod, the 4-4-2 model. But in return for paying that premium, the Hurst/Olds buyer got the optimum balance of luxury and performance available in an Oldsmobile muscle car.

Power was transmitted from the engine through a heavy-duty Turbo Hydra-Matic or the buyer's choice of a close- or wide-ratio four-speed manual transmission, all Hurst-shifted, of course. The package was finished off with an eye-popping White-and-Gold color scheme and featured an attention-grabbing, strut-mounted rear deck spoiler.

The hot 4-4-2 was as notable for its handling ability and
road manners as it was for its good looks and raw power.

OLDSMOBILE

Jerry Heasley

1970 4-4-2

The W-30-equipped 4-4-2 was Oldsmobile's response to the lifting of General Motors' ill-conceived mandate prohibiting the use of engines exceeding 400-cid in its A-bodied automobiles.

On a limited scale—and well beyond the reach of GM's authority—this wall of separation had already been breached by the Hurst Corp.'s 1969 Hurst/Olds. Either in a "bandit" Hurst or a W-30-optioned Olds 4-4-2, the division's 455-cid V-8 represented a major advance in straight-line performance. And it did not adversely affect the 4-4-2's handling, since it weighed about the same as the smaller and less-powerful 400-cid V-8 used in 1969 Olds 4-4-2s.

The 4-4-2 had, since its introduction in 1964, enjoyed a deserved reputation for handling far above the existing norm for American supercars. The W-30 version, along with its stature as a powerful 370-hp automobile, maintained the tradition of being a handler. There was nothing magical or exotic about the W-30 Olds 4-4-2 suspension, which consisted of front coil and rear leaf springs. Like all 4-4-2 Oldsmobiles, the W-30 was equipped with a rear stabilizer bar. *Car Life* magazine, in its March 1970 issue said, "At last people who want more power, but still want their car to handle, have a car that does both."

Also adding to the W-30 Olds 4-4-2's performance profile were standard 10.88-inch front power disc brakes that were optional for standard 4-4-2s. At the rear, 9.5 x 2.0-inch drum

brakes were utilized. This setup wasn't flawless, but *Car Life* noted that on its W-30 test car, "The front disc brakes came through the brake fade test smoking, but working well."

The source of all the kinetic energy in the W-30 was, at least officially, only slightly different from the standard 4-4-2 engine. Both engines displaced 455 cubic inches and had 10.5:1 compression ratios, but the standard 4-4-2 engine developed 365 hp at 5000 rpm and the W-30 was said to put out 370 hp at 5400 rpm.

Virtually identical to the one used on the 1969 Hurst/Olds was the 1970 W-30 model's fiberglass hood. Unlike the air ducts installed on the W-31, which were mounted under the front bumper, those for the W-30 were mounted on the hood. The twin intakes rammed a flow of cool air through a mesh filter and were linked to a low-restriction air intake by a sponge-like material that acted as a gasket seal with the hood.

The W-30's standard transmission was identified by Oldsmobile as the "Muncie Close Ratio." *Car Life* described it as "Oldsmobile's version of Chevy's M22 'Rock Crusher.'" For an additional $227, the M40 version of the Turbo Hydra-Matic 400 was available. Compared to a normal Turbo Hydra-Matic transmission, the M40 had higher rpm shift positions and sharper shifts.

The W-30 was capable of 0-to-60 times of under 6 seconds and quarter-mile runs of 14.36 seconds at 100.22 mph.

There was no mistaking the Rallye 350. Only 3,547 of these cars were
assembled, making them a pretty cool collector prize.

OLDSMOBILE

Jerry Heasley

1970 Rallye 350

If looks alone counted in a street race or drag race, the Rallye 350 had the image that it could send feathers flying like a "screaming yellow honker." And the car had more than looks. "Beneath that gaudy paint and wing lurks bargains in performance and handling," said *Car Life* magazine.

While not the brawniest muscle car ever built, the Oldsmobile Rallye 350 was surely one of the brightest. Its smart Sebring Yellow paint makes it stand out wherever it's seen. So does the fact that its urethane-clad bumpers and Rallye spoke wheels are done in the same color. In addition, it's trimmed with bold orange and black stripes along the tops of rear fenders and over the backlight.

Introduced in February 1970, the car was initially planned as a Hurst/Olds, but Lansing wound up marketing it as a new option that combined the looks of a limited-edition muscle car with a more "streetable" power-train package. It could be added to either the F-85 coupe or the Cutlass 'S' coupe or hardtop.

The base engine, of course, was the 350-cid V-8 with a 4.057 x 3.385-inch bore and stroke. This version developed 310 hp at 4200 rpm. A W-31 Force Air package was available for cars with the Rallye 350 option. It boosted compression from 10.25:1 to 10.5:1 and gave 325 hp at 5400 rpm. Also included on W-31s were aluminum intake manifolds, a heavy-duty clutch, front disc brakes, a special hood and decorative touches such as decals, paint stripes and specific emblems.

When the Rallye 350 equipment was added to an F-85 or Cutlass 'S,' the following extras were mandatory: Rallye sport suspension, Force Air fiberglass hood, dual sport mirrors and a sport steering wheel. Retail price for the F-85 option package was $3,163. The Cutlass 'S' based editions were $3,283 (coupe) and $3,346 (hardtop).

Transmission attachments included three-on-the-floor or four-on-the-floor, the latter available with wide- or close-ratio choices (all with Hurst shifters). Three-speed Turbo Hydra-Matic could be had with regular column shift or optional console shift. Axle ratios were 3.23:1 (manual) or 3.42:1 (automatic), with 3.42:1 and 3.91:1 options.

Like the GTO "Judge," this trendy-looking Olds was aimed at a market niche that proved to be smaller than sales projections forecasted. Only 3,547 of these cars were assembled: 2,527 were Cutlass S-based and 1,020 were F-85s. Many of the cars came with a rear deck lid spoiler, which cost $74 extra.

In February 1970, *Motor Trend* tested a Rallye 350 with the 310-hp engine, three-speed manual transmission and 3.23:1 rear axle. It did 0-to-60 mph in 7.7 seconds and covered the quarter-mile in 15.4 seconds at 89 mph.

The 4-4-2, one of the most refined muscle cars of its day, was a separate model for the last time in 1971.

OLDSMOBILE

1971 4-4-2

This was the last year that Oldsmobile would have the 4-4-2 as a separate model. In 1972, the 4-4-2 would become an appearance and handling option for the Cutlass "S."

For its last year as a separate series, the 4-4-2's standard equipment included a special 455-cid engine, a dual exhaust system, carpeting, special springs, stabilizer bars, special engine mounts, Strato bucket seats, heavy-duty wheels, special emblems and a deluxe steering wheel. Oldsmobile offered a choice of vinyl or cloth upholstery. The standard tires were G70-14s.

The W-31 version of the 350-cid 1970 Cutlass V-8 had to be discontinued in 1971 since it couldn't pass emission control tests that were coming online at the time, but W-30-optioned 4-4-2 models were continued in 1971. The W-30s had an 8.5:1 compression ratio, accomplished by using a piston with a dished-out top.

The 455-cid engine used in the 4-4-2 had a net horsepower rating of 260. The gross horsepower rating shown in the *Standard Catalog of American Cars 1946-1975* is 340 at 4600 rpm. While Oldsmobile was reluctant to give out the W-30's ratings for 1971, the 1970 rating was 470 gross hp.

A unique 1971 feature was the use of valve rotators on the exhaust valves of 4-4-2 and W-30 engines. In addition, valve rotators were fitted on the intake valves. Special alloy exhaust

valve seats were installed in the cylinder heads and the valves themselves had aluminum seats and hardened tips.

The rear ends on all Cutlass-based cars were given larger pinion bearings and stronger pinion shafts while the clutches in limited-slip differentials were such that they developed higher maximum friction torque. Optional on the W-30 cars was a dual-disc, dual-plate clutch that offered 10 percent greater torque capacity, 40 percent less pedal effort and a 100 percent increase in clutch life.

Hot Rod magazine drove a dual-disc equipped W-30 Olds 4-4-2 with a 455-cid engine and four-speed gearbox and found the shifts "startlingly quick and effortless." The writers said, "You really have to get used to using a light foot." A heavy-duty close-ratio four-speed gearbox could be ordered on the W-30 machines. *Hot Rod* magazine went on record saying, "It isn't recommended for sustained street driving."

On balance, *Hot Rod* concluded that the 1971 version of the 4-4-2 and its W-30 variant represented no appreciable performance sacrifice. As the last of the special series, the '71 4-4-2 is worth collecting. *Car & Driver* once characterized it as, "strictly speaking, a muscle car, but one … too gentlemanly to display the gutter habits of its competitors." Among the '71s, the 4-4-2 convertible is definitely the rarer piece with 1,304 produced. Oldsmobile also made 6,285 two-door hardtops.

GM photo

Oldsmobile was back in the muscle car business in 1979 with the new-generation Hurst/Olds.
It wasn't nearly the fire-breathing machine that its predecessors had been,
but its one-year run was a breath of fresh air for performance car fans.

OLDSMOBILE

1979 Hurst/Olds

By the mid-1970s, everyone though that cars like the Hurst/Olds had gone the way of the dodo bird. The government and the insurance companies had teamed up to give muscle cars the one-two punch of restrictive safety/emissions regulations and unaffordable insurance premiums. However, as the decade wound to its close, the domestic automakers gradually began growing bolder. All of a sudden, they were openly offering specialty performance cars again. Oldsmobile took the leap early in calendar year 1979, when it introduced the Hurst/Olds option for its Cutlass Calais coupe.

The first Hurst/Olds model had been built in 1968, when Oldsmobile used the back-door approach and hired George Hurst's company to stuff the big 455-cid engine into the intermediate Cutlass model. Later versions ended up being more for dress than speed, with the last offering prior to 1979 being the 1975 model.

For 1979, the downsized Cutlass Calais needed some extra dressing and excitement. Uncle George went back to the drawing board and supplied the much-needed ingredients with a Hurst/Olds package. For an extra $2,054 tacked on to the $5,631 base price you got option W-30. There was decal calling out this option kit on each front fender. The extra-cost package included Gold paint trim, Gold aluminum wheels, Gold sport mirrors, Hurst/Olds emblems on the sail panels, a Hurst Dual-Gate shifter on the mandatory Turbo Hydra-Matic 350 and the Oldsmobile 350-cid V-8 (which was not available on some other models at the time). The output of 170 net hp was nothing to brag about, but it bettered by far the 130 hp being put out by the 305-cid V-8 used in most other GM vehicles at the time.

In the past, Hurst/Olds cars had been shipped to a separate factory for the Hurst conversion, but the 1979 examples were set up for conversion right at the Oldsmobile factory. That didn't seem to bother the buyers in 1979, since a total of 2,499 were made, just a hair short of the 2,535 record set by the 1975 model. Of the 1979 total, 1,334 were finished in black and 1,165 were done in white. Optional T-top roofs ended up on 537 Hurst/Oldsmobiles.

Despite little promotion, the sales tally wasn't enough for the Hurst/Olds to return immediately and the Hi-Po model wasn't seen again until the 1983 model year. A second so-called energy crisis in the 1979-'80 period also was a factor.

The Hurst/Olds nameplate was taken out of mothballs in 1984 with a flashy new 180-hp coupe.

OLDSMOBILE

1984 Hurst/Olds

Too bad that Mercury had the Cougar name and GTO had the Tiger nickname, because both identities would have fit well on the specialty models that George Hurst built for Oldsmobile. The Hurst/Olds was truly like the cat that had nine lives. Every few years it would die and before long it would come back to life again.

The ninth edition of the Hurst/Olds brought the nameplate back to life again in model year 1984. And, for the first time in this reincarnation, the Hurst/Olds was not a middle-of-the-year model. It was announced along with the rest of the Oldsmobile lineup on September 14, 1983. Hurst's parent company—Cars & Concepts—started production of the package in December at the aftermarket company's Brighton, Michigan, facility.

Black and silver exterior colors were reversed from the 1983 model, with red trim continuing. The hood bulge and the front and rear spoilers from the previous year were also carried over. Returning, too, was the next best thing to a video arcade in the front seat, the Lightning Rod Automatic Shifter. Instead of the usual single lever popping up from the center console, there were three shifters between the seats. They controlled the overdrive automatic transmission. The

extra levers gave you manual control of first and second gear selections.

Helen Early, the wonderful lady who served as Oldsmobile's historian for many years and recently passed away, brought one of these cars to the Iola Old Car Show in 1984. Helen and her sister drove the car from Michigan and I think they battled the Lightening Rods all the way. After arriving, they got in the car and could not figure which shifter to move to make it go again! The set up could be a little tricky until you mastered it.

Power still came from the Olds-built 307-cid V-8, which was rated at 180 hp, the same as the Chevrolet Monte Carlo SS. A Rochester 4MV Quadrajet carb and aluminum intake manifold did the best job they could muster under the stringent emission and CAFE requirements of the time. A heavy-duty suspension, front and rear sway bars, chrome-plated super stock wheels and Goodyear Eagle GT P215/65R15 rubber got the power to the ground.

The price of the package on the Cutlass Supreme Calais coupe was $1,997 above the base price of $10,649. About 3,500 of the 1984 model were produced, making it the most popular car in the Hurst/Olds series.

PLYMOUTH

**By 1958 the Fury had established itself as a performance car,
although it evolved into more of a family car in the 1960s.**

1958 Fury

Model year 1958 was the third for Plymouth's top-of-the-line performance model, the Fury two-door hardtop. It was the first of the then traditional gold-trimmed Buckskin Beige speedsters to come out with the rest of the lineup at the start of the model year and the last to be a single model with its status unquestioned.

The 1956 Fury and the totally redesigned 1957 offering took giant steps in establishing the Plymouth name in performance circles.

Even though the domestic manufacturers banded together in 1957 to cut back on racing and performance promotion, the '58s were well along in the plans and too late to change.

As a result, Plymouth had several solid go-fast options for 1958.

Engine nomenclature gets a bit confusing, so here is an explanation. The 225-hp/318-cid Fury V-8 was not available on the Fury. Neither was the Fury V-8 with Super-Pak, which had a four-barrel carb and other modifications for a rating of 250 hp. Next up was the Dual Fury V-8, which had a pair of four-barrels, 9.25:1 compression and a rating of 290 hp. This engine was standard on the Fury, as it was for 1957.

Optional on all models, Fury included, was Plymouth's first crack at the new B-block, which came in at 350 cubes, two more than Chevrolet and two fewer than Ford big blocks for 1958. Two Carter four-barrels were on top, compression was 10:1 and the advertised horsepower rating was 305. This engine package was dubbed Golden Commando.

A very limited number of Furys were ordered with the Bendix electronic fuel-injection system, which raised the rating to 315 hp. Most were replaced with dual-carb setups when the injection proved troublesome.

Motor Trend tested an automatic equipped Fury with the 305 hp Golden Commando and got a 7.7 second 0-to-60 mph run. This was far faster than the Ford 352 cid at 10.2 seconds and the Chevrolet Impala's 348-cid run of 9.1.

With a $3,032 base price, the 1958 Fury was the most expensive Plymouth that year. Its production of 5,303 was down from the 7,438 for 1957, but up from the short 1956 run of 4,485. After 1958, the Fury name would be put on Plymouths of all types ranging from station wagons to police cars.

1962 Max Wedge 413

My friend Bruce Davis' family's car was a white '62 Plymouth sedan with a Slant Six. His father Jack used to drive a taxicab in New York City and that's where his love of the marque sprang from. From the '30s to the '60s, with a couple of exceptions, the Plymouth was a car for taxi enthusiasts. But the world was changing and the Mayflower marque was starting to feel pressured to go with some of the more modern trends.

During early 1962, Plymouth sales were really hurting. Then an announcement in *Motor Trend's* "Spotlight on Detroit" column in May 1962 publicized a new engine option that would help turn things around. "A new 410-hp/413-cubic inch V-8 engine with ram-tube manifolding will be available as a factory-installed option on many Plymouths and Dodge Darts beginning this month," said the brief photo caption. "The big power plant will have an 11-to-1 compression ratio, a newly designed short ram-tube intake manifold, two four-barrel carburetors and high-velocity exhausts."

A closer look at the 413-cid engine written up in *Motor Trend's* August 1962 issue was described as "the first report on the Plymouth-Dodge Super Stock engine." Technical editor Roger Huntington got his hands on a Super Stock Dodge Dart two-door sedan with the Ramcharger V-8. In his story, he explained that this engine was the same as the Plymouth version.

Amazingly, the big monster motor cost only $374.40 more than a base 230-hp V-8. With that option you got a big-block V-8 with a 4.19 x 3.75-inch bore and stroke, an 11.0:1 compression ratio and two 650-cfm Carter AFB four-barrel carburetors mounted on a newly designed cross-ram intake manifold. The Max Wedge V-8 was linked to a three-speed TorqueFlite automatic transmission. In the 3,440-lb. car, this combination was good for 5.8-second 0-to-60 times and a standing-start quarter mile in 14.4 seconds at 101 mph. Talk about a quick change in image!

Max Wedge racing cars with some aftermarket enhancements and other tweaking could do even better than that, and did. On July 15, at a drag strip in Fremont, California, Tom Grove became the first Super Stock driver to run the quarter-mile in under 12 seconds. His 413-powered 500-hp "Melrose Missile" ran down the drag strip in 11.93 seconds with a trap speed of 118.57 mph. After this crucial year in its history, Plymouth was never quite the taxicab-only car it had been before.

1963 Max Wedge 426

A Max Wedge was not something you squeezed into your shoes to make them as big as they could be. On the other hand, it had to do with wedging a massive engine into an under-hood space often occupied by off-center inline sixes in earlier years. "Wedge" also indicated the design of the engine. Its cylinder heads had wedge-shaped combustion chambers that greatly enhanced Plymouth's reputation as a muscular automobile.

In 1963, the National Hot Rod Association (NHRA) and the National Association for Stock Car Auto Racing (NASCAR) and several other groups that sanctioned automobile racing established an engine displacement limit of 7 liters or 427 cubic inches. As a reaction to this, in June of 1963, Plymouth announced its development of a 426-cid "Max Wedge" V-8 engine for Super Stock class drag racing. The 426-cid engine block had been introduced only in upper-level Chryslers in 1962 and had not been tuned for drag racing.

This changed in 1963. The so-called Stage II version of the motor brought out that year was intended for sale only to those competing in supervised drag racing and stock car racing. At 1 cubic inch under the new limit, this engine increased Chrysler's ability to win in both drag and oval-track racing. By the end of the year, a total of 2,130 Plymouths and Dodges with this motor would be built.

The new Max Wedge 426 engine looked identical to the previous Max Wedge 413 V-8 on the outside, but it had a larger bore size of 4.25 inches. The power plant came in three different versions. The first version, fitted with a single four-barrel carburetor, was designed to be "legal" under stock-car racing rules. It put out 400 hp. The second version, with an 11.0:1 compression ratio, was made for dragging. It had dual four-barrel carburetors on a cross-ram manifold and produced 415 hp at 5600 rpm and 470 ft.-lbs. of torque at 4400 rpm. The third version (also for drag racing) had a 13.5:1 compression ratio and dual four-barrel carburetors, also on the cross-ram intake. It produced 425 hp at 5600 rpm and 480 lbs.-ft. of torque at 4400 rpm.

Many of the Max Wedge 426s also carried a new Super/Stock package designed for drag racing. It included lightweight aluminum front-end sheet metal, a large air scoop for the hood and some trim deletions designed to shave off pounds.

PLYMOUTH

The 1963 Max Wedge (above and below) had three 426 engine options that all produced more than 400 hp.
Such an engine "Wedged" into a Belvedere/Savoy body was a race-ready combination.

PLYMOUTH

PLYMOUTH

The Barracuda unveiled a radical new body design in 1964, but the styling never caught on enough to make a challenger to the Mustang.

1964 Barracuda

The Barracuda was as unique a fish as a Hammerhead Shark or a Manta Ray. There was nothing else like it. There were other fastbacks of course, but none had the fish bowl-like piece of curved glass that characterized the rear end of the car. It was a love-it-or-leave-it type of design that was meant to created a distinctive sports-compact car aimed at the booming youth market.

"We are sure the Plymouth Barracuda is just right for young, sports-minded Americans who want to enjoy the fun of driving a car that also fills their general transportation needs," said Plymouth's general manager P.N. Buckminster, when the Barracuda arrived in April 1, 1964.

The Barracuda was a reaction to the Ford Mustang and the Corvair Monza. It was based on the Valiant's 106-inch stance and shared most of its front sheet metal with that compact-size Plymouth. The rear of the body was turned into a dramatic fastback roofline that was created primarily through the use of a very large, lift-up rear window.

Like the Valiant, the Barracuda featured front torsion bars and leaf springs at the rear. Power brakes were standard equipment. Tires were size 6.50 x 13. Chrome-plated lugs for the 13 x 4 1/2-inch safety-rim wheels were optional, as were finned wheel covers with simulated knock-off hubs.

Barracuda buyers had a choice of three engines, and two of them were in-line version of the Chrysler "slant six." The third was a 273-cid V-8 that produced 180 hp at 4200. This small-block engine had solid valve lifters, a 3.62 x 3.312-inch bore and stroke, an 8.8:1 compression ratio and a Carter Type BBS two-barrel carburetor. You could settle for the standard three-speed manual transmission, but muscle-car fans usually opted for a new four-speed manual gearbox with a Hurst shift linkage. You could also order a three-speed TorqueFlite automatic at extra cost.

The Barracuda had a base price of $2,365 and weighed 2,740 lbs. Some popular options included racing stripes for $31, a Transaudio radio for $59, and performance group equipment for $156. The latter included a four-barrel carburetor for the 273-cid V-8 plus a heavy-duty suspension package. While it was a neat package, the 1964 Barracuda did not strike a hit with buyers like Ford's Mustang did. In the 8 months that it was on the market, only 23,443 copies were built.

PLYMOUTH

Jerry Heasley

The 426-R or 426-S engine options could turn any Plymouth, like this Sport Fury, into a real pavement pounder. The "Street" option was conservatively rated at 365 hp. The "Race" version was even hairier.

1964 426-R/426-S

"Motown" stands for Motor City which stands for Detroit. The term is common to music buffs, but little used by car enthusiasts. Yet in the early '60s, Detroit was really a motor town. The guys who worked at Chrysler got caught up racing Chevys, Fords and Pontiacs on Woodward Ave. and put the pressure on MoPar to build a racecar for the streets. And it was a racecar. As *Musclecar Review* said about the Plymouth Max Wedge in February 1989: "The Super Stock was not designed for milk and egg runs to the 7-11."

In 1964, Plymouth continued offering the "Super Stock" Max Wedge Stage III 426-cid engine. Dodge offered the same motor of course, the only difference being the Plymouth version had a black cooling fan and the Dodge engine had a chrome-plated fan blade. It was a competition-only option and carried the code 426-R, with the "R" indicating "racing." It had an option price in the $500 range.

The 426-R engine was again available in 415- and 425-hp versions. The former had the 11.0:1 compression ratio and the latter had the 13.5:1 ratio. The more powerful version also had nifty "Tri-Y" exhaust headers.

New this year was a 426-S "street" version of the 426-cid V-8 that was rated for 365 advertised horsepower, but actually produced around 410 hp. This engine did not include most of the Max Wedge hardware, but because of the similar displacement numbers, many buyers thought it was nearly the same engine. It ran a single four-barrel carburetor on a cast-iron intake and a 10.3:1 compression ratio. It used a standard type exhaust system. With 470 lbs.-ft. of torque at 3200 rpm, it was no slouch and it was far more "streetable" than the race versions of the 426.

Most of the 426-R engines went into cheap Savoy two-door sedans because they were the lightest-weight full-size models made by Plymouth and thus went the fastest with the big engine. The NASCAR racing cars carried four-barrel carburetors. The drag racers went for the dual-quad setups and many had the lightweight aluminum front-end sheet metal, large hood scoops, etc. They were plain-Jane machines, but amazingly fast with performance in the same range as 1963.

The street version of the 426 could be had in any model from the Savoy to the Sport Fury hardtop or convertible. A 1964 Sport Fury two-door hardtop with the 426-cid/365-hp V-8 carried about 9.5 lbs. per horsepower and could turn in 6.8-second 0 to 60-mph runs. The same combination was good for a 15.2-second quarter-mile run.

The awesome Stage III Race Hemi was a pure performance engine without a factory warranty and wasn't "recommended for general driving," so most racers took them straight to the track.

PLYMOUTH

1965 Belvedere Satellite Max Wedge Stage III/Race Hemi

Promoted as "the roaring '65s," mid-sized Plymouths boasted new lower body styling, carryover roof lines, a return to single headlamps and a new high-performance line called Satellite. Starting at $3,045, this 116-inch wheelbase, Belvedere-based intermediate assumed the muscle car role heretofore filled by Sport Furys (which had become sports/luxury cars). A four-section aluminum grille and a crisp, tapering body-side feature line dominated the round-cornered, but mostly square styling. Rear fenders had a set of dummy louvers for image.

Bucket seats, a center console and all-vinyl upholstery were standard in two-door hardtops and ragtops. Chrysler's top trim levels had a glittery, rich look and the Satellite filled the bill. Sales literature showed the 426-cid 425-hp "Max Wedge" on the options list, as well as the 426-cid/365-hp "Street Wedge," the 383-cid/360-hp big-block V-8, the 361-cid/265-hp V-8 and the 318-cid/230-hp V-8.

Often confused with the Hemi due to similar displacement and horsepower numbers, the 426 Max Wedge Stage III was a race-bred engine with a different combustion chamber configuration. It had 12.5:1 compression, a NASCAR "Tri-Y" exhaust system, a cam with 320 degrees of overlap, reworked combustion chambers, notched valves and big, twin Carter four-barrels with giant air cleaners. Chrysler did not warranty this engine as it was "not recommended for general driving."

The tamer, 426-cid/365-hp Street Wedge, with 10.3:1 compression and a single four-barrel on a cast-iron intake had better street driveability, due to its lower state of tune.

A rare Plymouth engine was the 426-cid "Race Hemi." Introduced in 1964, it was intended for off-road (race) use only. It used a cast-iron block with 4.25 x 3.75-inch bore and stroke, a forged and shotpeened crankshaft, impact extruded pistons, cross-bolted main bearing caps, forged rods and solid lifters, all of which would be carried over for "Street Hemis." But, the Race Hemi also had a magnesium dual-four-barrel intake manifold, aluminum cylinder heads, a header-type exhaust system, a 328-degree cam (with 112-degree overlap), bigger valves with stiffer springs and 12.5:1 compression. Chrysler built 360 Race Hemi engines in 1965. Typically, 60 percent went into Plymouths. Most likely, the majority of Hemis went into base Belvedere coupes—the lightest model in the lineup. A '65 Hemi Satellite would, however, be a rare possibility. Chrysler was known to do just about anything to sell a car.

A Hemi-powered '65 Plymouth racing car, competing in S/SA drag classes with "Drag-On-Lady" Shirley Shahan behind the wheel, went 129.30 mph in the quarter-mile. While NASCAR issued a temporary ban on the $1,800 engine, Hemi Belvederes won many events in USAC, NHRA and AHRA competition during 1965.

The Barracuda continued to gain fans and performance for the 1966 model year.

PLYMOUTH

1966 Barracuda "S"

By 1966, the Plymouth Barracuda "S" fastback had clawed its way to the championship in the Sports Car Club of America's (SCCA) national rallying class. That was not bad for a car that had suffered through its first half year, in 1964, as a "pretty face" without much real performance behind it. Things had not improved a great deal during 1965.

For 1966, the heated-up "Golden Commando" version of the Chrysler 273-cid V-8 was the "hot-ticket" engine option once again. It had a new unsilenced air cleaner, but there were no real serious changes in this power plant's basic specifications.

Prices for the 1966 Barracuda V-8 started at $2,655. There was not a whole lot that was really new about the car's body design, although it did get the year's new split radiator grille with criss-cross inserts, which was also used on the 1966 Valiant.

When the Barracuda "S" package was added, the presence of this option was noted with small, circular model identification badges below the Barracuda name on each of the front fenders. New pin striping decorated the body and a vinyl-covered roof was a new option. Six types of optional racing stripes were available to Barracuda buyers.

Motor Trend decided to test a Barracuda "S" with $400 worth of options to prove the fact that "Barracudas can bite." The test car had the following extras: a 235-hp V-8 ($97.30), an automatic transmission ($177.30), a heavy-duty suspension ($13.60), front disc brakes ($81.95), a power brake system ($41.75), power steering ($80.35), an AM radio ($57.35), tinted glass ($27.90) and a tachometer ($48.70). Some of these add-ons were also included in the Barracuda 'S' model's price.

The resulting car was featured in the February 1966 edition of *Motor Trend*. It had an as-tested price of $3,616.50. In the test, it achieved 0-to-60 in 8.9 seconds and did the quarter-mile in 16.5 seconds at 84 mph. In production terms, the 1966 Barracuda's popularity leveled off at 38,029 units.

1966 Satellite "Street Hemi"

"That the Hemi Satellite accelerates in a straight line in astonishing fashion cannot be disputed, " *Car Life* magazine gushed in July 1966. Richard Petty's eight NASCAR wins created great demand for the engine—as well as for the Satellite. A USAC championship didn't hurt Plymouth's reputation on the street either.

According to Chrysler's historical archives, 844 Hemi-powered Plymouth Satellites were built in 1966. Hardtops accounted for 817 of these, including 503 with four-speeds and 314 with TorqueFlite. Ragtops with Hemis installed totaled 27 units. All had the "Street Hemi" engine. Although similar to a race Hemi, this 426-cid engine used a dual four-barrel aluminum intake, milder valve-train specs, different 10.25:1 pistons and a big single air cleaner. A pair of tubes were added to the right-hand exhaust manifold to handle heat riser functions. Chrysler rated the engine for 425 hp at 5,000 rpm and 490 lbs.-ft. of torque at 4,000 rpm.

Like other Plymouth Belvederes, the Satellite featured a major restyling for 1966, highlighted by a slab-sided body with crisper fenders and mild body side sculpturing. Satellites had bucket seats, consoles, full wheel covers and vinyl trim. Prices began at $2,695 for the hardtop with a 273-cid V-8 and $2,910 for the similarly powered ragtop. The Hemi package was about $1,105 extra.

Early in the season, the biggest engine for Satellites was the 383-cid big-block V-8 with 325 hp. Use of a new 440-cid 365-hp V-8 was limited to Plymouth Furys. Dodges got the Hemi first, a few months into the season. Then, Plymouth released it.

Hemi Satellites were good for 7.4-second 0-to-60 runs and 14.5-second ETs. Eight wins by Richard Petty announced the engine's induction into NASCAR circles. USAC saw the Hemi-powered cars take its annual championship. In professional drag racing, A/Stock class Belvederes were going 122 mph in 11.6-second quarter-miles, so the Satellites should be in the same bracket.

Production of Hemi Belvederes was a bit lower with 136 coupes, 531 hardtops and 10 convertibles recoded.

The fact that you could get a 383-cid/280-hp "B" block V-8 in the restyled 1967 Barracuda was big news for Plymouth fans. The Barracuda's good looks and improving performance kept it right in the middle of the escalating muscle car sweepstakes in the late '60s.

1967 Barracuda

Magazines of the era compared the sexy styling of the Gen II Barracuda to that of the classic Buick Riviera. In December 1966, *Car Life* said, "The game is pony car poker and Plymouth raises one—who'll call?"

Plymouth's sports compact really came of age for 1967. It was no longer just a fastback version of the Valiant. It was now a separate sub-make. It grew to three distinct models, including a much smoother looking fastback two-door hardtop, a uniquely styled notchback two-door hardtop and a convertible.

It officially bowed on November 26, 1966, about two months after the rest of the 1967 Plymouth lineup. In so doing it avoided being buried by the hoopla surrounding two other new sports compacts introduced in early fall, the Chevrolet Camaro and Mercury Cougar.

Barracuda basics were still Valiant-related, like a longer 108-inch wheelbase, but the relationship was far less apparent from the outside package. Curved side glass, mostly its own body panels and unique rooflines, plus a 4.4-inch greater overall length (192.8 inches) all added to the impression of the Barracuda as its own car line.

The fastback (sports) hardtop continued the interior with fold-down rear seats and access to the trunk area. The new notchback hardtop featured a small greenhouse area with a concave rear window. It looked a little like the 1960-'64 Corvair coupes. The notchback did serve as a basis for the convertible, which came out a few weeks later than the hardtops. It featured a glass rear window and power top. A split grille with directional and parking lights inside added to the Barracuda's sporty flair.

Power plants were the same used in the earlier models,

with one big exception—for the first time you could get a production B-block V-8 in a Barracuda. This was the 383-cid engine, which came with a Carter four-barrel carburetor and a 10:1 compression ratio. It was advertised at 280 hp.

One way to assure that all the right stuff showed up when you ordered your Barracuda was to order the Formula S package. Just as on the earlier Barracudas, it included the Commando 273 engine, wide oval 14-inch tires, heavy-duty suspension, anti-sway bar and appropriate S badges. Actually, there were two Formula S options for 1967, the second coming on stream a bit later and including the 383—the only way you were supposed to be able to get it.

Base prices for V-8-powered Barracudas were competitive with the fastback at $2,270, notchback at $2,530 and convertible at $2,860. The buying public responded, calling for a production run of 62,534 (30,110 fastbacks, 28,196 notchbacks and 4,228 convertibles). It was the most popular Barracuda model year ever. Only the restyled 1970 models would come close (55,499).

Today, 1967 Barracuda prices reach into five figures in No. 1 condition, with Formula S models commanding a 10 percent premium and 383s a whopping 40 percent.

An available 426 Street Hemi was one of a host of options that made the new GTX a formidable machine.
Surviving Hemi-equipped GTXs are high-dollar trophies today.

1967 Plymouth Belvedere GTX

Having a big-inch performance model in your lineup was mandatory if you wanted to market your muscle in the mid-1960s. Pontiac started it with its GTO option for the intermediate Tempest in 1964. One by one the competition

followed: GT, GTA and so on. One of the last to arrive was the 1967 Plymouth Belvedere GTX. The mid-size Belvedere already had a hot-car image, thanks to race driver Richard "The King" Petty. The GTX took it one step further as an official factory street machine with all the show-them-off-at-the-drive-in goodies on the outside and under the hood.

With its lightweight Super Stock models and its big Wedge and Hemi V-8 engines, Plymouth built limited-production cars that were far faster than the GTO. But the company dragged its feet on doing up an all-inclusive package that put the full range of parts together in one model.

Two vital elements of the Plymouth GTX story resided under the hood. In the middle of the 1966 model year, the company introduced the 426-cid Street Hemi and it then followed up with the release of the 440-cid "Super Commando" Wedge V-8 in 1967. When either of these powerful motors was combined with the Belvedere's 116-inch wheelbase and lighter weight, you had a potent combination. When you tossed in top-of-the-line front bucket seats, a couple of fake hood scoops and stripes, the GTX was ready to go cruising the boulevard.

For $3,178 in two-door hardtop form and $3,418 in convertible format, you got a 375-hp/440-cid V-8. Also on the GTX model's standard equipment list were TorqueFlite automatic transmission, a heavy-duty suspension and even a pit-stop type gas filler cap. If you plunked down an extra $564, you got the Street Hemi. The monstrous motor was fed by a pair of Carter AFB four-barrel carburetors and carried a conservative 425-hp rating. Magazine tests proved that the Super Commando GTX was capable of 0-to-60 mph spurts in 7 seconds or less.

The exact number of GTXs sold during the model year is not known, since that total was combined with the output of Satellite models. What is known is that the Hemi-optioned GTXs are rare, with only 720 of the approximately 12,500 GTXs that were built being equipped with a Hemi. Of those, 312 had four-speed transmissions and 408 were attached to TorqueFlite automatics. Estimates put the number of Hemi convertibles built at only 17.

The Hemi Under Glass, one of the most well-known drag race exhibition cars, used various Barracuda body shells to cover mid-ships Hemi race engine during its long life.

GEORGE H. HURST

93

Hurst Hemis couldn't necessarily make a Barracuda stand on end like the "Hemi Under Glass" exhibition car, but they were still drag-racing demons.

1968 Barracuda "Hurst Hemi"

This was a fish that could stand on its tail, which is a neat trick for just about any undersea creature. Most fish want to stand on their tail about as much as my cat wants to use his scratching post instead of the furniture, but there was a method to Plymouth's madness. The people watching the tail-standing Barracuda at the drag strip on Sunday

PLYMOUTH

might possibly stop by a dealership on Monday to order a Hemi-powered Mayflower car. That's called marketing and Plymouth was right on top of the "fish market."

The original '64 Barracuda was one of the first fish cars —in fact one of the first muscle cars of any type—to utilize a Hurst shifter as *standard* equipment on cars with an optional four-speed manual gear box. To help promote this product association, in 1965, Hurst Performance Research Co. built the famous "Hemi Under Glass" exhibition drag racer.

Using a modified Chrysler Hemi mounted amidships below the large Barracuda back window, this gold-colored "funny car" could stand on its bumper to reveal the words "Bear of a 'Cuda" written on its modified belly pan. In 1967, the racing car was updated to second-generation Barracuda styling.

Then, for 1968, Chrysler came up with the idea of stuffing the 426-cid/425-hp Street Hemi into Plymouth Barracudas and Dodge Darts. The purpose was to build the ultimate, big-engined, lightweight, production-based muscle car. These cars were made with the help of George Hurst and his company.

Hemi production totals at the Chrysler Historical Archives do not include the 1968 Hemi Barracudas and Hemi Darts, since they were not considered factory-built vehicles. However, in this case, the Hurst association with the cars increases their collectibility. Former employees of Hurst Performance Products estimate that 70 Hemi Barracudas and 80 Hemi Darts were made.

The cars were built by Hurst mainly for professional drag racers, so they did not get a standardized cosmetics package. After all, the pros were only going to decorate them in their own colors and graphics. Hurst did replace some stock steel body panels with fiberglass replicas. The interiors were gutted and fitted with lightweight truck bucket seats.

Hurst added headers to the cars. Of course, the company's own shifter kits went in, too. Hefty S/S axles were used, with various gear ratios available. All of the cars had either modified TorqueFlite transmissions or four-speed manual gearboxes.

When delivered, the cars were finished in primer and wore standard E70-14 street tires. It was up to the individual buyers to paint and decorate the cars and bolt on racing slicks.

With about 500 actual hp and low 3,400-lb. weights, the cars could fly down a drag strip. One, piloted by Judy Lilly, was christened "Miss Mighty MoPar" and campaigned in NHRA and SS/AA class racing.

1968 Barracuda "Savage GT"

Auto Craft Co., of Milwaukee, Wisconsin tried to become Chrysler's answer to Carroll Shelby, years before Chrysler decided it was best to go with the "real thing." How far the Wisconsin company got is unknown, but the Savage GT did get past the thinking stage, with body and engineering modifications done to a '68 Barracuda fastback.

Design specifications for both coupe and ragtop versions of the car were worked out. Both were based on the 108-inch wheelbase Plymouth pony car. They called for competition style upgrading at prices from $4,600 to $4,850, depending on whether the 340-, 383- or 440-cid power plant was ordered.

Engine enhancements included a bigger-than-stock carburetor mounted atop a high-rise intake manifold. Four-speed manual transmission was standard. A three-speed TorqueFlite automatic was extra.

A clean, blacked-out grille, fiberglass scooped hood with locking pins and fiberglass deck lid with integral spoiler were among body modifications. Savage GT nameplates appeared on the grille and rear beauty panel.

Race-inspired interior upgrades included a roll bar and inertia reel shoulder harness. Dunlop 205 x 14 radial tires, 14 x 6.5 inch Trans American alloy wheels and front disc brakes with sintered metallic linings were part of the conversion.

Auto Craft utilized the factory heavy-duty suspension with added stabilization up front and a pair of rear control arms in back. Curb weight varied from 3,300 lbs. for the 340-cid conversion to 3,600 lbs. for the 100 cube bigger model.

Conceived as a Shelby-type production-based racecar, the Savage GT was harsh, noisy and fast. It accelerated with the best of the supercars and handled well. Early prototypes experienced steering and braking problems, however. The fact that neither of these functions was power-assisted seemed a drawback. The reason for this was that Auto Craft experienced problems fitting power boosters below the hood with the massive MoPar engines.

Jerry Heasley

PLYMOUTH

The GTX probably never received its due as a great supercar of the late-1960s. It was one of the fiercest machines around, but was ultimately overshadowed by its Road Runner sibling.

1968 Belvedere GTX

The GTX was more like the GTO than any other member of Plymouth's muscle car fleet. It started out hot and got even hotter as you added more and more extras. Even the Hemi was available under the hood. "The Hemi GTX will appeal to the acceleration enthusiast who wants the ultimate," said *Car Life* magazine, which also referred to this version as "the fastest standard car on the market."

Plymouth's intermediate-size performance model should have been one of the more popular muscle machines in its market segment as the 1960s waned, but that just didn't turn out to be the case. Instead, the potent high-performance model was forced to play second fiddle in the Plymouth lineup to the Spartan-looking, lower-priced, but more imaginative Road Runner.

The Belvedere GTX never wavered from its mission of being a high-content muscle car with a nice assortment of big-block power plant offerings. However, since it was only a year old when the redesigned 1968 Plymouth models were introduced, it didn't have a loyal following to see it through. It shared the new Belvedere body—including the special high-performance hood—with the Road Runner.

For 1968, the Super Commando 440-cid V-8 again came

as *standard* equipment in the GTX. Even this was a mighty mill with a 4.32 x 3.75-inch bore and stroke, hydraulic valve lifters, a 10.1:1 compression ratio and a single Carter AFB four-barrel carburetor (model No. 4326S). This engine developed 375 hp at 4600 rpm.

Car Life (you can tell what magazines I read in the '60s) road tested a 440-powered GTX with automatic transmission and reported a 0-to-60 time of 6.8 seconds. It did the quarter-mile in 14.6 seconds with a 96-mph terminal speed. Its top speed was about 121 mph.

Base prices were $3,329 for the coupe and $3,590 for the soft top. Production figures were kept and with 17,914 hardtops and 2,026 ragtops built, the numbers were surely higher than those for the 1967 GTX models. However, these figures paled by comparison to the 44,599 Road Runners that came off the assembly line.

For $605 extra, you could get the 426-cid Street Hemi stuffed into your GTX. Hemi-equipped GTXs continued to be rare, with only 410 hardtops and about 36 convertibles believed to have been made. The Hemi shaved a half a second off the 0-to-60 time and shrunk the quarter-mile time to 14 seconds with a 96.5-mph terminal speed.

PLYMOUTH

Jerry Heasley

The Road Runner provided a lot of bang for the buck and was an instant hit for Plymouth in 1968.

1968 Road Runner

Chuck Jones, the Warner Brothers cartoonist who created the Road Runner character, said the bunnys, pigs, ducks and other animals were all based on the bosses that Jones and his co-workers labored for each day. I assume that Chuck's boss was a real big success, because the Road Runner character was a winner for Plymouth.

That company, once best known for making cheap taxicabs, may have been about the last nameplate to bring out a midsize muscle car when it introduced the 1967 Belvedere GTX. However, it was the first automaker to exploit the potential market for a low-buck performance car when it introduced the 1968 Road Runner.

The idea of putting a powerful engine in the cheapest, lightest model available was not a new one and wise users of the option list had been ordering "Q-Ships" for years. What Plymouth did with the Road Runner was to do all the work for the customer. The company gave the car a low price that youthful buyers could more easily afford and wrapped it all up in a gimmicky fashion—using a popular Warner Bros. cartoon character as the car's namesake.

Using Road Runner identification and a cheap horn that emulated the cartoon bird's well-known "beep-beep" got attention in the marketplace. The lowest-priced Belvedere two-door sedan was the basis for the Road Runner and came "complete" with such standard fleet items as plain bench seat and rubber floor mats.

The first Road Runner's standard engine was a 335-hp version of the 383-cid Chrysler B-block. It was rated at only 5 hp more than the regular 383, but it probably had more power than that due to the use of cylinder heads, intake and exhaust manifolds and a camshaft from the Chrysler 440-cid V-8. Added to the mechanical goodies were a standard four-speed manual transmission, a heavy-duty suspension, 11-inch drum brakes and Red Stripe tires.

The kicker for the Road Runner was its low $2,870 price. If you wanted some interior niceties such as carpeting and bright trim, you had to invest $79.20 for the Road Runner Decor Group. If you wanted to kick the toy image, you had to ante up $714.30 extra for the 426-cid/425-hp Street Hemi.

A two-door hardtop was added midyear and its 15,359 production run was added to the coupe's 29,240 tally to make the Road Runner a winner. Of those, 1,019 were Hemi-powered.

Car Life said that the Road Runner "emulates what a young, performance-minded buyer might do on his own if properly experienced and motivated." It was the car you would have had, back in the '60s, if old J.C. Whitney sent you every goodie he had in his catalog. Even with its base 383-cid/335-hp V-8, the Road Runner turned a 7.3-second 0-to-60 times and a 15.37-second quarter-mile at 91.4 mph. Now remember, there were three better engine options to go from that point on. Awesome!

GTX Hardtop
(also available as Convertible)

The 1969 GTX was lightning fast, even without the optional Street Hemi.

PLYMOUTH

1969 Belvedere GTX

"No matter how you may try to camouflage it by loading a car with power and comfort options, when you get down to the nitty gritty of supercar existence, an inescapable, basic fact always remains on the surface," said *Motor Trend's* Bill Sanders in January 1969. "One primary purpose of a supercar is to get from here to there, from this light to the next, in the shortest elapsed time. To this end, the Plymouth GTX is the flat out, best qualifier of all."

Sander's magazine test car had the 440-cid base engine, rather than the Street Hemi. It produced the same 375 hp at 4600 rpm and 480 lbs.-ft. of torque at 3200 rpm that it had in 1968. The test car was also equipped with a TorqueFlite automatic transmission and a 4.10:1 rear axle. Sanders managed to achieve 0-to-60 mph in 5.8 seconds. The car did the quarter-mile in a mere 13.7 seconds at 102.8 mph.

The GTX two-door hardtop Model RS23 had a dealer cost of $2,710.82 and retailed for $3,329. The convertible, Model RS27, cost dealers $2,924.89 and sold for $3,590. Sanders listed the base price of his test car as $3,433, which included federal excise tax.

Standard GTX equipment included a heavy-duty rear suspension, heavy-duty front torsion bars, anti-sway bars, the 440-cid Super Commando V-8, foam padded front bucket seats, simulated woodgrain trim on the doors, simulated woodgrain trim on the instrument panel, floor carpeting, F70 x 14 red streak or F70 x 14 white streak tires, body side accent stripes, heavy-duty brakes, a heavy-duty 70-amp battery, roof drip-rail moldings, firm-ride shocks, custom body sill moldings, front foam seat cushions, arm rests with ashtrays and dual horns.

Sander's test car also included a Super Performance axle for $271.50, a center console for $54.45, TorqueFlite transmission for $40.40 (on the GTX), the famous "Air Grabber" hood scoop for $55.30, and some other options. If he had ordered the Street Hemi it would have cost $604.75 extra.

For 1969, Plymouth made only 17,914 GTX hardtops and just 1,026 GTX convertibles. Survivors are not plentiful, but they do bring plenty of money today.

PLYMOUTH

The 426 Street Hemi gave the Road Runner head-snapping power, and the more traditional 440-cid V-8 option wasn't bad, either. The standard engine was a 383.

1969 Road Runner

New grilles and new rear-end styling characterized the 1969 Plymouth Road Runner models, which were now available in three different body styles. The original coupe version Model RM21 carried at $2,945 window sticker and weighed the least at 3,435 lbs. It attracted 33,743 buyers. The hardtop Model RM23 raced to the head of the pack with 48,549 assemblies. It cost a bit more at $3,083 and weighed 15 additional lbs., but customers liked its styling. The $3,313 convertible, Model RM27, was a rarity with only 2,128 of the 3,790-lb. ragtops being turned out.

Standard features of the 1969 Road Runner included a heavy-duty suspension, heavy-duty brakes, heavy-duty shocks, a dash nameplate, a deck lid nameplate, door nameplates, top-opening hood scoops, chrome engine parts, an un-silenced air cleaner, Hemi Orange paint treatment, red- or white-streak tires, a four-speed manual transmission with a Hurst gear shifter, a fake walnut shift knob, back-up lights and a deluxe steering wheel.

The standard engine for the Road Runner was the 383-cid V-8, which had a 4.250 x 3.375-inch bore and stroke. With a Carter AVS four-barrel carburetor and 10.0:1 compression

ratio, the Road Runner engine produced 335 hp at 4600 rpm. Engine options included the 440-cid V-8 or the 426-cid Street Hemi.

Car and Driver magazine included a Hemi Road Runner coupe in its comparison test of six "econo-racers" in January 1969. The Street Hemi also had a 4.25 x 3.75-inch bore and stroke, but the Hemi heads, a 10.25:1 compression ratio and dual four-barrel Carter carburetors helped boost its output up to 425 hp at 5000 rpm and 490 lbs.-ft. at 4000 rpm.

The Hemi Road Runner coupe was on a 116-inch wheelbase and had a curb weight of 3,938 lbs. It had a 3.54:1 rear axle. *Car and Driver* recorded 0-to-60 mph in 5.1 seconds. The quarter-mile was covered in 13.54 seconds with a trap speed of 105.14 mph. It had an estimated top speed of 142 mph.

"To say that the Road Runner scored heavily in the performance part of the test is Anglo Saxon understatement in the best tradition," said the writer. "It was the quickest in acceleration, stopped in the shortest distance and ranked second in handling. That's a pretty tough record."

The AAR 'Cuda was a one-year wonder that was hard to miss. About 1,900
were built, but by 1971 the racing-inspired package was discontinued.

PLYMOUTH

Jerry Heasley

1970 AAR 'Cuda

The Plymouth AAR 'Cuda was one very fast small-block muscle car. Though its name evolved from Trans-Am racing, the AAR had a split personality. "Everything makes sense if you forget all about Dan Gurney and think of it in terms of the Burbank Blue Bombers," said the July 1970 issue of *Car and Driver*. "The new AAR 'Cuda is every inch a hot rod."

Having a player in the Sports Car Club of America (SCCA) Trans-American sedan racing series was a must for the Detroit purveyors of pony cars in 1970. There were factory-backed efforts from American Motors, Ford, Dodge and Plymouth. Chevrolet and Pontiac had back-door programs.

Open Plymouth and Dodge participation was new. It came together because there were new Plymouth Barracuda and Dodge Challenger designs and because rules changed so that the 5.0-liter engines used in the racing cars didn't have to be exactly the same size as the production engines they were derived from.

This meant that Chrysler's potent 340-cid small-block could be de-stroked to 303.8 inches to meet the limit. Plymouth could legalize its Trans-Am racing equipment by building 1,900 or more special models. The result was the 1970 AAR 'Cuda.

The new option package for the Barracuda two-door hardtop was named after Dan Gurney's All-American Racers

(AAR) team. Gurney was signed for 1970 after driving the previous few seasons for Mercury. He would enter a 'Cuda in the Trans-Am series with Swede Savage as the driver.

Powering the AAR 'Cuda was a 340-cid small-block V-8 with high-performance heads and thicker webbing in the block to allow the racing team to use four-bolt mains. Even though only a single four-barrel carb was allowed in racing, that didn't prevent triple two-barrel Holleys from being used in the production model. A fiberglass, cold-air-induction hood let the carburetors breathe fresh air.

Other parts of the package for Plymouth's E-body model were a rear spoiler, front and rear sway bars, exhaust that exited in front of the rear tires, rally wheels with E40 x 15 tires up front and large G60 tires in the back. Transmission choices included the A-833 four-speed manual gearbox with a Hurst gear shifter or the Chrysler 727 TorqueFlite automatic. AAR decals and striping identified the package.

Compared to other specialized offerings of the time, the AAR 'Cuda was plentiful, with 2,724 being built.

Despite Gurney's efforts, Barracuda did not win a Trans-Am race in 1970. Factory support for racing was quickly eroding at the time and there was no 1971 AAR 'Cuda or racing team.

PLYMOUTH

The hardtop was the only GTX model available for 1970.

1970 Belvedere GTX

The difference between Priority Mail and Parcel Post is a matter of money and speed—kind of like the GTX version of Plymouth's midsize muscle machinery. My buddy Paul Zazarine summed the car up in the November '86 issue of *Musclecar Review*: "The Plymouth GTX was always considered an upscale version of the Road Runner—it could still boil the hides, but in a classy sort of way."

A redesigned grille, a new hood and restyled front fenders characterized all of Plymouth's intermediate models in 1970. The Belvedere GTX featured much of the same standard equipment as the Road Runner, including a heavy-duty suspension, heavy-duty brakes, a dual exhaust system, a high-performance hood with the "air grabber" hood scoop, front and rear bumper guards, a 150-mph speedometer, F70-14 red stripe or white stripe tires, three-speed windshield wipers, heavy-duty shock absorbers, bright roof moldings and bright door moldings. In addition, it also had the 440-cid Super Commando V-8, a deluxe vinyl interior, foam seat

padding on its new-for-1970 high-back front bucket seats and rear bench seat, body-side reflective tape stripes, side markers, dual (non-beep-beep) horns, a 70-amp battery and bright exhaust trumpets.

The Belvedere GTX lineup lost its convertible for 1970. The only body style left was the two-door hardtop, which Chrysler sold to Plymouth dealers for $2,703.36. The dealers then retailed the car to the public for around $3,535. The 1970 model wound up drawing only 7,748 orders, with a mere 72 of the cars getting Street Hemi V-8s installed at a cost of $710.60. In addition, Belvedere GTX buyers could also get the 440-cid Six-Pack option (with three two-barrel carburetors) for just $119.05 above the price of the base 440. "A GTX six-barrel is no slouch in the performance department either," said *Motor Trend* in its fall 1969 review of the hot '70s models.

The TorqueFlite automatic transmission was standard in the 1970 Belvedere GTX. A four-speed manual transmission was also available at no extra cost.

The 'Cuda 340 wasn't quite as fast as its Hemi sibling, but at least one industry magazine thought it was a better all-around car.

PLYMOUTH

Phil Kunz

1970 'Cuda 340

If you are an "I'll-drive-my-muscle-car-everyday-and-die-with-a-smile-on-my-face" type of guy, you should probably check out the Plymouth 'Cuda 340. Its small-block V-8 is a little more suitable for hops to the 7-11 than a 440 Wedge or a Hemi, but don't get the idea that the 340 is wimpy. Nothing could ever be further from the truth.

Barracuda entered its third and final generation for the 1970 model year, when the distance between the front wheels was upped to comfortably swallow any power plant from a Slant-Six to a Hemi. The fastback coupe body style that originated with the Barracuda name was axed, but attractive two-door hardtop and convertible versions remained in the model lineup

All 'Cudas sat on a 108-inch wheelbase and had an overall length of 186.7 inches. The width was 74.9 inches and the height was 5.9 inches. At 59.7 inches the front track was a bit narrower than the 60.7-inch rear track.

Attracting less media attention than the big-block 'Cudas was the 'Cuda 340, which continued as an option for the 'Cuda (which actually came standard with a 383-cid V-8). The 340-cid V-8, with its 4.04 x 3.31-inch bore and stroke,

was a nice alternative, especially for youthful muscle car buyers who couldn't quite hack the price of a 440 or a Hemi. It ran with a 10.5:1 compression ratio and a single four-barrel carburetor and that was enough to generate 275 hp at 5000 rpm and 340 lbs.-ft. of torque at 3200 rpm.

Motor Trend ran a comparison test between 'Cudas with all three available engines. In the 0-to-60-mph category, the 340-powered version needed 6.4 seconds compared to the 440's 5.9 seconds and the Hemi's 5.8 seconds. Its quarter-mile performance was 14.5 seconds (96 mph) compared to 14.4 seconds and 100 mph for the 440 version and 14 seconds and 102 mph for the Hemi 'Cuda. The 440-powered test car had a four-speed manual gearbox, while the 'Cuda 340 and the Hemi 'Cuda had automatic transmission.

For all-around use, the 'Cuda 340 was really a quite nicely balanced package. After driving all three cars, *Motor Trend's* A.B. Shuman admitted to his readers, "From the foregoing you may have detected a 'slight' preference for the 340 'Cuda. This was intentional. It was the best of the lot!" There are many Mopar maniacs who were glad they listened to A.B. and even more who wished they had!

PLYMOUTH

**The Duster was a tremendously popular car in 1970, and the 340 version proved
to be a terrific bargain for members of the muscle crowd who were on a budget.**

1970 Duster 340

New for 1970, the Duster was a derivative of Plymouth's
Valiant compact. Both cars were built on the same platform
and shared the same front end sheet metal, but they were
different from the cowl back. The Duster came only as a
two-door sedan or coupe. Prices for the new model started
at $2,172. It cost $11 to add a V-8, but the high-performance
340-cid engine brought the base price up by $375.

Plymouth certainly didn't anticipate the public's response
to the redesigned compact. Valiant production increased from
107,218 in 1969 to 268,002 in 1970. Of that number, most of
the cars that sold were Duster models. The regular Valiant
Duster found 192,375 buyers, while the Duster 340 appealed
to 24,817 customers. The Duster 340 had a distinct role to fill
in Plymouth's "Rapid Transit System"—it was the entry-level
muscle car for young enthusiasts.

The Duster replaced the rather staid two-door sedan
in the Valiant lineup. Its body styling was characterized by
a contemporary look, with bulging lines from the firewall
back. This was known as the "Coke bottle" shape, of course.
The same 108-inch wheelbase unitized chassis was used for
both models and both were 188.4 inches long. Standard V-8
for these cars was the 318-cid V-8. The Duster 340 weighed

3,110 lbs.—considerably more than the 2,865-lb. Duster with
a 318-cid V-8.

Doing for compact cars what the Road Runner did for
mid-sized cars, the Duster 340 was the low-priced performance
machine. It came standard with a 340-cid/275-hp V-8 that
had been used in Plymouths since 1968. It again had a 4.04
x 3.31-inch bore and stroke. The five-main-bearings engine
had hydraulic valve lifters, a 10.5:1 compression ratio and a
Carter Type AVS four-barrel carburetor. The engine produced
275 hp at 1500 rpm. More goodies included a three-speed
manual gear box with a floor-mounted shifter, a heavy-duty
suspension, E70 x 14 fiberglass belted tires, styled steel
wheels, body striping and the obligatory cartoon character—
in this case a friendly dust devil.

The Duster 340's bottom-line base price was only $2,547.
Front bucket seats and other dress-up items were optional, ala
Road Runner. *Car Life* tested an automatic-equipped Duster
340 and found that it could go from 0-to-60 mph in only 6.2
seconds and that it was a great buy. The buying public felt
the same, which made the Duster a success in general and the
340 version a particular hit.

The redesigned 1970 'Cuda and the 426 Hemi were a match made in muscle car heaven.

1970 Hemi 'Cuda

Plymouth had …. uh … let's say "nerve." The company's resounding message in the case of the Hemi 'Cuda was: "Damn the insurance company torpedos— full speed ahead!" The car tested out like a rocketship, as you'll see in the performance figures at the end of this essay. As Chrysler maven Cliff Gromer's Mopar Muscle magazine put it, "The new E-bodies offered a home for ol' King Kong hisself—the 426 Hemi."

When the redesigned 1970 Plymouth Barracuda came to the muscle-car market, there would be no excuses for not putting a big engine in the gaping crater under its wide hood. Design engineers had stretched the car sideways by more than 5 inches and increased both the front and rear tracks by 3 inches. As a result, any Chrysler Corporation engine would fit in the engine bay, right up to the street version of the "Monster Masher" racing power plant—the 426-cid Hemi.

The Hemi was an $871.45 option for the muscular 'Cuda sport coupe (which was base priced at $3,164) and the convertible (which carried a $3,433 window sticker total). The 'Cuda came standard with another big-block mill—the 383-cid 355-hp V-8. No wonder Chrysler listed the 'Cuda as a member of its "Rapid Transit System."

Street Hemis got new hydraulic valve lifters for 1970,

but a new cam profile gave the Mopar engineers no reason to alter the 425 advertised hp rating. The Hemi's two Carter AFB four-barrel carburetors breathed through the Air Grabber "shaker" hood scoop.

In order to get the horses to the pavement, Hemi-powered 'Cudas and other big-engined Barracudas relied on heavy-duty drive-line parts. There was a choice of the New Process A-833 four-speed manual gearbox or the 727 TorqueFlite automatic. A Dana 9 3/4-inch differential was kept in place by a leaf-spring rear suspension with six leaves on the right and five leaves plus two half-leaves on the left. Fifteen-inch-diameter, 7-inch-wide wheels held F60 x 15 tires

In short, power was the Hemi 'Cuda's long suit. Not long was the list of buyers. Insurance companies did not look kindly on Hemi 'Cudas and did not care if they could do 0-to-60 mph in 5.8 seconds and run down the quarter-mile in 14.1 seconds at 103.2 mph. By the time the 1970 run came to an end, only 652 hardtops had left the factory with Hemi power and 284 of them had four-speed transmissions. Far more spectacular in terms of rarity was the convertible with only 14 being made, five with a manual gearbox.

Only 652 Hemi 'Cuda hardtops left the factory for 1970.

PLYMOUTH

PLYMOUTH

The Road Runner was becoming a more refined car by 1970, but it
was still a bargain compared to its performance car competitors.

1970 Road Runner

Plymouth's "beep-beep" bomb still did a great job of kicking its feathers up in the stoplight grand prix in 1970, "It's no longer just a stripped down Belvedere with a big engine and heavy suspension" A. B. Shuman pointed out in *Motor Trend*. Like the GTO, the Road Runner got a few more creature comforts each year to widen its market niche, but the underhood hardware remained impressive, as did the performance figures. With the optional 440 engine you could nail down 6.6-second 0-to-60 runs and a 14.4-second quarter at 99 mph.

Plymouth's Spartan muscle car did continue its traditional use of the same basic Belvedere body. Standard Road Runner equipment was listed in *Car Fax* as: a three-speed manual transmission with floor-mounted gear shift, front armrests, rear armrests, a cigar lighter, a glove box light, the famous "beep-beep" horn, a high-performance hood, front bumper guards, a 150-mph speedometer, Road Runner emblems, the 383-cid/335-hp Road Runner V-8, F70-14 white-line tires on wide safety rim wheels, three-speed windshield wipers, roof-drip rail and upper door-frame moldings and heavy-duty shock absorbers all around. Power train options included a 440 four-barrel V-8 with 375 hp, the 440 "Six-Pak" V-8 with 390 hp and a 426-cid/425-hp Hemi.

There were again three Road Runner models. The dealer price on the coupe was only $2,210.28 and it carried a $2,896 suggested retail price. The two-door hardtop was dealer priced at $2,316.23 and sold for $3,034. The convertible cost the dealer $2,513 and retailed for $3,298 including federal excise tax.

To a degree, it seemed as if Plymouth was gradually losing sight of the Road Runner's original concept of being a "real" muscle car with a low price tag. Replacing the four-speed manual transmission with a three-speed gearbox was one sign of this. Another was the use of hydraulic valve lifters on the Hemi, which cost $841.05 extra. The 440-cid Six-Pack engine was a $249.55 extra and required the driver to get along without air conditioning. It also required either the four-speed manual gearbox or an automatic transmission.

Another option for Road Runner owners with drag racing in mind was the A33 Super Trak Pak package, which included a heavy-duty 9 3/4-inch Dana Sure-Grip 3.55:1 rear axle, a dual breaker-point distributor, a woodgrained gear shift knob and recess warning light and the heavy-duty four-speed manual gearbox with Hurst shifter. It cost $142.85 extra. Or they could order the Super Trak Pak version, which included all of the same extras with a 4.10:1 ratio Dana rear axle and power front disc brakes for $235.65.

The muscle car era reached crazy new heights with the arrival of the Superbird.

PLYMOUTH

1970 Road Runner Superbird

"The Superbird concept is a vehicle for the raw competition of NASCAR tracks," suggested *Road Test* magazine in 1970. "But in street versions, it is also a fun car when you get used to being stared at." We had a neighbor in 1970 who had a true "street": version of the car. He bought it at a clear out price and let it sit out on the street all winter. Naturally, it went downhill fast. If only we had known then what the Mopar fans know now.

The 1970 Plymouth Road Runner Superbird was the final volley in the battle of muscle car aerodynamics. With a 7.0-liter engine-displacement limit, competing automakers armed themselves with more wind-cheating body designs, culminating with the "winged warriors" from Chrysler— the 1969 Dodge Charger Daytona and 1970 Plymouth Road Runner Superbird. Designed for use on the NASCAR Grand National superspeedway oval tracks, these Mopars featured a long, peaked nose and a high airfoil on struts above the rear deck.

Though similar in concept, the 1970 Plymouth Superbird and 1969 Dodge Daytona shared little in the way of specialized parts. The noses, airfoil and the basic sheet metal of the Charger and Road Runner two-door hardtops differed. The nose added 19 inches of length.

Rules in 1969 called for only 500 copies of each model to be made to make it "legal" for racing. For 1970, manufacturers had to build one for each dealer. Experts believe that, when it was all over, a total of 1,971 Superbirds were built.

The most popular engine was the 440-cid Super Commando V-8 with a single four-barrel carburetor. It was rated at 375 hp and priced at $4,298. A total of 1,120 Superbirds came this way. Another 716 cars were equipped with the 440-cid/390-hp V-8 with three two-barrel carburetors. That leaves just 135 cars that were equipped with the 426-cid/425-hp, twin four-barrel Street Hemi (77 with automatic transmission and 58 with four-speed manual transmission). The racing cars used the Hemi racing engine.

Speaking of racing, the Superbird was big enough bait to lure Richard Petty back to racing Plymouths after his one-year hiatus with Ford. Petty Engineering hired Pete Hamilton to run a second Superbird at selected events in 1970 and he promptly won the big one—the Daytona 500.

Plymouth intermediates were redesigned for 1971 and, with the performance market shrinking and budgets for racing being shifted to meeting Federal safety and emission standards, there was no follow-up to the Superbird. That made the limited-edition Mopar winged machines among the first muscle cars to start climbing in collector value.

The GTX was still a fabulous car in 1971, whether you had a 440 (green car) or Hemi (red) in it.

PLYMOUTH

1971 Belvedere GTX

The fancy pants "Road Runner" —the GTX—often went unappreciated in its own era. However, with the same styling, the same engines and a little more bright work, it is starting to attract the attention of collectors today. A pair of 440s were offered for the hole under the GTX hood and the Hemi could be had, though it rarely was ordered. On paper, the optional Six-Pak version of the 440 lost a few horsepower, but this was nothing to bite your nails about. "Obviously a slight drop in horsepower had not hurt the big wedge engine," wrote Greg Rader in the February 1988 edition of *Musclecar Review* magazine.

With annual sales of the upscale high-performance model running much below expectations for several years, many people were surprised when the Belvedere-based, mid-sized GTX showed up for one more appearance in the 1971 Plymouth lineup. This year it once again came only as the Model RS23 two-door hardtop. At the beginning of the model year it had a $3,707 window sticker and weighed 3,675 lbs. By May, the price was increased to $3,733.

As usual, the GTX's list of standard equipment picked up where the Road Runner's list left off. Additional items included with the 1971 GTX were the 440-cid/375-hp Super Commando V-8, the TorqueFlite automatic transmission, high-back front bucket seats, a low-restriction dual exhaust system with chrome exhaust trumpets, dual horns, vinyl interior trims (cloth-and-vinyl interiors were a no-cost option), a 70-amp 12-volt battery, custom body sill moldings, front and rear wheel opening moldings, drip rail moldings, an extra-heavy-duty suspension (front and rear) and G70 x 14 black

sidewall tires with raised white letters.

A bench seat with cloth-and-vinyl trim and a center armrest was a no-charge option and white sidewall tires could be substituted in place of the white-lettered style at no extra cost. GTX buyers could also opt for a floor-mounted three-speed manual gearbox in place of the TorqueFlite automatic. The Hemi engine was still available for $746.50.

The Air Grabber hood was standard with the Hemi and the four-speed manual gearbox was a no-charge item on Hemi GTXs. This was the last year for the Street Hemi and Chrysler built only 356 of the engines for all of its lines. In the GTX series, only 30 cars were Hemis and of those, a mere 11 units had the four-speed manual transmission.

In the eyes of some enthusiasts, the 'Cuda 340 was the best muscle car on the block in 1971.

PLYMOUTH

Phil Kunz

1971 'Cuda 340

Some people confuse the term "muscle car" with "race car," and they shouldn't. Race cars have one purpose in life and muscle cars have many. For many enthusiasts in the '60s, a muscle car took them to work all week, to the supermarket on Saturday and to the drag strip on "Sunday . . . Sunday. . . Sunday!" One of the best of these multi-purpose muscle machines was the 'Cuda 340.

"The 'Cuda 340 is the kind of car a person could like," said auto writer Steve Kelly in the January 1971 issue of *Hot Rod* magazine. "It runs low-14 without breathing hard, takes corners without yelling and is big enough to be seen." Kelly admitted that the 'Cuda 340 was not the ultimate Trans-Am racer, but he also pointed out that it could beat a stock Camaro Z/28 or Mustang Boss 302 through the quarter-mile.

Early in model year 1971, the 'Cuda sport coupe cost Plymouth dealers $2,508.57 and retailed for $3,134. The ragtop had a $2,716.34 dealer cost and a $3,391 window sticker. In May, the dealer costs were increased to $2,525.67 and $2,733.44 respectively, and the window stickers rose to $3,155 for the two-door hardtop and $3,412 for the ragtop.

That compared to $253.20 extra for a 440 engine or $883.90 for the Hemi.

Standard equipment on the 'Cuda included all Barracuda features plus a performance hood, chrome wheel lip and body-sill moldings, a color-keyed grille, a black-out-style rear deck panel, a heavy-duty suspension front and rear, heavy-duty brakes, 'Cuda ornamentation and whitewall tires as a no-cost option. The 383-cid V-8 was again standard and the 340-cid four-barrel V-8 was a $44.35 option.

Production of 'Cudas in general was very low this year. Plymouth made only 6,228 hardtops and 374 convertibles. It is known that a total of 153 cars had Hemis. Although we have never seen production breakouts for 340s, 383s and 440s, with so many options available, the number made of each is probably fairly low, and since the 383-cid V-8 was bigger and less expensive, it's likely that it drew the bulk of orders.

Hot Rod managed to turn in a best run of 14.18 seconds for the quarter-mile (100.33 mph) with its 1971 'Cuda 340 after emptying the trunk and removing the air cleaner element. In addition, it also proved to be a superior road car.

PLYMOUTH

Jerry Heasley

**Only 115 'Cudas got the Hemi engine in 1971, including just seven convertibles.
These great cars are among the most prized muscle cars on the planet these days.**

1971 Hemi 'Cuda

"The '71 Hemi 'Cuda is pretty beyond comparison and potent beyond imagination," according to Paul Zazarine, a name well known to muscle car lovers. In *Musclecar Review* magazine, he wrote: "If you're looking for the ultimate Mopar, look no further than the Hemi 'Cuda."

Drag racers like Sox & Martin and PeeWee Wallace were burning up the drag strips in Barracudas back in 1971 and also helping to generate interest in Plymouth's "fish car." A lot of that interest went to non-Hemi-powered cars, however, as the $884 Hemi option was ordered for just 108 hardtops (60 with four-speed manual transmissions) and a mere seven convertibles. Two of the ragtops also had the four-speed gearbox.

Seven other engines were offered for 1971 Barracudas and a number of those mills fit into the muscle car category. The three smallest engines did not fill the bill. They included the 198-cid/125-hp slant six, the 225-cid/145-hp slant six and the 318-cid 230-hp V-8. These engines were aimed at the "Walter Mitty" buyers who wanted to experience the muscle car lifestyle without the ponies or price tag.

The 340-cid V-8 with a four-barrel carburetor was a little hotter, generating 275 hp and 340 lbs.-ft. of torque at 3200 rpm. Then came the 383-cid big-block V-8, which was offered in two versions. The 383 with a two-barrel and carb was good for 275 hp and 375 lbs.-ft. of torque at 2800 rpm. Even better for speed was the four-barrel edition that just hit the 300-hp bracket and pumped up 410 lbs.-ft. of power at 3400 rpm.

That still left two V-8 engines for the true muscle car crowd. The 440-cid "Six Pak" version climbed up to 385 hp and 490 lbs.-ft. at 3200 rpm, which wasn't bad. Then came the snortier, top-of-the-hill Hemi, which had 426 cubic inches, 425 hp and 490 lbs.-ft. of twisting power at 4000 rpm.

The 1971 Hemi engine featured a 10.2:1 compression ratio and a single four-barrel carburetor. It came attached to either a four-speed manual gearbox or an automatic transmission. The standard rear axle had a 3.23:1 ratio. Sure-Grip-only options included 3.55:1, 3.54:1 and 4.10:1. Plymouth's nifty S15 heavy-duty suspension package was standard with Hemi 'Cudas.

After model year 1971, Plymouth continued to offer Barracudas, but Hemi versions and convertibles didn't make the cut after the season came to its end.

Jerry Heasley

The beloved Plymouth Road Runner had a cartoon character on the outside, but it was a serious muscle car on the inside. The base engine was the 383, but the 440 Magnum and 425 Hemi kicked up even more dust.

1971 Road Runner

Youth of all ages took a fancy to the Road Runner's budget muscle car concept in the late '60s and they had been beep-beeping at each other ever since. By 1971, the Coyote clobberer had bred its own cult of Road Runner owners. "When the performance-minded think Plymouth they think Road Runner," said *Road Test* magazine, which selected the '71 Road Runner as its "U.S. Car of the Year."

High-performance cars of all sizes continued to be available in many models and with a long list of factory options during the 1971 model year. However, high insurance rates were keeping the buyers at bay. The low sales numbers put several models on the endangered species list.

The only body style returning for 1971 in Plymouth's Road Runner line was the two-door hardtop version. Its new grille looked like a big loop around the front of the car. The Road Runner's totally revised sheet metal was shared with the Sebring and Sebring Plus coupes. The sedan and convertible did not get translated onto the newly designed Mopar mid-size body shell.

With the more expensive GTX still around, the Road Runner again filled its low-priced muscle car niche with its trick "beep-beep" horn, hot graphics and other solid performance. Standard in the Road Runner model was a 300-hp version of the trusty 383-cid V-8. It had a 4.25 x 3.38-inch bore and stroke and a single four-barrel carburetor and developed 400 lbs.-ft. of torque at 2400 rpm. The Road Runner listed for $3,120 early in the year. Around May 31, the price increased to $3,147.

In all, the production of 14,218 was not that bad. As for the rare variety, that was the Hemi option, which went into only 55 Road Runners this year.

1972 Plymouth 'Cuda 340

The popularity of Plymouth's sporty compact car, the Barracuda, was in a tailspin by model year 1972. Insurance companies had upped the premiums for anything thought of as a high-performance machine and the government watchdogs joined them in ganging up on the muscle car makers from the safety and emissions angles. It was a year in which car salesmen did not get fat selling Barracudas.

As the sales charts turned red, the Barracuda convertible disappeared, as did the optional 383-, 440-, 440-Six-Pak and 426 Hemi engines for 'Cudas. Luckily, the 340-cid V-8 managed to slip by the gatekeepers.

Plymouth dealers had to part with $2,371.77 (and those were *1972* dollars) to floor plan a Model BH23 Barracuda hardtop with the base 318-cid V-8. The car had a suggested retail price of $2,808. Its standard equipment included dual

headlights, dual horns, hub caps, an inside day-night mirror, a brake warning light, an outside rear view mirror, bucket seats, a cigar lighter, fuel, temperature and ammeter gauges and 7.35 x 14 black sidewall tires. A dealer cost of $2,495 applied to the year's only other Barracuda, which was the Model BS23 'Cuda two-door hardtop. It retailed for $2,953.

In addition to Barracuda equipment, the 'Cuda included a 340-cid V-8 with a two-barrel carburetor, chrome front and rear wheel lip moldings, chrome body sill moldings, a performance hood, a color-keyed grille, a black rear deck panel, heavy-duty suspension and brakes, an electronic ignition system and F70 x 14 white sidewall tires.

A four-barrel version of the 340 was the only engine option. It was available for the special price of $209.70 in the 'Cuda. It cost $276.60 for other Barracudas. The A36 performance axle package could be ordered for all cars with 340-cid four-barrel engines. A four-speed manual gearbox was available only for 340-cid four-barrel cars for $192.85. TorqueFlite was $223.30 extra for cars with that same engine. Other than stripes, styled chrome rims or rallye road wheels and front disc brakes ($68.05), there was little left in the way of high-performance options.

Plymouth records show that 7,858 'Cudas were produced in 1972. All of them were 'Cuda 340s, but the numbers do not indicate how many were 340s with four-barrel carburetors. The 1970 340 with the four-barrel carburetor was rated for 240 net SAE hp. Weighing in at around 3,625 lbs., it carried about 15.1 lbs. per horsepower and could do 0-to-60 mph in 8.5 seconds. The quarter-mile took 16.3 seconds. Hey, it was 1972!

The Road Runner still had 400- and 440-cid engine options, but even the "Beep-Beep" car was losing a little steam by 1972.

1972 Plymouth Road Runner

This "momentum muscle car" struggled valiantly to keep alive the dwindling interest in high-performance motoring. For 1972, the Road Runner received minor cosmetic changes. A new radiator grille design made it look a little different than it had in 1971. Although Plymouth offered buyers a choice of 16 hues, the psychedelic colors of the past few years were gone. The standard bench seat came trimmed in blue, green or black vinyl.

As in 1971, the model RM23 Road Runner was offered in only a single body style. The two-door hardtop had a $3,080 list price and a 3,495-lb. curb weight. Production dropped nearly 50 percent to 7,628 cars.

The Road Runner equipment list started with all features that were considered standard on the Plymouth satellite, plus the following additions or substitutions: three-speed manual transmission with floor-mounted gear shifter, heavy-duty suspension, heavy-duty brakes, front and rear sway bars, pile carpets, a performance hood, a low-restriction dual exhaust system, a beep-beep horn, a rallye instrument cluster with a 150-mph speedometer, Road Runner trim and ornamentation, F70-14 white sidewall tires and a 400-cid four-barrel V-8.

The Code E86 440-cid V-8 with a single four-barrel carburetor was optional in the Road Runner for $152.70, but could not be ordered in combination with the three-speed manual transmission. You had to add either a four-speed manual gearbox for $201.85 extra or TorqueFlite automatic for $231.65. Plymouth sales literature did not list the output for this engine, but other sources put it at 280 net hp at 4800 rpm and 375 net lbs.-ft. of torque at 3200 rpm.

An "Air-Grabber" hood scoop could be substituted for the regular style when buyers were willing to pay $67.40 extra. In this case, a different tape stripe treatment (a $22 option) was used.

Performance numbers were published for the '72 Road Runner with the 340-cid/240-hp V-8. It went from a standing start to 60 mph in 7.8 seconds. The quarter-mile was eaten up in 15.5 seconds at 90 mph.

Tom Glatch

PONTIAC

With a reported top speed of 130 mph, the stylish fuel-injected 1957 Bonneville was a splendid fast-moving cruiser that helped kick off the first generation of Pontiac muscle cars.

1957 Custom Star Chief Fuel-Injected Bonneville

For 1957, Pontiac increased the size of its V-8 to 347 cid. The company introduced a limited-production Bonneville convertible powered by a fuel-injected engine. Pontiac had used the Bonneville name for a Motorama dream car and the publicity, plus images of record-smashing Pontiacs streaking across the Utah salt flats, backdropped the new model's introduction.

The Bonnevilles had sleek, distinctive lines with a bold chrome side body sweep-spear resembling a rocket ship's profile. It also had anodized aluminum rear fender trim similar to that on the Safari sport wagon, pseudo side fender louvers and tri-star spinner hubcaps. Four-ply 8.50 x 14 whitewall tires were standard, but the most sensational element of the Bonneville's trim was the words "Fuel-Injected" on its front fenders and rear deck.

Chevrolet's introduction of fuel-injection preceded the February 1957 introduction of the Bonneville, but the customized ragtop's exclusive nature guaranteed it plenty of attention. The Rochester FI system used by Pontiac differed in several ways from its Chevrolet counterpart. A significant distinction involved longer air pipes. Pontiac did not release an official power rating for the FI V-8, which had the same 10.25:1 compression ratio as other Pontiac engines. Instead, Pontiac offered a vague statement reporting that it produced "in excess of 300 horsepower."

Many historians believe the Tri-Power (three two-barrel carburetors) engines, especially those with dealer-installed solid lifter cams, were superior performers. Still, the Bonneville's primary attraction was not as a quarter-mile terror, but as a luxurious high-powered highway cruiser. Motor Trend magazine tested a pre-production Bonneville that netted a 0-to-60 mph time of 8.1 seconds and top speed of 130 mph. The Bonneville needed no apologies for its performance.

The Bonneville's $5,782 list price also included a long list of standard equipment features. Among these were Strato-Flight Hydra-Matic, power steering, power brakes, dual exhausts, eight-way power seat, electric wipers and washers, under the seat heater and defroster, deluxe Wonderbar radio, electric antenna, Custom Lounge latex foam front seat cushions, oil bath air cleaner, full flow oil filter, external mirror, non-glare interior mirror, passenger side visor vanity, deluxe steering wheel, padded dash, deluxe floor carpets, parking brake warning light, back-up lights, plus lights for the trunk, ashtray and glove box, and parking lights.

Only 630 Bonneville convertibles were produced for the 1957 model year. The following year the Bonneville name was applied to a full range of top-of-the-line Pontiacs.

The result of Pontiac's Bonneville venture was a revolution in how the car-buying public perceived Pontiac, plus the creation of a very rare, very desirable and very exciting automobile.

PONTIAC

The Tri-Power Bonneville convertible was hot enough to be named the 1958 Indy 500 Pace Car.

1958 Bonneville

The 1958 Pontiac had an aircraft look and all 16 models carried "guided-missile" side trim and "jet-pod" rear fenders. "It's a wholly new car, with nothing left over from '57 except the wheels," said Motor Trend.

And it was. The cars were longer and lower looking, with a new honeycomb grille, dual headlights, dual taillights and a new Bonneville series. A stronger tubular X frame allowed lower recessed floors. A new ball-joint suspension was used up front and optional "Ever-Level" rear air suspension was available. A Safe-T-Track no-spin differential added $54 to the Pontiac's price.

"Bonneville" became the name of a line instead of a single model in 1958. A convertible and sport coupe were offered. Base power plant was the Star Chief V-8. Both models used the shorter Chieftain wheelbase, but with a special longer, ribbed rear deck lid also used on Chieftain convertibles. There were "Bonneville" fender scripts and hood and deck lettering, four chevrons on the lower front fenders, four stars on the rear fenders and rocket-shaped, ribbed semi-cylindrical moldings on the "guided missiles."

Standard equipment included a Deluxe steering wheel, chrome wheel discs and special upholstery. The Bonneville coupe sold for $3,481 and the convertible was $3,586. Pontiac built 9,144 hardtops and 3,096 convertibles.

New options included a deluxe "Electromatic" radio and, for Bonnevilles, bucket seats. Tri-Power carburetion on standard blocks was $93.50 on Bonnevilles. The "standard" Tri-Power setup used three two-barrel Rochester carburetors, 10.5:1 cylinder heads, and a high-lift camshaft for 300 hp at 4600 rpm. Rochester fuel-injection was a $500 option. This setup included 10.5:1 compression ratio cylinder heads and gave 310 hp at 4800 rpm. Pontiac experts believe that 200 Bonnevilles carried this option. A Bonneville hardtop with the 300-hp engine was road tested by a magazine. Zero-to-60 mph took 7.6 seconds and the quarter-mile took 16 seconds.

In March 1958, two NASCAR-certified "extra hp" (Tempest 395-A) V-8s were released. The "PK" option was $233 on Bonnevilles. It included a four-barrel carburetor, 10.5:1 cylinder heads, higher-lift camshaft, low-restriction dual exhausts and other special components good for 315 hp. The "PM" option was $331 on lower-priced lines and $320 on upper lines and it combined special high-performance hardware with Tri-Power induction to generate 330 hp.

To celebrate General Motors' 50th anniversary, a Tri-Power Bonneville convertible was picked to be the Official Pace Car for the Indy 500 race in May 1958.

Tom Glatch

A long line of Pontiac muscle cars would follow in the footsteps of the 1961 Tempest.

1961 Tempest

The performance potential of Pontiac's first Tempest was perceived by *Hot Rod* magazine as early as November 1960. It said the Tempest "promises to offer outstanding performance if for no other reason than it has the same blood lines as one of the hot-test full-sized cars on the road." Pontiac said putting the transmission at the rear provided room for an engine, not a "putt-putt."

Pontiac helped the typical new car viewer focus on the torrid Wide-Track heritage of the "Tempest" name (once applied to hot V-8 engines) by using a virtually unchanged '59 Pontiac grille on the Tempest. This hint of performance was transferred into reality by the Tempest's technical specs. It was one of the most innovative and unconventional American vehicles of modern times. It had a front engine, but the transmission and differential were joined in a rear-mounted transaxle linked by a flexible drive shaft with a three-inch bow at its center. The drive shaft was enclosed in a stamped steel housing and was constructed of high-tensile steel.

The front and rear wheels were independently sprung. The suspension design followed that of the Corvair. Front coil springs with unequal length A-arms were used. The rear suspension had coil springs, but with a swing axle and semi-trailing control arms. Large 15-inch wheels and nine-inch brake drums were standard. A tread of 56.8 inches gave it a Pontiac "Wide Track." Other major dimensions included a 112-inch wheelbase and overall length of 189 inches.

Pontiac offered the Tempest with the 215 cid aluminum V-8 available in the Buick Special and Olds F-85. Of greater interest to enthusiasts who held Pontiac's "Trophy 389" V-8 in high regard was Tempest's "Trophy 4." It was essentially the left bank of the V-8. New components such as the crankshaft, cam, intake manifold, and block were used. The pistons, rods, cylinder head, valve train and oil pan were V-8-interchangeable. The size of this big four was 194.5 cid. The most potent version, with a 10.25:1 compression ratio, used a four-barrel carburetor and was rated for 155 hp at 4800 rpm and 215 lbs.-ft. of torque at 2800 rpm. A two-speed automatic transmission was standard. The standard axle ratio was 3.55:1, with 3.31 and 3.73:1 optional.

PONTIAC

PONTIAC

Jerry Heasley

Pontiac took its 1962 Catalina and made it into a potent drag racer
by lightening the body and shoving a 405-horse engine under the hood.

1962 Super-Duty Catalina

I once went to photograph one of these rare cars owned by Dimitri Toth of Pontiac, Michigan. He "lit it up" early on a Sunday morning and all of his neighbors woke up immediately. The Super-Duty Catalina shook the asphalt like a barrel of maniacal monkeys playing catch with a can of ammonium nitrate. "The '62 Catalina lightweight sings precious memories from the pre-GTO performance era," said Jerry Heasley in the December 1985 issue of *Car Review*.

Pontiac Motor Division was the first automaker to build factory lightweight drag racing cars. Ever since its NASCAR engine options were issued in mid-1957, the company found that racing on Sunday sold cars on Monday. By 1960, the "Poncho" performance image had made Pontiac the third-most popular American car nameplate for the first time in history. Chevy's new-for 1962 409-cid engine was a threat, though. Pontiac's best match for a 409-powered Chevy was the 1961 Super-Duty 389 Catalina, which had 368 hp with Tri-Power. Perhaps 25 of these cars were built.

More power and less weight was needed to keep the Pontiacs competitive, so Pontiac put its lightest, most powerful car on a diet with a horsepower supplement. Extensive use of aluminum body parts and a special 421-cid/405-hp V-8 created the 3,600-lb. 1962 Super-Duty Catalina.

The new 421-cid V-8 featured four-bolt main bearing caps, forged pistons and twin Carter four-barrel carburetors on a special intake manifold linked to either a Borg-Warner T-85 three-speed manual transmission or a T-10 four-speed manual gear box. Actual output from this massive motor was over 500 hp.

Lightweight parts, in addition to the front-end sheet metal like the fenders, hood and grille sections, included an aluminum back bumper and dealer-optional Plexiglas windows. Many of the Super-Duty Catalinas used a functional hood scoop that was actually a Ford truck part that Pontiac purchased in quantity and issued a GM parts number for. An unusual Super-Duty option was a set of cast aluminum Tri-Y exhaust headers.

Pontiac promotional expert and racing personality Jim Wangers found the 1962 Super-Duty Catalina to his liking and turned in performances like a 12.38-second quarter-mile at 116.23 mph at Detroit Dragway. In all, 225 of the 421-cid motors were built in 1962. They went into 162 cars and 63 engines were made as replacement motors. Not all cars that got the 421-cid Super-Duty engines had factory lightweight body parts.

PONTIAC

Jerry Heasley

The 1963 Super-Duty Catalina might not have been much to look at, but it was a serious
factory lightweight straight-line machine with tons of power and no extra baggage.

1963 Super-Duty Catalina

For 1963, Pontiac Motor Division took the Super-Duty Catalina 421 program a few steps further. The cylinder heads got higher intake ports and oval-shaped exhaust ports, plus larger valves and higher-compression (12.5:1) cylinder heads. A new McKellar No. 10 solid lifter camshaft was released for use in engines with dual valve springs. A transistorized ignition system was added. A few cars even had 13.0:1 compression ratios. Official ratings for the hottest setup went to 410 hp, but the actual output of the 421-cid Super-Duty engine was somewhere between 540 hp and 550 hp.

The 1963 factory lightweight cars lost about another 100 lbs. through the use of Plexiglas windows and aluminum trunk lids. Also available were aluminum splash pans, radiator core supports and bumper-attaching parts. In addition, some Catalina frames were "Swiss cheesed" by drilling large holes through them. They weighed in at about 3,325 lbs. in ultimate lightweight form.

Drag racer Arnie "Farmer" Beswick campaigned one of the 15 "Swiss cheese" Catalinas that was built before General Motors management issued an all-out ban on factory racing efforts in January 1963. His "passionate Poncho" racked up a low elapsed time of 11.91 seconds in the quarter mile. With their low production numbers, the "Swiss cheese" cars did not qualify for S/S "super stock" drag racing classes. Instead, they competed in the F/SX "factory experimental" class.

In addition to 77 Super-Duty Catalinas and Grand Prixs (including the "Swiss cheese" units) 11 Super-Duty Tempests were also constructed. The late Mickey Thompson dreamed up this combination for A/FX competition. Another pair of A/FX-class 421-powered Tempests—a coupe and a station wagon—were campaigned by Beswick.

After General Motors issued its anti-racing edict, Jim Wangers and a group of Pontiac Motor Division engineers known as the "Young Turks" turned their energies in a new and very successful direction. Wrapping up a package of performance extras as a LeMans option package, they snuck the first GTO onto the streets in 1964 and the rest is history.

The Super-Duty Catalinas helped Pontiac spin its racing reputation into a winning production vehicle that became a champion in the sales race and lasted for 10 glorious years. Today, a Super-Duty 421 Catalina factory lightweight car is worth a bundle. A Swiss cheese car is even more prized.

Pontiacs come as fine as you'd want—or as fierce.

Our Catalina 2+2 is both. Ease yourself into that cushy bucket seat. Grasp the custom steering wheel firmly. Lay a hand on the console-mounted shifter. Then leave. Abruptly. Our standard Trophy V-8 in a Catalina 2+2 puts out 283 hp coupled to a four-speed gearbox*; 267 hp with three-speed Hydra-Matic*. If neither's audacious enough for you, we're ready with engines up to 370 hp*—depending on how eager you are to get where you're aimed. Catalina 2+2 comes as convertible or sports coupe, complete with Wide-Track and pure, sweet Pontiac style. Buckle one on, sometime, at your Pontiac dealer.

'64 WIDE-TRACK PONTIAC

The 1964 Catalina 2+2 was pretty luxurious, but it was also plenty fast for a full-sized car.

1964 Catalina 2+2

The 1964 Pontiac lineup included seven Catalinas, two Star Chiefs and four Bonnevilles. However, this did not count the various model-options, which were base cars with specific extra-equipment packages. Important new full-size option-created-models introduced that year included the Catalina Ventura and the Catalina 2+2.

A more-rounded Pontiac front end kept the split grille and vertical headlamps of previous years. The new front fender line was squared off flush with the headlamps instead of being cut back. The tail lamps were boomerang-shaped and vertical.

Catalinas were Pontiac's "small" full-sized cars. The sport coupe and convertible body styles could be ordered with the 2+2 sports option package for the first time. Catalina 2+2s had identification badges below the Catalina name on the front fenders. The option included a 389-cid V-8 that generated 267 hp with Hydra-Matic transmission or 283 hp with a four-speed manual gearbox plus bucket seats, a center

console with a vacuum gauge, a special Morrokide interior and fender and rear deck identification badges for $291 extra. Only 7,998 Catalinas were built with the 2+2 option in 1964.

Picture a big GTO and you've got the 1964 Catalina 2+2. This was a model option designed to give the family a real sports car that was big enough for five passengers. Convertibles with the option will go for more than hardtops, but as automotive investments, both body styles will appreciate in price at about the same strong rate.

The 421 HO—a hot street version of the big-block Pontiac V-8—was also available in Catalina 2+2s. It came in three versions with 320-, 350- and 370-hp. The most powerful was equipped with Tri-Power and generated 460 lbs.-ft. of torque at 3800 rpm. This was the real muscle car edition and even though it had a curb weight of 4000 lbs., it carried just 10.8 lbs. per horsepower. It did 0-to-60 mph in only 7.2 seconds and covered the quarter-mile in 16.1 seconds.

The 1964 GTO is often recognized as the first legitimate muscle car. It was born when the Gran Turismo Omologato (GTO) package was added to the LeMans Tempest.

PONTIAC

1964 GTO

Often regarded by automotive enthusiasts as the first true muscle car, in the sense of being a midsize car with a big-block V-8 engine, the original GTO was not really a model at all. Due to General Motor's fall 1963 ban on divisional participation in high-performance marketing, Pontiac was prevented from putting an engine with more than 300 cubic inches into an intermediate-size model. That's why Pontiac's "Young Turk" executives and an ad man named Jim Wangers snuck the GTO into existence as an extra-cost package for the Tempest LeMans.

Late in October of 1963 the Grand Turismo Omologato package was announced for the LeMans coupe, hardtop and convertible as a $295 option. GTO equipment included a 325-hp/389-cid V-8 with a special camshaft, special hydraulic lifters and 421-style cylinder heads. It had a single Carter four-barrel carburetor. Also included in the option were specially valved shock absorbers, a seven-blade, 18-inch cooling fan with a cut-off clutch, a dual exhaust system, special 6-inch-

wide wheel rims, red-stripe nylon low-profile tires, GTO identification medallions, twin-simulated hood scoops, six GTO emblems, an engine-turned dash insert, bucket seats, special high-rate springs and longer rear stabilizers.

Desirable GTO options included a center console, Hurst-Campbell four-speed manual shift linkage, custom exhaust splitters, no-cost whitewall tires, special wheel covers and a Tri-Power engine option with three two-barrel carburetors. The Tri-Power version of the 389-cid V-8 produced 348 hp at 4900 rpm.

In January 1964, *Motor Trend* magazine found a four-speed GTO convertible capable of doing the quarter-mile in 15.8 seconds at 93 mph. The same car's 0-to-60 performance was 7.7 seconds and it had a 115-mph top speed.

By the year's end, the GTO was considered a huge sales success. Pontiac records showed production of 7,384 GTO coupes, 18,422 two-door hardtops and 6,644 convertibles.

PONTIAC

The 1965 Catalina 2+2 was tough to beat as an all-around driving machine.

1965 Catalina 2+2

Pontiac originally offered a 2+2 option for its 1964 Catalina sport coupe and convertible. Modest sales of the original bucket-seats-and-badges package were taken in stride by Pontiac Motor Division, which made the 2+2 a "sports option" for 1965. This blossoming of the 2+2 coincided with new styling and a chassis redesign for all full-sized Pontiacs. The result was an extremely attractive automobile with outstanding performance.

The second 2+2 was available again in either two-door hardtop or convertible body form. The 2+2's performance was given a strong starting point thanks to the 1965 Pontiac's bold "ship's prow" front end with its stacked headlights and a fresh variation on the neo-classic divided grille. Providing sufficient identification were front fender louvers and 2+2 emblems on the hood, rear fenders and rear deck.

The Catalina 2+2 base engine was now Pontiac's 421-cid V-8 with a 10.5:1 compression ratio and four-barrel carburetor. Its ratings were 338 hp at 4600 rpm and 459 lbs.-ft. of torque at 2800 rpm. The standard transmission was an all-Synchromesh close-ratio four-speed. Pontiac specified a 3.42:1 standard axle ratio for the 2+2. It provided excellent all-around performance as reflected in the car's 0-to-60 time of 7.2 seconds, its 0-to-100 time of 20.5 seconds and a standing-start quarter-mile completed in 15.8 seconds at 88 mph.

If a Catalina 2+2 of this caliber didn't satisfy a buyer's performance desires, Pontiac offered a 421 HO version. *Car Life*, April 1965, quoted one happy 421 HO owner as saying "I will say this is the finest road machine I have ever driven— foreign cars included. It has comfort, performance and, in

my opinion, handling that should satisfy anyone but a road course driver." The 421 HO had ratings of 376 hp at 5000 rpm and 461 lbs.-ft. of torque at 3600 rpm. Replacing the standard Carter AFB four-barrel carburetor was Pontiac's Tri-Power setup featuring three two-barrel carburetors. The 421 HO also benefited from its quick-bleed hydraulic valve lifters, which made 5400 rpm a realistic rev limit.

It was possible to equip the Catalina 2+2 with a "ride and handling package" consisting of extra-stiff front and rear springs, heavier-duty shock absorbers, a front sway bar, aluminum wheel hubs, quicker-ratio power steering, a tachometer, a gauge package and a close-ratio four-speed manual transmission.

A Catalina 2+2 so equipped (and running a 4.11:1 "Saf-T-Track" limited-slip differential) was tested by *Car Life* in April 1965. Although its 0-to-60 performance of 7.2 seconds and its quarter-mile time of 15.5 seconds (at 95 mph) were impressive, *Car Life* said the car fell short of true 2+2 potential. "Optimum time for the quarter-mile," said *Car Life*, "should fall into the low 14-second category when the car is more suitably tuned and equipped."

With a list price of $3,287, the Catalina 2+2 was a tremendous performance bargain. Even when equipped in its Royal Oak form, it listed for just over $4,200.

Along with the GTO, the 2+2 further contributed to Pontiac's mid-1960s performance image that has become a modern day legend. Exciting to look at, exciting to drive and, most of all, exciting to own, the Catalina 2+2 was in a class by itself among American automobiles.

Adding Tri-Power would jack the GTO's horsepower up from 335 to 360. Either way, it was a fun, fast car.

PONTIAC

Jerry Heasley

1965 GTO

I went to buy one of these cars once — a hardtop. It had a little too much Wisconsin rust to take it home, but the car ran terrific and it was a barrel of fun just to give it a test drive. That GTO didn't know the meaning of the word s-l-o-w. Another fan of the '65 was contemporary road tester Roger Huntington. "Pontiac Tempest GTO order blank building produces a winner," he said.

Huntington was referring to the fact that the 1965 Pontiac GTO remained an option package for three body styles in the Tempest LeMans series: the coupe, the two-door hardtop and the convertible. This year the car had vertically stacked dual headlights and the front fenders had small hoods. While sales of the original 1964 model had been held down by autoworker strikes and an abbreviated model year (after the GTO option's midyear introduction), this year Pontiac was ready to open the flood gates.

Advertising promotions included five huge 26 x 11 1/2-inch full-color photos of the so-called "GeeTO Tiger" in action for only 25 cents and a GeeTO Tiger record for 50 cents. The latter captured the sounds made as a company test driver put a 1965 GTO through its paces at the GM Proving Ground in Milford, Michigan. At the same time, Hurst Performance Products Co., of Glenside, Pennsylvania, sponsored a GTO pace car for *Motor Trend* magazine's Riverside 500 race.

Pontiac Motor Division held the price of the GTO option at $295.90 for 1965. The package included most of the same items it did in 1964, except that a single dummy hood scoop was used in place of two. The 421-style cylinder heads were re-cored to improve the flow of gases.

The standard 389-cid GTO V-8 was a four-barrel-carburetor job with 10.75:1 compression and 335 hp. It was good for 16.1-second quarter-mile acceleration runs at 89 mph. Its 0-to-60-mph time was 7.2 seconds. For only $115.78 extra buyers could add Tri-Power carburetion with a special 288-degree camshaft that provided 360 hp from the same block.

The GTO convertible was available for as little as $3,092.90 and 11,311 were made. The coupe had a base price of $2,786.90 and 8,319 assemblies. The sales leader was the two-door hardtop, which could be had for as little as $2,854.90. It was the choice of 55,722 buyers.

PONTIAC

Phil Kunz

A Tri-Power 421 HO engine could launch the big Catalina 2+2 up to 95 mph in the quarter-mile.

1966 Catalina 2+2

Throughout the late 1960s, Pontiac Motor Division did a good job of holding onto its new-found role as America's No. 3 automaker. The company had built its post-1957 image on the youth-market appeal of full-sized performance cars. Under-the-table factory support of drag and stock car racing helped move the big, "brutaful" Pontiacs out of showrooms across the United States. In the mid-1960s, big-car sales started to gradually decline and the performance emphasis switched to the midsize cars where the Pontiac GTO ruled the roost.

Pontiac Motor Division's big cars continued to come on two wheelbases in 1966 (as they had since 1958). From 1965-1969, the smaller stance—which measured 121 inches—was used for Catalinas and all Safari station wagons (regardless of trim line). The larger 124-inch stance was reserved for Star Chiefs, Executives and Bonnevilles.

Sporty luxury, smooth performance and high style were the keynotes of Pontiac's larger cars during this 6-year period. Playing off the glory of the Super-Duty high-performance engine series, big-cube, multi-carbureted engines and 300-plus-hp ratings continued to be offered. However, 0-to-60 acceleration suffered due to added weight. The big-boat Bonnevilles were super cars to drive on superhighways, but rarely did much at a drag strip. The opposite was true of the

Catalina 2+2, which became Pontiac's full-sized performance car.

One of Pontiac's top full-size collector cars of the era, the Catalina 2+2 has a mystique of its own. It came—on either hardtop coupes or convertibles—as a pre-packaged group of equipment. Individual options could also be added. For 1966, small changes were the rule. An industry-first plastic grille was among them. A two-stage exhaust system with resonators was new. Added options included manually inflatable Super-Lift air shocks, Strato bucket or Strato bench seats and headrests.

The package included all-vinyl bucket seats, louvered fender trim, 2+2 badges, a 421-cid V-8, a three-speed transmission with a Hurst floor shifter, heavy-duty shocks and springs, chrome engine parts, full wheel discs and special fender pin striping.

With a weight in the over-2-ton range, the 2+2 with the Tri-Power 421 HO engine and four-speed gearbox could hit an incredible 95 mph in the quarter-mile. Pontiac installed the 2+2 option on 6,383 Catalinas in 1966, but Pontiac's records do not indicate how many cars with the option were sport coupes or convertibles. Of the total, 2,208 cars had manual transmissions and 4,175 had Hydra-Matic drive.

The "Goat" had some styling changes in 1966, but was still largely the
same midsized powerhouse that had blazed new muscle car trails.

PONTIAC

1966 GTO

Smooth new styling touches, added power under the hood and some outstanding new exterior paint colors made the '66 "Goat" the "King of the Hill" in muscle car land for another 12 months. "The GTO always surprises *Car Life* drivers with its ability to perform well," said *Car Life* magazine in its May 1966 road test.

Pontiac's mid-size A-body cars had a new, smoother and rounder appearance for 1966 with wide wheel openings and a recessed split grille. GTOs were in their own series. It was the last year for the Tri-Power three two-barrel-carb option.

A distinctive new mesh-style grille incorporating rectangular parking lamps characterized 1966 GTOs. Standard features of the high-performance model included front bucket seats, a single hood scoop, walnut grain dashboard inserts, specific ornamentation, dual exhausts, a heavy-duty suspension and 7.75 x 14 red-line or white-stripe tires.

Coupe prices started at $2,783 and 10,363 were built. Hardtop prices started at $2,847 and 73,798 were built. The $3,082 convertible found 12,798 buyers. Sales included 77,901 cars with the base 335-hp V-8, 18,745 with Tri-Power 360-hp engines and about 30 with 360-hp Ram Air Tri-Power engines. Most GTOs (61,279) had manual gear boxes.

Car Life magazine (May 1966) asked for and almost got a "standard" GTO to test drive. Pontiac supplied a two-door hardtop or sport coupe with the 389-cid/335-hp four-barrel engine, four-speed manual gearbox, a console, tinted glass, rally gauges, a tachometer, rally wheels, a radio, a remote rearview mirror and air conditioning. It booked out at $3,589, a bit more than the coupe's base price of $2,763. The car had a 3.08:1 rear axle and a dual reverse-flow exhaust system with mufflers and resonators.

The 389-cid V-8 had a 4.064 x 3.75-inch bore and stroke. It featured a single Carter four-barrel carburetor, a 10.75:1 compression ratio and hydraulic valve lifters. Its output was rated at 335 hp at 5000 rpm and 431 lbs.-ft. of torque at 3200 rpm. *Car Life's* 3,950-lb. GTO carried 11.6 lbs. per horsepower and delivered outstanding performance. It went from 0-to-60 mph in 6.8 seconds and did the quarter-mile in 15.4 seconds at 92 mph. Another publication test drove a heavier '66 GTO convertible with the heftier 360-hp Tri-Power V-8 and did not do any better, running 0-to-60 in the same 6.8 seconds and using 15.5 seconds to cover the quarter-mile.

Phil Kunz

The 325-hp/400-cid engine option made the Firebird a pretty fast mover in its debut season of 1967. This car has had its factory wheels and rubber replaced.

PONTIAC

1967 Firebird 400

Pontiac's general manager, John DeLorean, gave the Firebird a strong send off. On January 27, 1967 he noted, "The personal sports car field is probably the most rapidly growing in the industry. With the introduction of the Firebird we hope to attract new buyers who want to step up to something extra in styling as well as performance in this segment of the market."

The most potent of the five new Pontiacs, the Firebird 400, boasted a 400-cid engine with a single four-barrel carburetor and 10.75:1 compression ratio. It developed 325 hp at 4800 rpm and 410 lbs.-ft. of torque at 3400 rpm. A heavy-duty three-speed transmission was standard with a four-speed or automatic transmission optional. The Firebird 400 model had twin traction bars that helped minimize the negative impact of the single leaf spring rear suspension.

Since the Firebird 400 and GTO engines had identical specs, enthusiasts wondered why the Firebird developed 325 hp compared to the GTO's 350. The answer was a small steel tab positioned on the linkage between the Rochester carburetor's primary and secondary barrels. It limited the second venturi's opening to 90 percent of capacity. This restrictive act, performed in the name of corporate policy prohibiting any GM product to leave the factory with less than 10 lbs. per horsepower, was easily circumvented by removing or bending this innocent-looking, but power-robbing tab.

The Firebird 400's styling left no doubt that it was pure Pontiac. Most apparent was its divided front grille, which successfully continued a Pontiac styling theme dating back to the original Wide-Tracks of 1959. At the rear, horizontally

divided tail lamps linked the Firebird to the GTO. The most audacious of the several instrument packages offered for the Firebird was the hood-mounted tachometer. This had been introduced on the GTO and it further reinforced the Firebird's performance image.

Car Life dubbed the Firebird 400 "the enthusiast's choice" and discovered that it could deliver a 0-to-60-mph time of 6.5 seconds with the four-speed all-synchromesh transmission and a 3.36:1 axle. Aside from its engine, the 400 option included (as standard equipment) a chrome air cleaner, chrome rocker covers, a chrome oil cap, a dual exhaust system, red or white E70 x 14 wide-oval tires, a heavy-duty battery, a heavy-duty starter, a de-clutching engine fan and dual hood scoops.

When the Ram Air option was ordered it added direct-air induction, a longer-duration cam with more overlap, a more efficient cast-iron exhaust manifold and different valve springs with flat metal dampers. The carburetor was also recalibrated. Power ratings with the Ram Air option were deliberately understated at 325 hp at 5200 rpm and 410 lbs.-ft. of torque at 3600 rpm. Firebirds with this option were truly rare birds, as only 65 400s were so equipped.

The 400 convertible listed for $3,346.53 and the coupe for $3,109.53. With the rare Ram Air option the prices were $3,609.39 and $3,372.36, respectively. Prices for the Firebird 400 included installation of either a four-speed manual or Turbo Hydra-Matic transmission. If a heavy-duty three-speed manual gearbox was selected, the Firebird 400 price differential was $358.09.

PONTIAC

Jerry Heasley

**The 400 HO was the hottest engine for the 1967 GTO. It generated
360 hp and helped the Goat crack 100 mph in the quarter-mile.**

1967 GTO

Minor trim revisions and wide, bright body underscores identified 1967 GTOs. The Model 24207 coupe was the lowest-priced body style, costing dealers $2,174.04 and having a suggested retail price of $2,871. It saw 7,029 assemblies. The Model 24217 hardtop's dealer price was $2,222.64 and it retailed for $2,935. Its production was 65,176 units. A total of 9,517 customers bought the Model 24267 convertible, which wholesaled for $2,399.22 and sold for $3,165 at showroom level. This year, stick-shift cars totaled 39,128 versus 42,594 with Pontiac's new three-speed Turbo Hydra-Matic transmission.

GTOs included all LeMans equipment plus a specific base engine, bucket seats, body paint striping, a walnut-grain-style dash panel, dual exhausts, heavy-duty shocks, heavy-duty springs, heavy-duty stabilizer bars and red line or whitewall tires.

A new 400 cid V-8 replaced the 389-cid. It had a 4.12 x 3.75-inch bore and stroke. A two-barrel "economy" version with an 8.6:1 compression ratio and a Carter AFB carburetor went into 2,967 GTOs. This motor was available at no extra cost only in cars with automatic transmission. It produced 255 hp at 4400 rpm and 397 lbs.-ft. of torque at 4400 rpm.

The base GTO engine was put under 64,177 hoods. This version of the 400-cid V-8 had a 10.75:1 compression ratio and a Rochester four-barrel carburetor. It generated 335 hp at 5000 rpm and 441 lbs.-ft. of torque at 3400 rpm.

Another option was the 400 HO engine, which was factory installed in 13,827 cars. With manual transmission attachment this engine was $76.89 extra whether or not the car had the RPO 612 air injection exhaust control system. The price was the same for cars with automatic transmission. The HO engine had a 10.75:1 compression ratio. It developed 360 hp at 5100 rpm and 438 lbs.-ft. of torque at 3600 rpm.

The Ram Air I engine was installed in 751 cars (only 138 with automatics). This version of the 400-cid V-8 was $263.30 extra with both manual or automatic transmissions and with or without RPO 612. It had the same basic specs as the HO engine, except that the horsepower curve peaked at 5400 rpm and the torque curve peaked at 3800 rpm.

Motor Trend did a comparison test of two Ram Air 400 GTOs. One car had a four-speed manual gearbox and the other had Turbo Hydra-Matic. The manually shifted car was faster from 0-to-60 mph, doing the run in 4.9 seconds versus 5.2 seconds for the car with automatic. With standard tires, the stick-shift GTO did the quarter-mile in 14.21 seconds at 102.97 mph, while the second one took 14.09 seconds at 101 mph. Both cars were then fitted with M & H drag tires and tested again. The stick version took 13.09 seconds at 106.5 mph and the THM version took 13.36 seconds at 105 mph.

PONTIAC

Jerry Heasley

The press loved the 1968 GTO, and *Motor Trend* named it the "Car of the Year."

1968 GTO

When the 1968 Pontiacs hit the market in the fall of 1967, it was clear that the "King of Woodward Avenue" was back on the throne for another 12 months. "If press reaction to the '68 model is any indication, Pontiac's third place in sales is in no jeopardy for another year," raved the editors of *Car Life* magazine.

A long hood and short deck highlighted a more streamlined-looking Tempest line. Two-door models, including all GTOs, were on a shorter 112-inch wheelbase. GTOs added dual exhaust, a three-speed transmission with a Hurst shifter, heavy-duty underpinnings, red line tires, bucket or notchback bench seats, a cigar lighter, carpeting, disappearing windshield wipers and a 400-cid/350-hp V-8. New and highly touted was the unique Endura rubber-clad front bumper (a GTO exclusive). GTO emblems, distinctive taillights and hood scoops rounded out the GTO goodies.

Base prices for the two 1968 models (there was no more "post" coupe) were $3,101 for the two-door hardtop and $3,996 for the convertible. Production of these body styles was 77,704 and 9,980, respectively. Although the Endura bumper was a hit of the year, those who didn't like it could get the standard 1968 Tempest chrome bumper as a delete

option on GTOs. Engine options for 1968 were the same as in 1967.

The 1967 GTO production figures included 2,841 hardtops and 432 ragtops with the 400-cid/255-hp two-barrel V-8 and automatic, 39,215 hardtops and 5,091 convertibles with the 400-cid/335-hp four-barrel V-8 and automatic, 25,371 hardtops and 3,116 ragtops with the 400-cid/335-hp four-barrel V-8 and manual transmission, 3,140 hardtops and 461 ragtops with the 360-hp 400 HO V-8 and automatic, 6,197 hardtops and 766 ragtops with the 360-hp 400 HO V-8 and stick shift, 183 hardtops and 22 convertibles with the Ram Air 400 V-8 and automatic, and 757 hardtops and 92 ragtops with the Ram Air 400 V-8 and a stick shift.

Motor Trend named the 1968 GTO as its "Car of the Year" and tested two different versions. The first car had the 400-cid/350-hp V-8, a 3.23:1 rear axle and Turbo Hydra-Matic transmission. It did 0-to-60 mph in 7.3 seconds and the quarter-mile in 15.93 seconds at 88.32 mph. The second car was a 360-hp Ram Air model with a four-speed manual gearbox and a 4.33:1 rear axle. It went from 0-to-60 mph in 6.5 seconds and covered the quarter-mile in 14.45 seconds at 98.20 mph.

The flashy debut Trans Am was outfitted in white with blue stripes, and marked the start
of a long-running Firebird package for Pontiac.

PONTIAC

Jerry Heasley

1969 1/2 Firebird Trans Am

This muscle machine version of Pontiac's Firebird sports-compact started out as a sports-racing car. It was originally conceived of as a sedan racer that could compete in the Sports Car Club of America (SCCA) Trans-American Cup series. The racing version was supposed to be powered by an ultra-high-performance, low-compression 303-cid small-block V-8.

The new engine's displacement figure of 303 cubic inches came in under the 305-cid maximum that the Trans-Am racing formulas allowed. However, only 25 of these engines were ever made. They were sold to competitors to replace the 400-cid big-block V-8s their cars left the factory with. Production versions of the Trans Am (the car name is spelled without the hyphen) stuck with the 400-cid engine size.

The base 400 HO engine (which Pontiac engineers called the "Ram Air III" V-8) was used in 634 cars (including all convertibles, which was a rare body style with only eight assemblies). Of these Ram Air III cars, 114 units (including four of the convertibles) had a four-speed manual gearbox. Fifty-five other cars (all coupes) came with a Ram Air IV engine, which cost $390 extra. Of these, nine cars had Turbo Hydra-Matic transmissions and all of the others had stick shift.

The WS4 Trans Am package for base Firebirds included the Ram Air III engine, a three-speed heavy-duty floor shifter, functional hood scoops, heavy-duty running gear, special interior and exterior trim, a rear deck lid airfoil, full-length body stripes and front fender air extractors. A prototype Trans Am that was fitted with a 303-cid V-8 and used for extensive road testing by *Motor Trend* was finished in solid silver. All other '69 1/2 Trans Ams were Cameo White with blue stripes.

The Ram Air III V-8 produced 335 hp at 5000 rpm and 430 lbs.-ft. of torque at 3400 rpm. The Ram Air IV engine cranked up 345 hp at 5400 rpm and 430 lbs.-ft. at 3700 rpm. With its higher output and lower production, the Ram Air IV is definitely the engine preferred by most muscle car collectors.

Big-block-powered Trans Ams were found to be better suited for drag racing than road racing. They could do the quarter-mile in 14.1 seconds at 101 mph.

Prices for the WS4 option varied by body style and transmission, but were around $725. That put the Trans Am sport coupe's window sticker at around $3,556. Only eight convertibles (base priced around $3,770) were built.

Base Trans Ams came with standard steel disc wheels. Some had their stripes running over the rear spoiler, some below it. A rare option is the Code 293 special custom interior with gold genuine leather seat bolsters.

Jerry Heasley

The attention-grabbing "The Judge" GTO originally came only in
orange with tri-colored striping, but other colors were added later.

1969 GTO "The Judge"

Any muscle car inspired by the "Here Come 'de Judge" skits on Rowan & Martin's "Laugh In" TV show was sure to be a bit crazy and the GTO Judge was crazy in a very fast way. As *Car Life* magazine once put it, "Pontiac inspired the supercar for this generation . . . and The Judge is one of the best."

"Born Great" was the catchy sales slogan that Pontiac Motor Division used for the 1969 GTO "The Judge." The new model of the GTO was designed to be what *Car and Driver* magazine called an "econo racer." In other words, it was a heavily optioned up muscle car with a price that gave you a lot for your money! It was a machine that you could take racing, pretty much "as is," and for a lot less money than a purpose-built drag racing car cost. It was seen in many street races, too.

Pontiac Motor Division's release of the "The Judge" option packager was made on December 19, 1968. At first, "The Judge" came only in bright orange with tri-color striping, but it was later made available in the full range of colors that were available for other '69 GTOs. Special standard features of the Judge package included a blacked-out radiator

grille, Rally II wheels (minus bright trim rings), functional hood scoops and "The Judge" decals on the sides of the front fenders and "Ram Air" decals on the hood scoops. At the rear of the car there was a 60-inch wide "floating" deck lid airfoil with a "The Judge" decal emblem on the upper right-hand surface.

The standard "The Judge" engine was the Pontiac-built 400-cid/366-hp Ram Air III V-8. It came linked to a three-speed manual transmission with a floor-mounted Hurst T-handle shifter and a 3.55:1 rear axle. A total of 8,491 GTOs and Judges were sold with this motor and only 362 of them were convertibles. The more powerful 400-cid/370-hp Ram Air IV engine was installed in 759 cars in the same two lines and 59 of these cars were convertibles.

"The Judge" option was added to 6,725 GTO two-door hardtops and only 108 GTO ragtops. The editors of *Car Life* magazine whipped a Judge through the quarter-mile at 14.45 seconds and 97.8 mph. *Supercars Annual* covered the same distance in a Judge with Turbo Hydra-Matic transmission and racked up a run of 13.99 seconds at 107 mph!

The 1970 Formula Firebird looked tough, and it was. With Ram
Air and twin hood scoops, the muscular Pontiac turned out 335 hp.

1970 1/2 Firebird Formula 400

While the 1970 Trans Am was probably the hottest of the second-generation Firebirds introduced during the last week in February, the Formula 400 was right up there in terms of performance and had more of the street-racer look that said "muscle car" from the word go.

In addition to all the federally mandated GM safety features, the Formula models included a 330-hp/400-cid V-8 with a single four-barrel carburetor, a three-speed manual gearbox with a heavy-duty Hurst shifter, a 1 1/8-inch front and 5/8-inch rear stabilizer bar, high-rate springs, special wind-up rear axle controls, F70 x 14 bias-belted tires, 7-inch-wide wheel rims, Formula 400 trim, a deluxe steering wheel, carpets, a vinyl bucket seat interior, dual sport mirrors, concealed windshield wipers and manual front disc and rear drum brakes.

All Formulas had a special, tough-looking hood with long twin air scoops that opened at the front end, just above the grille. These scoops became functional when the L74 Ram Air V-8 was ordered for $168.51 extra. This was called the 400 Ram Air option and it put out 335 hp at 5000 rpm.

Pontiac's 400-cid V-8 had a 4.122 x 3.75-inch bore and stroke, a 10.25:1 compression ratio and a single four-barrel Rochester carburetor. It generated 330-hp at 4800 rpm and 430 lbs.-ft. of torque at 3000 rpm. *Car and Driver* charted a 6.4-second 0-to-60 run and a 14.7-second quarter-mile at 98.9 mph. That wasn't as fast as the Trans Am the magazine also tested, which also cost less ($4,663.63).

But the Formula's appeal was image. While the Trans Am looked like an exotic European road-racing car, the Formula had the look of a winner in the "Stoplight Grand Prix."

1970 Pontiac-Hurst Grand Prix SSJ

One thing that kept Pontiac on the highest rungs of the muscle car ladder in the '60s and early '70s was the fact that many people who worked for the company were dyed-in-the-wool car enthusiasts. Known in the industry as the "Young Turks," they cruised Woodward Avenue, won drag racing titles and read all the car magazines of the day. When retrospect sections of those publications featured the fabulous Duesenberg SSJ, the story served as inspiration for a new high-performance Grand Prix.

Car Life magazine referred to the 1969 Grand Prix as "a stretched GTO" and named it the best-engineered car of the year. The factory took things as far as a J model. For muscle-car enthusiasts, the big news for 1970 was the SSJ, which was a Grand Prix SJ with Hurst modifications.

The SSJ could be ordered through Pontiac dealers. Pontiac built and painted 272 of the cars. They were then shipped to Hurst for the conversion work. They were based on the 'J' model (the vinyl accent stripes used on factory-issued SJs were incompatible with Hurst SSJ features). The SSJs were painted either Cameo White (code CC) or Starlight Black (code AA). Interiors were ivory, black or sandalwood in cloth or all-Morrokide. Mandatory options included body-color sport mirrors, G78 x 14 whitewalls and Rally II wheels. The space-saver spare and ride and handling package were recommended.

After assembly, these cars were shipped to a Hurst plant in Southfield, Michigan, where frost gold accents were applied to the hood, side window frames, front of the roof and

Rally II wheels. A landau-style half-top (antique white, white or black) was installed, as was a steel, electrically operated sunroof like those used in Cadillac Eldorados.

Engines for 1970 included the same base power plant as in 1969 or a 265-hp regular-fuel economy version of the 400-cid V-8 at no extra charge. However, the 428-cid V-8 was replaced with a 455-cid/370-hp big block.

In *Popular Science*, a road-tested Grand Prix proved faster than a Dodge Hemi Charger and Ford Fairlane GT around the road racing circuit at Bridgehampton.

Instead of the 370-hp engine, a code LS5 455 HO V-8 could be had as an option. The SSJ conversion work took about 10 days. Special die-cast model SSJ emblems were featured for identification.

The GT-37 was a sportier version of the stripped-down, bargain basement T-37. Only 1,419 were built, making these cars interesting collector pieces.

1970 Tempest GT-37

An economy wave swept the American auto industry in 1970, with cheap, six-cylinder cars seeing renewed popularity. Pontiac Motor Division—with its 1960s performance image—was a little out of step with the new trend that inspired cars like Chevrolet's Vega, Ford's Maverick and Plymouth's Duster. In fact, Plymouth was able to knock PMD out of third place in sales.

By midyear, Pontiac simplified its Tempest hardtop to give it a more competitive price. It was released as the T-37, which was aimed at entry-level buyers. Although the "37" part of the designation was based on General Motors' code for a two-door hardtop model, Pontiac soon bent the rules a bit and released a T-37 coupe (two-door sedan) as well as the hardtop. With a $2,683 price tag, the cheap T-37 generated 20,883 sales in half a year.

It wasn't long after the T-37 appeared that somebody decided to issue a sporty variation. To create such a budget-priced muscle car, it was decided to dress up the plain-looking coupe with GTO-like extras and call it the GT-37. The new model was a stripped-down muscle car with a V-8 engine. The fastest production car that Pontiac built in 1970 turned out to be the Tempest GT-37 two-door sedan with the Ram Air

III engine.

Standard equipment for the GT-37 included any Tempest V-8 with low-restriction dual exhaust, a three-speed heavy-duty manual transmission with floor shift, G70-14 raised-white-letter tires, Rally II wheel rims, 1969 Judge-style stripes and a hood pin kit. A rear deck airfoil was optional, but bucket seats were not available.

According to Pontiac's Official Historian John Sawruk, some radical weight reduction was done on the T-37 and carried through on the sporty GT-37 versions. Sawruk, an expert on these models and owner of a GT-37, noted: "Almost all sound deadening treatment was deleted. This saved about 120 pounds all by itself. A long list of other features and equipment was also deleted. For example, there is only one coat hook and there is no Pontiac nameplate in the grille, although the holes are still there! Even the trunk mat was almost left off."

The hot GT-37 engine was the 400 cid V-8 that came in 1970 1/2 models with stick shift. This was actually the Ram Air III V-8, without a Ram Air hood and dual-snorkel air cleaner. It did have the bigger Ram Air III valves.

Pontiac built 1,419 of the 1970 1/2 GT-37 coupes.

**With a base 350-hp/400-cid V-8, and optional 455-cid and
Ram Air 400 mills, every 1970 Goat on the street was fast.**

1970 GTO

Prominent styling changes on the 1970 Pontiac GTO included smaller, split oval grilles, dual rectangular headlight housings (with round lenses) and creased body sides. The hood had twin air scoops and a GTO nameplate was seen on the left-hand grille. The rear end also sported flared fenders and the exhaust pipes exited through a valance panel below the rear bumper.

Standard hardware for the two GTOs included: front bucket seats, a padded dashboard, a functional air-scoop with a handle under the dash for manual control, a heavy-duty clutch, sports-type springs and shock absorbers, courtesy lights, a dual exhaust system, a 350-hp V-8, a heavy-duty three-speed transmission with floor-mounted gear shifter and G78-14 fiberglass-belted tires. The "Goat" featured a total Endura nosepiece without a metal bumper and had cleaner styling than other Tempests.

It was $3,267 for the base hardtop and 32,737 were built. The base 400-cid/350-hp V-8 was put in 27,496 of these cars, including 9,348 with stick shifts. Priced at $3,492, the convertible saw only 3,615 assemblies. The base engine went into 3,058 of the ragtops, including 887 with stick shifts.

The 1970 GTO engines had several innovations, including special spherical-wedge cylinder heads and a computer-perfected camshaft design. Ram Air III engines with 366 hp were used in 1,302 hardtops and 114 convertibles with stick shifts and 3,054 hardtops and 174 convertibles with Turbo Hydra-Matics. Ram Air IV engines with 370 hp were used in 140 hardtops and 13 convertibles with stick shifts and 627 hardtops and 24 convertibles with Turbo Hydra-Matic. Also available in non-Judges was a 455-cid/360-hp V-8. This engine was installed in 2,227 stick-shift cars (241 ragtops) and 1,919 cars with Turbo Hydra-Matics (including 158 ragtops).

A 1970 GTO hardtop with the 400-cid/366-hp V-8 did 0-to-60 mph in 6 seconds flat and covered the quarter-mile in 14.6 seconds. With a 455-cid/360-hp V-8 the same model was actually slower, requiring 6.6 seconds for the 0-to-60 run and 14.8 seconds to cover the quarter mile. *Car and Driver* tested a 455-cid GTO coupe in its January 1970 issue. The car had a four-speed manual gearbox and 3.31:1 rear axle. The chart accompanying the article showed a 6.6-second 0 to 60-mph time and a quarter-mile run in 15 seconds at 96.5 mph.

The bottom line was that the 455 was enough engine for a "daily driver" GTO. Though big, it was docile enough to take the family out to dinner at McDonald's. But the Ram Air 400 was the engine you wanted when you went to the drag strip. *Car Life* pointed out: "It got to the end of the drag strip first and it was going faster when we arrived, so the Ram Air 400 does have more power than the 455."

PONTIAC

Jerry Heasley

For Pontiac fans, a Judge convertible was about as good as it got during the golden age of the muscle car.

1970 GTO Judge

Pontiac Motor Division advertised that the GTO "Judge" was born great and enthusiasts like John DeLorean and Jim Wangers were there to make sure that the delivery went without complications. It was a newborn that hit the ground running and a return appearance for 1970 resulted in few product changes. In March 1970, *Road Test* magazine described the latest version of the GTO Judge by saying, "It's a fun car built by people who had a good idea and weren't afraid the carry it out."

The Judge option package was once again available for the GTO two-door hardtop (sport coupe) and the GTO convertible. It was listed on options sheets as the code 332-WT1 accessory group. This package included the 400-cid/366-hp Ram Air V-8, Rally II wheels less bright trim rings, G70-14 black sidewall fiberglass-belted tires, a T-handle-shifted manual gearbox, a rear deck lid airfoil, specific body side stripes, "The Judge" body decals and stripes and a black-textured radiator grille.

Contrary to some people's beliefs, the GTO Judge was not cheaper than a base model GTO. It was less expensive than a base model GTO that had all of the same options and accessories installed (and paid for) individually.

The 366-hp engine package added $337.02 to the price of the cars that it was ordered for, regardless of whether the car was a hardtop or a ragtop. That put the base price of a hardtop with "The Judge" equipment at about $3,604.02, although there may have been some mandatory options that added a little more to that. Prices on the convertible version started at about $3,829.02.

Those buyers who wanted to get their GTO Judge with a more powerful Ram Air IV engine had to shell out $558.20 extra. In addition, Ram Air IV cars could only be built with either a three-speed Turbo Hydra-Matic transmission or a four-speed manual gear box.

Pontiac Motor Division engine production records show that 42 GTO hardtops and 288 ragtops were built with Ram Air V-8s. As for the Ram Air IV V-8, it was used in 767 hardtops and just 37 convertibles. (These combined production figures are for both plain GTOs and cars with "The Judge" option lumped together.)

Pontiac's base 455-cid/360-hp 1970 GTO "The Judge" two-door hardtop was good for 0-to-60 mph in 6.6 seconds. It did the quarter-mile in 14.6 seconds.

The 1970 1/2 Trans Am was a terrific performance car, with a powerful engine list that started with the 400-cid four-barrel and topped out with a 370-hp Ram Air IV option that made it into only 88 cars. Whatever engine was under the hood, these cars were fabulous all-around machines.

1970 1/2 Firebird Trans Am

The 1970 Trans Am is one of my favorite muscle cars and I'd buy one if the prices didn't keep climbing just out of my range every time I get close. While I like the car mainly for its smooth, clean look, it is also a true high-performance machine. As *Road Test* magazine said in March 1970, "The standard Trans Am engine transforms the Firebird into a true muscle car."

The introduction of 1970 Firebirds was delayed until the winter of 1970. When they appeared they had a sleek new, half-inch-longer body shell on the same 108-inch wheelbase. There were now four separate Firebird series called Firebird, Espirit, Formula 400 and Trans Am. A Maserati-like, semi-fastback body made the second-generation Trans Am a sophisticated muscle car.

The No. 22887 Trans Am hardtop coupe had a base sticker price of $4,305. It weighed 3,550 lbs. and 3,196 were made. The Trans Am suspension was upgraded and big-block engines were carried over with Ram Air induction. The least-powerful engine option was the Ram Air 400-cid four-barrel V-8 connected to a four-speed, wide-ratio gearbox with a floor-mounted Hurst shifter.

Convertibles were no longer available. In addition to white paint with blue stripes, Pontiac offered blue cars with white stripes. Standard equipment included all mandatory safety features, a front air dam, front and rear spoilers, a shaker hood, side air extractors, a rear spoiler, aerodynamic mirrors (left-hand remote controlled), 1 1/4-inch front and 7/8-inch rear stabilizer bars, heavy-duty shocks and springs, an engine-turned aluminum instrument panel with a rally gauge cluster, concealed windshield wipers, bucket seats, carpets, all-vinyl upholstery, power brakes and steering and 15-inch Rally II wheels.

A higher 10.5:1 compression ratio gave the base 400-cid Ram Air III V-8 in 1970 1/2 models 345 hp. This engine went into 1,339 cars with automatic and 1,769 with stick. In addition to the standard four-speed manual transmission, Turbo Hydra-Matic, also with a floor shift, was a no-cost extra. Fifty-nine automatics and 29 sticks were built with the 370-hp Ram Air IV option. A Ram Air III-equipped Trans Am could do the quarter-mile in 14.5 seconds at 99 mph. *Car and Driver* (June 1970) road tested an Espirit, a Formula 400 and a Trans Am. The latter was the hottest of the three and moved from 0-to-60 mph in just 5.7 seconds. The standing-start quarter-mile took only 14.1 seconds at 103.2 mph.

PONTIAC

The 1971 Formula Firebird could be equipped with a 350-, 400- or 455-cid engine. This car had the 400.

1971 Formula Firebird

While the name of this Pontiac muscle machine may appeal to mathematicians or chemists, it actually comes from the same pursuit that inspired many other Pontiac car names—racing. Pontiac was keen on building its repuation as GM's high-performance branch and racing words like Bonneville, LeMans, GTO, Grand Prix and Trans Am were often chosen to identify the company's car. In racing, a "formula" establishes the specifications of a race car from limits on cubic inches to vehicle weight. When it came to the Formula Firebird, the cubes were big and the car was a "heavyweight" in performance.

In 1971, GM made few alterations to the outside of its F-cars, but installed new high-back bucket seats and adopted some under-hood changes dictated by forthcoming anti-pollution rules. A 350-cid small-block V-8 was made standard equipment and a 455-cid V-8 replaced the venerable 400-cid V-8 as the largest Pontiac engine. As a result of all these "engine swaps," the third-rung model in the Firebird line could be had as a Formula 350, a Formula 400 or a Formula 455. However, most people started to call it simply the "Formula Firebird."

Standard equipment on this model included vinyl bucket seats, a custom cushion steering wheel, a flame chestnut wood-grain-appearance dash panel, right- and left-hand body-color outside rear-view mirrors (with a remote-control mechanism for the left mirror), an Endura rubber front bumper, a fiberglass hood with simulated dual air scoops, a black-textured grille with bright moldings, standard hubcaps, narrow rocker panel moldings, Formula 350/400/455 identification, a heavy-duty three-speed transmission with floor shifter, a high-performance dual exhaust system with chrome exhaust pipe extensions and a Power Flex cooling fan (with 400- and 455-cid engines).

Muscle car lovers were most interested in the Formula 455 version in 1971, although not all buyers understood that there were two 455-cid engine options. Both had the same 4.15 x 4.21-inch bore and stroke, but the least-powerful version used an 8.2:1 compression ratio. This engine, which cost $157.98 extra, produced 325 hp at 4400 rpm and 455 lbs.-ft. of torque at 3200 rpm. The option was the same 455 HO version that Trans Ams got as standard equipment. It was good for 335 hp at 4800 rpm and 480 lbs.-ft. of torque at 3600 rpm. This motor cost $236.97 extra in Formulas.

The Formula 455 with a four-speed manual gearbox and a 3.42:1 rear axle could go from 0-to-60 mph in 7.6 seconds and did the quarter-mile in 15.5 seconds at 89.5 mph.

**The big 1971 Grand Prix SSJ arrived on the muscle car scene
a little too late, and only 157 cars rolled out of showrooms.**

1971 Grand Prix SSJ

With the longest hood in the entire automobile industry, the Grand Prix had lots of room to stuff massive cubic inches into the engine bay. It's too bad this super-sized GTO came along at the end of the muscle car era, when big-car horsepower was trending down instead of up. Fortunately, Pontiac was smart enough to farm out a limited number of cars to Hurst Performance Products for the heated-up SSJ treatment.

For 1971, the regular Grand Prix received a beauty treatment that enhanced it both up front and at the rear. There were single headlights, a separate bumper (running across the grille) and a semi-boattail rear end that gave a dramatic new appearance to the back of the car. Two inches were added to the Grand Prix's overall length. Although it remained on a 126-inch wheelbase, it now stretched 230.2 inches end to end.

Hurst once again marketed its semi-custom SSJ option package through Pontiac dealers. The basic package was about the same as it had been in 1970, although gold honeycomb wheels or American mag wheels could now be substituted for the factory-type Rally II rims. The Hurst sunroof was now described as "the same German type used in Mercedes-Benz." SSJ nameplates were located on the car's front fender tips. Hurst Fire Frost Gold accents highlighted the body.

Engines were the base 400-cid/300-hp L78 V-8 (that was standard in Grand Prix Js) and the 455-cid/325-hp LS5 V-8 (which was standard in SJ models and optional in Js). Only 116 stick-shift cars were made and half of them had four-speed manual transmissions. Sales of Hurst SSJs dwindled to about 157 units. Apparently, the base price of the conversion ($1,147.25) remained the same as in 1970. It didn't include destination charges.

PONTIAC

The GT-37 was sort of a poor man's version of the GTO Judge,
and was the lowest-priced car in the 1971 Pontiac lineup.

1971 Tempest GT-37

Styling revisions to Pontiac Motor Division's 1971 Tempest intermediate-size models included redesigned grilles and a reworked nose and hood for GTOs. The year's lowest-priced Pontiacs were the Tempest T-37 models, which now included a four-door sedan that retailed for $2,795, a two-door coupe that sold for $2,747 and a two-door hardtop priced at $2,807.

With its longer 116-inch wheelbase, the Tempest four-door sedan was not suited for the muscle market, since the extra-long stance added up to additional weight. The two-door body styles had a four-inch shorter wheelbase and were just 202 1/2 inches long overall. That made them lighter. The coupe weighed 3,445 lbs. (with a V-8) and the hardtop was five pounds heavier. Cars with the GT option were heavier of course, but in the same proportion.

In 1971, the GT-37 option was supposed to be made available for T-37 hardtops and coupes with a V-8 engine. However, no 1971 Tempest GT-37 coupes were ever made. According to Official Pontiac Historian John Sawruk, that is because the sport mirrors that were added to the package would have prevented the opening of the front vent windows on cars of that particular body style.

The GT-37 package cost Pontiac dealers $187.47 and retailed for $236.97. It included vinyl accent stripes, Rally II wheels less trim rings, fat G70-14 white-letter tires, a dual exhaust system with chrome exhaust pipe extensions, a heavy-duty three-speed manual transmission with a floor-mounted gear shifter, body color outside rearview mirrors (with a remote-control left-hand mirror), hood locking pins, GT decals and a GT-37 nameplate.

Changes for 1971 included the use of 1971 GTO "The Judge" stripes and a minor redesign of the hood locking pins. A third variation of the GT-37 package, which came with sword-shaped body stripes made of reflective foil, was introduced in mid-1971.

For 1971, engines available in GT-37s started with a 350-cid two-barrel V-8 that had an advertised 250 hp. Options included a two-barrel 400-cid/265-hp V-8 for $52.66 extra, a four-barrel 400-cid 300-hp V-8 for $221.17 additional, a four-barrel 455-cid/335-hp V-8 for $279.10 more and the four-barrel 455 HO with 335 hp, which added $358.09 to the price of the GT-37 with a standard V-8.

The 1971 GT-37s had a 5,802-unit production run, of which about 50 were 1971 1/2 models with foil stripes. About seven of these cars had a distinctive black-and-gold paint and interior trim combination.

Only 661 GTO convertibles were assembled for 1971.

1971 GTO

For 1971, Pontiac's legendary GTO was marketed as a part of the Series 42 Tempest line up. The famous "Goat" still came in two-door hardtop and soft-top models. Pontiac factory dealers paid $2,612.25 to get a Model 24237 hardtop with a suggested retail price of $3,446. The Model 24267 convertible wholesaled to dealers for $2,788.83 and went on the lots for as little as $3,676. Both models shared a 112-inch wheelbase and an overall length of 202.3 inches. The two-door hardtop weighed 3,619 lbs. and the convertible tipped the scales at 3,664 lbs.

Larger grille cavities and round front parking lamps were changes seen in the front end of the '71 GTO. The hood now had twin air slots at the front. The GTO came with all features of the LeMans Sport model plus an engine-turned aluminum instrument panel insert, special front-end styling with an Endura front bumper, a special hood with forward-mounted simulated air-intake scoops, a 400-cid four-barrel V-8, a heavy-duty three-speed manual transmission with floor-mounted gear shifter, dual exhausts with extensions exiting through the rear valance panel, a Power-Flex cooling fan, a 1-1/8-inch diameter front stabilizer bar, a rear stabilizer bar, high-rate shock absorbers, high-rate springs, G70-14 black

sidewall tires and GTO identification emblems.

The number of engine and transmission combinations available in the GTO was cut from 17 to 10. The base 400-cid V-8 was installed in 6,421 hardtops and 508 convertibles with a manual gear box and 2,011 hardtops and 79 convertibles with automatic transmission. It had an 8.2:1 compression ratio and a single four-barrel carburetor and was good for 300 hp at 4800 rpm and 400 lbs.-ft. of torque at 3600 rpm.

The 455-cid V-8 went into 534 hardtops and 43 convertibles, all with the four-speed manual gear box. This engine also had an 8.2:1 compression ratio and a Rochester 4MV four-barrel carburetor. It developed 325 hp at 4400 rpm and 455 lbs.-ft. of torque at 3200 rpm.

A 455-cid HO engine was used in some non-Judge-optioned GTOs. This engine had an 8.4:1 compression ratio and a four-barrel carburetor. It produced 335 nhp at 4800 rpm and 480 lbs.-ft. of torque at 3600 rpm. It was used in 412 hardtops and 23 convertibles with stick shift and 476 hardtops and 21 convertibles with Turbo-Hydra-Matic.

The regular GTO hardtop had a 9,497-unit production run. Only 661 GTO convertibles were made this year.

PONTIAC

The Judge option for 1971 gave the GTO a bigger 455-cid HO
motor and a laundry list of other go-fast and look-fast goodies.

Jerry Heasley

1971 Pontiac GTO Judge

In 1971, the jury may have been out on whether the muscle car era would survive the onslaught of high insurance rates and restrictive government regulations, but there was no denying that the judge knew how to make rulings with decisive zeal. "This 455 HO Judge can still deal out some judicial action on the street," said Paul Zazarine in the November 1990 issue of *Musclecar Review*.

Pontiac dealers didn't earn much of a mark-up on the 1971 GTO "The Judge" option. The package, which had the code No. 332, carried a dealer cost of $312.45 and a suggested retail price of $394.95. That certainly wasn't a bad deal for the buyer, considering all he or she got for the money.

The GTO was based on the LeMans Sport, which included all LeMans equipment plus dual horns, pedal trim plates, a lamp package, carpeted lower door panels, a custom cushion steering wheel and wheel opening moldings. Moving up to the GTO series got buyers an engine-turned aluminum instrument panel, an exclusive Endura front end treatment, a special scooped hood, a 400-cid 300-hp four-barrel V-8, a heavy-duty three-speed transmission with a floor shifter, a dual exhaust system, a power-flex fan, a 1 1/8-inch-thick

front stabilizer bar, a beefed-up rear stabilizer, high-rate shock absorbers and springs, G70-14 black sidewall tires and GTO badges. Cars with this engine were road tested through the quarter mile. The acceleration run took 14.4 seconds and left the car traveling 98 mph at the end.

The "The Judge" option—available for the two-door hardtop and the convertible only—added a bigger engine (the 455-cid HO four-barrel V-8), Rally II wheels less trim rings, a hood air inlet, a T-handle shifter (with manual transmission), a rear deck lid airfoil, specific body side stripes, "The Judge" decals, Ram Air decals and a black texture in the grille.

Adding the option price to the base price of the hardtop gives you a total of $3,840 for "The Judge" of that body style. The very rare ragtop version (only 17 1971 GTO "The Judge" convertibles were actually built) went out the door for as little as $4,070 when no extras were added on. Actually, the price was about $10 higher for both body styles because the RPO 621 "ride & handling" shock absorber and spring package, which had a suggested retail price of $9.48, was a mandatory option.

It was tough to criticize the 1971 Trans Am. It looked great, had all the bells and whistles, and went like crazy.

PONTIAC

Jerry Heasley

1971 Firebird Trans Am

The 1971 Pontiac Firebird Trans Am Sport Coupe looks like an Italian-made Maserati sport coupe with a star spangled paint job and a "made in the USA" big-block V-8 under its air-scooped hood. "It probably wouldn't be a good idea to drive it to next week's meeting of the Sierra Club," wrote Paul Zazarine in *Car Review* (March 1986). "They still don't like Trans Ams."

The 1971 Pontiac Firebirds were very close to a direct carryover of the late-arriving 1970 1/2 models. The most obvious change between cars of the two years was the new high-back bucket seats used on the 1971 models. The lower-level models like the Firebird, Espirit and Formula also had new front fender air extractors and a few other detail changes, but the 1970 and 1971 Trans Ams looked virtually identical, except for the new bucket seat design.

The style No. 22887 Trans Am hardtop coupe had a base sticker price of $4,590. It weighed 3,578 lbs. and only 2,116 were made. Standard equipment in Trans Ams included: all mandatory safety features, vinyl bucket seats, rally gauges, a clock, a tachometer, a Formula steering wheel, an Endura front bumper, body-colored mirrors, honeycomb wheels, functional front fender air extractors, a rear deck lid spoiler,

a black textured grille with bright moldings, front and rear wheel opening flares, concealed wipers, identification badges, a performance dual exhaust system, a special air cleaner, a rear-facing cold-air hood intake with throttle control, a Power Flex fan, dual horns, front power disc brakes and rear drum brakes, F60-15 white-lettered tires, a close-ratio four-speed manual transmission with floor shift and—most important of all—a big 455 HO four-barrel V-8.

With a change to lower compression ratios in 1971 (thanks to future leaded gas requirements), Pontiac found it prudent to substitute the 455-cid V-8 for the 400-cid engine. The 455 HO version had a 4.15 x 4.21-inch bore and stroke and used a single four-barrel Rochester carburetor. With 8.4:1 compression, it developed 335 hp at 4800 rpm and 480 lbs.-ft. of torque at 3600 rpm. Trans Am buyers who preferred an automatic transmission could substitute a three-speed Turbo Hydra-Matic for the Hurst-shifted close-ratio four-speed manual gearbox at no charge.

According to one enthusiast magazine of the '70s, the 445-cid/335-hp Trans Am could move from 0-to-60 mph in just 5.92 seconds and did the quarter in 13.90 seconds at 103 mph.

PONTIAC

Phil Kunz

Like all the new cars of the day, the 1972 Firebird was affected by changing rules and insurance rates, but it was still a pretty nice all-around muscle car.

1972 Formula Firebird

The one-two punch of government regulation and restrictive liability insurance rates pounded the pony car market niche pretty hard in 1972. This was the very marketplace that Pontiac had aimed the sporty Firebird at. As a result of the pounding, sales got very slow by 1972 and PMD cut the prices on all Firebird models to try to lure customers into the showrooms.

With lower window stickers and increased customer traffic, dealers were hoping to increase Firebird sales, but a crippling United Auto Workers Union strike at GM's Norwood, Ohio, assembly plant (where F-cars were made) caused production lines to grind to a premature halt. As a result, only 5,249 Formula Firebirds were built for the 1972 model year.

The possibility of stopping production of the Firebird was raised for the first time this year. With the model's future in question, annual styling and equipment changes were kept to a minimum. There was a new honeycomb mesh grille insert, new interior trims, redesigned hubcaps and restyled wheel covers.

Formula Firebirds had the same equipment features as the base Firebird, plus a fiberglass hood with forward-mounted twin air scoops, a custom cushion steering wheel, body-color outside rearview mirrors, special Formula identification, a 1 1/8-in. front stabilizer bar, firm control shock absorbers, a dual exhaust system with chrome tailpipe extensions, a 1 1/8-in. front stabilizer bar, a 5/8-in. rear stabilizer bar and F70-14 tires. A power-flex fan was standard with the 400- and 455-cid engines.

There was only one 455-cid engine option in 1972. This power plant now used an 8.4:1 compression ratio and produced 300 hp at 4000 rpm and 415 lbs.-ft. of torque at 3200 rpm. It sold for $231 over the price of the base 400-cid/250-hp engine. The Formula 455 with a four-speed manual gearbox and a 3.42:1 rear axle could go from 0-to-60 mph in 7.6 seconds and did the quarter-mile in 15.5 seconds at 89.5 mph.

PONTIAC

Tom Glatch

The Grand Prix SSJ took its final bow in 1972. The '72s were identified by their "egg-crate" radiator grilles and triple-segment taillights.

1972 Grand Prix SSJ

I remember the ad that ran in *Motor Trend*. The Pontiac copywriters said it like this, "the 1972 Grand Prix lacks the 1909 Tudhope-McIntyre's runningboards, but has the same enduring styling, innovations, exceptional engineering and construction." The ads also said that these cars were built only in Pontiac, Michigan, and Lakewood, Georgia, "By a select group of dedicated men." They promoted the Grand Prix as if it was a capital "C" Classic approved by the Classic Car Club of America and designed by a custom coachbuilder.

Meanwhile, out in Warminster, Pennsylvania, George Hurst and his crew at Hurst Performance Products were virtually hand-building some high-performance versions of the personal-luxury car in very small numbers. It was the last year for the Hurst-made Grand Prix SSJ and, apparently, only a few dozen cars got the special conversion.

New Grand Prix styling elements for 1972 were modest. At the front end there was a new "egg-crate" radiator grille with multiple fins between its main bars. At the rear end of the car there were new triple-segment tail lamps at the rear. New full wheel covers of a finned design also appeared this year.

Returning to the product lineup once more was the SJ with twin body-color sport style outside rearview mirrors,

vinyl pin stripes, a luggage compartment light, door courtesy lamps, a rally gauge cluster and the 455-cid/300-hp V-8. This engine had a 4.15 x 4.21-inch bore and stroke. It used an 8.4:1 compression ratio and a single four-barrel carburetor. It developed peak horsepower at 4000 rpm.

All Grand Prixs had Turbo-Hydra-Matic transmissions and more than 90 percent of them had front bucket seats. With a carryover 118-inch wheelbase, the Grand Prix stretched 213.6 inches end to end.

The 1972 Hurst SSJ is very hard—in fact, near impossible—to find today. Hurst Performance Products Company had no record of producing any such cars, but some are claimed to exist. In their book *The Hurst Heritage*, Bob Lichty and Terry Boyce estimated that 60 examples of the 1972 Hurst SSJ were built. This estimate was based on an interview with a former company employee who recalled delivering about that many cars to Pontiac Motor Division for shipping.

According to the research conducted by Lichty and Boyce, Hurst SSJs were priced at about $5,132 in 1970, about $5,461 in 1971 and around $5,617 in 1972. During the last year of production they apparently came only with a dual-gate automatic transmission.

PONTIAC

Doug Mitchel

**As sad proof the muscle car era was winding to a close in 1972,
the GTO returned to being an option package for the LeMans.**

1972 LeMans Sports GTO

The clean air Gestapo and the insurance industry ganged up to bring an end to the muscle car market niche that Pontiac had started back in the middle of 1964. You may recall that ad man Jim Wangers had the basic concept and John Z. DeLorean helped him sneak it onto the market. It had to be done under cover, because the big-block 389-cid V-8 wasn't allowed in a mid-sized car according to rules laid down by The General (General Motors). The only way to get a muscle car to market was to make it the GTO option for the LeMans. It worked, and the GTO became the icon for all muscle car built later on.

As the muscle-car era drew near its close in 1972, it was perhaps somewhat fitting that the GTO returned to being an option for the LeMans. This change was part of a general de-emphasis of the GTO, which actually helped it survive a few more years. But even though the '72 GTO made the cut as an add-on package for the LeMans coupe, the GTO convertible bit the dust along with the eye-catching "The Judge" option.

In terms of appearance, the 1972 GTO was very 1971-like. It had a revised grille mesh and new front-fender air extractors. It was still characterized by an Endura front end and a special hood with dual air scoops opening at the front. However, this treatment was no longer exclusive to the "Goat." You could order it as an option for any LeMans or LeMans sport model with a V-8.

The base engine for the new GTO was the 400-cid with a 4.12 x 3.75-inch bore and stroke. It had an 8.2:1 compression ratio and a single four-barrel carburetor. This motor generated 250 hp at 4400 rpm and 325 lbs.-ft. of torque at 3200 rpm.

There were two 455-cid engine options, both with a 4.15 x 4.21-inch bore and stroke. The first had a single four-barrel carburetor and an 8.2:1 compression ration and cranked out 250 hp at 3700 rpm and 325 lbs.-ft. of torque at 2400 rpm. The most powerful option was the 455 HO, which had an 8.4:1 compression ratio and a four-barrel. It was good for 300 hp at 4000 rpm and 415 lbs.-ft. of torque at 3200 rpm.

A 1972 GTO hardtop with the 455 HP V-8 was base priced at about $2,968 and weighed 3,885 lbs. It carried 13 lbs. per horsepower and its performance really suffered for it. It required 7.1 seconds to scoot from 0-to-60 mph and the quarter-mile took 15.4 seconds. No wonder GTO orders dropped to only 5,807.

Not many Trans Ams were built in 1972, making them very nice collector trophies today.

PONTIAC

1972 Firebird Trans Am

Late in model year 1971, rumors were heard circulating around the auto industry in Detroit that the Pontiac Firebird and Chevrolet Camaro were going to disappear from the General Motors product lineup. "The General" was very close to dropping both models because sales were down and it was getting expensive to build them.

In the end, this did not happen because a number of enthusiasts who worked for Pontiac Motor Division fought very hard to keep both of the models alive. As it turned out, both cars turned out to be big successes. So in the long run, the company was just as glad as the "Young Turks" at PMD that the kill order was rescinded.

Still, PMD came very close to dropping the Firebird and as a result, very few styling changes were made for the model year. The 1972 Trans Am looked virtually identical to the 1971 model—which certainly wasn't a "bad" thing. It takes a real expert to tell the cars of the two model years apart from each other.

For 1972, the No. 22887 Trans Am hardtop coupe had a lower base sticker price of $4,255. It weighed a little less,

too—3,564 lbs. Production was extremely low, with only 1,286 cars leaving the factory. If you want to collect Trans Ams and you like the 1970-1972 "Maseratiacs," the '72 is definitely a vintage to seek.

Standard equipment in Trans Ams included: all mandatory safety features, vinyl bucket seats, rally gauges, a clock, a tachometer, a Formula steering wheel, an Endura front bumper, body-colored mirrors, honeycomb wheels, functional front-fender air extractors, a rear deck lid spoiler, a black textured grille with bright moldings, front and rear wheel opening flares, concealed wipers, identification badges, a performance dual-exhaust system, a special air cleaner, a rear-facing cold-air hood intake with throttle control, a Power Flex fan, dual horns, front power disc brakes and rear drum brakes, F60-15 white-lettered tires and a close-ratio four-speed manual transmission with floor shift.

Only one V-8 engine was used in 1972 Trans Ams. It was the 455-cid HO version with the 4.15 x 4.21-inch bore and stroke.

PONTIAC

Phil Kunz

Adding the Super-Duty 455 to the Formula Firebird created a throwback muscle car that was tough to beat in 1973, but only 43 cars left the factory with the top-shelf engine.

1973 Formula SD 455

While many enthusiasts prefer the sano-looking '70-'71 versions of the Gen II Firebird, it was the '73-and-up models with all the bells and whistles that sent the sales charts into the black. Those who drove these cars thought they were buying a true sedan racer, but those who wanted the real McCoy added the required sizzle by popping the SD 455 V-8 below the Formula's double-scooped hood. As Paul Zazarine once pointed out in *Muscle Car Review*: "When every other maker had forgotten about muscle cars, Pontiac introduced the '73 455 Super-Duty."

In the early 1970s, the Formula was Pontiac's street racing version of the Firebird. As a result of this model's image and reputation, the Formula Firebird was a great platform for the hottest options available from Pontiac Motor Division. This was obvious and the hottest engine was what Pontiac decided to make available under the Formula model's hood. It wasn't a cheap option, but for those who wanted to keep the muscle car magic going, it was one of the few choices left.

The SD 455 mill was a very special big-block V-8. This awesome engine had actually been a spin-off of Pontiac's small-block racing program of 1970. PMD had put a lot of effort into developing a powerful small-displacement motor that would be legal under Sports Car Club of America sedan racing formulas, which had a 305 cubic inch limit. Only a few of these engines were sold on an in the crate basis. However,

much of the racing technology embodied in them was then transferred to the RPO LS2 455-cid V-8.

The optional super-duty engine was the same one used in Trans Ams. All SD 455 V-8s featured a special block with reinforced webbing, large forged-steel connecting rods, special aluminum pistons, a heavy-duty oiling system, a high-lift camshaft, four-bolt main bearing caps, a special intake manifold, a dual exhaust system and upgraded valve train components. It had an 8.4:1 compression ratio and 310-hp rating.

A dual-scoop fiberglass hood characterized the third-step-up Formula Firebird, which came in Formula 350 (150 hp), Formula 400 (230 hp) and Formula 455 (250 hp) editions. The front fenders carried Formula lettering behind a Firebird emblem and engine call-out badge. Formulas also sported a new black-textured grille, high-rate rear springs and other high-performance equipment. A dual exhaust system was standard on all Formula models. Radial tires were a new option.

The Formula 350 hardtop coupe had a base price of $3,276. Late in the 1973 model year, the SD 455 was offered as a $675 option for the Formula. A total of 10,166 Formulas were made in 1973, but only 43 of those cars were actually sold with the ultra-high-performance engine.

The 1973 GTO was a much different car than its mid-60s ancestors, but for its vintage it was a nice performer, especially with the optional 400-cid/230-hp V-8.

1973 LeMans GTO

The 1973 GTO kit is a muscle car package of great interest to car collectors. Only 4,806 LeMans or LeMans Sport Colonnade coupes left the Pontiac factory with this option. The GTO goodies added approximately $368 to the base prices of the two LeMans models.

For many years, the 1973 GTOs were virtually ignored by purist muscle car collectors. Now, their rarity and high-performance characteristics, coupled with a dwindling supply of early GTOs in general, are beginning to change their collector car status.

The code 341 GTO option included a standard 400-cid V-8 engine with a four-barrel carburetor, a blacked-out grille, dual NASA-type air scoops in a special hood, fat tires, a dual exhaust system, a three-speed manual transmission with a floor-mounted gear shifter, super-firm shock absorbers, a rear sway bar, "baby moon" hubcaps, 15 x 7-inch wheels and specific body striping.

The base 400-cid Pontiac V-8 had an 8.0:1 compression ratio. It developed 230 net horsepower at 4400 rpm and 325 lbs.-ft. of torque at 3200 rpm. Also available was an optional 455-cid four-barrel V-8 with an 8.0:1 compression ratio. This engine developed 250 net horsepower at 4000 rpm and its advertised torque rating was 370 lbs.-ft. at 2800 rpm.

Pontiac sales catalogs also listed the 455 Super-Duty V-8 as a GTO option in 1973. However, this engine was only installed in a handful of pre-production units. Last minute management decisions prevented it from being installed in assembly line cars. But one of these SD 455 GTOs showed up at Pontiac's long-lead press conference in the summer of 1972. It was very powerful and amazingly fast. Too bad the Super-Duty option was later canceled.

According to factory production totals, only 544 cars that left the assembly line with the GTO option were sold with the regular 455 V-8 under the hood. This batch included 25 LeMans two-door Colonnade coupes and 519 LeMans Colonnade two-door hardtops. All had of these cars had Turbo-Hydra-Matic transmission.

According to experts, with all things considered, the 400-cid/230-net horsepower GTO engine was the best choice for all-around performance. GTOs with the 400-cid V-8 came standard with a 3.42:1 ratio rear axle. Optional axle ratios were 3.08:1 and 3.23:1. When the 455-cid V-8 was added, the standard ratio was 3.08:1 with air conditioning and 3.23:1 without it. The 3.08:1 axle was also optional in 455-powered cars without air.

PONTIAC

Jerry Heasley

The 250-horse 455 Super-Duty mill kept the mildly redesigned Trans Am at the head of the dwindling muscle car field in 1973.

1973 Trans Am

During the 1960s, Pontiac Motor Division had made great strides in popularity and rose to the rank of third best selling American car brand. To a large degree, its success was built upon its image as General Motors' high-performance division. When the muscle car market began to evaporate in the mid-1970s, PMD realized that it was going to be a big loser unless it did something to keep its performance car image alive.

Firebirds for 1973 had new exterior colors, redesigned interiors, new hubcaps and a longer list of optional equipment. The bumpers on the F-cars were redesigned to meet new federal crashworthiness standards. This gave the cars a slightly longer overall length, which in turn resulted in the new Firebird grille being slightly less recessed than the 1970-1972 design. The grille insert had an "egg-crate" pattern.

Like other Trans Ams that came before it, the 1973 model had special front fender air extractors, a rear deck lid spoiler, body flares and air inlet openings. The hood scoops were now sealed and no longer functional. A new feature was a large hood decal showing the American Indian Firebird icon that the base car was named for. Enthusiasts soon dubbed this graphic the "screaming chicken" and most Trans Ams displayed it. On 1973 models, the flaming bird was always

black in color, but the hue of the background varied. The background was Orange on Red cars, Black on White cars and Light Green on dark Brewster Green Trans Ams.

The base engine used in the Trans Am was a big-block 455-cid V-8 with a single four-barrel carburetor. With an 8.0:1 compression ratio, it produced 250 net horsepower. Pontiac built 4,550 cars with this engine and 1,420 of them had a manual gear box. For real muscle, buyers could add a 455-cid super-duty engine derived from Pontiac's experience in Trans-Am racing. The SD 455 V-8 featured a special engine block with reinforced webbing, large forged-steel connecting rods, special aluminum pistons, a heavy-duty oiling system, a high-lift camshaft, four-bolt main bearing caps, a special intake manifold, a dual exhaust system and upgraded valve train components. It had an 8.4:1 compression ratio and cranked out 310 hp.

The SD 455 Trans tested by *Hot Rod* magazine turned the quarter-mile in 13.54 seconds at 104.29 mph. Going from 0-to-60 mph took all of 7.3 seconds. *Car and Driver* also tested an SD 455 and registered a 13.75-second quarter-mile at 103.56 mph. The SD 455 engine designation appeared on the side of the hood scoop on these cars. Only 252 SD 455 Trans Ams were built and 72 had stick shifts.

PONTIAC

Tom Glatch

Only 48 Formula Firebirds went out the door with 290-hp 455 Super-Duty V-8s under the hood.
The less-muscular versions had a 250-horse 455 V-8, or an even milder 350-cid two-barrel.

1974 Formula Firebird

The 1974 Pontiacs were introduced at showroom level on September 20, 1973. This was a time in which Detroit was struggling to meet new government safety and emissions regulations that came with a stiff price tag. By the time the engineers in the smog lab made the cars "legal," there was little leftover to pay for styling alterations.

The 1974 model U 87 Formula Firebird was basically the same as its '73 counterpart, but Pontiac decided it had to do something to differentiate the two cars. Like a book publisher looking for that hot-selling cover design, PMD worked out a new front-end treatment that gave quite a different look to Firebirds. Also like a book cover, not everyone liked the results.

Inspired more or less by the Vega's early popularity, this rear-slanting "shovel nose" grille cap was made of the same Endura rubber material that Pontiac had pioneered in the late 1960s. It had an "electric shaver" style insert that was easy to spot. The Firebird's rear end styling was also slightly revised.

Pontiac dealers had to send the factory $3,092.75 to get a Formula into their showroom. They could then hope to sell the car for its suggested retail price of $3,614.20. In many cases, with demand for muscle cars on the wane, the dealer had to sweeten the deal to get a buyer to plunk down some of his or her hard-earned cash.

Basic Firebird equipment included bucket seats, narrow rocker panel moldings, a deluxe two-spoke steering wheel, E78-14 black sidewall tires and a 250-cid inline six-cylinder engine. The Formula model option also included a custom cushion steering wheel, hubcaps, a fiberglass hood with dual air scoops, dual outside rearview mirrors, a special heavy-duty suspension, a black textured grille, F70-14 tires, dual exhausts and a 350-cid V-8 with a two-barrel carburetor. Automatic transmission was required on cars sold in California.

There were two 455-cid V-8s available in 1974 Formula Firebirds. The L75 version had a four-barrel carburetor with dual exhausts. It produced 250 nhp at 4000 rpm and 330 lbs.-ft. of torque at 2400 rpm. Its price was $154 and the M40 Turbo Hydra-Matic transmission was mandatory. The 455-cid Super-Duty V-8 was a bit more expensive in Formulas than in Trans Ams. It cost $675 extra. The 1974 version was rated for 290 nhp at 4000 rpm and 395 lbs.-ft. of toque at 3200 rpm. Only 58 Formulas were built with this engine during the 1974 model run.

PONTIAC

Phil Kunz

Pontiac kept the GTO badge alive with its Ventura-based rendition of the car in 1974, but the Goat bought the farm at the end of the model year.

1974 Pontiac Ventura GTO

The problem with the "last" GTO (at least until modern times) was that the world wasn't ready for it. For the most part, the GTO had been a serious-looking muscle car for most of its existence. At least until the "Judge" package came along in mid-1969, most GTOs were "adult-looking" machines with subdued colors, a cleanliness of line and a mature use of chrome tinsel. Then came the Ventura-based '74 model. It was a different breed of tiger!

Somehow you could tell that this car was made for youngsters, rather than the young at heart. It was small. It looked like a Nova with a Pontiac nose. GTO goodies like the fog lights and hood scoop had more of an add-on look than an integrated design flavor. Don't get me wrong, the car was a very neat package, it just didn't have a lot of appeal to the traditional GTO buyer.

Had this little GTO come out in the days of DeLorean and Wangers, it probably would have gone places. The "Young Turks" at Pontiac were brassy enough to stuff it with countless cubes when the GM big wigs weren't looking. Unfortunately, by 1974, the best the engineering staff could do was to stuff in the J-code 350-cid V-8. It wasn't enough!

The people most likely to buy a "Goat" remembered the GTO as major player in the 1960s muscle car era. They knew the legend of how it had bowed as an under-the-table high-powered option for the mid-size '64 Tempest. They also grasped the reality that by the early 1970s, it had become a different car.

For 1974, the GTO name labeled a $195 sports package for the '74 Ventura two-door sedan. This 111-inch wheelbase car was one of seven Chevy Nova clones. As mentioned above, Pontiac's J-code 350-cid was included in the option. This 165-net horsepower V-8 breathed through an open-at-the-rear "shaker" hood scoop. A three-speed manual transmission with a floor-mounted gear shifter was standard. Buyers could add a four-speed manual transmission for $207 over the GTO's base price of $3,212.

The little GTO's other mechanical systems were also fairly adept. The beefy suspension featured front and rear stabilizer bars, heavy-duty shock absorbers, heavy-duty springs, 6-inch-wide Rally II wheels with no extraneous trim, a 3.08:1 rear axle and E70-14 tires, all as standard equipment. A radial-tuned suspension cost extra.

For the first time, the standard GTO interior included a bench seat. Options ranged all the way up to all-Morrokide front bucket seats and a center console.

While it was different, the 1974 GTO was not a bad car and customers seemed to agree somewhat. A total of 7,058 were built. While that doesn't sound like the "good old days" it was an approximate 75 percent increase in production over the Lemans-based 1973 GTO. However, it was not enough to warrant another try in 1975.

Today the 1974 GTO is easily the most valuable of the Ventura compacts from Pontiac, but its value is a far cry from the five-digit prices that the early GTOs generate in the collectors' marketplace.

The 1974 Trans Am Super-Duty 455 was faster than the
Corvette and certainly one of the hottest things on the road.

PONTIAC

Jerry Heasley

1974 Pontiac Trans Am SD 455

It was all over but the church service! Fortunately, no one told Pontiac Motor Division that "the day the muscle car music died" had arrived. The company didn't know it didn't have a prayer of keeping the hot-as-a-pistol SD 455 around much longer. In the November 1985 issue of *Car Review*, Jerry Heasley interviewed a big-time muscle car collector named Dan Werner. "The '74s with the big HO and SD engines kept the muscle car era going another year," Werner told our ace photographer.

Extensive front-end styling revisions and an improvement in showroom sales made headlines in the Firebird niche of the American muscle car marketplace in 1974. The base Firebird ($2,895), the fancier Espirit ($3,295), the Formula Firebird street machine ($3,276) and the boy-racer Trans Am ($4,204) models were carried over from 1973. The SD 455 engine option also remained in limited availability for the Formula Firebird and Trans Am models.

The new front end created by well-known Pontiac designer John Schinella introduced an integrated "soft" bumper treatment, which was repeated at the rear of the F-cars. The front of all Firebirds carried a new, slanting "shovel-nose" grille cap with an "electric shaver" grille insert made

up of slanting, vertical blades. Black rubber bumper-face bars were featured. An air-scoop-like front valance panel contributed to a more massive overall look. Slimmer, wider front parking lamps without chrome protective grids were used. They carried textured, amber-colored lenses.

The Trans Am model option included a Formula steering wheel, rally gauges with a clock and a dash panel tachometer, a swirl-finish dash panel trim plate, a full-width rear deck lid spoiler, power steering, power front disc/rear drum brakes, a limited-slip differential, wheel opening air deflectors, front-fender air extractors, a dual exhaust system with chrome extensions, Rally II wheels with bright trim rings, a special heavy-duty suspension, dual outside rear view sports mirrors, F60-15 white-letter tires, a four-speed manual gearbox and a 400-cid/225-hp V-8.

The regular 455-cid/215-hp V-8 was $55 above the price of the 400-cid engine and the SD 455 V-8 was $578 extra. The SD 455 was installed in 212 Trans Ams with four-speed manual gearboxes and 731 with automatic transmission. Although it was relatively rare, the engine was popular with the editors of enthusiast magazines, who said it made the Firebird the hottest car of the year and slightly faster than the Corvette!

Tom Glatch

The Can Am was short-lived, but it was a flashy car that definitely got noticed while it was around.

1977 Can Am

Can Ams were constructed on an off-line basis by a specialty car company named Motortown Corp. The overall design was taken from a Pontiac factory concept car, exhibited in 1975. The show car was called the All-American Grand Am. Motortown started with a specifically equipped Lemans sport coupe and handled the conversion process.

The Can Ams had a flamboyant and competition-like appearance. Just one body style—the Colonnade coupe—was available with Can Am features. The package constituted a model option, rather than a separate series. It was introduced as a midyear addition to the line and was available for only a few months. This makes the Can Am a rare find.

Some ingredients of the Can Am option package were the same as Grand Am equipment, such as: a Grand Prix instrument cluster and clock, power front disc brakes, variable-ratio power steering, front and rear stabilizer bars, twin body-color sport mirrors, the RTS handling package, GR70-15 steel-belted radial tires, rubber bumper strips and a 400-cid V-8.

The 400-cid V-8 engine was not the two-barrel version used for base Grand Ams. Instead, the Trans Am's "T/A 6.6-liter" four-barrel V-8 was used. It was rated at 200 nhp. The Can Am had about the same 10-second 0-to-60 time as a 1975 midsized Pontiac with the 455-cid V-8.

Can Ams that were sold in California and in high-altitude counties used a different 403-cid 6.6-liter V-8 built by Oldsmobile.

Other elements of the $1,589 Can Am model-option included: Cameo White body paint, a blacked-out grille assembly, black-finished rocker panel moldings and window moldings, special identification badges and a "shaker" style hood scoop. Also included were a space-saver spare, body-color Rally II wheels, a black lower-body side with accent striping and Turbo Hydra-Matic transmission (a manual gearbox was not available).

The graphics package for the Can Am was really an eye catcher. It used fade-away lettering and stripes with an orange base, red lower accents and yellow upper accents. The model name appeared in these colors on the front fenders behind the wheel openings and on the right-hand side of the deck lid. Similar stripes were used along the upper belt line's forward section, on the rear spoiler, on the mirrors, on the hood scoop and front spoiler and around the rear license recess. Engine call-outs in the same colors decorated the shaker hood scoop.

As the story goes, just when the production process was getting smoothed out, a machine that stamped out the special rear spoiler broke down. Motortown was unable to solve the problem cost effectively and, therefore, decided to cancel the model option after 1,130 cars had been assembled.

PONTIAC

Pontiac's search for a slipprier race car produced the 2+2 Aerocoupe.

1986 1/2 Grand Prix 2+2 Aerocoupe

Pontiac, like Chevrolet, had a tough time beating Ford Thunderbirds in general and Bill Elliott in particular in NASCAR Winston Cup stock car racing during 1985. In fact, Pontiac didn't win a single Winston Cup event that year. One of the reasons for this was unfavorable aerodynamics caused by the brick-like frontal design and nearly vertical rear window of the Pontiac Grand Prix, which was the model raced.

While the Chevrolet Monte Carlo SS had a sleek nose and only needed a rear window design modification, Pontiac had to make changes front and rear in order to make its package "slipperier." The resulting high-performance model arrived on January 3, 1986, when the Pontiac 2+2 was announced. Even though the Grand Prix name was absent from early publicity, the 2+2 equipment was an option package (RPO Y97) for the Grand Prix.

The 2+2 option included a rounded front fascia that was similar to that of the Monte Carlo SS, but not quite as sleek, a bubble-back rear window, a smaller-than-stock fiberglass deck lid with a spoiler, styled steel wheels, silver paint with medium gray lower trim and two-tone red accent striping around the perimeter. A gray interior was featured.

Mechanically, the LG4 305-cid Chevy small-block V-8 was rated at 165 hp, up 15 from the regular 305 in the Grand Prix. A four-speed automatic overdrive transmission and 3.08:1 rear end gearing kept things on the calm side. Front and rear stabilizer bars, stronger shocks and 215/65R15 Goodyear Eagle GT tires firmed up the ride and handling.

Not cheap, the $17,800 2+2 came loaded with air conditioning, AM/FM/cassette radio, cruise control, power locks and windows and full tinted glass. Sales to the public started in early March and except in the Southeast, the 2+2 was a slow mover. Only 200 are believed to have been built. A 1987 2+2 was announced at the start of the model year, but was never put into production, making the 1986-1/2 models rare indeed.

Pontiac racers didn't have to worry about production schedules as for $1,512.50, Pontiac Motorsports offered the 2+2 Race Body Pac (PN 100449830), which contained all the 2+2 pieces. The parts were also available to racers individually. Unfortunately, the 2+2 didn't prove all that successful on the track with only two wins in 1986-1987. Most NASCAR Winston Cup Pontiac competitors switched to the 1988 Grand Prix front-wheel-drive body for 1988.

PONTIAC

The Trans Am was a dressed-up sports car that had a dose of throwback performance in 1987.

1987 Trans Am/GTA

Starting with cars built to 1987 model specifications, Pontiac began offering Firebird buyers more model options, more aerodynamic styling and more performance. The release of a powerful new 5.7-liter (350-hp) V-8 with Tuned Port Injection (TPI) brought the Trans Am and other Firebird models back into the "muscle car" category.

The Trans Am version of the Firebird represented Pontiac's "driving excitement" car. It included a body aero package, an aero rear deck spoiler, "bird" decals, fog lamps, hood air extractors, hood louvers, neutral-density smooth contour taillights, deep-dish 15 x 7-inch Gold or Silver Hi-Tech Turbo Cast wheels and added gauges.

The Trans Am power train offerings started with a base 165-hp V-8 and included a 5.0-liter TPI V-8 featuring a high-output cam good for 206 hp and 285 lbs.-ft. of torque. Of course, if you wanted a muscle machine, the 5.7-liter TPI engine was a must. It featured roller valve lifters, a hardened steel camshaft, fast-burn combustion chambers, a remote mounted coil and dual cooling fans. Essentially a slightly modified Corvette engine, the 5.7-liter TPI V-8 produced 210 hp and 315 lbs.-ft. of torque.

Third-generation Firebirds had not had this kind of power in years. The 1982 model with the 5.0-liter V-8 had been tested for 9.2-second 0-to-60 mph runs and 17-second quarter-miles at 80.5 mph. This was great performance in context of the time, but it was not really "muscular" go power. By 1986, the performance figures had been slightly improved to an 8.4-second 0-to-60 time and a 15.2-second quarter-mile. However, with the 5.7-liter TPI motor, *High Performance Pontiac* magazine reported a 0-to-60 time of 6.2 seconds and a 14.2-second quarter-mile at 94 mph.

The GTA package was an option for the Trans Am and came in a choice of two content levels: W61 at $1,701 and W63 at $1,958. It was primarily a luxury performance option including monochromatic exterior finish, a dressed-up interior, fancier wheels, a WS6 suspension upgrade, a 3.27:1 limited-slip rear axle and the 5.7-liter V-8 as standard equipment. So it gave you a pre-packaged muscle Trans Am, but you could make the regular Trans Am just as fast by selecting all the right options from the extra-cot equipment list.

Pontiac Motor Division built a grand total of 88,623 Firebirds in the 1987 model year. About half of them were Trans Ams or GTAs.

Jerry Heasley

The third-generation Firebird continued to evolve and was one of the hottest cars around with the 225-hp 5.7-liter TPI motor as motivation.

1988 Formula Firebird

For 1988, Pontiac enhanced the performance strengths that had been given to the 1987 Firebirds. The basic offerings remained the same, but each model or model-option gained some power train, trim and equipment features that underlined its role in the product mix.

After its well-received revival as an option package in 1987, the Formula package returned.

Formulas had new 16 x 8 in. High-Tech Turbo cast-aluminum wheels and a new 5.0-liter EFI/TBI V-8 engine that was also standard in the Trans Am. The switch from a four-barrel carburetor to a throttle-body injection system added five additional hp. The high-output 5.0-liter EFI/TPI V-8 was available at extra cost. With air-induction improvements, this motor delivered 190 hp with a four-speed automatic transmission and 215 hp with a five-speed manual transmission. Once again, the 225-hp 5.7-liter automatic-only V-8 was a must for muscle-car mavens.

Formula Firebirds got new colors, revised interior trim and a different speedometer. All cars with TPI engines now came with full-gauge analog clusters and a 140-mph speedometer. Formula Firebirds also featured a body-color aero rear deck lid spoiler, a dome hood, Formula graphics and other goodies.

The Formula's role in the product mix was to offer the acceleration and handling characteristics of the Trans Am and the GTA at a more attractive base price of $11,999, which represented a substantial savings to the buyer.

In 1987, Carroll Supercharging Co., of Wyckoff, New Jersey, advertised an aftermarket conversion called the VHO Formula in 1987. It added a belt-driven Paxton supercharger to the Formula 350. The blower provided a 5-psi pressure-boost raising output to 400 hp at 2500 rpm and torque to 475 lbs.-ft. at 4000 rpm. *High Performance Pontiac* magazine tested the VHO Formula 350 and found that it did 0-to-60 mph in 6 seconds and the quarter-mile in 13 seconds. The Carroll supercharging package retailed for $8,500. The conversion voided the Pontiac factory warranty, but engineer Greg Carroll said he would guarantee the VHO Formula 350 for 12 months or 12,000 miles. Very few of these cars were built.

PONTIAC

The TPI V-8 delivered 235 horsepower and was standard on the GTA and optional on the Trans Am for 1989.
The big motor gave the sleek high-end Pontiacs a great blend of power and looks.

1989 Trans Am/GTA

The 1989 Pontiac Trans Am cost $15,999 and weighed 3,337 lbs. That compared to a sticker price of $12,399 for the 3,300-lb. base Firebird. Even that base Trans Am had a few GTA-like extras. Engine choices were the same for both the Formula and the Trans Am as far as V-8s were concerned (the base model was also available with a V-6).

A 5.0-liter (305-cubic inch) TBI engine with 170 hp was the standard V-8 in both the Trans Am and Formula and was available in the base model. A 5.0-liter 190-hp TPI V-8 was available in Firebirds and Formulas and could be had in the GTA as a delete option. The 5.7-liter "Corvette" TPI V-8 was standard in the GTA and optional in Formulas and TransAms with automatic transmission. It had a 4.00 x 3.48-inch bore and stroke and a 9.3:1 compression ratio. This engine generated 235 hp at 4400 rpm and 330 lbs.-ft. of torque at 3200 rpm. A limited-slip differential was standard with the 5.7-liter V-8.

Added equipment on all Trans Ams and GTAs included body skirting, an aero fascia, hood air extractors, front fender air extractors, hood louvers, fog lamps and Soft-Ray tinted glass. Also standard was the F41 heavy-duty suspension with a 34-mm front anti-roll bar, a 23-mm rear anti-roll bar and recalibrated spring and shock absorber rates. Firestone Firehawk GTX tires were mounted on 15 x 7-inch cast-aluminum wheels.

With its $20,339 price tag, the 5.7-liter GTA was Pontiac's muscle car of the year. Finally released for this model was an optional new notchback hatch rear window. This was designed to provide a more individual profile, as well as a cooler interior. With 330 lbs.-ft. of torque, the big-engined 1989 GTA was 0.2 to 0.3 seconds faster in the 0-to-60-mph sprint than ever before.

New deflected-disc valving for the gas shocks and struts gave the GTA's WS6 performance suspension a more comfortable ride. It had 36mm front and 24mm rear anti-roll bars, P245/50ZR16 Goodyear tires and lightweight 16 x 8-inch cross-lace aluminum wheels.

The 1989 1/2 Indy Pace Cars carried turbo V-6s that churned out
250 horses. These were fabulous cars and definite collector gems.

1989 1/2 Trans Am Indy 500 Pace Car

Back in 1989, my friend Jane Schuman and I wangled a brief spin in one of the three actual Indy Pace Cars for that year. The car had the strobes and all the track equipment, plus the already hot factory-issued Turbo V-6 package. The cars went like V-6 jets and it was obvious that this was a very special Trans Am. "It might be a good idea to get in the Turbo Trans Am line now," *Road & Track* recommended in its January '89 issue.

Sometimes a new car is an instant collectible. No experts are needed to debate its pros and cons or its future value. Such was the case with the 1989 1/2 20th Anniversary Firebird Trans Am. It had all the bases covered. Trans Ams have general collector value and the limited-production 20th Anniversary Edition was a plus, but topping this off was its Indy 500 Official Pace Car status.

For these reasons alone, the 20th Anniversary Trans Am is worthy of admiration, but the icing on the cake is its standard 231-cid/250-nhp Buick turbo V-6—the same V-6 used in the very hot 1987 Buick Regal Grand National.

Technically, the 20th Anniversary model was an option on the Trans Am GTA, which itself was a $4,340 option on the $15,999 Trans Am. Prices on the 20th Anniversary Indy 500 edition often passed $30,000. Pontiac said it would build only 1,500 copies.

Visuals included monotone white paint with a camel interior. There was a 20th Anniversary emblem on the nose, a similar emblem on each sail panel plus Turbo Trans Am and Indianapolis Motor Speedway emblems on the front fenders. Cars used at the speedway had hatch roofs, but this extra was optional on production models.

Road and Track tested a 20th Anniversary Trans Am Indy 500 Pace Car and found it could do 0-to-60 mph in 5.3 seconds and 0-to-100 in 13.9 seconds.

Three actual Pace Cars were outfitted with strobe lights and other special equipment by Dave Doern of Chicago, Illinois. They had been driven to his shop from different points and one car was actually wrecked by a PR man, who had it fixed on the hush-hush. After the strobes were added, the cars went to Indy. Bobby Unser drove one of them on the Indy 500 pace laps. The others were backups. Emerson Fittipaldi took one home after his win.

PONTIAC

Tom Glatch

Pontiac and SLP Engineering built only a handful of the 1992 Firehawks, which were blazing fast and cost nearly $50,000.

1992 Formula SLP Firehawk

In 1992, Pontiac Motor Division and SLP Engineering teamed up to make the hot new Formula Firehawk available through the factory dealer network as a special 1992 Firebird model-option. Representatives of Pontiac and SLP Engineering exhibited one of these cars at the Boston "World of Wheels" show during the first week of January 1992. They explained that Firehawks would be offered in "street" and "competition" versions. The street version produced 350 hp at 5500 rpm and 390 lbs.-ft. of torque at 4400 rpm.

The factory-built Formula Firebird that served as the basis for SLP's Firehawk carried the 5.0-liter TPI V-8 and a four-speed automatic transmission (both upgraded to 1LE specs) plus air conditioning. Externally, the main difference from a stock Formula model was the use of five-spoke aluminum alloy wheels and a Firehawk decal on the right-hand side of the rear fascia.

The factory Formula had a $19,242 base price and the Firehawk street package was $20,753 for a total delivered price of $39,995. The Firehawk Competition package was $9,905 additional, raising the total bill to $49,990.

When a Firehawk was ordered, Pontiac shipped a new Formula from its Van Nuys, California, factory to SLP Engineering in Toms River, New Jersey. The aftermarket company then extracted the entire drive train and added a Corvette ZF six-speed gearbox with computer-aide gear selection (CAGS), a Dana 44 rear axle with 3.54:1 gears, a shortened input shaft and a 16-lb. flywheel. A heavy-duty block fitted with four-bolt mains then got a forged steel crank, Gen II cast pistons, Ed Pink Racing con rods and a hydraulic roller cam. Bolted to this were aluminum heads with 2-inch intake and 1.56-inch stainless-steel exhaust valves.

A special downdraft port-injection manifold was also employed. Designed by Ray Falconer, it featured 11 1/2-inch runners, a 52-mm throttle body, high-flow dual filter system

and stainless-steel exhaust headers and exhaust pipes with dual catalytic converters.

Firehawk suspension modifications included revised spring rates, a lowered ride height, new struts, new rear shocks, larger front and rear anti-roll bars, special bushings and Corvette 11.85-inch disc brakes. Firestone 275/40ZR17 Firehawk tires were mounted on the 17 x 9.5-inch Ronal wheels. Recaro seats were extra for $995 and the center console inside the cars was modified to give more space for shift throws.

The competition version of the Firehawk included the Recaro seats as standard equipment, plus 13-inch Brembo vented disc brakes with four-piston calipers, a roll cage and an aluminum hood. The rear seat was also left out.

High Performance Pontiac magazine reported that only 250 copies of what it called the "Quickest Street Pontiac Ever" were going to be made. The magazine found that its test car did 0-to-60 mph in 4.6 seconds and covered the quarter-mile in 13.20 seconds at 107 mph.

SLP Engineering targeted production of five cars per week starting in July 1991, but only produced actual cars on a build-to-order basis. A preproduction version of the Competition Firehawk was entered in the Bridgestone Petenza Supercar Series at Lime Rock Race Course on May 27, 1991. It took third place and the company soon had orders for three or four additional competition models.

The SLP kit was also available through GM Service Parts Organization, but it was not shown in sales literature because there was some initial uncertainty about its 1992 EPA certification. In the end, SLP Engineering wound up building only 25 street versions, at least one of which was a Trans Am convertible with serial No. 27. That could raise questions in the future, but the reason for the high number was that cars 18 and 25 were ordered but never built.

The Firebird family for 1994: (clockwise from left) Trans Am, base coupe, Formula and GTA.

1994 Trans Am

Pontiac's theme for its Firebird 1994 lineup could have been the "return of the ragtop." Each of its series—including Trans Am—had its 1993 coupe-only offering bolstered with the addition of a convertible. The Trans Am convertible was part of its GT series, while the coupe version was offered both as a Trans Am and a Trans Am GT. New features for the Trans Am included a new Dark Aqua Metallic exterior color, flood-lit interior door switches, visor straps, a Delco 2001 Series radio, a compact disc player (without graphic equalizer), a 5.7-liter SFI V-8, a Mass Air Flow Control System, a four-speed electronically-controlled automatic transmission, driver-selectable automatic transmission controls, a six-speed manual transmission with a 1-4 gear skip shift feature, a 3.42:1 axle ratio, a traction-control system (V-8 automatic only) and two-component clearcoat paint.

Pontiac said the 1994 Trans Am had "the power to change minds" and suggested that it represented a mature approach to power, because its performance capabilities were "properly managed." It was much the same as the Formula, except for its speed-rated, high-performance P245/50ZR16 Goodyear Eagle GSC tires.

Externally, the "TA" gained a new, uniquely styled front end without Pontiac's traditional twin-air-slot grille. Instead, the nose had a blunter look, broken by round, sunken running lights on each side of center. The Trans Am name appeared on the body sides, and between the tail lamps (along with a

"screaming-chicken" emblem).

A new Trans Am GT was added to the top of the Trans Am lineup. It featured body-color side moldings as standard equipment, plus a special GT spoiler (it looked more like an air foil than the other spoiler). Also standard on this car was an electric rear-window defogger, a remote keyless-entry system, rear carpet mats, a Delco 2001 Series sound system, a four-way manual driver's seat, and a leather-wrapped steering wheel, shift knob and parking-brake handle.

On Feb. 4, 1994, at the Chicago Auto Show, PMD announced that it was introducing a Firebird convertible in the spring. A press kit indicated that the ragtop would be available "on Firebird, Formula and Trans Am models," but only the Trans AM GT came in the open-air-driving style.

All convertibles featured a flush-folding power top that could be stored beneath an easily assembled three-piece tonneau cover. They included a glass rear window and electric rear-window defogger. "These Firebird convertibles weren't an afterthought," revealed Pontiac chief engineer Byron Warner. Warner said that 13 structural parts were added to the Firebird, and front cross member structural stiffness was increased. Structural adhesive was also utilized on 15 key areas, such as the cowl, pillar and rocker reinforcements. Convertibles were built on the St. Therese assembly line, to ensure high quality. Warner said that ragtop drivers "will think they're driving one of our coupes when the top is up."

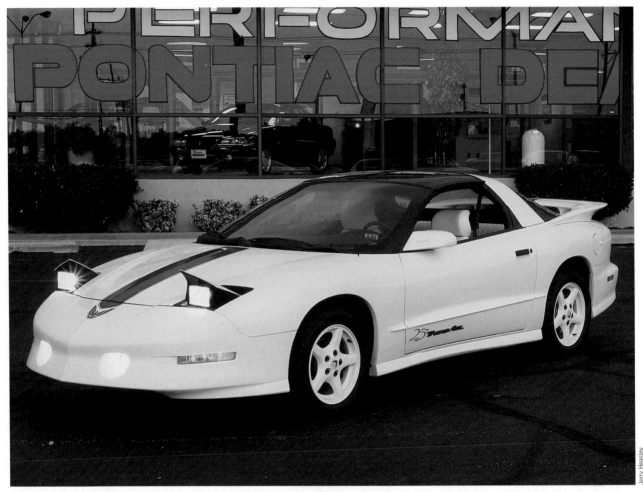

The bright white exterior and blue stripe down the center made the 25th Anniversary Trans Am easy to spot.

1994 25th Anniversary Trans Am

Pontiac Motor Division hasn't done very much to mark milestones years for its "Firebird" brand of pony cars, which started life in 1967. However, the automaker has been very faithful about marking anniversaries of its Trans Am model, which first became available in the middle of model year 1969.

Over the years, there had been 10th anniversary (1979), 15th anniversary (1984) and 20th anniversary (1989) anniversary editions of the sporty T/A. All were built in fairly limited numbers and most, if not all of them, are considered collector items. In fact, it is common to run across car collectors who own one of each.

When model year 1994 came along, Pontiac watchers just knew something would go up the flagpole and they were hoping that PMD management would salute the products planners' ideas. The 25th Anniversary Trans Am arrived on January 7, 1989.

At first, the 25th Anniversary package was announced as something available only for the Trans Am GT coupe. About a month later, at the Chicago Auto Show, the Firebird convertible was introduced and a 25th Anniversary Trans Am GT convertible was also put on display. From then on, the Pontiac fans had two special edition Trans Ams to choose from.

The cars' theme was obviously taken from the original 1969 1/2 Trans Am, since the package featured a Bright White exterior that was decorated with a Bright Blue stripe down the center. There were also anniversary logos and door badges. The special 16-inch aluminum wheels were done in White, as were the Prado leather seating surfaces with blue embroidery logos that matched those on the door panels. Owners also got a special portfolio commemorating their purchase.

The price for all of this was only $995. Of course, you had to come up with the base price $22,309 for the GT coupe or $27,279 for the GT convertible. "The result is a white-on-white stunner of a car, with the highest profile in traffic this side of a presidential motorcade," said *Car & Driver*.

Despite its 3,668-lb. curb weight and automatic transmission, the 25th Anniversary convertible was good for a 0-to-60 run in 6.1 seconds.

While certainly not as rare as the first Trans Am convertible (only eight of those were made), the 1994 ragtop is certainly a keeper. Its production was low. Seeing that it is part of a set of special editions, its collector value is still fairly high.

The 1995 SLP Formula Firehawk came in 300- and 315-hp versions.

PONTIAC

1995 Pontiac/SLP Formula Firehawk

To Firebird muscle model fans, the letters "SLP" stand for "Street Legal Performance." That was the goal of SLP Engineering. This Toms River, New Jersey, firm was what General Motors called an "aftermarket partner company." It converted new Firebirds that Pontiac shipped to its Garden State shop into super high-performance cars.

Promoted as "an irresistible force that moves you," the 1995 Formula Firehawk version of the Firebird offered 300- and 315-hp versions of the 5.7-liter LT1 V-8, plus all-new features like optional chrome wheels. In addition, Ed Hamburger and his SLP engineers added a Hurst six-speed gear shifter. About 750 Formula Firehawks were sold this year.

Twin air scoops on the Formula Firehawk's snout were part of a special air-induction system that added 25 to 35 hp. The suspension was upgraded from Formula specifications to increase handling limits. Coupes benefited from bigger, better-handling Firestone 275/40/17 tires and 17-inch wide wheels. Firehawk convertibles, however, came only with Firestone 16-inch tires and closed-lug 16-inch-wide alloy wheels.

Other Formula Firehawk features included megaphone-style polished stainless-steel tailpipe tips, special exterior graphics and a sequentially numbered dash plaque. A sport suspension and performance exhaust system were optional.

A six-speed Firehawk coupe with the performance exhaust system went from 0 to 60 mph in 4.9 seconds and did the quarter mile in 13.5 seconds at 103.5 mph. Its top speed was 160 mph. The Formula Firehawk was available as an SLP alteration on '95 Formulas, which buyers had to order through Pontiac dealers. The Firehawks came with a three-year, 36,000-mile limited warranty. The base price for the alteration was $6,495, an increase of $500 over the 1993 and 1994 versions.

Since the six-speed Hurst shifter was a new accessory for the high-performance 1995 Formula Firehawk model, SLP Engineering promoted this feature by photographing a Firehawk coupe alongside a 1965 Pontiac Catalina 2 + 2—an earlier high-performance Pontiac that also came with a Hurst shifter.

PONTIAC

The Formula Firebird was again the less-flashy sibling of the ultra-cool Trans Am in 1995.

Jerry Heasley

1995 Formula Firebird/Trans Am

As the world raced towards a new Millennium, the number of V-8 powered muscle machines being turned out by Detroit was declining each year. There were cars with turbocharged fours and supercharged V-6s that could go very fast, but if you wanted the pavement-pounding pulse that the '60s supercars were famous for (instead of the whine of a turbo), there was nothing like having a big-cube V-8 and the choices remaining were few indeed. Pontiac Motor Division's Firebird series was one of them and the Trans Am was the image-car of the line.

"Firebird is styled to be noticed, equipped for outstanding performance and handling, and priced to be accessible," said general manager John Middlebrook at the Chicago Auto Show. "A lot of people are taking notice, because for the 1994 model year, Firebird sales were up 143 percent over the previous year. We look for the exciting lineup of 1995 Firebirds to continue a hot sales pace."

The top-of-the-line Trans Am had a number of added or replacement standard features over those included with Formulas. They were: fog lamps, body-color body-side moldings, P245/50ZR16 speed-rated all-weather tires, cruise control, automatic power door locks, and an upgraded Delco sound system. Rear-seat courtesy lamps and a trunk lamp were deleted, however.

The 1995 Trans Am coupe had a suggested retail price of $21,184, while the convertible listed for $27,239 in standard equipment form. Both models were powered by the Chevrolet-built 5.7-liter LT1 V-8 with sequential fuel injection. Traction control was now offered for Firebird V-8 models equipped with a four-speed automatic or six-speed manual transmission.

Three new exterior colors were introduced: blue green chameleon, medium dark purple metallic, and bright silver metallic. Inside, a new bright red leather interior option was offered for all models, while a bright white leather interior was an extra limited to convertibles.

Other new features included 16-inch five-spoke wheels for V-8 models, all-weather speed-rated P245/50Z16 tires, a power antenna, and a four-spoke sport steering wheel. Firebird models with optional up-level sound systems were factory pre-wired to receive a Delco 12-disk CD changer, which was available as a new dealer-installed option. All 1995 Firebirds also had maintenance-free lower control-arm ball joints and "lubed-for-life" front-end components. Because Pontiac wheels were designed to show the wheel-and-brake mechanical parts, all Firebird models got a special coating to keep the brake rotors looking new. A new 16-inch, five-spoke wheel was available in chrome for Trans Ams.

Jerry Heasley

The fiercest 1996 Formula came with the 305-horse WS6 engine option.

PONTIAC

1996 Formula Firebird

Pontiac Motor Division's Firebird offerings for 1996 included the base Firebird, the Formula and the Trans Am models. All three versions of the Firebird came in Sport Coupe and Convertible body styles. The Formula Firebird model shared availability of the new WS6 Ram Air performance and handling package with the Trans Am.

The Model V87S Formula Firebird Coupe had a base price of $19,464, while prices for the Model V67S Formula Convertible started at $23,135. As on the flagship Trans Am, exhaust system improvements boosted the output of the Formula Firebird's standard 5.7-liter LT1 V-8 to 285 hp. If you added the WS6 options, you got a whopping 305 hp at 5400 rpm and 335 lbs.-ft. of torque at 3200 rpm.

Pontiac said that the hairy-looking WS6 Formula Firebird, with its twin-nostril hood, "bridged the gap between the raw power of the Muscle Car Era and today's sophisticated performance and safety technology." The business department of the WS6-equipped Formula was under the hood, where

the LT1 V-8 engine featured sequential-port fuel injection and an Opti-Spark ignition system. While providing 1960s-like acceleration, this power plant could run smoothly on 91-octane gas.

The 1996 Formula Firebird with the WS6 option came with fat 17-inch Goodyear Eagle GS-C tires. The front and rear springs were both stiffened. The WS6 suspension upgrades included 32-mm/19-mm rear sway bars, unique shock absorber valving, stiffer transmission mounts and stiffer Panhard-bar bushings.

The 1996 Formula's V-8 was OBD II compliant (meaning that it met stage II on-board-diagnostic system regulations to assure proper emission controls). OBD II was designed to monitor the EGR valve, oxygen sensor, and crankshaft and camshaft position sensors to detect any misfiring condition.

Pontiac said of the 1996 Firebird: "If it were in your blood, it'd be adrenaline. If it were more advanced, it'd be from NASA. If it came from Italy, it'd be way too expensive!"

PONTIAC

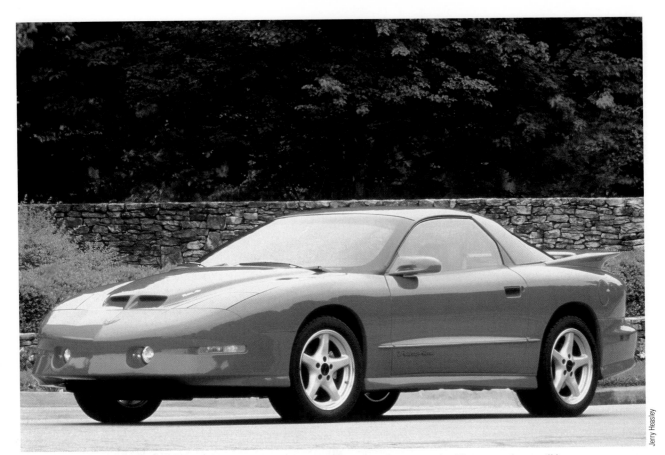

Jerry Heasley

The Ram Air Trans Am of 1996 was another standout Pontiac performer. It came in either coupe of convertible varieties, but the WS6 Performance & Handling package was not available on the ragtop, making the coupe the more potent car.

1996 Trans Am

Pontiac Motor Division's Firebird sports-personal car roared into 1996 with more excitement and more powerful engine options. There were several new high-performance packages for V-8 models. Trans Am coupes had a new WS6 Pontiac Ram Air performance-and-handling option that was instantly desirable and appealed to many late-model muscle car collectors. The Ram Air-equipped Trans Ams were promoted almost as if they were separate models.

The 1996 Trans Am convertible was the highest-priced Firebird available for this model year. Designated as the Model V67S + Y82 Trans Am, the ragtop retailed for $27,364. Structural adhesives were again used on 15 key areas of every convertible body that Pontiac built, including the cowl, windshield pillar and rocker reinforcements. The Model V87S + Y82 Trans Am Coupe had a base price of $21,414.

The horsepower of the LT1 V-8 (again sourced from the Chevrolet Corvette) was increased to 285, thanks to some exhaust system improvements. When the WS6 Ram Air option package was added, the car's top performing engine option leaped to 305 hp at 5400 rpm, while torque was 335 lbs.-ft. at 3200 rpm. The WS6 package also included a special twin-port hood scoop with Ram Air logos below each

"nostril," 17 x 9-inch-wide cast-aluminum five-spoke wheels, P275/40ZR17 tires, a dual-pump catalytic converter system, aluminum exhaust tips and specific suspension tuning.

On the Trans Am, the twin-snout hood was combined with the twin-fog-lamp front fascia. The WS6 Performance & Handling package could not be ordered for the Trans Am convertible. PMD described the WS6 Trans Am as an "open-snouted, fire-breathing dragon made for serious driving enthusiasts who want the response of an I-Ain't-Kiddin' 305-hp V-8 when they press on the accelerator."

A special Firebird model offered in 1996 was called the Harley-Davidson Edition Trans Am. The Milwaukee, Wisconsin motorcycle maker took a black Trans Am equipped with the WS6 Ram Air package (without factory upholstery) and added leather-and-fabric seats with the famous Harley-Davidson logo embroidered on them. The Harley-Davidson Edition Trans Am also had Harley decals on the front quarter panels just behind the tires. Only 40 such cars are believed to have been produced. Most of them were sold in Southern California. Also produced in 1996 were 10 Comp T/A hardtops and 35 Comp T/A T-tops. All Comp T/As had the WS6 Ram Air package.

The 1997 Trans Am could be ordered several ways, from mild to
wild, depending on the buyer's personality and bank account.

Jerry Heasley

PONTIAC

1997 Trans Am

You could get a 1997 Firebird in a variety of flavors, from affordable to expensive, from economical to guzzler, and from sports car to muscle car.

The typical buyer of a V-6 Firebird coupe was a 36-year-old person making $55,000 a year. Just over half were married and just below half were male college graduates working in a professional field. At the other end of the Firebird spectrum, Trans Am buyer demographics indicated a median age of 40, average household income of $75,000 and that slightly over 50 percent of buyers were married males with a college degree and professional occupation.

Air conditioning and the PASS-Key II theft-deterrent system became standard equipment for all 1997 Firebirds, including Trans Ams. Also standard was a four-way seat adjuster located on the left-hand side of the driver's seat.

Starting this year, all Trans Am convertibles incorporated a number of standard features, including power mirrors, power windows, power door locks, cruise control and rear-seat courtesy lamps. The ragtops included a flush-folding power top that stored beneath an easily assembled three-piece hard tonneau cover. When the top was raised, the standard rear-glass window with electric defogger helped give a clear view out the back of the car. A fully trimmed headliner contributed to a quieter ride.

The Trans Am featured a distinctive fog-lamp front fascia that added 1.4 inches to its overall length and 1.2 inches to its front overhang. It also had slightly more overhang at the rear. The standard 5.7-liter V-8 produced 285 hp at 5000 rpm and 325 lbs.-ft. of torque at 2400 rpm. With the WS6 Ram Air Package, these ratings changed to 305 hp at 5400 rpm and 335 lbs.-ft. at 3200 rpm. Cars with the $3,000 WS6 option were again characterized by the use of a twin-nostril hood with a Ram Air logo on each air-inlet opening.

The Trans Am coupe, Model V87S + Y82, now had a suggested retail price of $22,884 and prices for the Model V67S + Y82 Trans Am convertible began at $28,444. Trans Am coupes included power sport mirrors, cruise control, power door locks, an electric rear-window defogger, leather-wrapped interior and power windows. Trans Am convertibles also had a power antenna, P245/50ZR16 all-weather speed-rated tires, a Delco 2001 series stereo, remote-keyless entry and a leather-wrapped interior with steering wheel radio controls.

PONTIAC

It was hard to argue Pontiac's claims that the potent 1998 Formula Firebird was "a modern muscle car."

1998 Formula Firebird

"The automotive family tree includes the branch that bore muscle cars — those revered, big-engined road rockets of yore," said the promotional copy in Pontiac Motor Division's 1998 full line sales catalog. "As often happens when a species evolves, the strong get stronger," PMD added. Was this just hype? The departure of the Formula Firebird convertible certainly didn't make the Formula model look stronger; however, this "street-fighting" version of the Firebird did get a new, all-aluminum LS1 5.7-liter 305-hp V-8 with a six-speed manual transmission.

Leading PMD's stable of aggressively styled cars, the bold new Firebird had a new outer appearance guaranteed to turn heads and continue its legendary status among sports car enthusiasts. The hot Formula Firebird showcased numerous functional improvements, including V-8 engines with more horsepower and more torque.

The Formula Firebird now shared its front fascia design with the base Firebird. The front-end design incorporated twin center ports below the hood and restyled, round, outboard-mounted fog lamps. Two new paint colors, Navy

Metallic and Sport Gold Metallic were available. The Formula Firebird also had new styling lines on its rear end. Inside there were new gauges with clear white characters on black analog faces to help keep drivers informed of what was going on with their car.

In addition to standard Firebird features, the Formula model added or substituted a power radio antenna, power operated door locks, dual power sport type outside rearview mirrors with blue glass, a 500-watt peak-power "Monsoon" radio with CD and seven-band graphic equalizer (including a clock, touch control, seek up/down, search-and-replay, Delco theft lock and a high-performance 10-speaker system.

A beefed-up LS1 5.7-liter V-8 engine generated 305 hp at 5200 rpm and 335 lbs.-ft. of torque at 4000 rpm. Revisions to this power plant provided enhanced mid-range responsiveness. That translated into 20 more horsepower and 10 more lbs.-ft. of torque than the previous Firebird V-8 delivered. The WS6-equipped Ram Air LS1 V-8 boasted 320 hp. Pontiac Motor Division called it "a modern muscle car."

The mildly redesigned 1998 Trans Am had looks to kill and 320 horses turning the rubber when the WS6 engine was ordered.

1998 Trans Am

The 1998 Trans Am had a distinctive front end design. Like base Firebirds and Formula Firebirds, the Trans Am had center twin ports below the hood and round fog lamps. However, on Trans Ams, the fog lamps were located near the center, while the base Firebird and Formula Firebird fog lamps were located further outboard.

The aggressive-looking hood design provided smoother contours and also improved underhood air flow. The standard hood had two openings with a Ram Air look that were actually non-functional. A revised 320-hp Ram Air (UPC code WS6) package did arrive at the middle of the year. The Ram Air nose had two large "ant eater" air scoops that were divided, in front, by a horizontal fin or blade. This was a very, very racy-looking design. Small "Ram Air" lettering appeared on the sides of the hood scoops.

New pop-up headlights had a "mini-quad" design that enhanced the appearance of the car when they were in use. The new headlights also provided significantly improved road lighting. GM bean counters wanted Pontiac to drop flip-up headlights, because they're costly, but market researchers determined that they were a trademark of the Firebird, so they were not discontinued.

An aggressive new fender design, with air extractors (or brake-cooling ducts), was common to all Firebird models. A new 16-inch wheel rim was used on cars with the base V-8. Optional chrome wheels were carried over from 1997, as were the 17-inch wheels on Ram Air cars. Trans Am models also had new rear-end styling.

Mechanical upgrades included larger brakes at all four corners. Up front, dual-piston aluminum brake calipers replace the old cast-iron jobs that had only single-piston bores. The parking brake was reworked, too. Organic pads replaced the previous "semi-mets" and the ABS hardware was also improved with a new Bosch solenoid.

Trans Ams came with all standard Formula Firebird equipment, plus an audible theft-deterrent system, a remote keyless entry system and a six-way power front driver's seat.

The 5.7-liter 305-hp V-8 was the same used in Formula Firebirds. The WS6-equipped Ram Air LS1 V-8 boasted 320 hp. In October 1997, *High Performance Pontiac* magazine featured the 1988 Firebird on its cover and in a story titled "Perfecting Excellence." It explained the improvements that had been made to the LS1 V-8 in great detail and gave a positive, seat-of-the-pants impression of the performance of the '98 over the already-hot '97.

PONTIAC

The 1999 Firehawk was a pavement scorcher that was a relative
bargain new with a window price of about $31,000.

1999 Trans Am Firehawk

Motor Trend's Jack Keebler (April 1999) described his bright red SLP Trans Am Firehawk as "All Detroit muscle all the time." The "Street Legal Performance" Firebird's 16-valve 5.7-liter V-8 produced 327 hp at 5200 rpm and 345 lbs.-ft. of torque at 4400 rpm. The car could do 0-to-60 mph in 5.3 seconds and covered the quarter-mile in 13.6 seconds at 105.6 mph.

Keebler was comparing the $31,000 heated-up Firebird to nine other super cars, including the $140,000 Mercedes Benz CL600 and the $299,900 Bentley Continental R. It was the lowest-priced car in the pack, but was right up there with the top performing models.

The reworked 346-cid LS1 block was attached to a Borg-Warner T-56 six-speed manual transmission. A set of meaty P275/40ZR17 Firestone tires "attached" it to the road and helped it slide through a slalom course at 66 mph while pulling a strong 0.89 Gs on a skid pad. The car built by SLP Engineering could still be ordered directly through Pontiac factory dealers.

The contents of the WU6 Firehawk package included the 327-hp LS1 V-8, a composite hood with fiunctional air scoops, hood-mounted heat extraxtors, an underhood forced-air induction system, a Firehawk badge on the front fascia, a Cat-Back stainless steel performance exhaust system with twin dual tips, upgraded suspension components, 17 x 9-inch painted lightweight aluminum wheels, 275/40ZR17 SZ50 Firestone Firehawk tires, Firehawk exterior graphics on the doors and rear fascia, a Firehawk dash plaque and two Firehawk key fobs.

A handful of options were available for the 1999 Firehawk. They included a custom car cover, premium floor mats with embroidered Firehawk graphics, a Black (Code 41) exterior color and a Dark Pewter Cartenga cloth (Code 14B9) upholstery selection.

A total of 719 Firehawks were assembled in 1999. This includes 622 cars for the U.S. market and 97 for Canada. The total included 34 Formula coupes, 72 Formulas with T-tops, 538 Trans Ams with T-Tops and 75 Trans Am convertibles. The MN6 manual transmission was fitted to 317 Trans Am T-Tops, 40 Trans Am convertibles, 22 Formula coupes and 39 Formula T-tops. The MXO automatic transmission was used in 221 Trans Ams with T-tops, 35 Trans Am convertibles, 12 Formula coupes and 33 Formulas with T-tops.

In terms of color, of the 719 cars 38 were Artic White, 311 were Black, 169 were Bright Red, 37 were Bright Silver, 84 were Navy Blue and 80 were Pewter Metallic.

The 2002 Firehawk package kicked out either 330 or 345 hp, and there were lots of go-fast options that helped the racy Pontiac run as good as it looked.

PONTIAC

2002 Firehawk

SLP Engineering, of Troy, Michigan, produced the Firehawk version of the Pontiac Firebird at its special assembly facility in Montreal, Canada. The SLP plant was located 20 minutes away from the General Motors F-Car assembly facility in Ste. Therese, Canada, where the last Firebirds and Camaros were built. GM shipped the cars to SLP for the performance modifications and they were then returned to the GM factory to be shipped to Pontiac dealerships in the U.S. and Canada.

SLP promoted its 2002 Firehawk with the slogan "It doesn't get any better" and few could argue with that claim. The 11th edition of this modern muscle car offered more muscle and more excitement. With well over 300 hp, the 2002 Firehawk could pull up to .90 gs on a skidpad.

New for the 2002 Firehawk was a heated-up version of the LS1 V-8, an engine derived from the famous Corvette LS1. The 2002 version developed 345 hp and 350 lbs.-ft. of torque. It came coupled to an SLP (Steet Legal Performance) high-flow induction system, as well as SLP's proprietary Dual-Dual Performance Exhaust system. To handle the added power, the cars could be shod with new and improved 17-inch Firestone SZ50 extended performance tires.

Special Firehawk features included an optional IROC-inspired deck-lid spoiler, a super-wide composite hood with air scoops and engine heat extractors, a Firehawk front fascia badge, Firehawk graphics and the extra-cost 17 x 9-inch five-spoke, painted aluminum wheels.

To build a Firehawk, a customer had to order a V87X Trans Am Coupe, a V67X Trans Am Convertible or a V87X Firebird Coupe coupled with the W66 Formula option from a Pontiac dealer. The customer could then check option WU6, which added a GM RPO V12 power-steering cooler, plus the QLC tires and 16-inch wheels required for a basic Firehawk.

Buyers could get the 2002 Firehawk package in a 330-hp version for $3,999 or in the 345-hp version for $4,299. Available options included the all-new rear deck lid spoiler for $699, 17-inch wheels for $799, a Bilstein performance suspension for $1,099, a 1LE performance suspension for $1,899, an Auburn high-torque performance differential with AAM cast-aluminum cooling cover for $899, premium front floor mats embroidered with the Firehawk logo for $99, a custom rear deck mat with embroidered logo for $99, a commemorative portfolio for $59 and a custom-fitted car cover with a locking cable and tote bag for $159.

Wieck Media

The GTO was back in 2004, at least as a show car, after a three-decade absence.

2004 Pontiac GTO Show Cars

The 2004 Pontiac GTO was based on the Holden (GM Austrailia) Monaro, a modern car that shares many traits with the legendary GTOs of the '60s and '70s. The Monaro was the first all-Australian performance coupe when it was introduced in 1968.

Bob Lutz, the ex-Chrysler exec and car collector who is now Chairman of GM's North American Operations (and perhaps the only enthusiast left in the corporate hierarchy) played the key role in turning the Monaro into the 2004 GTO. It has been reported that Lutz drove a Holden Monaro while in Australia. He liked the car and felt that it was a machine that could live up to the original GTO's genuine high-performance image.

To give America's car-buying public its first look at the rebirth of the legend, Pontiac introduced show-car versions of the 2004 GTO to audiences at the Los Angeles Auto Show, the North American International Auto Show in Detroit and the Chicago Auto Show early in 2003. Production versions of the GTO became available in Pontiac showrooms later in the year.

"The public's interest in the GTO has been everything we hoped it would be and more," Lutz said. "This car is a strong statement from both Pontiac and GM that we are determined to re-energize the car market with vehicles that command attention and excite the customer's senses." The introduction of the show-car came just seven months after GM announced it was bringing back the GTO. Lutz said the "GTO will carry on the proud tradition of a legendary line."

Later, when GTO enthusiasts criticized the Los Angeles show car for not being "retro" styled, Lutz posted answers to the critics on the Internet. He told them that the idea behind the car was not to go down the retro road like Ford's T-Bird, but to develop a modern counterpart to the '60s American muscle car. Lutz did add that a hood scoop, needed for GTO identity, was coming.

Sporting special high-gloss paint, the GTO exhibited a strong Pontiac brand character with its dual-port grille and a wide and aggressive stance. Under the hood was a specially tuned LS1 5.7-liter V-8 aluminum-block engine that produced an estimated 340 hp at 5200 rpm and 360 lbs.-ft. of torque at 4000 rpm. The throaty V-8 was said to have had "an appropriately-tuned Pontiac exhaust note." While sharing its basic configuration with the first-level Corvette, the GTO V-8 has been modified with a high-lift camshaft and increased air induction. These changes provide the Monaro with greater horsepower and low-end torque to meet the needs of American drivers.

The GTO had an under-7-second 0-to-60 time and could run the quarter-mile in approximately 14 seconds with a terminal speed of 105 mph. The top speed was about 160 mph.

Transmission choices included an electronically controlled Hydra-Matic 4L60-E four-speed automatic or a six-speed, close-ratio manual transmission like that currently available in Corvette ZO6 models. Both drove to the same low-geared 3.46:1 rear axle. Maximum off-the-line performance was assured with a limited-slip differential and a three-channel traction control system that enhanced the driver's control of the car. The GTO had power-assisted four-wheel ventilated disc brakes and a standard four-channel anti-lock braking system.

The new-generation GTO has its critics, but the 2005 model definitely left no doubt
that Pontiac could still produce a stylish rear-drive coupe that could really fly.

2005 GTO

The Pontiac GTO returned in 2005 with more power and style. A new LS2 6.0-liter V-8 was introduced and lowered 0-to-60 times to less than 5 seconds. The modern muscle car also had new badging and a revised rear fascia incorporating a new dual-exhaust system. Also available was a new hood incorporating a pair of stylish air scoops to draw fresh air into the engine bay.

The badges identifying the '05 GTO's bigger V-8 included a "6.0" badge on the trunk lid and revised GTO fender badges (with 1964-like "6.0 Litre" designations). Along with the power increase came larger brake rotors, calipers and pads. The calipers were painted red and the front calipers featured the GTO logo. Also new were Blue and Gray body colors and a driver foot rest.

A line of regular production accessories, based on the 2004 GTO Performance Plus SEMA concept vehicle, was available by the start of 2005 production. The accessories included a tall rear spoiler, front and rear fascia extensions, rocker molding extensions and grille inserts. As part of GM's program, the accessories could be ordered and installed on the vehicle prior to delivery.

Compared to the Gen III-based LS1, the 2005 GTO's LS2 V-8 incorporated several significant changes to help improve performance. The block was an all-new casting with cylinder bores measuring 4.00 inches (101.6 mm) in diameter. The cylinder heads and camshaft were revised, too, to deliver the airflow necessary to complement the engine's larger displacement. Other changes included a new aluminum block casting with revised oil galleries and provisions for external knock sensors to improve serviceability, a higher-lift cam to take advantage of increased cylinder head flow, the camshaft sensor relocated from the rear of the block to the front of the block to allow room for new oil galleries, new flat-top pistons with lower ring tension to reduce friction, floating wrist pins, a more efficient ignition system, higher (10.9:1) compression, a larger 90-mm single-blade throttle body, a reduced-mass water pump with improved sealing capability and a revised and more powerful engine controller that incorporated all electronic throttle control functions. Some of the changes helped give the engine a high 6500-rpm redline.

The 2005 GTO delivered impressive cornering abilities, a smooth ride and surprising comfort. The car had a 109.8-inch wheelbase with a low stance that enhanced its behind-the-wheel "wide-track" feel. The suspension had MacPherson struts in front and a semi-trailing arm design in the rear, with specially tuned strut valving and spring rates. The direct-acting stabilizer bars and variable-ratio power steering were tuned to provide a sporty feel and increased driver feedback. Seventeen-inch alloy wheels and performance tires were matched to the performance-tuned suspension. Traction control and a limited slip differential also became standard.

The interior had full-leather seating, a leather-covered steering wheel and shifter knob, stainless steel sill plates, a metallic-look steering wheel styling, satin nickel-look accent trim and racing-inspired drilled metallic pedals. The 2+2 interior had the "GTO" name embroidered on the front seats. Interior seat and trim colors could be coordinated to the exterior color with red, blue, purple and black interiors available. A host of creature comforts was standard or optional.

The Shelby Series 1 was a wildly fast cutting-edge supercar with a sky-high price to match its lofty performance. Only about 280 Series 1 Shelbys were reportedly built, and they became instant collector cars for enthusiasts with deep pockets.

SHELBY

2000 Shelby Series 1

In the late 1990s, Carrol Shelby came up with a new idea: to build a sleek, lightweight roadster with the performance of a real muscle car. Okay, so it wasn't a new idea, but the car was great looking and the use of an Oldsmobile engine was a little bit of a twist on history.

Shelby's $174,975 Series 1 roadster took a long time to become a reality, but when it finally debuted, many people were happy they had filled their penny jar, instead of buying a used Sunbird convertible to run around in.

The non-supercharged version of the Oldsmobile Aurora V-8 delivered 320 hp and 290 lbs.-ft. of torque at 5000 rpm. The engine sported double overhead camshafts and four valves per cylinder. It was linked to a six-speed manual gearbox.

A Vortec supercharger was merchandised as a dealer-installed extra. The system included special camshafts, a larger-than-stock throttle body and tweaked engine control system software. It brought the Series 1 roadster's price up to around $195,000.

With the supercharger and related goodies installed, the 244-cid Oldsmobile Aurora V-8 produced 450 hp at 6800 rpm and 400 ft. lbs. at 5300 rpm. In the lightweight (2,650-pound) Series 1 roadster it produced amazing performance figures. The Shelby could rocket from 0-to-60 mph in an amazing 3.71 seconds. The quarter-mile required 12.14 seconds. In that brief amount of time, the roadster could get all the way up to about 120 mph. The car could pull .98gs on the skid pad. Top speed was 175 mph.

The Series 1 roadster was 168.9 inches long, 76.5 inches wide and 47 inches high. Underneath the Series 1's sleek, race-car-style body was a competition-style suspension with upper and lower control arms, coil springs and front and rear anti-roll bars. Vented disc brakes were used front and rear with 13-inch vented discs up front and 12-inchers at the rear. Braking from 60 mph to 0 required 129 feet. In front the car wore 18 x 10-inch cast-aluminum rims, with 18 x 12-inch wheels in the rear. The tires were Goodyear Eagle F1 Supercar models, 265/40ZR18 in front and P315/40ZR18 in the rear. Production of the Series 1 was originally supposed to have been limited to 500 cars.

Eventually, the price of the Series 1 soared over $200,000, a factor that drove away some potential buyers. According to reliable sources, 280 cars were eventually assembled. But, knowing Carroll Shelby, there might be a few tucked away for the future. A prototype Series 1 roadster is part of the Auto Collections at the Imperial Palace Hotel & Casino in Las Vegas, Nevada. According to their Web site, it can be yours for a cool $260,000 or so.

The 1963 Avanti R2 was a truly unique vehicle and ahead of its time in many ways.

1963 Studebaker R2 Avanti

As a symbol of change and fresh thinking, the Studebaker Avanti was intended as a prime factor in an effort to save Studebaker from oblivion by shaking it loose from its rather musty and stodgy image. Although this effort ended in failure, the Avanti has gained recognition as an outstanding example both of styling excellence and performance competence.

Three engine alternatives were offered for the 1963 Avanti: the base R1 power plant, the supercharged R2 and the seldom-seen and expensive R3. The R1 was a nice, if somewhat unexciting, 280-cid/240-hp V-8. The R3, although garnering a great deal of publicity, was an extremely rare commodity. The R2 was readily available and (at $210) not terribly expensive. It offered a brand of performance rather different from that of the 400-plus-cid V-8s generally available in the mid-1960s.

While the R2 lacked the brute force of other muscle cars, the use of a supercharged and relatively small V-8, along with clever and resourceful use of existing Studebaker components, resulted in an American car that needed no apologies or alibis for either its acceleration or handling.

Officially listed as a 1963 model, the Avanti received a tremendous publicity boost through the successful assault upon existing American records by an R3-engineered Avanti in August. Among the new marks established was a two-way Flying Mile mark of 168.15 mph. Early in 1963, a four-speed-equipped R2 Avanti that was almost completely stock, except for its exhaust system, averaged 158.15 mph through the measured mile.

The R2 Avanti engine was based on Studebaker's V-8, which had entered production in 1951 with a displacement of 232 cid and 120 hp. By 1963, this V-8 had evolved through several displacement changes and for the R2 had reached 289

cid. A sealed Carter AFB four-barrel carburetor was used in conjunction with a Paxton SN-60 centrifugal supercharger. Due to the supercharger, the compression ratio of the R2 was at 9.0:1—lower than the R1's 10.25:1. Output of the R2 was impressive: 289 hp at 5200 rpm and 330 lbs.-ft. of torque at 3600 rpm.

Aside from having an engine that developed 1 hp per cubic inch, the Avanti was the first full-size American car to be endowed with front caliper disc brakes. These 11.5-inch units were supplied by Bendix and were produced under license from Dunlop. In their basic design they were similar to those used by Jaguar. Finned drums were used at the rear.

Neither the Avanti's standard three-speed manual transmission nor its optional air conditioning were available with the R2 engine. Instead, customers selected either a four-speed Warner Gear T-10 all-synchromesh gearbox or a three-speed "power-shift" automatic produced by Borg-Warner, which permitted manual shifting if desired. Overall length of the Avanti was 192.4 inches and curb weight was approximately 3,400 lbs.

The performance and top-speed capability of the R2 was superb. *Road and Track*, October 1962, reported a 0-to-60 time for the four-speed model of 7.3 seconds. *Motor Trend*, July 1962, noted that a power-shift model needed 8 seconds for the same run.

With a total 1963 model year run of just 3,834 units, the Avanti was truly a limited-edition vehicle. The subsequent output of an additional 809 units in 1964—as well as the regeneration of the Avanti in its various Avanti II permutations—has not diluted the appeal of the 1963 R2 Avanti.

The 1964 Studebaker Daytona conceded little to any fast-moving midsize car on the street, and their low production numbers make them scarce collector vehicles today.

1964 Studebaker Daytona

Designer Brooks Stevens effected more than a facelift when he created the new Studebaker Daytona hardtop in 1964. The crisp, squared-off roof that Stevens grafted onto the now 4-year-old Lark body looked every bit as up to date as Chevy's equally angular Impala. Of course, the Daytona was narrower than a full-size Chevy (Studebaker's basic body stampings dated back to 1953 and most American cars had grown substantially wider over the intervening decade), but its size fit nicely with the new intermediates.

What really made the Daytona stand out were the performance options available. Lacking money for frequent styling changes, Studebaker had attempted to garner attention through performance with its Hawk coupes and the stunning Avanti. Studebaker's overhead-valve V-8, first introduced in 1951, had been a farsighted enough design that more than a dozen years later it was being boosted to outputs exceeding 1 hp per cubic inch.

Studebaker designated its high-output V-8s as the R-series engines. The "base" R1 engine developed 240 hp from a 289-cid displacement. Next came the R2, also a 289, but equipped with a supercharger for a rated 289 hp. The R3, also supercharged and with a slightly larger displacement of 304.5 cid, gave a power rating of 335 hp. The final engine in this series, dubbed the R4, ran two four-barrel carburetors without supercharging for a rated 280 hp. It was this engine that Studebaker selected to create a street "sleeper" from its

docile-looking Daytona hardtop.

With a top speed of 132 mph and 0-to-60 acceleration of 7.8 seconds, Studebaker's R4 Daytona could show its taillights to any production sedan. Its performance was rivaled only by that of the Pontiac GTO, which was also released in 1964. As might be expected, performance carried a mileage penalty. An R4 Daytona owner could expect little more than 12 to 14 mpg. With a total carburetor venturi area of 13 inches, the Daytona's 304.5-cid engine was capable of gulping plenty of fuel.

Performance cars of the 1950s and 1960s have a great reputation for going like lightning in a straight line, but come to a corner and watch out. To give the Daytona some measure of road-handling ability, Studebaker fit it with an Avanti suspension package that consisted of stiffer springs and shocks, anti-roll bars front and rear, and front disc brakes. To glue the engine's power to the pavement, these performance cars came standard with traction bars and a limited-slip differential. To put the R4's power to pleasurable use, Studebaker fitted its hot Daytona model with a Borg-Warner T-10 four-speed transmission.

Not many performance Daytonas were built (besides the R4, other R series engines could also be optioned) making them one of the least known and rarest of muscle cars—a real "sleeper" even today.

STUDEBAKER